Bavaria
p104

Stuttgart & the Black Forest
p213

Munich
p42

Salzburg & Around
p185

D1052648

THIS EDITION WRITTEN AND RESEARCHED BY

Marc Di Duca, Kerry Christiani

welcome to Munich, Bavaria
& the Black Forest

Southern Comfort

The Germans have a word, *Gemütlichkeit*, that untranslatable blend of cosiness, well-being and a laid-back attitude. Nowhere does this mood permeate deeper than in the prosperous south where fairy-lit beer gardens, Alpine views, medieval towns, rousing hilltop castles and many a red-faced village brass band awaits you. But there's another facet to *Gemütlichkeit*: it's also a marble-smooth autobahn of luxury cars speeding to gourmet restaurants and chic Alpine spas, Munich's high-brow cultural scene robed in black, and cappuccinos at dawn on intercity expresses. The two southern Germanys coexist, an incongruous mix packed with the unexpected.

Alpine Air & Munich Flair

Bavaria is definitely a place for those who prefer their air fresh rather than freshened. Though the Alps only tickle Germany's underbelly, locals know how to get the most out of their peaks, stringing cable cars up the vertical reality of the Alps; marking out entire atlases of cycling, hiking and cross-country skiing trails; even running a train up the inside of the Zugspitze, Germany's highest mountain. Yet all this is just a short ride from the urban *joie de vivre* of Munich, a sexy, sophisticated and self-confident city with a nonchalant, almost Mediterranean feel.

Hilltop castles and green energy, beer halls and luxury cars, Alpine peaks and cutting edge art – southern Germany blends thigh-slapping tradition with clear-headed modernity like nowhere else on earth.

(left) Traditional Bavarian house
(below) Munich fairground

Of Cuckoo Clocks & Lederhosen

If you're coming here in search of strapping Alpine types in lederhosen, big-bosomed wenches juggling platters of roast pork, tipsy oompah bands and Hänsel-and-Gretel cottages, you'll be pleased to hear that Germany's south keeps all its clichéd promises. Nowhere is this truer than on the Romantic Road, a 350km-long route from Würzburg to the Alps stringing centuries' worth of quaint walled towns on a ribbon of history and tweeness. And if you think all the folksy fuss is just for the tourists you'd be wrong – many Bavarians turn out en masse for traditional festivals and celebrations in their lederhosen or dirndl.

King of the Castle

Southern Germany is also famed for its castles, from medieval fortresses to the 19th-century follies commissioned by Bavaria's most celebrated king, Ludwig II. Mad about Versailles (and some claim just plain mad) he 'single-handedly' launched Bavaria's tourist industry and even stirred Walt Disney with his story-book Neuschwanstein Castle. You could spend a month zig-zagging between sugary palaces, stuccoed baroque residences, wind-cracked Gothic ruins and vista-rich chateaux. Palace fatigue? Then there's nothing simpler in these parts than retreating to a cosy tavern and raising a tankard to this marvellous corner of Europe.

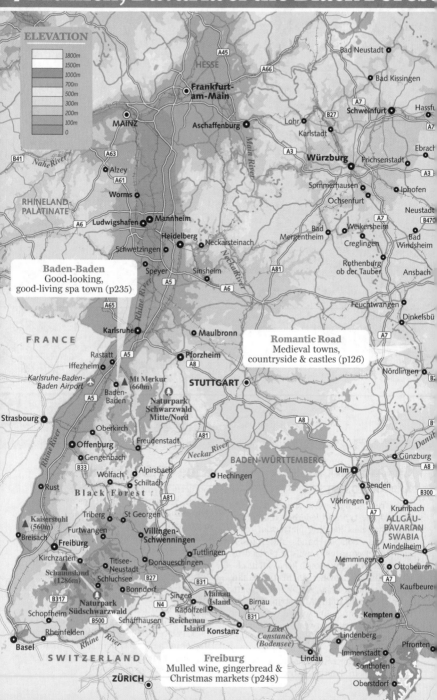

ELEVATION

1800m
1500m
1000m
700m
500m
300m
200m
100m
0

HESSE

A45

A66

Frankfurt-am-Main

MAINZ

Aschaffenburg

Lohr

Karlstadt

Schweinfurt

Hassfu

Ebrach

Würzburg Prichsenstadt

Sommerhausen Iphofen

Ochsenfurt

Bad Weikersheim Neustadt
Mergentheim Creglingen Bad
Windsheim

Rothenburg
ob der Tauber Ansbach

Feuchtwangen

Dinkelsbü

Nördlingen

B41 NaheRiver

A63

Alzey

A61

Worms

RHINELAND-
PALATINATE

A6

Ludwigshafen Mannheim

Heidelberg Neckarsteinach

Schwetzingen

Speyer Sinsheim

A5 A6

NeckarRiver

A81

A7

A3

B27

A7

B470

A7

Baden-Baden
Good-looking,
good-living spa town (p235)

A65

Karlsruhe Maulbronn

FRANCE

Rastatt A5

Iffezheim

Karlsruhe-Baden-
Baden Airport

A5

Baden-
Baden

Mt Merkur
(660m)

Naturpark
Schwarzwald
Mitte/Nord

Pforzheim

A8

STUTTGART

Romantic Road
Medieval towns,
countryside & castles (p126)

A7

Nördlingen

B2

B

Strasbourg

Oberkirch

Offenburg Freudenstadt

Gengenbach

B33

Wolfach Alpirsbach

Rust Schiltach

Black Forest A81

Hechingen

A81

BADEN-WÜRTTEMBERG

Ulm

A8

Günzburg

A8

Senden

B300

Vöhringen

A7

Krumbach

ALLGÄU-
BAVARIAN
SWABIA

Neckar River

Danu

Triberg St Georgen

Kaiserstuhl
(560m)

Furtwangen

Breisach

Freiburg

Kirchzarten

Schauinsland
(1286m)

Schluchsee

**Villingen-
Schwenningen**

Tuttlingen

Titisee-
Neustadt

Donaueschingen

B27

Bonndorf

Singen

B31

Mainau
Island

Birnau

Naturpark
Südschwarzwald

Schopfheim

B317

B500

Schäffhausen

Radolfzell

Reichenau
Island

Konstanz

B31

Mindelheim

Memmingen Ottobeuren

A7

Kaufbeure

Kempten

Rheinfelden

Basel

Rhine River

SWITZERLAND

N4

Lake
Constance
(Bodensee)

Lindenberg

Lindau

Immenstadt

Sonthofen

Pfronten

ZÜRICH

Freiburg
Mulled wine, gingerbread &
Christmas markets (p248)

Oberstdorf

Nuremberg
The south's most
kid-friendly city (p144)

Munich
Explore Bavaria's exciting
capital city (p42)

Salzburg
Visit Mozart and Maria's
Alpine home (p187)

Bavarian Alps
Outdoor frolics amid
mountain peaks (p108)

Schloss Neuschwanstein
Explore the world's most
famous castle (p109)

10 TOP
EXPERIENCES

Munich

1 Confident and cutting edge, traditional and twee, Bavaria's capital (p42) takes all the state's quirky variety and condenses it into one of Europe's most intriguing destinations. The 'city of art and beer' wows with its world-beating collections of old masters, Gothic sculpture and pop art; but when the high-brow day ends, Munich retreats to the beer hall to savour a hop-infused culture like no other. Factor in some intense nightlife, world-class museums and easy-going locals and it's plain to see there's much more to Munich than just Oktoberfest. Neues Rathaus, Marienplatz, Munich

Oktoberfest

2 Social barriers evaporate, strangers become friends and everybody sings too loudly, drinks in excess and has way too much fun at the world's biggest beer bash in Munich (p22). The event lures a global mob of hedonists, but there's a quieter, folksier side, with less raucous beer tents and time-honoured traditions taking visitors back to its early 19th-century beginnings. So squeeze into your lederhosen or dirndl and get on down to the Theresienwiese – it's an experience you won't forget, if you can remember it at all, that is. Beer tent at Theresienwiese

OLIMPIO FANTUZ/SIME 4CORNERS©

Beer Halls & Gardens

3 Munich and Bavaria are synonymous with the beer hall, a time-warped institution of towering tankards; tightly trussed, strong-armed waitresses; and resident umpah bands. The (grand)daddy of all beer halls is central Munich's Hofbräuhaus (p52), but there are plenty of equally characterful, and perhaps less touristy, spots throughout the south. If you prefer your watering holes al fresco, Munich celebrated 200 years of the beer garden in 2012, and this summertime passion certainly has another two centuries' worth of elbow bending to come. Hofbräuhaus tent at Oktoberfest

Schloss Neuschwanstein

4 Bavaria's best-known castle (p109) emerges from hilltop woodland above Füssen like a bedtime storybook vision. Commissioned by Ludwig II, 19th-century king of Bavaria, Neuschwanstein is top of the league when it comes to Germany's tourist attractions and it's easy to see why. What would have been a private royal residence is a reflection of Ludwig II's longing to retreat into his own cloistered fantasy world, a secluded realm in which the operas of Richard Wagner played a pivotal role. No wonder Walt found inspiration here for his Disney World creations.

Hiking

5 If you're a fan of *wandern* (hiking), boy are you in for a treat – the hiking in southern Germany is about as good as it gets. Whether you want to ramble among the mythical mountains of Berchtesgaden (p123), splashed with jewel-coloured lakes; crest the country's highest peak, 2962m Zugspitze (p115); or trek from hut-to-hut in the Alps, there is a trail with your name on it. Edging west brings you to the wonderful solitude, bristling spruce forests and mile after glorious mile of footpaths in the Black Forest.

CRAIG PERSHOUSE/GETTY IMAGES©

Romantic Road

6 As roads go, Western Bavaria's Romantic Road (p126) is something pretty special – a 350km-long ribbon of higgledy-piggledy walled towns and soothing countryside. However, it's not all medieval quaintness; the route passes blockbuster Harburg castle, the Unesco-listed baroque Wieskirche and Ludwig II's Schloss Neuschwanstein. Yes, it's tourist-clogged, and yes, the renovation can be more Technicolor than Teutonic, but come in the snow, stroll after the tourist buses depart or tackle the route by bike, and the Romantic Road begins to live up to its name.
Marktplatz, Rothenburg

Baden-Baden

7 Some 2000 years ago the Romans raved about *baden* (bathing) in Baden-Baden's therapeutic waters (p235), and the spring-fed town still hasn't lost its touch. Royalty and celebrities from Queen Victoria to Victoria Beckham have put this classy Black Forest spa town on the global map, but its merits speak for themselves. Nestled smugly at the foot of thickly wooded hills, this is a good-looking, good-living town of pristine belle époque villas and sculpture-strewn gardens, cupola-crowned spas, and ritzy boutiques, cafes and restaurants.
Bavarian health spa

Salzburg

8 At times Salzburg (p185) can feel like a Hollywood film set, with its theatrical alpine backdrop, exuberant baroque architecture, and Mozart and Maria everywhere. But here's the good news: it's real. History seeps through the Altstadt's maze of narrow lanes, crowned by a formidable fortress and sprinkled with churches and abbeys. Pathways thread along river banks and cliff ridges, allowing you to survey the city from every photogenic angle. By night, locals pour into palatial concert halls for chamber concerts, and chestnut-canopied beer gardens for monastic brews.
Schloss Hellbrunn

Nuremberg

9 The beer is as dark as the tourism in buzzing Nuremberg (p144), where some of the region's most evocative Nazi heritage sites, including the mammoth rally grounds where the faithful came en masse to Heil Hitler, draw those on the Third Reich trail. So with all its Nazi and WWII associations, you may be surprised to hear that Bavaria's second city is also its most child-friendly, with heaps for the kids to do. It's also sticky flypaper for Renaissance art fans, enticed to the city by Dürer, who was born here. Stage coach, Nuremberg

Christmas Markets

10 It's Advent so pull on your woollies, grab a mug of mulled wine and a wedge of festive gingerbread and set out to discover southern Germany's fabled Yuletide markets (p21). Sprawled across ancient town squares in a Christmassy ruck of fairy lights, handmade ornaments, live nativity scenes and irresistible treats, they arouse a bagful of season's cheer as you hunt down those not-made-in-China (though look to make sure) gifts for folks back home. Nuremberg, Munich and Freiburg hold the biggest markets.

SHAWN HEMPEL/ALAMY®

TOM BONAVENTURE/GETTY IMAGES®

need to know

When To Go

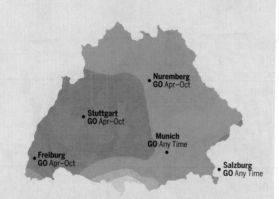

Nuremberg
GO Apr–Oct

Stuttgart
GO Apr–Oct

Munich
GO Any Time

Freiburg
GO Apr–Oct

Salzburg
GO Any Time

High Season
(May–Sep)

» Best time to travel: skies are bright and temperatures comfortable.

» Good for hiking and other outdoor pursuits; hanging out in beer gardens; attending festivals.

Shoulder
(Mar–May & Oct)

» Fewer tourists means lower prices and less crowded sights.

» Surprisingly pleasant weather and a riot of colour: wildflowers in spring, foliage in autumn.

Low Season
(Nov–Feb)

» With the exception of winter sports, activities focus more on culture and city life.

» Reduced opening hours or seasonal closures at museums, other sights and smaller guesthouses.

Your Daily Budget

Budget less than
€70

» Dorm beds: €15-30

» Lots of relatively cheap supermarkets for self-caterers; avoid overpriced markets

» In Munich, visit museums and galleries on Sundays when many charge €1 admission

Midrange
€70– €130

» Double room in a midrange hotel: around €80

» Main course in a midrange restaurant: €8-17

» Economy car rental: from around €30 per day (less if booked online in advance)

Top End over
€130

» Luxury hotel room: from €150

» Three-course meal in a good restaurant: around €45

Money

» ATMs widely available. Credit and debit cards accepted at most hotels and shops but not all restaurants.

Visas

» Generally not required for stays of up to 90 days; some nationalities will need a Schengen visa.

Mobile Phones

» Phones from most other countries work in Germany but attract roaming charges. Local SIM cards cost as little as €10.

Transport

» Drive on the right; steering wheels are on the left.

Websites

» **City of Munich** (www.muenchen.de) Official tourism site.

» **Bavarian Tourism Association** (www.bayern.by)

» **Black Forest Tourism** (www.blackforest-tourism.com)

» **Castles in Bavaria** (www.schloesser.bayern.de) Bavaria's palaces and castles.

» **State of Bavaria** (www.bayern.de) Official Bavarian government site.

» **Lonely Planet** (www.lonelyplanet.com/Germany) Travel news, forum, booking and more.

Exchange Rates

Australia	A$1	€0.80
Canada	C$1	€0.80
Japan	¥100	€1
New Zealand	NZ$1	€0.65
UK	UK£1	€1.25
USA	US$1	€0.80

For current exchange rates see www.xe.com

Important Numbers

Omit the area code if you are inside that area. Drop the initial 0 if calling from abroad.

Country code	+49
International access code	00
Emergency (police, fire, ambulance, mountain rescue)	112

Arriving in the Region

» **Munich Airport** Shuttle bus every 20 minutes to the Hauptbahnhof from 5am to 8pm. S-Bahn every 20 minutes, almost 24 hours. Taxi to city centre €50 to €70

» **Nuremberg Airport** U-Bahn every few minutes to the city centre. Taxi to city centre €16.

» **Salzburg Airport** City bus every 10 to 20 minutes to the Hauptbahnhof from 5.30am to 11pm. Taxi to city centre €20.

Packing for Southern Germany

Trips to Germany's south are often varied experiences, one day inspiring you to hike a trail in the Alps, another to enjoy Munich's cycle paths, the next to splurge on a fancy city centre restaurant – pack accordingly. Sturdy walking boots or trail shoes are a must, both for Alpine tracks and old town sightseeing, as well as a waterproof outer layer when the rain falls. Germans are quite easy-going about formal dress, but you may attract a few sour looks if you turn up to a fancy Munich eatery or the theatre in hiking gear, so crumple something smart casual into your case as well. Winters are bitterly cold so layers and woollens are essential between November and March; summers are often sweltering, though have a sweater or fleece handy for cool evenings in the Alps.

first time

Everyone needs a helping hand when they visit a country for the first time. There are phrases to learn, customs to get used to and etiquette to understand. The following section will help demystify southern Germany so your first trip goes as smoothly as your fifth.

Language

It's just about possible to get by in Germany's south without speaking any German whatsoever, but learning a few simple words and phrases will pay dividends in all kinds of situations from the restaurant table to the booking office. In big cities, such as Munich and Nuremberg, English is spoken by those who come into regular contact with foreigners, but this may not be the case in rural locations.

Booking Ahead

Booking a room in a foreign language can be a daunting task, so here are some phrases to see you through a call to the place you'd like to stay.

I would like to book a room.	Ich möchte bitte ein Zimmer reservieren.
a single room	ein Einzelzimmer
a double room	ein Doppelzimmer
My name is...	Mein Name ist …
from...to... (date)	vom … bis zum…
How much is it per night/person?	Wie viel kostet es pro Nacht/Person?
Thank you very much.	Vielen Dank.

What to Wear

In general, Germans are fairly laid back about clothing and you'll only need to think about apparel in certain specific situations. Smart casual will do for the vast majority of evening occasions and outside of more fashion-conscious Munich, you may be surprised how informally Germans dress for smart restaurants, the theatre and other special occasions. Only the most upmarket establishments may insist on jackets for men, but these are rare. Ties are only required in casinos and by flashier establishments. For sightseeing take sturdy shoes for all those cobbled streets and a waterproof coat; walking boots or trail shoes are essential if you are heading to the Alps or even for a walk around one of the region's many lakes. Even at the height of summer long sleeves are a must in the evenings, especially at altitude.

What to Pack

» Passport
» Credit/debit cards
» Driving licence
» Mobile phone charger
» Prescription medicines
» European plug adaptor
» Earplugs
» Spare glasses
» Hiking boots
» Camera
» Travel first-aid kit
» Penknife
» Sunhat
» Umbrella
» Waterproofs
» Phrasebook
» Bathing suit
» Flip-flops
» Sunglasses
» Sewing kit

Checklist

» Ensure your passport is valid for another four months after arrival in Germany.

» Check airline baggage restrictions.

» Inform your bank/ credit card company you'll be travelling in Germany.

» Make any necessary advance bookings (accommodation, transport etc).

» Make sure your travel insurance covers all planned activities.

» Check if your mobile/ cell phone will work in Germany.

» Find out what you need to provide to hire a car.

Etiquette

Southern Germans are a pretty rigid bunch with elderly people in particular expecting lots of set behaviour and stock phrases. It's easy to make a mistake, but the following should help you avoid red-faced moments.

» Greetings

Until noon say '*Guten Morgen*'; from noon until early evening this becomes '*Gruss Gott*'. '*Guten Abend*' is used from around 6pm onwards until it's time to say '*Gute Nacht*'. Use the formal '*Sie*' with strangers, and the informal '*du*' and first names if invited to do so. If in doubt, use '*Sie*'.

» At the table

Tucking into food before the '*Guten Appetit*' starting gun is fired is regarded as bad manners. Place your knife and fork parallel across your plate to show you've finished. When drinking wine, the toast is '*Zum Wohl*', with beer it's '*Prost*'.

» Other dos & don'ts

Always give your name at the beginning of a phone call. When visiting someone's home, bring a small gift such as flowers or wine. Punctuality is appreciated – never arrive more than 15 minutes late.

Tipping

» Essentials

You could get through an entire trip around southern Germany without giving a single tip. Few service industry employees expect them these days, although most still appreciate a little extra when it comes their way.

» Restaurants

Round up the bill (which already includes a service charge) to the nearest €5 (or €10) if you were satisfied with service.

» Taxis

Round up the fare to the nearest €5 so the driver doesn't have to hunt for change.

Money

Cash is still king in Germany's south with credit and debit cards used far less frequently than in Britain or the US. Most hotels, upmarket eateries and car rental companies normally take cards, but it's a good idea to check beforehand that this is the case with yours. Mastercard and Visa are the most widely accepted cards; businesses willing to take American Express and Diner's Club are rare indeed. Chip-and-pin is the normal way to validate a payment, though you may still be asked for a signature in some places. ATMs are ubiquitous in urban areas, and even smaller towns and villages will have a couple. Not all ATMs take all types of card, and some are reserved solely for the customers of the bank in which they are situated.

what's new

For this new edition of Munich, Bavaria & the Black Forest, our authors have hunted down the fresh, the transformed, the hot and the happening. These are some of our favourites. For up-to-the-minute recommendations, see lonelyplanet.com/Germany.

Museum of the Bavarian Kings

1 As if two of Germany's dreamiest castles, Neuschwanstein and Hohenschwangau, weren't enough, someone's gone and opened a must-see museum a short stroll away! Perched on the edge of the picturesque little Alpsee, this former lakeside hotel is full of Wittelsbach memorabilia and provides a bit more background on the castles you've probably just toured. (p108)

Museum Brandhorst
2 The biggest, brashest characters of pop art rule at the Brandhorst, an edgy addition to Munich's Kunstareal. Warhol, Hirst, Wombly, Flavin... the name-dropping list is long (p57).

Cuvilliés-Theater
3 One of Europe's finest rococo theatres reopened recently after a much-needed facelift. Wander the auditorium on a tour or dip into the programme of regular classical music concerts (p54).

Segway Tours
4 Strap on your helmet, climb aboard your whirring Segway and sweep effortlessly around the sights of Munich (p78) and Salzburg (p198).

Schweinemuseum
5 Probably only Germany could get away with opening the world's biggest pig museum...in a former slaughterhouse! But we won't *boar* you with the details of Stuttgart's newest attraction (p221).

Hotel Herrnschlösschen
6 The most characterful hotel to open on the Romantic Road in years occupies a 900-year-old mansion in Rothenburg's old town (p134).

Badeparadies
7 Saunas, palm-wafted lagoons, a wellness area, Black Forest views and aquafun with the kids at this new Titisee water park (p257).

Regensburg's Golf Museum
8 Humbly claiming to be Europe's second most important golf museum, this new repository of sporting tweed and yellowing scorecard is a must for the hole-in-one crowd (p171).

World Heritage Visitors Centre
9 With its interactive exhibitions and knowledgeable staff, Regensburg's impressive new Unesco World Heritage Visitors Centre is the place to kick off a wander through this fascinating city (p174).

Italian Jobs
10 No, we're not talking southern Europe's economic woes but the multitudo of Italian eateries that have opened in Munich in recent years, led by the superb La Baracca (p84) and XII Apostel (p87).

if you like...

Castles & Palaces

If castles are your thing, Bavaria is your place with some blockbuster piles hugging hilltops and hogging priceless city centre plots. Three cheers for King Ludwig II for commissioning the region's most charming chateaux, hardly any of which he saw completed.

Neuschwanstein King Ludwig's (and the world's) most celebrated castle is Bavaria's top must-see (p109).

Residenz (Munich) Revived from the rubble of WWII, the former residence of the Bavarian royal family is essential viewing (p52).

Linderhof Versailles-inspired Linderhof occupies a remote site surrounded by snow-capped peaks and pine forests (p113).

Herrenchiemsee Another of Ludwig II's 'Versailles in miniature' located on his own private island in the Chiemsee (p121).

Nymphenburg Munich's grandest pile is famous for its 'Gallery of the Beauties' and stately gardens (p65).

Residenz (Würzburg) One of Bavaria's most impressive palaces, Würzburg's Residenz was home to the local Prince-Bishops and boasts the largest ceiling fresco on earth (p127).

Cars & Trains

Germany and Bavaria are synonymous with high-tech industries and skilled engineering, particularly when it comes to cars. Explore the past and present of Bavaria's motor industry and discover its railway heritage at high-velocity museums.

BMW Welt & Museum Get up close and personal with BMW's high-octane present then hop across the bridge to what may just be the world's most exciting car museum (p63).

Deutsche Bahn Museum A wonderful repository of Germany's choo-choo past containing some of its best-known locos (p144).

Audi Museum Mobile Ingolstadt's Audi Museum will get a petrolhead's pulse racing (p176).

Bayerisches Eisenbahnmuseum Retirement home for Deutsche Bahn's steam locos of yesteryear, follow a tour of Nördlingen's railway museum with a ride on a heritage line along the Romantic Road (p137).

Mercedes-Benz Museum Complete your luxury car museum collection at this shrine to the Mercs of yesterday in Stuttgart (p217).

Museums

Bavaria's ruling Wittelsbach family certainly liked their art and their world-class collections now pack Munich's museums and galleries. Countless other repositories of the past tell southern Germany's tale with imagination and flair.

Münchner Stadtmuseum An innovatively conceived overview of the Bavarian capital's past created in 2008 to mark the city's 850th birthday (p50).

Alte Pinakothek One of Germany's finest art exhibitions from the Wittelsbachs' extensive collections and the high-brow highlight of Munich's Kunstareal (p56).

Pinakothek der Moderne Heaps of chunky retro design and artwork, plus temporary shows, pack out this minimalist, purpose-built Munich museum (p57).

Deutsches Museum If science normally shuts down your grey matter, head to this great museum where experiments and demonstrations bring out the boffin in everyone, especially kids (p70).

Germanisches Nationalmuseum Nuremberg's contribution to the Bavarian museum scene is this journey through Germany's cultural past (p147).

» Munich's Englischer Garden has plenty of the unexpected, including the opportunity to surf some waves (p61)

WWII Heritage

Southern Germany certainly has its fair share of dark tourism attractions, most of which date from the recent past. Visit sites made infamous by the Nazis during their rise to power and subsequent demise at the hands of the Allies.

Hitler's Eagle's Nest Soar into the Alps to this high perch built as Hitler's mountain retreat (p123).

Dachau Concentration Camp The Nazis' first concentration camp is a moving memorial that relates the inmates' stories in a particularly harrowing manner (p98).

Memorium Nuremberg Trials Visit the courtroom where many top-ranking Nazis were tried and sentenced for their crimes against humanity (p145).

Reichsparteitagsgelände Ever wondered where all that footage of a ranting Hitler and Sieg-Heiling masses was filmed? One of Nuremberg's most popular attractions (p145).

White Rose Memorial This small memorial within Munich's Ludwig-Maximilians-Universität commemorates students executed for anti-Nazi activities (p59).

Churches

From baroque riots to Gothic restraint, round-arched Romanesque to red-brick marvels, southern Germany's steadfast Catholic tradition has bequeathed the region a posse of show-stopping churches, often bejewelled with exquisite works of art.

Freiburg Münster A sandstone colossus presiding over Freiburg's historical core. Climb the tower for views as far as France (p248).

Wieskirche This Unesco-listed barrage of baroque ornamentation enjoys a pretty setting amid idyllic Alpine meadows (p113).

Frauenkirche No building in the city centre may rise higher than the bulbous spires of Munich's most recognizable temple (p55).

St Martin Church Talk about dominating a skyline! The spire of Landshut's basilica is the world's tallest brick structure at 130m (p179).

Ulmer Münster Ulm's massive cathedral may just prove that size *is* everything (p231).

Spas & Pools

Perhaps not instantly synonymous with spas and pools, southern Germany offers a surprising number of places to get pampered and pummelled, tossed around by a wave machine or just wet during a relaxing dip.

Baden-Baden The grand dame of central Europe's traditional spa towns and still a magnet for royalty, celebrities and wannabes, who come to strut along the promenades, pose in the casino and (perhaps) take the waters (p235).

Watzmann Therme Berchtesgaden's spa complex offers wellness, sport and saunas galore against a pristine Alpine backdrop (p124).

Alpamare No scary white coats or painful-sounding procedures at the spa town of Bad Tölz; just Europe's longest waterslide and an indoor surfing wave (p120).

Badeparadies Palm trees in the Black Forest? That's not the only surprise at this great new spa and water park (p257).

Müller'sches Volksbad Snap on your goggles and belly flop into Munich's most characterful swimming pool still bedecked in original Jugendstil (art nouveau) decoration (p76).

If You Like... Surfing
Pack your stick and head for Munich's Englischer Garten (p76) where the Eisbach canal forms a natural surfing wave. Hang ten here for the crowds if you can stand the cold outside the summer months.

Local Food & Drink

Dark and wheat, Bock and Doppelbock, light and smoked: it would seem Bavaria has a beer for every day of the year. Add a ker-sizzle of sausages and possibly the world's most scrumptious cake for an epic south German feast (p296).

Beer Every tipple has its true home – whisky belongs to Scotland, wine to France and beer to Bavaria.

Sausages You could easily put together a sausage-themed tour of southern Germany, from the *Weisswurst* of Munich, to the 30cm Coburg sausage to the finger-size links of Nuremberg.

Snowballs & gingerbread Rothenburg's sugar-dusted snowballs and Nuremberg's peppery gingerbread are just two of the region's tooth-rotters.

Black forest gateau Europe's tastiest cake is a mouth-watering combination of rich chocolate sponge, whipped cream and black cherries, infused with a splash of cherry brandy.

Wine Southern Germany's finest wines come from the south-facing slopes around Würzburg.

Lakes & Mountains

Bavaria claims just a sliver of the Alps but packs a lot into its mountain ranges. Between the peaks glisten glacier-fed lakes providing stop-and-stare vistas and ample opportunities for messing about on the water.

Zugspitze You won't need ropes or crampons to tackle Germany's highest peak – just a ticket for the train! (p115)

Starnbergersee A watery weekend destination for Munich city dwellers and the place where King Ludwig II drowned in unexplained circumstances (p100).

Garmisch-Partenkirchen The German Alps' premier resort with the state's longest skiing season and a spider's web of gentle hiking and cross-country skiing trails (p114).

Königssee Bavaria's most picturesque lake is cupped by bare peaks and is a great starting point for flits into the Alpine backcountry (p123).

Lake Constance Shared between Germany, Switzerland and Austria and by millions of snap-happy tourists who flock to its shores every year (p262).

Shopping

For every chain store and out-of-town megamall in Germany's south there's an independent boutique or family-run emporium selling those special items you just won't find back home.

Christmas markets Southern Germany's Yuletide bazaars are legendary with an international horde of shoppers packing the city centres of Munich (p79), Nuremberg (p149) and Salzburg (p199) to seek out those quirky gifts and to warm extremities with mulled wine and grilled sausages.

Dirndl & lederhosen If you're planning a session in a beer hall or garden, you may as well look the part. Plenty of outlets in Munich can squeeze you into the local tight-fitting traditional garb (p208).

Yuletide decorations It's Christmas every day of the year at Rothenburg's Weihnachtsdorf (Christmas Village) where you can buy a nativity scene in July or a Christmas tree at Easter time (p135).

Cuckoo clocks Triberg in the Black Forest is cuckoo central, though you can buy these inimitable timepieces across the region (p258).

month by month

Top Events

1 **Oktoberfest**, September

2 **Tollwood Festival**, July

3 **Christmas Markets**, December

4 **Salzburger Festspiele**, August

5 **Wagner Festival**, July

January

With the last corks of New Year popped, it's time to clear your head on the ski slopes of the Alps. Winter bites coldest in January so wrap up snug while sightseeing.

Hornschlittenrennen

Fun celebration on 6 January in Garmisch-Partenkirchen with locals racing downhill on period sleds once used for bringing hay and wood down to the valleys.

Mozartwoche

Since 1956 Salzburg has held a Mozart Week (p199) in late January to mark the great composer's birthday on 27th of the month. The event lures a spectacular list of internationally renowned conductors, soloists and orchestras.

February

The skiing season reaches its zenith with clogged pistes and queues at the ski lifts. Down in the valleys and on the plains you can probably kiss goodbye to the snow as the very first hints of spring appear.

Fasching (Carnival)

During the six-week pre-Lent period (January to February) preceding Ash Wednesday, many towns celebrate with silly costumes, waving parades, incomprehensible satirical shows and drunken revelry, especially in Munich (p78). Rio it ain't.

May

Spring has well and truly *gesprungen!* The cable cars are heaving hikers instead of skiers up the mountainsides and the beer garden season kicks off under flowering chestnut trees.

Maifest

On the eve of 1 May, the May Festival celebrates the end of winter with villagers chopping down a tree to make a *Maibaum* (maypole), painting, carving and decorating it, then partying around it.

Africa Festival

Bongo drums, hot rhythms and fancy costumes turn the banks of the Main River in Würzburg into Europe's largest international festival of black music. The event is held in late May and draws around 100,000 visitors.

July

Fleeing the city heat is as easy as buying a train ticket to the cooler air of the Alps. Return to an urban setting in the evenings as the festival season swings into action.

Tollwood Festival

Crowds flock to Munich's Olympiapark for this popular month-long world-culture festival (p78) with concerts, theatre, circus acts, readings and other fun events. Held from late June to late July, and also has a winter incarnation in December.

Christopher Street Day

Gay, lesbian, straight or transgender – everybody comes out to party at Munich's flashy gay parade (p78) held over two days in mid-July and attracting 50,000 revellers. Provocative costumes, rainbow flags, techno music and naked torsos guaranteed.

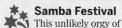

Samba Festival

This unlikely orgy of song and dance in mid-July draws a quarter of a million people to Coburg for three days of exotically colourful costumes, high-energy music and a procession of gyrating backsides (p163).

Wagner Festival

This prestigious festival (p160) held in Bayreuth from late July to August is *the* Wagner event of the year attracting opera-goers from every continent. Tickets are hard to come by and the opera house is a hot and hard-seated ordeal.

August

Summer is at its peak, the kids are off school, campsites fill with an international fleet of campervans, and the Alpine meadows reach their floral peak.

Sommerfest

Join in four days of gigs, food and partying by the River Neckar in Stuttgart (p218). Held in early August, if the weather is hot the event attracts half a million revellers.

Salzburg Festival

One of the most important classical-music festivals in Europe (p199), this premier event runs from late July to early September and features everything from Mozart to contemporary music, opera and theatre. Special performances for children also dot the programme.

Gäubodenvolksfest

This epic Oktoberfest-style drink-up and occasion for much red-faced revelry draws about a million people to little Straubing (p176) for 11 days starting on the second Friday of August. Expect lots of oompah music and traditional costumes as well as a fun fair for the little 'uns.

September

Autumn delivers its first nip, especially at altitude. Pupils return to their schools, students to uni and small-town Germany reverts to its predictable central European normality.

Oktoberfest

Oktoberfest (p22) should be under October, right? Wrong. It actually takes place more in September than October. The world's most celebrated guzzle fest is Bavaria's top event with five million raising a tankard or ten. *Prost!*

Cannstatter Volksfest

Very similar to Oktoberfest, Stuttgart's biggest beer festival (p219) takes place for two weeks from late September to mid-October and features processions, a fairground and a huge firework display to round things off.

Munich Marathon

Bavaria's top mass-participation running event wisely takes place just after Oktoberfest, keeping at least the runners sober in the weeks leading up to the race. The course skips through the historical centre before ending in a grandstand finish at the Olympic Stadium.

December

An eventful month with the ski season beginning in earnest and the 5 December visit by St Nick. Bavarian New Year's Eve celebrations see fireworks launched by thousands of amateur pyromaniacs.

Christmas Markets

Celebrate the holidays at glittery Christmas markets with mulled wine, gingerbread cookies and shimmering ornaments. The markets in Munich, Nuremberg, Freiburg and Salzburg are the most famous, but smaller ones sometimes have more local flavour. Open from late November to 24 December.

Oktoberfest

Need to Know

Where?
At the Theresienwiese to the west of the city centre. Poccistrasse and Theresienwiese are the nearest U-Bahn stations.

When?
For 16 days up to the first Sunday in October.
2013: 21 September to 6 October.
2014 & 2015: subtract a day from the start/finish of the previous year.

Hours?
Beer is served from 10am to 10.30pm Monday to Friday, 9am to 10.30pm Saturday and Sunday.
Other attractions and facilities open longer hours.

How Much?
Admission to the Oktoberfest: free
Price of a 1L *Mass* of beer: €9.50
Half a roast chicken: around €8

How Many?
Visitors: 6.5 million
Amount of beer consumed: over 7.5 million litres
Beer tents: 34 (14 large, 20 small)

Mass Hysteria

The world's largest drink-a-thon, the traditional highlight of Bavaria's annual events calender, is one of the best-known fairs on earth, aped the world over from Prague to Palestine. No other event manages to mix such a level of crimson-faced humour, drunken debauchery, excessive consumption of alcohol, and public peeing (known as *wildes Bieseln* in German) with so much tradition, history and oompah music.

As early as mid-July the brewery crews move in to start erecting the tents which almost fill the Theresienwiese, a gravelly open space in the western reaches of Munich city centre known locally as the Wiesn. When the canvas is taut, the space-age technology is in place to deliver millions of litres of beer to the taps, the Ferris wheel is ready to roll and tens of thousands of chickens are rotating on grills, the Wiesn is ready to welcome the 6.5 million people who arrive annually to toast Germany's 'city of beer'.

During the 16 days of festivities, most travellers dip in for a few days or perhaps a week, taking time off from the *Mass* (the towering 1L mugs of beer) to see Munich's sights and perhaps a castle or two. Whatever you decide to do, be sure to book everything up to a year in advance. And if you can't make it for Oktoberfest, fear not. Throughout the summer and autumn the region hosts countless other fests, often with more traditional, less commercial atmospheres (and cheaper beer). Erding and Straubing (p176) have particularly good events.

TOP 10 TIPS

» No cash changes hands within the beer tents – to be served beer, buy special metal tokens (*Biermarken*) from outside the tents. If you have tokens left over at the end of your session, you can spend them in some Munich pubs.

» From 2012 no more glass bottles are allowed at the Oktoberfest due to countless injuries in recent years.

» Food at Oktoberfest is as pricey as the beer, so bring your own snacks. These can be consumed on the outside terraces of the beer tents but not inside.

» Beer tents are elbow to elbow all day on Saturday and Sunday, but for lighter traffic try a weekday afternoon. Until Friday of the first week the evenings tend to be slightly less swamped as well.

» Don't even think of lighting up in any of the beer tents. 2010 new anti-smoking laws mean your time in the tent will be up and you could face a fine.

» If you pop out of a beer tent during the busy times, don't expect your seat to be free when you return.

» Don't drink in excess – the beer at Oktoberfest is strong stuff, and probably much more potent than your local brew.

» The vast majority of the beer tents have their last call at 10.30pm.

» The Wiesn has its own post office, left luggage office and childcare centre.

» You can reserve a seat at some of the beer tents up to a year in advance – see the tents' individual websites to find out how.

A Bit of History

The world's biggest foam fest has its origins in a simple horse race. In 1810 Bavarian crown prince Ludwig, later King Ludwig I, married Princess Therese of Saxe-Hildburghausen, and following the wedding a horse race was held at the city gates. The six-day celebration was such a galloping success that it became an annual event, was extended and moved forward to start in September so that visitors could enjoy warmer weather and lighter nights. The horse race, which quickly became a sideshow to the suds, ended in 1960, but an agricultural show is still part of the Oktoberfest.

Ozapft ist's!

Starting at 10.45am on the first day, the brewer's parade (the Festzug) travels through the city centre from the River Isar to the fairgrounds. This involves many old, brightly decorated horse-drawn carriages once used to transport kegs from brewery to pub and countless felt-hatted tag alongs. When the procession reaches the Wiesn, focus switches to the Schottenhamel beer tent and the mayor of Munich who, on the stroke of noon, takes a mallet and knocks the tap into the first keg. As the beer flows forth and the thirsty crowds cheer, the mayor exclaims: '*Ozapft ist's!*' (literally 'It's tapped' in Bavarian dialect). If you want to witness this ceremonial opening of the Oktoberfest, be sure to get there as early as 9am to bag a seat.

The Beer

Let's get down to the real reason most come to Oktoberfest – the beer. All the suds pulled at Oktoberfest must have been brewed within Munich's city limits which restricts the number of breweries permitted to wet your whistle to six: Hofbräu-München (of Hofbräuhaus fame), the world famous Paulaner, Löwenbräu, Augustiner, and the less well-known Hacker-Pschorr and Spaten.

The famous 1L *Mass* brought to your table by a dirndl-trussed waitress, contains pretty strong stuff as the breweries cook up special concoctions for the occasion (usually known as *Oktoberfestbier*). The percentage of alcohol starts at around 5.8% which makes a single *Mass* the equivalent of almost 3.5 pints of most regular ales in Britain, Australia and the US. Traditionally the most potent brews are piped to the Wiesn by Hofbräu, the weakest by Hacker Pschorr.

OKTOBERFEST'S ASTOUNDING STATS

» The biggest ever beer tent was the Bräurosl of 1913 which held a whopping 12,000 drinkers.

» Munich's biggest bash of the year has been cancelled an amazing 24 times, mostly due to cholera epidemics and war. There was no Oktoberfest during either world wars and in 1923 and 1924 inflation put paid to the festivities.

» If you are your party's nominated driver, don't think you're getting off lightly when it comes to the bill. A litre of water costs almost as much as a *Mass* of beer!

» Some 90,000L of wine are supped over the 16 days of Wiesn frolics.

» It takes around 10 weeks to erect the beer tents and five weeks to dismantle them.

» Around 12,000 waiters and waitresses are employed at Oktoberfest.

» Around 75% of the Munich Red Cross' annual workload occurs during Oktoberfest.

Not Just Beer

The Oktoberfest is not called the world biggest fair for nothing, and while most visitor's focus is on the *Bier*, there's quite a lot going on away from the tents.

The funfair with its big wheel, ye-olde test-your-strength booths and scarier 21st-century rides are obvious attractions but magic performances, an agricultural show (it's more interesting than it sounds) and stalls selling everything from Oktoberfest souvenirs to waffles constitute other minor diversions. The first Sunday sees an impressive costumed procession wend its way through Munich city centre, a tradition going back to 1835, and the customary religious Oktoberfest mass is held in the Hippodrom beer tent on the first Thursday. A brass band concert huffs and puffs beneath the Bavaria statue on the morning of the second Sunday near the spot from where the gun salute is fired on the last Sunday. These events are mostly attended by locals, but give a more traditional insight into the origins and customs of this blockbuster fair for those with a deeper, less inebriated interest.

Sleeping It Off

Your chances of scoring a room in Munich once the mayor has driven the tap into the famous first keg are next to nil, and even a bed in the dingiest of dorms will come with an absurd price tag. However, with Munich's excellent transport links to the rest of Bavaria, and the proximity of the Hauptbahnhof to the Theresienwiese, commuting in from Augsburg, Garmisch-Partenkirchen or In-golstadt, or even Salzburg and Nuremberg, is feasible. This secret got out long ago, and accommodation providers across Bavaria hitch up their rates from mid-September, but not as much as in Munich. Book accommodation just as the previous Oktoberfest is finishing if possible. If you decide to stay out of town, make sure you know when the last train back is, or you'll be spending a potentially chilly night at the Hauptbahnhof!

Camping is a fun and relatively inexpensive way to get around the accommodation shortage. **Wiesn Camp** (www.munich-oktoberfest .com) sets up shop every year at the Olympic Equestrian Centre in München-Riem, a 20-minute S-Bahn ride from the Hauptbahnhof. The site offers four-man tent hire for a between €59 and €69 a night. Another place you won't need your own rustling nylon is **The Tent** (www.the-tent.com) where you can bed down in the communal FloorTent for as little as €14 a night!

Family Fun

The two Tuesday afternoons (from noon to 6pm) are dedicated family days with reduced charges for funfair rides, special family oriented events, and lots of balloons and roasted almonds. Away from these days, the Augustiner Festhalle is regarded as the most family-friendly beer tent, but children are allowed into all the others. All tots under six must be out by 8pm every day. The tents have become better places for children since the music was turned down (until 6pm) and smoking was banned.

Dirnd...
Led...

Part o...
parh...
led...

» (above) Fairground, Oktoberfest
» (left) Marching band in traditional
dress, Oktoberfest

&
rhosen

the fun at the Wiesn is looking the
traditional Bavarian dirndl for the gals,
erhosen and felt hat for the guys. Dirndl
onsists of a figure-squeezing bodice, a frilly
blouse, a skirt that ends just below the knee
and an apron. The real deal costs a Hellenic
bailout of euros but Munich has countless
Trachten (folk costume) shops where cheaper versions can be bought. For second-hand
dirndl and lederhosen, try Holareidulijö
(p94).

Top Beer Tents

Here is our selection of the Wiesn's finest
marquees:

» **Hippodrom** (www.hippodrom-oktoberfest.de)
Seating 3200 inside, this popular tent attracts
a young crowd and the odd German celebrity.
Spatenbräu and Löwenbräu beers and top-notch
Bavarian food, plus lots of gobsmackingly pricey
champagne.

» **Hofbräu-Festzelt** (www.hb-festzelt.de)
Including the beer garden and standing room, this
tent can accommodate almost 10,000 drinkers. A
favourite among English-speaking visitors.

» **Schottenhamel** (www.festzelt.schottenhamel.
de) Where Munich's mayor kicks off the whole
caboodle with a little mallet.

» **Käfers Wiesen Schänke** Exellent food, longer
opening hours (to 12.30am) and Paulaner beer
make this a popular tent with partying celebs and
wannabes.

» **Glöckle Wirt** (www.gloeckle-wirt.de) If you
fancy something a bit different, this is one of the
most attractive, most intimate and the smallest of
the beer tents, bedecked with antiques and knick-
knacks of yesteryear.

Online Resources

» **Oktoberfest** (www.oktoberfest.de) The
definitive Oktoberfest website containing a wealth
of facts, figures and maps.

» **City of Munich** (www.muenchen.de) Click
through to the official Oktoberfest pages.

» **Oktoberfest-TV** (www.oktoberfest-tv.de)
Webcam coverage of the event plus heaps of info.

IMPORTANT OKTOBERFEST NUMBERS

Don't forget that when calling from a
mobile, the dialling code for Munich
is 089.
» **Security point** ☎5022 2366
» **First-aid post** ☎5022 2424
» **Oktoberfest police station** ☎500
3220
» **Guided tours of the Oktoberfest**
☎232 3900
» **Oktoberfest lost & found office**
☎2338 2825
» **Taxi** ☎21 610

» **Oide Wiesn** (www.oide-wiesn.de) Online
magazine (in German) providing a sober, more
high-brow view of the Oktoberfest and other
traditional celebrations.

» **Wiesn Countdown** (www.wiesn-countdown.
com) Find out exactly how many seconds remain
until the next Oktoberfest.

Dangers & Annoyances

Over seven million litres of strong Oktoberfest beer equates to a lot of intoxicating
ethanol and, as you might expect, drunkenness is the main source of danger during
Oktoberfest. Things tend to be pretty calm
within the beer tents themselves, but it's late
at night, when the elbow bending is over,
that trouble can flare up as the inebriated
masses stagger to the Hauptbahnhof and
other stations. Stay well clear of any bother.

For problems at the Wiesn itself, the
Oktoberfest has its own dedicated police
force, lost and found office, first-aid post and
fire brigade.

**Aktion Sichere Wiesn für Mädchen
und Frauen** (http://wiesn.amyna.de) offers
free multilingual assistance at Oktoberfest
to women who have been sexually harassed
or feel otherwise unsafe. It is located below
the Bavaria statue in the Service Centre
(Servicezentrum in German) and is open
from 6pm to 1am.

There have been rare cases of drink spik-
ing at Oktoberfest.

itineraries

Whether you've got six days or 60, these itineraries provide a starting point for the trip of a lifetime. Want more inspiration? Head online to lonelyplanet. com/thorntree to chat with other travellers.

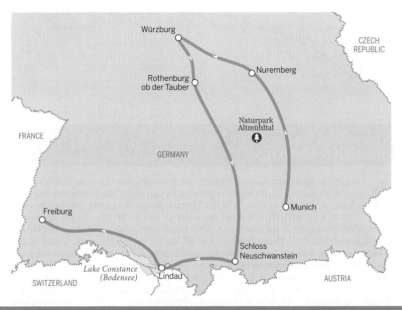

Ten Days
Southern Germany Highlights

Kick off your south German odyssey in **Munich** where three days is barely enough time to sample the Bavarian capital's museums, nightlife and celebrated brews. A short hop north by train brings you to **Nuremberg**, the bustling capital of Franconia and a major draw for fans of both dark tourism and dark beer. Another train, another historic city, this time university town **Würzburg** where fine wine has flowed for centuries and the prince-bishop's residence constitutes one of Bavaria's most impressive palaces. You're now at the northern terminus of the Romantic Road, which runs south for 350km. The most engaging stop along the route is **Rothenburg ob der Tauber**, a labyrinth of medieval streets and lanes with heaps of eye-candy architecture. The Romantic Road ends at the gates of **Schloss Neuschwanstein**, Bavarian King Ludwig II's fairytale pad and one of the world's most iconic 19th-century follies. Perhaps stopping off at **Lindau** on the shores of Lake Constance on the way, next stop is **Freiburg** in the southern Black Forest, where you can follow a tour of the mammoth Münster with a slab of the famous local gâteau.

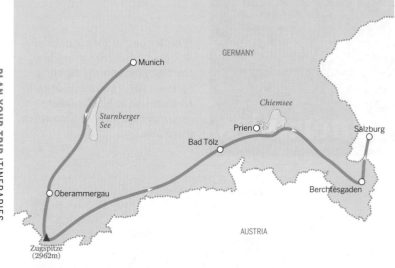

Ten Days
Munich & the Alps

> The following itinerary can be tackled as a point-to-point trip or as individual day trips from Munich; the bracing air, cobalt skies and glassy lakes of the German Alps are easily reachable by train from the Bavarian capital. Beginning in **Munich**, you'll need at least three days to cover the essential viewing in this vibrant metropolis, perhaps reserving a bit of time for a spot of shopping and to visit some of the city's lesser known sights such as the Olympiapark and BMW Welt. If there's time, make a dash on the S-Bahn for gobsmackingly beautiful **Starnberger See** to enjoy a relaxing stroll along the pebbly shore. Pretty **Oberammergau**, famous for its once-a-decade passion play, is just over two hours (with changes) on the train from Munich's Hauptbahnhof and makes a superb base for visiting King Ludwig II's Schloss Linderhof, an easy going 12km hike. Then it's time to stand on the roof of Germany: the **Zugspitze** above Garmisch-Partenkirchen, the Bundesrepublik's highest peak. If you don't have your own wheels you'll have to backtrack all the way to Munich to reach the pleasant spa town of **Bad Tölz**, the heart of the Tölzer Land and home to Alpamare, the region's best water park. Heading east, more train connections will have you on the shores of the **Chiemsee** in no time. Water sports are one of the big draws here, though most come to ogle at another of Ludwig II's palaces, Schloss Herrenchiemsee, set on an island (the Herreninsel) in the lake and accessible by ferry from the town of Prien. After a day of messing around on the *wasser*, it's back into the mountains, this time the ranges around **Berchtesgaden** in Germany's extreme southeastern tip. Drawing in many visitors is the area's intriguing Nazi history, particularly Hitler's mountain perch, the Eagle's Nest, now a seasonal restaurant. For an equally photogenic escapade, take one of the electric boats from Berchtesgaden along the stunningly picturesque Königssee, surrounded by the Berchtesgaden National Park. From Berchtesgaden it's a short bus ride across the border into Austria and a day or two of *Sound of Music*–mania in achingly beautiful **Salzburg**.

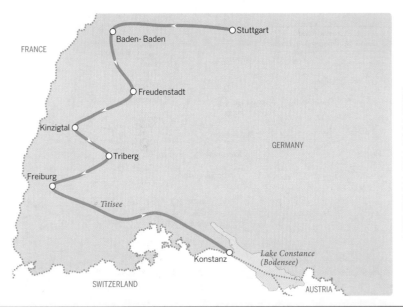

One Week
Stuttgart & Black Forest

Begin with a couple of days exploring the galleries, stately plazas and vibrant nightlife of regional capital **Stuttgart**. High on your agenda should be the city's regal heart, Schlossplatz, the Staatsgalerie's art treasures and evenings spent sampling local rieslings in a *Weinstube* (wine tavern) or hanging out in Theodor-Heuss-Strasse's lounge bars. Car fans should race to the space-age Mercedes-Benz and Porsche museums. On day three, head west to **Baden-Baden**, a swish art nouveau spa town picturesquely nestled at the foot of the Black Forest's spruce-cloaked hills. Here you can wallow in thermal waters as the Romans once did, saunter through the sculpture-speckled Lichtentaler Allee gardens and try your luck in the ever-grand casino. Day four takes you south along the serpentine Schwarzwald-Hochstrasse, or B500, with tremendous forest and mountain panoramas at every bend. Stop to glimpse Germany's largest square in **Freudenstadt** on your way to the curving **Kinzigtal**, the prettiest valley in this neck of the woods, with its orchards, vineyards and cluster of half-timbered villages waiting to be ticked off like rosary beads. Your fifth day takes you to the Black Forest's most storied town, **Triberg**, where Germany's highest waterfall flows, the world's biggest cuckoo clock calls, and Claus Schäfer bakes *the* best black forest gateau using the original 1915 recipe. Work off the cake with a walk or cross-country ski in the wooded heights of Martinskapelle or Stöcklewaldturm. A scenic hour's drive from Triberg brings you to the sunny university city of **Freiburg**, close to the French border. Spend the day absorbing its easygoing flair in the Altstadt's quaint lanes, watched over by a monster of a medieval minster. Wind out your final day by the lake. Swinging east brings you to forest-rimmed **Titisee** en route to the watery expanse of **Lake Constance**, Central Europe's third largest lake, flanked by quaint villages, vineyards, wetlands and beaches. An afternoon in **Konstanz** is just long enough to get a taste of this Roman-rooted city, where the historic alleys of the Altstadt wend down to a relaxed lakefront promenade.

One Week
Romantic Road

The Romantic Road begins its 350km way through Bavaria's western reaches at **Würzburg** where you should take at least two days to tour the impressive Baroque Residenz and sample the wines produced within view of the city centre. From here carve your way south to magical **Rothenburg ob der Tauber** where you can lose yourself in the tangle of medieval lanes and celebrate Christmas every day. Perhaps with a stop-off at Feuchtwangen, your next destination is quaint little **Dinkelsbühl**, a medieval gem ringed by a complete set of town walls. More medieval defences ring **Nördlingen**, a less touristy but equally attractive stopover. Then set aside some time to check out the storybook castle guarding the half-timbered village of **Harburg**, and to stroll through twee **Donauwörth** before hitting the energetic city of **Augsburg**. Countless churches grace the Romantic Road but, to Augsburg's south, the one packing the mightiest punch is the luminous Wieskirche. Contemplate King Ludwig II's flights of fancy at his whimsical castle, **Schloss Neuschwanstein**, where Germany's most popular tourist route comes to a fittingly fairytale climax.

One Week
Nuremberg & Franconia

With the exception of the Naturpark Altmühltal, this itinerary is best tackled as a series of excursions from **Nuremberg**, using Bavaria's excellent railways. The lively capital of Franconia has bags to see and do – including the Nuremberg trials courtroom, the Germanisches Nationalmuseum and the Deutsche Bahn Railway Museum – and an embarrassment of eateries to choose from when you return from exploring the region. A close second in Franconia's pecking order is Unesco-listed **Bamberg**, a confusion of ancient bridges, winding cobbled streets and riverside cottages, the air perfumed by numerous breweries producing the town's unique smoked beer. An hour's train ride brings you to **Bayreuth**, famous for its annual Wagner Festival but a pleasant place to stroll any time of year. Around 100km north of Nuremberg, **Coburg** is memorable for its fortress, its British Royal family connections and the longest sausages you'll ever eat served in the smallest bread buns. Round off your time in Franconia with a hike, bike or canoe trip (requiring more time) through the glorious **Altmühltal Nature Park**.

Outdoor Activities

Best...

Skiing
Garmisch-Partenkirchen (p114) A holy grail for downhill skiers, with titanic peaks, groomed slopes and an impeccable snow record.

Hiking
Black Forest (p235) Mile after pine-scented mile of trails weaving through forests, mist-enshrouded valleys and half-timbered villages freshly minted for a fairy tale.

Mountaineering
Bavarian Alps (p108) Grapple with limestone peaks in this mountaineering wonderland.

Windsurfing
Walchensee (p120) Let your sail catch the breeze on this jewel-coloured, mountain-rimmed lake.

Cycling
Altmühltal Radweg (p164) A 'Best of Bavaria' bike ride, taking in river bends and dense forests, ragged limestone cliffs and castle-topped villages.

Bavaria and the Black Forest live up to their reputations as splendid outdoor playgrounds. There's plenty to do year-round, with each season offering its own special delights, be it hiking among spring wildflowers, swimming in an Alpine lake warmed by the summer sun, biking among a kaleidoscope of autumn foliage or celebrating winter by skiing through deep powder.

Hiking & Mountaineering

Der Weg ist das Ziel (the journey is the reward) could be the perfect strapline for Bavaria and the Black Forest. No matter whether you want to peak-bag in the Alps, stroll gently among fragrant pines with the kids or embark on multiday treks over hill and forested dale, this region is brilliant for exploring on foot.

Trails are usually well signposted, sometimes with symbols quaintly painted on tree trunks. To find a route matching your fitness level and timeframe, pick the brains of local tourist office staff, who can also supply you with maps and tips. Many offer multiday 'hiking without luggage' packages that include accommodation and luggage transfer between hotels.

The sky-scraping peaks of the Bavarian Alps are Germany's mountaineering heartland. Here you can pick between day treks and multiday hut-to-hut clambers, though you'll need to be reasonably fit and come equipped with the right gear and topographic maps or GPS. Trails can be steep and

STAR TREKS FOR...

» **Alpine hikers** Swoon over views of colossal mountains and jewel-coloured lakes hiking in the Berchtesgaden National Park (p124) and Oberstdorf (p118).

» **Family ramblers** Kiddies love the wondrous **Partnachklamm gorge** (www. partnachklamm.eu; adult/child €3/1.50; ⊙9am-5pm Oct-Easter, 8am-6pm Easter-Sep) and red squirrel-spotting on the trail shadowing the 163m **Triberger Wasserfall** (adult/concession €3.50/3; ⊙Mar–early-Nov, 25-30 Dec) Germany's highest waterfall.

» **Serious mountaineers** One word: Zugspitze (p115). The tough ascent and phenomenal four-country views are breathtaking in every sense of the word.

» **Long-distance hikers** Trek Bavaria's beautiful 200km Altmühltal Panoramaweg (p164) or the 280km Westweg (p242), the ultimate walk in the Black Forest.

» **Wildlife spotters** Wander silently for the chance to see deer, otters, and woodpeckers in the Bavarian Forest National Park (p183) and eagles, chamois, marmots and salamanders in Berchtesgaden National Park (p124).

» **Escapists** Seek solace hiking in the fir-cloaked hills of the Black Forest (p235) and the Bavarian Forest National Park (p183).

narrow, with icy patches lingering even in summer. Before heading out, seek local advice on routes, equipment and weather. If you're inexperienced, ask tourist offices about local outfitters offering instruction, equipment rental and guided tours.

The **Deutscher Alpenverein** (DAV; ☑089-140 030; www.alpenverein.de) is a goldmine of information on hiking and mountaineering, and has local branches in practically every town. It maintains hundreds of Alpine mountain huts, where you can spend the night and get a meal. Local DAV chapters also organise courses (climbing, mountaineering etc), as well as guided treks. If you're planning multiday treks, becoming a member of the organisation can yield a 30% to 50% discount on Alpine huts and other benefits, including insurance.

For climbing routes, gear, walls and more, visit www.dav-felsinfo.de, www.klettern.de and www.climbing.de (all in German).

When to Walk

The summer months are the best for walking in the Alps, when snow retreats to the highest peaks, and wildflowers carpet the slopes. Rush hour is from July to August when you'll need to book hut accommodation well in advance. Autumn has its own charm, with fewer crowds and a riot of colour in deciduous forests. Snow makes it impossible to undertake high-altitude walks during the rest of the year. Many of the big resorts, however, are criss-crossed with winter walking trails, and crunching through

snow with a crisp blue sky overhead certainly has its own magic.

Resources

» **German National Tourist Office** (www. germany.travel) Your first port of call, with information in English on walking in Bavaria and the Black Forest.

» **Kompass** (www.kompass.de, in German) Has a reliable series of 1:25,000 scale walking maps, which come with booklets listing background information on trails.

» **Wanderbares Deutschland** (www. wanderbares-deutschland.de) Features the lowdown on dozens of walking trails and has a handy interactive map. Some routes are also detailed in English.

» **Wandern ohne Gepäck** (www.wandern-ohne -gepaeck-deutschland.de, in German) Touch base with the 'hiking without luggage' specialists.

Winter Sports

Modern lifts, primed ski runs from easy-peasy blues to death-wish blacks, solitary cross-country trails, log huts, steaming mulled wine, hearty dinners by a crackling fire – these are the hallmarks of a German skiing holiday.

The Bavarian Alps, only an hour's drive south of Munich, offer the best downhill slopes and most reliable snow conditions. The most famous and ritzy resort is **Garmisch-Partenkirchen** (☑4931, 74260; www .skischule-gap.de; Am Hausberg 8; 1-day group lessons €35, ski gear €25), which hosted the FIS

» (above) Mountain biking, Garmisch-
Partenkirchen
» (left) Skiiers, Upper Bavaria

Alpine Skiing World Championship 2011 and is but a snowball's throw from Germany's highest peak, 2962m Zugspitze. The resort has 60km of slopes to pound, mostly geared towards intermediates, and a one-day ski pass costs €36.

Picture-book pretty Oberstdorf (p118) in the Allgäu Alps forms the heart of the Oberstdorf-Kleinwalsertal ski region, where 125km of slopes are covered by a one-day ski pass costing €41.50. It's a good pick for boarders, with snow parks and a half-pipe to play on, and cross-country skiers who come to glide along 75km of classic and 55km of skating tracks. For low-key skiing and stunning scenery, there is **Jenner** (✆958 10; www.jennerbahn.de; daily pass adult/child €29.20/15.50) near Berchtesgaden, with vertical drops up to 600m and truly royal vistas of the emerald Königssee, and family-magnet Kranzberg in Mittenwald (p118).

Elsewhere in the country, the mountains may not soar as high as in the Alps, but assets include cheaper prices (with day passes hovering between €25 and €30), smaller crowds, and resorts with a low-key atmosphere suited to families. The Bavarian Forest (p182) and the Black Forest (p235) have the most reliable snow levels, with moderate downhill action on the Grosser Arber and Feldberg mountains respectively.

At higher elevations, the season generally runs from late November/early December to March. Resorts have equipment-hire facilities. Skis, boots and poles cost around €20 or 12 for downhill or cross-country gear. Group lessons cost €30 to €45 per day.

Resources

» **Bergfex** (www.bergfex.com) A handy website with piste maps, snow forecasts of the Alps and details of German ski resorts.

» **On the Snow** (www.onthesnow.co.uk) Reviews of Germany's ski resorts, plus snow reports, webcams and lift pass details.

» **Skiresort** (www.skiresort.de) Ski resorts searchable by map and region, with piste details, pass prices and more.

Cycling & Mountain Biking

Strap on your helmet! Bavaria and the Black Forest are superb cycling territory, whether you're off on a leisurely lakeside spin or a multiday bike touring adventure. Practically every town and region has a network of signposted bike routes. For day tours, staff at the local tourist offices can supply you with ideas, maps and advice.

Mountain biking is hugely popular in the Black Forest and in the Alpine region,

---

THE BIG CHILL

If climbing mountains or whizzing down slopes has left you frazzled and achy, a trip to a day spa may be just the ticket. Every place has its own array of massages and treatments. Not a stitch of clothing is worn in German saunas, so leave your modesty in the locker, and always bring or hire a towel.

» **Friedrichsbad** (✆275 920; www.roemisch-irisches-bad.de; Römerplatz 1; 3hr ticket €23, incl soap-and-brush massage €33; ⊗9am-10pm, last admission 7pm) The crown jewel of Baden-Baden's spas, with its Roman Irish bath and Carrera marble pool.

» **Watzmann Therme** (✆946 40; www.watzmann-therme.de; Bergwerkstrasse 54; 2hr/4hr/day €9.70/12.20/13.90; ⊗10am-10pm) Perfect for a soak in the Bavarian Alps.

» **Sanitas Spa** (✆860 20; www.sanitas-spa.de; Gartenstrasse 24; admission half-/full-day €24/40; ⊗9.30am-8pm) Snuggled in the Black Forest, this Triberg spa has first-class treatments, a pool with views of forest-draped hills and, ahhh… blissfully few crowds.

» **Kaiser-Friedrich-Therme** (Langgasse 38-40; per hr May-Aug €4.50, Sep-Apr €6; ⊗10am-10pm, to midnight Fri & Sat Sep-Apr) Splash around as the Romans once did at this regal-looking spa in Wiesbaden, where spring water bubbles up at 66.4°C.

» **Rupertustherme** (✆01805-606 706; Friedrich-Ebert-Allee 21; 4hr ticket €14, incl sauna €19; ⊗9am-10pm) Saline-spring day spa with big Alpine views.

» **Alpamare** (✆509 999; www.alpamare.de; Ludwigstrasse 14; day pass adult/child €34/24; ⊗9.30am-10pm) Great family all-rounder with surfing, water slides and a wave pool for kids, mineral baths, saunas and treatments for grown-ups.

TOP FIVE BIKE TOURING TRAILS

» **Altmühltal Radweg** (160km) Easy to moderate route from Rothenburg to Beilngries, following the Altmühl River through the Altmühltal Nature Park.

» **Donauradweg** (434km) Travelling from Neu-Ulm to Passau, this is a delightful, easy to moderate riverside trip along one of Europe's great streams.

» **Romantische Strasse** (359km) Würzburg to Füssen; this easy to moderate route is one of the nicest ways to explore Germany's most famous holiday route, though it can get busy during the summer peak season.

» **Bodensee-Königssee Radweg** (418km) Lindau to Berchtesgaden; a moderate route running along the foot of the Alps with magnificent views.

» **Bodensee Cycle Path** (273km) Mostly flat, well-marked, tri-country route, which does a loop of Europe's third largest lake, taking in vineyards, meadows, orchards, wetlands, historic towns and Alpine vistas.

especially around Garmisch-Partenkirchen (p114), Berchtesgaden (p123) and Freudenstadt (p243). The Bavarian Forest is another top destination for mountain bikers with more than 450km of challenging routes and climbs. The mountain-bike elite comes to the Black Forest for several international MTB races, including the Black Forest **Ultra Bike Marathon** (www.ultra-bike.de) in June, the **Worldclass MTB Challenge** (www.womc.de) in July and the **Vaude Trans Schwarzwald** (www.trans-schwarzwald.com) in August.

Southern Germany is criss-crossed by dozens of long-distance trails, making it ideal for *Radwandern* (bike touring). Routes are well signposted and are typically a combination of lightly travelled back roads, forestry tracks and paved highways with dedicated bike lanes.

Bike Rental

Most towns have at least one bike-hire station (often at or near the train station), usually with a choice of city, mountain, electro and children's bikes. Depending on the model, you'll pay between €8 to €40 per day or €50 to €120 per week, plus a deposit.

Route Planning

For inspiration and route planning, check out www.germany-tourism.de, which provides (in English) an overview of routes, helpful planning tips, a route finder and free downloads of route maps and descriptions. For more detailed route descriptions German readers can consult www.schwarzwald-bike.de, www.blackforest-tourism.com and www.bayernbike.de. The **Galli Verlag** (www.galli-verlag.de) publishes a variety of bike guides sold in bookshops and by the publisher.

Maps & Resources

For basic route maps, order or download the free *Bayernnetz für Radler* (Bavarian Cycling Network) from www.bayerninfo.de. For on-the-road navigating, the best maps are those published by the national cycling organization **Allgemeiner Deutscher Fahrrad Club** (www.adfc.de). They indicate inclines, track conditions and the location of repair shops. GPS users should find the UTM grid coordinates useful.

ADFC also publishes a useful online directory called Bett & Bike (p315) that lists thousands of bicycle-friendly accommodations. Bookstores carry the printed version.

Water Sports

There's no sea for miles but southern Germany's lakes and rivers offer plenty of water-based action. The water quality is high, especially in the glacier-fed Alpine lakes, but the swimming season is relatively short (June to September) since water temperatures rarely climb above 21°C. Steady breezes, deep water and good visibility attract windsurfers and divers to the dazzlingly turquoise, mountain-backed Walchensee in Tölzer Land (p120). Starnberger See (p100), Lake Constance (p262), the fjordlike Schluchsee (p257) and Chiemsee (p121) offer great windsurfing, sailing and boating in lovely surroundings.

Kayaking and canoeing are great fun and easy to get the hang of. One of the most popular areas to absorb the slow, soothing rhythm of waterways is the Altmühltal Nature Park (p164), where the mellow Altmühl River meanders past steep cliffs, willow-fringed banks and little beaches.

Travel with Children

Best Places for Kids

Nuremberg
Bavaria's most child-friendly city with attractions as diverse as the Deutsche Bahn Museum, a school museum and a zoo.

Munich
Plenty of hands-on and high-octane diversions as well as a classic toy museum and fantastic trams to ride all day.

Rothenburg ob der Tauber
Edible snowballs and Christmas tree lights in the heat of the summer holidays – pure magic if you're six.

Europa-Park
Europe in miniature and Welt der Kinder (Children's World) at Germany's biggest theme park.

Ulm
Most kids love Lego and most adults love the fact Legoland keeps them occupied for a few hours.

Triberg
Some kids will burst into tears at the sight of a titchy bird lurching out of a clock, others will go cuckoo at the very thought.

With its tradition of lager and beer halls, lederhosen and tipsy oompah ensembles, you'd be excused for thinking southern Germany is a wholly unsuitable place to bring the little'uns. But you'd be wrong. Germany's south, especially its larger cities, lays on lots of tot-focused activities. In fact, having kids on board can make your holiday a more enjoyable experience and bring you closer to the locals than a few tankards of ale ever would.

On the Ground

In Transit

Trains are preferable to buses when travelling with toddlers as they can leave their seats and wander around quite safely. All trains have at least half a carriage dedicated to carrying prams (and bikes and wheelchairs) and copious amounts of luggage.

Most forms of city transport – such as Munich's trams, trains and underground – are pram-friendly and lifts are ubiquitous. Various discounts are available for families.

Most car-hire companies provide child booster and baby seats. They are often free but must be reserved in advance.

Feeding Frenzy

When it comes to feeding the pack, Germany's south is one of Europe's easier destinations. Most restaurants welcome young diners with smaller portions, special menus and perhaps even a free balloon.

Youngsters under 16 are allowed into pubs and bars at any time, as long as they are accompanied by a parent. This includes beer halls and gardens, the latter being particularly popular with families who can bring their own picnics. Thanks to Germany's smoking ban, fume-filled premises are a thing of the past.

Breastfeeding in public is perfectly acceptable.

All Change

City centres can be a headache for parents of nappy-wearing children – your best bet is to dip into a department store, though these usually position their toilets as far away from the entrance as possible, on the very top floor. Things are better at places of interest, and at child-centric attractions nappy-changing amenities are first rate.

The Best...

Family tickets are available at the vast majority of sights. It's always worth asking if there's a discount, even if none is advertised.

Museums

» **Deutsches Museum, Munich** The KinderReich at Munich's science museum is hands-on fun.

» **Deutsche Bahn Museum, Nuremberg** Germany's top railway museum has a huge interactive section for choo-choo enthusiasts.

» **Children & Young People's Museum, Nuremberg** Heaps of hands-on experiments.

» **Weihnachtsdorf, Rothenburg ob der Tauber** This Romantic Road institution houses a hands-off museum meaning kids are usually more interested in the adjacent Yuletide superstore.

» **Spielzeugmuseum, Munich** An I-had-that-in-1974 kinda museum, so not just for kids.

» **Bayerisches Eisenbahnmuseum, Nördlingen** Retired locos to clamber around on and seasonal steam train rides.

» **Spielzeugmuseum, Salzburg** Classic toy museum with Punch and Judy shows and free tea for the adults.

Fresh-Air Fun

» **Playground of the Senses, Nuremberg** Education by stealth at this large open-air experiment park.

KINDERLAND BAVARIA

Overseen by the Bavarian tourist board, the Kinderland Bavaria programme guarantees the good standard of children's facilities as well as rating amenities used by holidaying families. Businesses sporting the Kinderland Bavaria logo have been checked for everything from toy safety to availability of pram storage.

» **Englischer Garten, Munich** Large playground, ice creams, boat rides and acres of grass.

» **Steinwasen Park, Black Forest** Alpine animals, rides and a huge hanging bridge.

» **Tierpark Hellabrunn, Munich** Themed playgrounds, a cafe, feeding sessions and a special children's zoo.

Rainy Day Sights

» **Playmobil, Nuremberg** Headquartered in Zindorf just outside Nuremberg, the adjoining fun park is one of the city's best family attractions.

» **Münchner Marionettentheater, Munich** Bavaria's top puppet theatre.

» **BMW Welt, Munich** Grip the wheel of BMW's latest models and wish you were old enough to have a driver's licence.

» **Alpamare, Bad Tölz** Aqua-fun for all the family at Bavaria's best water park.

Planning
When to Go

The best times to visit are spring and early autumn. Summer temperatures see the niggle factor climb and central Europe's sub-zero winters are no fun.

Sleeping

The majority of hotels and guesthouses are pretty kid-friendly and the higher up the food chain you ascend, the more facilities (baby-sitting, laundry) there are likely to be. Small-hotel and guesthouse owners are generally willing to supply extra beds and even cots for babies. Of course campsites are the most entertaining places to stay; some have playgrounds and kids' clubs.

regions at a glance

Munich

History ✓✓✓
Museums ✓✓✓
Beer ✓✓✓

History
As the capital of Bavaria for the last five centuries, Munich has naturally played a pivotal role in its history and is the best place to explore the region's narrative. Losing yourself in the House of Wittelsbach's opulent Residenz, taking a guided tour of Nazi-related sites or discovering the city's recent sporting past at the Olympiapark and Allianz Arena are just some of the experiences on offer.

Museums
From the hands-on fun of the Deutsches Museum to the high-brow, hands-off masterpieces of the Alte Pinakothek; the outrageous pop art of the Museum Brandhorst to the waxed classics of the BMW Museum; and the exotic loot displayed at the Staatliches Museum für Völkerkunde (Museum of Ethnology) to the vats and steins of the Bier & Oktoberfestmuseum, Munich has a repository of the past for every rainy day, and one for most days when the sun's out, too.

Beer
Mammoth beer halls swaying to the oompah beat; chestnut-canopied beer gardens with tradition going back two centuries; proud breweries constantly striving to out-brew their rivals; breakfasts of Weissbier, *Weisswurst* and pretzel; an annual per capita ale consumption of almost 200L; and the world's biggest booze-up, the Oktoberfest – Munich, is the unchallenged beer capital of the world.

p42

Bavaria

Castles ✓✓✓
Romance ✓✓✓
Mountains ✓✓

Castles
From spectacular hilltop follies such as Neuschwanstein to medieval strongholds like Nuremberg's Kaiserburg, visits to castles and palaces provide some of Bavaria's most memorable experiences.

Romance
Whether it be the panorama from an Alpine peak or a lazy cruise along the Danube, Bavaria packs in a lot of dreamy encounters. But the biggest chunk of romance comes in the form of the Romantic Road, a mostly rural route meandering from one time-warped medieval town to the next.

Mountains
Compared to its neighbours, Bavaria possesses but a scant sliver of the Alps, but there's still bags of dramatic scenery out there to enjoy. Clearly visible and easily reachable from Munich, winter skiing and summer hiking are the main draws.

p104

Salzburg & Around

Art & Music ✓✓✓
Baroque Rocks ✓✓✓
Mythical Mountains ✓✓

Art & Music
In the city that sired Mozart, music is in Salzburg's blood. *Sound of Music* bike tours rattle through the tangled lanes, while classical music climaxes during August's Salzburg Festival. Find world-class art in cutting-edge galleries, baroque palaces and out on the street.

Baroque Still Rocks
The joke 'If it's not baroque, don't fix it' is a perfect maxim for Salzburg, and it's all thanks to the high-minded prince-archbishops. Ramble among architectural riches like the lordly Residenz and Dom in the Unesco World Heritage–listed Altstadt.

Mountains of Myth
Mother Superior sang about climbing every mountain, but now cable cars zip up Salzburg's peaks. Take in the full sweep of the city from Mönchsberg and Kapuzinerberg, hike, ski and paraglide at Untersberg and Gaisberg, or delve into the Alps for serious outdoor action.

p185

Stuttgart & the Black Forest

Lyrical Landscapes ✓✓✓
Outdoor Activities ✓✓✓
Cultured Cities ✓✓✓

Lyrical Landscapes
The Black Forest is fairy-tale Germany in a nutshell. This forested patchwork of hills and valleys, where waterfalls and brooks run swift and clear, is one of the region's greatest escapes. Tiptoe off the beaten track to half-timbered villages and tucked-away farmhouses.

Outdoor Activities
Big views, bracing air and well-marked trails lure you outdoors. Strap on boots for some of Germany's best hiking or swish through snowy woodlands while cross-country skiing. Lake Constance is perfect cycling terrain.

Cultured Cities
Stuttgart woos with outstanding galleries, concert halls and high-tech temples to the automobile, but there's more. Soak in the spas of Baden-Baden, hang out in Roman-rooted Konstanz, and spy the world's tallest steeple in Ulm.

p213

> **Every listing is recommended by our authors, and their favourite places are listed first**

> **Look out for these icons:**

 Our author's top recommendation

 A green or sustainable option

 No payment required

See the Index for a full list of destinations covered in this book.

On the Road

Munich

🎵089 / 1.38 MILLION / 310 SQ KM

Best Places to Eat

» Fraunhofer (p86)

» Königsquelle (p84)

» Tantris (p85)

» Prinz Myshkin (p84)

» Marais (p86)

Best Places to Stay

» Bayerischer Hof (p79)

» La Maison (p80)

» Hotel Laimer Hof (p80)

» Anna Hotel (p81)

» Cortiina (p80)

Why Go?

The natural habitat of well-heeled power dressers and leder-hosen-clad thigh-slappers, Mediterranean-style street cafes and Mitteleuropa beer halls, high-brow art and high-tech in-dustry, Germany's second city is a flourishing success story that revels in its own contradictions. If you're looking for Alpine clichés, they're all here, but the Bavarian metropolis sure has many an unexpected card down its dirndl.

Statistics show Munich is enticing more visitors than ever, especially in summer and during Oktoberfest. Munich's walkable centre retains a small-town air but holds some world-class sights, especially its art galleries and museums. Throw in a king's ransom of royal Bavarian heritage, an en-tire suburb of Olympic legacy and a kitbag of dark tourism and you can see why it's such a favourite among those who seek out the past, but like to hit the town once they're done.

When To Go

Stark Bier Zeit, in February and March, is the time to sup strong ale local monks once brewed for Lent. Temperatures climb high in summer, so this is the best season to escape to the lakes south of Munich. October and November are perfect for an amble in the English Garden as its trees fire off an autumnal salute. During Advent, central Marienplatz fills with Christmas stalls, Yuletide cheer and a gaggle of in-ternational shoppers. Welcome in the New Year at the foot of the Friedensengel statue.

Art Attack

'Munich nestles between art and beer like a village between hills', wrote 19th-century German poet Heinrich Heine, and his words ring as true today as they did back then. Visit any of Munich's galleries (especially on Sundays) and you'll find them packed to the gift shop with well-informed locals, rightly proud of their city's reputation for blockbuster art collections and leading galleries. It was the Wittelbachs, Bavaria's ruling family for over 700 years, who gathered much of the city's enviable collection under several roofs. This led to the creation of the Kunstareal, an entire quarter of the city centre given over to galleries. Two 21st-century additions to the Kunstareal include the Pinakothek der Moderne and the Museum Brandhorst, with more on the way.

CITY OF BEER

Other cities such as Pilsen and Brussels occasionally launch weak bids, but few can rival Munich when it comes to claiming the title of 'beer capital of the world'. Countless beer gardens; Oktoberfest (and several other minor beer festivals); some of central Europe's best known breweries such as Paulaner and Augustiner; myriad beers in all shades and strengths; and of course, the famous Hofbräuhaus, the mothership of all beer halls, all form part of the hop-based culture that makes Munich to the drinker what Las Vegas is to the gambler. Munich's beer halls set a high bar for all others across the world, and the unofficial franchise can be found everywhere from Tenerife to Siberia. Despite high ale consumption, public drunkenness and disorder (among locals at least) is rarely seen and most beer halls and gardens are family friendly, with kids' playgrounds and high chairs. And even if you're devoutly teetotal back home, non-alcoholic brews enable you to relish the colour of Munich's frothy traditions minus the falling over.

Best...

- » **Beer hall:** Augustiner Bräustuben (p89)
- » **Bavarian food:** Fraunhofer (p86)
- » **Vegetarian food:** Prinz Myshkin (p84)
- » **Partying:** Kultfabrik (p91)
- » **Views:** Tower of St Peterskirche (p47)
- » **Escape from the city:** Starnberger See

SET YOUR BUDGET

- » Budget hotel room: €60 to €80
- » Two course meal: €11 to €16
- » *Mass* of beer (1L): €7.50
- » Single-trip Zone 1 transport ticket: €2.50
- » Museum/gallery tickets around: €7

Need to Know

- » Many museums close on Mondays.
- » Booking accommodation during Oktoberfest (late September to early October) can be almost impossible, and expensive.
- » Most major museums charge just €1 admission on Sundays

Fast Facts

- » **Munich Time** (GMT/ USC +1)
- » **Number of students:** 94,783
- » **Number of theatres:** 61

Resources

- » **Munich's Official Tourism Website** (www.muenchen-tourist.de)
- » **Munich's Museum Portal** (www.museen-in-muenchen.de)
- » **MUNICHfound, Expat Magazine** (www.munichfound.de)
- » **Toytown Germany Community Website** (www.toytowngermany.com)

Munich Highlights

1 Toast the town with a tankard of *Weissbier* at an authentic beer hall, such as the **Augustiner Bräustuben** (p89)

2 Feel your brow getting higher among the world-class art collections at the **Alte Pinakothek** (p56)

3 Experience an incredible adrenaline rush while clambering around the roof of the Olympic Stadium, **Olympiapark** (p62)

4 Get under the high-octane hood of the **BMW Welt** (p63)

5 Crawl the bars and clubs of the **Gärtnerplatzviertel** (p88) for a night of fun

6 Revel in the bling-fest that is the **Schatzkammer der Residenz** (p53)

7 Squeeze Alpine style into lederhosen or a dirndl at a folk costume emporium such as **Holareidulijö** (p94)

8 Watch daredevil surfers negotiate an urban wave in the **English Garden** (p61)

History

It was the Benedictine monks, drawn by fertile farmland and the closeness to Catholic Italy, who first settled present-day Munich over eight and a half centuries ago. They also gave the city its name – München is medieval German for monk.

In 1240 the city passed to the Wittelsbach dynasty who would run Munich (as well as Bavaria) until the 20th century. Munich prospered as a centre for the salt trade but was hit hard by the outbreak of plague in 1349. When the epidemic finally subsided 150 years later, the *Schäffler* (coopers) began a ritualistic dance to remind residents of their good fortune. The *Schäfflertanz* is re-enacted daily by the little figures on the city's glockenspiel on Marienplatz.

By the early 19th century, furious monument building gave Munich its spectacular architecture and wide Italianate avenues. Culture and the arts flourished, but when Ludwig II ascended the throne his grandiose projects for example, bankrupted the royal house and threatened the government. Ironically, today they are the biggest money-spinners in Bavaria's booming tourism industry.

By 1901 Munich had a population of half a million souls but last century was a hard time for most of them. WWI practically starved the city; the Nazis first rose to prominence here and the next world war nearly wiped the city off the map. The 1972 Olympic Games ended in tragedy when 17 people were killed in a terrorist hostage-taking incident. In 2006 the city won a brighter place in sporting history when it hosted the opening game of soccer's World Cup.

Today Munich's claim to being the secret capital of Germany is alive and well. The city is recognised for its high living standards, the most millionaires per capita in Germany after Hamburg and for an appreciation of the good life.

◉ Sights

ALSTADT

MARIENPLATZ & AROUND

The heart and soul of the Altstadt, Marienplatz is a popular gathering spot that packs a lot of personality into its relatively small frame. It's anchored by the **Mariensäule** (Mary's Column; Map p48), built in 1638 to celebrate victory over Swedish forces during the Thirty Years' War; it's topped by a golden statue of the Virgin Mary balancing on a crescent moon. At 11am and noon (also 5pm March to October), the square jams up with tourists craning their necks to take in the animated Glockenspiel in the Neues Rathaus.

MUNICH IN...

One Day

Spend your first day exploring Munich's historic Altstadt. Get your bearings from the St Peterskirche tower, peruse the colourful bounty at the Viktualienmarkt, then keep a tab on the city's evolution at the Münchner Stadtmuseum, where the Third Reich exhibit makes a poignant transition to the nearby Jüdisches Museum. Duck into the lavishly baroque Asamkirche, then compare it to the Gothic starkness of the landmark Frauenkirche. Time for lunch and perhaps some shopping in the Fünf Höfe arcade. In the afternoon, pick your favourite Pinakothek museum, then cap the day off with a classic Bavarian meal, for instance in the Augustiner Bräustuben.

Two Days

Tour the royal splendour of the Residenz, then relax in the English Garden. Follow up with a coffee break in a Schwabing cafe, then treat your ears to a concert at the Kulturzentrum Gasteig. Finish the night with a bar hop around the Gärtnerplatzviertel.

More Days

If you've got more time, head out to Schloss Nymphenburg, visit the Deutsches Museum, browse the funky boutiques in the Gärtnerplatzviertel and confront the ghosts of Dachau Concentration Camp. If you need a break from urbanity, head to the Fünf-Seen-Land.

Neues Rathaus
HISTORICAL BUILDING

(New Town Hall; Map p48; Ⓢ Marienplatz, Ⓡ Marienplatz) The coal-blackened façade of the neo-Gothic Neues Rathaus, New Town Hall, is festooned with gargoyles and statues, including a dragon scaling the turrets. Inside, six grand courtyards host festivals and concerts throughout the year. For a good view of the city, ascend the 85m **tower** (Map p48; Neues Rathaus; adult/child €2/€1; ⏱ 9am-7pm Mon-Fri, 10am-7pm Sat & Sun).

The highlight of the building is the **Glockenspiel** (carillon; Map p48). Note the three levels: two portraying the Schäfflertanz and another the Ritterturnier, a knights' tournament held in 1568 to celebrate a royal marriage. The night scene featuring the *Münchener Kindl* (a girl in a monk's robe) and *Nachtwächter* (night watchman) runs at 9pm.

Altes Rathaus
HISTORICAL BUILDING

(Old Town Hall; Map p48; Marienplatz; Ⓢ Marienplatz, Ⓡ Marienplatz) The eastern side of Marienplatz is dominated by the Altes Rathaus. Lightning got the better of the medieval original in 1460 and WWII bombs levelled its successor, so what you see is really the third incarnation of the building designed by Jörg von Halspach of Frauenkirche fame. On 9 November 1938 Joseph Goebbels gave a hate-filled speech here that launched the nationwide *Kristallnacht* pogroms.

Today it houses the adorable **Spielzeugmuseum** (Toy Museum; Map p48; www.toymuseum.de; Marienplatz 15; adult/child €4/1; ⏱ 10am-5.30pm) with its huge collection of rare and precious toys from Europe and the US. The oldest ones – made of paper, tin and wood – are on the top floor; from the 3rd floor you have a great view of Marienplatz and Tal street.

St Peterskirche
CHURCH

(Church of St Peter; Map p48; Rindermarkt 1; admission free, tower adult/child €1.50/1; ⏱ tower 9am-5.30pm Mon-Fri, from 10am Sat & Sun; Ⓢ Marienplatz, Ⓡ Marienplatz) Some 306 steps divide you from the best view of central Munich from the 92m tower of St Peterskirche, Munich's oldest church (1150). Also known as *Alter Peter* (Old Peter), it's a virtual textbook of art through the centuries, from the Gothic St-Martin-Altar to Johann Baptist Zimmermann's baroque ceiling fresco and Ignaz Günther's rococo sculptures.

Try to find the ghoulish relics of an obscure saint named Munditia (located to the left as you look at the altar).

VIKTUALIENMARKT & AROUND

Viktualienmarkt
OUTDOOR MARKET

(Map p48; ⏱ Mon-Fri & Sat morning; Ⓢ Marienplatz, Ⓡ Marienplatz) Fresh fruits and vegetables, piles of artisan cheeses, tubs of exotic olives, hams and jams, chanterelles and truffles – Viktualienmarkt is a feast of flavours and one of central Europe's finest gourmet markets. The market moved here in 1807 when it outgrew the Marienplatz and many of the stalls have been run by generations of the same family.

Prices are high, naturally, but so is the quality and many items sold here are hard to find elsewhere. Generally speaking, stalls along the main walkways are more expensive than those a little off to the side. Put together a picnic and head for the market's very own beer garden for an al fresco lunch with a brew and to watch the traders in action.

Heiliggeistkirche
CHURCH

(Church of the Holy Spirit; Map p48; Im Tal 77; ⏱ 7am-6pm; Ⓢ Marienplatz, Ⓡ Marienplatz) Gothic at its core, this baroque church on the edge of the Viktualienmarkt has fantastic ceiling frescos created by the Asam brothers in 1720, depicting the foundation of a hospice that once stood next door. The hospice was demolished to make way for the new Viktualienmarkt.

Bier & Oktoberfestmuseum
MUSEUM

(Beer & Oktoberfest Museum; Map p48; www.bier-und-oktoberfestmuseum.de; Sterneckerstrasse 2; adult/concession €4/2.50; ⏱ 1-5pm Tue-Sat; Ⓢ Isartor, Ⓡ Isartor) Head to this popular museum to learn all about Bavarian suds and the world's most famous booze-up. The four floors heave with old brewing vats, historic photos and some of the earliest Oktoberfest regalia. The 14th-century building has some fine medieval features, including painted ceilings and a kitchen with an open fire. There's an earthy pub downstairs (evenings only).

JÜDISCHES MUSEUM & AROUND

Jüdisches Museum
MUSEUM

(Jewish Museum; Map p48; www.juedisches-museum-muenchen.de; St-Jakobs-Platz 16; adult/child €6/3; ⏱ 10am-6pm Tue-Sun; Ⓢ Sendlinger Tor, Ⓡ Sendlinger Tor) Coming to terms with its Nazi past has not exactly been a

Central Munich

0 400 m
0 0.2 miles

MAXVORSTADT

Karl-Scharnagl-Ring

Königinstr
Von-der-Tann-Str
Galeriestr
Hofgarten
Ludwigstr
Maximilianstr
Hildegardstr
Neuturmstr
Amplatz
Marstallplatz
Lion Statues
Max-Joseph-Platz
Residenzstr
Schrammerstr
Hofgraben
Pfisterstr
Sparkassenstr
Münzstr
Ledererstr
Castles & Museums
Infopoint
Altenhofstr
Tourist Office
Marienplatz
Brenner Str
Odeonsplatz
Theatinerstr
Salvatorstr
Kardinal-Faulhaber-Str
Maffeistr
Schäfflerstr
Frauenplatz
Kaufinger Str
Altheimer Eck
Jägerstr
Oskar-von-Miller-Ring
Maximiliansplatz
Promenadeplatz
Löwengrube
Maxburgstr
Neuhauser Str
Herzogspitalstr
Adolf-Kolping-Str
Ottostr
Lenbachplatz
Barer Str
Karlstr
Karlsplatz
Palace of Justice
Elisenstr
Alter Botanischer Garten
Schützenstr
Zweigstr
To Hauptbahnhof (100m)
Karolinenplatz

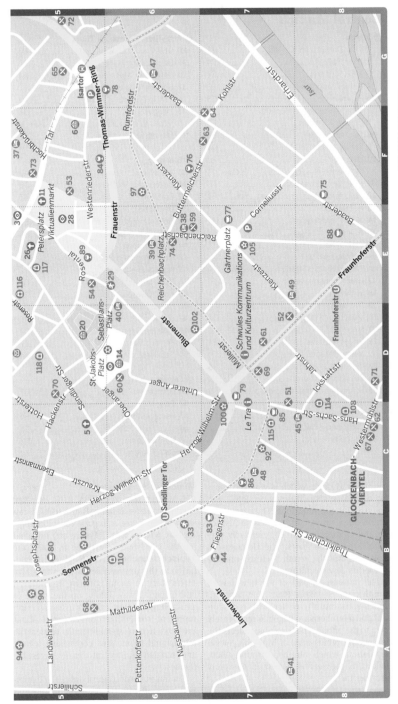

Central Munich

priority in Munich, which is why the opening of the Jewish Museum in 2007 was hailed as a major milestone. The permanent exhibit offers an insight into Jewish history, life and culture in Munich, creatively presented over three floors. The Holocaust is dealt with, but the accent is clearly on contemporary Jewish culture.

The museum is part of the new Jewish complex on St-Jakobs-Platz that also includes a community centre with a restaurant and a bunkerish synagogue that's rarely open to the public. The ensemble reflects the burgeoning renaissance of Munich's Jewish population, which numbers around 9300, making it the second largest in Germany after Berlin.

Münchner Stadtmuseum MUSEUM
(City Museum; Map p48; ☑2332 2370; www.stadt museum-online.de; St-Jakobs-Platz 1; adult/concession/child €6/3/free, audioguide €3; ☺10am-6pm Tue-Sun; ⑤Marienplatz, ⓡMarienplatz) Installed for the city's 850th birthday in 2008, the **Typisch München** (Typical Munich) exhibition at this unmissable museum tells Munich's story in an imaginative, uncluttered and engaging way. Taking up the whole of a rambling building, exhibits in each section represent something quintessential about the city; a booklet-audioguide relates the tale behind them, thus condensing a long and tangled history into easily digestible themes.

Set out in chronological order, the exhibition kicks off with the founding monks and ends in the post-war boom decades. The first of five sections, **Old Munich**, contains a scale model of the city in the late 16th century (one of five commissioned by Duke Albrecht V; the Bayerisches Nationalmuseum displays the others) but the highlight here is the *Morris Dancers*, a series of statuettes gyrating like 15th-century ravers. It's one of the most valuable works owned by the City of Munich

Next comes **New Munich**, which charts the Bavarian capital's 18th- and 19th-century transformation into prestigious royal capital and the making of the modern city. The *Canaletto View* gives an idea in oil paint of how Munich looked in the mid-18th century, before the Wittelsbachs launched their makeover. The section also takes a fas-

cinating look at the origins of Oktoberfest and Munich's cuisine, as well as the phenomenon of the 'Munich Beauty' – Munich's womenfolk are regarded as Germany's most attractive.

City of Munich takes a look at the weird and wonderful late 19th and early 20th century, a period known for Jugenstil architecture and design, Richard Wagner and avantgarde rumblings in Schwabing. Munich became the 'city of art and beer', a title many might agree it still holds today.

The fourth **Revue** hall becomes a little obscure, but basically deals with the aftermath of WWI and the rise of the Nazis. The lead up to war and the city's sufferings during WWII occupy the Feuchtwangersaal where a photo of a very determined

Chamberlain stands next to the other culprits of the Munich Agreement. This is followed by a couple of fascinating rooms that paint a portrait of the modern city, including nostalgic TV footage from the last 40 years.

What could not be boiled down for the Typical Munich exhibition is the city's role in the rise of the Nazis, and this notorious chapter has been rightly left as a powerful separate exhibition called **Nationalsozialismus in München**. This occupies an eerily windowless annex of the main building.

The Stadtmuseum's gift shop includes a real antique-junk shop.

Asamkirche   CHURCH

(Map p48; Sendlinger Strasse 34; ⓈSendlinger Tor, ⓇSendlinger Tor) Though pocket-sized, the late baroque Asamkirche, built in 1746, is as rich and epic as a giant's treasure chest. Its creators, the brothers Cosmas Damian and Egid Quirin, dipped deeply into their considerable talent box to swathe every inch of wall space with paintings, *putti* (cherubs), gold leaf and stucco flourishes.

The crowning glory is the ceiling fresco illustrating the life of St John Nepomuk to whom the church is dedicated (lie down on your back in a pew to fully appreciate the complicated perspective). The brothers lived next door and this was originally their private chapel; the main altar could be seen through a window from their home.

HOFBRÄUHAUS & AROUND

FREE **Hofbräuhaus**   BEER HALL

(Map p48; www.hofbraeuhaus.de; Am Platzl 9; ⓈMarienplatz, ⓇMarienplatz) Even teetotalling, ubercool kitsch-haters will at some point gravitate, out of simple curiosity, to the Hofbräuhaus, the world's most celebrated beer hall. The writhing hordes of tourists tend to overshadow the sterling interior, where dainty twirled flowers and Bavarian flags adorn the medieval vaults.

Beer guzzling and pretzel snapping has been going on here since 1644 and the ballroom upstairs was the site of the first large meeting of the National Socialist Party on 20 February 1920.

Alter Hof   PALACE

(Map p48; Burgstrasse 8; ⓈMarienplatz, ⓇMarienplatz) The starter home of the Wittelsbach family with origins in the 12th century, the Bavarian rulers moved out of this super central palace as long ago as the 15th century. Visitors can only see the central courtyard where the bay window on the southern facade was nicknamed Monkey Tower in honour of a valiant ape that saved an infant Ludwig the Bavarian from the clutches of a ferocious market pig. Local lore at its most bizarre.

Münzhof   FORMER MINT

(Map p48; Hofgraben 4; ⓈMarienplatz, ⓇMarienplatz) The former Münzhof (mint) has a pretty courtyard, remarkable for its three-storey Renaissance arcades dating from 1567. An inscription on the western side of the building reads *Moneta Regis* (Money Rules), particularly apt words for this well-heeled part of Europe. The building now houses the agency charged with protecting Bavaria's many historical monuments.

RESIDENZ

The **Residenz** (Map p48; Max-Joseph-Platz 3; Schatzkammer Treasure Chamber adult/child €6/free) is a suitably grand palace that reflects the splendour and power of the Wittelsbach clan, the Bavarian rulers who lived here from 1385 to 1918. The edifice dwarfs Max-Joseph-Platz along with the grandiose Nationaltheater, home to the Bavarian State Opera. Its museums are among the jewels in Munich's cultural crown and an unmissable part of the Bavarian experience.

A quadriga of giant bronze lion plaques guards the entrance to the palace on Residenzstrasse, supported by pedestals festooned with a half-human, half-animal face. Note the creature's remarkably shiny noses. If you wait a moment, you'll see the reason for the sheen: scores of people walk by and casually rub one or all four noses. It's supposed to bring you wealth and good luck.

TOP FIVE VIEWS OF MUNICH

Here are our top five places from which to get a bird's eye view of the Bavarian capital:

» Bavaria (p70) – see the Oktoberfest through the statue's eyes

» Frauenkirche (p55) – put the Alps and Altstadt at your feet

» Monopteros (p61) – survey the charms of the English Garden

» Olympiaturm (p63) – ogle panoramic views of up to 100km

» St Peterskirche (p47) – survey all of Munich's major landmarks

Tram 19 halts outside the Residenz, though the stop is called Nationaltheater.

Residenzmuseum   MUSEUM
(Map p48; ☏290 671; www.residenz-muenchen.de; adult/child €7/free, combination ticket for the museum, Schatzkammer and Cuvilliés-Theater €13/free; ◉9am-6pm Apr–mid-Oct, 10am-5pm mid-Oct–Mar) Home to Bavaria's Wittelsbach rulers from 1508 until WWI, the Residenz is Munich's number one attraction. The amazing treasures, as well as all the trappings of their lifestyles over the centuries, are on display at the Residenzmuseum, which takes up around half of the palace. Allow at least two hours to see everything at a gallop.

Tours are in the company of a rather long-winded audioguide (free), and gone are the days when the building was divided into morning and afternoon sections, all of which means a lot of ground to cover in one go. It's worth fast forwarding a bit to where the prescribed route splits into short and long tours, taking the long route for the most spectacular interiors. Approximately 90 rooms are open to the public at any one time, but as renovation work is ongoing, closures are inevitable and you may not see all the highlights.

When wandering the Residenz, don't forget that only 50 sq meters of the building's roof remained intact at the end of WWII. Most of what you see today is a meticulous post-war reconstruction.

The tours kick off at the **Grottenhof** (Grotto Court), home of the wonderful **Perseusbrunnen** (Perseus Fountain), with its namesake holding the dripping head of Medusa. Next door is the famous **Antiquarium**, a barrel-vaulted hall smothered in frescos and built to house the Wittelsbach's enormous antique collection. It's widely regarded as the finest Renaissance interior north of the Alps.

Further along the tour route, the neo-Byzantine **Hofkirche** was built for Ludwig I in 1826. After WWII only the red-brick walls were left; it reopened as an atmospheric concert venue in 2003.

Upstairs are the **Kurfürstenzimmer** (Electors Rooms), with some stunning Italian portraits and a passage lined with two dozen views of Italy, painted by local romantic artist Carl Rottmann. Also up here are François Cuvilliés' **Reiche Zimmer** (Rich Rooms), a six-room extravaganza of exuberant rococo carried out by the top stucco and fresco artists of the day; they're a definite

DON'T MISS

MAXIMILIANSTRASSE

It's pricey and pretentious, but no trip to Munich would be complete without a saunter down Maximilianstrasse, one of the city's grandest boulevards. Starting at Max-Joseph-Platz, it's a 1km-long ribbon of style where doe-eyed shoppers browse for Escada and Prada, and suits sip champagne in pavement cafes, with nary a hair out of place. Several of Munich's finest theatrical venues, including the Nationaltheater, the Kammerspiele and the Kleine Komödie am Max II, are also here.

Built between 1852 and 1875, Maximilianstrasse was essentially an ego trip of King Max II. He harnessed the skills of architect Friedrich von Bürklein to create a unique stylistic hotchpotch ranging from Bavarian rustic to Italian Renaissance and English Gothic. It even became known as the Maximilianic Style. That's the king gazing down upon his boulevard – engulfed by roaring traffic – from his perch at the centre of the strip. Clinging to the base are four rather stern-looking children holding the coats of arms of Bavaria, Franconia, Swabia and the Palatinate.

highlight. More rococo magic awaits in the **Ahnengallery** (Ancestors Gallery), with 121 portraits of the rulers of Bavaria in chronological order.

The **Hofkapelle**, reserved for the ruler and his family fades quickly in the memory when you see the exquisite **Reichekapelle** with its blue and gilt ceiling, inlaid marble and 16th-century organ. Considered the finest rococo interiors in southern Germany, another spot to linger longer is the **Steinzimmer** (Stone Rooms), the emperor's quarters awash in intricately patterned and coloured marble.

Schatzkammer der Residenz   MUSEUM
(Residence Treasury; Map p48; adult/concession/under 18yr with parents €7/6/free; ◉9am-6pm Apr–mid-Oct, 10am-5pm mid-Oct–Mar) The Residenzmuseum entrance also leads to the Schatzkammer der Residenz, a veritable banker's bonus worth of jewel-encrusted bling of yesteryear, from golden toothpicks to finely crafted swords, miniatures in ivory to gold entombed cosmetics trunks.

The 1250 incredibly intricate and attractive items on display come in every precious material you could imagine, including rhino horn, lapis lazuli, crystal, coral and amber.

Definite highlights are the Bavarian crown insignia and the ruby-and-diamond–encrusted jewellery of Queen Therese.

Cuvilliés-Theater
THEATRE

(Map p48; adult/child €3.50/free; ☺2-6pm Mon-Sat, from 9am Sun Apr-Jul & mid-Sep–mid-Oct, 9am-6pm daily Aug–mid-Sep, shorter hours mid-Oct–Mar) Commissioned by Maximilian III in the mid-18th century, François Cuvilliés fashioned one of Europe's finest rococo theatres. Famous for hosting the premiere of Mozart's opera *Idomeneo*, restoration work in the mid-naughties revived the theatre's former glory and its stage once again hosts highbrow musical and operatic performances.

Access is limited to the auditorium where you can take a seat and admire the four tier of loggia, dripping with rococo embellishment, at your leisure.

Hofgarten
GARDEN

(Map p48; enter from Odeonsplatz) Office workers catching some rays during their lunch break, stylish mothers pushing prams, seniors on bikes, a gaggle of chatty nuns – *everybody* comes to the Hofgarten. The formal court gardens with fountains, radiant flower beds, lime-tree-lined gravel paths and benches galore sits just north of the Residenz. Paths converge at the **Dianatempel**, a striking octagonal pavilion honouring the Roman goddess of the hunt.

Bavaria's governor keeps his office in the humongous **Bayerische Staatskanzlei**, which takes up the entire eastern flank of the Hofgarten. It's a strikingly modern glass palace built around the restored centre section of the Army Museum that for years stood as a ruined antiwar memorial.

Staatliches Museum Ägyptischer Kunst
MUSEUM

(Egyptian Art Museum; www.aegyptisches-museum-muenchen.de) This old-school museum of late 19th-century Egyptian finds was closed at the time of research, but due to reopen in a purpose-built structure at Gabelsbergerstrasse 35 (near the Alte Pinakothek) in the summer of 2013.

ODEONSPLATZ & AROUND

Odeonsplatz marks the beginning of the Maxvorstadt, a 19th-century quarter built to link central Munich with Schwabing to the north. Leo von Klenze masterminded its overall design and several of the buildings, including the **Leuchtenberg-Palais** (Map p48; to Odeonsplatz), a stately town palace modelled after a Roman palazzo and now home of the Bavarian Finance Ministry. There are several nice, if pricey, cafes, including the plushly furnished **Cafe Tambosi** (Map p48; Odeonsplatz 18), which has a pedigree going back more than 200 years and used to be popular with Munich's high society.

Feldherrnhalle
HISTORIC BUILDING

(Field Marshalls Hall; Map p48; Residenzstrasse 1; ⓈOdeonsplatz) Corking up Odeonsplatz's south side is Friedrich von Gärnter's Feld-

---

MUNICH'S MUSEUMS

Munich has almost 50 museums, some so vast and containing so many exhibits you could spend a whole day shuffling through a single institution. Gallery fatigue strikes many a visitor and it's easy to get your *pinakotheks* in a twist. Here we list Munich's best museums – be selective and take your time.

Best For...

» **Curious kids** KinderReich at the Deutsches Museum (p70)

» **Petrol heads** BMW Welt (p63)

» **Tech heads** Deutsches Museum (p70)

» **Design devotees** Pinakothek der Moderne (p57)

» **Dino hunters** Paläontologisches Museum (p59)

» **Sovereign stalkers** Residenzmuseum (p53)

» **Art-ficionados** Alte Pinakothek (p56)

» **History groupies** Bayerisches Nationalmuseum (p71)

herrnhalle, modelled on the Loggia dei Lanzi in Florence. It honours the Bavarian army and positively drips with testosterone; check out the statues of General Johann Tilly, who kicked the Swedes out of Munich during the Thirty Years' War; and Karl Phillip von Wrede, an ally turned foe of Napoleon.

It was here on 9 November 1923 that police stopped the so-called Beer Hall Putsch, Hitler's attempt to bring down the Weimar Republic. A fierce skirmish left 20 people, including 16 Nazis, dead. A plaque in the pavement of the square's eastern side commemorates the police officers who perished in the incident.

Hitler was subsequently tried and sentenced to five years in jail, but ended up serving a mere nine months, during which he penned his hate-filled manifesto *Mein Kampf*.

Theatinerkirche   CHURCH
(Map p48; Theatinerstrasse 22; ⑤Odeonsplatz) The mustard-yellow Theatinerkirche, built to commemorate the 1662 birth of Prince Max Emanuel, was dreamed up by Swiss architect Enrico Zuccalli. Also known at St Kajetan's, it's a voluptuous design with two massive twin towers flanking a giant cupola. Inside, an intensely ornate dome lords over the *Fürstengruft* (royal crypt), the final destination of several Wittelsbach rulers, including King Maximilian II.

Fünf Höfe   NOTABLE BUILDING
(Map p48; www.fuenfhoefe.de; Theatinerstrasse 15; ⓖTheatinerstrasse) Munich usually feels more cosy than cosmopolitan, but one exception is the Fünf Höfe, a ritzy shopping arcade whose modernist design is as interesting as the fancy flagship and concept stores lining its passageways. The building also houses the **Kunsthalle der Hypo-Kulturstiftung** (Map p48; www.hypo-kunsthalle.de; Theatinerstrasse 8; admission varies; ⊙10am-8pm) an art space with high-calibre changing installations. Entrances to the Fünf Höfe are on Theatinerstrasse, Salvatorstrasse, Maffeisstrasse and Kardinal-Faulhaber-Strasse.

FRAUENKIRCHE & AROUND
Frauenkirche   CHURCH
(Church of Our Lady; Map p48; Frauenplatz 1; €2; ⊙7am-7pm Sat-Wed, 7am-8.30pm Thu, 7am-6pm Fri) The landmark Frauenkirche, built between 1468 and 1488, is Munich's spiritual heart and the Mt Everest among its churches. No other building in the central city may stand taller than its onion-domed twin tow-

ⓘ SUNDAY BEST

Save yourself a bailout of euros by visiting the Pinakotheken, Bayerisches Nationalmuseum, Museum Brandhorst, the Glyptothek, Sammlung Schack, Archäologische Staatssammlung or the Staatliches Museum für Völkerkunde on a Sunday when admission is reduced to a symbolic €1 at each.

ers, which reach a sky-scraping 99m. From April to October, you can enjoy panoramic city views from the **south tower**.

Bombed to bits in WWII, the reconstruction is a soaring passage of light but otherwise fairly spartan. Of note is the epic cenotaph of Ludwig the Bavarian just past the entrance and the bronze plaques of Pope Benedict XVI and his predecessor John Paul II affixed to nearby pillars.

Michaelskirche   CHURCH
(Church of St Michael; Map p48; Kaufingerstrasse 52; crypt admission €2; ⊙crypt 9.30am-4.30pm Mon-Fri, 9.30am-2.30pm Sat & Sun; ⑤Karlsplatz, ⓖKarlsplatz, ⓔKarlsplatz) It stands quiet and dignified amid the retail frenzy out on Kaufingerstrasse, but to fans of Ludwig II, the Michaelskirche is the ultimate place of pilgrimage. Its dank **crypt** is the final resting place of the Mad King, whose humble tomb is usually drowned in flowers.

Completed in 1597, St Michael was the largest Renaissance church north of the Alps and boasts an impressive unsupported barrel-vaulted ceiling. The massive bronze statue between the two entrances shows the Archangel finishing off a dragonlike creature, a classic Counter Reformation–era symbol of Catholicism triumphing over Protestantism. The building has been, and is set to be, under heavy renovation for years.

MAXVORSTADT
'Museums and universities' pretty much sums up Maxvorstadt, meaning that you'll likely be spending some time in this delightful district. The Pinakotheken and Brandhorst art museums form the unrivalled **Kunstareal**, the Glyptothek displays its precious antiquities, and the hallowed **Ludwig-Maximilians-Universität** and venerable **Kunstakademie** (Art Academy) bustle with studious activity. The area has been a hotbed of culture since the early 20th century; painters Franz Marc and Wassily

MUNICH SIGHTS

THE WHITE ROSE

Open resistance to the Nazis was rare during the Third Reich, where arbitrary terror meted out by the SA and Gestapo served as powerful disincentives. In 1942, however, a group of medical students, led by Hans and Sophie Scholl, formed Die Weisse Rose (The White Rose), which aimed to encourage Germans to wake up to what was happening around them.

Members acted cautiously at first, creeping through the streets of Munich and smearing slogans such as Freedom! or Down With Hitler! on walls. Growing bolder, they printed and distributed anti-Nazi leaflets, reporting on the mass extermination of the Jews and other Nazi atrocities. One read: We shall not be silent – we are your guilty conscience. The White Rose will not leave you in peace.

In February 1943 Hans and Sophie were caught distributing leaflets at the university. Together with their best friend, Christian Probst, the Scholls were arrested and charged with treason. After a summary trial, all three were found guilty and beheaded the same afternoon. Their extraordinary courage inspired the award-winning film *Sophie Scholl – Die Letzten Tage* (*Last Days of Sophie Scholl*; 2005).

Kandinsky had their studios here and Thomas Mann used to talk literature with kindred colleagues in smoky coffeehouses. Today students shape the neighbourhood feel, and cafe-, bar- and boutique-lined streets such as Türkenstrasse and Schellingstrasse are places to catch the boho spirit.

Maxvorstadt was the first city expansion, conceived by Maximilian I around 1805 but not really taking shape until his son, Ludwig I, put his mind – and money – to it some 20 years later. Flashy Ludwigstrasse is just one reminder of the legacy of this king who dreamed of turning Munich into a city of art and culture, an Athens on the Isar. The grand boulevard links Odeonsplatz with the Siegestor, where Maxvorstadt spills over into Schwabing. The remarkably uniform and well- proportioned row of neoclassical piles is a credit to court architects Klenze and Gärtner.

Alte Pinakothek ART MUSEUM
(Map p64; www.pinakothek.de; Barer Strasse 27; adult/child €7/5, Sun €1, audio guide €4.50; ☺10am-8pm Tue, to 6pm Wed-Sun; ⓰Pinakotheken, ⓰Pinakotheken) Munich's main repository of Old European Masters is crammed with all the major players that decorated canvases between the 14th and 18th centuries. This neoclassical temple was masterminded by Leo von Klenze and is a delicacy even if you can't tell your Rembrandt from your Rubens. Nearly all the paintings were collected or commissioned by Wittelsbach rulers; it fell to Ludwig I to unite them in a single museum.

The collection is world famous for its exceptional quality and depth, especially when it comes to German masters. The oldest works are altar paintings, of which the *Four Church Fathers* by Michael Pacher and Lucas Cranach the Elder's *Crucifixion* (1503), an emotional rendition of the suffering Jesus, stand out.

A key room is the Dürersaal upstairs. Here hangs Albrecht Dürer's famous Christ-like *Self-Portrait* (1500), showing the gaze of an artist brimming with self-confidence. His final major work, *The Four Apostles*, depicts John, Peter, Paul and Mark as rather humble men in keeping with post-Reformation ideas. Compare this to Matthias Grünewald's *Sts Erasmus and Maurice*, which shows the saints dressed in rich robes like kings.

For a secular theme, inspect Albrecht Altdorfer's *Battle of Alexander the Great* (1529), which captures in dizzying detail a 6th-century war pitting Greeks against Persians.

There's a choice bunch of Dutch masters, including an altarpiece by Rogier van der Weyden called *The Adoration of the Magi*, plus *The Seven Joys of Mary* by Hans Memling, *Danae* by Jan Gossaert and *The Land of Cockayne* by Pieter Bruegel the Elder. Rubens fans also have reason to rejoice. At 6m in height, his epic *Last Judgment* is so big that Klenze custom-designed the hall for it. A memorable portrait is *Hélène Fourment* (1631), a youthful beauty who was the ageing Rubens' second wife.

The Italians are represented by Botticelli, Rafael, Titian and many others, while the French collection includes paintings by Nicolas Poussin, Claude Lorrain and François Boucher. The Spaniards field such heavy hitters as El Greco, Murillo and Velázquez.

Allow at least two hours for a visit, and when you're finished digesting the art, take on refreshments at the wonderfully vaulted museum cafe.

Pinakothek der Moderne   ART MUSEUM
(www.pinakothek.de; Barer Strasse 40; adult/child €10/7, Sun €1; ⊙10am-6pm Tue, Wed & Fri-Sun, 10am-8pm Thu; ▣Pinakotheken, ▣Pinakotheken) Germany's largest modern art museum opened in 2002 in a blockbusting building by Stephan Braunfels that sets the perfect stage for artists and designers who have dominated their respective fields throughout the last century. The spectacular four-storey interior centres on a vast eye-like dome, which spreads soft natural light throughout blanched white galleries.

The museum unites four significant collections under a single roof. The **State Gallery of Modern Art** has some exemplary modern classics by Picasso, Klee, Dalí, Kandinsky and many lesser-known works that will be new to many visitors. More recent big shots include Georg Baselitz, Andy Warhol, Cy Twombly, Dan Flavin and the late enfant terrible Joseph Beuys.

In a world obsessed by retro style, the **New Collection** is the busiest section of the museum. Housed in the basement it focuses on applied design from the industrial revolution via art nouveau and Bauhaus to today. VW Beetles, Eames chairs and early Apple Macs stand alongside more obscure interwar items that wouldn't be out of place in a Kraftwerk video. There's lots of 1960s furniture, the latest spool tape recorders and an exhibition of the weirdest jewellery you'll ever see.

The **State Graphics Collection** boasts 400,000 pieces of art on paper, including drawings, prints and engravings by such craftsmen as Leonardo da Vinci and Paul Cézanne. Because of the light-sensitive nature of these works, only a tiny fraction of the collection is shown at any given time.

Finally, there's the **Architecture Museum**, with entire studios of drawings, blueprints, photographs and models by such top practitioners as baroque architect Balthasar Neumann, Bauhaus maven Le Corbusier and 1920s expressionist Erich Mendelsohn.

Neue Pinakothek   ART MUSEUM
(www.pinakothek.de; Barer Strasse 29; adult/child €7/5, Sun €1; ⊙10am-6pm Thu-Mon, to 8pm Wed; ▣Pinakotheken, ▣Pinakotheken) Picking up where the Alte Pinakothek leaves off, the Neue Pinakothek harbours a respected collection of 19th- and early 20-century paintings and sculpture, from rococo to Jugendstil (art nouveau). Its imposing original structure by Friedrich von Gärtner was destroyed during WWII and not rebuilt; since 1981 works are housed in a modernist structure by Alexander von Branca.

All the world-famous household names get wall space here, including crowd-pleasing French impressionists such as Monet, Cézanne and Degas as well as Van Gogh, whose bold pigmented *Sunflowers* (1888) radiates cheer. There are also several works by Gauguin, including *Breton Peasant Women* (1894); and by Manet, including *Breakfast in the Studio* (1869). Turner gets a look-in with his dramatically sublime *Ostende* (1844).

Perhaps the most memorable canvases, though, are by Romantic painter Caspar David Friedrich, who specialised in emotionally charged, brooding landscapes such as *Riesengebirge Landscape with Rising Mist.*

Local painters represented in the exhibition include Carl Spitzweg and Wilhelm von Kobell of the so-called Dachau School; and Munich society painters such as Wilhelm von Kaulbach, Franz Lenbach and Karl von Piloty. Another focus is on the works by the Deutschrömer (German Romans), a group of neoclassicists centred on Johann Koch, who stuck mainly to Italian landscapes.

Museum Brandhorst   GALLERY
(www.museum-brandhorst.de; Theresienstrasse 35a; adult/child €7/5, Sun €1; ⊙10am-8pm Tue, to 6pm Wed-Sun; ▣Maxvorstadt/Sammlung Brandhorst, ▣Pinakotheken) A big, bold and aptly abstract building, clad entirely in vividly multi-hued ceramic tubes, the Brandhorst jostled its way into the Munich Kunstareal in a punky blaze of colour in mid-2009. Its walls, floor and occassionally ceiling provide space for some of the most challenging works of art in the city, some of them instantly recognisable 20th-century images by Andy Warhol who dominates the collection.

In fact it's Warhol who kick starts proceedings right at the entrance with his bolshie *Hammer and Sickle* (1976). Pop Art's 1960s poster boy pops up throughout and even has an entire room dedicated to pieces such as his punkish *Self Portrait* (1986), *Marilyn* (1962) and *Triple Elvis* (1963).

The other prevailing artist at the Brandhorst is the lesser known Cy Wombly. His arrestingly spectacular splash-and-dribble canvasses are a bit of an acquired taste, but this is the place to acquire it if ever there was one.

Elsewhere Dan Flavin floodlights various corners with his eye-watering light installations and other big names such as Mario Merz, Alex Katz and Sigmar Polke also make an appearance. Surprisingly Damian Hirst hardly gets a look in with just a single installation called *Pill Wall*.

Museum Reich der Kristalle — MUSEUM

(☑2180 4312; Theresienstrasse 41; adult/concession €4/2; ☉1-5pm, closed Mon; 🚇Maxvorstadt/Sammlung Brandhorst, 🚇Pinakotheken) If diamonds are your best friends, head to the Museum Reich der Kristalle, with its Fort Knox–worthy collection of gemstones and crystals, including a giant Russian emerald and meteorite fragments from Kansas.

Königsplatz — SQUARE

(Map p64; 🚇Königsplatz, ⑤Königsplatz) Nothing less than the Acropolis in Athens provided the inspiration for Leo von Klenze's imposing Königsplatz, commissioned by Ludwig I and anchored by a Doric-columned **Propyläen** gateway and two temple-like museums. The Nazis added a few buildings of their own and used the square for their mass parades. Only the foundations of these structures remain at the eastern end of the square, rendered unrecognisable by foliage. Peaceful and green today, the square comes alive in summer during concerts and open-air cinema.

Glyptothek — ART MUSEUM

(Map p64; www.antike-am-koenigsplatz.mwn.de; Königsplatz 3; adult/concession €3.50/2.50, Sun €1; ☉10am-5pm, to 8pm Thu, closed Mon; 🚇Königsplatz, ⑤Königsplatz) If you're a fan of classical art or simply enjoy the sight of naked guys without noses (or other pertinent body parts), make a beeline to the Glyptothek. One of Munich's oldest museums, it's a feast of art and sculpture from ancient Greece and Rome amassed by Ludwig I between 1806 and 1830, and opens a surprisingly naughty window onto the ancient world.

An undisputed highlight is the marble *Barberini Faun* (220 BC), a sleeping satyr rendered in meticulous anatomical detail and striking a pose usually assumed by

Playgirl centrefolds. Rooms X to XII contain superb busts, including one of a youthful Alexander the Great and several of Emperor Augustus. Also of note is the tomb relief of Mnesarete, a Greek courtesan. Don't miss the sculptures from the Aphaia Temple in Aegina with extensive supportive displays to lend context.

The inner courtyard has a calm and pleasant cafe where, in summer, classical theatre takes place under the stars.

Antikensammlungen — MUSEUM

(Map p48; ☑5998 8830; www.antike-am-koenigsplatz.mwn.de; Königsplatz 1; adult/concession €3.50/2.50, Sun €1; ☉10am-5pm, 10am-8pm Wed, closed Mon; 🚇Königsplatz, ⑤Königsplatz) Complementing the Glyptothek, the Antikensammlungen is an engaging showcase of exquisite Greek, Roman and Etruscan antiquities. The collection of Greek vases, each artistically decorated with gods and heroes, wars and weddings, is particularly outstanding. Other galleries present gold and silver jewellery and ornaments; figurines made from terracotta and more precious bronze; and super-fragile drinking vessels made from ancient glass.

Städtische Galerie im Lenbachhaus — GALLERY

(Municipal Gallery; Map p64; ☑2333 2000; www.lenbachhaus.de; Luisenstrasse 33; ☉10am-6pm Tue-Sun; 🚇Königsplatz, ⑤Königsplatz) Late 19th-century portraitist Franz von Lenbach used his fortune to build a fabulous Tuscan-style home, which his widow later sold to the city for a pittance but with the proviso that it be used as a museum. To get things going, she also threw in a bunch of hubbie's works. Today the gallery fills with fans of the expressionist *Blauer Reiter* (Blue Rider) group founded by Wassily Kandinsky and Franz Marc in 1911.

Soon joined by August Macke, Gabriele Münter, Alexej von Jawlensky and others, they rebelled against traditional academy art and instead pursued ground-breaking visions and themes. Ironically, Lenbach's portraits seem comparatively staid and retro.

Contemporary art is another focal point. The acquisition of Joseph Beuys installation *Show Your Wound* nearly caused a riot in the conservative city council, but the collection took off anyway. All the big names are here: Gerhard Richter, Sigmar Polke,

Anselm Kiefer, Andy Warhol, Dan Flavin, Richard Serra and Jenny Holzer among them.

Works are also shown in the nearby **Kunstbau**, a 120m-long underground tunnel above the U-Bahn station Königsplatz.

The Lenbachhaus closed in 2009 for a top-to-bottom renovation directed by stellar British architect Lord Norman Foster. By the time you read this the extended and renovated building should have reopened to the public.

FREE **Paläontologisches Museum** MUSEUM
(Palaeontological Museum; Map p64; ☑2180 6630; www.palmuc.de; Richard-Wagner-Strasse 10; admission free; ⊗8am-4pm Mon-Thu, to 2pm Fri; ᑭKönigsplatz, ⑤Königsplatz) The curatorial concept of the Paläontologisches Museum could use a little dusting up but otherwise this archaeological trove of prehistoric skulls and bones is anything but stuffy. The most famous resident is a fossilised archaeopteryx, a creature that forms the evolutionary link between reptile and bird.

Jurassic fans can check out the wicked horns on a triceratops skull or the delicate bone structure of a plateosaurus. What better place to bring the kids when they're passing through their 'dinosaur phase'?

Ludwig-Maximilians-Universität UNIVERSITY
(LMU; Map p60; ☑218 00; www.uni-muenchen. de; Geschwister-Scholl-Platz 1; ⑤Universität) Bavaria's oldest university, the Ludwig-Maximilians-Universität started out as political football for its rulers. Founded in Ingolstadt in 1472, it moved to Landshut in 1800 before being lassoed to Munich in 1826 by newly crowned King Ludwig I. It has produced more than a dozen Nobel Prize winners, including Wilhelm Röntgen in 1901 and Theodor Hänsch in 2005.

The main building, by Friedrich von Gärtner of course, has cathedral-like dimensions and is accented with sculpture and other art work. A flight of stairs leads to a light court with a memorial to *Die Weisse Rose,* the Nazi resistance group founded by Hans and Sophie Scholl. To get the full story visit the small **DenkStätte** (Map p60; Geschwister-Scholl-Platz 1; admission free; ⊗10am-4pm Mon-Fri, 11.30am-2.30pm Sat Apr-Oct) in the vaulted space behind.

Ludwigskirche CHURCH
(Church of St Ludwig; Map p60; Ludwigstrasse 20; ⊗8am-8pm; ⑤Universität) The somber twin-towered Ludwigskirche, built by Friedrich von Gärtner between 1829 and 1844, is a highly decorative, almost Byzantine affair with one major showpiece: the *Last Judgment* fresco by the Nazarene painter Peter Cornelius in the choir. It's one of the largest in the world and an immodest – and thoroughly unsuccessful – attempt to outdo Michelangelo's version.

Karlsplatz SQUARE
(Map p48; ⑤Karlsplatz, ᑭKarlsplatz, ᑫKarlsplatz) Karlsplatz and the medieval Karlstor form the western gateway to the Altstadt and the pedestrianised shopping precinct along Neuhauser Strasse and Kaufinger Strasse. The busy square was laid out in 1791 as an ego project of the highly unpopular Elector Karl Theodor.

When he named it for himself, locals were even less impressed and insisted on referring to the square as Stachus, possibly in memory of a pub that had been displaced by the square's construction. The huge fountain in the centre is a favoured meeting spot, but Karlsplatz is really at its most magical in winter when an outdoor ice-skating rink brings out young and old.

FREE **Justizpalast** COURTHOUSE
(Palace of Justice; Map p48; Prielmayerstrasse 7; admission free; ⊗9am-4pm Dec–mid-Apr & May–mid-Oct; ⑤Karlsplatz, ᑭKarlsplatz, ᑫKarlsplatz) The 1890s Justizpalast witnessed the Weisse Rose trial of Hans Scholl, Sophie Scholl and Christoph Probst on 22 February 1943. They were condemned to death by the notorious judge Roland Freisler. The verdict was read at 1pm. Four hours later they were dead. There's a permanent exhibit about the sham trial in the very courtroom (room 253) where it took place.

A second courthouse, the **Neuer Justizpalast** (New Palace of Justice) was built just a few years later and is more of a neo-Gothic confection.

Alter Botanischer Garten PARK
(Map p48; Sophienstrasse 7; ᑮ; ⑤Karlsplatz, ᑭKarlsplatz, ᑫKarlsplatz) The Old Botanical Garden is a pleasant place to soothe your heels after an Altstadt shopping spree or to see out a long wait for a train away from the grotty Hauptbahnhof. Created under King Maximilian in 1814, most of the tender specimens were moved in the early 20th century to the New Botanical Garden behind Schloss Nymphenburg, leaving this island of city-centre greenery.

Schwabing & the Englischer Garten

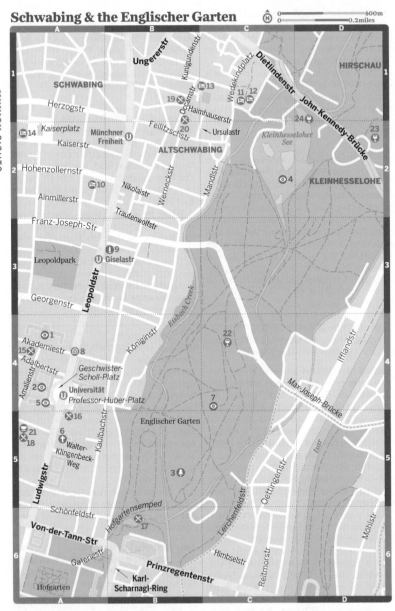

The ferocious *Neptunbrunnen* (Neptune Fountain), on the south side, dates from the Nazi period when the garden was turned into a public park. The neoclassical entrance gate is called the Kleine Propyläen and is a leftover from the original gardens.

Schwabing & the Englischer Garten

Take the U-Bahn to Münchner Freiheit, grab a table in a street-side cafe on Leopoldstrasse and watch the world on parade. What do you see? Bronzed Lotharios in

Schwabing & the Englischer Garten

deep-buttoned white shirts. Faux blondes in tiny tees. Teens in tight premium jeans. Chic mamas walking designer dogs. Yep, no matter what you've heard or read, Schwabing's reputation as a boho stronghold of artists and students is a thing of the past. Fact is, Schwabing is thoroughly gentrified, has some of the highest rents in town, and is populated by lawyers, editors, professors and well-heeled types. Some live in beautifully restored Jugendstil (art nouveau) buildings along such streets as Ainmillerstrasse and Gedonstrasse.

Through it all runs urban Leopoldstrasse. Like all grand boulevards, Leopoldstrasse is a catwalk for the masses, a wide and shady promenade in full view of passing traffic and perfect for showing off the goods – a new car, a new partner, a new outfit – especially on warm summer evenings. The task is made easier by the rows of street-side cafe tables packed with aspirants and arrivés. The tallest eye-catcher along here, though, is Jonathan Borofsky's **Walking Man** (Map p60), a white 17m-high alien captured in mid-stride.

Best of all, the English Garden is only a quick stroll away. The student quarter, meanwhile, is actually south of Schwabing, in Maxvorstadt. But don't worry; even locals get the two confused.

TOP
CHOICE ⟩ **Englischer Garten**   PARK
(Map p60; Ⓢ Universität) The sprawling English Garden is among Europe's biggest city parks, bigger than even London's Hyde Park and New York's Central Park and a favour-

ite playground for locals and visitors alike. Stretching north from Prinzregentenstrasse for about 5km, it was commissioned by Elector Karl Theodor in 1789 and designed by Benjamin Thompson, an American-born scientist working as an advisor to the Bavarian government.

Paths piddle around in dark stands of mature oak and maple before emerging into sunlit meadows of lush grass. Locals are mindful of its popularity and tolerate the close quarters of bicyclists, walkers and joggers. Street musicians dodge balls kicked by frolicking children, and students sprawl on the grass to chat about missed lectures.

Sooner or later you'll find your way to the Kleinhesseloher See (p76), a lovely lake at the centre of the park. Work up a sweat while taking a spin around three little islands, and then quaff a well-earned foamy one at the Seehaus beer garden (p89).

When the sun is out, many Münchners love to get naked and work on their tan, even during their lunch break when they stack their coats, ties and dresses neatly beside them. It's all perfectly legal and socially acceptable, so leave your modesty at home.

Several historic follies lend the park a playful charm. The wholly unexpected **Chinesischer Turm** (Chinese Tower), now at the heart of Munich's oldest beer garden (p88), was built in the 18th century during a pan-European craze for all things oriental. Further south, at the top of a gentle hill, stands the heavily photographed **Monopteros** (Map p60; 1838), a small Greek temple whose ledges are often knee-to-knee with dangling legs belonging to people admiring the view of the Munich skyline.

Another hint of Asia awaits further south at the **Japanisches Teehaus** (Japanese Teahouse; Map p60; ☑ info 224 319; English Garden; ⊘3pm, 4pm, 5pm Sat & Sun Apr-Oct), built for the 1972 Olympics beside an idyllic duck pond. The best time to come is for an authentic tea ceremony celebrated by a Japanese tea master.

Don't even think about spending the night in the park! Muggers, drug fiends and other ne'er-do-wells often keep the *polizei* busy till dawn.

Siegestor
HISTORIC BUILDING

(Victory Gate; Map p60; ⑤Universität) Munich's massive Siegestor was modelled on Constantine's arch in Rome and looks like a miniature version of the Arc de Triomphe in Paris. Built to honour the Bavarian army for sending Napoleon packing, it's crowned by a triumphant Bavaria piloting a lion-drawn chariot. Severely damaged in WWII, the arch was turned into a peace memorial. The inscription on the upper section reads: *Dem Sieg geweiht, vom Kriege zerstört, zum Frieden mahnend* (Dedicated to victory, destroyed by war, calling for peace).

Akademie der Bildenden Künste
ART SCHOOL

(Academy of Fine Arts; Map p60; ☑385 20; www.adbk.de; Akademiestrasse 2-4; ⑤Universität) The Academy of Fine Arts is housed in a three-storey neo-Renaissance building. Founded in 1808 by Maximilian I, it advanced to become one of Europe's leading arts schools in the second half of the 19th century and still has a fine reputation today.

Famous students included Max Slevogt, Franz von Lenbach and Wilhelm Leibl; and, in the early 20th century, Lovis Corinth, Paul Klee, Wassily Kandinsky, Franz Marc and others who went on to become modern art pioneers.

Olympiapark & Around

Olympiapark
OLYMPIC SITE

(Olympic Park; Map p64; www.olympiapark-muenchen.de; audio tour €7, plus €50 refundable deposit, adventure tour adult/concession €9.50/6.50, stadium tour adult/concession €7.50/5; ⊘stadium tour 11am Apr-Oct; ⑤Olympiazenturm) The area to the north of the city where soldiers once paraded and the world's first Zeppelin landed in 1909 found a new role in the 1960s as the Olympiapark. Built for the 1972 Olympic Summer Games, it has quite a small-scale feel and some may be amazed that the games could once have been held at such a petite venue.

The complex draws people year-round with concerts, festivals and sporting events; the swimming hall and the ice-skating rink are open to the public as well.

A good first stop is the **Info-Pavilion** (☑3067 2414; ⊘10am-5pm Mon-Fri, 10am-4pm Sat & Sun), which has information, maps, tour tickets and a model of the complex. Staff also rent MP3 players for a self-guided audiotour. Tickets to the 90-minute guided Adventure Tour that covers the entire Olympiapark on foot and by toy train are available, too.

'THE GAMES MUST GO ON'

The 1972 Summer Olympics presented Munich with an historic chance. It was the first time since 1936 that the Games would be held in the country. The motto was the Happy Games, the emblem a blue solar Bright Sun. The city built a shiny Olympic Park, including buildings with striking Plexiglas tents that, at the time, were revolutionary in design. It was the opportunity to present a new, democratic Germany full of pride and optimism.

In the final week of the Olympics, members of the Palestinian terrorist group Black September killed two Israeli athletes and took nine others hostage at the Olympic Village, demanding the release of political prisoners and escape aircraft. During a failed rescue attempt by German security forces at Fürstenfeldbruck, a military base west of Munich, all the hostages and most of the terrorists were killed. The competition was suspended briefly before Avery Brundage, the International Olympic Committee president, famously declared 'the Games must go on'. The bloody incident cast a pall over the entire Olympics and sporting events in Germany for years to follow.

The Munich Olympic tragedy is chronicled in an Oscar-winning documentary *One Day in September* (2000), by Kevin McDonald, and also inspired Steven Spielberg's searing *Munich* (2005). The killings prompted German security to rethink its methods and create the country's elite counter-terrorist unit, GSG 9.

UP ON THE ROOF

Can't make it to the Alps for a high-altitude clamber? No matter. Just head to the Olympic Stadium for a **walk on the roof** (adult/concessions €41/31; ☺2.30pm daily Apr-Oct). Yup, the roof; that famously contorted steel and Plexiglas confection is ready for its close-up. Just like in the mountains, you'll be roped and hooked up to a steel cable as you clamber around under the eagle-eyed supervision of an experienced guide showering you with fascinating details about the stadium's architecture and construction. Unusual perspectives are guaranteed, but the vertigo-prone might want to take a pass on this one. The minimum age is 10 and expeditions last two hours. Wear rubber-soled shoes.

True daredevils might also be tempted by the **abseiling tour** (adult/student & child €51/41; ☺4pm daily Apr-Oct), which has you scaling up the stadium north side to a height of 50m, then heading straight back down in a free rappel. Contact the Olympic Park Info-Pavilion (p62) for details.

Olympiapark has two famous eye-catchers: the 290m Olympiaturm and the warped **Olympiastadion** (Olympic Stadium; Map p64; adult/child €3/2; ☺9am-8pm mid-May-mid-Sep, shorter hours rest of the year). Germans have a soft spot for the latter because it was on this hallowed grass in 1974 that the national soccer team – led by the Kaiser Franz Beckenbauer – won the FIFA World Cup.

When the sky is clear you'll quite literally have Munich at your feet against the breathtaking backdrop of the Alps from the top of the **Olympiaturm** (Olympic Tower; Map p64; adult/child €4.50/3; ☺9am-midnight). Your lift ticket also buys access to the small, if quirky, Rock Museum, also up on top. Ozzie Osbourne's signed guitar, a poem penned by Jim Morrison, and Britney Spears' glitter jeans jostle for space with letters, photos and concert tickets, all the result of three decades of collecting by a pair of rock fans.

BMW-Welt, Museum & Plant NOTABLE BUILDING (Map p64; ⑤Olympiazenturm) Next to the Olympiapark, the glass-and-steel, double-cone tornado spiraling down from a dark cloud the size of an aircraft carrier holds **BMW-Welt** (BMW World; ☎0180-2118 822; www.bmw -welt.de; admission free, tours adult/child €7/5; ☺9am-6pm), truly a petrol head's dream. Apart from its role as a prestigious car pickup centre (new owners fork out €500 for the privilege), this king of showrooms acts as a shop window for BMW's latest models and a show space for the company as a whole.

Straddle a powerful motorbike, marvel at technology-packed saloons and estates (no tyre kicking please), browse the 'lifestyle' shop or take the 80-minute guided tour. On the Junior Campus, kids learn about mobility, fancy themselves car engineers and even get to design their own vehicle in workshops. Hang around long enough and you're sure to see motorbike stunts on the staircases and other petroleum-fuelled antics; the venue also hosts jazz and classical music concerts.

BMW Welt is linked via a bridge to BMW Headquarters, another stunning building of four gleaming cylinders, and to the silver-bowl-shaped **BMW Museum** (Map p64; www. bmw-welt.de; adult/child €12/6; ☺10am-6pm Tue-Sun). Redesigned from scratch and reopened in 2008, it's like no other car museum on the planet. The seven themed 'houses' examine the development of BMW's product line and include sections on motorcycles and motor racing. However, the interior design of this truly unique building, with its curvy retro feel, futuristic bridges, squares and huge backlit wall screens, almost upstages the exhibits.

With some planning you can also tour the belly of the beast, the adjacent **BMW Plant** (☎0180-2118 822; tours adult/child €8/5; ☺Mon-Fri). Reservations are required and can be made up to six months in advance. Tours (also in English) last 2½ hours, and children under four are not allowed.

NEUHAUSEN & NYMPHENBURG
One of Munich's oldest districts, Neuhausen has an air of relaxed confidence, Europe's largest beer garden (the Hirschgarten; p89) and pretty good nightlife and dining. It also has a long and cosy association with the royal family since becoming the servants' quarter for the newly built Schloss Nymphenburg in the 17th century. A couple of hundred years later, Neuhausen was revamped

Nymphenburg, Neuhausen & Olympiapark

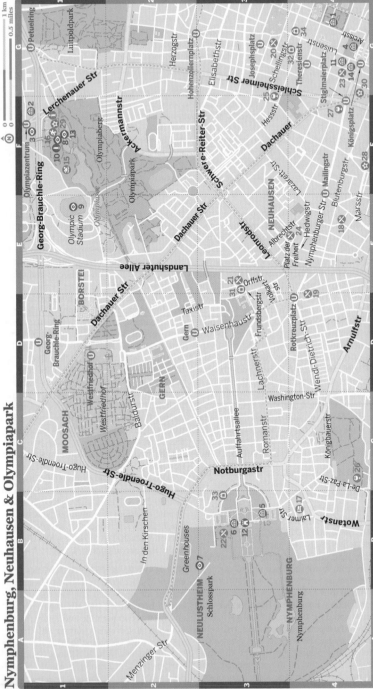

Nymphenburg, Neuhausen & Olympiapark

MUNICH SIGHTS

as a residential pad for the wealthy, with the villas along the Nymphenburg Canal resembling second-string royal residences. The canal, by the way, often freezes over in winter, luring skaters and curlers onto the ice.

The commercial heart of Neuhausen – bustling Rotkreuzplatz (nicknamed Stachus of Neuhausen) – may be an aesthetically challenged product of the 1960s, but at least it's home to Munich's best ice-cream parlour, the Eiscafé Sarcletti (p83). The square is also the gateway to low-key and tourist-free bars and restaurants in radiating side streets. On Thursday a farmers market brings out the locals from 10am to 7pm.

Schloss Nymphenburg   PALACE
(Map p64; www.schloss-nymphenburg.de; adult/child €6/5; ⊙9am-6pm Apr–mid-Oct, 10am-4pm mid-Oct–Mar; ⊡Schloss Nymphenburg) This commanding palace and its lavish gardens sprawl around 5km northwest of the Altstadt. Begun in 1664 as a villa for Electress Adelaide of Savoy, the stately pile was extended over the next century to create the royal family's summer residence. Franz Duke of Bavaria, head of the once royal Wit-

telsbach family, still occupies an apartment here.

The main palace building consists of a large villa and two wings of creaking parquet floors and sumptuous period rooms. Right at the beginning of the self-guided tour comes the highpoint of the entire Schloss, the **Schönheitengalerie** (Gallery of Beauties), housed in the former apartments of Queen Caroline. Some 38 portraits of attractive females chosen by an admiring King Ludwig I peer prettily from the walls. The most famous image is of Helene Sedlmayr, the daughter of a shoemaker, wearing a lavish frock the king gave her for the sitting. You'll also find Ludwig's beautiful, but notorious, lover Lola Montez (p286), 19th-century gossip-column celebrity Jane Lady Ellenborough, and English beauty Lady Jane Erskin.

Further along the tour route comes the **Queen's Bedroom**, which still contains the sleigh bed on which Ludwig II was born, and the **King's Chamber** resplendent with 3D ceiling frescoes.

Also in the main building is the **Marstall-museum** (Map p64; adult/concession €4.50/3.50; ⊙9am-6pm Apr-mid-Oct, 10am-4pm mid-Oct-Mar), displaying royal coaches and riding gear.

This includes Ludwig II's fairy tale–like rococo sleigh, ingeniously fitted with oil lamps for his crazed nocturnal outings. Upstairs is the world's largest collection of old porcelain made by the famous Nymphenburger Manufaktur. Also known as the Sammlung Bäuml, it presents the entire product palette from the company's founding in 1747 until 1930.

Gardens & Outbuildings GARDENS

The sprawling park behind Schloss Nymphenburg is a favourite spot with Münchners and visitors for strolling, jogging or whiling away a lazy afternoon. It's laid out in grand English style and accented with water features, including a large lake, a cascade and a canal popular for feeding swans, and ice-skating and ice-curling when it freezes over in winter.

The park is at its most magical without the masses, ie early in the morning and an hour before closing. But even in the daytime, you can usually commune in solitude with water lilies and singing frogs at the **Kugelweiher** pond in the far northern corner.

The park's chief folly – and quite frilly to boot – the **Amalienburg** is a small hunting lodge dripping with crystal and gilt decoration; don't miss the amazing Spiegelsaal.

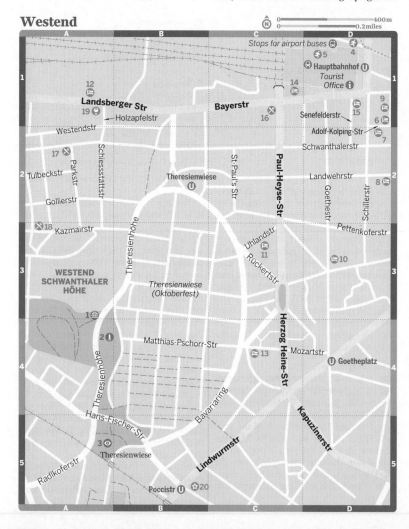

Westend

Stops for airport buses
Hauptbahnhof
Tourist Office

Landsberger Str
Bayerstr
Holzapfelstr
Westendstr
Senefelderstr
Adolf-Kolping-Str
Schwanthalerstr
Tulbeckstr
Parkstr
Schiessstättstr
Theresienwiese
St-Paul's Str
Paul-Heyse-Str
Landwehrstr
Goethestr
Schillerstr
Gollierstr
Kazmairstr
Theresienhöhe
Pettenkoferstr
Uhlandstr
Rückertstr

WESTEND SCHWANTHALER HÖHE

Theresienwiese (Oktoberfest)

Theresienhöhe
Matthias-Pschorr-Str
Herzog Heine-Str
Mozartstr
Goetheplatz

Hans-Fischer-Str
Bavariaring

Theresienwiese
Kapuzinerstr
Radlkoferstr
Lindwurmstr
Poccistr

The two-storey Pagodenburg was built in the early 18th century as a Chinese teahouse and is swathed in ceramic tiles depicting landscapes, figures and floral ornamentation. The Badenburg is a sauna and bathing house that still has its original heating system. Finally, the Magdalenenklause was built as a mock hermitage in faux-ruined style. A combination ticket to all four park buildings is €4.50/3.50 per adult/child.

Neuer Botanischer Garten BOTANICAL GARDEN
(New Botanical Garden; Map p64; 1786 1350; www .botmuc.de; Menzinger Strasse 65; adult/concession €4/2.50, Palmenhaus audioguide €3; 9am-7pm May-Aug, 9am-6pm Apr & Sep, 9am-5pm Feb-Mar & Oct, 9am-4.30pm Nov-Jan; Schloss Nymphenburg) Munich's verdant New Botanical Garden segues smoothly from the north side of the palace park and ranks among the most important in Europe. About a century old, it boasts some 14,000 plant species from around the world. Highlights include the Victorian-style *Palmenhaus* (glass palm house) with its famous collection of tropical and subtropical plants. Other greenhouses shelter cacti, orchids, ferns, carnivorous plants and other leafy treasures.

Museum Mensch und Natur MUSEUM
(Museum of Humankind & Nature; Map p64; 179 5890; www.musmn.de; Schloss Nymphenburg; adult/child €3/2, Sun €1; 9am-5pm Tue, Wed & Fri, to 8pm Thu, 10am-6pm Sat & Sun; Schloss Nymphenburg) Kids will have plenty of ooh and aah moments in the Museum of Humankind & Nature, in the Schloss Nymphenburg north wing. Anything but old school, it puts a premium on interactive displays, models, audiovisual presentations and attractive animal dioramas. Sadly it's all in German but few language skills are needed to appreciate the visuals.

LUDWIGSVORSTADT & WESTEND

Once a neglected working-class backwater scented by the hop-laden aroma wafting gently from its breweries, the Westend is gradually finding its groove and evolving into one of Munich's most vibrant and intriguing neighbourhoods. There are no major sights, which is just fine because its charms reveal themselves in subtler, often unexpected ways: on leafy Gollierplatz, for instance, or in hip cafes and pubs, in the growing number of artist's studios and indie boutiques, and the Turkish corner store with its artfully piled produce.

For contrast, head west of the Theresienwiese Oktoberfest grounds, where Ludwigsvorstadt basks in an air of bourgeois haughtiness, its leafy streets hemmed with grand old mansions looking as impeccable now as they did a century ago. However, the district's face changes drastically the further north, and closer to the Hauptbahnhof, you get where strip clubs, sex shops and made-in-China import stores dominate.

Theresienwiese OCTOBERFEST GROUNDS
(Theresienwiese) The Theresienwiese (Theresa Meadow), better known as Wiesn, just southwest of the Altstadt is the site of the Oktoberfest. At the western end of the meadow is the Ruhmeshalle (Hall of Fame) guarding solemn statues of Bavarian

MUNICH SIGHTS

Westend

1. Frauenkirche (p55)
The onion-domed twin towers on the left reach 99m above the city centre.

2. Glockenspiel, Neues Rathaus (p47)
The Marienplatz is packed with tourists watching the animated figurines perform.

3. Munich Residenz (p52)
Reflecting the splendour and power of the long-ruling Wittelsbach clan of Bavaria.

leaders, as well as the **statue of Bavaria** (☎290 671; adult/under 18/concession €3.50/free/2.50; ⊙9am-6pm Apr-mid-Oct, to 8pm during Oktoberfest), an 18m-high Amazon in the Statue of Liberty tradition, oak wreath in hand and lion at her feet.

This iron lady has a cunning design that makes her seem solid, but actually you can climb via the knee joint up to the head for a great view of the Oktoberfest. At other times, views are not particularly inspiring.

Deutsches Museum – Verkehrszentrum   MUSEUM
(Transport Museum; ☎500 806 500; www.deutsches-museum.de/verkehrszentrum; Am Bavariapark 5; adult/child €6/3; ⊙9am-5pm; ⑤Theresienwiese) An ode to mobility, the Transport Museum explores the ingenious ways humans have devised to transport things and each other. From the earliest automobiles to famous race cars and the high-speed ICE trains, the collection is a virtual trip through transport history.

The exhibit is spread over three historic trade-fair halls near Theresienwiese, each with its own theme – Public Transportation, Travel, and Mobility & Technology – and is a fun place even if you can't tell a piston from a carburettor. Classic cars abound, vintage bikes fill an entire wall and there's even an old petrol station.

GÄRTNERPLATZVIERTEL & GLOCKENBACHVIERTEL

Southeast of the Altstadt, the Gärtnerplatzviertel and Glockenbachviertel pack more personality into a fairly compact frame than most other Munich neighbourhoods. The trendiest bars, cafes and clubs are here; pretty streets teem with local designer boutiques and lifestyle stores; and creatives of all stripes scroll away on their iPads in stylish offices. Come nightfall the area is a haven of hip, not as studenty as Maxvorstadt, not as snooty as Schwabing, not as multicultural as Haidhausen. The epicentre of LGBT life is here as well, with rainbow flags flying out-and-proudly along Müllerstrasse and Hans-Sachs-Strasse. Further south is the up-and-coming Schlachthofviertel, an area where the slaughterhouses used to be located. The official name for all three quarters is Isarvorstadt.

Sooner or later everyone gravitates towards the circular Gärtnerplatz, where street cafes are lorded over by the splendid Staatstheater am Gärtnerplatz (p93). Found-ed by citizens in 1865, the theatre was taken over by Ludwig I after the owners went bankrupt.

The Glockenbachviertel (Bell Brook Quarter) derives its name from a foundry once located on a stream nearby. Many of the city's carvers and woodworkers lived here, giving rise to street names such as *Baumstrasse* (Tree St) and *Holzstrasse* (Wood St). A lovely spot for a walk is along the babbling Glockenbach creek, which runs south along Pestalozzistrasse. It's the sole survivor of a network of brooks that once crisscrossed Munich; the rest have been rerouted or paved over. This one parallels the Alter Südlicher Friedhof, a cemetery that's a favourite final destination for Munich's wealthy. Famous residents include the painter Carl Spitzweg, the physicist Joseph von Fraunhofer and the architect Friedrich von Gärtner. Look for a plaque with names and grave locations near the entrance.

LEHEL

Just east of the Altstadt proper, Lehel (prnounced *lay-hl*) has the second-highest concentration of museums after the art nexus in Maxvorstadt. It's the oldest Munich suburb, having been absorbed into the city in 1724, and a charismatic warren of quiet streets lined with late-19th-century buildings.

TOP CHOICE **Deutsches Museum**   SCIENCE MUSEUM
(Map p72; ☎21 791; www.deutsches-museum.de; Museumsinsel 1; adult/child €8.50/3; ⊙9am-5pm; ⓢDeutsches Museum) If you're one of those people for whom science is an unfathomable turn off, a visit to the Deutsches Museum might just show you that physics and engineering are more fun than you thought. Spending a few hours in this temple to technology is an eye-opening journey of discovery and the exhibitions and demonstrations will certainly be a hit with young minds.

There are tons of interactive displays (including glass blowing and paper-making), live demonstrations and experiments, model coal and salt mines, and engaging sections on cave paintings, geodesy, microelectronics and astronomy. In fact, it can be pretty overwhelming after a while, so it's best to prioritise what you want to see. The place to entertain little ones is the fabulous **Kinder-Reich** (Childrens Kingdom) where 1000 activities, from a kid-size mouse wheel to a fully explorable fire engine, await.

The museum's collection is so huge that some sections have been moved to separate locations. Vehicles are now in the Verkehrszentrum (p70), while aircraft are at the Flugwerft Schleissheim (p99). Combination tickets to all three museums cost €15 and may be used on separate days

Bayerisches Nationalmuseum MUSEUM
(Map p72; www.bayerisches-nationalmuseum.de; Prinzregentenstrasse 3; adult/child €5/free, Sun €1; ◎10am-5pm Tue, Wed & Fri-Sun, to 8pm Thu; 🚇Nationalmuseum/Haus Der Kunst, 🚇Nationalmuseum/Haus Der Kunst) Picture the classic 19th-century museum, a palatial neo-Classical edifice overflowing with exotic treasure and thought-provoking works of art, a repository of a nation's history, a grand purpose built display case for royal trinkets, Church baubles and state-owned rarities – this is the Bavarian National Museum, a good old-fashioned museum for no-nonsense museum lovers.

Filling 40 rooms over three floors, there's a lot to get through so be prepared for at least two hours' legwork.

Most start on the 1st floor where hall after hall is packed with Baroque, Mannerist and Renaissance sculpture, ecclesiastic treasures (check out all those wobbly Gothic 'S' figures), Renaissance clothing and one-off pieces such as the 1000-year-old St Kunigunde's chest fashioned in mammoth ivory and gold. Climb to the second floor to the Rococo, *Jugenstil* and Modern periods, represented by priceless collections of Nymphenburg and Meissen porcelain, Tiffany glass, Augsburg silver and precious items used by the Bavarian royal family. Also up here is a huge circular model of Munich in the first half of the 19th century, shortly after it was transformed into a capital fit for a kingdom.

It's easy to miss, but the building's basement also holds an evocative collection of *Krippen* (nativity scenes), some with a Cecil B DeMille–style cast of thousands. Retold in everything from paper to wood to resin, there are Christmas story scenes here from Bohemia, Moravia and Tyrol, but the biggest contingent hails from Naples. Also down here is the excellent museum shop.

Haus der Kunst ART MUSEUM
(House of Art; Map p72; ✆2112 7113; www.hausderkunst.de; Prinzregentenstrasse 1; ◎10am-8pm Mon-Sun, to 10pm Thu; 🚇Nationalmuseum/Haus Der Kunst, 🚇Nationalmuseum/Haus Der Kunst) It was built in 1937 to showcase Nazi art, but now the Haus der Kunst presents works by exactly the artists whom the Nazis rejected and deemed degenerate. The focus is on contemporary art and design supplemented by hip events, including an after-work party that includes a tour, nibbles snacks and drinks.

**Staatliches Museum
für Völkerkunde** MUSEUM
(State Museum of Ethnology; Map p72; ✆210 136 100; www.voelkerkundemuseum-muenchen.de; Maximilianstrasse 42; adult/concession €5/4, Sun €1; ◎9.30am-5.30pm Tue-Sun; 🚇Maxmonument) A bonanza of art and objects from Africa, India, the Americas, the Middle East and Polynesia, the State Museum of Ethnology has one of the most prestigious and complete ethnological collections anywhere. Sculpture from West and Central Africa is particularly impressive, as are Peruvian ceramics, Indian jewellery, mummy parts, and artefacts from the days of Captain Cook.

DEGENERATE ART

Expressionism, Surrealism, Dadaism...modern art of all stripes was anathema to Hitler and his honchos. Internationally renowned artists like Klee, Beckmann and Schlemmer were forced into exile, their work was removed from museums and confiscated from private collections. The Nazis then sold them off to rake in foreign currency; about 4000 of them were publicly burned in Berlin.

However, in July 1937 Goebbels gathered about 650 paintings, sculptures and prints in the crammed and poorly lit Galerie am Hofgarten, calling it an exhibit of *Entartete Kunst* (Degenerate Art). Organised into such themes as Mockery of God and Insult to German Womanhood, it was intended to portray modern art as debauched and decadent. The propaganda show opened on 19 July 1937, just one day after the Great German Art Exhibition of Nazi-approved works premiered in the nearby, custom-built Haus der Deutschen Kunst. Ironically, the Nazi art was largely reviled by the public, while over two million people came to see the *Entartete Kunst*, more than any other modern art show in history.

Lehel, Haidhausen & Bogenhausen

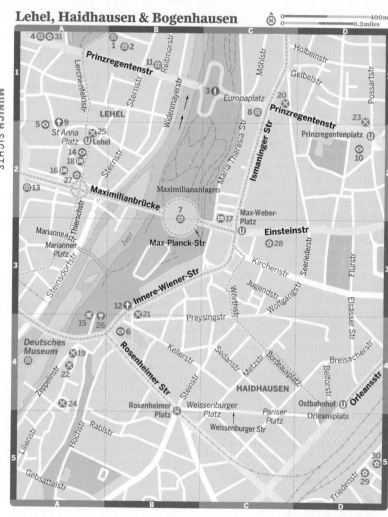

Archäologische Staatssammlung MUSEUM
(State Archaeological Collection; Map p72; ☎211
2402; www.archaeologie-bayern.de; Lerchenfeld-
strasse 2; adult/concession €7.50/5.50, Sun €1;
⌚9.30-5pm Tue-Sat, 10am-6pm Sun; ☐National-
museum/Haus der Kunst, ☐Nationalmuseum/
Haus der Kunst) Turns out Bavaria has been
a popular place of residence for 120,000
years. Prehistoric Stone Age people came
first, then the Romans, the Celts and finally
various Germanic tribes. The Archäologische Staatssammlung opens up a window
on these long-gone civilisations with cult

objects, floor mosaics, jewellery, medical
equipment and scores of other items.

Sammlung Schack ART MUSEUM
(Map p72; www.sammlung-schack.de; Prinzregentenstrasse 9; adult/concession €4/3; ⌚10am-6pm
Wed-Mon; ☐Reitmorstrasse/Sammlung Schack)
Count Adolf Friedrich von Schack (1815–94)
was a great fan of 19th-century Romantic
painters such as Böcklin, Feuerbach and Moritz von Schwind. His collection is housed
in the former Prussian embassy, now the
Schack-Galerie. A tour of the intimate space

Lehel, Haidhausen & Bogenhausen

is like an escape into the idealised fantasy worlds created by these artists.

St-Anna-Platz SQUARE
(Map p72; S Lehel, 🚊 Lehel) The Asamkirche may be more sumptuous, but the **Klosterkirche St Anna** (Map p72; St-Anna-Platz 21; ⊙6am-7pm) is actually a collaboration of the rococo era's top dogs; Johann Michael Fischer designed the building, Cosmas Damian Asam painted the stunning ceiling fresco and altar.

The rather pompous neo-Romanesque **Pfarrkirche St Anna im Lehel** (Map p72; St-Anna-Platz 5; ⊙8am-5pm Mon-Sat, to 8pm Sun) arrived on the scene in 1892 when the Klosterkirche St Anna im Lehel became too small. Conceived by locally-born architect Gabriel von Seidl, it's worth a spin for the huge Byzantine-style painting behind the altar and little art nouveau touches throughout.

HAIDHAUSEN

Haidhausen is hip, eclectic and leagues away from its 19th-century working-class roots. Major gentrification since the late 1970s has made the district desirable for artsy professionals, professional artists and all urban types, although there are still plenty

of upwardly hopeful immigrants, artists and students and ageing lefties left. For visitors, the main draw is a congenial mix of sceney bars and boundary-pushing restaurants, the Gasteig Culture Centre, fun streets like Metzstrasse and gorgeously restored late-19th-century buildings in the French quarter around Pariser Platz. Munich's biggest party zone can be found near the Ostbahnhof.

Kulturzentrum Gasteig CULTURAL CENTRE
(Gasteig Culture Centre; Map p72; ☎480 980; www.gasteig.de; Rosenheimer Strasse 5; 🚊 Am Gasteig) Haidhausen is home to one of Munich's finest cultural venues, the Kulturzentrum Gasteig, whose postmodern, boxy, glass-and-brick design caused quite a controversy a generation ago. The name is derived from the Bavarian term *gaacher Steig*, meaning steep trail. The complex harbours four concert halls, including the 2400-seat Philharmonie, which is the permanent home of the Münchner Philharmoniker.

St Nikolaikirche CHURCH
(St Nicholas Church; Map p72; Innere-Wiener-Strasse; 🚊 Am Gasteig) St Nikolai was first built in 1315 in Gothic style only to go all baroque three centuries later. Outside the prim church ensemble of St Nikolai and

Lorettokapelle, the covered walkway protects some pretty nifty 'Stations of the Cross' made of Nymphenburg porcelain. Today the church is used by a Ukrainian Orthodox congregation.

Maximilianeum   HISTORIC BUILDING
(Map p72; Max-Planck-Strasse 1; 🚇Maximilianeum) Maximilianstrasse culminates in the glorious Maximilianeum, completed in 1874, a decade after Max II's sudden death. It's an imposing structure, drawn like a theatre curtain across a hilltop, bedecked with mosaics, paintings and other artistic objects. It's framed by an undulating park called the Maximiliananlagen, which is a haven for cyclists in summer and tobogganists in winter.

BOGENHAUSEN

Bogenhausen is not shy about flaunting its wealth. Elegant villas sprang up here from the 1870s onwards and the area is peppered with gilded art nouveau–buildings. Just take a wander along Möhlstrasse, a chic avenue branching northeast from the Europaplatz near the Friedensengel, which is lined with mansions for the super-rich, foreign consulates and law offices. East of here (via Siebertstrasse and Ismaninger Strasse), Holbeinstrasse is a treasure chest of listed art nouveau–houses, with the one at No 7 being an especially fine specimen. Prinzregentenstrasse, the main artery, divides Bogenhausen from Haidhausen to the south.

Museum Villa Stuck   ART MUSEUM
(Map p72; ☑455 5510; www.villastuck.de; Prinzregentenstrasse 60; adult/concession €6/3; ☺11am-6pm Tue-Sun; 🚇Friedensengel/Villa Stuck) Franz von Stuck was a leading light in Munich's art scene around the turn of the 20th century and his residence is one of the finest Jugendstil homes you'll ever see. Stuck came up with the intricate design, which forges tapestries, patterned floors, coffered ceilings and other elements into a harmonious work of art. Today his pad is open as a museum with changing exhibitions.

Friedensengel   STATUE
(Map p72; 🚇Friedensengel/Villa Stuck) Just east of the Isar River, the *Friedensengel* (Angel of Peace) statue stands guard from its perch atop a 23m-high column. It commemorates the 1871 Treaty of Versailles, which ended the Franco-Prussian War, and the base contains some shimmering golden frescos. On New Year's Eve the steps around the monu-

ment are party central, hence all the popped corks that litter the ground when the snow thaws.

Prinzregententheater   THEATRE
(Map p72; ☑218 502; www.prinzregententheater .de; Prinzregentenplatz 12; ⑤Prinzregentenplatz) One of Bogenhausen's main landmarks is the Prinzregententheater. Its dramatic mix of art nouveau and neoclassical styles was conceived under Prince-Regent Luitpold as a festival house for Richard Wagner operas.

After WWII it became the temporary home of the Bavarian State Opera for a couple of decades, but then was left to crumble for a quarter-century. A theatre director named August Everding eventually rode to the rescue and raised the funds for its renovation. In 1996 it reopened to the strains of Wagner's *Tristan und Isolde*. Today the beautiful venue is used for drama, concerts and other events, and is also the seat of the Bavarian Theatre Academy.

OUTER DISTRICTS

Allianz Arena   SOCCER STADIUM
(☑tour 01805-555 101; www.allianz-arena.de; Werner-Heisenberg-Allee 25, Fröttmaning; tour adult/child €10/6.50; ☺tours 1pm, in English; ⑤Fröttmaning) Sporting and architecture fans alike should take a side trip to the northern suburb of Fröttmaning to see the ultraslick €340 million Allianz Arena, Munich's dramatic football stadium. The 75-minute stadium tours are hugely popular (no tours on match days); tickets are sold in the 3rd-floor gift shop.

Nicknamed the life belt and rubber boat, it has walls made of inflatable cushions that can be individually lit to match the colours of the host team (red for 1 FC Bayern, blue for TSV 1860, and white for the national side).

Tierpark Hellabrunn   ZOO
(Hellabrunn Zoo; ☑625 080; www.tierpark-hellab runn.de; Tierparkstrasse 30; adult/child €11/4.50; ☺9am-6pm Apr-Sep, to 5pm Oct-Mar; 🚇52 from Marienplatz) Some 6km south of the city centre, Tierpark Hellabrunn has 5000 furry, feathered and finned friends that rarely fail to enthral the little ones. It was one of the first to be set up with spacious natural habitats dividing animals by continent.

Kids can get all touchy-feely with the animals at the large petting zoo where tots get to feed deer and goats. Other crowd-pleasers include the Villa Dracula (inhabited by bats,

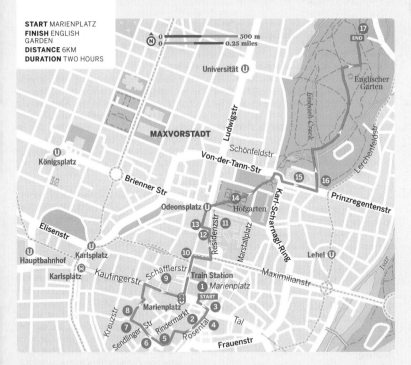

START MARIENPLATZ
FINISH ENGLISH GARDEN
DISTANCE 6KM
DURATION TWO HOURS

0   500 m
0   0.25 miles

Universität Ⓤ

Englischer Garten

MAXVORSTADT

Königsplatz Ⓤ

Schönfeldstr
Von-der-Tann-Str
Ludwigstr
Brienner Str

Prinzregentenstr

Odeonsplatz Ⓤ   Hofgarten   ⑮   ⑯

⑭

Elisenstr   ⑬   ⑪
⑫
Residenzstr   Marstallplatz   Karl-Scharnagl-Ring

Hauptbahnhof Ⓤ   Karlsplatz Ⓤ   ⑩   Lehel Ⓤ

Karlsplatz   Kaufingerstr   Schäfflerstr   Train Station   Maximilianstr
⑨
Marienplatz
① Marienplatz
START

Kreuzstr   Marienplatz   ③
⑧   Rindermarkt   ②   Tal   ④
⑦   Sendlinger Str   ⑥   Rosental
Frauenstr

Walking Tour
Historic Centre & the English Garden

❯ Kick off at central Marienplatz where the glockenspiel chimes from the ① **Neues Rathaus**, the impressive Gothic town hall. The steeple of the ② **St Peterskirche** affords great views of the old town, including the ③ **Altes Rathaus**. Turn left as you leave St Peters and walk down Petersplatz to the ④ **Viktualienmarkt**. Head south from here to Sebastiansplatz and the well-curated ⑤ **Münchner Stadtmuseum**. The big cube opposite on St-Jakobs-Platz is Munich's synagogue, flanked by the ⑥ **Jüdisches Museum**.

From here follow Unterer Anger, turn right on Klosterhofstrasse, which continues as Schmidstrasse and reaches Sendlinger Strasse. Turn right for a peek inside the ⑦ **Asamkirche**. Backtrack a few steps on Sendlinger Strasse, turn left on Hackenstrasse, right on Hotterstrasse, past the tiny ⑧ **Hundskugel**, the city's oldest restaurant, left on Altheimer Eck and immediately right on Färbergraben. This takes you to Kaufinger Strasse, the Altstadt's pedestrianised shopping strip. Continue on Augustinerstrasse to the twin-onion-domed ⑨ **Frauenkirche** with great views from the top. Lanes behind the church lead to Weinstrasse; turn left and continue on Theatinerstrasse, taking a break at the postmodern ⑩ **Fünf Höfe** shopping arcade. Backtrack a few steps on Theatinerstrasse, then turn left on tiny Perusastrasse, which delivers you to the grand ⑪ **Residenz**.

Continue north on Residenzstrasse to reach Odeonsplatz, dominated by the ⑫ **Feldherrnhalle**, a shrine to war heroes. The mustard-yellow ⑬ **Theatinerkirche** contains the Wittelsbach's crypt. Cross the neoclassical ⑭ **Hofgarten** and take the underpass, then turn right on Prinzregentenstrasse and proceed past the ⑮ **Haus der Kunst**, a gallery. Just beyond, don't miss the ⑯ **surfers** riding the artificial wave on the Eisbach creek. Across the creek, turn left into the English Garden and the multitiered ⑰ **Chinesischer Turm** for a well-deserved beer.

what else?), the penguins and polar bears in the Polarium, and the Orang-utan Paradise.

Bavaria FilmStadt FILM STUDIOS
(☑6499 2000; www.bavaria-filmtour.de; Bavaria-filmplatz 7; all attractions adult/child €25/19; ☺9am-3pm Apr-Oct, 10am-2pm Nov-Mar; ☐Bavariafilmplatz) Movie magic is the draw of the Bavaria Filmstadt, a theme park built around Bavaria Film, one of Germany's oldest studios, founded in 1919. The top-grossing German film of all time, *Das Boot,* was among the classics shot here but today's German audience is more interested in sets of the family soap *Marienhof.*

Films and TV are still produced today, and you might see a star during the guided 90-minute tours. The 1pm tour is in English.

The crash-and-burn Stunt Show is a runaway hit as well, while kids are particularly fond of the wacky 4D cinema, with seats that lurch and other special effects from silly to spooky. The Filmstadt is in the southern suburb of Geiselgasteig, about 14km from the Altstadt. Take the U1 to Wettersteinplatz, then tram 25 to Bavariafilmplatz.

🏃 Activities

Boating
A lovely spot to take your sweetheart for a spin is on the **Kleinhesseloher See** (Map p60) in the English Garden. Rowing or pedal boats cost around €8 per half-hour for up to four people. Boats may also be hired at the Olympiapark.

Cycling
Munich has excellent cycling, particularly along the Isar River. Some 1200km of cycle paths within the city limits make it one of Europe's friendliest places for two-wheelers.

The holy grail for mountain- and downhill bikers is the **Bombenkrater** (www.bombenkrater.de), a unique terrain of hillocks, dips, roots, ridges, holes and ramps created by WWII bombs. It's in a woody area on the southern city edge, right on the Isar River. Take the S7 to Höllriegelskreuth.

Hiking
For information about hiking and climbing as well as gear rental, swing by the Munich chapter of the **Deutscher Alpenverein** (German Alpine Club; Map p48; ☑551 7000; www.davplus.de; Bayerstrasse 21; ☺9am-7pm Mon-Fri, 8am-5pm Sat), near the Hauptbahnhof. See Shopping section (p94) for details of city-centre outdoor gear outlets.

Skating
From May to August, thousands of skaters take to Munich streets every Monday during **Blade Night** (www.aok-bladenight.de), organised rolls through various parts of the city. Check the website for routes and other details. The Olympiapark and the English Garden are also popular blader destinations.

Ice-skaters can glide alongside future medallists in the **Olympia-Eissportzentrum** (Map p64; ☑306 70; www.olympiapark.de; Spiridon-Louis-Ring 21; adult/child per session €4/2.80; ☺check website for times), hit the frozen canals in Nymphenburg (free) or twirl around at the **Münchner Eiszauber** (Map p48; www.muenchnereiszauber.de; per person €4; ☺mid-Nov–mid-Jan) ice rink on Karlsplatz.

Swimming
Bathing in the Isar River isn't advisable due to strong and unpredictable currents (especially in the English Garden), though many locals do. Better to head out of town to one of the many nearby swimming lakes, including the popular **Feringasee** (Take the S8 to Unterföhring then follow signs), where the party never stops on hot summer days; the pretty **Feldmochinger See** (S1 to Feldmoching), which is framed by gentle mounds and has a special area for wheelchair-bound bathers; and the **Unterföhringer See**

NO WAVE GOODBYE

Possibly the last sport you might expect to see being practiced in Munich is surfing, but go to the southern tip of the English Garden at Prinzregentenstrasse and you'll see scores of people leaning over a bridge to cheer on wetsuit-clad daredevils as they hang on an **artificially created wave in the Eisbach** (Prinzregentenstrasse, Eisbach). It's only a single wave, but it's a damn fine one. A few years ago park authorities attempted to ban this watery entertainment, but a successful campaign by surfers saw plans to turn the wave off shelved. Now some of the board riders have even put in an application for their sport (river surfing) to be included in the 2016 Olympics!

To find out more about Munich's urban surfers log on to www.eisbachwelle.de.

MUNICH FOR CHILDREN

(Tiny) hands down, Munich is a great city for children with plenty of activities, including parks for romping around, swimming pools and lakes for cooling off and beer gardens with childrens' playgrounds for making new friends. Many museums have special kid-oriented programs, but the highly interactive **KinderReich** at the Deutsches Museum (p70) specifically lures the single-digit set.

Kids love animals, of course, making the zoo Tierpark Hellabrunn (p74) a sure bet. Petting baby goats, feeding pelicans, watching falcons and hawks perform, or even riding a camel should make for some unforgettable memories. For a fishy immersion head to the new **SeaLife München** (Map p64; Willi-Daume-Platz 1; adult/child 3-14yr €15.95/10.50; ☺10am-7pm; ⑤Olympiazentrum) in the Olympic Park. Dino fans gravitate to Paläontologisches Museum (p59), while budding scientists will find plenty to marvel at in the Museum Mensch und Natur (p67) in Schloss Nymphenburg. The Spielzeugmuseum (p47) is of the look-but-don't-touch variety, but kids might still get a kick out of seeing the toys grandma used to pester for.

The adorable singing and dancing marionettes performing at the **Münchner Marionetten Theater** (Map p48; ☎265 712; www.muenchner-marionettentheater.de; Blumenstrasse 32; tickets €8-18; ☺3pm Wed-Sun, 8pm Sat) have enthralled generations of wee ones. At the **Münchner Theater für Kinder** (Map p64; ☎594 545; www.muenchner-theater-fuer-kinder.de; Dachauer Strasse 46; tickets €8-11) budding thespians can enjoy fairy tales and childrens classics à la *Max & Moritz* and *Pinocchio*. In winter, a show at the venerable Circus Krone (p94) is a magical experience.

For hands-on fun head to the **Dschungelpalast** (☎7248 8441; www.dschungelpalast.de; Hansastrasse 41), which organises low-cost arts and crafts workshops and a Sunday family brunch.

If you happen to be in Neuhausen, near Schloss Nymphenburg, swing by **Brauseschwein** (Map p64; ☎1395 8112; Frundsbergstrasse 52; ☺10am-1pm & 3pm-6.30pm Mon-Fri, 11am-2pm Sat), a wacky toy shop selling everything from penny candy to joke articles and wooden trains. Another great little shop for kids and nostalgic parents alike is **Puppenstube** (Map p64; Luisenstrasse 68), an entire emporium hung with dolls and puppets of yesteryear and this year.

German readers can find lots more tips and useful information at www.pomki.de and www.spiellandschaft.de.

(S8 to Unterföhring, via the Isarradweg), which has warm water and is easily reached by bicycle via the Isarradweg.

The best public swimming pool options, both indoors, are the **Olympia Schwimmhalle** (Map p64; www.swm.de; Coubertinplatz 1; 3hr pass adult/concession €4.20/3.20; ☺7am-11pm; ⑤Olympiazentrum), where Mark Spitz famously won seven gold medals in 1972; and the spectacular **Müller'sches Volksbad** (Map p72; Rosenheimer Strasse 1; adult/child €4/3.10; ☺7.30am-11pm; 🚋Am Gasteig), where you can swim in art nouveau splendour, then sweat it out in the Roman–Irish bath. Alternatively you could head to the **Dante-Winter-Warmfreibad** (Postillonstrasse 17; adult/child €3.70/2.70; ☺9am-6pm; 🚋Westfriedhof), a modern heated outdoor pool open from autumn to spring, for an invigorating dip in the depths of winter.

☞ Tours

Radius Tours　　　GUIDED TOURS
(☎543 487 7720; www.radiustours.com; opposite track 32, Hauptbahnhof; ☺8.30am-6pm Apr-Oct, to 2pm Nov-Mar) Entertaining and informative English-language tours include the two-hour **Priceless Munich Walk** (☺10am daily) where you pay the guide as much as you think the tour was worth; the fascinating 2½-hour **Hitler & The Third Reich Tour** (adult/student €12/10; ☺3pm Apr-mid-Oct, 11.30am Fri-Tue mid-Oct-Mar); and the three-hour **Prost! Beer & Food tour** (adult/student €29/27; ☺6pm selected days). The company also runs popular excursions to Neuschwanstein, Salzburg and Dachau as well as a range of other themed tours.

Mike's Bike Tours　　　BIKE TOURS
(Map p48; ☎2554 3987; www.mikesbiketours.com; departs Altes Rathaus, Marienplatz; tours from €24)

This outfit runs guided bike tours of the city from the Altes Rathaus on Marienplatz. The standard tour is around four hours long (with a one-hour beer garden break; lunch not included); the extended tour goes for seven hours and covers 15km.

Segway Tour Munich — SEGWAY TOURS
(STM; www.seg-tour-munich.com; €75; ☺tours at 9am, 10am, 2pm, 3pm, 7pm & 8pm) Three-hour, 12km segway tours led by English-speaking guides. Great way to see a lot in a short period of time without wearing your soles thin, though it comes with hefty price tag. Driving license required; weight limit between 45 and 117kg.

New Munich — WALKING TOURS
(www.newmunich.com; ☺walking tour 10.45am & 1pm) Departing from Marienplatz, these English-language walking tours tick off all Munich's central landmarks in three hours. Guides are well-informed and fun though they seem under pressure at the end of the tour to get as much as they can in tips. The company runs a number of other tours to Dachau (€21) and Neuschwanstein (€35) as well as a four-hour pub crawl (€14) from the Hauptbahnhof.

Munich Walk Tours — WALKING TOURS
(☑2423 1767; www.munichwalktours.de; Arnulfstrasse 2; tours from €12) This tour company runs tours around Munich, Dachau and Neuschwanstein. They also rent out bicycles (€15 per 24 hours) and offer internet access at Thomas-Wimmer-Ring 1 (€1 per 45 minutes).

Grayline Hop-On-Hop-Off Tours — BUS TOURS
(www.grayline.com/Munich; adult/child from €13/7; ☺every 20min) This tour bus company offers a choice of three tours from one-hour highlights to the 2.5-hour grand tour, as well as excursions to Ludwig II's castles, the Romantic Road, Dachau, Berchtesgaden, Zugspitze and Salzburg. All tours can be booked online and buses are of recent vintage. The main departure point (Map p48) is outside the Karstadt department store opposite the Hauptbahnhof.

★ Festivals & Events

Beer to opera, film to Christmas, Munich has a year-round calendar of fun goings-on. We've picked through the pile for our faves, but www.muenchen-tourist.de has the full rundown. Check individual websites for line-ups and ticket information.

January–March
Fasching — FESTIVAL
A carnival time beginning on 7 January and ending on Ash Wednesday involving all kinds of merriment such as costume parades and fancy-dress balls.

Starkbierzeit — BEER FESTIVAL
Salvator, Optimator, Unimator, Maximator and Triumphator are not the names of gladiators but potent *doppelbock* brews dekegged only between Shrovetide and Easter. Monks allegedly invented them to ease hunger pangs during Lent. The Paulaner am Nockherberg (☑459 9130; Hochstrasse 77) and Löwenbräukeller (Map p64; ☑089 526 021; Nymphenburger Strasse 2; ☺10am-midnight; U1 Stiglmaierplatz) are the places to experience festivities, though many others also serve the beer.

April–June
Frühlingsfest — BEER FESTIVAL
This mini-Oktoberfest kicks off the outdoor festival season with two weeks of beer tents and attractions starting around 20 April. Highlight: the mammoth flea market on the first Saturday.

Maidult — FESTIVAL
The first of three traditional dult fairs held on the Mariahilfplatz. Starts on the Saturday preceding 1 May.

Stustaculum — FESTIVAL
(www.stustaculum.de) This giant open-air festival in Europe's largest student quarter, the Studentenstadt Freimann in northern Schwabing, consists of four days of theatre, music and general merriment, usually in early June. Take the U6 to Studentenstadt.

Tollwood Festival — CULTURAL FESTIVAL
(www.tollwood.de) Major world-culture festival with concerts, theatre, circus, readings and other fun events held from late June to late July. Also throughout December on the Theresienwiese.

July–September
Filmfest München — FILM FESTIVAL
(www.filmfest-muenchen.de) Not as glamorous as Cannes or Venice, this flick festival presents intriguing and often high-calibre fare by newbies and masters from around the world in the first week of July.

Christopher Street Day — FESTIVAL
(www.csd-munich.de) Gay festival and parade culminating in a big street party on Marien-

platz. Usually held on the second weekend in July.

Jakobidult FESTIVAL
The second dult starts on the Saturday following 25 July and continues for one week.

Opernfestspiele MUSIC FESTIVAL
(Opera Festival; www.muenchner-opern-festspiele.de) The Bavarian State Opera brings in top-notch talent from around the world for this month-long festival which takes place at numerous venues around the city throughout July.

Tanzwerkstatt Europa CULTURAL FESTIVAL
(www.jointadventures.net) Performances and workshops for modern dance, drama and readings held over 10 days in early August.

October–December

Oktoberfest BEER FESTIVAL
(www.oktoberfest.de) Legendary beer-swilling party running from mid-September to the first Sunday in October, held on the Theresienwiese (p22).

Kirchweihdult FAIR
A traditional fair that opens on the third Saturday in October.

Munich Marathon MARATHON
(www.muenchenmarathon.de) More than 10,000 runners from around the world take to the streets in mid-October, finishing after just over 42km at the Olympic Stadium.

Christkindlmarkt CHRISTMAS MARKET
(www.christkindlmarkt.de; ⊘late-Nov–Christmas Eve) Traditional Christmas market on Marienplatz and a visual stunner.

🛏 Sleeping

Munich's excellent public transport system puts you within easy reach of everything. If you prefer being steps from the trophy sights, find a place in the Altstadt, although you'll pay a premium for the priviledge. Choices are greater and rates more reasonable in Ludwigsvorstadt near the Hauptbahnhof and the Oktoberfest grounds. Party people will enjoy Schwabing, Maxvorstadt and the Gärtnerplatzviertel-Glockenbachviertel area. Lodging options are thinner on the ground in slower-paced residential neighbourhoods such as Haidhausen and Lehel, but are often the most charming and authentic.

Room rates skyrocket during Oktoberfest and other major events and trade shows. Book well ahead to avoid disappointment.

Long-Term Rentals

If you're staying in Munich for a week or longer, it usually works out cheaper to rent a room, flat or apartment.

Statthotel ACCOMMODATION AGENCY
(☑08709-926 00; www.statthotel.de) Rooms here start at €180 per week and €350 per month, while studio flats will set you back about €300 per week and €600 per month, all excluding the 25% commission and 19% VAT.

**Mitwohnzentrale –
Mr Lodge** ACCOMMODATION AGENCY
(☑340 8230; www.mrlodge.de; Barer Strasse 32; 🚇Karolinenplatz) Flats across Munich starting at around €700 per month.

**Gästehaus Englischer Garten
Apartments** APARTMENTS
(Map p60; ☑383 9410; www.hotelenglischergarten.de; Liebergesellstrasse 8; ⑤Münchner Freiheit) This guesthouse has 20 self-contained studio flats on the edge of the English Garden for €1500 per month.

ALTSTADT

TOP CHOICE **Bayerischer Hof** HOTEL €€€
(Map p48; ☑212 00; www.bayerischerhof.de; Promenadeplatz 2-6; r €250-450; ❋@🛜🏊; 🚇Theatinerstrasse) One of the grande dames of the Munich hotel trade, rooms at the Hof come in a number of styles, from busy Laura Ashley to minimalist cosmopolitan. The super-central location, pool and on-site cinema come in addition to impeccably behaved staff. Marble, antiques and oil paintings abound, and with ample cash you can dine till you burst at any one of the five fabulous restaurants.

Hotel Mandarin Oriental Munich HOTEL €€€
(Map p48; ☑290 980; www.mandarinoriental.com; Neuturmstrasse 1; d €525-645; 🅿❋@🛜🏊; ⑤Marienplatz, 🚇Marienplatz) These magnificent neo-Renaissance digs lure the world's glamourous, rich, powerful and famous with opulently understated rooms and top-notch service. Paul McCartney, Bill Clinton and Prince Charles have crumpled the sheets here. Service is polite almost to a fault, but incredibly, breakfast and internet access are extra.

Hotel Blauer Bock
HOTEL €€

(Map p48; ☎231 780; www.hotelblauerbock.de; Sebastiansplatz 9; s €55-99, d €90-153; ☎; ⑤Marienplatz, ◍Marienplatz) A stuffed olive's throw away from the Viktualienmarkt, this simple hotel has succesfully slipped through the net of gentrification to become the Altstadt's best deal. The cheapest, unmodernised rooms have shared facilities, the updated en-suite chambers are of a 21st-century vintage and all are quiet, despite the location. Superb restaurant.

Cortiina
HOTEL €€€

(Map p48; ☎242 2490; www.cortiina.com; Ledererstrasse 8; s €165-270, d €225-345; P✿❋; ⑤Marienplatz, ◍Marienplatz) Tiptoeing between hip and haute, this hotel scores best with trendy, design-minded travellers. The street-level lounge usually buzzes with cocktail-swigging belles and beaus, but all traces of hustle evaporate the moment you step into your minimalist, Feng Shui–inspired room. Breakfast is an unappetising €19.50 extra.

Hotel am Viktualienmarkt
HOTEL €€

(Map p48; ☎231 1090; www.hotel-am-viktualienmarkt.de; Utzschneiderstrasse 14; d €50-120; ☎; ⑤Marienplatz, ◍Marienplatz) Owners Elke and her daughter Stephanie run this good-value property with panache and a sunny attitude. The best of the up-to-date 26 rooms have wooden floors and framed poster art. All this, plus the city centre location, makes it a superb deal.

SCHWABING & MAXVORSTADT

La Maison
DESIGN HOTEL €€

(Map p60; ☎3303 5550; www.hotel-la-maison.com; Occamstrasse 24; s/d from €109/119; P✿@; ⑤Münchner Freiheit) Discerningly retro and immaculate in shades of imperial purple and uber-cool grey, this sassy number wows with its rooms flaunting heated oak floors, jet-black basins and starkly contrasting design throughout, though they still can't resist the coy pack of gummi bears on the expertly ruffed pillows! Cool bar on ground level.

Pension am Kaiserplatz
GUESTHOUSE €

(Map p60; ☎395 231, 349 190; www.amkaiserplatz.de; Kaiserplatz 12; s €35-49, d €53-67; ☎; ◍Kurfürstenplatz) One of the best value places to stay in the city centre, this family-run B&B in a grand Jugendstil building has generously cut, high-ceiling rooms furnished with four decades' worth of furniture. Continental breakfast is served in your room by the always-around-to-help owners. Toilets are shared but there are in-room showers (literally). Cash only.

Gästehaus Englischer Garten
GUESTHOUSE €€

(Map p60; ☎383 9410; www.hotelenglischergarten.de; Liebergesellstrasse 8; s €68-177, d €79-177; P@☎; ⑤Münchner Freiheit) Cosily inserted into a 200-year-old ivy-clad mill, this small guesthouse on the edge of the English Garden offers a Bavarian version of the British B&B experience. Not all rooms are en-suite, but the breakfast is generous and there's cycle hire (€12 per day).

Hotel Marienbad
HOTEL €€

(Map p48; ☎595 585; www.hotelmarienbad.de; Barer Strasse 11; s/d from €55/105; ☎; ◍Ottostrasse) Back in the 19th century, Wagner, Puccini and Rilke shacked up in what once ranked among Munich's finest hotels. Still friendly and well maintained, it now flaunts an endearing alchemy of styles, from playful art nouveau to floral country Bavarian to campy 1960s utilitarian. Amenities, fortunately, are of more recent vintage.

Hotel Hauser
HOTEL €€

(☎286 6750; www.hotel-hauser.de; Schellingstrasse 11; s €88-148, d €118-230; P☎; ⑤Universität) The ageing woody rooms date back to the optimistic days of the economic miracle, but are pristinely maintained, if small. Unexpected extras include a sauna and solarium. Cash preferred.

Cosmopolitan Hotel
HOTEL €€

(Map p60; ☎383 810; www.cosmopolitan-hotel.de; Hohenzollernstrasse 5; d from €135; P☎; ⑤Münchner Freiheit) Almost Soviet in their no-frills functionality, the decor of hollow tubing, primary colours and fake veneer is all very 90s but rooms are clean and well-tended and breakfasts are generous. Sleep, wash, breakfast and surf, but if you want character, go elsewhere.

NYMPHENBURG, NEUHAUSEN & OLYMPIAPARK

TOP CHOICE Hotel Laimer Hof
HOTEL €€

(Map p64; ☎178 0380; www.laimerhof.de; Laimer Strasse 40; s/d from €65/85; P@☎; ◍Romanplatz) Just a five-minute amble from Schloss Nymphenburg, this tranquil refuge is run by a friendly team who take time to get to know their guests. No two of the 23 rooms are alike, but all boast antique touches, oriental carpets and golden beds. Popular with everyone from honeymooners to families, business travellers to round-the-world backpackers.

LUDWIGSVORSTADT & WESTEND

Anna Hotel
DESIGN HOTEL €€€
(Map p48; ☑599 940; www.geisel-privathotels.de; Schützenstrasse 1; s €160-215, d €175-235; ❋@; ⑤Karlsplatz, ⑩Karlsplatz, ⑩Karlsplatz) Urban sophisticates love this designer den where you can retire to rooms dressed in sensuous Donghia furniture and regal colours, or others with a more minimalist feel tempered by teakwood, marble and mosaics. The swanky restaurant-bar is a 24/7 beehive of activity.

Hotel Cocoon
DESIGN HOTEL €€
(Map p48; ☑5999 3907; www.hotel-cocoon.de; Lindwurmstrasse 35; s/d €79/99; ⑤Sendlinger Tor, ⑩Sendlinger Tor) If retro-design is your thing, you just struck gold. Things kick off in the reception with its faux '70s veneer and suspended '60s ball chairs, and continue in the rooms, all identical and decorated in cool retro oranges and greens. Every room has LCD TV, iPod dock, 'laptop cabin' and the hotel name above every bed in 1980s robotic lettering.

The glass showers actually stand in the sleeping area, with only a kitschy Alpine meadow scene veiling life's vitals. Another branch, **Cocoon Stachus** (Adolf-Kolping-Strasse 11), opened in 2012.

Sofitel Munich Bayerpost
HOTEL €€€
(☑599 480; www.sofitel.com; Bayerstrasse 12; s/d from €140/160; ⓟ❋@☀; ⑤Hauptbahnhof, ⑩Hauptbahnhof Süd, ⑩Hauptbahnhof) The restored Renaissance façade of a former post office hides this high-concept jewel that wraps all that's great about Munich – history, innovation, elegance, the art of living – into one neat and appealing package. Be sure to make time for the luxurious spa where the grotto-like pool juts into the atrium lobby lidded by a tinted glass roof.

Hotel Eder
HOTEL €€
(☑554 660; www.hotel-eder.de; Zweigstrasse 8; s €55-140, d €65-190; ☎; ⑤Hauptbahnhof, ⑩Hauptbahnhof) Like five storeys of small-town Bavaria teleported to the slightly seedy area south of the Hauptbahnhof, this rustic oasis has its chequered curtains, carved-wood chairs and Sisi/Ludwig II portraits firmly in place for those who didn't come all this way for the cocktails. The unevenly sized rooms are a bit vanilla, but when rates are mid to low this is a nifty deal.

Pension Westfalia
B&B €
(☑530 377; www.pension-westfalia.de; Mozartstrasse 23; s/d from €38/50; @; ⑤Goetheplatz) Literally a stumble away from the Oktoberfest meadow a stately four-storey villa conceals this cosy, family-run guesthouse, a serene base for sightseeing (outside the beer fest). Rooms are reached by lift and the cheaper ones have corridor facilities.

Alpen Hotel
HOTEL €€€
(☑559 330; www.alpenhotel-muenchen.de; Adolf-Kolping-Strasse 14; s/d from €115/145; ☎; ⑤Hauptbahnhof, ⑩Hauptbahnhof, ⑩Hauptbahnhof) Don't be fooled by the woodchipped wallpaper of the corridors here – rooms are of a very high business standard, parading big bathrooms and every amenity you could need. The downstairs restaurant is a lively spot.

Hotel Uhland
HOTEL €€
(☑543 350; www.hotel-uhland.de; Uhlandstrasse 1; s/d from €69/87; ⓟ☎; ⑤Theresienwiese) The Uhland is an enduring favourite with regulars who expect their hotel to feel like a home away from home. Three generations of family members are constantly finding ways to improve their guests' experience, be it with wi-fi, bathroom phones, ice cubes, bike rentals or mix-your-own organic breakfast muesli.

Schiller 5
HOTEL €€
(Map p48; ☑515 040; www.schiller5.com; Schillerstrasse 5; s/d from €102/144; ⓟ❋☎; ⑤Hauptbahnhof, ⑩Hauptbahnhof, ⑩Hauptbahnhof) Not only are the pads at this semi-apartment hotel smartly trimmed, you also get a lot for your euro here in the shape of a well-equipped kitchenette, sound system, coffee machine and extra large bed in every room. Some guests complain of street noise so try to bag a room away from the hustle below.

Hotel Müller
HOTEL €€
(Map p48; ☑232 3860; www.hotel-mueller-muenchen.de; Fliegenstrasse 4; s/d €119/139; ⓟ☎; ⑤Sendlinger Tor) This friendly hotel has big, bright, business-standard rooms and good price-to-quality ratio with five-star breakfasts and well-regimented staff. Despite the city-centre location, this side-street is pretty quiet.

Hotel Mariandl
HOTEL €€
(☑552 9100; www.mariandl.com; Goethestrasse 51; s €65-115, d €70-165; ⑤Sendlinger Tor, ⑩Sendlinger Tor) If you like your history laced with quirkiness, you'll find both aplenty in this

rambling neo-Gothic mansion. It's an utterly charming place where rooms convincingly capture the Jugendstil period with hand-selected antiques and ornamented ceilings. Breakfast is served until 4pm in the Vienna-style downstairs cafe, which also has live jazz or classical music nightly.

Hotelissimo Haberstock HOTEL €€
(Map p48; ☑557 855; www.hotelissimo.com; Schillerstrasse 4; s/d from €74/104; ☎; Ⓢ Hauptbahnhof, 🚇 Hauptbahnhof, 🚈 Hauptbahnhof) The cheery decor at this value-for-money pick reflects the vision of the owners, a husband-and-wife team with a knack for colour, fabrics and design. Easy-on-the-eye gold, brown and cream tones dominate the good-sized rooms on the lower floors, while upper ones radiate a bolder, Mediterranean palette.

Wombat's Hostel HOSTEL €
(☑5998 9180; www.wombats-hostels.com; Senefelderstrasse 1; dm €12-24, d from €70; @☎; Ⓢ Hauptbahnhof, 🚇 Hauptbahnhof, 🚈 Hauptbahnhof) Munich's top hostel is a professionally run affair with a whopping 300 dorm beds plus private rooms. Dorms are basic with no frill or theme, but with en-suite facilities, sturdy lockers and comfy pine bunks, all in a central location near the train station, who needs gimmicks. A free welcome drink awaits in the bar, but breakfast is €3.80 extra.

Meininger's HOSTEL/HOTEL €
(☑5499 8023; www.meininger-hostels.de; Landsbergerstrasse 20; dm/s/d without breakfast from €15/45/80; @☎; 🚇 Holzapfelstrasse.) About 800m west of the Hauptbahnhof, this energetic hostel-hotel has basic, clean, bright rooms with big dorms divided into two for a bit of privacy. Room rates vary wildly depending on the date, events taking place in Munich and occupancy. Breakfast is an extra €4, bike hire €12 per day.

Demas City Hotel HOTEL €€
(☑693 3990; www.demas-city.de; Landwehrstrasse 19; r from €89; ☎; Ⓢ Karlsplatz, 🚇 Karlsplatz, 🚈 Karlsplatz) The 54 rooms at this quiet sleeper near the Hauptbahnhof are done out in trendy greys and blacks, accentuated by flashes of lime and purple. Bathrooms are a snug fit and staff English is *nicht so gut*, but all in all a decent, if vibe-less, place for centrally-based snoozing, breakfasting and web surfing.

GÄRTNERPLATZVIERTEL & GLOCKENBACHVIERTEL

Pension Gärtnerplatz GUESTHOUSE €€
(Map p48; ☑202 5170; www.pensiongaertnerplatz.de; Klenzestrasse 45; s/d €80/110; ☎; Ⓢ Fraunhoferstrasse) Flee the urban hullabaloo to an Alpine fantasy land where rooms allure in carved wood, painted bedsteads, woollen rugs and crisp, quality bedding. In one room a portrait of Ludwig II watches you as you slumber; breakfasts are honestly organic.

H'Otello Advokat BOUTIQUE HOTEL €€
(Map p48; ☑4583 1200; www.hotel-advokat.de; Baaderstrasse 1; r from €135; ☎; 🚇 Isartor, 🚈 Isartor) Though now not as excitingly different as it once was, Munich's first boutique hotel is all about understated retro design and amiable service. Rooms won't fit a tonne of luggage but are nicely dressed in creamy hues, tactile fabrics and subtle lighting. Guests rave about the breakfast; a smorgasbord of fresh fruit, deli salads, smoked salmon and organic cheeses.

Hotel Olympic HOTEL €€€
(Map p48; ☑231 890; www.hotel-olympic.de; Hans-Sachs-Strasse 4; s €95-160, d €155-200; P@☎; 🚇 Müllerstrasse) If you're looking for a small, friendly, peaceful and well-run place to lay your head with a bit of simple, understated style, then this guesthouse-type hotel in a funky location might be for you. Rooms double up as mini art galleries and staff couldn't be more accommodating. Parking costs €15 a night.

Pension Eulenspiegel GUESTHOUSE €€
(Map p48; ☑266 678; www.pensioneulenspiegel.de; Müllerstrasse 43a; s €49-110, d €78-200; P☎; 🚇 Müllerstrasse) Tucked away in a courtyard off Müllerstrasse, this completely non-smoking, gay-friendly guesthouse offers nine rooms with sparkling wooden floors and newly renovated showers. Some rooms share a corridor shower and toilet.

Deutsche Eiche HOTEL €€
(Map p48; ☑231 1660; www.deutsche-eiche.com; Reichenbachstrasse 13; s/d from €79/139; ☎; 🚇 Reichenbachplatz) The rainbow flag flutters camply alongside the usual national pennants outside this traditionally gay outpost that invites style junkies of all sexual persuasions to enjoy the slick rooms and first-class restaurant. There's a gay sauna and gay tourist information stand on the premises.

LEHEL

Hotel Splendid-Dollmann HOTEL €€€
(Map p72; ☑238 080; www.hotel-splendid-doll
mann.de; Thierschstrasse 49; s/d from €130/160;
☎; ⌂Lehel) This small but posh player delivers old-world charm and is sure to delight
romantically inclined. The mood is set
at check-in where fresh orchids, classical
music and friendly staff welcome you. Retire to antique-furnished rooms, the idyllic
terraced garden or the regally furnished
lounge. Rooms in front must deal with tram
noise.

Hotel Opéra HOTEL €€€
(Map p72; ☑210 4940; www.hotel-opera.de; St-An-
na-Strasse 10; d from €155; ⌂Maxmonument) Like
the gates to heaven, a white double door
opens at the touch of a tiny brass button. Beyond awaits a smart, petite cocoon of quiet
sophistication with peaches-and-cream
marble floors, a chandelier scavenged from
the Vatican and uniquely decorated rooms.
In summer, the serene arcaded courtyard
is perfect for alfresco breakfast, served à la
carte.

HAIDHAUSEN

Hotel Ritzi HOTEL €€€
(Map p72; ☑414 240 890; www.hotel-ritzi.de;
Maria-Theresia-Strasse 2a; s/d from €110/179; ☎;
⌂Maxmilianeum) At this charming art hotel
next to a little park, creaky wooden stairs
(no lift) lead to rooms that transport you to
the Caribbean, Africa, Morocco and other
exotic lands. But it's the Jugendstil features
of the building that really impress, as does
the much-praised restaurant downstairs.

Hotel am Nockherberg HOTEL €€
(☑623 0010; www.nockherberg.de; Nockherstrasse
38a; s €89-119, d €110-135; ℗☎; ⑤Kolumbusplatz)
This charming base of operation south of
the Isar puts you close to the Deutsches Museum, the bar- and restaurant-filled Gärtnerplatzviertel and the Gasteig Cultural Centre.
The decor of the 46 rooms is pleasing in a
generic kind of way but all major mod-cons
are accounted for, and there's a sauna to
boot.

✘ Eating

Munich's food was once described by Viennese actor Helmut Qualtinger as 'garnish for
the beer', and while that may still ring true
in traditional beer halls and restaurants,
where the menu rarely ventures beyond the
roast pork and sausage routine, elsewhere

Munich can claim to have southern Germany's most exciting cuisine scene. There's lots
of innovation going on in Munich's kitchens,
where the best dishes make use of fresh
regional, seasonal and organic ingredients.
The Bavarian capital is also the best place
between Vienna and Paris for a spot of internationally flavoured dining, especially when
it comes to Italian, Afghan and Turkish food,
and even vegetarians can look forward to
something other than noodles and salads.

Quick Eats

Pommes Boutique FAST FOOD €
(Map p60; Amalienstrasse 46; fries €2.50; ⊙10am-
10pm Mon-Sat; ⑤Universität) This funky lunch
halt serves cheap-as-chips, Belgian-style
fries made from organic potatoes, 30-odd
finger-licking dips to dunk them in and *Currywurst* to die for.

Bergwolf FAST FOOD €
(Map p48; Fraunhoferstrasse 17; ⊙noon-2am Mon-
Thu, noon-4am Fri & Sat, noon-10pm Sun, closed
3-6pm Sun-Fri; ⑤Fraunhoferstrasse) At this favourite pit stop for night owls, the poison of
choice is *Currywurst,* a sliced spicy sausage
provocatively dressed in a curried ketchup
and best paired with a pile of crisp fries.
Hangover prevention at its tastiest.

Eiscafé Sarcletti ICE CREAM €
(Map p64; Nymphenburger Strasse 155; ⊙9am-
11.30pm; ⌂Volkartstrasse) Ice-cream addicts
have been getting their gelato fix at this
Munich institution since 1879. Choose from
more than 50 mouth-watering flavours,
from not-so-plain vanilla to honey-yogurt or
caramel.

Küche am Tor GERMAN/ASIAN €
(Map p48; Lueg Ins Land 1; mains €8; ⊙noon-5pm
Mon-Fri; ☑; ⌂Isartor, ⌂Isartor) No-nonsense,
blink-and-you'd-miss-it lunch halt for local
office workers with a comfortingly short
menu of mostly German fair but containing
little subcontinental inflections such as red
lentils, mild curry and Ayurvedic soup.

Cafe Frischhut CAFE €
(Map p48; Prälat-Zistl-Strasse 8; pastries €1.70;
⊙7am-6pm Mon-Sat; ⑤Marienplatz, ⌂Marien-
platz) This incredibly popular institution
serves just four traditional pastries, one of
which – the *Schmalznudel* (an oily type of
doughnut) – gives the place its local nickname. Every baked goodie you munch here
is crisp and fragrant as they're always fresh
off the hot plate out front.

Wiener Cafe
CAFE €

(Map p48; cnr Reichenbachstrasse & Rumfordstrasse; snacks €1.50-5; ☺8.30am-6pm Mon-Fri, 8am-5pm Sat; ℗; ⓡReichenbachplatz) Serving cakes, snacks and drinks, the only cool thing about this delightfully old-fashioned central European coffeehouse is the marble table tops.

Best Back
BAKERY €

(Bayerstrasse 55; ☺6.30am-midnight Mon-Fri, 7am-midnight Sat; ⓡHolzkirchner Bahnhof) Forget the overpriced food at the station, just a few steps from the tracks is this no-frills bakery where the same sandwiches, savouries and cakes are on sale for half the price, and coffees go for a single euro.

Self-Catering

The dominant supermarket chains are Aldi, Penny, Tengelmann, Rewe and Lidl, with multiple branches scattered throughout the city. For a more upscale (and pricier) selection, head to the supermarket in the basement of the **Kaufhof** (Map p48; Karlsplatz 21-24) department store or the Viktualienmarkt (p47). Deep-pocketed gourmets have a couple of venerable destinations to look forward to: **Dallmayr** (Dienerstrasse 14) is famous for its coffee but has so much more, including cheeses, ham, truffles, wine, caviar and exotic foods from every corner of the earth. **Käfer** (Map p72; Prinzregentenstrasse 73) is just as good.

ALTSTADT

TOP
CHOICE **Prinz Myshkin**
VEGETARIAN €€

(Map p48; ☑265 596; www.prinzmyshkin.com; Hackenstrasse 2; mains €10-17; ☺11am-12.30am; ✐; ⓢMarienplatz, ⓡMarienplatz) Proof if any were needed that the vegetarian experience has left the sandals, beards and lentils era, Munich's premier meat-free dining spot fills out an open-plan, but strangely intimate vaulted dining space, a former brewery, with health-conscious eaters who come to savour imaginative dishes such as curry-orange-carrot soup, tofu stroganoff, 'Save the Tuna' pizza and unexpectedly good curries.

Daylesford Organic
ORGANIC €€

(Map p48; Ledererstrasse 3; mains from €9-17; ☺9am-8pm Mon-Sat; ✐; ⓢMarienplatz, ⓡMarienplatz) The Munich branch of this British organic food buffet enjoys a superb setting in the white-washed cellars of the Zerwirk building. The fish, meat and vegetarian dishes are superb, but it's the little British elements such as curry and chutney, plus the extensive organic wine list, that make this laid-back eatery something a bit different.

Bratwurstherzl
FRANCONIAN €

(Map p48; ☑295 113; Dreifaltigkeitsplatz 1; mains €6-10; ☺10am-11pm Mon-Sat; ⓢMarienplatz, ⓡMarienplatz) Cosy panelling and an ancient vaulted brick ceiling set the tone of this Old Munich chow house with a Franconian focus. Home-made organic sausages are grilled to perfection on an open beechwood fire, served on heart-shaped pewter plates and best enjoyed with a cold beer straight from the wooden keg.

Weisses Brauhaus
BAVARIAN €€

(Map p48; Tal 7; mains €8-15; ⓢMarienplatz, ⓡMarienplatz) The Weisswurst (veal sausage) sets the standard for the rest to aspire to; sluice down a pair with the unsurpassed Schneider Weissbier. Of an evening the dining halls are charged with red-faced, ale-infused hilarity with Alpine whoops accompanying the rabble-rousing oompah band.

La Baracca
ITALIAN €€

(Map p48; ☑4161 7852; www.labaracca.eu; Maxmiliansplatz 9; mains €5.50-14; ☺11.30am-1am; ⓢOdeonsplatz) At this great new Italian place homely spaces such as a library and a cushion-strewn chill-out area combine effortlessly with iPad menus, an automated ordering system and a marble bar with stainless steel stools. The ceiling is made entirely of huge lengths of driftwood and rustic knick-knacks decorate throughout. Free wine tasting but untypically small helpings for an Italian eatery.

Cafe Luitpold
CAFE €€

(Map p48; www.cafe-luitpold.de; Briennerstrasse 11; mains €10-18; ☺8am-7pm Mon, to 11pm Tue-Sat, 9am-7pm Sun; ⓢOdeonsplatz) A cluster of pillarbox red, streetside tables and chairs announces you've arrived at this stylish but not uber-cool retreat offering a choice of three spaces – a lively bar, a less boisterous columned cafe and a cool palm-leaved atrium. Good for a daytime coffee and cake or an evening blow-out with all the trimmings.

Königsquelle
ALPINE €€

(Map p48; ☑220 071; Baaderplatz 2; mains €9-18; ☺dinner; ⓢIsartor, ⓡIsartor) This Munich institution is well-loved for its attentive service, expertly prepared food, and dark, well-stocked hardwood bar containing what must be the Bavarian capital's best selection of malt whiskeys. The hardly decipherable, handwritten menu hovers somewhere mid-Alps with anything from schnitzel to linguine and goat's cheese to cannelloni to choose from.

Conviva INTERNATIONAL €€
(Map p48; Hildegardstrasse 1; 3-course lunch €8-10, dinner mains €10-15; ⊙11am-1am Mon-Sat; ⌨; ⏃Kammerspiele) The spartan interior and barely dressed tables means nothing distracts from the great food at this theatre restaurant. The daily changing menus make the most of local seasonal ingredients and are reassuringly short.

Einstein KOSHER €€
(Map p48; St-Jakobs-Platz 18; mains €9-17; ⊙noon-3pm & 6pm-midnight Sat-Thu, noon-3pm Fri; ⑤Marienplatz, ⏃Marienplatz) Reflected in the plate-glass windows of the Jewish Museum, this is the only kosher eatery in the city centre. The ID and bag search entry process is worth it for the restaurant's uncluttered lines, smartly laid tables and soothing ambience.

SCHWABING & MAXVORSTADT

Tantris FINE DINING €€€
(☎361 9590; www.tantris.de; Johann-Fichte-Strasse 7; menu from €75; ⊙lunch & dinner Tue-Sat; ⑤Dietlindenstrasse) Tantris means 'the search for perfection' and here, at one of Germany's most famous restaurants, they're not far off it. The interior design is full-bodied '70s – all postbox reds, truffle blacks and illuminated yellows – the food gourmet sublimity and the service sometimes as unintrusive as it is efficient. The wine cellar is probably Germany's best. Reservations and a fat wallet essential.

Potting Shed BAR, BURGERS €€
(Map p60; Occamstrasse 11; tapas €2.50-10.50, burgers €11.50-13.90; ⊙from 6pm; ⑤Münchner Freiheit) This relaxed hangout serves tapas, gourmet burgers and cocktails to an easy-going evening crowd. The burger menu whisks you round the globe, but it's the house speciality, the 'Potting Shed Special' involving an organic beef burger flambéed in whiskey, that catches the eye on the simple but well-concocted menu.

Café An Der Uni CAFE €
(Map p60; Ludwigstrasse 24; snacks & mains €5-9; ⊙8am-1am Mon-Fri, from 9am Sat & Sun; ☎⌨; ⑤Universität) Anytime is a good time to be at charismatic CADU. Enjoy breakfast (served until a hangover-friendly 11.30pm!), a cuppa Java or a Helles in the lovely garden hidden by a wall from busy Ludwigstrasse.

Tibet Kitchen TIBETAN €
(Map p60; www.tibetkitchen.de; Occamstrasse 4; mains €7.50-12.50; ⊙5-11pm Mon-Sat; ⑤Münchner Freiheit) Bavaria's first and only Tibetan restaurant is an informal affair, drooped in prayer flags and awash with bits of Buddhist paraphernalia. The English menu is a blessing as otherwise few would know what *Momos, Lugsha* and *Gyathung* were. And anyone who thought Tibetans are vegetarians will be taken aback by the choice of meat dishes, though yak (sadly) makes no appearance.

Chopan AFGHAN €€
(Map p64; Elvirastrasse 18A; €7-17.50; ⊙6pm-midnight; ⑤Maillingerstrasse) Munich has a huge Afghan community and their best respected eatery is this much-lauded restaurant done out Central Asian *caravanserai*-style in rich fabrics, multi-hued glass lanterns and geometric patterns. In this culinary Aladdin's cave you'll discover an exotic menu of lamb, lentils, rice, spinach and flat bread in various combinations, but no alcoholic beverages.

Il Mulino ITALIAN €€
(Map p64; Görresstrasse 1; mains €6-20; ⑤Josephsplatz) This neighbourhood classic has been feeding Italophiles for over three decades. All the expected pastas and pizzas are present and correct, though the daily specials will likely tickle the palate of more curious eaters.

Bar Tapas TAPAS €
(Map p60; Amalienstrasse 97; tapas €4.30 each; ⊙5pm-1am; ⌨; ⑤Universität) A phalanx of 30 tapas – *boquerones* (anchovies) to octopus salad to garlic chicken – reports to duty behind glass along the bar of this convivial Iberian outpost. Write down the numbers, then sit back with a jug of sangria and wait for your tasty morsels to arrive.

Schmock ISRAELI €€
(Map p64; ☎5235 0535; Augustenstrasse 52; mains €5.20-27.50; ⊙10am-1am; ⌨; ⑤Theresienstrasse) Israeli food gets a gourmet twist at this elegant restaurant with stucco ornamented ceiling, fresh flowers and complexion-friendly art-nouveau lamps. Kosher *Currywurst* anyone?

NEUHAUSEN

Ruffini
CAFE €

(Map p64; Orffstrasse 22; meals €7-10; ⊙10am-midnight Tue-Sun; ⎇; ⎇Neuhausen) Well worth the effort of delving deep into Neuhausen to find, this hip cafe is a fun place to be no matter where the hands of the clock are. On sunny days the self-service rooftop terrace gets busy with locals – few tourists make it out here. Regular music events from rock to classical.

Schlosscafé Im Palmenhaus
CAFE €€

(Map p64; mains €9-15; ⊙10am-5.30pm Tue-Sun; ⎇Schloss Nymphenburg) The glass-fronted 1820 palm house, where Ludwig II used to keep his exotic house plants warm in winter, is now a high-ceilinged and pleasantly scented cafe. It's just behind Schloss Nymphenburg.

Zauberberg
INTERNATIONAL €€

(Map p64; Hedwigstrasse 14; 3-course dinner menu €39, with wine €58; ⊙6.30pm-1am Tue-Sat; ⎇Albrechtstrasse) Far off the tourist track, this 40-seat locals' favourite will put your tummy into a state of contentment with its elegant, well-composed international creations. Single plates are available but in order to truly sample the chef's talents, you should order a multi-course menu.

LUDWIGSVORSTADT & WESTEND

TOP CHOICE Marais
CAFE €

(Parkstrasse 2; dishes €5-12; ⊙8am-8pm Mon-Sat, 10am-6pm Sun; ⎇; ⎇Holzapfelstrasse) Is it a junk shop, a cafe or a sewing shop? Well, Westend's oddest coffeehouse is in fact all three, and everything you see in this converted haberdashery – the knickknacks, the cakes and the antique chair you're sitting on – is for sale.

Müller & Söhne
MEDITERRANEAN €

(⎇4523 7867; Kazmairstrasse 28; mains €6-12; ⊙9am-11pm Mon-Fri; ⎇; ⎇Schwanthalerhöhe) In a former bakery, this sweet, unhurried cafe fits as comfortably as a well-worn shoe. Everyone from young mothers to office folks and local artists gather behind the big windows for breakfast, strong Java or tasty, Italian-flavoured sustenance.

La Vecchia Masseria
ITALIAN €€

(Map p48; Mathildenstrasse 3; mains €6-15; ⊙11.30am-12.30am; ⎇Sendlinger Tor, ⎇Sendlinger Tor) One of Munich's more typically Italian *osteria*, this loud but unquestionably romantic place has earthy wood tables, antique tin buckets, baskets, and clothing irons conjuring up the ambience of an Apennine farmhouse. If you're (un)lucky the chef might come out to greet you in his trademark straw hat.

GÄRTNERPLATZVIERTEL & GLOCKENBACHVIERTEL

TOP CHOICE Fraunhofer
BAVARIAN €€

(Map p48; Fraunhoferstrasse 9; mains €7-17.50; ⊙4pm-1am; ⎇; ⎇Müllerstrasse) With its screechy parquet floors, stuccoed ceilings, wood panelling and virtually no trace that the last century even happened, this wonderfully characterful brewpub is one of the city centre's best places to explore the region with a fork. The menu is a checklist of southern German favourites, but also features at least a dozen vegetarian dishes as well as Starnberg fish.

The tiny theatre at the back stages great shows and was among the venues that pioneered a modern style of *Volksmusik* (folk music) back in the 70s and 80s.

Sushi & Soul
SUSHI €€

(Map p48; Klenzestrasse 21; mains €10-20; ⊙6pm-1am; ⎇Reichenbachplatz) The sushi is tasty, other dishes can be hit or miss but the scene is fun anyway with a mixed crowd sluicing down piscine morsels with creative cocktails (Tokyopolitan anyone?) while getting showered with Japanese pop. A flirty *Sex & the City* vibe rules, especially during happy hour (6pm to 8pm and after 11pm) when drinks are half-price.

Joe Peña's
LATIN AMERICAN €€

(Map p48; Buttermelcherstrasse 17; mains €11-16; ⊙5pm-1am; ⎇Reichenbachplatz) If you came to southern Germany to eat food from Central America, do it here. Munich's best Tex-Mex joint gets busy during happy hour (5pm to 8pm) and the nosh is tasty and as authentic as you'd expect this side of the pond.

La Bouche
FRENCH €€€

(Map p48; ⎇265 626; Jahnstrasse 30, enter on Westermühlstrasse; mains €13.50-19.50; ⊙noon-3pm Mon-Fri, 6pm-midnight Mon-Sat; ⎇Fraunhoferstrasse) Expect good Gallic goings-on at this French-inspired port of call where tables are squished as tight as lovers and the accent is on imaginative but gimmick-free fare such as truffle ravioli, veal liver with caramelised apple, and plenty of fish. It's much bigger than first meets the eye – there's a second room at the back.

Bamyan
AFGHAN €€
(Map p48; Hans-Sachs-Strasse 3; mains €8.50-17; ⊙11am-2am; 🚇Müllerstrasse) The terms 'happy hour', 'cocktail' and a 'chilled vibe' don't normally go together with the word 'Afghan', but that's exactly the combination you get at this new and exotic hangout, named after the Buddha statues infamously destroyed by the Taliban in 2001. Central Asian soups, kebabs, rice and lamb dishes, and big salads are eaten at hand-made tables inlaid with ornate metalwork.

MC Müller
BURGERS €
(Map p48; cnr Müllerstrasse & Fraunhoferstrasse; burgers from €5; ⊙6pm-2am Mon-Thu, to 4am Fri & Sat; 🚇Müllerstrasse) Sixties looks and triple duty as bar, DJ lounge and burger joint until the wee hours.

Götterspeise
CAFE €
(Map p48; Jahnstrasse 30; snacks from €3; ⊙8am-7pm Mon-Fri, 9am-6pm Sat; 🚇Müllerstraße) The name of this place translates as 'food of the gods' and the food in question is that most sinful of treats, chocolate. This comes in many forms, both liquid and solid, but there are also teas, coffees and cakes and we love the little smokers' perches outside for puffing chocoholics.

LEHEL & HAIDHAUSEN

Wirtshaus in der Au
BAVARIAN €€
(Map p72; 📞448 1400; Lilienstrasse 51; mains €8-19; ⊙5pm-midnight Mon-Fri, from 10am Sat & Sun; 🚇Deutsches Museum) Though this traditional Bavarian restaurant has a solid 21st-century vibe, it's that time-honoured staple the dumpling that's been declared top speciality here (they even run a dumpling making course in English). Once a brewery, the space-rich indoor dining area has chunky tiled floors, a lofty ceiling and a crackling fireplace in winter. When spring springs, the beer garden fills.

Dreigroschenkeller
THEME RESTAURANT €€
(Map p72; 📞379 558 34; Lilienstrasse 2; mains €7.50-16.50; ⊙5pm-1am Sun-Thu, to 3am Fri & Sat; 🚇Deutsches Museum) A cosy and labyrinthine brick-cellar pub with rooms based upon Bertolt Brecht's *Die Dreigroschenoper* (*The Threepenny Opera*), ranging from a prison cell to a red satiny salon. There are nine types of beer to choose from and an extensive menu of hearty Bavarian soak-up material.

Vegelangelo
VEGETARIAN €€
(Map p48; 📞2880 6836; www.vegelangelo.de; Thomas-Wimmer-Ring 16; mains €9-19; ⊙6pm-late Mon-Sat, noon-2pm Tue-Thu; 🅿; 🚇Isartor, 🚋Isartor) Reservations are recommended at this petite vegie spot where Indian odds and ends, a piano and a small Victorian fireplace distract little from the superb meat-free cooking, all of which can be converted to suit vegans. There's a menu only (€24 to €30) policy Fridays and Saturdays. Cash only.

XII Apostel
ITALIAN €€
(Map p72; Thierschplatz 6; mains €6-17; ⊙11am-1am Mon-Fri & Sun, noon-2am Sat; 🚇Lehel) Despite the expensive, exclusive feel of the dramatic dining space at this brand new, somewhat over-styled Italian job, resplendent in high ceiling frescoes, wood panelling and Chesterfield-style seating, the pizza-pasta menu here will not overwhelm your wallet. The triangular upstairs bar is a cool night spot in its own right. Staff speak little English.

Showroom
FINE DINING €€€
(Map p72; 📞4442 9082; Lilienstrasse 6; five-course menu €95; ⊙6pm-1am Mon-Fri; 🚇Deutsches Museum) Andreas Schweiger's crossover creations strike just the right balance between adventure and comfort, which is why his restaurant is among the most respected in town. The finely crafted dishes on offer are beyond the means of most mortals so this is definitely one for very special occasions.

Swagat
INDIAN €€
(Map p72; Prinzregentenplatz 13; mains €10-20; ⊙11.30am-2.30pm & 5.30pm-1am; 🅿; 🚋Prinzregentenplatz) Though a touch shabby from the outside, inside Swagat fills every nook of an intimate cellar space with Indian fabrics, cavorting Hindu gods and snow-white table cloths. The curry is as hot as Bavarians can take it, and there's plenty to please noncarnivores.

Nektar
FUSION €€
(Map p72; 📞4591 1311; Stubenvollstrasse 1; mains €12-18.50, dinner menu €49; ⊙7pm-2am Tue-Sun; 🚇Am Gasteig) With its dramatic mood lighting and sexy crowd, this big-city spot delivers so much eye candy, it's hard to focus on the flavour-intense fusion food. More elite nightclub than restaurant at weekends.

☕ Drinking

Munich is a great place for boozers. Raucous beer halls, snazzy hotel lounges, chestnut-canopied beer gardens, hipster DJ bars, designer cocktail temples – the variety is so huge that finding a party pen to match your mood is not exactly a tall order. Generally speaking, student-flavoured places abound in Maxvorstadt and Schwabing, while traditional beer halls and taverns cluster in the Altstadt; Haidhausen goes for trendy types and the Gärtnerplatzviertel and Glockenbachviertel is a haven for gays and hipsters.

No matter where you are, you won't be far from an enticing cafe to get a Java-infused pick-me-up. Many also serve light fare and delicious cakes (often home-made) and are great places to linger, chat, write postcards or simply watch people on parade.

Bavaria's brews are best sampled in a venerable old *Bierkeller* (beer hall) and *Biergarten* (beer garden). People come here primarily to drink, and although food may be served, it is generally an afterthought. In beer gardens you are usually allowed to bring your own picnic as long as you sit at tables without tablecloths and order something to drink. Sometimes there's a resident brass band pumping oompah music. And don't even think about sitting at a *Stammtisch*, a table reserved for regulars (look for a brass plaque or some other sign)!

Beer costs €6 to €7.50 per litre. A deposit of €2 or so may be charged for the glass.

ALTSTADT

Hofbräuhaus   BEER HALL
(Map p48; Am Platzl 9; ⊗9am-11.30pm daily; ⑤Marienplatz, ⋒Kammerspiele, ⋒Marienplatz) The mothership of all beer halls, every visitor to Munich should at some point make a pilgrimage to this temple of ale, if only once. The swigging hordes of tourists, swaying to the inevitable oompah band, is like something from a film set.

Braunauer Hof   BEER GARDEN
(Map p48; ✐223 613; Frauenstrasse 42; ⊗11.30am-11pm Mon-Sat; ⋒Isartor, ⋒Isartor) Near the Isartor, this pleasingly twisted beer garden is centred on a snug courtyard. There's a hedge maze, a fresco with a bizarre bunch of historical figures and a golden bull that's illuminated at night.

Master's Home   BAR
(Map p48; ✐229 909; Frauenstrasse 11; ⋒Reichenbachplatz) Colonial era trappings such as zebra skins, African spears, dark wood panelling and random pieces of taxidermy, plus plenty of antique furnishings and oddities such as a dining space in a bathroom, make this a wholly incongruous place for a time-warped snifter. The food menu is Italian flavoured.

Schumann's Bar   BAR
(Map p48; ✐229 060; Odeonsplatz 6-7; ⊗8am-3am Mon-Fri, 6pm-3am Sat & Sun; ⑤Odeonsplatz) Urbane and sophisticated, Schumann's has been shaking up Munich's nightlife with libational flights of fancy in an impressive range of more than 220 concoctions. It's also good for weekday breakfasts.

Viktualienmarkt   BEER GARDEN
(Map p48; Viktualienmarkt 6; ⊗9am-10pm; ⑤Marienplatz, ⋒Marienplatz) After a day of sightseeing or shopping stock up on tasty nibbles at the Viktualienmarkt, then lug your loot a few steps further to this chestnut-shaded beer garden, a Munich institution since 1807. The breweries take turns serving here, so you never know what's on tap.

Café Cord   CAFE
(Map p48; Sonnenstrasse 19; ⊗11am-1am Mon-Sat; ⑤Karlsplatz, ⋒Karlsplatz, ⋒Karlsplatz) Set back from busy Sonnenstrasse in a modern precinct, clean-cut Cord is a good stop for a light lunch or coffee, or an ideal first stop on the club circuit. In summer, the super-delicious global fare tastes best in the romantic, twinkle-lit courtyard.

Isarpost   CAFE
(Map p48; ✐4111 8046; Sonnenstrasse 24-26; mains €5-10; ⑤Sendlinger Tor) Housed in a grand, mid-18th-century former postal office, this foyer cafe offers an Italian menu, or just unwind with a macchiato under the stylishly high, light-flooded vaulting.

SCHWABING & MAXVORSTADT

Alter Simpl   PUB
(Türkenstrasse 57; ⊗11am-3am Mon-Fri, 11am-4am Sat & Sun; ⋒Schellingstrasse) Thomas Mann and Hermann Hesse used to knock 'em back at this well-scuffed and wood-panelled thirst parlour. A bookishly intellectual ambience still pervades and this is an apt spot to curl up with a weighty tomb over a few Irish ales. The curious name is an abbreviation of the satirical magazine *Simplicissimus*.

Chinesischer Turm   BEER GARDEN
(Chinese Tower; Map p60; ✐383 8730; Englischer Garten 3; ⊗10am-11pm daily; ⋒Chinesischer Turm,

Tivolistrasse) This one's hard to ignore because of its English Garden location and pedigree as Munich's oldest beer garden (since 1791). Camera-toting tourists and laid-back locals, picnicking families and businessmen sneaking a sly brew clomp around the wooden pagoda, showered by the strained sounds of possibly the world's drunkest oompah band.

Salon Иркутск BAR
(Isabellastrasse 4; ☺5pm-late; §Josephsplatz) Escape the sugary cocktails and belly-inflating suds to one of Munich's more cultured watering holes, which touts itself as a Franco-Slavic evening bistro. You'll soon see this is no place to get slammed on Russian ethanol or cheap Gallic plonk – Monday is piano night, Wednesday French evening and the green-painted, wood-panelled interior hosts exhibitions of local art.

Hirschau BEER GARDEN
(Map p60; ☑322 1080; Gysslingstrasse 15; §Dietlindenstrasse) This monster beer garden accommodates 1700 drinkers and puts on live jazz almost daily in summer. Dispatch the kids to the playground and adjacent minigolf course while you indulge in some tankard caressing.

Eat the Rich BAR
(Map p64; Hessstrasse 90; ☺7pm-1am Tue-Thu, to 3am Fri & Sat; §Theresienstrasse) Strong cocktails served in half-litre glasses quickly loosen inhibitions at this sizzling meet market where wrinkle-free hotties mix it up with banker types halfway up the career ladder. A great spot to crash when the party's winding down everywhere else. Food is served till 2.30am on weekends.

Cafe Zeitgeist CAFE
(Türkenstrasse 74; ⊟Schellingstrasse) Simply the perfect spot to pore over caffeine and cake to watch, from a shady courtyard, the steady flow of students and trendoids pulsing along busy Türkenstrasse.

Black Bean CAFE
(Map p60; Amalienstrasse 44; ☺7.30am-8pm Mon-Fri, 9am-6.30pm Sat, 10am-6.30pm Sun; ☎; §Universität) If you thought the only decent brew Bavarians could mash was beer, train your Arabica radar to this regional retort to Starbucks. The organic coffee gets tops marks as do the muffins.

Seehaus BEER GARDEN
(Map p60; Kleinhesselohe 3; ☝; §Münchner Freiheit) Situated on the shores of the English Park's Kleinhesseloher See, the Seehaus is a family-friendly beer garden with attached folksy restaurant.

NEUHAUSEN & NYMPHENBURG

Hirschgarten BEER GARDEN
(Map p64; Hirschgartenallee 1; ☺11am-11pm daily; ⊟Kriemhildenstrasse, ☒Laim) The Everest of Munich beer gardens can accommodate up to 8000 Augustiner lovers, but still manages to feel airy and uncluttered. It's in a lovely spot in a former royal hunting preserve and rubs up against a deer enclosure and a carousel. Steer here after visiting Schloss Nymphenburg – it's only a short walk south of the palace.

Augustiner Keller BEER GARDEN
(☑594 393; Arnulfstrasse 52; ☺10am-1am Apr-Oct; ☝; ⊟Hopfenstrasse) Every year this leafy 5000-seat beer garden, about 500m west of the Hauptbahnhof, buzzes with fairy-lit thirst-quenching activity from the first sign that spring may have *gesprungen*. The ancient chestnuts are thick enough to seek refuge under when it rains, or else lug your mug to the actual beer cellar. Small playground.

WESTEND

Augustiner Bräustuben BEER HALL
(Landsberger Strasse 19; ☺10am-midnight daily; ⊟Holzapfelstrasse) Depending on the wind, an aroma of hops envelops you as you approach this ultra-authentic beer hall inside the actual Augustiner brewery, popular with the brewmeisters themselves (there's an entire table reserved just for them). The Bavarian grub here is superb, especially the *Schweinshaxe* (pork knuckle).

GÄRTNERPLATZVIERTEL & GLOCKENBACHVIERTEL

Baader Café CAFE
(Map p48; Baaderstrasse 47; ☺9.30am-1am daily; ⊟Fraunhoferstrasse) Around for over a quarter of a century, this literary think-and-drink place lures all sorts, from short skirts to tweed jackets who linger over daytime coffees and night-hour cocktails. Normally packed, even on winter Wednesday mornings. Popular Sunday brunch.

Trachtenvogl CAFE, LOUNGE
(Map p48; Reichenbachstrasse 47; ☺10am-1am Sun-Thu, to 2am Fri & Sat; ⊟Fraunhoferstrasse) At

OLYMPIAN SOUNDS

Munich summers simply would not be the same without free concerts in the Olympia-park. All through August, the **Theatron MusikSommer Festival** (www.theatron.de) brings international bands from hip-hop to gospel, pop to punk to the amphitheatre next to the Olympic Lake. Kids won't get bored at the **Lilalu Umsonst und Draussen Festival** (www.lilalu.org), which features circus acts, music from mostly local and regional bands, and readings for about two weeks late in the month.

Can't get (or afford) a concert ticket to the Rolling Stones, U2 or Robbie Williams at the Olympic Stadium? No sweat, don't fret – you can hear them for free (!) simply by climbing up the **Olympiaberg**. At 564m, it's a so-called *Trümmerberg*, meaning a pile of war debris that's been greened over. It happens to be right across from the open-air Olympic Stadium, with the sound travelling neatly across the little lake. How handy is that? Bring a blanket and beverage and join the local throngs for a free concert with, and under, the stars.

night you'll have to shoehorn your way into this buzzy lair favoured by a chatty, boozy crowd of scenesters, artists and students. Daytimes are mellower, all the better to slurp its hot chocolate menu and check out the cuckoo clocks and antlers, left over from the days when this was a folkoric garment shop.

Café am Hochhaus CAFE
(Map p48; www.cafeamhochhaus.de; Blumen-strasse 29; ⊗8pm-3am; ⊠Müllerstrasse) Nightly DJs keep this tiny, grungy joint happy till the wee hours with standing room only and pavement spill out early doors. Decor? Think chipped school chairs, black paint and funky photo wallpaper.

Box COFFEEHOUSE
(Map p48; Gärtnerplatz 1; ⊗9.30am-midnight Sun-Fri, to 1am Sat; Reichenbachplatz) Come to this buzzing Italian coffeehouse for the outdoor seating on the Gärtnerplatz where there's standing room only from the first rays of late winter to the last of autumn. Great people-watching possibilities all day long.

HAIDHAUSEN

Biergarten Muffatwerk BEER GARDEN
(Map p72; Zellstrasse 4; ⊗5pm-late Mon-Thu, noon-late Fri & Sat; ⊠Am Gasteig) Think of this one as a progressive beer garden with reggae instead of oompah, civilised imbibing instead of brainless guzzling, organic meats, fish and vegetables on the grill, and the option of chilling in lounge chairs. Plus opening hours are open-ended meaning some very late finishes.

BEYOND THE INNER CITY

Zum Flaucher BEER GARDEN
(☎723 2677; Isarauen 8; ⊠; ⑤Brudermühlstrasse) This congenial restaurant-cum-beer gar-

den in the Isar River meadows feels a like a microvacation from the city bustle. The spare ribs are fall-off-the-bone tender, kids can wear themselves out on the imaginative playground and soccer fans descend for big matches beamed onto a giant screen.

Waldwirtschaft Grosshesselohe BEER GARDEN
(☎7499 4030; Georg-Kalb-Strasse 3; ⊠; ⊠Grosshesselohe/Isartalbahnhof.) One of Munich's nicest beer garden oases, this one delivers Spaten beer, 2500 seats under shady chestnuts, idyllic views of the Isar valley and live jazz nightly in good weather from Easter through September. Kids can frolic in the big playground.

☆ Entertainment

As you might expect from a major metropolis, Munich's entertainment scene is lively and multifaceted, though not particularly edgy. You can hobnob with high society at the opera or the chic P1 disco, hang with the kids at an indie club, catch a flick alfresco or watch one of Germany's best soccer teams triumph in a futuristic stadium.

Listings

Websites useful for tuning into the local scene include www.munig.com, www.munichx.de, www.ganz-muenchen.de and www.muenchengehtaus.com. All are in German but are not too hard to navigate with some basic language skills.

FREE **In München** LISTINGS
(www.in-muenchen.de; free) This freebie mag available at bars, restaurants and shops is the most detailed print source for what's on in Munich.

Munich Found LISTINGS
(www.munichfound.de) English-language magazine geared towards expats and visitors.

Prinz München LISTINGS
(http://muenchen.prinz.de; €1) Weekly lifestyle and entertainment glossy.

Tickets & Reservations

Tickets to cultural and sporting events are available at venue box offices and official ticket outlets, such as **Zentraler Kartenvorverkauf** (Map p48; ☎292 540; www.zkv-muenchen.de) which has a handy kiosk within the Marienplatz U-Bahn station. They're also good for online bookings, as are **München Ticket** (Map p48; ☎0180-5481 8181; www.muenchenticket.de; Neues Rathaus, Marienplatz), which shares premises with the tourist office.

Clubbing

Munich has a thriving club scene, so whether your musical tastes run to disco or dance-hall, house or punk, noise pop or punk-folk, you'll find somewhere to get those feet moving. To get the latest from the scene, peruse the listings mags or sift through the myriad flyers in shops, cafes and bars. This being Munich, expect pretty strict doors at most venues. Dress to kill to get into the fanciest clubs. Dance floors rarely heat up before 1am, so showing up early may increase your chances of getting in without suffering the indignities of a ridiculous wait and possible rejection. If you look under 30, bring ID. Cover charges rarely exceed €15.

Kultfabrik CLUB COMPLEX
(Map p72; www.kultfabrik.de; Grafingerstrasse 6; ⌂Ostbahnhof) If you've been to Munich before, you may remember this one-stop nightlife shop near the Ostbahnhof as Kunstpark Ost. Now the former dumpling factory has a different name but it still has more than a dozen, mostly mainstream, venues as well as numerous fast-food eateries making it the best place in Munich to *carpe noctem*.

Electro and house beats charge up the crowd at the loungy **11er,** while hard rock hounds mash it up at **Titty Twister** and metal freaks bang on at **Refugium.** Nostalgic types can become dancing queens at such 70s and 80s emporia as **Noa, Rafael** and **Q Club** while central European rock-a-billies jive till the wee hours at **Eddy's.** For the latest line-ups, happy hours and other useful info, check the website or look around for KuFas own listings mag, the free *Das K-Magazin*.

Harry Klein NIGHTCLUB
(Map p48; www.harrykleinclub.de; Sonnenstrasse 8; ⌂from 11pm; ⑤Karlsplatz, ⌂Karlsplatz, ⌂Karlsplatz) Since its move out of the Optimolwerke to the city centre, Harry Klein has come to be regarded as one of the best elektroclubs in the world. Nights here are an amazing alchemy of electro sound and visuals, with live video art projected onto the walls Kraftwerk-style blending to awe-inspiring effect with the music.

Atomic Café CLUB
(Map p48; www.atomic.de; Neuturmstrasse 5; ⌂from 10pm Tue-Sat; ⌂Kammerspiele) This bastion of indie sounds with funky 60s décor is known for bookers with a knack for catching upwardly hopeful bands before their big break. Otherwise it's party time; long-running Britwoch is the hottest Wednesday club night in town.

Optimolwerke CLUB COMPLEX
(Map p72; www.optimolwerke.de; Friedenstrasse 10; ⌂Ostbahnhof) Just behind Kultfabrik, Optimol is another clubber's nirvana with about 15 different venues after dark. Latin lovers flock to **Do Brasil**, while newcomer **Die Burg** keeps the party hits and classics booming till 6am.

P1 NIGHTCLUB
(Map p72; www.p1-club.de; Prinzregentenstrasse 1; ⌂Nationalmuseum/Haus der Kunst) If you make it past the notorious face control at Munich's premier late spot, you'll encounter a crowd of Bundesliga reserve players, Q-list celebs, the odd lost piece of central European aristocracy and quite a few Russian-speakers too busy seeing and being seen to actually have a good time. But it's all part of the fun and the décor and summer terrace have their appeal.

Rote Sonne CLUB
(Map p48; www.rote-sonne.com; Maximiliansplatz 5; ⌂from 11pm Thu-Sun; ⌂Lenbachplatz) Named for a 1969 Munich cult movie starring It-Girl Uschi Obermaier, the Red Sun is a fiery nirvana for fans of electronic sounds. An international roster of DJs from the US, Berlin, Paris, London and elsewhere keeps the wooden dance floor packed and sweaty until the sun rises.

OUT & ABOUT IN MUNICH

Munich's gay and lesbian scene is the liveliest in Bavaria but tame if compared to Berlin, Cologne or Amsterdam. The rainbow flag flies especially proudly along Müllerstrasse and the adjoining Glockenbachviertel and Gärtnerplatzviertel. To plug into the scene, keep an eye out for the freebie mags *Our Munich* and *Sergej,* which contain up-to-date listings and news about the community and gay-friendly establishments around town. Another source is www.gaymunich.de, which has a small section in English. For help with lodging, check out www.gaytouristoffice.com.

Max & Milian (Map p48; Ickstattstrasse 2) is Munich's bastion for queer lit, nonfiction and mags. Sub ('the Sub'; ☎260 3056; www.subonline.org; Müllerstrasse 14; ☉7-11pm Sun-Thu, 7pm-midnight Fri & Sat) is a one-stop service and information agency; lesbians can also turn to Le Tra (☎725 4272; www.letra.de; Angertorstrasse 3; ☉2.30-5pm Mon & Wed, 10.30am-1pm Tue).

The festival season kicks off in April with the Verzaubert (www.liebefilme.com) film series featuring the best of international queer cinema at Atelier (Map p48; ☎591 1983; Sonnenstrasse 12; ⑤Karlsplatz, Ⓜ︎Karlsplatz, Ⓡ︎Karlsplatz). The main street parties are Christopher Street Day (p78) and the Schwules Strassenfest (www.schwules-strassenfest.de) held in mid-August along Hans-Sachs-Strasse in the Glockenbachviertel. During Oktoberfest, lesbigay folks invade the Bräurosl beer tent on the first Sunday and Fischer-Vroni on the second Monday.

Bars, Clubs & Cafes

Ochsengarten (Map p48; ☎266 446; www.ochsengarten.de; Müllerstrasse 47) The first bar to open in the Bavrian capital where you have to be clad in leather, rubber, lycra, neopren or any other kinky attire you can think of, to get in. Gay men only.

Backstage
CLUB

(www.backstage.eu; Reitknechtstrasse 6; ☉from 8pm; Ⓡ︎Hirschgarten) Refreshingly nonmainstream, this groovetastic *boîte* has a chilled night beer garden and a shape-shifting line-up of punk, nu metal, hip-hop, dance hall and other alt sounds, both canned and live.

Substanz
CLUB

(Ruppertstrasse 28; ⑤Poccistrasse) About as alternative as things get in Munich, this low-key, beery lair gets feet moving with house to indie to soul, tickles your funny bones during the English Comedy Club (first Sunday of the month) and brings out edgy wordsmiths for the SRO (standing-room-only) Poetry Slam (second Sunday).

Heart
NIGHTCLUB

(Map p48; www.h-e-a-r-t.me/; Lenbachplatz 2a; Ⓜ︎Lenbachplatz) New and exclusive dine-dance-flirt club for well-heeled over-25s who like their beef tatar served at 5am. Dress to impress for the cool, well-illuminated, mirror-ceilinged hall and other impressively designed chill spaces.

Jazz & Blues

Jazzclub Unterfahrt im Einstein BLUES, JAZZ
(Map p72; ☎448 2794; www.unterfahrt.de; Einsteinstrasse 42; ⑤Max-Weber-Platz) Join a diverse crowd at this long-established, intimate club for a mixed bag of acts ranging from old bebop to edgy experimental. The Sunday open jam session is legendary.

Jazzbar Vogler
JAZZ

(Map p48; Rumfordstrasse 17; Ⓜ︎Reichenbachplatz) This intimate watering hole brings some of Munich's baddest cats to the stage. You never know who'll show up for Monday's blues-jazz-Latin jam session. Cover is added to your final bill giving you the opportunity to listen in a bit before deciding to stay (so as not to 'buy a cat in a bag' as the Germans say).

Café am Beethovenplatz
JAZZ

(☎552 9100; Goethestrasse 51; ⑤Sendlinger Tor) Downstairs at the Hotel Mariandl, this is Munich's oldest music cafe with an eclectic menu of sounds ranging from bossa nova to piano to Italian *canzoni* (songs). Reservations advised.

Classical Music & Opera

Münchner Philharmoniker CLASSICAL MUSIC
(Map p72; ☎480 980; www.mphil.de; Rosenheimer Strasse 5; Ⓜ︎Am Gasteig) Munich's premier orchestra regularly performs at the Gasteig Cultural Centre. Book tickets early as performances usually sell out.

Kraftakt (Map p48; ☑2158 8881; www.kraftakt.com; Thalkirchner Strasse 4) Laid-back cafe where the only sign of gay-inclination during the day is the rainbow flag in the window. However on party nights you'll know soon enough you've come to the right/wrong address.

Nil (Map p48; www.cafenil.com; Hans-Sachs-Strasse 2; meals €3.50-8; ☉3pm-3am) A construct in wood and marble, this chill café-bar is open till 3am and a good place to crash after the party has stopped elsewhere. If you need a reality check, a plate of its kick-ass goulash soup (€4.90) should do the trick.

Deutsche Eiche (Map p48; ☑231 1660; www.deutsche-eiche.com; Reichenbachstrasse 13) A Munich institution and gay central, this was once filmmaker Rainer Werner Fassbinders favourite hang-out. It's still a popular spot and packs in a mixed crowd for its comfort food and fast service.

NY Club (Map p48; Sonnenstrasse 25; ☉Fri & Sat) It had been raining men at Munich's hottest gay dance temple until a water main burst in 2012 and almost destroyed the building. But it's expected to return soon and will fill once again with Ibiza-style abandon.

Bau (Map p48; ☑269 208; www.bau-munich.de; Müllerstrasse 41) Bilevel bar that's party central for manly men with nary a twink in sight but plenty of leather, Levis and uniforms. Foam parties in the small cellar darkroom.

Prosecco (Map p48; ☑2303 2329; www.prosecco-munich.de; Theklatstrasse 1) Fun venue for dancing, cruising and drinking that attracts a mixed bunch of party people with quirky decor and a cheesy mix of music (mostly 80s and charts).

Bei Carla (Map p48; ☑4187 4168; Buttermelcherstrasse 9) This energised scene staple has been keeping lesbians happy since, well, like forever. It's a popular spot with a good mixed-age crowd, lots of regulars and snack foods if you're feeling peckish.

Bayerische Staatsoper   OPERA
(Bavarian State Opera; Map p48; ☑218 501; www.bayerische.staatsoper.de; Max-Joseph-Platz 2) Considered one of the best opera companies in the world, the Bavarian State Opera puts the emphasis on Mozart, Strauss and Wagner but doesn't shy away from early baroque pieces by Monteverdi and others of the period. In summer it hosts the prestigious Opernfestspiele. Performances are at the Nationaltheater in the Residenz and often sell out. The opera's house band is the **Bayerisches Staatsorchester**, in business since 1523 and thus Munich's oldest orchestra. It's currently under the capable helm of Kent Nagano, who occasionally shakes up the tried-and-true repertory with contemporary and avant-garde works.

BR-Symphonieorchester   CLASSICAL MUSIC
Charismatic Lithuanian maestro Mariss Jansons has rejuvenated this orchestra's playlist and often performs with its choir at such venues as the Gasteig and the Prinzregententheater.

Staatstheater
am Gärtnerplatz   CLASSICAL MUSIC
(Map p48; ☑2185 1960; www.gaertnerplatztheater. de; Gärtnerplatz 3; ⓜReichenbachplatz) The light opera and musicals normally performed at this 19th-century theatre will be farmed out to other stages between 2012 and 2015 while the building is spruced up for its 150th birthday .

Theatre & Performing Arts

Bayerisches
Staatsschauspiel   THEATRE COMPANY
(☑218 501) This leading ensemble has a bit of a conservative streak but still manages to find relevance for today's mad mad world in works by Shakespeare, Schiller and other tried-and-true playwrights. Performances are in the **Residenztheater** (Map p48; Max-Joseph-Platz 2), the **Theater im Marstall** (Map p48; Marstallplatz 4) and the now fully renovated Cuvilliés-Theater (p54).

Münchener Kammerspiele   THEATRE
(Map p48; ☑2339 6600; www.muenchner -kammerspiele.de; Maximilianstrasse 26; ⓜKammerspiele) This stage has an edgy, populist bent and delivers provocative interpretations of the classics as well as works by contemporary playwrights. Performances are held in a beautifully refurbished art-nouveau theatre at Maximilianstrasse and in the Neues Haus, a new glass cube at Falckenbergstrasse 1.

Deutsches Theater
THEATRE

(Map p48; ☑5523 4444; www.deutsches-theater.
de; Werner-Heisenberg-Allee 11; ⓈFröttmaning)
Still occupying its impressive 'tent palace' in
Fröttmaning (near the Allianz Arena), Munich's answer to London's West End hosts
touring road shows such as *Grease*, *Mamma Mia* and *Tommy*.

GOP Varieté Theater
VARIETY

(Map p72; ☑210 288 444; Maximilianstrasse 47;
ⒶMaxmonument) Hosts a real jumble of acts
and shows from magicians to light comedies
to musicals.

Circus Krone
CIRCUS

(Map p64; ☑545 8000; www.circus-krone.de; Zirkus-
Krone-Strasse 1-6; tickets from €15; ⒶHackerbrücke)
No matter how you feel about circuses, the
venerable Circus Krone is unlike any other.
A Munich fixture for decades, its tent is
vast and the shows are dazzling. After three
months of performances, the circus goes on
tour, leaving the city in a grand procession
with elephants and camels driven along Arnulfstrasse towards the Hauptbahnhof.

The hall is left to host rock concerts and
other events for the rest of the year.

Spectator Sports

FC Bayern München
SOCCER

(☑6993 1333; www.fcbayern.de; ⓈFröttmaning)
Like it or not, the Germans can play football
and none do it better in the Bundesrepublik
than Bayern Munich, Germany's most successful team both nationally and on a European level. Home games are played at the
impressive, chameleon-like Allianz Arena,
built for the 2006 World Cup. Tickets can be
ordered online.

The Allianz Arena is also home turf for
Munich's other soccer team, the perennial
underdogs TSV 1860 (www.tsv1860.de). They
play in Germany's second league and have a
passionately loyal fan base.

EHC München
ICE HOCKEY

(Map p64; www.ehc-muenchen.de; Olympia Eishalle,
Olympiapark; ⓈOlympiazentrum) Not one of
Germany's premier ice-hockey outfits, but
games at the Olympic ice rink are exciting
spectacles nonetheless, plus the team features several Canadian and Swedish players.

🔒 Shopping

Munich is a fun and sophisticated place to
shop that goes far beyond chains and department stores. If you want those, head to
Neuhauser Strasse and Kaufingerstrasse.
East of there, Sendlinger Strasse has smaller
and somewhat more individualistic stores,
including a few resale and vintage emporia.

To truly unchain yourself, though, you
need to hit the Gärtnerplatzviertel and
Glockenbachviertel, the bastion of well-edited indie stores and local designer boutiques.
Hans-Sachs-Strasse and Reichenbachstrasse
are especially promising. Maxvorstadt, especially Türkenstrasse, also has an interesting
line-up of stores with stuff you won't find on
the high street back home.

Maximilianstrasse, meanwhile, is the
catwalk for the Prada and Escada brigade,
especially in the new, minimalist Maximilianhöfe in the Bürkleinbau just past the Nationaltheater. High-flying shoppers will also
be happy on Theatinerstrasse (home of the
Fünf Höfe arcade), on Residenzstrasse and
Brienner Strasse.

Manufactum
HOMEWARES

(Map p48; Dienerstrasse 12; ⊙9.30am-7pm Mon-
Sat; ⓈMarienplatz, ⒶMarienplatz) Anyone with
an admiration for top-quality German design classics should make a beeline for this
store. Last-a-lifetime household items compete for shelf space with retro toys, Bauhaus
lamps and times-gone-by stationary.

Munich Readery
BOOKSTORE

(Map p64; www.readery.de; Augustenstrasse 104;
⊙11am-8pm Mon-Fri, 10am-6pm Sat; ⓈTheresienstrasse) Germany's biggest collection of secondhand English-language titles.

Holareidulijö
CLOTHING

(Schellingstrasse 81; ⊙noon-6.30pm Tue-Fri, 10am-
1pm Sat; ⒶSchellingstrasse) Munich's only
secondhand traditional clothing store, and
worth a look even if you don't intend to buy
anything. The shop's name is a phonetic yodel
and apparently, wearing hand-me-down lederhosen greatly reduces the risk of chaffing.

Porzellan Manufaktur
Nymphenburg
CERAMICS

(Map p64; ☑179 1970; Nördliches Schlossrondell 8;
⊙10am-5pm Mon-Fri ; ⒶSchloss Nymphenburg)
Traditional and contemporary porcelain
masterpieces by the royal manufacturer.
Also in the Altstadt at Odeonsplatz 1 (☑282
428; Odeonsplatz 1; ⊙10am-6.30pm Mon-Fri,
10am-4pm Sat).

7 Himmel
CLOTHING

(Map p48; Hans-Sachs-Strasse 17; ⊙11am-7pm
Mon-Fri, 10am-6pm Sat; ⒶMüllerstrasse) Cool

hunters will be in seventh heaven (a translation of the boutique's name) when browsing the assortment of fashions and accessories by hip indie labels like Pussy de Luxe, Indian Rose and Religion, all sold at surprisingly reasonable prices.

Flohmarkt Riem   MARKET
(www.flohmarkt-riem.com; Willy-Brandt-Platz; ☺6am-4pm Sat; ⑤Messestadt-West) Play urban archaeologist and sift through heaps of junk and detritus to unearth the odd treasure at Bavaria's largest flea market. It's located outside the city centre by the trade fair grounds in Riem. Take the U2 to Messestadt-Ost.

Schuster   OUTDOOR, SPORTS
(Map p48; Rosenstrasse 1-5; ☺10am-8pm Mon-Sat; ⑤Marienplatz, ℝMarienplatz) Get tooled up for the Alps at this sports megastore boasting seven shiny floors of equipment, including cycling, skiing, travel and camping paraphernalia.

Sport Scheck   OUTDOOR, SPORTS
(Map p48; Sendlinger Strasse 6 ; ☺10am-8pm Mon-Sat; ⑤Marienplatz, ℝMarienplatz) First-rate outdoor and sports gear for flits into Bavarian backcountry.

Loden-Frey   TRADITIONAL CLOTHING
(Map p48; Maffeistrasse 5-7; ☺10am-8pm Mon-Sat; ℝTheatinerstrasse) Stocks a wide range of Bavarian wear. Expect to pay at least €300 for a good leather jacket, pair of lederhosen or dirndl.

Raritäten & Sammlungsobjekte   COLLECTABLES
(Map p48; Müllerstrasse 33; ☺10am-2pm Mon-Sat; ℝMüllerstrasse) Rummage through heaps of glass-eyed dolls, old beer steins, 1980s toy cars and even the odd traditional glass painting at this cosy emporium, well stocked with quirky collectibles gathered from Bavaria's forgotten drawers and dustiest attics. Great for sourcing unique souvenirs.

Foto-Video-Media Sauter   PHOTOGRAPHY
(Map p48; Sonnenstrasse 26; ☺9.30am-8pm Mon-Fri, to 7pm Sat; ⑤Sendlinger Tor) The largest camera and video shop in town.

Sebastian Wesely   SOUVENIRS
(Map p48; Rindermarkt 1; ☺9am-6.30pm Mon-Fri, to 6pm Sat; ⑤Marienplatz, ℝMarienplatz) If you're in the market for traditional souvenirs, this little shop (in business since 1557) has floor-to-ceiling shelves of carved angels, pewter

tankards, beer steins, carved figurines and handmade candles. The saleswomen are quick with a smile and happy to help.

FC Bayern Fan-Shop   SPORTS, SOUVENIRS
(Map p48; Stachus underground mall level 1, Karlsplatz; ☺9.30am-8pm Mon-Sat; ⑤Karlsplatz, ℝKarlsplatz, ℝKarlsplatz) One of seven FC Bayern outlets around the city selling shirts, scarves and myriad other kit belonging to southern Germany's premier soccer team.

❶ Information

Dangers & Annoyances

During Oktoberfest crime and staggering drunks are major problems, especially around the Hauptbahnhof. It's no joke: drunks in a crowd trying to get home can get violent, and there are about 100 cases of assault every year. Leave early or stay very cautious, if not sober, yourself.

Strong and unpredictable currents make cooling off in the Eisbach creek in the English Garden more dangerous than it looks. Exercise extreme caution: there have been deaths.

Even the most verdant öko-warrior would interrupt his/her yoghurt pot of rainwater to agree with you that fast-moving bikes in central Munich are a menace. Make sure you don't wander onto bike lanes, especially when waiting to cross the road and alighting from buses and trams.

Emergency

» **Ambulance** (☏192 22)

» **Fire** (☏112)

» **Lost & Found** (☏2339 6045; Ötztaler Strasse 17; ☺8am-noon Mon-Thu, 7am-noon Fri, 2-6pm Tue)

» **Police** (☏110; Arnulfstrasse 1) Police station right beside the Hauptbahnhof.

Internet Access

Most public libraries offer internet access to non-residents. Check www.muenchner-stadt bibliothek.de (in German) for details.

Coffee Fellows (Schützenstrasse 14; per hr €5; ☺7am-11pm Mon-Fri, from 8am Sat & Sun) Free web access if you spend €5 or more in the cafe.

Medical Services

The US and UK consulates can provide lists of English-speaking doctors.

» **Ärztlicher Hausbesuchdienst** (☏555 566) Doctor home and hotel visits.

» **Bereitschaftsdienst der Münchner Ärzte** (☏01805-191 212; ☺24hr) Evening and weekend nonemergency medical services with English-speaking doctors.

CITY TOUR CARD

The Munich **City Tour Card** (www.citytourcard-muenchen.com; 1/3 days €9.90/19.90) includes all public transport in the Innenraum (Munich city – zones 1 to 4; marked white on transport maps) and discounts of between 10% and 50% for over 50 attractions, tours, eateries and theatres. These include the Residenz, the BMW Museum and the Bier- und Oktoberfestmuseum. It's available at some hotels, tourist offices, Munich public transport authority (MVV) offices and U-Bahn, S-Bahn and DB vending machines.

» **Chirurgische Klinik und Poliklinik** (☑tel, info 5160 2611; Nussbaumstrasse 20) Emergency room.

» **Emergency Dental Assistance** (☑723 3093, 129 43)

» **Emergency Pharmacy** (☑tel, info 594 475; www.apotheken.de) Referrals to the nearest open pharmacy. Most pharmacies have employees who speak passable English, but there are several designated international pharmacies with staff fluent in English including **Ludwigs-Apotheke** (☑550 5070; Neuhauser Strasse 11) and **Bahnhof Apotheke** (☑5998 9040; Bahnhofplatz 2).

» **Schwabing Hospital** (☑3304 0302; Kölner Platz 1) Accident and Emergency department.

Money

ATMs abound in the city centre, though not all take every type of card.

Reisebank (Bahnhofplatz 2; ☺daily 7am-10pm) Best place to change and withdraw money at the Hauptbahnhof.

Post

Post Office (Sattlerstrasse 1; ☺9am-6pm Mon-Fri, 9am-12.30pm Sat, closed Sun) For additional branches, see the tourist office map or search www.deutschepost.de.

Tourist Information

Tourist Office (☑2339 6500; www.muenchen.de) **Hauptbahnhof** (Bahnhofplatz 2; ☺9am-8pm Mon-Sat, 10am-6pm Sun) **Marienplatz** (Marienplatz 8, Neues Rathaus; ☺10am-7pm Mon-Fri, to 5pm Sat, to 2pm Sun)

Castles & Museums Infopoint (☑2101 4050; www.infopoint-museen-bayern.de; Alter Hof 1; ☺10am-6pm Mon-Sat) Central information point for museums and palaces throughout Bavaria. Has a small exhibition on the Kaiserburg.

Getting There & Away

Air

Munich Airport (MUC; www.munich-airport.de), aka Flughafen Franz-Josef Strauss, is second in importance only to Frankfurt for international and domestic connections. The main carrier is Lufthansa (Terminal 2), but around 70 other companies operate from the airport's two runways, from major carriers such as British Airways and Emirates to minor operations such as Luxair and Carpatair.

Only one major airline from the UK doesn't use Munich's main airport – Ryanair flies into Memmingen's **Allgäu Airport** (www.allgaeu-airport.de), 125km to the west.

Bus

Europabus links Munich to the Romantic Road. For times and fares for this service and all other national and international coaches contact **Sindbad** (☑5454 8989; Arnulfstrasse 20) near the Hauptbahnhof.

The bold new **Zentraler Omnibusbahnhof** (Central Bus Station; ZOB; Arnulfstrasse 21) next to the Hackerbrücke S-Bahn station handles the vast majority of international and domestic coach services. There's a Eurolines/Touring office, a supermarket and various eateries on the first floor with buses departing from ground level.

BEX BerlinLinienBus (www.berlinlinienbus.de) runs daily between Berlin and Munich ZOB (one way/return €43/86, 8½ hours) via Ingolstadt, Nuremberg, Bayreuth and Leipzig.

A special Deutsche Bahn express coach leaves for Prague (€61, five hours, four daily) from the north side of the Hauptbahnhof.

Car & Motorcycle

Munich has autobahns radiating in all directions. Take the A9 to Nuremberg, the A8 to Salzburg, the A95 to Garmisch-Partenkirchen and the A8 to Ulm or Stuttgart.

Naturally Munich airport has branches of all major car hire companies. Book ahead for the best rates.

Train

Train connections from Munich to destinations in Bavaria are excellent and there are also numerous services to more distant cities within Germany and around Europe. All services leave from the Hauptbahnhof, which is set to undergo major modernisation in coming years.

Staffed by native English speakers, **Euraide** (www.euraide.de; Desk 1, Reisezentrum, Hauptbahnhof; ☺9.30-8pm Mon-Fri May-Jul, 10am-7pm Mon-Fri Aug-Apr) is a friendly agency based at the Hauptbahnhof that sells all DB products, makes reservations and can create personalised rail tours of Germany and beyond. EurAide's free newsletter, the *Inside Track*, is packed with practical info about the city and surroundings.

Connections from Munich:

» **Nuremberg** €52, 1¼ hours, twice hourly

» **Regensberg** €25.20, 1½ hours, hourly

» **Würzburg** €67, two hours, twice hourly

» **Freiburg** €88, 4½ hours, hourly (change in Mannheim)

» **Baden-Baden** €81, five hours, hourly, (change in Mannheim)

» **Frankfurt** €95, 3¼ hours, hourly

» **Berlin** €121, six hours, every two hours

» **Cologne** €134, 4½ hours, hourly

» **Vienna** €85.80, 4½ hours, every two hours

» **Prague** €66, five hours 50 minutes, two daily

» **Zürich** €75.20, 4¼ hours, three daily

» **Paris** from €143, 10¾ hours, daily (night train)

❶ Getting Around

Central Munich is compact enough to explore on foot. To get to the outlying suburbs make use of the public transport network, which is extensive and efficient, if showing its age slightly.

Over the next few years there is likely to be some disruption to Munich's public transport, especially to the S-Bahn system as a new tunnel is burrowed beneath the city centre to relieve the pressure on the *Stammstrecke* (the trunk route via which all S-Bahn trains travel).

To/From the Airport

Munich's airport is about 30km northeast of the city and linked by S-Bahn (S1 and S8) to the Hauptbahnhof. The trip costs €10, takes about 40 minutes and runs every 20 minutes almost 24 hours a day.

The Lufthansa Airport Bus shuttles at 20-minute intervals between the airport and Arnulfstrasse at the Hauptbahnhof between 5am and 8pm. The trip takes about 45 minutes and costs €10.50 (return €17).

If you've unfortunately booked a flight from Munich's 'other' airport at Memmingen (around 125km to the west) there's a special bus from Arnulfstrasse at the Hauptbahnhof that makes the trip up to seven times a day. The journey takes one hour 40 minutes and the fare is €13 (return €19.50).

A taxi from Munich Airport to the Altstadt costs in the region of €50 to €70.

Car & Motorcycle

Driving in central Munich can be a nightmare; many streets are one way or pedestrian only, ticket enforcement is Orwellian and parking is a nightmare. Car parks (indicated on the tourist office map) charge about €1.50 to €2 per hour.

Public Transport

Munich's efficient public transport system is composed of buses, trams, the U-Bahn and the S-Bahn. It's operated by **MVV** (www.mvv -muenchen.de), which maintains offices in the U-Bahn stations at Marienplatz, Hauptbahnhof, Sendlinger Tor, Ostbahnhof and Poccistrasse. Staff hand out free network maps and time-tables, sell tickets and answer questions. Automated trip planning in English is best done online. The U-Bahn and S-Bahn run almost 24 hours a day, with perhaps a short gap between 2am and 4am. Night buses and trams operate in the city centre.

TICKETS & FARES

The city of Munich region is divided into four zones with most places of visitor interest (except Dachau and the airport) conveniently falling within the white Innenraum (inner zone).

Short rides (Kurzstrecke; four bus or tram stops; or two U-Bahn or S-Bahn stops) cost €1.20, longer trips cost €2.50. Children aged six to 14 pay a flat €1.20 regardless of the length of the trip. Day passes are €5.60 for individuals and €10.20 for up to five people travelling together. Three-day passes are €13.80/23.70. There's also a weekly pass called IsarCard, which costs €18.20 but is only valid from Monday to Sunday – if you buy on Wednesday, it's still only good until Sunday. Bikes costs €2.50 and may only be taken aboard U-Bahn and S-Bahn trains, but not during the 6am to 9am and 4pm to 6pm rush hours.

Bus drivers sell single tickets and day passes but tickets for the U-/S-Bahn and other passes must be purchased from vending machine at stations or MVV offices. Tram tickets are available from vending machines aboard. Most tickets must be stamped (validated) at station platform entrances and aboard buses and trams

---

❶ BUS 100: MUSEENLINIE

Bus 100, known as the *Museenlinie*, links the Ostbahnhof with the Haupt-bahnhof via several major museums, galleries and other sights. These include the Bayerisches Nationalmuseum, the Kunstareal, the English Garden and Königsplatz. The service runs every 10 minutes during the day and is a handy way of getting between Munich's major places of interest, and to/from the stations.

before use. The fine for getting caught without a valid ticket is €40.

Taxi

Taxis cost €2.90 at flag fall (€3.90 if ordered by phone), plus €1.40 to €1.60 per kilometre and are not much more convenient than public transport. Luggage is charged at €0.50 per piece. Ring a taxi on 216 10 or 194 10. Taxi ranks are indicated on the city's tourist map.

AROUND MUNICH

Dachau
📞 08131 / POP 42,500

> 'There is a path to freedom. Its milestones are: obedience, honesty, cleanliness, sobriety, hard work, discipline, sacrifice, truthfulness and love of the Fatherland' Inscription from the roof of the concentration camp at Dachau.

Dachau was the Nazis' first concentration camp, built by Heinrich Himmler in March 1933 to house political prisoners. All in all it 'processed' more than 200,000 inmates, killing between 30,000 and 43,000, and is now a haunting memorial that will stay long in the memory. Expect to spend two to three hours here to fully absorb the exhibits. Note that children under 12 may find the experience too disturbing.

Officially called the **KZ-Gedenstätte Dachau** (Dachau Memorial Site; www.kz-gedenkstaette-dachau.de; Alte Römerstrasse 75; admission free; ⊘9am-5pm daily), start at the new visitors centre which houses a bookshop, cafe and tour booking desk where you can pick up an audioguide (€3.50). It's on your left as you enter the main gate. Two-and-a-half-hour tours (€3) also run from here Tuesday to Sunday at 11am and 1pm.

You pass into the compound itself through the Jourhaus, originally the only entrance. Set in wrought iron, the chilling slogan *'Arbeit Macht Frei'* (Work Sets You Free) hits you at the gate.

The **museum** is at the southern end of the camp. Here a 22-minute English-language documentary runs at 10am, 11.30am, 12.30pm, 2pm and 3pm and uses mostly post-liberation footage to outline what took place here. Either side of the small cinema extends an exhibition relating the camp's harrowing story, from relatively orderly prison for religious inmates, leftists and criminals to overcrowded concentration camp racked by typhus, and its eventual liberation by the US Army in April 1945.

Disturbing displays include photographs of the camp, its officers and prisoners (all male until 1944) and horrifying 'scientific experiments' carried out by Nazi doctors. Other exhibits include a whipping block, a chart showing the system of prisoner categories (Jews, homosexuals, Jehovah's Witnesses, Poles, Roma and other 'asocial' types) and documents on the persecution of 'degenerate' authors banned by the party. There's also a lot of information on the rise of the Nazis and other concentration camps around Europe, a scale model of the camp at its greatest extent and numerous uniforms and everyday objects belonging to inmates and guards.

Outside, in the former roll-call square, is the **International Memorial** (1968), inscribed in English, French, Yiddish, German and Russian, which reads 'Never Again'. Behind the exhibit building, the **bunker** was the notorious camp prison where inmates were tortured. Executions took place in the prison yard.

Inmates were housed in large barracks, now demolished, which used to line the main road north of the roll-call square. In the camp's northwestern corner is the **crematorium** and gas chamber, disguised as a shower room but never used. Several religious shrines, including a timber Russian Orthodox church, stand nearby.

Dachau is about 16km northwest of central Munich. The S2 makes the trip from Munich Hauptbahnhof to the station in Dachau in 21 minutes. You'll need a two-zone ticket (€5). Here change to bus 726 (direction Saubachsiedlung) to get to the camp. Show your stamped ticket to the driver. By car, follow Dachauer Strasse straight out to Dachau and follow the KZ-Gedenkstätte signs.

Schleissheim

When you've exhausted all possibilities in central Munich, the northern suburb of Schleissheim is well worth the short S-Bahn trip for its three regal palaces and a high-flying aviation museum, a great way to entertain the kids on a rainy afternoon.

The crown jewel of the palatial trio is the **Neues Schloss Schleissheim** (New Palace; 📞 315 8720; www.schloesser-schleissheim.de; Max-Emanuel-Platz 1; adult/concession €4.50/3.50, combination ticket for all three palaces €8/6;

Around Munich

concession €3.50/2.50; ☺9am-6pm Apr-Sep, 10am-4pm Oct-Mar, closed Mon year-round), on a little island in the eastern Schlosspark, providing an elegant setting for porcelain masterpieces from Meissen.

Nearby, the **Altes Schloss Schleissheim** (☎315 8720; Maximilianshof 1; adult/concession €2.50/1.50; ☺9am-6pm Apr-Sep, 10am-4pm Oct-Mar, closed Mon year-round) is a mere shadow of its Renaissance self. It houses paintings and sculpture depicting religious culture and festivals all over the world, including an impressive collection of more than 100 nativity scenes.

Only a short walk away, the **Flugwerft Schleissheim** (☎315 7140; www.deutsches -museum.de/flugwerft; Effnerstrasse 18; adult/child €6/3; ☺9am-5pm), the aviation branch of the Deutsches Museum, makes for a nice change of pace and aesthetics. Spirits will soar at the sight of the lethal Soviet MiG-21 fighter jet, the Vietnam-era F-4E Phantom and a replica of Otto Lilienthals 1894 glider, with a revolutionary wing shaped like Batman's cape. Another highlight is the open workshop where you can observe the restoration of historical flying machines. Kids can climb into an original cockpit, land a plane and even get their pilot's license.

To get to Schleissheim, take the S1 (direction: Freising) to Oberschleissheim (€5), then walk along Mittenheimer Strasse for about 15 minutes towards the palaces. On weekdays only, bus 292 goes to the Schloss Lustheim stop.

By car, take Leopoldstrasse north until it becomes Ingolstädter Strasse. Then take the A99 to the Neuherberg exit, at the south end of the airstrip.

☺9am-6pm Apr-Sep, 10am-4pm Oct-Mar, closed Mon year-round). This pompous pile was dreamed up by Prince-Elector Max Emanuel in 1701 in anticipation of his promotion to emperor. It never came. Instead he was forced into exile for over a decade and didn't get back to building until 1715. Cash flow problems required the scaling back of the original plans, but given the palace's huge dimensions (the façade is 330m long) and opulent interior, it's hard to imagine where exactly the cuts fell. Some of the finest artists of the baroque era were called in to create such eye-pleasing sights as the ceremonial staircase, the Victory Hall and the Grand Gallery. There are outstanding pieces of period furniture, including the elector's four-poster bed, intricately inlaid tables, and a particularly impressive ceiling fresco by Cosmas Damian Asam.

The palace is home to the **Staatsgalerie** (State Gallery), a selection of European baroque art drawn from the Bavarian State Collection, including works by such masters as Peter Paul Rubens, Antonis van Dyck and Carlo Saraceni. The most impressive room here is the Grand Galerie.

While construction was ongoing, the elector resided in the fanciful hunting palace of **Schloss Lustheim** (☎315 8720; adult/

Freising

☎08161 / 45,200

For a thousand years Freising was the spiritual and cultural epicentre of southern Bavaria. Now the nearest town to the airport, it's become something of a bedroom community for Munich but retains the feel of a traditional market town. In 1821 the bishop bowed to the inevitable and moved his seat to Munich. Freising sank in the ecclesiastical ranking but hung onto its religious gems, the main reasons to visit today. The town was a major way station in the life of Pope Benedict, who studied and taught at the university, was ordained as a priest and later became archbishop here.

◉ Sights & Activities

Dom St Maria und St Korbinian   CATHEDRAL
(⊙8am-6pm Sat-Thu, from 2pm Fri) Looming over the old town is the Domberg, a hub of religious power with the twin-towered Dom St Maria und St Korbinian as its focal point. The restored church interior in whitewash, ochre and delicate rose is a head-turning stucco masterpiece by the Asam brother megastars, whose baroque frescoes grace the most pious ceilings of Bavaria. Remnants from the Gothic era include the choir stalls and a *Lamentation of Christ* painting in the left aisle. The altar painting by Rubens is a copy of the original in the Alte Pinakothek museum in Munich.

Don't miss the crypt, not so much to view Korbinian's mortal remains as to admire the forest of pillars, no two of which are carved alike. The **Bestiensäule** (Beast Pillar) features an epic allegory of Christianity fighting the crocodile-like monsters of evil.

East of the Dom are the cloisters, where the halls drip with fancy stucco and a thousand years' homage in marble plaques to the bishops of Freising. The baroque hall of the **cathedral library** designed by François Cuvilliés, of Cuvilliés-Theatre fame, was under meticulous renovation at the time of writing.

Diözesan Museum   MUSEUM
(Domberg 21; adult/concession €6/4; ⊙10am-5pm Tue-Sun) At the western end of the Domberg you'll find Germany's largest ecclesiastical museum. The building contains a Fort Knox–worthy collection of bejewelled gold vessels, reliquaries and ceremonial regalia as well as some exquisite nativity scenes. Pride of place goes to the *Lukasbild*, a 12th-century Byzantine icon set in its own diminutive silver altar. Rubens and other masters await upstairs.

Staatsbrauerei Weihenstephan   BREWERY TOUR
(⊙5360; www.weihenstephaner.de; Alte Akademie 2; tours 60/120 min €6/9; ⊙10am-Wed & 1.30pm Tue) Southwest of the Domberg, a former Benedictine monastery hosts, among other university faculties, a respected college of beer brewing. Also here is the Staatsbrauerei Weihenstephan, a brewery founded in 1040, making it the world's oldest still in operation. Guided tours trace a millenium of brewery history in the museum, which is followed by a behind-the-scenes spin around the hallowed halls and concluded with a beer tasting (you get to keep the glass). Bookings are advised. Tours include a pretzel and a €2 voucher good for souvenirs or another brew served in the beer garden and the vaulted cellar of the Bräustüberl.

❶ Information

The bulk of Freising's sights are in the Altstadt on or around the Lehrberg, site of the cathedral complex, more popularly known as the Domberg. For information, visit the **tourist office** (⊙544 4111; www.freising.de; Marienplatz 7; ⊙9am-6pm Mon-Fri, to 1pm Sat) from which staff run guided tours in English, including one that follows in the steps of Pope Benedict. Book ahead.

❶ Getting There & Away

Freising is about 35km northeast of Munich at the northern terminus of the S1 (€7.50, 40 minutes) and is also frequently served by faster regional trains (€7.50, 25 minutes). The Domberg and Altstadt are a 10-minute walk from the train station. By car, take Leopoldstrasse north and turn right on Schenkendorfstrasse. Then take the A9 north and the A92 to the Freising-Mitte exit.

Starnberger Fünf-Seen-Land

Once a royal retreat and still a popular place of residence with the rich and famous, the Fünf-Seen-Land (Five Lakes District) is set in a glacial plain and makes a fast and easy escape from the urban bustle of Munich. Organised tourism in these parts is very much a seasonal affair, but any time is good for hiking and cycling.

The largest lake is the 21km-long, narrow and much-loved **Starnberger See (Lake Starnberg)**, nicknamed Munich's bathtub and ringed by a necklace of resorts, including Starnberg, Berg and Possenhofen. The road linking all these communities can get terribly clogged, especially on summer weekends. It also rarely skirts the lake shore, much of which is privately owned. There is, however, a paved trail dedicated to biking and walking along the shore. Circumnavigating the entire lake (50km) takes about 12 hours on foot and four hours by bike.

The other lakes – Ammersee, Pilsensee, Wörthsee and Wesslinger See – are smaller and offer more secluded charm. Swimming, boating and windsurfing are popular activities on all lakes, and the district is also criss-crossed by a whopping 493km network of bike paths and 185km of hiking trails.

This area has long been a favourite with Bavarian nobility. The 19th-century fairytale king Ludwig II had a soft spot for the Starnberger See. That is until he mysteriously drowned in the lake on the eastern shore. Ludwig's bosom buddy, Empress Sisi of Austria (1837–98), spent many a summer staying in Possenhofen on the western shore. The lakes area is still a favourite stomping ground for central Europe's estateless nobility. The present head of the Wittelsbach family, the art-loving Duke Franz, still uses Ludwig's former palace in Berg.

⊙ Sights

STARNBERG

The century-old town of Starnberg is the northern gateway to the lake district but lacks any lasting allure, meaning most visitors head straight on to other towns or sites along the lake's edge. The train station is just steps from the cruise-boat landing docks, pedal-boat hire, the regional tourist office and the **Museum Starnberger See** (☑08151-772 132; www.museum-starnberger-see. de; Possenhofener Strasse 5, enter on Bahnhofsplatz; adult/child €1.50/0.50; ☉10am-noon & 2-5pm Tue-Sun). You may have to duck your head when touring this 400-year-old farmhouse that offers a glimpse into yesteryear's life on the lake and also boasts a precious Ignaz Günther sculpture in the little chapel. A modern extension showcasing a fancy royal barge and a section on its construction are the most recent additions to its exhibits.

Starnberg is just 30 minutes on the S6 from Munich (€5).

BERG

It's about an hour's walk (5km) from Starnberg (starting on Nepomukweg and following the shingle) to Berg on the northeastern lake shore, where King Ludwig II spent summers at **Schloss Berg** and where he and his doctor died in 1886 under mysterious circumstances. The palace and its lovely gardens still belong to the Wittelsbach family and are closed to prying eyes, but you're free to walk through its wooded park to the **Votivkapelle** (☑08151-5276; Votive Chapel; admission free; ☉9am-5pm Apr-Oct). Built in honour of Ludwig and shrouded by mature trees, this neo-Romanesque memorial chapel overlooks the spot in the lake – marked by a simple cross, erected years later by his mother – where Ludwig's dead body was supposedly found.

POSSENHOFEN & FELDAFING

Austrian empress Sisi, cousin of Ludwig II, spent her childhood summers at **Schloss Possenhofen**, a chunky cream-coloured palace on the western shore of Lake Starnberg. It's since been converted into condos but the grounds are now a huge leisure park with lake access, volleyball nets and barbecue pits that swarm with city folk on hot summer weekends. To learn a bit more about the Sisi mystique, call in at the **Kaiserin-Elisabeth-Museum** (☑08151-164 79; Schlossbergstrasse 2; admission free; ☉2-6pm Fri-Sun Jun-early Oct or by appointment). It's a small exhibit in the grand surroundings of the former royal waiting rooms of the historic *Bahnhof* Possenhofen, now the S-Bahn station.

Sisi was so taken with the lake's beauty that she returned as an adult to summer in what is now a hotel, in the hamlet of Feldafing a couple of kilometres south. A larger-than-life sculpture in the garden shows her with a book in relaxed repose, gazing back at the hotel. You can eat in the rustic Ludwigstüberl or the silver-service restaurant where aproned waiters serve the Sisi Menu.

Fans of art-nouveau villas should take a spin around Feldafing, which also has a popular swimming beach, the **Strandbad Feldafing**.

From the Strandbad, it's an easy 10-minute walk to the Glockensteg, the place to catch a ferry to the **Roseninsel**. Sisi and Ludwig frequently met on this romantic island, where Ludwig also received other luminaries, Richard Wagner among them. Neglected for a century after the king's death, the island, rose garden and his summerhouse, called the **Casino,** have been restored and are now open to the public. A small exhibit in the garden house has displays of about 6000 years of the island's history.

Possenhofen and Feldafing are both stops on the S6 from Munich (€7.50, 40 minutes).

DIESSEN

To see one of the area's most magnificent baroque churches, you have to travel to Diessen, some 11km west of Andechs, which is home to the **Marienmunster**. Part of a

WORTH A TRIP

BUCHHEIM MUSEUM

A bronze statue of a BMW sprouting octopuslike tentacles is the mind-teasing overture to the full symphony of art and objects at the amazing **Buchheim Museum** (www. buchheimmuseum.de; Am Hirschgarten 1; adult/concession €8.50/3.50; ☺10am-6pm Tue-Sun Apr-Oct, to 5pm Nov-Mar), right on the Starnberger See about 1km north of the town of Bernried. The modernist structure by Olympia Stadium architect Günter Behnisch houses the private collection of Lothar-Günther Buchheim, author of *Das Boot*, the novel that inspired the famous film. The heart and soul of the museum are German expressionist works by members of *Die Brücke* (The Bridge), an artist group founded in Dresden in 1905. The bright, emotionally coloured canvasses by Ludwig Kirchner, Emil Nolde, Max Beckmann, Otto Dix and Karl Schmidt-Rottluff marked the beginning of modern art in Germany.

Other galleries present a fascinating hotchpotch of global arts and crafts, which justifies the museum's subtitle Museum of the Imagination. You'll see handsome art-nouveau vases, African masks, Japanese woodcuts, jewellery from India and a stunning collection of some 3000 paperweights.

The most scenic approach to the museum is by an hour-long boat trip from Starnberg. Alternatively, take the S6 or Regionalbahn to Tutzing, change to another RB train to Bernried, then walk north for about 15 minutes.

monastery complex, this festive symphony in white stucco, red marble and gold leaf involved some of the most accomplished artists of the 18th century, including the architect Johann Michael Fischer; François Cuvilliés, who designed a high altar; and Giovanni Battista Tiepolo, who was responsible for an altar painting.

Diessen also has the small **Carl-Orff-Museum** (☎08807-919 81; Hofmark 3; adult/concession €2/1; ☺2-5pm Sat, Sun & holidays), with a biographical exhibit, a cabinet of instruments and a video room where you can watch performances of his work.

To reach Diessen by train from Munich requires a change in either Geltendorf or Weilheim (€12.20, one hour).

🏃 Activities

From Easter to mid-October, **Bayerische-Seen-Schifffahrt** (☎08151-8061; www.seen schifffahrt.de) runs scheduled boat services on the Starnberger See and the Ammersee – a leisurely way to explore the region. In Starnberg, boats leave from the landing docks just south of the main station. For the Ammersee, Herrsching is the most convenient starting point.

If a cruise seems too tame, consider taking a spin around the lake under your own steam. Boat hire is available on the Starnberger See, the Ammersee and the Wörthsee. In Starnberg, **Paul Dechant** (☎08151-121 06;

Hauptstrasse 20), near the train station, has rowing, pedal and electric-powered boats for €15 per hour.

If the weather plays along, there's no better way to explore the area than by bicycle. **Radhaus Starnberg** (www.radhaus-starnberg. de; Hauptstrasse 6) in Starnberg and **Fahrradgeschäft Nandlinger** (www.nandlinger. de; Mühlfelder Strasse 5) in Herrsching have a decent selection of two wheelers. **Bike It** (www.bikeit.de; Bahnhofstrasse 1) in Starnberg runs guided bike tours from €25. There's a famous in-line skating stretch on the eastern shore between Berg and Ambach.

There's plenty of good hiking as well. A delightful half-day trip starts in Tutzing and goes via a moderate ascent to the Ilkahöhe, which is a 730m hill with a restaurant, beer garden and panoramic lake views.

An usual and visually stunning way to see the lakes and Alps to the south is suspended below one of the hot-air balloons belonging to **Landstettener Ballonfahrten** (☎08157-9014; www.landstettener-ballonfahrten. de; Klosterholzweg 1, Starnberg). A 90-minute flight for four people costs €175 with balloons leaving on request from near the village of Landstetten, halfway between Starnberg and Herrsching.

🛈 Information

The **Starnberger Fünf-Seen-Land tourist office** (☎08151-906 00; www.sta5.de;

Wittelsbacherstrasse 2c, Starnberg; ⊘8am-6pm Mon-Fri year round, 9am-1pm Sat May-mid-Oct), just north of Starnberg's Bahnhofs-platz, has a free room-finding service and trip planning to other lake towns. The website has links to all tourist offices in the local communities.

❶ Getting There & Away

Starnberg lies 25km southwest of central Munich – a half-hour's journey by car or S-Bahn. The S6 links Munich with Starnberg and Possenhofen, Feldafing and Tutzing on the western lake shore. The S8 goes from Munich to Herrsching am Ammersee in about 45 minutes.

MUNICH STARNBERGER FÜNF-SEEN-LAND

Bavaria

Includes »

Best Places to Eat

» Goldenes Posthorn (p153)

» Le Ciel (p125)

» Bürgerspital Weinstube (p130)

» Bürgerkeller (p135)

» Messerschmidt (p158)

Best Places to Stay

» Hotel Herrnschlösschen (p136)

» Hotel Elch (p150)

» Dom Hotel (p141)

» Hotel Deutscher Kaiser (p152)

» Hotel Elements (p172)

Why Go?

From the cloud-shredding Alps to the fertile Danube plain, the Free State of Bavaria is a place that keeps its clichéd promises. Story-book castles bequeathed by an oddball king poke through dark forest, cowbells tinkle in flower-filled meadows, the thwack of palm on lederhosen accompanies the clump of frothy stein on timber bench, and medieval walled towns go about their time-warped business.

But diverse Bavaria offers much more than the chocolate-box idyll. Learn about Bavaria's state-of-the-art motor industry in Ingolstadt, discover its Nazi past in Nuremberg and Berchtesgaden, sip world-class wines in Würzburg, get on the Wagner trail in Bayreuth or seek out countless kiddy attractions across the state. Destinations are often described as possessing 'something for everyone', but in Bavaria's case this is no exaggeration.

And, whatever you do in Germany's southeast, every occasion is infused with that untranslatable feel-good air of *Gemütlichkeit* (cosiness) that makes exploring the region such an easygoing experience.

When to Go

A winter journey along an off-season, tourist-free Romantic Road really sees the snow-bound route live up to its name. Come the spring, tuck into some seasonal fare as Bavaria goes crazy for asparagus during *Spargelzeit* (from late March). The summer months are all about the beer garden, and this is obviously the best time to savour the region's unsurpassed brews in the balmy, fairy-lit air. Autumn is the time to experience the dreamy haze of the Bavarian Forest and the bustle of Bavaria's cities, revived after the summer's time-out.

Fairy-Tale Castles

So just why do all those millions of visitors flock to Bavaria? If it's not for the beer then it's probably for the state's blockbuster castles and palaces. King Ludwig II's Neuschwanstein is the one everyone wants to tick off their list of '1000 things to see before I die', but did you know that Bavaria's most flamboyant monarch built two other country piles – Linderhof and Herrenchiemsee? And he was planning more when he drowned in Lake Starnberg. Away from Ludwig's marvels, others hot properties not to miss are Würzburg's Residenz, Veste Coburg and Landshut's Burg Trausnitz.

BODY & SOUL

Whether it's snowboarding in the Alps, striking a trail through the Bavarian Forest, pedalling your way through a city-centre sightseeing tour, wild swimming in Lake Starnberg, canoeing in the Altmühltal Nature Park or trying your hand at river surfing, Bavaria is definitely a place to get carbed up and kitted out for. Bavaria certainly provides ample opportunities to work off those dumplings, but if fresh-air antics seem like too much hard work, you can always retreat to a spa, water park or swimming pool.

Essential Food & Drink

» **Beer** From the proud breweries of Bamberg to tiny one-man producers in rural Franconia, from a quick summer beer-garden thirst-quencher to the millions of litres consumed at Oktoberfest, beer plays a bigger cultural role in Bavaria than almost anywhere else on earth.

» **Sausages** Almost every town in Bavaria has its own take on the banger, from the famous digit-sized bratwurst of Nuremberg to the 30cm-long Coburg whopper. Add a bun and a squirt of mustard, and a couple of these makes a respectable meal on the hop.

» **Snowballs** Unless you end up surviving in the mountains, eating snowballs is an experience you'd want to avoid, but not in Rothenburg ob der Tauber. The local sweet – strips of dough ravelled into a ball then deep fried and sprinkled with something sweet – are best eaten smashed up in their bag.

» **Wine** German wine sometimes gets bad press, but you'll forget the sceptics when you sip a glass of Franconian red or white. The main vine-cultivating areas can be found around Würzburg, with the vineyards visible from the city centre.

DISCOUNT PASSES

Staying in the Alps? Make sure your hotel or guesthouse gives you a free *Gästekarte* (guest card), which often gives you free access to public transport and discounts on sights and attractions.

BAVARIA

Need to Know

» Many museums close on Mondays

» Travelling by train? Get yourself a Bayern-Ticket for huge savings

» Nuremberg is Bavaria's most engaging city for young children

Fast Facts

» Population: 12.6 million

» Area: 70,549 sq km

Resources

» Bavarian Tourism Association (www.bayern.by)

» Castles in Bavaria (www.schloesser.bayern.de)

» State of Bavaria (www.bayern.de)

» Train and bus timetables (www.bahn.de)

Bavaria Highlights

1 Indulging your romantic fantasies at fairy-tale **Schloss Neuschwanstein** (p109)

2 Rack-and-pinioning your way to the top of the **Zugspitze** (p115), Germany's highest peak

3 Perching at the Eagle's Nest in **Berchtesgaden** (p123) to enjoy show-stopping Alpine vistas

4 Striking a trail through the tranquil wilds of the **Bavarian Forest** (p183)

5 Going full circle around the town walls of quaint **Dinkelsbühl** (p136)

6 Messing around on the waters of the achingly picturesque **Königssee** (p123)

7 Revisiting Bavaria's Nazi past in **Nuremberg** (p144)

8 Going frothy at the mouth in the hundreds of superb **beer gardens, breweries and brewpubs** across the region (p158)

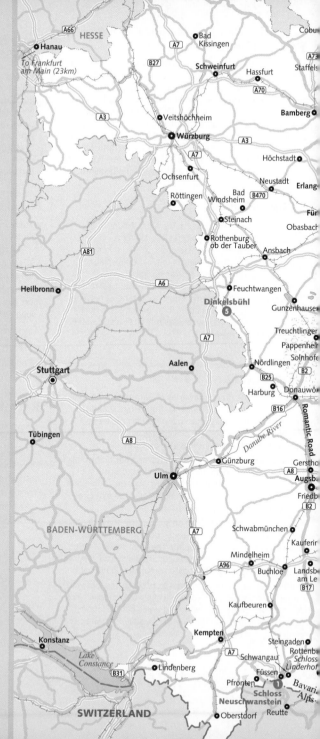

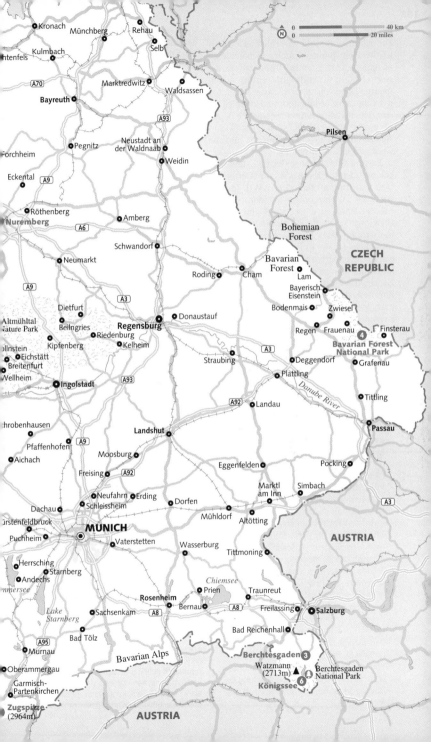

BAVARIA

History

For centuries Bavaria was ruled as a duchy in the Holy Roman Empire, a patchwork of nations that extended from Italy to the North Sea. In the early 19th century, a conquering Napoleon annexed Bavaria, elevated it to the rank of kingdom and doubled its size. The fledgling nation became the object of power struggles between Prussia and Austria and, in 1871, was brought into the German Reich by Bismarck.

Bavaria was the only German state that refused to ratify the Basic Law (Germany's near constitution) following WWII. Instead Bavaria's leaders opted to return to its pre-war status as a 'free state', and drafted their own constitution. Almost ever since, the *Land* (state) has been ruled by the Christlich-Soziale Union (CSU), the arch-conservative party that is peculiar to Bavaria. Its dominance of the politics of a single *Land* is unique in postwar Germany, though Bavarian state elections in 2008 saw the party lose 17% of its vote, forcing it to enter a coalition with the FDP. Its sister party, the CDU, operates in the rest of the country by mutual agreement.

ℹ Getting There & Around

Munich is Bavaria's main transport hub, second only to Frankfurt in flight and rail connections.

MUSEUM OF THE BAVARIAN KINGS

Palace-fatigued visitors to Füssen often head straight for the bus stop, coach park or nearest beer after a tour of the royal homes, most overlooking the area's third attraction, the worthwhile **Museum der Bayerischen Könige** (www.museumderbayerischenkoenige.de; Alpseestrasse 27; adult/concession €8.50/7; ⊙8am-7pm Apr-Sep, 10am-6pm Oct-Mar), installed in a former lakeside hotel 400m from the castle ticket office (heading towards Alpsee Lake). The big-window views across the lake to the Alps are almost as stunning as the Wittelsbach bling on show, including Ludwig II's famous blue and gold robe. The architecturally stunning museum is packed with historical background on Bavaria's first family and well worth the extra legwork.

Rail is the best way to reach Munich from other parts of Germany, and the best means of getting from the Bavarian capital to other parts of Bavaria. Air links within Bavaria are much less extensive.

Without your own set of wheels in Eastern Bavaria and the Alps, you'll have to rely on bus services, which peter out in the evenings and at weekends. Trips along the Romantic Road can be done by tour bus, although again a car is a better idea. Several long-distance cycling routes cross Bavaria and the region's cities are some of the most cycle friendly in the world, so getting around on two wheels could not be easier.

If you're travelling in a group, or can assemble one (as some people do pre-departure), you can make enormous savings with the **Bayern-Ticket** (www.bahn.de; €22, plus €4 per additional passenger). This allows up to five adults unlimited travel on one weekday from 9am to 3am, or from midnight to 3am the next day on weekends. The single version, costing €22, is also a good deal and means that all fares in Bavaria are capped at that price, as long as you don't leave before 9am. Both are good for 2nd-class rail travel across Bavaria (regional trains only, no ICs or ICEs), as well as most public transport.

BAVARIAN ALPS

Stretching west from Germany's remote southeastern corner to the Allgäu region near Lake Constance, the Bavarian Alps (Bayerische Alpen) form a stunningly beautiful natural divide along the Austrian border. Ranges further south may be higher, but these mountains shoot up from the foothills so abruptly that the impact is all the more dramatic.

The region is pocked with quaint frescoed villages, spas and health retreats, and possibilities for skiing, snowboarding, hiking, canoeing and paragliding – much of it year-round. The ski season lasts from about late December until April, while summer activities stretch from late May to November.

One of the largest resorts in the area is Garmisch-Partenkirchen, one of urban Bavaria's favourite getaways. Berchtesgaden, Füssen and Oberstdorf are also sound bases.

ℹ Getting Around

There are few direct train routes between main centres, meaning buses are the most efficient method of public transport in the Alpine area. If you're driving, sometimes a short cut via Austria works out to be quicker (such as between Garmisch-Partenkirchen and Füssen or Oberstdorf).

LUDWIG II, THE FAIRY-TALE KING

Every year on 13 June, a stirring ceremony takes place in Berg, on the eastern shore of Lake Starnberg. A small boat quietly glides towards a cross just offshore and a plain wreath is fastened to its front. The sound of a single trumpet cuts the silence as the boat returns from this solemn ritual in honour of the most beloved king ever to rule Bavaria: Ludwig II.

The cross marks the spot where Ludwig died under mysterious circumstances in 1886. His early death capped the life of a man at odds with the harsh realities of a modern world no longer in need of a romantic and idealistic monarch.

Prinz Otto Ludwig Friedrich Wilhelm was a sensitive soul, fascinated by romantic epics, architecture and music, but his parents, Maximilian II and Marie, took little interest in his musings and he suffered a lonely and joyless childhood. In 1864, at 18 years old, the prince became king. He was briefly engaged to the sister of Elisabeth (Sisi), the Austrian empress but, as a rule, he preferred the company of men. He also worshipped composer Richard Wagner, whose Bayreuth opera house was built with Ludwig's funds.

Ludwig was an enthusiastic leader initially, but Bavaria's days as a sovereign state were numbered, and he became a puppet king after the creation of the German Reich in 1871 (which had its advantages, as Bismarck gave Ludwig a hefty allowance). Ludwig withdrew completely to drink, draw up castle plans and view concerts and operas in private. His obsession with French culture and the Sun King, Louis XIV, inspired the fantastical palaces of Neuschwanstein, Linderhof (p113) and Herrenchiemsee (p121) – lavish projects that spelt his undoing.

Contrary to popular belief, it was only Ludwig's purse – and not the state treasury – that was being bankrupted. However, by 1886 his ever-growing mountain of debt and erratic behaviour had put him at odds with his cabinet. The king, it seemed, needed to be 'managed'.

In January 1886, several ministers and relatives arranged a hasty psychiatric test that diagnosed Ludwig as mentally unfit to rule (this was made easier by the fact that his brother had been declared insane years earlier). That June he was removed to Schloss Berg on Lake Starnberg. A few days later the dejected bachelor and his doctor took a Sunday evening lakeside walk and were found several hours later, drowned in just a few feet of water.

No one knows with certainty what happened that night. There was no eyewitness nor any proper criminal investigation. The circumstantial evidence was conflicting and incomplete. Reports and documents were tampered with, destroyed or lost. Conspiracy theories abound. That summer the authorities opened Neuschwanstein to the public to help pay off Ludwig's huge debts. King Ludwig II was dead, but the myth, and a tourist industry, were just being born.

Füssen

☑ 08362 / POP 14,200

Nestled at the foot of the Alps, tourist-busy Füssen is the southern climax of the Romantic Road, with the nearby castles of Neuschwanstein and Hohenschwangau the highlight of many a southern Germany trip. But having 'done' the country's most popular tourist route and seen Ludwig II's fantasy palaces, there are other reasons to linger longer in the area. The town of Füssen is worth half a day's exploration and, from here, you can easily escape from the crowds into a landscape of gentle hiking trails and Alpine vistas.

☉ Sights

TOP CHOICE Schloss Neuschwanstein CASTLE
(☑930 830; www.hohenschwangau.de; adult/concession €12/11, with Hohenschwangau €23/21; ☉8am-5pm Apr-Sep, 9am-3pm Oct-Mar) Appearing through the mountaintops like a misty mirage is the world's most famous castle, and the model for Disney's citadel, fairy-tale Schloss Neuschwanstein.

King Ludwig II planned this castle himself, with the help of a stage designer rather than an architect, and it provides a fascinating glimpse into the king's state of mind. Built as a romantic medieval castle, work started in 1869 and, like so many of Ludwig's grand schemes, was never finished. For all the coffer-emptying sums spent on it, the king spent just over 170 days in residence.

Ludwig foresaw his showpiece palace as a giant stage on which to recreate the world of Germanic mythology in the operatic works of Richard Wagner. Its epicentre is the lavish **Sängersaal** (Minstrels' Hall), created to feed the king's obsession with Wagner and medieval knights. Wall frescos in the hall depict scenes from the opera *Tannhäuser*. Concerts are held here every September.

Other completed sections include Ludwig's *Tristan and Isolde*–themed **bedroom**, dominated by a huge Gothic-style bed crowned with intricately carved cathedral-like spires; a gaudy artificial grotto (another allusion to *Tannhäuser*); and the Byzantine **Thronsaal** (Throne Room) with an incredible mosaic floor containing over two million stones. The painting on the wall opposite the (throneless) throne platform depicts another castle dreamed up by Ludwig that was never built. Almost every window provides tour-halting views across the plain below.

At the end of the tour visitors are treated to a 20-minute **film** on the castle and its creator, and there's a reasonably priced cafe and the inevitable gift shops.

For the postcard view of Neuschwanstein and the plains beyond, walk 10 minutes up to **Marienbrücke** (Mary's Bridge), which spans the spectacular Pöllat Gorge over a waterfall just above the castle. It's said Ludwig liked to come here after dark to watch the candlelight radiating from the Sängersaal.

Schloss Hohenschwangau CASTLE

(☎930 830; www.hohenschwangau.de; adult/concession €12/11, with Neuschwanstein €23/21; ◷8am-5.30pm Apr-Sep, 9am-3.30pm Oct-Mar) Ludwig spent his formative years at the sun-yellow Schloss Hohenschwangau. His father, Maximilian II, rebuilt this palace in a neo-Gothic style from 12th-century ruins left by Schwangau knights. With all this faux-medieval imagery filling his childhood, no wonder Ludwig turned out the way he did.

Far less showy than Neuschwanstein, Hohenschwangau has a distinctly lived-in feel and every piece of furniture is a used original. After his father died, Ludwig's main alteration was having stars, illuminated with hidden oil lamps, painted on the ceiling of his bedroom.

Here Ludwig first met Wagner, and the **Hohenstaufensaal** features a square piano where the hard-up composer would entertain Ludwig with excerpts from his latest oeuvre. Some rooms have frescos from German history and legend (including the story of the Swan Knight, *Lohengrin*). The swan theme runs throughout.

If visiting both Hohenschwangau and Neuschwanstein in the same day, timed tickets are always issued so that Hohenschwangau is first on your itinerary.

Hohes Schloss CASTLE, GALLERY

(Magnusplatz 10; adult/concession €6/4; ◷galleries 11am-5pm Tue-Sun Apr-Oct, 1-4pm Fri-Sun Nov-Mar) Füssen's compact historical centre is a tangle of lanes lorded over by the Hohes Schloss, a late-Gothic confection and onetime retreat of the bishops of Augsburg. The inner courtyard is a masterpiece of illusionary architecture dating back to 1499; you'll do a double take before realising that the gables, oriels and windows are not quite as they seem. The north wing of the palace contains the **Staatsgalerie**, with regional paintings and sculpture from the 15th and 16th centuries. The **Städtische Gemälde-**

ℹ CASTLE TICKETS & TOURS

Both castles must be seen on guided tours (in German or English), which last about 35 minutes each (Hohenschwangau is first). Timed tickets are only available from the **Ticket Centre** (☎930 40; www.hohenschwangau.de; Alpenseestrasse 12; ◷tickets 8am-5pm Apr-Sep, 9am-3pm Oct-Mar) at the foot of the castles. In summer, come as early as 8am to ensure you get in that day.

When visiting both castles, enough time is left between tours for the steep 30- to 40-minute walk between the castles. Alternatively, you can shell out €5 for a horse-drawn carriage ride, which is only marginally quicker.

All Munich's tour companies (p77) run day excursions out to the castles.

Füssen & Around

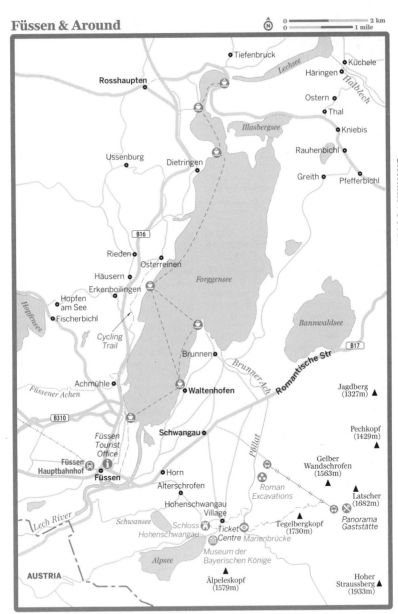

galerie (City Paintings Gallery) below is a showcase of 19th-century artists.

Museum Füssen   MUSEUM
(Lechhalde 3; adult/concession €6/4; ⊘11am-5pm Tue-Sun Apr-Oct, 1-4pm Fri-Sun Nov-Mar) Below

the Hohes Schloss, and integrated into the former Abbey of St Mang, this museum highlights Füssen's heyday as a 16th-century violin-making centre. You can also view the abbey's festive baroque rooms, Romanesque cloister and the St Anna Kapelle (AD 830).

Tegelbergbahn
CABLE CAR

(☑983 60; www.tegelbergbahn.de; one-way/return €11.50/18; ☺9am-5pm) For fabulous views of the Alps and the Forggensee, take this cable car to the top of the Tegelberg (1730m), a prime launch point for hang-gliders and parasailers. From here it's a wonderful hike down to the castles (two to three hours; follow the signs to Königsschlösser). To get to the valley station, take RVO bus 73 or 78 from Füssen Bahnhof.

🛏 Sleeping

Accommodation in the area is surprisingly good value and the tourist office can help track down private rooms from as low as €25 per person.

Altstadt Hotel zum Hechten
HOTEL €€

(☑916 00; www.hotel-hechten.com; Ritterstrasse 6; s €59-65, d €90-99; 🛜) This is one of Füssen's oldest hotels and a barrel of fun. Public areas are traditional in style but the bedrooms are mostly airy, light and brightly renovated. Children are welcome and one of Füssen's better eateries awaits downstairs.

Pension Kössler
GUESTHOUSE €€

(☑4069; www.pension-koessler.de; Zalingerstrasse 1; s/d €40/80) This three-storey Alpine guesthouse with a friendly family atmosphere offers outstanding value. Rooms are simple but comfortable and all have private bathroom, TV, phone and balcony - some overlook the attractive garden. Turning up unannounced is not recommended; call ahead.

Hotel Sonne
HOTEL €€

(☑9080; www.hotel-sonne.de; Prinzregentenplatz 1; s/d from €79/109; P🛜) Although traditional looking from outside, this Altstadt favourite offers an unexpected design-hotel experience within. Themed rooms feature everything from swooping bed canopies to heavy velvet drapes and antique-style furniture, all intended to make you feel as though you've bagged a royal residence for the night.

House LA
HOSTEL €

(☑evenings 607 366, mobile 0170 624 8610; www.housela.de; Welfenstrasse 39; dm from €18) A 15-minute walk west of the train station, this small, basic apartment hostel offers spacious rooms (some with balconies) and breakfast (€2 extra) on a rear patio with mountain views. Call ahead as it's unstaffed during the day.

✖ Eating

Beim Olivenbauer
ALPINE €€

(Ottostrasse 7; mains €6-16; ☺11.30am-11.30pm) Northern Italy meets Tyrol meets the Allgäu at this fun eatery, its interior a jumble of Doric columns, mismatched tables and chairs, multi-hued paint and assorted rural knick-knackery. Treat yourself to a wheel of pizza and a glass of Austrian wine, or go local with a plate of *Maultaschen* and a mug of Paulaner. There's a kids corner in the main dining room and a sunny beer garden out front. Takeaway pizza service available.

Zum Hechten
BAVARIAN €€

(Ritterstrasse 6; mains €7-16; ☺10am-10pm) Füssen's best hotel-restaurant keeps things regional with a menu of Allgäu staples like schnitzel and noodles, Bavarian pork-themed favourites, and local specialities such as venison goulash from the Ammertal. Post-meal, relax in the wood-panelled dining room caressing a König Ludwig Dunkel, one of Germany's best dark beers brewed by the current head of the Wittelsbach family.

Franziskaner Stüberl
BAVARIAN €€

(☑371 24; Kemptener Strasse 1; mains €5.50-15; ☺lunch & dinner) This quaint restaurant specialises in *Schweinshaxe* (pork knuckle) and schnitzel, prepared in more varieties than you can shake a haunch at. Non-carnivores go for the scrumptious *Käsespätzle* (rolled cheese noodles) and the huge salads.

❶ Information

Füssen Tourist Office (☑938 50; www.fuessen.de; Kaiser-Maximilian-Platz 1; ☺9am-6.30pm Mon-Fri, 10am-2pm Sat, 10am-noon Sun May-Oct, 9am-5pm Mon-Fri, 10am-2pm Sat Nov-Apr)

❶ Getting There & Away

BUS The Europabus (p126), which runs up and down the Romantic Road, leaves from stop 3 outside Füssen train station at 8am. It arrives in Füssen after 8pm.

TRAIN If you want to do the castles in a single day from Munich, you'll need to start early. The first train leaves Munich at 4.48am (€24, change in Kaufbeuren), reaching Füssen at 7.26am. Otherwise, direct trains leave Munich once every two hours throughout the day.

❶ Getting Around

BUS RVO buses 78 and 73 (www.rvo-bus.de) serve the castles from Füssen Bahnhof (€4 return), also stopping at the Tegelbergbahn valley station.

TAXI Taxis to the castles are about €10 each way.

Wieskirche

Known as 'Wies' for short, the **Wieskirche** (☎08862-932 930; www.wieskirche.de; ⊙8am-5pm) is one of Bavaria's best-known baroque churches and a Unesco-listed heritage site. About a million visitors a year flock to see this stuccoed wonder, the monumental work of the legendary artist brothers Dominikus and Johann Baptist Zimmermann.

In 1730, a farmer in Steingaden, about 30km northeast of Füssen, witnessed the miracle of his Christ statue shedding tears. Pilgrims poured into the town in such numbers over the next decade that the local abbot commissioned a new church to house the weepy work. Inside the almost circular structure, eight snow-white pillars are topped by gold capital stones and swirling decorations. The unsupported dome must have seemed like God's work in the mid-17th century, its surface adorned with a pastel ceiling fresco celebrating Christ's resurrection.

From Füssen, regional RVO bus 73 makes the journey up to six times daily. The Europabus also stops here long enough in both directions to have a brief look round then get back on. By car, take the B17 northeast and turn right (east) at Steingaden.

Schloss Linderhof

A pocket-sized trove of weird treasures, **Schloss Linderhof** (☎08822-920 30; adult/concession €8.50/7.50; ⊙9am-6pm Apr–mid-Oct, 10am-4pm mid-Oct–Mar) was Ludwig II's smallest but most sumptuous palace, and the only one he lived to see fully completed. Finished in 1878, the palace hugs a steep hillside in a fantasy landscape of French gardens, fountains and follies. The reclusive king used the palace as a retreat and hardly ever received visitors here. Like Herrenchiemsee (p121), Linderhof was inspired by Versailles and dedicated to Louis XIV, the French Sun King.

Linderhof's myth-laden, jewel-encrusted rooms are a monument to the king's excesses that so unsettled the governors in Munich. The **private bedroom** is the largest, heavily ornamented and anchored by an enormous 108-candle crystal chandelier weighing 500kg. An artificial waterfall, built to cool the room in summer, cascades just outside the window. The **dining room** reflects the king's fetish for privacy and inventions. The

king ate from a mechanised dining board, whimsically labelled 'Table, Lay Yourself', that sank through the floor so that his servants could replenish it without being seen.

Created by the famous court gardener Carl von Effner, the gardens and outbuildings, open April to October, are as fascinating as the castle itself. The highlight is the oriental-style **Moorish Kiosk**, where Ludwig, dressed in oriental garb, would preside over nightly entertainment from a peacock throne. Underwater light dances on the stalactites in the **Venus Grotto**, an artificial cave inspired by a stage set for Wagner's *Tannhäuser*. Now sadly empty, Ludwig's fantastic conch-shaped boat is moored by the shore.

Linderhof is about 13km west of Oberammergau and 26km northwest of Garmisch-Partenkirchen. Bus 9622 travels to Linderhof from Oberammergau 10 times a day. If coming from Garmisch-Partenkirchen, change in Ettal or Oberammergau. The last service from Linderhof is just before 7pm but, if you miss it, the 13km vista-rich hike back to Oberammergau is an easygoing amble along the valley floor through shady woodland.

Oberammergau

☎08822 / POP 5230

Quietly quaint Oberammergau occupies a wide valley surrounded by the dark forests and snow-dusted peaks of the Ammergauer Alps. The centre is packed with traditional painted houses, woodcarving shops and awestruck tourists who come here to learn about the town's world-famous Passion Play. It's also a great budget base for hikes and cross-country skiing trips into easily accessible Alpine backcountry.

A blend of opera, ritual and Hollywood epic, the **Passion Play** (www.passionplay-oberammergau.com) has been performed every year ending in a zero (plus some extra years for a variety of reasons) since the late 17th century as a collective thank you from the villagers for being spared the plague. Half the village takes part, sewing amazing costumes and growing hair and beards for their roles (no wigs or false hair allowed). The next performances will take place between May and October 2020, but tours of the **Passionstheater** (🎭945 8833; Passionswiese 1; theatre tour & Oberammergau Museum admission adult/child/concession €8/3/6; ⏰tours 9.30am-5pm Apr-Oct) enable you to take a peek at the costumes and sets anytime. The theatre doesn't lie dormant in the decade between Passion Plays – ask the tourist office about music, plays and opera performances that take place here over the summer.

The town's other claim to fame is **Lüftmalerei**, the eye-popping house facades painted in an illusionist style. Images usually have a religious flavour, but some also show hilarious beer-hall scenes or fairy-tale motifs, like *Little Red Riding Hood* at Ettalerstrasse 48 or *Hänsel und Gretel* at No 41 down the road. The pick of the crop is the amazing **Pilatushaus** (Ludwig-Thoma-Strasse 10; ⏰3-5pm Tue-Sat May-Oct), whose painted columns snap into 3D as you approach. It contains a gallery and several craft workshops.

Oberammergau is also celebrated for its intricate **woodcarvings**. Workshops abound around town, where skilled craftspeople can produce anything from an entire nativity scene in single walnut shell to a life-size Virgin Mary. Speciality shops and the **Oberammergau Museum** (🎭941 36; www.oberammergaumuseum.de; Dorfstrasse 8; ⏰10am-5pm Tue-Sun Apr-Oct) display fine examples of the art.

Oberammergau has a **DJH hostel** (🎭4114; www.oberammergau.jugendherberge.de; Malensteinweg 10; dm from €16.80) as well as several guesthouses, including the exceptionally good-value **Gästehaus Richter** (🎭935 765; www.gaestehaus-richter.de; Welfengasse 2; s €28-35, d €56-70; 🅿) with immaculate en-suite rooms, a guest kitchen and a filling Alpine breakfast. Recently updated **Hotel Turmwirt** (🎭926 00; www.turmwirt.de; Ettalerstrasse 2; s/d from €75/99) next to the church has pristine business-standard rooms, some with Alpine views from the balconies and bits of woodcarving art throughout.

The **tourist office** (🎭922 740; www.ammergauer-alpen.de; Eugen-Papst-Strasse 9a; ⏰9am-6pm Mon-Fri, 9am-1pm Sat) can help find accommodation.

Hourly trains connect Munich with Oberammergau (change at Murnau; €18.10, 1¾ hours). Hourly **RVO bus 9606** (www.rvo-bus.de) goes direct to Garmisch-Partenkirchen via Ettal; change at Echelsbacher Brücke for Füssen.

Ettal

Ettal would be just another bend in the road were it not for its famous monastery, **Kloster Ettal** (www.kloster-ettal.de; Kaiser-Ludwig-Platz 1). The highlight here is the sugary rococo basilica housing the monks' prized possession, a marble madonna brought from Rome by Ludwig der Bayer in 1330. However, some might argue that the real high point is sampling the monastically distilled Ettaler Klosterlikör, an equally sugary herbal digestif.

Ettal is 5km south of Oberammergau, an easy hike along the Ammer River. Otherwise take bus 9606 from Garmisch-Partenkirchen or Oberammergau.

Garmisch-Partenkirchen

🎭08821 / POP 26,000

An incredibly popular hang-out for outdoorsy types and moneyed socialites, the double-barrelled resort of Garmisch-Partenkirchen is blessed with a fabled setting a snowball's throw from the Alps. To say you 'wintered in Garmisch' still has an aristocratic ring, and the area offers some of the best skiing in the land, including runs on Germany's highest peak, the Zugspitze (2964m).

The towns of Garmisch and Partenkirchen were merged for the 1936 Winter Olympics and, to this day, host international skiing events. Each retains its own distinct character: Garmisch has a more cosmopolitan, 21st-century feel, while Partenkirchen has retained its old-world Alpine village vibe.

Garmisch-Partenkirchen also makes a handy base for excursions to Ludwig II's palaces, including nearby Schloss Linderhof (p113) and the lesser-known Jagdschloss Schachen (p115), as well as Oberammergau (p113) and even, at a push, Neuschwanstein (p109) and Hohenschwangau (p110) castles.

Around Garmisch-Partenkirchen

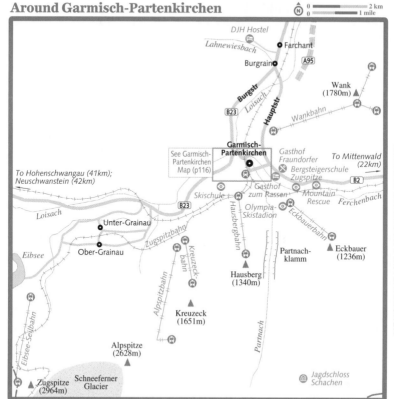

⊙ Sights

Zugspitze MOUNTAIN
(www.zugspitze.de) Views from Germany's rooftop are quite literally breathtaking and, on good days, extend into four countries. Skiing and hiking are the main activities here. The trip to the Zugspitze summit via the Zugspitzbahn is as memorable as it is popular; beat the crowds by starting early in the day and, if possible, skip weekends altogether. In Garmisch, board the **Zahnradbahn** (cogwheel train) at its own station behind the Hauptbahnhof. Trains first chug along the mountain base to the Eibsee, a forest lake, then wind their way through a mountain tunnel up to the Schneeferner Glacier (2600m). Here, you'll switch to the **Gletscherbahn** cable car for the final ascent to the summit. When you're done soaking in the panorama, board the **Eibsee-Seilbahn**, a steep cable car, that sways and swings its way back down to the Eibsee in about 10 minutes. It's not for vertigo sufferers, but the views surely are tremendous.

Most people come up on the train and take the cable car back down, but it works just as well the other way around. Either way, the entire trip costs €39/21.50 per adult/child in winter and €49.50/28 in summer. Winter rates include a day ski pass.

Partnachklamm GORGE
(www.partnachklamm.eu; adult/child €3/1.50; ⊙9am-5pm Oct-Easter, 8am-6pm Easter-Sep) One of the area's main attractions is the dramatically beautiful Partnachklamm, a narrow 700m-long gorge with walls rising up to 80m. A circular walk hewn from the rock takes you through the gorge, which is spectacular in winter when you can walk beneath curtains of icicles and frozen waterfalls.

Jagdschloss Schachen CASTLE
(☑920 30; adult/concession €4.50/3.50; ⊙Jun-Oct) A popular hiking route is to King

Garmisch-Partenkirchen

Ludwig II's hunting lodge, Jagdschloss Schachen, which can be reached via the Partnachklamm in about a four-hour hike. A plain wooden hut from the outside, the interior is surprisingly magnificent; the **Moorish Room** is something straight out of *Arabian Nights*.

🏃 Activities

Garmisch has two big ski fields: the Zugspitze plateau (2964m) and the Classic Ski Area (Alpspitze, 2628m; Hausberg, 1340m; Kreuzeck, 1651m; €33/18.50 day pass per adult/child). Local buses serve all the valley stations. Cross-country ski trails run along the main valleys, including a long section

from Garmisch to Mittenwald; call ☏797 979 for a weather or snow report (in German only). If you're a beginner, expect to pay around €60 per day for group ski lessons or €45 per hour for private instruction.

The area around Garmisch-Partenkirchen is also prime hiking and mountaineering territory. The website of the tourist office (p118) has a superbly interactive tour-planning facility to help you plot your way through the peaks on foot, and many brochures and maps are also available with route suggestions for all levels. Qualified Alpine guides are also on hand at the tourist office between 4pm and 6pm Monday and Thursday to answer questions and provide all kinds of information. Hiking to the Zugspitze (p115) summit is only possible in summer and is only recommended for those with experience in mountaineering.

Skischule   SKIING
(☏4931; www.skischule-gap.de; Am Hausberg 8) Ski hire and courses.

Alpensport Total   SKIING
(Map p116; ☏1425; www.alpensporttotal.de; Marienplatz 18) Winter ski school and hire centre that organises other outdoor activities in the warmer months.

Bergsteigerschule Zugspitze   HIKING
(☏589 99; www.bergsteigerschule-zugspitze.de; Am Kreuzeckbahnhof 12a) A mountaineering school, offering guided hikes and courses.

Deutscher Alpenverein   HIKING
(Map p116; ☏2701; www.alpenverein-gapa.de; Hindenburgstrasse 38) This outdoor organisation offers guided hikes and courses.

🛏 Sleeping

The tourist office operates a 24-hour out-door room-reservation noticeboard.

Hotel Garmischer Hof
HOTEL €€

(Map p116; ☎9110; www.garmischer-hof.de; Chamonixstrasse 10; s €59-94, d €94-136; 🕸🏊) Property of the Seiwald family since 1928, many a climber, skier and Alpine adventurer has creased the sheets at this welcoming inn. Rooms are simply furnished but cosy, breakfast is served in the vaulted cafe-restaurant and there's a sauna providing après-ski relief.

Reindl's Partenkirchner Hof
HOTEL €€€

(Map p116; ☎943 870; www.reindls.de; Bahnhofstrasse 15; s/d from €80/176; 🅿@🕸) Though Reindl's doesn't look worthy of its five stars from the outside, this elegant, tri-winged luxury hotel is stacked with perks, a wine bar and a top-notch gourmet restaurant. Rooms are studies in folk-themed elegance and some enjoy gobsmacking mountain views.

Hostel 2962
HOSTEL €

(Map p116; ☎957 50; www.hostel2962.com; Partnachauenstrasse 3; dm/d from €20/60; 🕸) Touted as a hostel, the former Hotel Schell is essentially a typical Garmisch hotel, but a good choice nonetheless. If you can get into one of the four-bed dorms, it's the cheapest sleep in town. Breakfast is an extra €6 if you stay in a dorm.

Gasthof zum Rassen
HOTEL €€

(☎2089; www.gasthof-rassen.de; Ludwigstrasse 45; s €32-53, d €52-90; 🅿) This beautifully frescoed 14th-century building is home to a great budget option where the simply furnished, contemporary rooms contrast with the traditionally frilly styling of the communal areas. The cavernous event hall, formerly a brewery, houses Bavaria's oldest folk theatre.

DJH Hostel
HOSTEL €

(☎967 050; www.garmisch.jugendherberge.de; Jochstrasse 10; dm €23.10; 🅿@) The standards at this smart, immaculately maintained hostel are as good as some chain hotels. Rooms have Ikea-style furnishings and fruity colour schemes, and there are indoor and outdoor climbing walls if the Alps are not enough.

🍴 Eating

Gasthof Fraundorfer
BAVARIAN €€

(☎9270; Ludwigstrasse 24; mains €8-20, breakfast €9.80; ☯7am-1am Thu-Mon, from 5pm Wed) If you came to the Alps to experience yodelling, knee slapping and red-faced locals in lederhosen, you just arrived at the right address. Steins of frothing ale fuel the increasingly raucous atmosphere as the evening progresses and monster portions of platted pig meat push belt buckles to the limit. Decor ranges from baroque cherubs to hunting trophies and the 'Sports Corner'. Unmissable.

Zum Wildschütz
BAVARIAN €€

(Map p116; ☎3290; Bankgasse 9; mains €6-17; ☯11am-10pm) The best place in town for fresh venison, rabbit, wild boar and other seasonal game dishes, this place is, not surprisingly, popular with hunters. The Tyrolean and south Bavarian takes on schnitzel aren't bad either. If you prefer your victuals critter free, look elsewhere.

Isi's Goldener Engel
BAVARIAN €€

(Map p116; ☎948 757; Bankgasse 5; mains €8-15; ☯11.30am-2.30pm & 5-10pm) The 'Golden Angel' is a rococo riot, complete with wacky frescos and gold-leaf-sheathed ceilings that wouldn't look out of place in a church. It's family run, neighbourhood adored and delivers classic Bavarian cooking, including a mean pork knuckle with the crust done just so.

Bräustüberl
GERMAN €€

(Map p116; ☎2312; Fürstenstrasse 23; mains €6-17) A short walk from the centre, this quintessentially Bavarian tavern is the place to cosy up with some local nosh, served by Dirndl-trussed waitresses, while the enormous enamel coal-burning stove revives chilled extremities. The dining room is to the right, the beer hall (with a little more ambience) to the left and the small beer garden out front.

Colosseo
ITALIAN €€

(Map p116; ☎528 09; Klammstrasse 7; mains €5.50-25.50; ☯11.30am-2.30pm & 5-11.30pm) If you fancy an Alpine take on la dolce vita, with mountain views and a bit of faux archaeology thrown in, this much-lauded pasta-pizza parlour with a mammoth menu is the place to head.

HAPPY SKIING

A **Happy Ski Card** (two days, adult/child €69/41.50) covers all the slopes, plus other ski areas around the Zugspitze, including Mittenwald and Ehrwald (an incredible 231km of pistes and 106 ski lifts).

BAVARIA GARMISCH-PARTENKIRCHEN

Zirbel PUB €€
(Map p116; ☑716 71; Promenadestrasse 2; mains €8-17; ☺5pm-1am) Guarded by a grumpy-looking wood-carved bear, this popular music pub serves noodle dishes, salads and schnitzel, all washed down with Czech Urquell beer on tap.

Saigon City VIETNAMESE €
(Map p116; Am Kurpark 17a; mains €6.50-11.50; ☺11am-2.30pm & 5-10.30pm) No-frills Vietnamese diner serving crispy duck, egg noodles and seafood. Cheap lunch menus.

ℹ Information

Hobi's Cyber Café (Zugspitzstrasse 2; per hr €3; ☺5.45am-5.30pm Mon-Fri, to noon Sat, 7-11am Sun) Internet cafe within the town's best bakery.

Mountain Rescue (☑112; www.bergwacht bayern.de; Auenstrasse 7) Mountain rescue station.

Post Office (Bahnhofstrasse 31)

Sparda Bank (Hauptbahnhof)

Tourist Office (☑180 700; www.gapa.de; Richard-Strauss-Platz 2; ☺8am-6pm Mon-Sat, 10am-noon Sun)

ℹ Getting There & Around

Garmisch-Partenkirchen has hourly connections from Munich (€19, 1½ hours), and special packages, available from Munich Hauptbahnhof (p96), combine the return trip with a Zugspitze day ski pass (around €45).

RVO bus 9606 (www.rvo-bus.de) leaves at 9.40am, reaching the Füssen castles at Neuschwanstein and Hohenschwangau two hours later. On the way back take the 4.13pm or 5.13pm bus 73 and change onto the 9606 at Echelsbacher Brücke. The 9606 also runs hourly to Oberammergau (40 minutes).

The A95 from Munich is the direct road route. The most central parking is at the Kongresshaus (next to the tourist office) for €1 per hour.

Bus tickets cost €1.50 for journeys in town. For bike hire, try **Fahrrad Ostler** (☑3362; Kreuzstrasse 1; per day/week from €10/50).

Mittenwald

☑08823 / POP 7400

Nestled in a cul-de-sac under snowcapped peaks, sleepily alluring Mittenwald, 20km southeast of Garmisch-Partenkirchen, is the most natural spot imaginable for a resort. Known far and wide for its master violin makers, the citizens of this drowsy village seem almost bemused by its popularity. The air is ridiculously clean, and on the main street the loudest noise is a babbling brook.

The **tourist office** (☑339 81; www.mitten wald.de; Dammkarstrasse 3; ☺8.30am-6pm Mon-Fri, 9am-noon Sat, 10am-noon Sun Jul & Aug, shorter hours Sep-Jun) has details of excellent hiking and cycling routes. Popular hikes with cable-car access will take you up the grandaddy Alpspitze (2628m), as well as the Wank, Mt Karwendel and the Wettersteinspitze. Return tickets to Karwendel, which boasts Germany's second-highest cable-car route, cost €22/13.50 per adult/child.

The Karwendel ski field has one of the longest runs (7km) in Germany, but it is primarily for freestyle pros. All-day ski passes to the nearby Kranzberg ski fields, the best all-round option, cost €24.50 per adult and €18.50 per child. For equipment hire and ski/snowboard instruction contact the **Erste Skischule Mittenwald** (☑3582; www. skischule-mittenwald.de; Bahnhofsplatz 14).

The only classic off-piste sight in town is the **Geigenbaumuseum** (☑2511; www.geigenbaumu seum-mittenwald.de; Ballenhausgasse 3; adult/concession €4.50/3.50; ☺10am-5pm Tue-Sun Feb–mid-Mar, mid-May–mid-Oct & mid-Dec–early Jan, other months 11am-4pm Tue-Sun), a collection of over 200 locally crafted violins and the tools used to fashion them. It's also the venue for occasional concerts.

Behind a very pretty facade, **Hotel-Gasthof Alpenrose** (☑927 00; www.alpenrose -mittenwald.de; Obermarkt 1; s €29-48, d €89-96) has cosy, old-style rooms, a cute restaurant and live Bavarian music almost nightly. Around 1km south of the Obermarkt, **Restaurant Arnspitze** (☑2425; Innsbrucker Strasse 68; mains €16.50-22.50; ☺Thu-Mon) serves award-winning gourmet fare.

Mittenwald is served by trains from Garmisch-Partenkirchen (€4.10, 20 minutes, hourly), Munich (€22.20, 1¾ hours, hourly) and Innsbruck (€11.10, one hour, seven daily), across the border in Austria. Otherwise RVO bus 9608 (www.rvo-bus.de) connects Mittenwald with Garmisch-Partenkirchen (30 minutes) several times a day.

Oberstdorf

☑08322 / POP 9900

Spectacularly situated in the western Alps, the Allgäu region feels a long, long way from the rest of Bavaria, both in its cuisine (more *Spätzle* than dumplings) and the dialect, which is closer to the Swabian of Baden-Württemberg. The Allgäu's chief draw is the car-free resort of Oberstdorf, a major skiing centre a short hop from Austria.

Activities

Oberstdorf is almost ringed by towering peaks and offers some top-draw hiking. In-the-know skiers value the resort for its friendliness, lower prices and less-crowded pistes. The village is surrounded by 70km of well-maintained cross-country trails and three ski fields: the **Nebelhorn** (half-day/day passes €32/37.50), **Fellhorn/Kanzelwand** (half-day/day passes €33.50/39) and **Söllereck** (half-day/day passes €21.50/26). For ski hire and tuition, try **Alpin Skischule** (☑952 90; www.alpinskischule.de; Am Bahnhofplatz 1a) opposite the train station or **Erste Skischule Oberstdorf** (☑3110; www.skischule-oberstdorf.de; Freiherr-von-Brutscher-Strasse 4).

Gaisalpseen   HIKING

For an exhilarating day walk, ride the Nebelhorn cable car to the upper station, then hike down via the Gaisalpseen, two lovely Alpine lakes (six hours).

Eislaufzentrum Oberstdorf   ICE SKATING

(☑700 510; Rossbichlstrasse 2-6) The Eislaufzentrum Oberstdorf, behind the Nebelhorn cablecar station, is the biggest ice-skating complex in Germany, with three separate rinks.

🛏 Sleeping

Oberstdorf is chock full with private guesthouses, but owners are usually reluctant to rent rooms for just one night, even in the quieter shoulder seasons.

Haus Edelweiss   APARTMENTS €€

(☑959 60; www.edelweiss.de; Freibergstrasse 7; apt from €103; P🐾) As crisp and sparkling as freshly fallen Alpine snow, this new apartment hotel just a couple of blocks from the tourist office has 19 pristine, self-contained flats with fully equipped kitchens, ideal for stays of three nights or more. Generally the longer you tarry, the fewer euros per night you kiss goodbye.

Weinklause   GUESTHOUSE €€

(☑969 30; www.weinklause.de; Prinzenstrasse 10; s €67, d €106-126; P) Willing to take one nighters at the drop of a felt hat, this superb lodge offers all kinds of rooms and apartments, some with kitchenette, others with jaw-dropping, spectacular Alpine views. A generous breakfast is served in the restaurant, which comes to life most nights with local live music.

DJH Hostel   HOSTEL €

(☑987 50; www.oberstdorf.jugendherberge.de; Kornau 8; dm €18.90) A relaxed, 200-bed chalet-hostel with commanding views of the Allgäu Alps. Take bus 9742 from the bus station in front of the Hauptbahnhof to the Reute stop; it's in the suburb of Kornau, near the Söllereck chairlift.

🍴 Eating & Drinking

Weinstube am Frohmarkt   TYROLEAN €€

(☑3988; Am Frohmarkt 2; mains €10-19; ⊙5pm-midnight) 'Where did Bavaria go?' you might exclaim at this intimate wine bar, where the musty-sweet aroma of wine, cheese and Tyrolean cured ham scents the air. Rub shoulders with locals downstairs over a plate of wild boar or Tessin-style turkey steak, or retreat upstairs for a quiet nip of wine.

Nordi Stüble   SWABIAN €€

(☑7641; cnr Walserstrasse & Luitpoldstrasse; mains €8.50-21.50; ⊙4pm-late Tue-Sat, from noon Sun) Family owned and run, this intimate neighbourhood eatery, a small wood-panelled dining room bedecked in rural junk of yesteryear, is the place to enjoy local takes on schnitzel and *Maultaschen*. All dishes are prepared fresh, so be prepared to wait; swab the decks afterwards with a Stuttgart Dinkelacker beer.

Oberstdorfer Dampfbierbrauerei   BREWERY

(Bahnhofplatz 8; ⊙11am-1am) Knock back a few 'steamy ales' at Germany's southernmost brewery, right next to the train station.

ℹ Information

The main **tourist office** (☑7000; www.oberstdorf.de; Prinzregenten-Platz 1; ⊙9am-5pm Mon-Fri, 9.30am-noon Sat) and its **branch office** (Bahnhofplatz; ⊙10am-5pm daily) at the train station run a room-finding service.

ℹ Getting There & Away

There are at least five direct trains daily from Munich (€30, 2½ hours), otherwise change in Buchloe.

Andechs

Founded in the 10th century, the gorgeous hilltop monastery of **Andechs** (☑08152-376 253; www.andechs.de; admission free; ⊙8am-6pm Mon-Fri, 9am-6pm Sat, 9.45am-6pm Sun) has long been a place of pilgrimage, though today more visitors come to slurp the Benedictines' fabled ales.

The church owns two relics of enormous importance: branches that are thought to come from Christ's crown of thorns, and a victory cross of Charlemagne, whose army overran much of Western Europe in the 9th century. In the Holy Chapel, the votive candles, some of them over 1m tall, are among Germany's oldest. The remains of Carl Orff, the composer of *Carmina Burana*, are interred here as well.

Outside, soak up the magnificent views of the purple-grey Alps and forested hills before plunging into the nearby **Bräustüberl** (☺10am-8pm), the monks' beer hall and garden. There are seven varieties of beer on offer, from the rich and velvety *Doppelbock* dark to the fruity unfiltered *Weissbier*. The place is incredibly popular and, on summer weekends, you may have to join a queue of day trippers at the door to get in.

The easiest way to reach Andechs from Munich is to take the S8 to Herrsching (€7.50, 49 minutes), then change to bus 951 or the private Ammersee-Reisen bus (€2.20, 11 times daily). Alternatively, it's a pleasant 4km hike south from Herrsching through the protected woodland of the Kiental.

Bad Tölz

☑08041 / POP 17,800

Situated some 40km south of central Munich, Bad Tölz is a pretty spa town straddling the Isar River. The town's gentle inclines provide a delightful spot for its attractive, frescoed houses and the quaint shops of the old town. At weekends thousands flock here from Munich to enjoy the ultramodern swimming complex, Alpine slide and hiking trips down the river. Bad Tölz is also the gateway to the Tölzer Land region and its emerald-green lakes, the Walchensee and the Kochelsee.

◉ Sights & Activities

Cobble-stoned and car-free, **Marktstrasse** is flanked by statuesque town houses with ornate overhanging eaves that look twice as high on the sloping street. Above the town, on Kalvarienberg, looms Bad Tölz' landmark, the twin-towered **Kalvarienbergkirche** (Cavalry Church). This giant baroque structure stands side by side with the petite **Leonhardikapelle** (Leonhardi Chapel; 1718), the destination of the Leonhardi pilgrimage.

Stadtmuseum   MUSEUM
(☑793 5156; Marktstrasse 48; adult/child €2/1; ☺10am-4pm Tue-Sun) The Stadtmuseum touches on virtually all aspects of local culture and history, with a fine collection of painted armoires (the so-called Tölzer Kas-

ten), a 2m-tall, single-stringed *Nonnengeige* (marine trumpet), examples of traditional glass painting and a cart used in the Leonhardifahrt.

Alpamare   SPA
(☑509 999; www.alpamare.de; Ludwigstrasse 14; day pass adult/child €34/24; ☺9.30am-10pm) In the spa section of town, west of the Isar River, you'll find the fantastic water complex Alpamare. This huge centre has heated indoor and outdoor mineral pools, a wave and surfing pool, a series of wicked water slides (including Germany's longest, the 330m-long Alpabob-Wildwasser), saunas, solariums and its own hotel. Bus 9570 from the train station stops 100m away.

Blomberg   HIKING
Southwest of Bad Tölz, the Blomberg (1248m) is a family-friendly mountain that has a natural toboggan track in winter, plus easy hiking and a fun Alpine slide in summer.

Unless you're walking, getting up the hill involves, weather permitting, a chairlift ride aboard the **Blombergbahn** (top station adult/child return €8/3.50; ☺9am-5pm May-Oct, 9am-4pm Nov-Apr). Over 1km long, the fibreglass Alpine slide snakes down the mountain from the middle station. You zip down at up to 50km/h through the 17 hairpin bends on little wheeled bobsleds with a joystick to control braking. A long-sleeved shirt and jeans provide a little protection. Riding up to the midway station and sliding down costs €4 per adult (€3.50 concession), with discounts for multiple trips.

To reach Blomberg, take RVO bus 9612 or 9591 from the train station to the Blombergbahn stop.

✿ Festivals & Events

Leonhardifahrt   PILGRIMAGE
Every year on 6 November, residents pay homage to the patron saint of horses, Leonhard. The famous Leonhardifahrt is a pilgrimage up to the Leonhardi chapel, where townsfolk dress up in traditional costume and ride dozens of garlanded horse carts to the strains of brass bands.

⎙ Sleeping & Eating

Posthotel Kolberbräu   HOTEL €€
(☑768 80; www.kolberbraeu.de; Marktstrasse 29; s/d from €54/94) Very well-appointed digs amid the bustle of the main street, with a classic Bavarian restaurant and a tradition going back over four centuries.

Gasthof Zantl BAVARIAN €€

(Salzstrasse 31; mains €8-18; ⊗lunch & dinner Sat-Thu Jun-Dec, Sat-Wed Jan-May) One of Bad Tölz' oldest buildings, this convivial tavern has a predictably pork-heavy menu, with ingredients sourced from local villages as much as possible. There's a sunny beer garden out front.

Solo BISTRO €€

(☑730 923; Königsdorfer Strasse 2; mains €8-16; ⊗9am-midnight) For a casual meal try Solo, right on the Isar, which draws an all-ages crowd with global bistro favourites (pasta, curries, enchiladas, salads).

❶ Information

Tourist Office (☑793 5156; www.bad-toelz.de; Marktstrasse 48; ⊗10am-4pm Tue-Sun)

❶ Getting There & Away

The private **Bayerische Oberlandbahn** (BOB; ☑08024-997 171; www.bayerischeoberland bahn.de) runs hourly trains between Bad Tölz and Munich Hauptbahnhof (€11.10, 50 minutes). Alternatively, take the S2 from central Munich to Holzkirchen, then change to the BOB. In Holzkirchen make sure you board the Bad Tölz–bound portion of the train.

Chiemsee

☑08051

Most foreign visitors arrive at the shores of the Bavarian Sea – as Chiemsee is affectionately known – in search of King Ludwig II's Schloss Herrenchiemsee. The lake's natural beauty and water sports make the area popular with de-stressing city dwellers, and many affluent Müncheners own weekend retreats by its shimmering waters.

The towns of Prien am Chiemsee and, about 5km south, Bernau am Chiemsee (both on the Munich–Salzburg rail line) are perfect bases for exploring the lake. Of the two towns, Prien is by far the larger and livelier. If you're day tripping to Herrenchiemsee, conveniently interconnecting transport is available. To explore further, you'll probably need a set of wheels.

⊙ Sights

Schloss Herrenchiemsee CASTLE

(☑688 70; www.herren-chiemsee.de; adult/child/concession €8/free/7; ⊗tours 9am-6pm Apr-Oct, 9.40am-4.15pm Nov-Mar) An island just 1.5km across the Chiemsee from Prien, Herreninsel is home to Ludwig II's Versailles-inspired Schloss Herrenchiemsee. Begun in 1878, it was never intended as a residence, but as a homage to absolutist monarchy, as epitomised by Ludwig's hero, the French Sun King, Louis XIV. Ludwig spent only 10 days here and even then was rarely seen, preferring to read at night and sleep all day.

The palace is typical of Ludwig's creations, its design and appearance the product of the Bavarian monarch's romantic obsessions and unfettered imagination. Ludwig splurged more money on this palace than on Neuschwanstein and Linderhof combined, but when cash ran out in 1885, one year before his death, 50 rooms remained unfinished.

The rooms that were completed outdo each other in opulence. The vast **Gesandtentreppe** (Ambassador Staircase), a double staircase leading to a frescoed gallery and topped by a glass roof, is the first visual knockout on the guided tour, but that fades in comparison to the stunning **Grosse Spiegelgalerie** (Great Hall of Mirrors). This tunnel of light runs the length of the garden (98m, or 10m longer than that in Versailles). It sports 52 candelabra and 33 great glass chandeliers with 7000 candles, which took 70 servants half an hour to light. In late July it becomes a wonderful venue for classical concerts.

The **Paradeschlafzimmer** (State Bedroom) features a canopied bed perching altarlike on a pedestal behind a golden balustrade. This was the heart of the palace, where morning and evening audiences were held. But it's the king's bedroom, the **Kleines Blaues Schlafzimmer** (Little Blue Bedroom), that really takes the cake. The decoration is sickly sweet, encrusted with gilded stucco and wildly extravagant carvings. The room is bathed in a soft blue light emanating from a glass globe at the foot of the bed. It supposedly took 18 months for a technician to perfect the lamp to the king's satisfaction.

Admission to the palace also entitles you to a spin around the **König Ludwig II Museum**, where you can see the king's christening and coronation robes, more blueprints of megalomaniac buildings and his death mask.

To reach the palace, take the hourly or half-hourly ferry from Prien-Stock (€7.10 return, 15 to 20 minutes) or from Bernau-Felden (€8.30, 25 minutes, May to October). From the boat landing on Herreninsel, it's about a 20-minute walk through pretty gardens to the palace. Palace tours, offered in German or English, last 30 minutes.

BAVARIA CHIEMSEE

Fraueninsel ISLAND

A third of this tiny island is occupied by **Frauenwörth Abbey** (www.frauenwoerth.de; admission free), founded in the late 8th century, making it one of the oldest abbeys in Bavaria. The 10th-century church, whose free-standing campanile sports a distinctive onion-dome top (11th century), is worth a visit.

Opposite the church is the AD 860 Carolingian **Torhalle** (admission €2; ☉10am-6pm May-Oct). It houses medieval objets d'art, sculpture and changing exhibitions of regional paintings from the 18th to the 20th centuries.

Return ferry fare, including a stop at Herreninsel, is €8.20 from Prien-Stock and €8.40 from Bernau-Felden.

⚡ Activities

The swimming beaches at Chieming and Gstadt (both free) are the easiest to reach, on the lake's eastern and northern shores respectively. A variety of boats are available for hire at many beaches, for €10 to €25 per hour. In Prien, **Bootsverleih Stöffl** (☎2000; www.stoeffl.de; Strandpromenade) is possibly the best company to turn to.

Prienavera SWIMMING

(☎609 570; Seestrasse 120; 4hr pass adult/child €9.90/5.50, day pass €11.90/6.50, sauna extra €3; ☉10am-9pm Mon-Fri, 9am-9pm Sat & Sun) The futuristic-looking glass roof by the harbour in Prien-Stock shelters Prienavera, a popular pool complex with a wellness area, water slides and a restaurant.

🛏 Sleeping

Hotel Bonnschlössl HOTEL €€

(☎965 6990; www.alter-wirt-bernau.de; Kirchplatz 9, Bernau; s/d €57/96) Built in 1477, this pocket-sized palace hotel with faux turrets once belonged to the Bavarian royal court. Rooms are stylish, if slightly overfurnished, and there's a wonderful terrace with a rambling garden.

Hotel Garni Möwe HOTEL €€

(☎5004; www.hotel-garni-moewe.de; Seestrasse 111, Prien; s/d from €61/99) This traditional Bavarian hotel right on the lakefront is excellent value, especially the loft rooms. It has its own bike and boat hire, plus a fitness centre, and the large garden is perfect for travellers with children.

DJH Hostel HOSTEL €

(☎687 70; www.prien.jugendherberge.de; Carl-Braun-Strasse 66; dm from €18.40) Prien's hostel organises lots of activities and has an environmental study centre for young people. It's in a bucolic spot, a 15-minute walk from the Hauptbahnhof.

Panorama Camping Harras CAMPGROUND €

(☎904 613; www.camping-harras.de; Harrasser Strasse 135; per person/tent/car from €5.50/3.60/2) This campsite is scenically located on a peninsula with its own private beach, and catamaran and surfboard hire. The restaurant has a delightful lakeside terrace.

🍴 Eating

Alter Wirt BAVARIAN €€

(☎965 6990; Kirchplatz 9, Bernau; mains €8-15; ☉closed Mon) This massive half-timbered inn with five centuries of history, situated on the main drag through Bernau, serves up Bavarian meat slabs and international favourites to a mix of locals and tourists.

Badehaus BAVARIAN €€

(☎970 300; Rathausstrasse 11; mains €6.50-17; ☉10am-late) Near the Chiemsee Info-Center and the lakeshore, this contemporary beer hall and garden has quirky decor and gourmet fare enjoyed by all. A special attraction is the 'beer bath', a glass tub (sometimes) filled with a mix of beer and water.

Westernacher am See MODERN BAVARIAN €€

(☎4722; Seestrasse 115, Prien; mains €8-16) This lakeside dining haven has a multiple personality, with a cosy restaurant, cocktail bar, cafe, beer garden and glassed-in winter terrace. Its speciality is modern twists on old Bavarian favourites.

ℹ Information

All the tourist offices have free internet for brief walk-in use.

Bernau Tourist Office (☎986 80; www.bernau-am-chiemsee.de; Aschauer Strasse 10; ☉8.30am-6pm Mon-Fri, 9am-noon Sat Jul–mid-Sep, shorter hours Mon-Fri & closed Sat mid-Sep–Jun)

Chiemsee Info-Center (☎965 550; www.chiemsee.de; ☉9am-6pm Mon-Fri) On the southern lake shore, near the Bernau-Felden autobahn exit.

Prien Tourist Office (☎690 50; www.tourismus.prien.de; Alte Rathausstrasse 11; ☉8.30am-6pm Mon-Fri, to 4pm Sat May-Sep, 8.30am-5pm Mon-Fri Oct-Apr)

❶ Getting There & Around

Trains run hourly from Munich to Prien (€16.40, one hour) and Bernau (€18.10, 1¼ hours). Hourly RVO bus 9505 connects the two lake towns.

Local buses run from Prien Bahnhof to the harbour in Stock. You can also take the historic **Chiemseebahn** (one-way/return €2.60/3.60) (1887), the world's oldest narrow-gauge steam train.

Chiemsee Schifffahrt (✆6090; www.chiemsee -schifffahrt.de; Seestrasse 108) operates half-hourly to hourly ferries from Prien with stops at Herreninsel, Fraueninsel, Seebruck and Chieming on a schedule that changes seasonally. You can circumnavigate the entire lake and make all these stops (getting off and catching the next ferry that comes your way) for €12.40. Children aged six to 15 get a 50% discount.

Chiemgauer Radhaus (✆4631; Bahnhofs-platz 6) and **Chiemgau Biking** (✆961 4973; Chiemseestrasse 84) hire out mountain bikes for between €12 and €22 per day.

Berchtesgaden

✆08652 / POP 7600

Wedged into Austria and framed by six formidable mountain ranges, the Berchtes-gadener Land is a drop-dead-gorgeous corner of Bavaria steeped in myths and legends. Local lore has it that angels given the task of distributing the earth's wonders were startled by God's order to get a move on and dropped them all here. These most definitely included the Watzmann (2713m), Germany's second-highest mountain, and the pristine Königssee, perhaps Germany's most photogenic body of water.

Much of the area is protected by law within the Berchtesgaden National Park, which was declared a 'biosphere reserve' by Unesco in 1990. The village of Berchtesgaden is the obvious base for hiking circuits into the park.

Away from the trails, the main draws are the mountaintop Eagle's Nest, a lodge built for Hitler and now a major dark-tourism destination, and Dokumentation Obersalz-berg, a museum that chronicles the region's sinister Nazi past.

◉ Sights

Eagle's Nest   HISTORIC SITE
(✆2969; www.kehlsteinhaus.de; ⊙mid-May–Oct) Berchtesgaden's most sinister draw is Mt Kehlstein, a sheer-sided peak at Obersalz-berg where Martin Bormann, a key hench-man of Hitler's, engaged 3000 workers to build a diplomatic meeting house for the Führer's 50th birthday. Perched at 1834m, the innocent-looking lodge (called Kehl-steinhaus in German) occupies one of the world's most breathtaking spots. Ironically, Hitler is said to have suffered from vertigo and rarely enjoyed the spectacular views himself. The Allies never regarded the site worth bombing and it survived WWII un-touched. Today the Eagle's Nest houses a restaurant that donates its profits to charity.

To get there, drive or take half-hourly bus 838 from the Hauptbahnhof to the Hotel Intercontinental then walk to the Kehlstein bus departure area. From here the road is closed to private traffic and you must take a special **bus** (adult/child €15.50/9) up the mountain (35 minutes). The final 124m stretch to the summit is in a luxurious brass-clad elevator.

Königssee   LAKE
Crossing the serenely picturesque, emerald-green Königssee makes for some unforget-table memories and once-in-a-lifetime photo opportunities. Contained by steep mountain walls some 5km south of Berchtesgaden, it's Germany's highest lake (603m), with drink-ably pure waters shimmering into fjordlike depths. Bus 841 makes the trip out here from the Berchtesgaden Hauptbahnhof roughly every hour.

Escape the hubbub of the bustling lake-side tourist village by taking an electric **boat tour** (www.seenschifffahrt.de; return adult/child €13.30/6.70) to St Bartholomä, a quaint onion-domed chapel on the western shore. At some point, the boat will stop while the captain plays a horn towards the Echo Wall – the sound will bounce seven times. Pure magic! The effect only fails during heavy fog. From the dock at St Bartholomä, an easy trail leads to the wondrous **Eiskapelle** (Ice Chapel) glacier cave in about one hour.

You can also skip the crowds by meander-ing along the lake shore. It's a nice and easy 3.5km return walk to the secluded **Maler-winkel** (Painter's Corner), a lookout famed for its picturesque vantage point.

Dokumentation Obersalzberg   MUSEUM
(www.obersalzberg.de; Salzbergstrasse 41, Ober-salzberg; adult/child & student €3/free; ⊙9am-5pm daily Apr-Oct, 10am-3pm Tue-Sun Nov-Mar) In 1933 the quiet mountain retreat of Ober-salzberg (3km from Berchtesgaden) be-came the southern headquarters of Hitler's government, a dark period that's given the

HITLER'S MOUNTAIN RETREAT

Of all the German towns tainted by the Third Reich, Berchtesgaden has a burden heavier than most. Hitler fell in love with nearby Obersalzberg in the 1920s and bought a small country home, later enlarged into the imposing Berghof.

After seizing power in 1933, Hitler established a part-time headquarters here and brought much of the party brass with him. They bought, or often confiscated, large tracts of land and tore down farmhouses to erect a 7ft-high barbed-wire fence. Obersalzberg was sealed off as the fortified southern headquarters of the NSDAP (National Socialist German Workers' Party). In 1938, British prime minister Neville Chamberlain visited for negotiations (later continued in Munich) which led to the infamous promise of 'peace in our time' at the expense of Czechoslovakia's Sudetenland.

Little is left of Hitler's Alpine fortress today. In the final days of WWII, the Royal Air Force levelled much of Obersalzberg, though the Eagle's Nest, Hitler's mountaintop eyrie, was left strangely unscathed. The historical twist and turns are dissected at the impressive Dokumentation Obersalzberg.

full historical treatment at the Dokumentation Obersalzberg. It's a fascinating exhibit that will probably make you queasy and uneasy, but the experience provides another piece in the region's historical jigsaw. You'll learn about the forced takeover of the area, the construction of the compound and the daily life of the Nazi elite. All facets of Nazi terror are dealt with, including Hitler's near-mythical appeal, his racial politics, the resistance movement, foreign policy and the death camps. A section of the underground bunker network is open for perusal. Half-hourly bus 838 from Berchtesgaden Hauptbahnhof will get you there.

Salzbergwerk   HISTORIC SITE
(www.salzzeitreise.de; Bergwerkstrasse 83; adult/child €15.50/9.50; ☉9am-5pm May-Oct, 11am-3pm Nov-Apr) Once a major producer of 'white gold', Berchtesgaden has thrown open its salt mines for fun-filled 90-minute tours. Kids especially love donning miners' garb and whooshing down a wooden slide into the depths of the mine. Down below, highlights include mysteriously glowing salt grottoes and crossing a 100m-long subterranean salt lake on a wooden raft.

🏃 Activities

Berchtesgaden National Park   HIKING
(www.nationalpark-berchtesgaden.de) The wilds of the 210-sq-km Berchtesgaden National Park offer some of the best hiking in Germany. A good introduction is a 2km trail up from St Bartholomä beside the Königssee to the notorious Watzmann-Ostwand, where scores of mountaineers have met their deaths. Another popular hike goes from the southern end of the Königssee to the Obersee. For details of routes visit the **national park office** (☏643 43; Franziskanerplatz 7; ☉9am-5pm), or buy a copy of the *Berchtesgadener Land* (sheet 794) map in the Kompass series.

Jenner-Königssee Area   SKIING
(☏958 10; www.jennerbahn.de; daily pass adult/child €29.20/15.50) The Jenner-Königssee area at Königssee is the biggest and most varied of five local ski fields. For equipment hire and courses, try **Skischule Treff-Aktiv** (☏979 707; www.treffaktiv.de; Jennerbahnstrasse 19).

Watzmann Therme   SPA
(☏946 40; www.watzmann-therme.de; Bergwerkstrasse 54; 2hr/4hr/day €9.70/12.20/13.90; ☉10am-10pm) The Watzman Therme is Berchtesgaden's thermal wellness complex, with several indoor and outdoor pools and various hydrotherapeutic treatment stations, a sauna and inspiring Alpine views.

👉 Tours

Eagle's Nest Tours   TOUR
(☏649 71; www.eagles-nest-tours.com; Königsseer Strasse 2; adult/child €50/35; ☉1.15pm mid-May–Oct) Experience the sinister legacy of the Obersalzberg area, including the Eagle's Nest and the underground bunker system, on a four-hour guided tour with Eagle's Nest Tours. Buses depart from the tourist office and reservations are advised.

🛏 Sleeping

Ask at the tourist office about private rooms in and around Berchtesgaden and campsites in Schönau near the Königssee. Advertised room rates normally don't include the local spa tax of €2.10 per adult per night.

Hotel Krone
HOTEL €€

(☏946 00; www.hotel-krone-berchtesgaden.de; Am Rad 5; s €44-54, d €82-108) Ambling distance from the town centre, this family-run gem provides almost unrivalled views of the valley and the Alps beyond. The wood-rich cabin-style rooms are generously cut affairs, with carved ceilings, niches and bedsteads all in fragrant pine. Take breakfast on the suntrap terrace for a memorable start to the day.

Hotel-Pension Greti
GUESTHOUSE €€

(☏975 297; www.pension-greti.de; Waldhauser Strasse 20; s €35-39, d €61-120) Warm and welcoming, and just a 15-minute walk from the Königssee, Greti's rooms are surprisingly voguish and all have balconies. The cellar bar and small sauna are perfect for some post-piste unwinding.

Hotel Bavaria
HOTEL €€

(☏660 11; www.hotelbavaria.net; Sunklergässchen 11; r €50-130; P) In the same family for over a century, this well-run hotel offers a romantic vision of Alpine life with rooms bedecked in frilly curtains, canopied beds, heart-shaped mirrors and knotty wood galore. Five of the pricier rooms have their own whirlpools. Breakfast is a gourmet affair, with sparkling wine and both hot and cold delectables.

Hotel Vier Jahreszeiten
HOTEL €€

(☏9520; www.hotel-vierjahreszeiten-berchtesgaden .de; Maximilianstrasse 20; s €50-68, d €85-101; P ☀) For a glimpse of Berchtesgaden's storied past, stay at this traditional in-town lodge where Bavarian royalty once entertained. Rooms are a bit long in the tooth but the spectacular mountain views (only from south-facing, ergo more expensive, rooms) more than compensate. Don't miss dinner in the atmospheric Hubertusstube restaurant.

DJH Hostel
HOSTEL €

(☏943 70; www.berchtesgaden.jugendherberge. de; Struberberg 6; dm from €17.60) This 265-bed hostel is situated in the suburb of Strub and has great views of Mt Watzmann. It's a 25-minute walk from the Hauptbahnhof or a short hop on bus 839.

✖ Eating

Farmers markets selling meats, cheese and other produce are held on the Marktplatz every Friday morning between April and October.

Le Ciel
INTERNATIONAL €€€

(☏975 50; www.restaurant-leciel.de; Hintereck 1; mains €30-40; ☺6.30-10.30pm Tue-Sat) Don't let the Hotel InterConti location turn you off: Le Ciel really is as heavenly as its French name suggests and it has the Michelin star to prove it. Testers were especially impressed by Ulrich Heimann's knack for spinning regional ingredients into such inspired gourmet compositions. Service is smooth and the circular dining room is magical. Only 32 seats, so book ahead if you can.

Gastätte St Bartholomä
BAVARIAN €€

(☏964 937; St Bartholomä; mains €7-16) Perched on the shore of the Königssee, and reached by boat, this is a tourist haunt that actually serves delicious food made with ingredients picked, plucked and hunted from the surrounding forests and the lake. Savour generous platters of venison in mushroom sauce with dumplings and red sauerkraut in the large beer garden or indoors.

Bräustübl
BAVARIAN €€

(☏976 724; Bräuhausstrasse 13; mains €8-14; ☺10am-1am) Enter through the arch painted in Bavaria's white and blue diamonds and pass the old beer barrels to reach the secluded beer garden belonging to the town's brewery. The vaulted hall is the scene of heel-whacking Bavarian stage shows every Saturday night.

Holzkäfer
CAFE, BAR €

(☏600 90; Buchenhöhe 40; dishes €4-9; ☺11am-1am Wed-Mon) This funky log cabin in the Obersalzberg hills is a great spot for a night out with fun-loving locals. Cluttered with antlers, carvings and backwoods oddities, it's known for its tender pork roasts, dark beer and Franconian wines.

Dalmacija
BISTRO €

(☏976 027; Marktplatz 5; dishes €5-9; ☺9am-late) Pizzas, pastas and a whiff of the Balkans in a contemporary-styled bistro-cafe.

ℹ Information

Post Office (Franziskanerplatz 2)

Tourist Office (www.berchtesgaden.de; Königsseer Strasse 2; ☺8.30am-6pm Mon-Fri, to 5pm Sat, 9am-3pm Sun Apr–mid-Oct, reduced hours mid-Oct–Mar)

ℹ Getting There & Away

Travelling from Munich by train involves a change at Freilassing (€30.90, three hours, five connections daily). The best option between Berchtesgaden and Salzburg is RVO bus 840 (45 minutes) which leaves from the train station in both towns roughly twice hourly. Berchtesgaden is south of the Munich–Salzburg A8 autobahn.

THE ROMANTIC ROAD

From the vineyards of Würzburg to the foot of the Alps, the almost 400km-long Romantic Road (Romantische Strasse) draws two million visitors every year, making it by far the most popular of Germany's holiday routes. This well-trodden trail cuts through a cultural and historical cross-section of southern Germany as it traverses Franconia and clips Baden-Württemberg in the north before plunging into Bavaria proper to end at Ludwig II's crazy castles. Expect lots of Japanese signs and menus, tourist coaches and kitsch galore, but also a fair wedge of *Gemütlichkeit* and geniune hospitality from those who earn their living on this most romantic of routes.

ℹ Information

The Romantic Road runs north–south through western Bavaria, covering 385km between Würzburg and Füssen near the Austrian border. It passes through more than two dozen cities and towns, including Rothenburg ob der Tauber, Dinkelsbühl and Augsburg.

ℹ Getting There & Away

Though Frankfurt is the most popular gateway for the Romantic Road, Munich is a good choice as well, especially if you decide to take the bus.

With its gentle gradients and bucolic flavour between towns, the Romantic Road is ideal for the holidaying cyclist. Bikes can be hired at many train stations; tourist offices keep lists of bicycle-friendly hotels that permit storage, or check out **Bett und Bike** (www.bettundbike.de) predeparture.

Direct trains run from Munich to Füssen (€24, two hours) at the southern end of the Romantic Road every two hours, more often if you change in Buchloe. Rothenburg is linked by train to Würzburg (€12.20, one hour), Munich (from €37.30, three hours), Augsburg (€29.70, 2½ hours) and Nuremberg (€18, 1¼ to two hours), with at least one change needed in Steinach to reach any destination.

ℹ Getting Around

It is possible to do this route using train connections and local buses, but the going is complicated, tedious and slow, especially at weekends. The ideal way to travel is by car, though many foreign travellers prefer to take Deutsche Touring's **Europabus** (☑069-790 3230; www.romanticroadcoach.de), which can get incredibly crowded in summer. From April to October the special coach runs daily in each direction between Frankfurt and Füssen (for Neuschwanstein); the entire journey takes around 12 hours. There's no charge for breaking the journey and continuing the next day.

Tickets are available for short segments of the trip, and reservations are only necessary during peak-season weekends. Reservations can be made through travel agents, Deutsche Touring, EurAide in Munich, and Deutsche Bahn's Reisezentrum offices in the train stations. If you stayed on the coach all the way from Frankfurt to Füssen (a pointless exercise), the total fare would be €158. The average fare from one stop to the next is around €3.

Coaches can accommodate bicycles (up to five stops cost €5; six to 11 stops, €8), but you must give three working days' notice. Students, children, pensioners and rail-pass holders qualify for discounts of between 10% and 50%.

For detailed schedules and prices, see www.romanticroadcoach.de.

Würzburg
☑0931 / POP 133,500

'If I could choose my place of birth, I would consider Würzburg', wrote author Hermann Hesse, and it's not difficult to see why. This scenic town straddles the Main River and is renowned for its art, architecture and delicate wines. A large student population guarantees a lively scene, and plenty of hip nightlife pulsates through its cobbled streets.

Würzburg was a Franconian duchy when, in 686, three Irish missionaries tried to persuade Duke Gosbert to convert to Christianity and ditch his wife. Gosbert was mulling it over when his wife had the three bumped off. When the murders were discovered decades later, the martyrs became saints and Würzburg was made a pilgrimage city and, in 742, a bishopric.

For centuries the resident prince-bishops wielded enormous power and wealth, and the city grew in opulence under their rule. Their crowning glory is the Residenz, one of the finest baroque structures in Germany and a Unesco World Heritage Site.

Decimated in WWII when 90% of the city centre was flattened, the authorities originally planned to leave the ruins as a reminder of the horrors of war. But a valiant rebuilding project saw the city restored almost to its pre-war glory.

◉ Sights

Residenz   PALACE
(Map p128; www.residenz-wuerzburg.de; Balthasar-Neumann-Promenade; adult/child €7.50/6.50; ⊙9am-6pm Apr-Oct, 10am-4.30pm Nov-Mar) The Unesco-listed Residenz is one of Germany's most important and beautiful baroque palaces and is a great way to kick off or end a journey along the Romantic Road.

Johann Philipp Franz von Schönborn, unhappy with his old-fashioned digs up in Marienberg Fortress, hired young architect Balthasar Neumann to build a new palace in town. Construction started in 1720. It took almost 60 years before the interior was completed, but the prince-bishops only used the palace for 20 years before they were incorporated into Bavaria. During the British bombing of WWII, the central section miraculously escaped unharmed; the rest required extensive restoration. Today the 350 rooms are home to government institutions, flats, faculties of the university and a museum, but the grandest spaces have been restored for visitors to admire.

Visits are by guided tour only. German-language groups leave every half an hour; English tours leave at 11am and 3pm year-round and, additionally, at 4.30pm April to October.

In 1750, the ceiling above Neumann's brilliant **Grand Staircase**, a single central set of steps that splits and zigzags up to the 1st floor, was topped by what still is the world's largest fresco (667 sq metres), by Tiepolo. It allegorically depicts the four then-known continents (Europe, Africa, America and Asia).

Take in the ice-white stucco of the **Weisser Saal** (White Hall), a soothing interlude in mind-boggling stucco and papier mâché, before entering the **Kaisersaal** (Imperial Hall), canopied by yet another impressive Tiepolo fresco. Other meticulously restored staterooms include the gilded stucco **Spiegelkabinett** (Mirror Hall), covered with a unique mirrorlike glass painted with figural, floral and animal motifs that make you feel as if you're standing inside a Fabergé egg. Destroyed in WWII, this room took eight years to recreate in the 1980s and contains 600 sq metres of gold leaf.

You're usually set free by the guide to explore the north-wing imperial apartments alone. Less impressive than the other parts of the palace, highlights include the velveteen-draped bed where Napoleon I slept in 1812 and a green lacquered room with an intricately inlaid parquet floor.

The bare corridors between the various restored rooms are given interest by fascinating exhibitions on the restoraion techniques used here in the postwar decades.

In the residence's south wing, the **Hofkirche** (Court Church) is another Neumann and Tiepolo co-production. Its marble columns, gold leaf and profusion of angels match the Residenz in splendour and proportions.

Behind the Residenz, the **Hofgarten** has whimsical sculptures of children, mostly by court sculptor Peter Wagner. Concerts, festivals and special events take place here during the warmer months. Enter through intricate wrought-iron gates into the French- and English-style gardens, partly built on the old baroque bastions.

Next to the main entrance, the **Martin-von-Wagner Museum** (Map p128; ☑312 288; Residenzplatz 2; admission free; ⊙Antikensammlung 1.30-5pm Tue-Sat, Gemäldegalerie 10am-1.30pm Tue-Sat, Graphische Sammlung 4-6pm Tue & Thu) is home to three collections. The **Antikensammlung** (Antiquities Collection) focuses on Greek, Roman and Egyptian ceramics, vases, figurines and marble sculptures from 1500 BC to AD 300. The **Gemäldegalerie** (Art Gallery) has primarily German, Dutch and Italian paintings from the 15th to the 19th centuries, including works by Tiepolo. Finally, the **Graphische Sammlung** (Graphics Collection) consists of drawings, copperplate etchings and woodcuts, including some by Albrecht Dürer.

Atmospherically housed in the cellar of the Residenz is a winery owned and run by the Bavarian government, **Staatlicher Hofkeller Würzburg** (Map p128; ☑305 0931; www.hofkeller.de; Residenzplatz 3; tours €7; ⊙tours 4.30pm & 5.30pm Fri, hourly from 10am Sat & Sun), Germany's second largest. It produces some exceptional wines; tours conclude with a tasting.

Festung Marienberg   FORTRESS
(Map p128) Panoramic views over the city's red rooftops and vine-covered hills extend from Festung Marienberg (Marienberg Fortress), which has presided over Würzburg

Würzburg

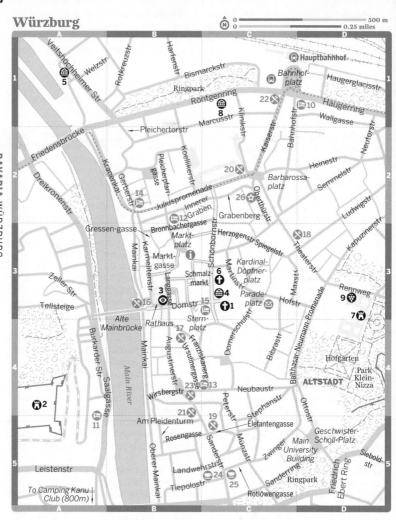

since the city's prince-bishops commenced its construction in 1201; they governed from here until 1719. At night floodlights dramatically illuminate the hulking structure, which has only been penetrated once, by Swedish troops in 1631 during the Thirty Years' War. In summer, the gently sloping lawns are strewn with picnickers.

The prince-bishops' pompous lifestyle is on show in the residential wing at the **Fürstenbaumuseum** (Map p128; adult/child €4.50/3.50; ⊙9am-6pm Tue-Sun mid-Mar–Oct), the highlight of which is a huge tapestry showing the entire family of Julius Echter

von Mespelbrunn. The city's history is laid out in the upper-level exhibition rooms.

A striking collection of Tilman Riemenschneider sculptures take pride of place in the **Mainfränkisches Museum** (Map p128; www.mainfraenkisches-museum.de; adult/child €4/2; ⊙10am-5pm Tue-Sun). In another section, porcelain, glass, furniture and other such objects illustrate life during the baroque and rococo eras; from the same period are the sketches and drawings by Neumann and Tiepolo.

The fortress is a 30-minute walk up the hill from the Alte Mainbrücke via the Tell-

Würzburg

steige trail, which is part of the 4km-long **Weinwanderweg** (Wine Hiking Trail) through the vineyards around Marienberg.

Neumünster CHURCH
(Map p128; Schönbornstrasse; ⊙6am-6.30pm Mon-Sat, from 8am Sun) In the Altstadt, this satisfyingly symmetrical church stands on the site where the three ill-fated Irish missionaries who tried to convert Duke Gosbert to Christianity in 686 met their maker. Romanesque at its core, it was given a baroque makeover by the Zimmermann brothers. The interior has busts of the three martyrs (Kilian, Colonan and Totnan) on the high altar and the tomb of St Kilian lurks in the crypt.

Dom St Kilian CHURCH
(Map p128; www.dom-wuerzburg.de) Würzburg's Romanesque Dom St Kilian was built between 1040 and 1237, although numerous alterations have added Gothic, Renaissance and baroque elements. The whole ecclesiatical caboodle was under heavy renovation at the time of writing, but was set to reopen in early 2013.

FREE **Grafeneckart** MEMORIAL
(Map p128; Domstrasse) Adjoining the **Rathaus**, the 1659-built Grafeneckart houses a scale model of the WWII bombing, which starkly depicts the extent of the damage to the city following the night of 16 March 1945, when 5000 citizens lost their lives. Viewing it before you climb up to the fortress overlooking the city gives you an appreciation of Würzburg's astonishing recovery.

Museum Am Dom ART MUSEUM
(Map p128; www.museum-am-dom.de; Kiliansplatz; adult/concession €3.50/2.50; ⊙10am-6pm Tue-Sun Apr-Oct, to 5pm Nov-Mar) Housed in a beautiful building by the cathedral, this worthwhile museum displays collections of modern art on Christian themes. Works of international renown by Joseph Beuys, Otto Dix and Käthe Kollwitz are on show, as well as masterpieces of the Romantic, Gothic and baroque periods.

Museum im Kulturspeicher ART MUSEUM
(Map p128; ☎322 250; www.kulturspeicher.de; Veitshöchheimer Strasse 5; adult/concession €3.50/2; ⊙1-6pm Tue, 11am-6pm Wed & Fri-Sun, 11am-7pm Thu) In a born-again historic granary right on the Main River, you'll find this absorbing art museum with choice artworks from the 19th to the 21st centuries. The emphasis is on German impressionism, neo-realism and contemporary art, but the building also houses the post-1945 constructivist works of the Peter C Ruppert collection, a challenging assembly of computer art, sculpture, paintings and photographs.

Röntgen Gedächtnisstätte MUSEUM
(Map p128; ☎351 1102; www.wilhelmconradroentgen.de; Röntgenring 8; admission free; ⊙8am-8pm Mon-Fri, 8am-6pm Sat) Nobel Prize–winner Wilhelm Conrad Röntgen discovered X-ray in 1895; his laboratory forms the heart of this small exhibition where illuminating multimedia displays chart the emergence of the X-ray process.

🎊 Festivals & Events

Mozart Fest
MUSIC

(📞372 336; www.mozartfest-wuerzburg.de; ☺Jun) Germany's oldest Mozart festival takes place at the Residenz throughout June.

Africa Festival
CULTURE

(📞150 60; www.africafestival.org; ☺late May) Held on the meadows northwest of the river at Mainwiesen, complete with markets, food stalls and, if it rains, lots of mud.

Hoffest am Stein
WINE & MUSIC

(www.weingut-am-stein.de; ☺early Jul) Wine and music festival held in the first half of July at the Weingut am Stein.

🛏 Sleeping

Sleep in Würzburg comes slightly cheaper than in other Bavarian cities.

Hotel Rebstock
HOTEL €€

(Map p128; 📞309 30; www.rebstock.com; Neubaustrasse 7; s/d from €101/120; ❊@🅿🛜) Don't be misled by the Best Western sign out front: Würzburg's top digs, in a squarely renovated rococo town house, has 70 unique, stylishly finished rooms, impeccable service and an Altstadt location. The list of illustrious former guests includes Franz Beckenbauer and Cliff Richard. Bike rental available.

Babelfish
HOSTEL €

(Map p128; 📞304 0430; www.babelfish-hostel. de; Haugerring 2; dm €17-23, s/d €45/70) With a name inspired by a creature in Douglas Adams' novel *The Hitchhiker's Guide to the Galaxy*, this uncluttered and spotlessly clean hostel has 74 beds spread over two floors, a sunny rooftop terrace, 24-hour reception (2nd floor), wheelchair-friendly facilities and little extras like card keys and a laundry room. The communal areas are an inviting place to down a few beers in the evening and there's a well-equipped guest kitchen.

Hotel Zum Winzermännle
GUESTHOUSE €€

(Map p128; 📞541 56; www.winzermaennle.de; Domstrasse 32; s €56-70, d €86-100; 🅿@) This former winery in the city's pedestrianised heart was rebuilt in its original style after the war as a guesthouse by the same charming family. Well-furnished rooms and communal areas are bright and often seasonally decorated. Breakfast and parking are an extra €5 and €8 respectively.

Hotel Dortmunder Hof
HOTEL €€

(Map p128; 📞561 63; www.dortmunder-hof.de; Innerer Graben 22; s €42-65, d €76-100) This bike-friendly hotel occupies a brightly renovated building with spotless en-suite rooms with cable TV. Parking can be arranged close by, and there's live music in the cellar bar.

Hotel Residence
HOTEL €€

(Map p128; 📞3593 4340; www.wuerzburg-hotel. de; Juliuspromenade 1; s/d from €75/95; 🅿) The grandly named Residence has box-ticking rooms, some in pale shades others warmer, plusher affairs. It could do with a bit of an update, but it's comfortable enough and very central.

DJH Hostel
HOSTEL €

(Map p128; 📞425 90; www.wuerzburg.jugendherberge.de; Fred-Joseph-Platz 2 ; dm from €21.30) At the foot of the fortress, this well-equipped, wheelchair-friendly hostel has room for 238 snoozers in three- to eight-bed dorms.

Camping Kanu Club
CAMPGROUND €

(📞725 36; www.kc-wuerzburg.de; Mergentheimer Strasse 13b; per person/tent €2.50/3.50) The closest campsite to the town centre. Take tram 3 or 5 to the Judenbühlweg stop, which is on its doorstep.

Eating

For a town of its size, Würzburg has an enticing selection of pubs, beer gardens, cafes and restaurants, with plenty of student hang-outs among them.

Bürgerspital Weinstube
WINE RESTAURANT €€

(Map p128; 📞352 880; Theaterstrasse 19; mains €7-23; ☺lunch & dinner) The cosy nooks of this labyrinthine medieval place are among Würzburg's most popular eating and drinking spots. Choose from a broad selection of Franconian wines (declared Germany's best in 2011) and wonderful regional dishes, including *Mostsuppe,* a tasty wine soup.

Alte Mainmühle
FRANCONIAN €€

(Map p128; 📞167 77; Mainkai 1; mains €7-21; ☺10am-midnight) Accessed straight from the old bridge, tourists and locals alike cram onto the double-decker terrace suspended above the Main River to savour modern twists on old Franconian favourites. Summer alfresco dining is accompanied by pretty views of the Festung Marienberg; in winter retreat to the snug timber dining room.

Backöfele FRANCONIAN €€
(Map p128; ☑590 59; Ursulinergasse 2; mains €10-22; ☺noon-1am) Begin a memorable meal at this cobble-floored, candlelit restaurant with *Fränkische Mostsuppe* (frothy Franconian wine soup with cinnamon croutons) and follow up with Backöfele's innovative twists on traditional game, steak and fish dishes. Popular with the uni crowd and almost always full, so bookings are recommended.

Juliusspital WINE RESTAURANT €€
(Map p128; ☑540 80; Juliuspromenade 19; mains €8-21; ☺10am-midnight) This attractive *Weinstube* (traditional wine tavern) features fabulous Franconian fish and even better wines. Ambient lighting, scurrying waiters and walls occupied by oil paintings make this the place to head to for a special do.

Uni-Café CAFE €
(Map p128; ☑156 72; Neubaustrasse 2; snacks €2.50-7; ☺8am-1am) Hugely popular contemporary cafe strung over two levels, with a student-priced, daily-changing menu of burgers and salads and a buzzy bar.

Natur-Feinkostladen VEGETARIAN €
(Map p128; Sanderstrasse 2a; dishes from €4; ☺8.30am-7.30pm Mon-Fri, 10am-2pm Sat) Come here for wholesome snacks and healthy fare enjoyed around simple wooden tables. Also runs the adjacent specialist grocery.

Capri & Blaue Grotto ITALIAN €€
(Map p128; Elefantengasse 1; pizzas €6-8, other mains €6.50-14; ☺lunch & dinner) This outpost of the *bel paese* has been plating up pronto pasta and pizza since 1952, making it Germany's oldest Italian eatery.

Starback BAKERY €
(Map p128; Kaiserstrasse 33; snacks from €0.69) No German-language skills are required to put together a budget breakfast or lunch at this no-frills self-service bakery opposite the train station.

🍷 Drinking & Entertainment

For more options, grab a copy of the monthly listing magazine *Frizz* (in German). Look out for posters and flyers advertising big-name concerts that take place on the Residenzplatz.

Kult CAFE, BAR
(Map p128; Landwehrstrasse 10; ☺9am-late Mon-Fri, 10am-late Sat & Sun) Enjoy a tailor-made breakfast, munch on a cheap lunch or party into the wee hours at Würzburg's hippest cafe. The unpretentious interior, with its

salvaged tables and old beige benches, hosts regular fancy-dress parties, table-football tournaments and other off-beat events. DJs take over at weekends.

MUCK CAFE, BAR
(Map p128; Sanderstrasse 29) One of the earliest openers in town, and serving a mean breakfast from 7am, the cafe morphs into something of an informal party after nightfall.

Standard LIVE MUSIC
(Map p128; Oberthürstrasse 11a) Soulful jazz spins beneath a corrugated-iron ceiling and stainless-steel fans, while bands and DJs play a couple of times or more a week in a second, dimly lit downstairs bar.

ℹ Information

Ferial Internet Cafe (Sanderstrasse 6a; per hr €1.80; ☺10am-11pm Mon-Fri, from 11am Sat & Sun) Cheap web access.

Post Office (Paradeplatz 4)

Tourist Office (☑372 398; www.wuerzburg.de; Marktplatz; ☺10am-6pm Mon-Fri, 10am-2pm Sat Apr-Dec, plus 10am-2pm Sun May-Oct, reduced hours Jan-Mar)

ℹ Getting There & Away

BUS The Romantic Road Europabus stops at the main bus station next to the Hauptbahnhof, and at the Residenzplatz.

TRAIN Train connections from Würzburg:

» **Bamberg** €19, one hour, twice hourly

» **Frankfurt** €33, one hour, hourly

» **Nuremberg** €19.20 to €27, one hour, twice hourly

» **Rothenburg ob der Tauber** Change in Steinach; €12.20, one hour, hourly

ℹ Getting Around

The most useful service is bus 9 (€1.60) which shuttles roughly hourly between the Residenz and the Festung Marienberg. Otherwise Würzburg can be easily tackled on foot.

Rothenburg ob der Tauber

☑09861 / POP 11,000

A well-polished gem from the Middle Ages, Rothenburg ob der Tauber (meaning 'above the Tauber River') is the main tourist stop along the Romantic Road. With its web of cobbled lanes, higgledy-piggledy houses and towered walls, the town is impossibly charming. Preservation orders here are the

Rothenburg ob der Tauber

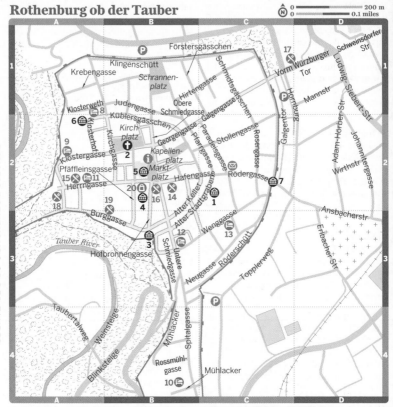

strictest in Germany – and at times it feels like a medieval theme park – but all's forgiven in the evenings, when the yellow lamplight casts its spell long after the last tour buses have left.

◎ Sights

Jakobskirche CHURCH
(Map p132; Klingengasse 1; adult/child €2/0.50; ⊗9am-5pm) One of the few places of worship in Bavaria to charge cheeky admission, Rothenburg's Lutheran parish church was begun in the 14th century and finished in the 15th. The building sports some wonderfully aged stained-glass windows, but its real pièce de résistance is Tilman Riemenschneider's carved **Heilig Blut Altar** (Sacred Blood Altar). The gilded cross above the main scene depicting the Last Supper incorporates Rothenburg's treasured reliquary: a capsule made of rock crystal said to contain three drops of Christ's blood.

**Mittelalterliches
Kriminalmuseum** MUSEUM
(Map p132; ☑5359; www.kriminalmuseum.rothen burg.de; Burggasse 3-5; adult/child €4.20/2.60; ⊗10am-6pm May-Oct, shorter hours Nov-Apr) Brutal implements of torture and punishment from medieval times are on show at this gruesomely fascinating museum. Exhibits include chastity belts, masks of disgrace for gossips, a cage for cheating bakers, a neck brace for quarrelsome women and a beer-barrel pen for drunks, and there are also displays on local witch trials. Visitors can have their photo taken in the stocks outside.

Deutsches Weihnachtsmuseum MUSEUM
(Map p132; ☑409 365; www.weihnachtsmuseum. de; Herrngasse 1; adult/child/family €4/2/7; ⊗10am-5.30pm daily Easter-Christmas, 11am-4pm Sat & Sun mid-Jan–Easter) If you're glad Christmas comes but once every 365 days, then stay well clear of the Käthe Wohl-

Rothenburg ob der Tauber

fahrt Weihnachtsdorf (p135), a Yuletide superstore that also houses the Christmas Museum. This repository of all things 'Ho! Ho! Ho!' traces the development of various Christmas customs and decorations, and includes a display of 150 Santa figures, plus lots of retro baubles and tinsel – particularly surreal in mid-July when the mercury outside is pushing 30°C. Not as big a hit with kids as you might predict, as they can't get their hands on anything.

Town Walls HISTORIC SITE
With time and fresh legs, a 2.5km circular walk around the unbroken ring of the town walls gives a sense of the importance medieval man put on defending his settlements. There are views from the eastern tower, the **Röderturm** (Map p132; Rödergasse; adult/child €1.50/1; ⊙9am-5pm Mar-Nov), though it's staffed by volunteers and is often closed. For the most impressive views head to the west side of town, where a sweeping view of the Tauber Valley includes the **Doppelbrücke**, a double-decker bridge.

Reichsstadt Museum MUSEUM
(Map p132; www.reichsstadtmuseum.rothenburg.de; Klosterhof 5; adult/concession €4/3.50; ⊙10am-5pm Apr-Oct, 1-4pm Nov-Mar) Highlights of the Reichsstadt Museum, housed in a former Dominican convent, include the *Rothen-burger Passion* (1494), a cycle of 12 panels by Martinus Schwarz, and the oldest convent kitchen in Germany, as well as weapons and armour. Outside the main entrance (on your right as you're facing the museum), you'll see a spinning barrel, where the nuns distributed bread to the poor – and where women

would leave babies they couldn't afford to keep. For a serene break between sightseeing, head to the **Klostergarten** behind the museum (enter from Klosterhof).

Rathaus HISTORIC BUILDING
(Map p132; Marktplatz; Rathausturm adult/concession €2/0.50; ⊙Rathausturm 9.30am-12.30pm & 1-5pm daily Apr-Oct, noon-3pm daily Dec, shorter hours Sat & Sun Nov & Jan-Mar) The Rathaus on Marktplatz was begun in Gothic style in the 14th century, and was completed during the Renaissance. Climb the 220 steps to the viewing platform of the **Rathausturm** to be rewarded with widescreen views of the Tauber.

**Alt-Rothenburger
Handwerkerhaus** HISTORIC BUILDING
(Map p132; ☑5810; Alter Stadtgraben 26; adult/child €2.50/1; ⊙11am-5pm Mon-Fri, from 10am Sat & Sun Easter-Oct, 2-4pm daily Dec) Hidden down a little alley is the Alt-Rothenburger Handwerkerhaus, where numerous artisans – including coopers, weavers, cobblers and potters – have their workshops today, and have had their workshops for the house's more than 700-year existence.

Puppen-und Spielzeugmuseum MUSEUM
(Map p132; ☑7330; Hofbronnengasse 13; adult/child €4/2.50; ⊙9.30am-6pm Mar-Dec, 11am-5pm Jan & Feb) A nostalgic collection of dollhouses, teddy bears, toy carousels, tin soldiers and infinite glass-eyed dolls awaits at this comprehensive museum, the work of collector Katharina Engels. All the exhibits are presented in traditional glass display cases.

Tours

The tourist office runs 90-minute walking tours (€7; in English) at 11am and 2pm from April to October. Every evening a lantern-toting *Nachtwächter* dressed in traditional costume leads an entertaining tour of the Altstadt; English tours (€7) meet at the Rathaus at 8pm.

Festivals & Events

Historisches Festspiel 'Der Meistertrunk' FOLK DANCE
The Historisches Festspiel 'Der Meistertrunk' takes place each year on Whitsuntide, with parades, dances and a medieval market. The highlight, though, is the re-enactment of the mythical *Meistertrunk* story. The *Meistertrunk* play itself is performed three more times: once during the Reichsstadt-Festtage in early September, when the entire city's history is re-enacted in the streets, and twice during the Rothenburger Herbst, an autumn celebration in October.

Historischer Schäfertanz DANCE
(Marktplatz) The Historischer Schäfertanz (Historical Shepherds' Dance), featuring colourfully dressed couples, takes places on Marktplatz several times between April and October.

Christmas Market MARKET
Rothenburg's Christmas market is one of the most romantic in Germany. It's set out around the central Marktplatz during Advent.

Sleeping

Hotel Herrnschlösschen HOTEL €€€
(Map p132; ☎873 890; www.herrnschloesschen.de; Herrngasse 20; r from €195) The most recent addition to Rothenburg's hotel stock has breathed life back into a 900-year-old mansion. The whole place is a blend of ancient and new, with Gothic arches leaping over faux-retro furniture and ageing oak preventing ceilings from crashing down onto chic 21st-century beds. The hotel's restaurant has established itself as one of the town's most innovative dining spots.

Altfränkische Weinstube HOTEL €
(Map p132; ☎6404; www.altfraenkische-wein stube-rothenburg.de; Klosterhof 7; r €59-89; ☎) Hiding in a quiet side street near the Reichsstad Museum, this enchantingly characterful inn has six atmosphere-laden rooms, all with bathtubs and most with four-poster or canopied beds. The restaurant (open for dinner only) serves up sound regional fare with a dollop of medieval cheer.

Hotel Raidel HOTEL €
(Map p132; ☎3115; www.gaestehaus-raidel.de; Wenggasse 3; s/d €45/69; ☎) With 500-year-old exposed beams studded with wooden nails, antiques throughout and a welcoming owner, as well as musical instruments for the guests to play, this is the place to check in if you're craving some genuine romance on the Romantic Road.

BOTTOMS UP FOR FREEDOM

In 1631 the Thirty Years War – pitching Catholics against Protestants – reached the gates of Rothenburg ob der Tauber. Catholic General Tilly and 60,000 of his troops besieged the Protestant market town and demanded its surrender. The town resisted but couldn't stave off the onslaught of marauding soldiers, and the mayor and other town dignitaries were captured and sentenced to death.

And that's about where the story ends and the legend begins. As the tale goes, Rothenburg's town council tried to sate Tilly's bloodthirstiness by presenting him with a 3L pitcher of wine. Tilly, after taking a sip or two, presented the men with an unusual challenge, saying 'If one of you has the courage to step forward and down this mug of wine in one gulp, then I shall spare the town and the lives of the councilmen!' Mayor Georg Nusch accepted – and succeeded! And that's why you can still wander though Rothenburg's wonderful medieval lanes today.

It's pretty much accepted that Tilly was really placated with hard cash. Nevertheless, local poet Adam Hörber couldn't resist turning the tale of the *Meistertrunk* into a play, which, since 1881, has been performed every Whitsuntide (Pentecost), the seventh Sunday after Easter. It's also re-enacted several times daily by the clock figures on the tourist office building.

Burg-Hotel
HOTEL €€
(Map p132; ✆948 90; www.burghotel.eu; Kloster-gasse 1-3; s €100-135, d €100-170; 🅿🛜) Each of the 15 elegantly furnished guest rooms at this boutique hotel built into the town walls has its own private sitting area. The lower floors shelter a decadent spa with tanning beds, saunas and rainforest showers, and a cellar with a Steinway piano; while phenomenal valley views unfurl from the breakfast room and stone terrace. Garaged parking costs €7.50.

Kreuzerhof Hotel Garni
GUESTHOUSE €
(Map p132; ✆3424; www.kreuzerhof-rothenburg.de; Millergasse 2-6; s €45, d €59-72) Away from the tourist swarms, this quiet family-run B&B has charming, randomly furnished rooms with antique touches in a medieval town house and annexe. There's free tea and coffee and the generous breakfast is an energy-boosting set-up for the day.

DJH Hostel
HOSTEL €
(Map p132; ✆941 60; www.rothenburg.jugendher berge.de; Mühlacker 1; dm from €21.60) Rothenburg's youth hostel occupies two enormous old buildings in the south of town. It's agreeably renovated and extremely well equipped, but you can hear the screams of noisy school groups from outside.

✗ Eating

Bürgerkeller
FRANCONIAN €
(Map p132; ✆2126; Herrngasse 24; mains €6.80-12.80; ☺dinner) Down a short flight of steps in a frescoed 16th-century cellar, this hidden spot serves local, seasonal produce, such as autumn mushrooms and spring asparagus, as part of classic Franconian mains. Service is clued up about the wines on offer and the food is some of the most authentically German you'll experience on the Romantic Road.

Zur Höll
GERMAN €€
(Map p132; ✆4229; Burggasse 8; dishes €6.50-18; ☺dinner) This medieval wine tavern, with an appreciation for slow food, is in the town's oldest original building, dating back to the year 900. The menu of regional specialities is limited but refined, though it's the wine, some from nearby Würzburg, that people really come for.

Villa Mittermeier
FRANCONIAN €€€
(Map p132; ✆945 40; www.villamittermeier.de; Vorm Würzburger Tor 9; mains €18-26; ☺dinner

Tue-Sat, lunch Sat) The kitchen ninjas at this classy establishment serve top-notch Michelin-starred cuisine in five settings, including a black-and-white tiled 'temple', an alfresco terrace and a barrel-shaped wine cellar. The artistic chefs rely on locally harvested produce, and the wine list (400-plus varieties) is probably Franconia's best.

Weinstube zum Pulverer
FRANCONIAN €€
(Map p132; ✆976 182; Herrngasse 31; mains €5-16.50; ☺call ahead for hours) The ornately carved timber chairs in this ancient wine bar (allegedly Rothenburg's oldest) are works of art. Its simple but filling dishes, like soup in a bowl made of bread, gourmet sandwiches and cakes, are equally artistic.

Bosporus Döner
KEBABS €
(Map p132; Hafengasse 2; dishes €3-8) You haven't really been to Germany until you've devoured a takeaway kebab in a twee medieval setting.

🛍 Shopping

Käthe Wohlfahrt Weihnachtsdorf
CHRISTMAS DECORATIONS
(Map p132; ✆4090; www.wohlfahrt.com; Herrngasse 1) With its mind-boggling assortment of Yuletide decorations and ornaments, this huge shop lets you celebrate Christmas every day of the year (to go with the local snowballs). Many of the items are handcrafted with amazing skill and imagination; prices are accordingly high.

ℹ Information

Post Office (Rödergasse 11)

Tourist Office (✆404 800; www.rothenburg. de; Marktplatz 2; ☺9am-6pm Mon-Fri, 10am-5pm Sat & Sun Apr-Oct, 9am-5pm Mon-Fri, 10am-1pm Sat Nov-Mar) Offers free internet access.

❶ Getting There & Away

BUS The Europabus (p126) stops in the main bus park at the Hauptbahnhof and on the more central Schrannenplatz.

CAR The A7 autobahn runs right past town.

TRAIN You can go anywhere by train from Rothenburg, as long as it's Steinach. Change there for services to Würzburg (€12.20, one hour and 10 minutes). Travel to and from Munich (from €37.30, three hours) can involve up to three different trains.

❶ Getting Around

The city has five car parks right outside the walls. The town centre is closed to non-resident vehicles from 11am to 4pm and 7pm to 5am weekdays, and all day at weekends; hotel guests are exempt.

Dinkelsbühl

☏ 09851 / POP 11,500

Some 40km south of Rothenburg, immaculately preserved Dinkelsbühl proudly traces its roots to a royal residence founded by Carolingian kings in the 8th century. Saved from destruction in the Thirty Years' War and ignored by WWII bombers, this is arguably the Romantic Road's quaintest and most authentically medieval halt. For an overall impression of the town, walk along the fortified walls with their 18 towers and four gates.

❂ Sights

Haus der Geschichte   MUSEUM
(☏902 440; Altrathausplatz 14; adult/child €4/2; ⊙9am-6pm Mon-Fri, 10am-5pm Sat & Sun May-Oct, 10am-5pm daily Nov-Apr) Near the Wörnitzer Tor, Dinkelsbühl's history comes under the microscope at the Haus der Geschichte, which occupies the old town hall. There's an interesting section on the Thirty Years' War and a gallery with paintings depicting Dinkelsbühl at the turn of the century. Audioguides are included in the ticket price.

Münster St Georg   CHURCH
(Marktplatz 1) Standing sentry over the heart of Dinkelsbühl is one of southern Germany's purest late-Gothic hall churches. Rather austere from the outside, the interior stuns with an incredible fan-vaulted ceiling. A curiosity is the **Pretzl Window** donated by the bakers' guild; it's located in the upper section of the last window in the right aisle.

Museum of the 3rd Dimension   MUSEUM
(☏6336; www.3d-museum.de; Nördlinger Tor; adult/concession/under 12yr €10/8/6; ⊙10am-6pm daily Jul & Aug, 11am-5pm daily Apr-Jun, Sep & Oct, 11am-5pm Sat & Sun Nov-Mar) Located just outside the easternmost town gate, this is probably the first museum dedicated entirely to simulating acid trips. Inside there are three floors of holographic images, stereoscopes and attention-grabbing 3D imagery (especially in the nude section on the 3rd floor). The you-gotta-be-kidding admission includes a pair of red–green-tinted specs.

✦ Festivals & Events

Kinderzeche   FESTIVAL
(www.kinderzeche.de; ⊙Jul) In the third week of July, the 10-day Kinderzeche celebrates how, during the Thirty Years' War, the town's children persuaded the invading Swedish troops to spare Dinkelsbühl from a ransacking. The festivities include a pageant, re-enactments in the festival hall, lots of music and other merriment.

⌂ Sleeping

The tourist office can help find private rooms from around €30.

TOP CHOICE/ Dinkelsbühler Kunst-Stuben   GUESTHOUSE €€
(☏6750; www.kunst-stuben.de; Segringer Strasse 52; s €60, d €80-85, ste €90; @) Personal attention and charm by the bucketload make this guesthouse, situated near the westernmost gate (Segringer Tor), one of the best on the entire Romantic Road. Furniture (including the four-posters) is all handmade by Voglauer, the cosy library is perfect for curling up in with a good read, and the new suite is a matchless deal for travelling families. The artisan owner will show his Asia travel films if enough guests are interested.

Gasthof Goldenes Lamm   HOTEL €€
(☏2267; www.goldenes.de; Lange Gasse 26-28; s €47-62, d €76-90; ℗) Run by the same family for four generations, this stress-free, bike-friendly oasis has pleasant rooms at the top of a creaky staircase, and a funky rooftop garden deck with plump sofas. The attached wood-panelled restaurant plates up Franconian–Swabian specialities, including a vegie selection.

Deutsches Haus
HOTEL €€

(☎6058; www.deutsches-haus-dkb.de; Weinmarkt 3; s €79-90, d €129; ☎) Concealed behind the town's most ornate and out-of-kilter facade, the 19 elegant rooms at this central inn opposite the Münster St Georg flaunt antique touches and big 21st-century bathrooms. Downstairs Dinkelbühl's hautiest restaurant serves game and fish prepared according to age-old recipes.

Campingpark 'Romantische Strasse'
CAMPGROUND €

(☎7817; www.campingplatz-dinkelsbuehl.de; Kobeltsmühle 6; per tent/person €6.15/4.10) This camping ground is set on the shores of a swimmable lake 1.5km northeast of Wörnitzer Tor.

DJH Hostel
HOSTEL €

(☎9509; www.dinkelsbuehl.jugendherberge.de; Koppengasse 10; dm from €19; ☉closed Nov-Feb) Dinkelsbühl's hostel in the western part of the Altstadt occupies a beautifully restored 15th-century granary.

✕ Eating

Haus Appelberg
BAVARIAN €

(☎582 838; www.haus-appelberg.de; Nördlinger Strasse 40; dishes €5.20-10.50; ☉6pm-midnight Mon-Sat) At Dinkelsbühl's best-kept dining secret, owners double up as cooks to keep tables supplied with traditional dishes such as local fish, Franconian sausages and *Maultaschen* (pork and spinach ravioli). On warm days swap the rustic interior for the secluded terrace, a fine spot for some evening idling over a local Hauf beer or a Franconian white wine. There are well-appointed rooms upstairs for sleeping off any overindulgences.

Weib's Brauhaus
PUB €

(☎579 490; Untere Schmiedgasse 13; mains €5-13.50; ☉11am-1am Thu-Mon, 6pm-1am Wed; ☎) A female brewmaster presides over the copper vats at this sage-green half-timbered pub-restaurant, which has a good-time vibe thanks to its friendly crowd of regulars. Many dishes are made with the house brew, including the popular *Weib's Töpfle* ('woman's pot') – pork in beer sauce with croquettes.

ⓘ Information

Tourist Office (☎902 440; www.dinkelsbuehl.de; Altrathausplatz 14; ☉9am-6pm Mon-Fri, 10am-5pm Sat & Sun May-Oct, 10am-5pm daily Nov-Apr)

ⓘ Getting There & Away

Despite a railway line cutting through the town, Dinkelsbühl is not served by passenger trains. Regional bus 501 to Nördlingen (50 minutes, six daily) stops at the derelict train station. Reaching Rothenburg is a real test of patience without your own car. Change from bus 805 to a train in Ansbach, then change trains in Steinach. The Europabus stops right in the Altstadt at Schweinemarkt.

Nördlingen

☎09081 / POP 19,000

Charmingly medieval, Nördlingen sees fewer tourists than its better-known neighbours and manages to retain an air of authenticity, which is a relief after some of the Romantic Road's kitschy extremes. The town lies within the Ries Basin, a massive impact crater gouged out by a meteorite more than 15 million years ago. The crater – some 25km in diameter – is one of the best preserved on earth, and has been declared a special 'geopark'. Nördlingen's 14th-century walls, all original, mimic the crater's rim and are almost perfectly circular.

Incidentally, if you've seen the 1970s film *Willy Wonka and the Chocolate Factory,* you've already looked down upon Nördlingen from a glass elevator.

⊙ Sights

You can circumnavigate the entire town in around an hour by taking the sentry walk (free) on top of the walls all the way.

St Georgskirche
CHURCH

(tower adult/child €2.50/1.70; ☉tower 9am-6pm Apr-Jun, Sep & Oct, to 7pm Jul & Aug, to 5pm Nov-Mar) Dominating the heart of town, the immense late-Gothic St Georgskirche got its baroque mantle in the 18th century. To truly appreciate Nördlingen's circular shape and the dished-out crater in which it lies, scramble up the 350 steps of the church's 90m-tall **Daniel Tower**.

Bayerisches Eisenbahnmuseum
MUSEUM

(www.bayerisches-eisenbahnmuseum.de; Am Hohen Weg 6a; adult/child €6/3; ☉noon-4pm Tue-Sat, 10am-5pm Sun May-Sep, noon-4pm Sat, 10am-5pm Sun Oct-Mar) Half museum, half junkyard retirement home for locos that have puffed their last, this trainspotter's paradise occupies a disused engine depot across the tracks from the train station (no access from the platforms). The museum runs steam and old diesel trains up to Dinkelsbühl, Feuchtwangen and Gunzenhausen several times a year; see the website for details.

Rieskrater Museum   MUSEUM

(📷847 10; www.rieskrater-museum.de; Eugene-Shoemaker-Platz 1; adult/child €4/1.50; ⏰10am-4.30pm Tue-Sun May-Oct, 10am-noon Nov-Apr) Situated in an ancient barn, this unique museum explores the formation of meteorite craters and the consequences of such violent collisions with earth. Rocks, including a genuine moon rock (on permanent loan from NASA), fossils and other geological displays shed light on the mystery of meteors.

Stadtmuseum   MUSEUM

(Vordere Gerbergasse 1; adult/concession €4/1.50; ⏰1.30-4.30pm Tue-Sun Mar-early Nov) Nördlingen's worthwhile municipal museum covers an ambitious sweep of human existence on the planet, from the early Stone Age to 20th-century art, via the Battle of Nördlingen during the Thirty Years' War, Roman endeavours in the area and the town's once-bustling mercantile life.

Stadtmauermuseum   MUSEUM

(Löpsinger Torturm; adult/concession €2/1; ⏰10am-4.30pm Apr-Oct) A fascinating exhibition on the history of the town's defences is on show at this tower-based museum, the best place to kick off a circuit of the walls.

🛏 Sleeping & Eating

Hotel Altreuter   HOTEL €

(📷4319; www.hotel-altreuter.de; Marktplatz 11; s/d from €36/52; 🅿) Perched above a busy cafe and bakery, the bog-standard rooms here are of the could-be-anywhere type, but the epicentral location next to the Daniel Tower cannot be beaten. Bathrooms are private and breakfast is served downstairs in the cafe.

Jugend & Familengästehaus   GUESTHOUSE €

(📷275 0575; www.jufa.at/noerdlingen; Bleichgraben 3a; s/d €50/70; 🅿@📶) Located just outside the town walls, this shiny, 186-bed hostel-guesthouse is spacious and clean-cut. There are two- to four-bed rooms, ideal for couples or families, and facilities include bicycle hire, a cafe with internet terminals and even a small cinema. Unless you are travelling with an entire handball team in tow,

dorms are off limits to individual travellers, no matter how hard you plead.

Kaiserhof Hotel Sonne   HOTEL €€

(📷5067; www.kaiserhof-hotel-sonne.de; Marktplatz 3; s €55-65, d €75-120; 🅿) Right on the main square, Nördlingen's top digs once hosted crowned heads and their entourages, but have quietly gone to seed in recent years. However, rooms are still packed with character, mixing modern comforts with traditional charm, and the atmospheric regional restaurant downstairs is still worth a shot.

Café Radlos   CAFE €€

(📷5040; www.cafe-radlos.de; Löpsinger Strasse 8; mains €4.50-14; ⏰10am-1am Thu-Tue; 📷) More than just a place to tuck into tasty Bavarian dishes, this convivialy random cafe, Nördlingen's coolest haunt, parades cherry-red walls that showcase local art and photography exhibits. Kids have their own toy-filled corner, while you while away the hours with board games, soak up the sunshine in the beer garden, or surf the web (€2 per hour).

Sixenbräu Stüble   BAVARIAN €€

(Bergerstrasse 17; mains €5-17; ⏰10am-2pm Tue & Wed, 10am-2pm & 5pm-midnight Thu-Sat, 10am-10pm Sun) An attractive gabled town house near the Berger Tor houses this local institution, which has been plonking wet ones on the bar since 1545. The pan-Bavarian menu has heavy carnivorous leanings, and there's a beer garden where, in the words of the menu, you can take on some *bayerisches Grundnahrungsmittel* (Bavarian nutritional staple).

ℹ Information

Geopark Ries Information Centre (www.geopark-ries.de; Eugene-Shoemaker-Platz; ⏰10am-4.30pm Tue-Sun) Free exhibition on the crater.

Tourist Office (📷841 16; www.noerdlingen.de; Marktplatz 2; ⏰9.30am-6pm Mon-Thu, to 4.30pm Fri, 10am-2pm Sat Easter-Oct, plus 10am-2pm Sun Jul & Aug, Mon-Fri only mid-Nov–Easter) Staff sell the Nördlinger Tourist-Card (€9.95) that saves you around €8 if you visit everything in town.

ℹ Getting There & Away

BUS The Europabus stops at the Rathaus. Bus 501 goes to Dinkelsbühl (45 minutes, five daily).

TRAIN Train journeys to and from Munich (€24.50, two hours) and Augsburg (€14.40, 1¼ hours) require a change in Donauwörth.

Donauwörth

☎ 0906 / POP 18.240

Sitting pretty at the confluence of the Danube and Wörnitz rivers, Donauwörth rose from its humble beginnings as a 5th-century fishing village to its zenith as a Free Imperial City in 1301. Three medieval gates and five town wall towers still guard it today, and faithful rebuilding – after WWII had destroyed 75% of the medieval old town – means steep-roofed houses in a rainbow of colours still line its main street, Reichstrasse.

Reichstrasse is around 10 minutes' walk north of the train station. Turn right onto Bahnhofstrasse and cross the bridge onto Ried Island.

◉ Sights

Liebfraukirche   CHURCH
(Reichstrasse) At the western end of Reichstrasse rises this 15th-century Gothic church with original frescos and a curiously sloping floor that drops 120cm. Swabia's largest church bell (6550kg) swings in the belfry.

Käthe-Kruse-Puppenmuseum   MUSEUM
(Pflegstrasse 21a; adult/child €2.50/1.50; ⊙11am-5pm daily May-Sep, 2-5pm Tue-Sun Apr & Oct, Wed, Sat & Sun Nov-Mar,) This nostalgia-inducing museum fills a former monastery with old dolls and dollhouses by world-renowned designer Käthe Kruse (1883–1968).

Rathaus   HISTORIC BUILDING
(Rathausegasse) Work on Donauwörth's landmark town hall began in 1236, but it has seen many alterations and additions over the centuries. At 11am and 4pm daily, the carillon on the ornamented step gable plays a composition by local legend Werner Egk (1901–83) from his opera *Die Zaubergeige* (The Magic Violin). The building also houses the tourist office.

Heilig-Kreuz-Kirche   CHURCH
(Heilig-Kreuz-Strasse) Overlooking the grassy banks of the shallow Wörnitz River, this soaring baroque confection has for centuries lured the faithful to pray before a chip of wood, said to come from the Holy Cross, installed in the ornate-ceilinged Gnadenkappelle.

⌂ Sleeping & Eating

Drei Kronen   HOTEL €€
(☎706 170; www.hotel3kronen.com; Bahnhofstrasse 25; s/d €82/115; [P][?]) Situated opposite the train station a little way along Bahnhofstrasse, the 'Three Crowns' has the town's most comfortable rooms and a lamplit restaurant. The reception is, inconveniently, closed in the evenings and all weekend, but staff are around in the restaurant.

Posthotel Traube   BAVARIAN €€
(Kapellstrasse 14-16; mains €5.50-17; ⊙11am-2pm & 5-10pm Mon-Fri & Sun, closed Sat) Choose from a cafe, coffee house, restaurant or beer garden at this friendly, multitasking hotel where Mozart stayed as a boy in 1777. The schnitzel, cordon bleu and local carp in beer sauce are where your forefinger should land on the menu.

Cafe Rafaello   ITALIAN €€
(Fischerplatz 1; mains €6.50-23.50) On Ried Island, this Italian job specialising in seafood uses Apennines kitsch to recreate *La Dolce Vita* to southern-German tastes.

❶ Information

Tourist Office (☎789 151; www.donauwoerth. de; Rathausgasse 1; ⊙9am-noon & 1-6pm Mon-Fri, 3-6pm Sat & Sun May-Sep, shorter hours Mon-Fri, closed Sat & Sun Oct-Apr)

❶ Getting There & Away

BUS The Europabus stops by the Liebfraukirche.

CAR & MOTORCYCLE Donauwörth is at the crossroads of the B2, B16 and B25 roads.

TRAIN Train connections from Donauwörth:

DESTINATION	FARE	DURATION	FREQUENCY
Augsburg	€6	30 minutes	twice hourly
Harburg	€3.40	10 minutes	hourly
Ingolstadt	€11.10	45 minutes	hourly
Nördlingen	€5.50	30 minutes	hourly

Augsburg

☎ 0821 / POP 264.700

The largest city on the Romantic Road (and Bavaria's third largest), Augsburg is also one of Germany's oldest, founded by the stepchildren of Roman emperor Augustus over 2000 years ago. As an independent city state from the 13th century, it was also one of its

BAVARIA DONAUWÖRTH

WORTH A TRIP

HARBURG

Looming over the Wörnitz River, the medieval covered parapets, towers, turrets, keep and red-tiled roofs of the 12th-century **Schloss Harburg** (www.burg-harburg.de; adult/child €5/3; ⊙10am-5pm Tue-Sun mid-Mar–Oct) are so perfectly preserved they almost seem like a film set. Tours tell the building's long tale and evoke the ghosts that are said to use the castle as a hang-out.

From the castle, the walk to Harburg's cute, half-timbered **Altstadt** takes around 10 minutes, slightly more the other way as you're heading uphill. A fabulous panorama of the village and castle can be admired from the 1702 **stone bridge** spanning the Wörnitz.

The Europabus stops in the village (outside the Gasthof Grüner Baum) but not at the castle. Hourly trains run to Nördlingen (€4.10, 18 minutes) and Donauwörth (€3.40, 10 minutes). The train station is about a 30-minute walk from the castle. Harburg is on the B25 road.

wealthiest, free to raise its own taxes, with public coffers bulging from the proceeds of the textile trade. Banking families such as the Fuggers and the Welsers even bankrolled entire countries and helped out the odd skint monarch. However, from the 16th century, religious strife and economic decline plagued the city. Augsburg finally joined the Kingdom of Bavaria in 1806.

Shaped by Romans, medieval artisans, bankers, traders and, more recently, industry and technology, this attractive city of spires and cobbles is an easy day trip from Munich or an engaging stop on the Romantic Road, though one with a grittier, less quaint atmosphere than others along the route.

⊙ Sights

Fuggerei   HISTORIC SITE
(www.fugger.de; Jakober Strasse; adult/concession €4/3; ⊙8am-8pm Apr-Sep, 9am-6pm Oct-Mar) The legacy of Jakob Fugger 'The Rich' lives on at Augsburg's Catholic welfare settlement, the Fuggerei, which is the oldest of its kind in existence.

Around 200 people live here today and their rent remains frozen at 1 Rhenish guilder (now €0.88) *per year,* plus utilities and three daily prayers. Residents wave to you as you wander through the car-free lanes of this gated community flanked by its 52 pinneat houses (containing 140 apartments) and little gardens.

To see how residents lived before running water and central heating, one of the apartments now houses the **Fuggereimuseum**, while there's a modern apartment open for public viewing at Ochsengasse 51. Interpretive panels are in German but you can ask for an information leaflet in English or download it from the website before you arrive.

Rathausplatz   SQUARE
The heart of Augsburg's Altstadt, this large, pedestrianised square is anchored by the **Augustusbrunnen**, a fountain honouring the Roman emperor; its four figures represent the Lech River and the Wertach, Singold and Brunnenbach brooks.

Rising above the square are the twin onion-domed spires of the Renaissance **Rathaus**, built by Elias Holl from 1615 to 1620 and crowned by a 4m-tall pine cone, the city's emblem (also an ancient fertility symbol). Upstairs is the **Goldener Saal** (Rathausplatz; adult/concession €3/2; ⊙10am-6pm), a huge banquet hall with an amazing gilded and frescoed coffered ceiling.

For panoramic views over Rathausplatz and the city, climb to the top of the **Perlachturm** (Rathausplatz; adult/child €1.50/1; ⊙10am-6pm daily Apr-Nov), a former guard tower, and also an Elias Holl creation.

St Anna Kirche   CHURCH
(Im Annahof 2, off Annastrasse; ⊙10am-12.30pm & 3-6pm Tue-Sat, 10am-12.30pm & 3-4pm Sun) Often regarded as the first Renaissance church in Germany, the rather plain-looking (and well-hidden) St Anna Kirche contains a bevy of treasures, as well as the sumptuous **Fuggerkapelle**, where Jacob Fugger and his brothers lie buried, and the lavishly frescoed **Goldschmiedekapelle** (Goldsmiths' Chapel; 1420). The church played an important role during the Reformation. In 1518 Martin Luther, in town to defend his beliefs before the papal legate, stayed at what was then a Carmelite monastery. His rooms have been

turned into the **Lutherstiege**, a small museum about the Reformation, under renovation at the time of writing.

Maximilianmuseum — MUSEUM
(☑324 4102; Philippine-Welser-Strasse 24; adult/child €7/5.50; ⊙10am-5pm Wed-Sun, to 8pm Tue) The Maximilianmuseum occupies two patrician town houses joined by a statue-studded courtyard covered by a glass-and-steel roof. Highlights include a fabulous collection of Elias Holl's original wooden models for his architectural creations, and a collection of gold and silver coins that can be viewed through sliding magnifying glass panels. Opening to the courtyard is a chic cafe where kids won't want to miss turning the pages of the 'magic book' that brings Augsburg's history to life.

Bertolt-Brecht-Haus — MUSEUM
(☑324 2779; Auf dem Rain 7; adult/concession €2.50/2; ⊙10am-5pm Wed-Sun, to 8pm Tue) Opened in 1998 to celebrate local boy Bertolt Brecht's 100th birthday, this house museum is the birthplace of the famous playwright and poet, where he lived for the first two years of his life (from 1898 to 1900) before moving across town. Among the displays are old theatre posters and a great series of life-size chronological photos, as well as his mother's bedroom.

Dom Mariä Heimsuchung — CHURCH
(Hoher Weg; ⊙7am-6pm) Augsburg's cathedral, the Dom Mariä Heimsuchung, has its origins in the 10th century but was Gothicised and enlarged in the 14th and 15th centuries. The star treasures here are the so-called 'Prophets' Windows'. Depicting David, Daniel, Jonah, Hosea and Moses, they are among the oldest figurative stained-glass windows in Germany, dating from the 12th century. Look out for four paintings by Hans Holbein the Elder, including one of Jesus' circumcision.

Jüdisches Kulturmuseum — JEWISH MUSEUM
(www.jkmas.de; Halderstrasse 8; adult/concession €4/2; ⊙9am-6pm Tue-Thu, to 4pm Fri, 10am-5pm Sun) About 300m east of the main train station, as you head towards the Altstadt, you'll come to the Synagoge Augsburg, an art-nouveau temple built between 1914 and 1917 and housing a worthwhile Jewish museum. Exhibitions here focus on Jewish life in the region, presenting religious artefacts collected from defunct synagogues across Swabia.

🛏 Sleeping

Augsburg is a good alternative base for Oktoberfest, though hotel owners pump up their prices just as much as their Munich counterparts.

TOP CHOICE › Dom Hotel — HOTEL €€
(☑343 930; www.domhotel-augsburg.de; Frauentorstrasse 8; s €70-135, d €90-155; P@🕸🖃) Augsburg's top choice packs a 500-year-old former bishop's guesthouse (Martin Luther and Kaiser Maxmilian I stayed here) with 57 rooms, all different but sharing a stylishly understated air and pristine upkeep; some have cathedral views. However the big pluses here are the large swimming pool, fitness centre and solarium, as well as the inviting lobby offering free English-language press, coffee and fruit. Parking is an extra €6.

Hotel am Rathaus — HOTEL €€
(☑346 490; www.hotel-am-rathaus-augsburg.de; Am Hinteren Perlachberg 1; s €79-98, d €98-125; 🕸) Just steps from Rathausplatz and Maximilianstrasse, this central boutique hotel hires out 31 rooms with freshly neutral decor and a sunny little breakfast room. Attracts a business-oriented clientele, so watch out for special weekend deals.

Jakoberhof — GUESTHOUSE €
(☑510 030; www.jakoberhof.de; Jakoberstrasse 41; s/d with shared bathroom from €27/39, with private bathroom from €49/64; P) This friendly *Pension* spans a collection of three buildings near the Fuggerei. Rooms are clean-cut if unimaginative, there's a decent Bavarian restaurant on the premises, and free parking and bike storage are available.

Steigenberger Drei Mohren Hotel — HOTEL €€€
(☑503 60; www.augsburg.steigenberger.de; Maximilianstrasse 40; r €125-280; P🌼@🕸) A proud Leopold Mozart stayed here with his prodigious kids in 1766 and it remains Augsburg's oldest and grandest hotel. Recently renovated, the fully refreshed rooms are the last word in soothing design in these parts and come with marble bathrooms and original art. Dine in-house at the gastronomic extravaganza that is **Maximilians**, a great place to swing by for Sunday brunch.

Augsburger Hof — HOTEL €€
(☑343 050; www.augsburger-hof.de; Auf dem Kreuz 2; s €90-115, d €99-140; 🕸) All rooms are business standard, staff are well regimented

and there are two on-site eateries at this pretty window-boxed hotel near the Dom. The higher-priced rooms look out into the quiet courtyard.

✖ Eating

In the evening, Maximilianstrasse is the place to tarry, with cafes tumbling out onto the pavements and Augsburg's young and beautiful watching the world go by.

Bayerisches Haus am Dom   BAVARIAN €€
(☏349 7990; Johannisgasse 4; mains €7-16) Enjoy an elbow massage from the locals at chunky timber benches while refuelling on Bavarian and Swabian dishes, cheap lunch options (€6) or a sandwich served by Dirndl-clad waitresses. Erdinger and Andechser are the frothy double act that stimulates nightly frivolity in the beer garden.

Barfüsser Café   CAFE €
(☏450 4966; Barfüsserstrasse 10; snacks €1-6; ⏱11am-6pm Mon-Sat) Follow a short flight of steps down from the street through a covered passageway to uncover this pretty snack stop by a little canal. It's run by a team of staff with disabilities, for whom it provides work opportunities as part of a community project, and serves delectable homemade cakes, pastries, salads and light lunches.

Bauerntanz   GERMAN €€
(Bauerntanzgässchen 1; mains €7-16; ⏱11am-11.30pm) Belly-satisfying helpings of creative Swabian and Bavarian food (*Spätzle,* veal medallions, and more *Spätzle*) are plated up by friendly staff at this prim Alpine tavern with lace curtains, hefty timber interior and chequered fabrics. When the sun makes an appearance, everyone bails for the outdoor seating.

Fuggereistube   BAVARIAN €€
(☏308 70; Jakoberstrasse 26; mains €10-19; ⏱lunch & dinner Tue-Sat, lunch Sun) Old-fashioned fine dining involving expertly crafted Bavarian and Swabian dishes in an understated dining space with arching ceilings and terracotta-tiled floors. The reassuringly short and seasonal menu reboots on a daily basis.

Anno 1578   CAFE €
(Fuggerplatz 9; mains €4-10; ⏱8.30am-7pm Mon-Sat) Munch on blockbuster breakfasts, lunchtime burgers and sandwiches, or just pop by for a cappuccino or ice cream at this slick cafe under ancient neon-uplit vaulting.

♟ Drinking

Elements   CAFE, BISTRO
(☏508 0759; Frauentorstrasse 2) Knock back a cocktail or five at this trendy cafe-bistro which attracts the beautiful people of an eve. Weekend breakfast is ideal for those who rise at the crack of lunchtime.

Thing   BEER GARDEN
(☏395 05; Vorderer Lech 45) Augsburg's coolest beer garden sports totem poles and often gets crowded in the evenings.

☆ Entertainment

Augsburger Puppenkiste   THEATRE
(☏450 3450; www.augsburger-puppenkiste.de; Spitalgasse 15) The celebrated puppet theatre holds performances of modern and classic fairy tales that even non–German speakers will enjoy. Advance bookings essential.

❶ Information

Post Office (Halderstrasse 29) At the Hauptbahnhof.

Tourist Office (☏502 070; www.augsburg-tourismus.de; Rathausplatz; ⏱9am-6pm Mon-Fri, 10am-5pm Sat, 10am-3pm Sun)

❶ Getting There & Away

BUS The Romantic Road Europabus stops at the Hauptbahnhof and the Rathaus.

CAR & MOTORCYCLE Augsburg is just off the A8 northwest of Munich.

TRAIN Augsburg rail connections:

» **Füssen** €19.20, two hours, every two hours

» **Munich** €12.20 to €20, 30 to 45 minutes, three hourly

» **Nuremberg** €34, one hour, hourly

» **Ulm** €16.40 to €23, 45 minutes to one hour, three hourly

---

Landsberg am Lech

☏08191 / POP 28,100

Lovely Landsberg am Lech is often overlooked by Romantic Road trippers on their town-hopping way between Füssen to the south and Augsburg to the north. But it's for this very absence of tourists and a less commercial ambience that this walled town on the River Lech is worth a halt, if only a brief one.

Landsberg can claim to be the town where one of the German language's best-selling books was written. Was it a work by Goethe,

Remarque, Brecht? No, unfortunately, it was Hitler. It was during his 264 days of incarceration in a Landsberg jail, following the 1923 beer-hall putsch, that Adolf penned his hate-filled *Mein Kampf*, a book that sold an estimated seven million copies when published. The jail later held Nazi war criminals and is still in use; the rights to the text of *Mein Kampf* are owned by the Free State of Bavaria, but these run out in 2015, 70 years after the author's demise.

◉ Sights

Landsberg's hefty medieval defensive walls are punctuated by some beefy gates, the most impressive of which are the 1425 **Bayertor** to the east and the Renaissance-styled **Sandauer Tor** to the north. The tall **Schmalztor** was left centrally stranded when the fortifications were moved further out and still overlooks the main square and the 500 listed buildings within the town walls.

**Stadtpfarrkirche
Mariä Himmelfahrt**   CHURCH
(Georg-Hellmair-Platz) This huge 15th-century church was built by Matthäus von Ensingen, architect of Bern Cathedral. The barrel nave is stuccoed to baroque perfection, while a cast of saints populates the columns and alcoves above the pews. Gothic-era stained glass casts rainbow hues on the church's most valuable work of art, the 15th-century *Madonna with Child* by local sculptor Lorenz Luidl.

Johanniskirche   CHURCH
(Vorderer Anger) If you've already seen the Wieskirche (p113) to the south, you'll instantly recognise this small baroque church as a creation by the same architect, Dominikus Zimmermann, who lived in Landsberg and even served as its mayor.

Heilg-Kreuz-Kirche   CHURCH
(Von-Helfenstein-Gasse) Head uphill from the Schmalztor to view this beautiful baroque Jesuit church, the interior a hallucination in broodily dark gilding and glorious ceiling decoration.

Neues Stadtmuseum   MUSEUM
(www.museum-landsberg.de; Von-Helfenstein-Gasse 426; adult/concession €3.50/2; ⊙2-5pm Tue-Fri, from 10am Sat & Sun May-Jan, closed Feb-Apr) Housed in a former Jesuit school, Landsberg's municipal museum chronicles the area's past from prehistory to the 20th century, and displays numerous works of local art, both religious and secular in nature.

🛏 Sleeping & Eating

Stadthotel Augsburger Hof   HOTEL €
(☑969 596; www.stadthotel-landsberg.de; Schlossergasse 378; s €32-43, d €69-72; P🐕) The 14 ensuite rooms at this highly recommended traditional inn are a superb deal, and have chunky pine beds and well-maintained bathrooms throughout. The owners and staff are a friendly bunch and the breakfast is a filling set-up for the day. Cycle hire and cycle friendly.

Schafbräu   INTERNATIONAL €€
(Hinterer Anger 338; mains €5-15) This cosy Bavarian-styled tavern has an international menu that leans firmly towards southern Europe. If you don't feel like moving far afterwards, there are rooms upstairs (€75).

Altstadt Cafe   CAFE €
(Ludwigstrasse 164; mains €5-8; ⊙8am-5pm) Munch on the mainstays of central European cuisine amid brass statuary and mock Chinese vases at this central cafe.

❶ Information

Tourist Office (☑128 246; www.landsberg.de; Rathaus, Hauptplatz 152; ⊙8am-6pm Mon-Fri May-Oct, 10am-5pm Sat & Sun Apr-Oct, shorter hours & closed weekends Nov-Mar)

❶ Getting There & Away

BUS The Europabus stops on request at the train station across from the old town.

TRAIN Landsberg has the following rail connections:

» **Augsburg** €7.50, 50 minutes, hourly

» **Füssen** Change at Kaufering; €14.40, 1½ hours, every two hours

» **Munich** Change at Kaufering; €12.20, 50 minutes, twice hourly

NUREMBERG & FRANCONIA

Somewhere between Ingolstadt and Nuremberg, Bavaria's accent mellows, the oompah bands play that little bit quieter and wine competes with beer as the local tipple. This is Franconia (Franken) and, as every local will tell you, Franconians, who inhabit the wooded hills and the banks of the Main River in Bavaria's northern reaches, are a breed apart from their brash and extrovert cousins to the south.

In the northwest, the region's winegrowers produce some exceptional whites, sold in a distinctive teardrop-shaped bottle, the *Bocksbeutel*. For outdoor enthusiasts, the Altmühltal Nature Park offers wonderful hiking, biking and canoeing. But it is Franconia's old royalty and incredible cities – Nuremberg, Bamberg and Coburg – that draw the biggest crowds.

Nuremberg

📞0911 / POP 503,000

Nuremberg (Nürnberg), Bavaria's second-largest city and the unofficial capital of Franconia, is an energetic place where the nightlife is intense and the beer is as dark as coffee. As one of Bavaria's biggest draws it is alive with visitors year-round, but especially during the spectacular Christmas market.

For centuries, Nuremberg was the undeclared capital of the Holy Roman Empire and the preferred residence of most German kings, who kept their crown jewels here. Rich and stuffed with architectural wonders, it was also a magnet for famous artists, though the most famous of all, Albrecht Dürer, was actually born here. 'Nuremberg shines throughout Germany like a sun among the moon and stars,' gushed Martin Luther. By the 19th century, the city had become a powerhouse in Germany's industrial revolution.

The Nazis saw a perfect stage for their activities in working class Nuremberg. It was here that the fanatical party rallies were held, the boycott of Jewish businesses began and the infamous Nuremberg Laws outlawing German citizenship for Jewish people were enacted. On 2 January 1945, Allied bombers reduced the city to landfill, killing 6000 people in the process.

After WWII the city was chosen as the site of the war crimes tribunal, now known as the Nuremberg Trials. Later, the painstaking reconstruction – using the original stone – of almost all the city's main buildings, including the castle and old churches in the Altstadt, returned the city to some of its former glory.

⊙ Sights

Most major sights are within the Altstadt.

Kaiserburg　　　　　　　　　　　CASTLE
(Map p146; www.schloesser.bayern.de; adult/child incl museum €7/6; ⊙9am-6pm Apr-Sep, 10am-4pm Oct-Mar) Construction of Nuremberg's

landmark, the immensely proportioned Kaiserburg, began during the reign of Hohenstaufen King Konrad III in the 12th century and dragged on for about 400 years. The complex, for centuries the receptacle of the Holy Roman Empire's treasures, consists of three parts: the Kaiserburg and Stadtburg (the Emperor's Palace and City Fortress), as well as the Burggrafenburg (Count's Residence), which was largely destroyed in 1420. Wedged between its surviving towers are the Kaiserstallung (Royal Stables), which today house the DJH hostel (p153).

The **Kaiserburg Museum** chronicles the history of the castle and provides a survey of medieval defence techniques. Other Tardis-like sections open to visitors include the royal living quarters, the Imperial and Knights' Halls, and the **Romanesque Doppelkapelle** (Twin Chapel). The latter poignantly illustrates the medieval hierarchy: common folk sat in the dimly lit lower section, with the royals entering up above directly from the palace.

Enjoy panoramic city views from atop the **Sinwellturm** (Sinwell Tower; 113 steps) or peer into the amazing 48m-deep **Tiefer Brunnen** (Deep Well) – guides lower a platter of candles so you can see its depth; it still yields drinking water.

The grassy knoll at the southeast corner of the **castle gardens** (open seasonally) is **Am Ölberg**, a favourite spot to sit and gaze out over the city's rooftops.

Deutsche Bahn Museum　　　　　　MUSEUM
(Map p146; 📞0180-444 2233; www.db-museum. de; Lessingstrasse 6; adult/child €5/2.50, free with InterRail pass; ⊙9am-5pm Tue-Fri, 10am-6pm Sat & Sun) Forget Dürer and Nazi rallies, Nuremberg is a railway town at heart. Germany's first passenger trains ran between here and Fürth, a fact reflected in the unmissable German Railways Museum, which explores the history of Germany's legendary rail system.

If you have tots aboard, head straight for the **Eisenbahn-Erlebniswelt** (Railway World), where lots of hands-on, interactive choo-choo–themed attractions await. Here you'll also find a huge model railway, one of Germany's largest, set in motion every hour by a uniformed controller.

The main exhibition charting almost two centuries of rail history starts on the ground floor and continues with more recent exhibits on the first. Passing quickly through the historically inaccurate beginning (as every rail buff knows, the world's first railway was the Stockton–Darlington, not the Liverpool–Manchester), highlights include Germany's oldest railway carriage dating from 1835 and lots of interesting Deutsche Reichsbahn paraphernalia from East Germany.

However the real meat of the show are the two halls of locos and rolling stock. The first hall contains Ludwig II's incredible rococo rail carriage, dubbed the 'Versailles of the rails', as well as Bismarck's considerably less ostentatious means of transport. There's also Germany's most famous steam loco, the *Adler*, built by the Stephensons in Newcastle upon Tyne for the Nuremberg–Fürth line. The second hall across the road from the main building houses some mammoth engines, some with their Nazi or Deutsche Reichsbahn insignia still in place.

Hauptmarkt   SQUARE

This bustling square in the heart of the Altstadt is the site of daily markets as well as the famous Christkindlesmarkt. At the eastern end is the ornate Gothic **Pfarrkirche Unsere Liebe Frau** (Map p146; Hauptmarkt 14), built from 1350 to 1358, and also known simply as the **Frauenkirche**. The work of Prague cathedral builder Peter Parler, it's the oldest Gothic hall church in Bavaria and stands on the ground of Nuremberg's first synagogue. It was built as a repository for the crown jewels of Charles IV who, fearing theft, sent them instead to Prague for safe keeping. The western facade is beautifully ornamented and is where, every day at noon, crowds crane their necks to witness a spectacle called *Männleinlaufen*. It features seven figures, representing electoral princes, parading clockwise three times around Emperor Karl IV to chimed accompaniment.

Rising from the square like a Gothic spire, the gargoyle-adorned, 19m-tall **Schöner Brunnen** (Beautiful Fountain; Map p146) is a gilded replica of the 14th-century original, though it no longer spouts water. Look for the seamless golden ring in the ornate wrought-iron gate on the southwestern side. Local superstition has it that if you turn it three times, your wish will come true. (Be careful not to confuse it with the gold ring on the opposite side of the gate, which, it's claimed, will make you conceive – if you're female, of course.)

Memorium
Nuremberg Trials   HISTORIC BUILDING

(☑3217 9372; www.memorium-nuremberg.de; Bärenschanzstrasse 72; adult/concession €5/3; ☉10am-6pm Wed-Mon) Nazis were tried from 1945 to 1946 for crimes against peace and humanity in Schwurgerichtssaal 600 (Court Room 600) of what is still Nuremberg's regional courthouse. These became known as the Nuremberg Trials, and were held by the Allies in the city for obvious symbolic reasons. Another factor in their choice of venue was that there was (and still is) a secure underground tunnel between the courthouse and adjacent prison (though today it only has female prisoners).

The initial and most famous trial, conducted by international prosecutors, saw 24 people accused, of whom 19 were convicted and sentenced. Following trials also resulted in the conviction, sentencing and execution of Nazi leaders and underlings until 1949. Hermann Göring, the Reich's field marshal, cheated the hangman by taking a cyanide capsule in his cell hours before his scheduled execution.

In addition to viewing the courtroom (if not in use), a new exhibition provides comprehensive background to the trials and their significance to the world today.

To get here, take the U1 towards Bärenschanze (get off at Sielstrasse). It's about 2km from the centre of the Altstadt.

Reichsparteitagsgelände   HISTORIC SITE

(Luitpoldhain) If you've ever wondered where the infamous black-and-white images of ecstatic Nazi supporters hailing their Führer were filmed, it was here in Nuremberg. This orchestrated propaganda began as early as 1927 but, after 1933, Hitler opted for a purpose-built venue, the **Reichsparteitagsgelände**. Much of the outsize grounds were destroyed during Allied bombing raids, but 4 sq km remain, enough to get a sense of the megalomania behind it.

At the northwestern edge was the **Luitpoldarena**, designed for mass SS and SA parades. The area is now a park. South of here, the half-built **Kongresshalle** (Congress Hall) was meant to outdo Rome's Colosseum in both scale and style.

A visit to the **Dokumentationszentrum** (☑231 7538; Bayernstrasse 110; adult/concession €5/3; ☉9am-6pm Mon-Fri, 10am-6pm Sat & Sun) in the north wing of the Kongresshalle helps to put the grounds into some historical context. A stunning walkway of glass cuts diagonally through the complex, ending with an interior view of the congress hall. Inside, the *Fascination and Terror* exhibit examines the rise of the NSDAP, the Hitler cult, the party rallies and the Nuremberg Trials.

Nuremberg

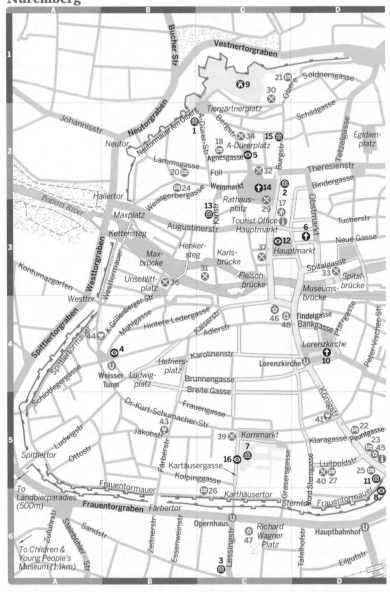

East of the Kongresshalle, across the artificial Dutzendteich (Dozen Ponds), is the **Zeppelinfeld**, fronted by a 350m-long grandstand, the **Zeppelintribüne**, where most of the big Nazi parades, rallies and events took place. It now hosts sport-ing events and rock concerts, though this rehabilitation has caused controversy.

The grounds are bisected by the 60m-wide **Grosse Strasse** (Great Road), which culminates 2km to the south at the **Märzfeld** (March Field), which was planned as a mili-

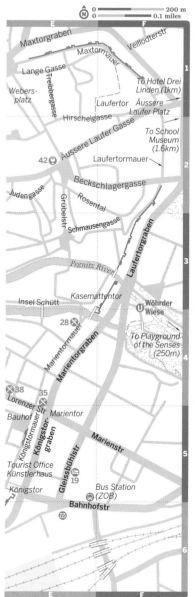

The Reichsparteitagsgelände is about 4km southeast of the centre. Take tram 9 from the Hauptbahnhof to Doku-Zentrum.

Germanisches Nationalmuseum MUSEUM

(Map p146; www.gnm.de; Kartäusergasse 1; adult/child €6/4; ⊙10am-6pm Tue & Thu-Sun, to 9pm Wed) Spanning prehistory to the early 20th century, the Germanisches Nationalmuseum is the country's most important museum of German culture. It features works by German painters and sculptors, an archaeological collection, arms and armour, musical and scientific instruments and toys. Among its many highlights is Dürer's anatomically detailed *Hercules Slaying the Stymphalian Birds*. The research library has over 500,000 volumes and 1500 periodicals.

At the museum's entrance is the inspired **Way of Human Rights** (Map p146), a symbolic row of 29 white concrete pillars (and one oak tree) bearing the 30 articles of the Universal Declaration of Human Rights. Each pillar is inscribed in German and, in succession, the language of peoples whose rights have been violated, with the oak representing languages not explicitly mentioned.

Neues Museum MUSEUM

(Map p146; www.nmn.de; Luitpoldstrasse 5; adult/child €4/3; ⊙10am-8pm Tue-Fri, to 6pm Sat & Sun) The aptly named Neues Museum showcases contemporary art and design, with resident collections of paintings, sculpture, photography, video art and installations, as well as travelling shows. Equally stunning is the building itself, with a dramatic 100m curved glass facade that, literally and figuratively, reflects the stone town wall opposite.

Albrecht-Dürer-Haus MUSEUM

(Map p146; Albrecht-Dürer-Strasse 39; adult/child €5/2.50; ⊙10am-5pm Fri-Wed, to 8pm Thu) Dürer, Germany's most famous Renaissance draughtsman, lived and worked at the Albrecht-Dürer-Haus from 1509 until his death in 1528. After a multimedia show there's an audioguide tour of the four-storey house, which is narrated by 'Agnes', Dürer's wife. Highlights are the hands-on demonstrations in the recreated studio and print shop on the 3rd floor and, in the attic, a gallery featuring copies and originals of Dürer's work.

Special tours led by an actress dressed as Agnes take place at 6pm Thursday, 3pm Saturday and 11am Sunday; there's an English-language tour at 2pm on Saturday.

tary exercise ground. The **Deutsches Stadion**, with a seating capacity of 400,000, was to have stood west of the Grosse Strasse. Things never got beyond the first excavation when the hole was filled with groundwater – today's Silbersee.

Nuremberg

Altes Rathaus   HISTORIC BUILDING
(Map p146; Rathausplatz 2) Beneath the Altes Rathaus (1616–22), a hulk of a building with lovely Renaissance-style interiors, you'll find the macabre **Lochgefängnisse** (Medieval Dungeons; Map p146; ☎231 2690; adult/concession €3.50/1.50; ⊙tours 10am-4.30pm Tue-Sun Apr-Oct). This 12-cell death row and torture chamber must be seen on a 30-minute guided tour (held every half-hour) and might easily put you off lunch.

Stadtmuseum Fembohaus   MUSEUM
(Map p146; ☎231 2595; Burgstrasse 15; museum adult/child €5/3, Noricama €4/2.50; ⊙10am-5pm Tue-Fri, 10am-6pm Sat & Sun) Offering an entertaining overview of the city's history, highlights of the Stadtmuseum Fembohaus include the restored historic rooms of this 16th-century merchant's house. Also here, **Noricama** takes you on a flashy Hollywoodesque multimedia journey (in German and English) through Nuremberg's history.

Jüdisches Museum Franken   JEWISH, MUSEUM
(☎770 577; www.juedisches-museum.org; Königstrasse 89; adult/concession €3/2; ⊙10am-5pm Wed-Sun, to 8pm Tue) A quick U-Bahn ride away in the neighbouring town of Fürth is the Jüdisches Museum Franken. Fürth once had the largest Jewish congregation of any city in southern Germany and this museum, housed in a handsomely restored building, chronicles the history of Jewish life in the region from the Middle Ages to today. To reach the museum, take the U1 to the Rathaus stop in Fürth.

St Sebalduskirche   CHURCH
(Map p146; www.sebalduskirche.de; Albrecht-Dürer-Platz 1; ⊙from 9.30am) Nuremberg's oldest church was built in rusty pink-veined sandstone in the 13th century. Its exterior is replete with religious sculptures and

symbols; check out the ornate carvings over the **Bridal Doorway** to the north, showing the Wise and Foolish Virgins. Inside, the bronze shrine of St Sebald (Nuremberg's own saint) is a Gothic and Renaissance masterpiece that took its maker, Peter Vischer the Elder, and his two sons more than 11 years to complete (Vischer is in it too, sporting a skullcap). The church is free to enter, despite the misleading sign on the door.

Felsengänge   HISTORIC SITE
(Underground Cellars; Map p146; www.felsengaenge-nuernberg.de; Bergstrasse 19; tours adult/concession €5/4; ⊗tours 11am, 1pm, 3pm & 5pm Mon-Fri, plus noon, 2pm & 4pm Sat & Sun) Beneath the Albrecht Dürer Monument on Albrecht-Dürer-Platz are the chilly Felsengänge. Departing from the brewery shop at Burgstrasse 19, tours descend to this four-storey subterranean warren, which dates from the 14th century and once housed a brewery and a beer cellar. During WWII it served as an air-raid shelter. Tours take a minimum of three people. Take a jacket against the chill.

Spielzeugmuseum   MUSEUM
(Toy Museum; Map p146; Karlstrasse 13-15; adult/child €5/3; ⊗10am-5pm Tue-Fri, to 6pm Sat & Sun) Nuremberg has long been a centre of toy manufacturing, and the Spielzeugmuseum presents toys in their infinite variety – from innocent hoops to blood-and-guts computer games, historical wooden and tin toys to Barbie et al. Kids and kids at heart will delight in the play area.

Ehekarussell Brunnen   FOUNTAIN
(Map p146; Am Weissen Turm) At the foot of the fortified Weisser Turm (White Tower; now the gateway to the U-Bahn station of the same name) stands this large and startlingly grotesque sculptural work depicting six interpretations of marriage (from first love to quarrel to death-do-us-part), all based on a verse by Hans Sachs, the medieval cobbler-poet. You soon realise why the artist faced a blizzard of criticism when the fountain was unveiled in 1984; it really is enough to put anyone off tying the knot.

Lorenzkirche   CHURCH
(Map p146; Lorenzplatz) Dark and atmospheric, the Lorenzkirche has dramatically downlit pillars, taupe stone columns, sooty ceilings and many artistic highlights. Check out the 15th-century tabernacle in the left aisle – the delicate carved strands wind up to the vaulted ceiling. Remarkable also are the stained glass (including a rose window 9m in diameter) and Veit Stoss' *Engelsgruss* (Annunciation), a wooden carving with life-size figures suspended above the high altar.

Handwerkerhof   MARKET
(Map p146; www.handwerkerhof.de; Am Königstor; ⊗9am-6.30pm Mon-Fri, 10am-4pm Sat mid-Mar–Dec) A recreation of an old-world Nuremberg crafts quarter, the Handwerkerhof is a self-contained tourist trap by the Königstor. It's about as quaint as a hammer on your thumbnail, but if you're cashed up you may find some decent merchandise (and the bratwurst aren't bad here either).

☞ Tours

English-language **Old Town walking tours** (Map p146; adult/child €10/free; ⊗1pm May-Oct) are run by the tourist office (p155) and include admission to the Kaiserburg. Tours leave from the Hauptmarkt branch and take 2½ hours.

Geschichte für Alle   CULTURAL TOUR
(☑307 360; www.geschichte-fuer-alle.de; adult/concession €7/6.) Intriguing range of themed English-language tours by a nonprofit association. The 'Albrecht Dürer' and 'Life in Medieval Nuremberg' tours come highly recommended.

Nuremberg Tours   WALKING TOUR
(www.nurembergtours.com; adult/concession €18/16; ⊗11.15am Mon, Wed & Sat Apr-Oct) Four-hour walking and public transport tours taking in the city centre and the Reichsparteitags-gelände (p145). Groups meet at the entrance to the Hauptbahnhof.

✦✦ Festivals & Events

Christkindlesmarkt   CHRISTMAS MARKET
(www.christkindlesmarkt.de) From late November to Christmas Eve, the Hauptmarkt is taken over by the most famous Christkindlesmarkt in Germany. Yuletide shoppers descend on the 'Christmas City' from all over Europe to seek out unique gifts at the scores of colourful timber trinket stalls that fill the square. The aroma of *Lebkuchen* (large, soft, spicy biscuits), mulled wine and roast sausages permeates the chilly air, while special festive events take place on the square and at other venues around town.

🛏 Sleeping

Accommodation gets tight and rates rocket during the Christmas market and the toy

NUREMBERG FOR KIDS

No city in Bavaria has more for kids to see and do than Nuremberg. In fact keeping the little 'uns entertained in the Franconian capital is child's play.

Museums

» **Children & Young People's Museum** (☑600 040; www.kindermuseum-nuernberg.de; Michael-Ende-Strasse 17; adult/family €7/19; ⊘2-5.30pm Sat, 10am-5.30pm Sun Sep-Jun) Educational exhibitions and lots of hands-on fun – just a pity it's not open more often.

» **School Museum** (☑231 3875; Äussere Sulzbacher Strasse 62; adult/child €5/3; ⊘9am-5pm Tue-Fri, 10am-6pm Sat & Sun) Recreated classroom plus school-related exhibits from the 17th century to the Third Reich.

» **Deutsche Bahn Museum** (p144) Feeds the kids' obsession with choo-choos.

Play

» **Playground of the Senses** (☑231 5445; www.erfahrungsfeld.nuernberg.de; Untere Talgasse 8; adult/child €6.10/4.40; ⊘9am-6pm Mon-Fri, 1-6pm Sat, 10am-6pm Sun May–mid-Sep) Some 80 hands-on 'stations' designed to educate children in the laws of nature, physics and the human body. Take the U2 or U3 to Wöhrder Wiese.

Toys

» **Playmobil** (☑9666 1700; www.playmobil-funpark.de; Brandstätterstrasse 2-10; admission €10; ⊘9am-7pm May-Sep, 9am-6pm Oct) This theme park has life-size versions of the popular toys. It's located 9km west of the city centre in Zirndorf; take the S4 to Anwanden, then change to bus 151. Free admission if it's your birthday. Special 'Kleine Dürer' (Little Dürer; €2.99) figures are on sale here and at the tourist office.

» **Käthe Wohlfahrt Christmas shop** (Map p268; www.bestofchristmas.com; Königstrasse 8) The Nuremberg branch of this year-round Christmas shop.

» **Spielzeugmuseum** (p149) Some 1400 sq metres of Matchbox, Barbie, Playmobil and Lego, plus a great play area.

» **Germanisches Nationalmuseum** (p147) Has a toy section and holds occasional tours for children.

Zoo

» **Nuremberg Zoo** (☑545 46; www.tiergarten.nuernberg.de; Am Tiergarten 30; adult/child €13.50/6.50; ⊘8am-7.30pm) An open-air zoo and dolphinarium, with enclosures as close as possible to the animals' natural habitats. Take tram 5 from the Hauptbahnhof.

fair (trade only) in late January to early February. At other times, cheap rooms can be found, especially if you book ahead.

TOP CHOICE Hotel Elch HOTEL €€

(Map p146; ☑249 2980; www.hotel-elch.com; Irrerstrasse 9; s/d from €75/95; ☏) Tucked up in the antiques quarter, this 14th-century, half-timbered house has morphed into the snuggest, most romantic 12-room gem of a hotel you could imagine. A couple of rooms (2 and 7) have half-timbered walls and ceilings, but modern touches include contemporary art, glazed terracotta bathrooms, rainbow-glass chandeliers and trendy multicoloured elk heads throughout (the name means 'elk'). The tiny, original wood-beamed

Schnitzelria restaurant downstairs serves guests breakfast in the morning, followed by numerous types of – yep, you guessed it – schnitzel later in the day. Rather surprisingly, rates come *down* at weekends.

Hotel Deutscher Kaiser HOTEL €€

(Map p146; ☑242 660; www.deutscher-kaiser-hotel. de; Königstrasse 55; s/d from €89/108; @☏) Epicentral in its location, aristocratic in its design and service, this treat of a historic hotel has been in the same family since the turn of the 20th century. Climb the castle-like granite stairs to find rooms of understated simplicity, flaunting oversize beds, Italian porcelain, silk lampshades and real period furniture (Biedermeier and Jugendstil). The

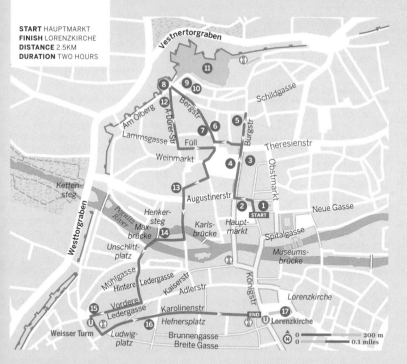

START HAUPTMARKT
FINISH LORENZKIRCHE
DISTANCE 2.5KM
DURATION TWO HOURS

Walking Tour
Nuremberg Altstadt

❯ This circuit covers the historic centre's
key sights. With visits to all the attractions
listed, it could take the best part of two days.

The tour starts at the Hauptmarkt, the
main square. At the eastern end is the ornate
Gothic ❶ **Pfarrkirche Unsere Liebe Frau**,
also called the Frauenkirche. The church
clock's figures spring into action every day at
noon. Also here, the ❷ **Schöner Brunnen**
rises up from the cobblestones like a buried
cathedral. Walk north to the Altes Rathaus, the
old town hall, with its ❸ **Lochgefängnisse**,
the medieval dungeons. Opposite stands
the 13th-century ❹ **St Sebalduskirche**,
with the bronze shrine of St Sebald inside.
Just up Burgstrasse, the ❺ **Stadtmuseum
Fembohaus** covers the highs and lows of
Nuremberg's past.

Backtrack south to Halbwachsengässchen
and turn right into Albrecht-Dürer-Platz, with
the ❻ **Albrecht Dürer Monument**. Directly
beneath are the ❼ **Felsengänge**, tunnels
once used as a beer cellar and air-raid shelter.
Up Bergstrasse you'll reach the ❽ **Tiergärt-
nertor**, a 16th-century tower. Nearby is the

half-timbered ❾ **Pilatushaus** and a strange,
glassy-eyed hare dedicated to Dürer. A few
steps east is the ❿ **Historischer Kunstbun-
ker** where precious art was stored in WWII.
Looming over the scene is the ⓫ **Kaiserburg**
castle of medieval knights. Go south to the
⓬ **Albrecht-Dürer-Haus**, where the Renaissance genius lived and worked. Continue
south along Albrecht-Dürer-Strasse, turn left
on Füll and skirt the back of Sebalduskirche
to Karlsstrasse, where you'll reach the
⓭ **Spielzeugmuseum**, with generations of
nostalgia-inducing playthings.

Cross the Karlsbrücke to enjoy a view of the
⓮ **Weinstadel**, an old wine depot by the river.
Continue across the Henkersteg (Hangman's
Bridge) and south to Vordere Ledergasse,
which leads west to the ⓯ **Ehekarussell
Brunnen**, with its shocking images of married life. Head east on Ludwigplatz past the
⓰ **Peter-Henlein-Brunnen**, with a statue
of the first watchmaker, and proceed along
Karolinenstrasse to the massive ⓱ **Lorenzkirche**, with its 15th-century tabernacle and
suspended carving of the Annunciation.

club-like reading room with newspapers and magazines in German and English is a welcome extra and the breakfast room is a study in soothing, early-morning elegance. Renovation work is ongoing.

Art & Business Hotel
HOTEL €€

(Map p146; ☑232 10; www.art-business-hotel.com; Gleissbühlstrasse 15; s/d €89/115; 🌐) You don't have to be an artist or a business person to stay at this new, up-to-the-minute place, a retro sport shoe's throw from the Hauptbahnhof. From the trendy bar area to the latest in slate bathroom styling, design here is bold, but not overpoweringly so. From reception follow the wobbly carpet to your room, a well-maintained haven uninfected by traffic noise despite the city-centre frenzy outside. Local Technicolor art and design brings cheer to the communal spaces and there's a small sculpture garden out back. Rates tumble at weekends.

Probst-Garni Hotel
PENSION €

(Map p146; ☑203 433; www.hotel-garni-probst.de; Luitpoldstrasse 9; s/d €56/75; 🌐) A creaky lift from street level takes you up to this realistically priced, centrally located guesthouse, run for 65 years by three generations of Probsts. The 33 gracefully old-fashioned rooms are multi-hued and high-ceilinged but some are more renovated than others. Furniture in the breakfast room is family made.

Burghotel
HOTEL €€

(Map p146; ☑238 890; www.burghotel-nuernberg. de; Lammsgasse 3; s/d from €56/100; @🌐🏊) The mock-Gothic reception area and lantern-lit corridors (watch your head) indicate you're in for a slightly different hotel experience here. The small singles and doubles have strange '50s-style built-in timber furniture reminiscent of yesteryear train carriages, old-fashioned bedhead radios and chunky TVs, while some much larger 'comfort' rooms under the eaves have spacious sitting areas and more up-to-date amenities. However the big draw here is the basement heated swimming pool, where all guests are free to make a splash.

Hotel Drei Raben
HOTEL €€€

(Map p146; ☑274 380; www.hotel3raben.de; Königstrasse 63; s/d €130/150; 🌐) The design of this original hotel builds upon the legend of the three ravens perched on the building's chimney stack, who tell stories from Nuremberg lore. Each of the 'mythology' rooms uses

decor and art including sandstone-sculpted bedheads and etched-glass bathroom doors to reflect a particular tale, from the life of Albrecht Dürer to the history of the local football club. Junior suites have claw-foot tubs.

Agneshof
HOTEL €€

(Map p146; ☑214 440; www.agneshof-nuernberg. de; Agnesgasse 10; s/d from €73/86; P@) Tranquilly located in the antiques quarter near the St Sebalduskirche, the Agneshof's public areas have a sophisticated, artsy touch. The box-ticking rooms have whitewashed walls and '90s furniture; some at the top have views of the Kaiserburg. There's a state-of-the-art wellness centre, and a pretty summer courtyard garden strewn with deckchairs. Parking (by reservation) costs €15 per day and the farmhouse breakfast is a cheeky extra €7.

Lette'm Sleep
HOSTEL €

(Map p146; ☑992 8128; www.backpackers.de; Frauentormauer 42; dm €16-20, r from €50; @🌐) A backpacker favourite, this independent hostel is just five minutes' walk from the Hauptbahnhof, with a laundry, colourfully painted dorms and some groovy self-catering apartments. The retro-styled kitchen and common room are great areas to chill; internet, tea and coffee are free, and staff are wired into what's happening around town.

Hotel Victoria
HOTEL €€

(Map p146; ☑240 50; www.hotelvictoria.de; Königstrasse 80; s/d from €78/99; P@🌐) A hotel since 1896, the Victoria is a solid option with a central location. With its early 21st-century bathrooms and now ever-so-slightly dated decor, the price is about right. Popular with business travellers. Parking costs €11.

Hotel Drei Linden
HOTEL €

(☑506 800; www.hotel-drei-linden-nuernberg.de; Äussere Sulzbacher Strasse 1-3; s/d €40/60; 🌐) Persistently the cheapest deal in town, rooms are comfortable though not at all chic, and there's round-the-clock free tea and coffee. Breakfast is a whopping €9.50 extra. Located 1km east of the Altstadt; take tram 8 to Deichlerstrasse.

Knaus-Campingpark
CAMPGROUND €

(☑981 2717; www.knauscamp.de; Hans-Kalb-Strasse 56; per tent/person €5.30/6.30; 🌐) A camping ground near the lakes in the Volkspark, southeast of the city centre. Take the U1 to Messezentrum, then walk about 1km.

DJH Hostel
HOSTEL €

(Map p146; ✆230 9360; www.nuernberg.jugendher berge.de; Burg 2; dm from €21.90) A 20-minute walk north of the Hauptbahnhof, this spotless, recently renovated youth hostel in the former castle stables has 382 beds in bright airy dorms. Open year-round.

✕ Eating

TOP CHOICE Goldenes Posthorn
FRANCONIAN €€

(Map p146; ✆225 153; Glöckleinsgasse 2, cnr Sebalder Platz; mains €6-19; ⊘11am-11pm; ✐) Push open the heavy copper door to find a real culinary treat that has been serving the folk of Nuremberg since 1498. The miniature local sausages are big here, but there's plenty else on the menu including many an obscure rural dish and some vegie options. The choice of dining spaces ranges from formal to folksy, chunky wood to wood panelled. Cash only.

TOP CHOICE Bratwursthäusle
GERMAN €€

(Map p146; http://die-nuernberger-bratwurst.de; Rathausplatz 2; meals €6-14; ⊘closed Sun) Seared over a flaming beech-wood grill, the little links sold at this rustic inn arguably set the standard for *Rostbratwürste* across the land. You can dine in the timbered restaurant or on the terrace with views of the Hauptmarkt. Service can be flustered at busy times.

Hütt'n
GERMAN €€

(Map p146; Bergstrasse 20; mains €5.50-15; ⊘4pm-midnight Mon-Fri, 11am-12.30am Sat, 11am-10.30pm Sun) Successfully and confusingly relocated from Burgstrasse to Bergstrasse, this local haunt perpetually overflows with admirers of *Krustenschäufele* (roast pork with crackling, dumplings and sauerkraut salad) and the finest bratwurst put to work in various dishes, though menus change daily (Friday is fish day). It's also not the worst place to try a tankard or three of Franconian *Landbier*.

Heilig-Geist-Spital
BAVARIAN €€

(Map p146; ✆221 761; Spitalgasse 16; mains €7-17; ⊘lunch & dinner) Lots of dark carved wood, a herd of hunting trophies and a romantic candlelit half-light make this former hospital, suspended over the Pegnitz, one of the most atmospheric dining rooms in town. Sample the delicious, seasonally changing menu inside or out in the pretty courtyard, where the tinkle of cutlery on plate competes with a dribbling fountain.

Marientorzwinger
GERMAN €€

(Map p146; Lorenzer Strasse 33; mains €8-17; ⊘lunch & dinner) The last remaining *Zwinger* eatery (taverns built between the inner and outer walls when they relinquished their military use) in Nuremberg is an atmospheric place to chomp on sturdy Franconian staples or a vegie dish in the simple wood-panelled dining room or the leafy beer garden. Swab the decks with a yard of Fürth-brewed Tucher.

Restaurant Oberkrainer
FRANCONIAN €€

(Map p146; Hauptmarkt 7; mains €7-21.50; ⊘lunch & dinner) Blending tradition and nutrition for 35 years, central Oberkrainer is the place to explore Franconia with a knife and fork. You might want to skip a meal before tackling the strapping portions of goose, beef steak, *Schäufele*, schnitzel and the house speciality of tenderloin in paprika and garlic sauce, all served in the timber-rich dining room.

Café am Trödelmarkt
CAFE €

(Map p146; Trödelmarkt 42; dishes €4-8.50; ⊘9am-6pm Mon-Sat, 11am-6pm Sun) A gorgeous place on a sunny day, this multilevel waterfront cafe overlooks the covered Henkersteg bridge. It's especially popular for its continental breakfasts, and has fantastic cakes, as well as good blackboard lunchtime specials between 11am and 2pm.

Burgwächter
FRANCONIAN, INTERNATIONAL €€

(Map p146; ✆222 126; Am Ölberg 10; mains €9-15; ⊘11am-11pm; ✐) Refuel after a tour of the Kaiserburg with prime steaks, bratwurst with potato salad, and vegetarian-friendly Swabian filled pastas and salads, as you feast your eyes on the best terrace views from any Nuremberg eatery or drinking spot. With kiddies in tow, ask for *Kloss*, a simple dumpling with sauce.

Sushi Glas
SUSHI €

(Map p146; ✆205 9901; Kornmarkt 5-7; sushi from €5; ⊘noon-11pm Mon-Wed, noon-midnight Thu-Sat, 6-10pm Sun) Take a pew in this 21st-century sugar cube to watch the sushi chef deftly craft your order. When the mercury climbs high, enjoy your nigiri, sashimi and American sushi beneath the huge sunshades on the Kornmarkt.

Schäufelewärtschaft
BAVARIAN €

(Schweiggerstrasse 19; mains €6-8.50; ⊘noon-2pm & 5-10pm Mon-Fri, 5-10pm Sat, 11am-10pm Sun) It's easy to maintain best-kept-secret status with such an unpronounceable name and a dodgy location on the wrong side of the tracks behind the Hauptbahnhof. But most Nürnbergers agree that this rough-hewn eatery plates up the best shoulder of pork in the business. Take tram 6, 7, 8 or 9 from the train station to the Schweigger-strasse stop.

Naturkostladen Lotos
ORGANIC, BUFFET €

(Map p146; www.naturkostladen-lotos.de; Unschlittplatz 1; dishes €3-6; ⊙noon-6pm Mon-Fri; ☑) Unclog arteries and blast free radicals with a blitz of grain burgers, spinach soup or vegie pizza at this health-food shop. The fresh bread and cheese counter is a treasure chest of nutritious picnic supplies.

Souptopia
SOUP €

(Map p146; ☑240 6697; Lorenzer Strasse 27; soups €3-7.50; ⊙closed Sun) This fragrantly spicy place has a weekly changing menu, outdoor seating and a choice of non-liquid mains (sandwiches, salads) if you don't fancy a bowl of broth. Very popular lunch spot, so get there early.

American Diner
AMERICAN €€

(Map p146; Gewerbemuseumsplatz 3; burgers €9-12; ⊙11am-1am Sun-Thu, 11am-2am Fri & Sat) For the juiciest burgers in town, head for this retro diner in the Cinecitta Cinema, Germany's biggest multiplex.

Wurst & Durst
GERMAN €

(Map p146; Luitpoldstrasse 13; dishes €3-5; ⊙11am-6pm Tue & Wed, 11am-6pm & 9pm-3am Thu, 1-6pm & 9pm-5am Fri & Sat) Wedged between the facades of Luitpoldstrasse, this tiny snack bar offers munchies relief in the form of Belgian fries, sausages and trays of *Currywurst*.

🍷 Drinking

Landbierparadies
PUB

(☑468 882; www.landbierparadies.com; Wodanstrasse 15; mains €6-9; ⊙evenings Mon-Fri, from noon Sat, from 10am Sun) This spit 'n sawdust saloon stocks an incredible wellspring of obscure country ales, some of which are only available here and in the village where they are brewed.

Barfüsser Brauhaus
BEER HALL

(Map p146; Königstrasse 60) This beer hall is a popular spot to hug a mug of site-brewed ale, bubbling frothily in the copper kettles that occupy the cavernous vaulted cellar. Traditional trappings have been done away with, yellow polo shirts having replaced Dirndl and local kitsch kept to a minimum.

Treibhaus
CAFE

(Map p146; ☑223 041; Karl-Grillenberger-Strasse 28; snacks €3.80-8.20; ☎) Well off the path of most visitors, this bustling cafe is a Nuremberg institution. It serves breakfast till evening and caffeinated comfort to students and weary-legged shoppers.

Sausalitos
BAR

(Map p146; ☑200 4889; Färber Strasse 10) This busy Santa Fe–themed bar draws all sorts, from mums with prams and business people during the day to a slicker crowd the later the hour, who come for the long cocktail menu.

Meisengeige
BAR

(Map p146; Am Laufer Schlagturm 3) This long-established hole-in-the-wall bar draws an intense crowd of film intellectuals.

☆ Entertainment

The excellent *Plärrer*, available at newsstands throughout the city, is the best source of information on events around town. Otherwise the free monthly listings magazine *Doppelpunkt* (www.doppelpunkt.de), found in bars, restaurants and the tourist office, does an adequate job.

Hirsch
LIVE MUSIC

(☑429 414; www.der-hirsch.de; Vogelweiherstrasse 66) This converted factory, 2.5km south of the Hauptbahnhof, hosts live alternative music almost daily, both big-name acts and local names. Take the U1 or U2 to Plärrer, then change to tram 4, alighting at Dianaplatz.

Staatstheater
THEATRE

(Map p146; www.staatstheater-nuernberg.de; Richard-Wagner-Platz 2) Nuremberg's magnificent state theatre serves up an impressive mix of dramatic arts. The renovated art-nouveau opera house presents opera and ballet, while the Kammerspiele offers a varied program of classical and contemporary plays. The Nürnberger Philharmoniker also performs here.

Filmhaus
CINEMA

(Map p146; ☑231 5823; www.kubiss.de; Königstrasse 93) This small indie picture house shows foreign-language movies, plus reruns of cult German flicks and films for kids.

Loop Club
CLUB

(☑686 767; www.loopclub.de; Klingenhofstrasse 52) With three dance areas and a languid chill-out zone with lounge music, this place attracts a slightly more mature crowd, meaning

'80s and '90s hits plus student nights. Take the U2 to Herrnhütte, turn right and it's a five-minute walk.

Mach1 CLUB
(Map p146; ☑246 602; www.mach1-club.de; Kaiserstrasse 1-9; ⊙Thu-Sat) This legendary dance temple has been around for decades, but still holds a spell over fashion victims. Line up and be mustered.

Roxy CINEMA
(☑488 40; www.roxy-nuernberg.de; Julius-Lossmann-Strasse 116) This cinema shows first-run films in the original English version, a rarity in Nuremberg. Take tram 8 to the Südfriedhof stop.

Rockfabrik CLUB
(☑565 056; Klingenhofstrasse 56; ⊙Thu-Sat; ☎) Safely out of earshot of the centre, 3.5km to the northeast, this citadel of rock heaves with longhairs, who flock here for the weekend 'AC/DC', 'Oldies' and 'Heroes of Rock' nights. Take the U2 to Herrnhütte.

ℹ Information

Main Post Office (Bahnhofplatz 1)
ReiseBank (Hauptbahnhof)
S-Flat (Hauptbahnhof; per 15min €1; ⊙24hr) Web access upstairs in the train station.
Tourist Office (www.tourismus.nuernberg.de) Künstlerhaus (☑233 60; Königstrasse 93; ⊙9am-7pm Mon-Sat, 10am-4pm Sun) Hauptmarkt (Hauptmarkt 18; ⊙9am-6pm Mon-Sat, 10am-4pm Sun May-Oct)

ℹ Getting There & Away

AIR Nuremberg airport (NUE; www.airport-nuernberg.de), 5km north of the centre, is served by regional and international carriers, including Lufthansa, Air Berlin and Air France.

BUS Buses to destinations across Europe leave from the **main bus station** (ZOB) near the Hauptbahnhof. There's a Touring/Eurolines office nearby. Special Deutsche Bahn express coaches to Prague (€50, 3½ hours, seven daily) leave from outside the Hauptbahnhof.

TRAIN Rail connections from Nuremberg:

» **Berlin** €93, five hours, at least hourly

» **Frankfurt** €51, two hours, at least hourly

» **Hamburg** €122, 4½ hours, nine daily

» **Munich** €52, one hour, twice hourly

» **Vienna** €94.20, five hours, every two hours

ℹ **NÜRNBERG + FÜRTH CARD**

Available to those staying overnight in the two cities, the Nürnberg + Fürth Card (€21) is good for two days of public transport and admission to all museums and attractions in both cities. It can only be purchased from tourist offices or online from Nuremberg's official tourism website.

ℹ Getting Around

TO/FROM THE AIRPORT U-Bahn 2 runs every few minutes from the Hauptbahnhof to the airport (€2.40, 12 minutes). A taxi to the airport will cost you about €16.

BICYCLE Nuremberg has ample bike lanes along busy roads and the Altstadt is pretty bike friendly. For bike hire, try the excellent **Ride on a Rainbow** (☑397 337; www.ride-on-a-rainbow. de; Adam-Kraft-Strasse 55; per day from €10).

PUBLIC TRANSPORT The best transport around the Altstadt is at the end of your legs. Timed tickets on the VGN bus, tram and U-Bahn/S-Bahn networks cost from €1.60. A day pass costs €4.80. Passes bought on Saturday are valid all weekend.

Bamberg
☑0951 / POP 70,000

A disarmingly beautiful architectural masterpiece with an almost complete absence of modern eyesores, Bamberg's entire Altstadt is a Unesco World Heritage Site and one of Bavaria's unmissables. Generally regarded as one of Germany's most attractive settlements, the town is bisected by rivers and canals, and was built by archbishops on seven hills, earning it the sobriquet of 'Franconian Rome'. Students inject some liveliness into its streets, pavement cafes and pubs and no fewer than 10 breweries cook up Bamberg's famous smoked beer, but it's usually wide-eyed tourists who can be seen filing through its narrow medieval streets. The town can be tackled as a day trip from Nuremberg but, to really do it justice and to experience the romantically lit streets once most visitors have left, consider staying the night.

Bamberg

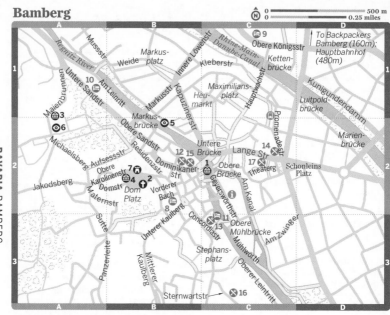

◉ Sights

Bamberger Dom
CATHEDRAL

(Map p156; www.erzbistum-bamberg.de; Domplatz; ⊙8am-6pm Apr-Oct, to 5pm Nov-Mar) The quartet of spires of Bamberg's Dom soars above the cityscape. Founded by Heinrich II in 1004, its current appearance dates to the early 13th century and is the outcome of a Romanesque-Gothic duel between church architects after the original and its immediate successor burnt down in the 12th century. The pillars have the original light hues of Franconian sandstone thanks to Ludwig I, who eradicated all postmedieval decoration in the early 19th century.

The interior contains superb and often intriguing works of art. In the north aisle, you'll spot the **Lächelnde Engel** (Smiling Angel), who smirkingly hands the martyr's crown to the headless St Denis.

In the west choir is the marble tomb of **Pope Clemens II**, the only papal burial place north of the Alps. Of the several altars, the **Bamberger Altar**, carved by Veit Stoss in 1523, is worth closer inspection. Because its central theme is the birth of Christ, it's also called the Christmas Altar.

However, the Dom's star attraction is the statue of the knight-king, the **Bamberger Reiter**. Nobody has a clue as to either the name of the artist or the young king on the steed. The canopy above the statue represents the heavenly Jerusalem, suggesting the mysterious figure may have been revered as a saint.

Altes Rathaus
HISTORIC BUILDING

(Map p156; Obere Brücke) The best views of the Gothic 1462 Altes Rathaus, which perches on a tiny artificial island between two bridges like a ship in dry dock, are from the small Geyerswörthsteg footbridge across the Regnitz. Look for the cherub's leg sticking out from the fresco on the east side.

For closer views, turning at the end of the Geyerswörthsteg then right again onto Obere Brücke brings you face to facade with the imposing tower, a baroque addition by Balthasar Neumann. It provides access to the precious porcelain and faiences – mostly from Strasbourg and Meissen – housed in the **Sammlung Ludwig Bamberg** (Map p156; ☑871 871; Obere Brücke 1; adult/concession €3.50/2.50; ⊙9.30am-4.30pm Tue-Sun).

Historisches Museum
MUSEUM

(Map p156; ☑519 0746; www.museum.bamberg. de; Domplatz 7; adult/concession €5/4.50; ⊙9am-5pm Tue-Sun May-Oct) Bamberg's main museum fills the **Alte Hofhaltung** (Old Court Hall), a former prince-bishops' palace near

Bamberg

the cathedral, with a mixed bag of exhibits. These include a model of the pilgrimage church Vierzehnheiligen and the Bamberger Götzen, ancient stone sculptures found in the region. Often of greater interest are the expertly curated special exhibitions (some of which run through the winter), which examine aspects of the region's past in more detail.

Neue Residenz PALACE
(Map p156; ☑519 390; www.schloesser.bayern.de; Domplatz 8; adult/child €4.50/3.50; ⊙9am-6pm Apr-Sep, 10am-4pm Oct-Mar) Home to Bamberg's prince-bishops from 1703 until secularisation in 1802, 45-minute guided tours of Neue Residenz take in some 40 stuccoed rooms crammed with furniture and tapestries from the 17th and 18th centuries.

The palace also hosts a small branch of the **Bayerische Staatsgalerie** (Bavarian State Gallery). Its strengths are in medieval, Renaissance and baroque paintings, with works by Anthony Van Dyck, Hans Baldung Grien and Cranach the Elder.

The third attraction here is the small but exquisite baroque **Rosengarten** (Rose Garden), from where the Altstadt's sea of red rooftops spread out below.

Fränkisches Brauereimuseum MUSEUM
(Map p156; ☑530 16; www.brauereimuseum.de; Michaelsberg 10f; adult/concession €3/2.50; ⊙1-5pm Wed-Fri, 11am-5pm Sat & Sun Apr-Oct) Located next to the Kloster St Michael, this comprehensive brewery museum exhibits heaps of period mashing, boiling and bottling implements, as well as everything to do with local suds, such as beer mats, tankards, enamel beer signs and lots of photos and documentation. If the displays have left you dry mouthed, quench your thirst in the small pub.

Kloster St Michael MONASTERY
(Map p156; Franziskanergasse 2; ⊙9am-6pm) Above Domplatz, at the top of Michaelsberg, is the Benedictine Kloster St Michael, a former monastery and now an aged people's home. The monastery **church** is a must-see, both for its baroque art and the meticulous depictions of nearly 600 medicinal plants and flowers on the vaulted ceiling. The manicured garden terrace boasts a splendid city panorama.

🏃 Tours

BierSchmecker Tour WALKING TOUR
(adult €20) Possibly the most tempting tour of the amazingly varied offerings at the tourist office (p159) is the self-guided BierSchmecker Tour. The price includes entry to the Franconian Brewery Museum (depending on the route taken), plus five beer vouchers valid in five pubs and breweries, an English information booklet, a route map and a souvenir stein.

🛏 Sleeping

Hotel Sankt Nepomuk HOTEL €€
(Map p156; ☑984 20; www.hotel-nepomuk.de; Obere Mühlbrücke; r €95-145; 🛜) Aptly named after the patron saint of bridges, this is a classy establishment in a half-timbered former mill right on the Regnitz. It has a superb restaurant (mains €15 to €30) with a terrace, 24 comfy rustic rooms and bikes for rent.

Barockhotel am Dom HOTEL €€
(Map p156; ☑540 31; www.barockhotel.de; Vorderer Bach 4; s/d from €77/99; 🅿🛜) The sugary facade, a sceptre's swipe from the Dom, gives a hint of the baroque heritage and original details within. The 19 rooms have sweeping views of the Dom or the roofs of the Altstadt, and breakfast is served in a 14th-century vault.

BAVARIA BAMBERG

DON'T MISS

KLEIN VENEDIG

A row of diddy, half-timbered cottages once inhabited by fishermen and their families makes up Bamberg's **Klein Venedig** (Little Venice; Map p156), which clasps the Regnitz' east bank between Markusbrücke and Untere Brücke. The little homes balance on poles set into the water and are fronted by tiny gardens and terraces (wholly unlike Venice, but who cares). Klein Venedig is well worth a stroll but looks at least as pretty from a distance, especially when red geraniums tumble from the many window boxes.

Hotel Residenzschloss HOTEL €€€
(Map p156; ☎609 10; www.residenzschloss.com; Untere Sandstrasse 32; r €109-199; P⊖🛜) Bamberg's grandest digs occupy a palatial building formerly used as a hospital. But have no fear, as the swanky furnishings – from the Roman-style steam bath to the flashy piano bar – have little in common with institutional care. High-ceilinged rooms are business standard though display little historical charm. Bus 916 from the ZOB stops nearby.

Hotel Europa HOTEL €€
(Map p156; ☎309 3020; www.hotel-europa-bamberg.de; Untere Königstrasse 6-8; r €89-119) The Europa is a spick-and-span but unfussy affair above the town's most respected Italian restaurant, just outside the Altstadt. Ask for a room at the front with views of the Dom and the red-tiled roofs of the Altstadt. Breakfast is in the restaurant or out in the sunny courtyard.

Backpackers Bamberg HOSTEL €
(☎222 1718; www.backpackersbamberg.de; Heiliggrabstrasse 4; dm €15-18, s/d €27/40; 🛜) Bamberg's backpacker hostel is a funky but well-kept affair, with clean dorms, a fully functional kitchen and a quiet, family-friendly atmosphere. Make sure you let staff know when you're arriving, as it's left unmanned for most of the day. Located around 400m north along Luitpoldstrasse from the Luitpoldbrücke.

Campingplatz Insel CAMPGROUND €
(☎563 20; www.campinginsel.de; Am Campingplatz 1; tents €4-8, adult/car €5/4) If rustling nylon is your abode of choice, this well-equipped site, in a tranquil spot right on the river, is the sole camping option. Take bus 918 to Campingplatz.

Eating & Drinking

Messerschmidt FRANCONIAN €€
(Map p156; ☎297 800; Lange Strasse 41; mains €12-25; ⏲lunch & dinner) This stylish gourmet eatery may be ensconced in the house where aviation engineer Willy Messerschmidt was born, but there's nothing 'plane' about dining here. The place oozes old-world charm, with dark woods, white linens and traditionally formal service. Sharpen your molars on platters of roast duck and red cabbage out on the alfresco terrace overlooking a pretty park, or in the attached wine tavern.

Schlenkerla FRANCONIAN €
(Map p156; ☎560 60; Dominikanerstrasse 6; dishes €5-10; ⏲9.30am-11.30pm) At the foot of the cathedral, this local legend is a dark, rustic 14th-century tavern with hefty wooden tables groaning with scrumptious Franconian fare and its own superb *Rauchbier,* poured straight from oak barrels.

Kornblume ORGANIC €€
(☎917 1760; Kapellenstrasse 22; mains €7-22; ⏲5.30pm-midnight Wed-Mon, plus 11.30am-2pm Sun; 🖉) Don't be deterred by the somewhat style-absent decor at this family-run place 1.5km east of the centre, as the tasty food is lovingly prepared and strict organic and ecofriendly principles impeccably upheld. The menu reads like a vegetarian's antioxidant bible, though the occasional meat dish also makes an appearance. Take bus 905 to Wunderburg.

Zum Sternla FRANCONIAN €
(Map p156; ☎287 50; Lange Strasse 46; mains €4-12.50; ⏲10am-11pm) Bamberg's oldest *Wirtshaus* (inn), Zum Sternla was established in 1380 and the camaraderie among its patrons has seemingly changed little in the intervening years. Bargain-priced staples include pork dishes, steaks, dumplings and sauerkraut, as well as specials, but it's a great, non-touristy place for traditional *Brotzeit* (snack) or just a pretzel and a beer. The menu is helpfully translated from Franconian into German.

Spezial-Keller BREWERY €
(Map p156; ☎548 87; Sternwartstrasse 8; dishes €5-12; ⏲3pm-late Tue-Sat, from 10am Sun) Quite a hike out of town, but the superb *Rauchbier* served here is your reward, along with

great views of the Dom and the Altstadt from the beer garden.

Klosterbräu BREWERY €
(Map p156; ☑522 65; Obere Mühlbrücke 1-3; mains €6-12; ☉10.30am-11pm Mon-Fri, 10am-11pm Sat, 10am-10pm Sun) This beautiful half-timbered brewery is Bamberg's oldest. It draws *Stammgäste* (regular local drinkers) and tourists alike who wash down filling slabs of meat and dumplings with its excellent range of ales. English-language brewery tours on request.

Ambräusianum PUB €
(Map p156; ☑509 0262; Dominikanerstrasse 10; dishes €7-15; ☉11am-11pm Tue-Sat, 11am-9pm Sun) Bamberg's only brewpub does a killer *Weisswurst* breakfast – parsley-speckled veal sausage served with a big freshly baked pretzel and a *Weissbier* – as well as schnitzel, pork knuckle and *Flammkuchen* (Alsatian pizza) that'll have you waddling out the door like a Christmas goose.

❶ Information

Post Office (Ludwigstrasse 25)

Tourist Office (☑297 6200; www.bamberg.info; Geyerswörthstrasse 5; ☉9.30am-6pm Mon-Fri, to 4pm Sat, to 2.30pm Sun) Slightly visitor-weary office in a new purpose-built complex. Staff sell the three-day Bambergcard (€12) which provides admission to city attractions, use of city buses and a Unesco-themed walking tour.

❶ Getting There & Around

BUS Several buses, including 901, 902 and 931, connect the train station with the **central bus station** (ZOB). Bus 910 goes from the ZOB to Domplatz.

TRAIN Bamberg has the following rail connections:

» **Berlin** €76, 4¼ hours, every two hours

» **Munich** €59, two to 2½ hours, every two hours

» **Nuremberg** €12 to €21, 40 to 60 minutes, four hourly

» **Würzburg** €19, one hour, twice hourly

Bayreuth

☑0921 / POP 72,600

Even without its Wagner connections, Bayreuth would still be an interesting detour from Nuremberg or Bamberg for its baroque architecture and curious palaces. But it's for the annual Wagner Festival that 60,000 opera devotees make a pilgrimage to this neck of the *Wald*.

Bayreuth's glory began in 1735 when Wilhelmine, sister of King Frederick the Great of Prussia, was forced to marry stuffy Margrave Friedrich. Bored with the local scene, the cultured Anglo-oriented Wilhelmine invited the finest artists, poets, composers and architects in Europe to court. The period bequeathed some eye-catching buildings, still on display for all to see.

⊙ Sights

Outside of the Wagner Festival (see box, p160) from late July to the end of August, the streets of Bayreuth slip into a kind of provincial slumber, although the town's strong musical traditions ensure there are good dramatic and orchestral performances all year.

Markgräfliches Opernhaus OPERA HOUSE
(☑759 6922; Opernstrasse 14; tours adult/concession €5.50/4.50; ☉tours 9am-6pm daily Apr-Sep, occasional weekends Oct-Mar) Designed by Giuseppe Galli Bibiena, a famous 18th-century architect from Bologna, Bayreuth's opera house is one of Europe's most stunningly ornate baroque theatres. Germany's largest opera house until 1871, it has a lavish interior smothered in carved, gilded and marbled wood. However, Richard Wagner considered it too modest for his serious work and conducted here just once. The 45-minute sound-and-light multimedia show is in German only but, even if you don't speak the local lingo, tours are still worth it just to ogle at the show-stopping auditorium.

Neues Schloss PALACE
(☑759 6920; Ludwigstrasse 21; adult/concession €5.50/4.50; ☉9am-6pm daily Apr-Sep, 10am-4pm Tue-Sun Oct-Mar) The Neues Schloss, which opens into the vast **Hofgarten** (admission free; ☉24hr), lies a short distance to the south of the main shopping street, Maxmilianstrasse. A riot of rococo style, the margrave's residence after 1753 features a vast collection of 18th-century porcelain made in Bayreuth. The annual VIP opening of the Wagner Festival is held in the Cedar Room. Also worth a look is the Spiegelscherbenkabinett (Broken Mirror Cabinet), which is lined with irregular shards of broken mirror – supposedly Wilhelmine's response to the vanity of her era.

Richard Wagner Museum – Haus Wahnfried MUSEUM
(www.wagnermuseum.de; Richard-Wagner-Strasse 48) In the early 1870s King Ludwig II, Wagner's most devoted fan, gave the great composer

WAGNER FESTIVAL

The **Wagner Festival** (www.bayreuther-festspiele.de) has been a summer fixture in Bayreuth for over 130 years and is generally regarded as the top Wagner event anywhere in the world. The festival lasts for 30 days (from late July to late August), with each performance attended by an audience of just over 1900. Demand is insane, with an estimated 500,000 fans vying for less than 60,000 tickets. Until recently all tickets were allocated in a shady lottery with preference given to 'patrons' and 'Wagner enthusiasts'. Ordinary, unconnected fans sometimes had to wait five to 10 years before 'winning' a seat. However, in a bid to introduce a bit more transparency into proceedings, the festival organisers recently decided to release some tickets onto the open market through travel agencies, making the procedure of bagging a seat considerably less frustrating and angering many a Wagner society in the process. Alternatively, it is still possible to lay siege to the box office two and a half hours before performances begin in the hope of snapping up cheap returned tickets, but there's no guarantee you'll get in.

Once in the Festspielhaus, ticket holders to one of Germany's premier classical music festivals face uncomfortable hard wood seats and poor ventilation – all part of the experience, diehards claim.

the cash to build Haus Wahnfried, a minimansion on the northern edge of the Hofgarten. The building now houses the Richard Wagner Museum, but at the time of research it was closed for renovation and would remain that way until at least 2013.

Despite the ongoing building work, you can still sneak around the back of the house to see the unmarked, ivy-covered tomb containing Wagner and his wife Cosima. The sandstone grave of his loving canine companion Russ stands nearby.

Festspielhaus OPERA HOUSE
(☎787 80; www.bayreuther-festspiele.de; Festspielhügel 1-2; adult/concession €5/3) North of the Hauptbahnhof, the main venue for Bayreuth's annual Wagner Festival is the Festspielhaus, constructed in 1872 with King Ludwig II's backing. The structure was specially designed to accommodate Wagner's massive theatrical sets, with three storeys of mechanical works hidden below stage. It's still one of the largest opera venues in the world. Tours are available daily most of the year; check the website for details. Take bus 305 to Am Festspielhaus.

Eremitage PARK
Around 6km east of the centre lies the Eremitage, a lush park girding the **Altes Schloss** (☎759 6937; adult/concession €4.50/3.50; ⊙9am-6pm Apr-Sep), Friedrich and Wilhelmine's summer residence. Visits to the palace are by guided tour only and take in the Chinese Mirror Room where Countess Wilhelmine penned her memoirs.

Also in the park is horseshoe-shaped Neues Schloss (not to be confused with the one in town), which centres on the amazing mosaic Sun Temple with gilded Apollo sculpture. Around both palaces you'll find numerous grottoes, follies and gushing fountains. To get there take bus 302 from Markt.

Maisel's Brauerei-und-Büttnerei-Museum MUSEUM, BREWERY
(☎401 234; www.maisel.com/museum; Kulmbacher Strasse 40; tours adult/concession €4/2; ⊙tours 2pm daily) For a fascinating look at the brewing process, head to this enormous museum next door to the brewery of one of Germany's top wheat-beer producers. The 90-minute guided tour takes you into the bowels of the 19th-century plant, with atmospheric rooms filled with 4500 beer mugs and amusing artefacts. Visits conclude with a glass of cloudy *Weissbier* (wheat beer).

🛏 Sleeping

Don't even think of attempting a sleepover in Bayreuth during the Wagner Festival as rooms are booked out months in advance.

Hotel Goldener Anker HOTEL €€€
(☎787 7740; www.anker-bayreuth.de; Opernstrasse 6; s €98-128, d €148-198; P⊙) The refined elegance of this hotel, owned by the same family since the 16th century, is hard to beat. It's just a few metres from the opera house, in the pedestrian zone. Many of the rooms are decorated in heavy traditional style with swag curtains, dark woods and antique touches. Parking is €15 a day.

Hotel Goldener Hirsch HOTEL €€
(☑1504 4000; www.bayreuth-goldener-hirsch.de; Bahnhofstrasse 13; s €65-85, d €85-110; P@�)
Just across from the train station, the 'Golden Reindeer' looks a bit stuffy from the outside, but once indoors you'll discover crisp, well-maintained rooms with contemporary furniture and unscuffed, whitewashed walls. Some of the 40 rooms have baths. Parking is free.

Gasthof Hirsch GUESTHOUSE €
(☑267 14; St Georgen Strasse 6; dm/d €25/50)
Though a bit of a hike from the train station, some of it uphill, this guesthouse is a decent budget option with well-furnished doubles or a three-bed dorm with its own piano. Bathrooms are shared but there are hot- and cold-water basins in all rooms. Calling ahead is advised as there's no reception.

DJH Hostel HOSTEL €
(☑764 380; www.bayreuth.jugendherberge.de; Universitätsstrasse 28; dm €17.60) This excellent 140-bed hostel near the university has comfortable, fresh rooms, a relaxed atmosphere and heaps of guest facilities.

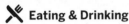

✗ Eating & Drinking

Oskar FRANCONIAN, BAVARIAN €€
(☑516 0553; Maximilianstrasse 33; mains €6-15; ☺8am-1am Mon-Sat, from 9am Sun) At the heart of the pedestrianised shopping boulevard, this multitasking, open-all-hours bar-cafe-restaurant is Bayreuth's busiest eatery. It's good for a busting Bavarian breakfast, a light lunch in the covered garden cafe, a full-on dinner feast in the dark-wood restaurant, or a *Landbier* and a couple of tasty Bayreuth bratwursts anytime you feel.

Kraftraum CAFE €
(Sophienstrasse 16; mains €6-8; ☺8am-1am Mon-Fri, from 9am Sat & Sun; ☑) This vegetarian eatery has plenty to tempt even the most committed meat eaters, including pastas, jacket potatoes, soups and huge salads. The retroish, shabby-chic interior empties on sunny days when everyone plumps for the alfresco seating out on the cobbles. Tempting weekend brunches (€12.50) always attract a large crowd.

Rosa Rosa BISTRO, BAR €
(☑685 02; Von-Römer-Strasse 2; mains €3-7.50; ☺5pm-1am Mon-Fri, from 11am Sat, from 4pm Sun; ☑) Join Bayreuth's chilled crowd at this bistro-cum-pub for belly-filling portions of salad, pasta and vegie fare, as well as seasonal dishes from the big specials board, or just a Friedenfelser beer in the evening. The poster-lined walls keep you up to date on the latest acts to hit town.

Hansl's Wood Oven Pizzeria PIZZERIA €
(☑543 44; Friedrichsstrasse 15; pizzas from €4.30)
The best pizza in town is found at this hole in the wall. A checklist menu lets you choose your own toppings and, voila, you can name your creation.

BAVARIA BAYREUTH

RICHARD WAGNER

With the backing of King Ludwig II, Richard Wagner (1813–83), the gifted, Leipzig-born composer and notoriously poor manager of money, turned Bayreuth into a mecca of opera and high-minded excess. Bayreuth profited from its luck and, it seems, is ever grateful.

For Wagner, listening to opera was meant to be work and he tested his listeners wherever possible. *Götterdämmerung, Parsifal, Tannhäuser* and *Tristan and Isolde* are grandiose pieces that will jolt any audience geared for light entertainment. Four days of *The Ring of the Nibelung* are good for limbering up.

After poring over Passau and a few other German cities, Wagner designed his own festival hall in Bayreuth. The unique acoustics are bounced up from a below-stage orchestra via reflecting boards onto the stage and into the house. The design took the body density of a packed house into account, still a remarkable achievement today.

Wagner was also a notorious womaniser, an infamous anti-Semite and a hardliner towards 'non-Europeans'. So extreme were these views that even Friedrich Nietzsche called Wagner's works 'inherently reactionary, and inhumane'. Wagner's works, and by extension Wagner himself, were embraced as a symbol of Aryan might by the Nazis and, even today, there is great debate among music lovers about the 'correctness' of supporting Wagner's music and the Wagner Festival in Bayreuth.

Underground
BAR

(☑633 47; Von-Römer-Strasse 15; ☺from 7pm Tue-Sun Sep-May, Mon-Sun Jun-Aug) Squeezed into a cellar space shaped like a London Underground train, and decked out as such with hard seats and Tube logos, this bar-cafe has a gay clientele, though the crowd's usually as mixed as the cocktails.

❶ Information

Bayreuth Card (72hr €11.50) Good for unlimited trips on city buses, museum entry and a two-hour guided city walk (in German).

Post Office (Hauptbahnhof)

Sparkasse (Opernstrasse 12)

Tourist Office (☑885 748; www.bayreuth-tourismus.de; Opernstrasse 22; ☺9am-7pm Mon-Fri, 9am-6pm Sat year-round, plus 10am-2pm Sun May-Oct) Has a train ticket booking desk and a worthwhile gift shop.

❶ Getting There & Away

Most rail journeys between Bayreuth and other towns in Bavaria require a change in Nuremberg:

» **Munich** Change in Nuremberg; €65, 2½ hours, hourly

» **Nuremberg** €19, one hour, hourly

» **Regensburg** Change in Nuremberg; €26 to €41, 2¼ hours, hourly

Coburg

☑09561 / POP 41,000

If marriage is diplomacy by another means, Coburg's rulers were surely masters of the art. Over four centuries, the princes and princesses of the house of Saxe-Coburg intrigued, romanced and ultimately wed themselves into the dynasties of Belgium, Bulgaria, Denmark, Portugal, Russia, Sweden and, most prominently, Great Britain. The crowning achievement came in 1857, when Albert of Saxe-Coburg-Gotha took his vows with first cousin Queen Victoria, founding the present British royal family. The British royals quietly adopted the less-German name of Windsor during WWI.

Coburg languished in the shadow of the Iron Curtain during the Cold War, all but closed in by East Germany on three sides, but since reunification the town has undergone a revival. Its proud Veste is one of Germany's finest medieval fortresses. What's more, some sources contend that the original hot dog was invented here.

BAVARIA COBURG

◉ Sights & Activities

Coburg's epicentre is the magnificent Markt, a beautifully renovated square radiating a colourful, aristocratic charm. The fabulous Renaissance facades and ornate oriels of the **Stadthaus** (town house) and the **Rathaus** vie for attention, while a greening bronze of Prince Albert, looking rather more flamboyant and Teutonic medieval than the Brits are used to seeing him, calmly surveys the scene.

Veste Coburg
FORTRESS, MUSEUM

(www.kunstsammlungen-coburg.de; adult/concession €5/2.50; ☺9.30am-5pm daily Apr-Oct, 1-4pm Tue-Sun Nov-Mar) Towering above Coburg's centre is a story-book medieval fortress, the Veste Coburg. With its triple ring of fortified walls, it's one of the most impressive fortresses in Germany but, curiously, has a dearth of foreign visitors. It houses the vast collection of the **Kunstsammlungen**, with works by star painters such as Rembrandt, Dürer and Cranach the Elder. The elaborate Jagdintarsien-Zimmer (Hunting Marquetry Room) is a superlative example of carved woodwork.

Protestant reformer Martin Luther, hoping to escape an imperial ban, sought refuge at the fortress in 1530. His former quarters have a writing desk and, in keeping with the Reformation, a rather plain bed.

The **Veste-Express** (one-way/return €3/4; ☺10am-5pm Apr-Oct), a tourist train, leaves from the tourist office and makes the trip to the fortress every 30 minutes. Otherwise it's a steep 3km climb on foot.

Schloss Ehrenburg
CASTLE

(☑808 832; www.sgvcoburg.de; Schlossplatz; adult/child free; ☺tours hourly 9am-5pm Tue-Sun Apr-Sep, 10am-4pm Tue-Sun Oct-Mar) The lavish Schloss Ehrenburg was once the town residence of the Coburg dukes. Albert spent his childhood in this sumptuous, tapestry-lined palace, and Queen Victoria stayed in a room with Germany's first flushing toilet (1860). The splendid **Riesensaal** (Hall of Giants) has a baroque ceiling supported by 28 statues of Atlas.

Coburger Puppenmuseum
MUSEUM

(www.coburger-puppenmuseum.de; Rückerstrasse 2-3; adult/child €4/2; ☺10am-4pm daily Apr-Oct, 11am-4pm Tue-Sun Nov-Mar) Spanning 33 rooms, this delightfully old-fashioned museum displays a collection of 2000 dolls, dollhouses, miniature kitchens and chinaware, some from as far away as England and all dating from between 1800 and 1956. Aptly named 'Hallo Dolly', the stylish cafe next door is ideally situated for restoring calm after all those eerie glass eyes.

 Festivals & Events

Samba Festival
DANCE

(www.samba-festival.de) Believe it or not, Coburg hosts Europe's largest Samba Festival every year in mid-July, an incongruous venue if ever there was one. This orgy of song and dance attracts almost 100 bands and up to 200,000 scantily-clad, bum-wiggling visitors. Now what would Queen Vic have made of that?

🛏 Sleeping & Eating

Romantik Hotel Goldene Traube
HOTEL €€

(📞8760; www.goldenetraube.com; Am Viktoriabrunnen 2; s €89-99, d €109-129; [P] 🛜) Owner Bernd Glauben is president of the German Sommelier's Union, and you can taste and buy over 400 wines in the charming hotel **wine bar**. These can also be sampled in the two eateries, the Michelin-starred Esszimmer and the less fancy Victora Grill. Rooms are splashed with bright Mediterranean yellows and oranges or else decked out Laura Ashley style. Located in the Altstadt.

Hotelpension Bärenturm
GUESTHOUSE €€

(📞318 401; www.baerenturm-hotelpension.de; Untere Anlage 2; s €85, d €110-130; [P] 🛜) For those who prefer their complimentary pillow pack of gummy bears served with a touch of history, Coburg's most characterful digs started life as a defensive tower that was expanded in the early 19th century to house Prince Albert's private tutor. Each of the 15 rooms is a gem boasting squeaky parquet floors, antique-style furniture and regally high ceilings.

DJH Hostel
HOSTEL €

(📞153 30; www.coburg.jugendherberge.de; Parkstrasse 2) Housed in a mock redbrick castle, Schloss Ketschendorf (some 2km from town), Coburg's youth hostel was receiving a comprehensive makeover at the time of research and it wasn't clear when it would be back online. Check the website for details.

Café Prinz Albert
CAFE €

(Ketschengasse 27; snacks & cakes €2-5; ⊙7.30am-6pm Mon-Fri, from 8am Sat, from 1pm Sun) Coburg's links with the British royals are reflected here in both the decor and menu.

The Prince Albert breakfast (€7.60) – a cross-cultural marriage of sausage, egg and Bamberger croissants – is fit for a queen's consort.

Tie
VEGETARIAN €€€

(Leopoldstrasse 14; mains €15-23; ⊙from 5pm Tue-Sun; 🍴) Heavenly (if pricey) food is crafted from fresh organic ingredients at this vegetarian restaurant, where the focus is firmly on the food and not gimmicky decor. Dishes range from vegetarian classics to Asian inspirations, with the odd fish or meat dish for the unconverted.

Ratskeller
FRANCONIAN €

(Markt 1; mains €4.50-13.50; ⊙10am-midnight) Munch on regional dishes from Thuringia and Franconia while kicking back on well-padded leather benches under the heftily vaulted ceiling of Coburg's spectacular town hall.

ℹ Information

Tourist Office (📞898 000; www.coburg -tourist.de; Herrengasse 4; ⊙9am-6.30pm Mon-Fri, 10am-3pm Sat, 10am-2pm Sun Apr-Oct, 9am-5pm Mon-Fri, 10am-3pm Sat Nov-Mar) Helpful office where staff sell the CObook (€14.90), a five-day ticket good for 13 sights in Coburg and around as well as local public transport. English audioguides (€3.50) to the city are also available here.

ℹ Getting There & Away

Coburg has the following rail connections:

» **Bamberg** €11.10, 40 minutes, hourly

» **Bayreuth** €16.40, 1½ hours, hourly

» **Nuremberg** €21.50, 1¾ hours, hourly

Altmühltal Nature Park

The Altmühltal Nature Park is one of Germany's largest nature parks and covers some of Bavaria's most eye-pleasing terrain. The Altmühl River gently meanders through a region of little valleys and hills before joining the Rhine–Main Canal and eventually emptying into the Danube. Outdoor fun on well-marked hiking and biking trails is the main reason to head here, but the river is also ideal for canoeing. There's basic camping in designated spots along the river, and plenty of accommodation in the local area.

The park takes in 2900 sq km of land southwest of Regensburg, south of Nuremberg, east of Treuchtlingen and north of

Eichstätt. The eastern boundaries of the park include the town of Kelheim.

North of the river, activities focus around the towns of Kipfenberg, Beilngries and Riedenburg.

🏃 Activities

Canoeing & Kayaking

The most beautiful section of the river is from Treuchtlingen or Pappenheim to Eichstätt or Kipfenberg, about a 60km stretch that you can do lazily in a kayak or canoe in two to three days. There are lots of little dams along the way, as well as some small rapids about 10km northwest of Dollnstein, so make sure you are up for little bits of portaging. Signs warn of impending doom, but locals say that, if you heed the warning to stay to the right, you'll be safe.

You can hire canoes and kayaks in just about every town along the river. Expect to pay about €15/25 per day for a one-/two-person boat, more for bigger ones. Staff will sometimes haul you and the boats to or from your embarkation point for a small fee.

You can get a full list of boat-hire outlets from the Informationszentrum Naturpark Altmühltal.

San-Aktiv Tours　　　　CANOE RENTAL
(☑09831-4936; www.san-aktiv-tours.com; Otto-Dietrich-Strasse 3, Gunzenhausen) San-Aktiv Tours are the largest and best-organised of the canoe-hire companies in the park, with a network of vehicles to shuttle canoes, bicycles and people around the area. Trips through the park run from April to October, and you can canoe alone or join a group. Packages generally include the canoe, swim vests, maps, instructions, transfer back to the embarkation point and, for overnight tours, luggage transfer and lodgings.

Cycling & Hiking

With around 3000km of hiking trails and 800km of cycle trails criss-crossing the landscape, foot and pedal are the best ways to strike out into the park. Cycling trails are clearly labelled and have long rectangular brown signs bearing a bike symbol. Hiking-trail markers are yellow. The most popular cycling route is the Altmühltal Radweg, which runs parallel to the river for 166km. The Altmühltal-Panoramaweg stretching 200km between Gunzenhausen and Kelheim is a picturesque hiking route that crosses the entire park from west to east.

You can hire bikes in almost every town within the park, and prices are more or less uniform. Most bike-hire agencies will also store bicycles. Ask for a list of bike-hire outlets at the Informationszentrum Naturpark Altmühltal.

In Eichstätt, **Fahrradgarage** (☑08421-2110; www.fahrradgarage.de; Herzoggasse 3) hires out bicycles for €10 per day. Staff will bring the bikes to you or take you and the bikes to anywhere in the park for an extra fee.

Rock Climbing

The worn cliffs along the Altmühl River offer some appealing terrain for climbers of all skill levels. The medium-grade 45m-high rock face of Burgsteinfelsen, located between the towns of Dollnstein and Breitenfurt, has routes from the fourth to eighth climbing levels, with stunning views of the valley. The Dohlenfelsen face near the town of Wellheim has a simpler expanse that's more suitable for children. The Informationszentrum Naturpark Altmühltal can provide more details on the region's climbing options.

ℹ Information

The park's main information centre is in Eichstätt, a charmingly historic town at the southern end of the park that makes an excellent base for exploring.

For information on the park and for help with planning an itinerary, contact the **Information-szentrum Naturpark Altmühltal** (☑08421-987 60; www.naturpark-altmuehltal.de; Notre Dame 1; ⊙9am-5pm Mon-Sat, 10am-5pm Sun Apr-Oct, 8am-noon & 2-4pm Mon-Thu, 8am-noon Fri Nov-Mar) in Eichstätt. The website is tricky to navigate but does have a lot of brochures for free download.

ℹ Getting There & Around

There are bus and train connections between Eichstätt and all the major milestones along the river including, from west to east, Gunzenhausen, Treuchtlingen and Pappenheim.

BUS From mid-April to October the FreizeitBus Altmühltal-Donautal takes passengers and their bikes around the park. Buses normally run three times a day from mid-April to early October (see www.naturpark-altmuehltal.de to download the timetable). Route 1 runs from Regensburg and Kelheim to Riedenburg on weekends and holidays only. Route 2 travels between Eichstätt, Beilngries, Dietfurt and Riedenburg, with all-day service on weekends and holidays and restricted service on weekdays. All-day tickets, which cost €10.50/7.50 for passengers with/without

BAVARIA ALTMÜHLTAL NATURE PARK

bicycles, or €23.50/17.50 per family, are bought from the driver.

TRAIN Hourly trains run between Eichstätt Bahnhof and Treuchtlingen (€5.50, 25 minutes), and between Treuchtlingen and Gunzenhausen (€4, 15 minutes). RE trains from Munich that run through Eichstätt Bahnhof also stop in Dollnstein, Solnhofen and Pappenheim.

Eichstätt

☑ 08421 / POP 13,800

Hugging a tight bend in the Altmühl River, Eichstätt radiates a tranquil Mediterranean-style flair. Cobbled streets meander past elegantly Italianate buildings and leafy piazzas, giving this sleepy town a general sense of refinement. Italian architects, notably Gabriel de Gabrieli and Maurizio Pedetti, rebuilt the town after Swedes razed the place during the Thirty Years' War (1618–48) and it has since remained undamaged. Since 1980 many of its baroque facades have concealed faculties belonging to Germany's sole Catholic university.

Eichstätt is pretty enough, but is really just a jumping off and stocking up point for flits into the wilds of Altmühltal Nature Park. You'll be chomping at the bit, eager to hit a trail or grab a paddle, if you stay more than a day.

☉ Sights

Dom　　　　　　　　　　　　　　CHURCH
(www.bistum-eichstaett.de/dom; Domplatz; ⊙7.15am -7.30pm) Eichstätt's centre is dominated by the richly adorned Dom. Standout features include an enormous 16th-century stained-glass window by Hans Holbein the Elder, and the carved sandstone **Pappenheimer Altar** (1489–97), depicting a pilgrimage from Pappenheim to Jerusalem. The seated statue is of St Willibald, the town's first bishop.

The adjoining **Domschatzmuseum** (Cathedral Treasury; ☑507 42; Residenzplatz 7; adult/concession €3/1.50, Sun €1; ⊙10.30am-5pm Wed-Fri, 10am-5pm Sat & Sun Apr-Nov) includes the robes of 8th-century English-born bishop St Willibald and baroque Gobelin tapestries.

Willibaldsburg　　　　　　　　CASTLE
(☑4730; Burgstrasse 19; ⊙9am-6pm Tue-Sun Apr-Oct, 10am-4pm Tue-Sun Nov-Mar) The walk or drive up to the hilltop castle of Willibaldsburg (1355) is worth it for the views across the valley from the formally laid-out **Bastiongarten**; many locals also head

up here on sunny days for the nearby beer garden. The castle itself house two museums, the most interesting of which is the **Jura-Museum** (Burgstrasse 19; adult/concession €4.50/3.50; ⊙9am-6pm Apr-Sep, 10am-4pm Oct-Mar, closed Mon) specialising in fossils and containing a locally found archaeopteryx (the oldest-known fossil bird), as well as aquariums with living specimens of the fossilised animals.

Kloster St Walburga　　　　　CONVENT
(www.abtei-st-walburga.de; Westenstrasse; ⓘ) The final resting place of St Willibald's sister, the Kloster St Walburga is a popular local pilgrimage destination. Every year between mid-October and late February, water oozes from Walburga's relics in the underground chapel and drips down into a catchment. The nuns bottle diluted versions of the so-called *Walburgaöl* (Walburga oil) and give it away to the faithful. A staircase from the lower chapel leads to an off-limits upper chapel where you can catch a glimpse through the grill of beautiful ex-voto tablets and other trinkets left as a thank you to the saint. The main **St Walburga Church** above has a glorious rococo interior.

Residenz　　　　　　　　　　　PALACE
(Residenzplatz; admission €1; ⊙tours 10.15am, 11am, 11.45am, 2pm, 2.45pm & 3.30pm Sat & Sun Apr-Oct) The prince-bishops lived it up at the baroque Residenz, built between 1725 and 1736 by Gabriel de Gabrieli. Inside the stunning main staircase and a hall of mirrors stick in the mind, though you'll have to arrive on a weekend to see them. In the square outside rises a late 18th-century golden statue of the Madonna atop a 19m-high column.

🛏 Sleeping & Eating

Hotel Adler　　　　　　　　　HOTEL €€
(☑6767; www.adler-eichstaett.de; Marktplatz 22; s €67-75, d €91-115; ℗) A superb ambience reigns in this ornate 300-year-old building, Eichstätt's top digs. Sleeping quarters are bright and breezy, and the generous breakfast buffet a proper set up for a day on the trail or river. Despite the posh feel, this hotel welcomes hiker and bikers.

Fuchs　　　　　　　　　　　　HOTEL €
(☑6789; www.hotel-fuchs.de; Ostenstrasse 8; s €40-48, d €60-80; ⊛) This central, family-run hotel, with under-floor heating in the

BAVARIA EICHSTÄTT

Southern Germany's Finest

Slither down a mountain, go full circle around an idyllic walled town, raise a tankard at Oktoberfest, explore an opulent chateau and gaze in awe at a highly-strung cathedral interior – only then can you say you've experienced the essence of Germany's south.

Castles

1 You could spend a month or more castle-hopping from fairy-tale pile to hilltop fortress to lavish palace. Versailles-crazy King Ludwig II commissioned some of the most opulent, but wherever you find yourself in the region, you're never far away from a Schloss.

Old Towns

2 Quaint, time-warped little towns are what travelling in rural areas of the south is all about. Magnificent town halls, medieval towers, cobbled squares and countless Gothic and baroque facades deliver a mega dose of Teutonic civic pride.

Churches

3 From baroque mastery to austere red brick, from uplifting cathedrals to the tiniest onion-domed village chapel, southern Germany boasts a pope's ransom of churches, the most valuable of which have been recognised by Unesco as World Cultural Heritage Sites.

Traditions

4 From Oktoberfest to cuckoo clocks, lederhosen to Christmas markets, Germany's south is a place that takes its customs and traditions seriously. Folk celebrations pepper the calendar so whatever time of year you arrive, you can always join in the fun.

Landscapes

5 Bavaria has just a sliver of the Alps but crams a lot into its peaks. Summer hiking and winter skiing are the main draws, but you can enjoy a stroll in the foothills, especially around the many lakes in the area, at any time of year.

1. Schloss Hohenschwangau (p110) 2. Altes Rathaus, Bamberg (p156)
3. Wieskirche (p113) 4. Christmas Market stall, Nuremberg (p149)

bathrooms, adjoins a cake shop with a sunny dining area. It's convenient to a launch ramp on the river where you can put in, and you can lock your canoe or kayak in the garage.

DJH Hostel HOSTEL €
(☑980 410; www.eichstaett.jugendherberge.de; Reichenaustrasse 15; dm from €19, d €46.60) This comfy, 122-bed youth hostel provides pretty views of the Altstadt. The double rooms, if available, have their own shower and toilet.

Municipal Camp Site CAMPGROUND €
(☑908 147; www.eichstaett.info/wohnmobilstell platz; Pirkheimerstrasse; per site €7) This basic campground is on the northern bank of the Altmühl River, about 1km southeast of the town centre. It's open year-round but closes for 10 days during the Volksfest (a mini-Oktoberfest) in late August or early September.

Café im Paradeis CAFE €€
(☑3313; Markt 9; mains €5-17; ⊗8am-midnight) This open-all-hours cafe on Markt is a prime spot for people watching wherever the hands of the clock may be. Recharge with a home-cooked meal or just a coffee, either in the antique-lined interior or out on the terrace.

Gasthof Krone BAVARIAN €€
(☑4406; Domplatz 3; mains €7-18; ⊗lunch & dinner) Traditionally garbed waitresses bang down monster platters of local nosh in the beer garden and two-tiered dining room of this lively tavern. Altmühltaler lamb is the speciality here, its meat infused with special flavour by the park's herb-rich meadows.

❶ Information

Post Office (Domplatz 7)
Raiffeisenbank (Domplatz 5)
Tourist Office (☑600 1400; www.eichstaett. info; Domplatz 8; ⊗9am-6pm Mon-Sat, 10am-1pm Sun Apr-Oct, 10am-noon & 2-4pm Mon-Thu, 10am-noon Fri Nov-Mar)

❶ Getting There & Away

Eichstätt has two train stations. Mainline trains stop at the Bahnhof, 5km from the centre, from where coinciding diesel services shuttle to the *Stadtbahnhof* (town station). Trains run hourly between Ingolstadt and Eichstätt (€5.50, 25 minutes) and every two hours to Nuremberg (€18.10, 1½ hours).

REGENSBURG & THE DANUBE

The sparsely populated eastern reaches of Bavaria may live in the shadow of Bavaria's big-hitting attractions, but they hold many historical treasures to rival their neighbours. Top billing goes to Regensburg, a former capital, and one of Germany's prettiest and liveliest cities. From here the Danube gently winds its way to the Italianate city of Passau. Landshut was once the hereditary seat of the Wittelsbach family, and the region has also given the world a pope, none other than incumbent Benedict XVI who was born in Marktl am Inn. Away from the towns, the Bavarian Forest broods in semi-undiscovered remoteness.

Eastern Bavaria was a seat of power in the Dark Ages, ruled by rich bishops at a time when Munich was but a modest trading post. A conquering Napoleon lumped Eastern Bavaria into river districts, and King Ludwig I sought to roll back these changes by recreating the boundaries of a glorified duchy from 1255. Though it brought a sense of renewed Bavarian identity, the area remained very much on the margins of things, giving rise to the odd and appealing mixture of ancient Roman cities, undulating farmland and rugged wilderness that it is today.

Regensburg

☑0941 / POP 135,500
A Roman settlement completed under Emperor Marcus Aurelius, Regensburg was the first capital of Bavaria, the residence of dukes, kings and bishops, and for 600 years an Free Imperial City. Two millennia of history bequeathed the city some of the region's finest architectural heritage, a fact recognised by Unesco in 2006. Though big on the historical wow factor, today's Regensburg is a laid-back and unpretentious sort of place, and a good springboard into the wider region.

◉ Sights

Schloss Thurn und Taxis CASTLE
(Map p169; www.thurnundtaxis.de; Emmeramsplatz 5; tours adult/concession €11.50/9; ⊗tours 11am, 1pm, 2pm, 3pm, 4pm Mon-Fri, additionally 10am & noon Sat & Sun, closed Dec-Mar) In the 15th century, Franz von Taxis (1459–1517) assured his place in history by setting up the first

Regensburg

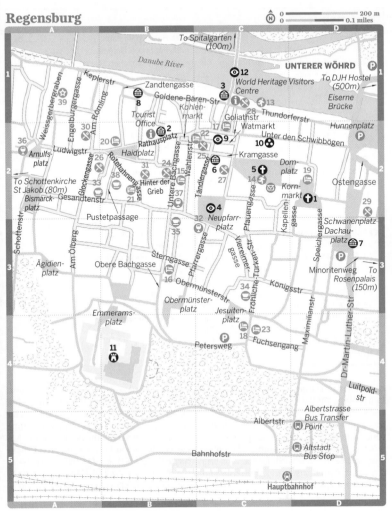

European postal system, which remained a monopoly until the 19th century. In recognition of his services, the family was given a new palace, the former Benedictine monastery St Emmeram, henceforth known as Schloss Thurn und Taxis. It was soon one of the most modern palaces in Europe and featured such luxuries as flushing toilets, central heating and electricity. Tours include a look into the Basilika St Emmeram.

The palace complex also contains the **Schatzkammer** (Map p169; adult/concession €4.50/3.50; ⊘11am-5pm Mon-Fri, 10am-5pm Sat & Sun). The jewellery, porcelain and precious furnishings on display belonged, for many years, to the wealthiest dynasty in Germany. The fortune, administered by Prince Albert II, is still estimated at well over €1 billion.

Dom St Peter CHURCH
(Map p169; Domplatz; ⊘6.30am-6pm Apr-Oct, to 5pm Nov-Mar) It takes a few seconds for your eyes to adjust to the dim interior of Regensburg's soaring landmark, the Dom St Peter, one of Bavaria's grandest Gothic cathedrals. Impressive features inside are the kaleidoscopic stained-glass windows above the choir and in the south transept, and the intricately

Regensburg

gilded altar. Construction dates from the late 13th century, but the distinctive filigree spires weren't added until the 19th century; the extravagant western facade also dates from this period and is festooned with sculptures.

The **Domschatzmuseum** (Map p169; adult/child €2/1; ⊙10am-5pm Tue-Sat, noon-5pm Sun) brims with monstrances, tapestries and other church treasures.

Altes Rathaus & Reichstagsmuseum
HISTORIC BUILDING

(Map p169; Rathausplatz; adult/concession €7.50/4; ⊙English tours 3pm Apr-Oct, 2pm Nov-Mar) The seat of the Reichstag for almost 150 years, the Altes Rathaus is now home to Regensburg's mayors and the **Reichstagsmuseum**. Tours take in not only the lavishly decorated **Reichssaal** (Imperial Hall), but also the original **torture chambers** in the basement. The interrogation room bristles with tools such as the rack, the Spanish donkey (a tall wooden wedge on which the victim was made to sit naked) and spiked chairs. Ask at the nearby tourist office about tickets and times of German-language tours.

Steinerne Brücke
BRIDGE

(Map p169) An incredible feat of engineering for its day, Regensburg's 900-year-old Steinerne Brücke (Stone Bridge) was at one time the only fortified crossing of the Danube. Ensconced in its southern tower is the **Brückturm-Museum** (Map p169; Weisse-Lamm-Gasse 1; adult/concession €2/1.50; ⊙10am-7pm Apr-Oct), a small historical exhibit about the bridge.

Historisches Museum
MUSEUM

(Map p169; ⌀507 2448; Dachauplatz 2-4; adult/concession €2.20/1.10; ⊙10am-4pm Tue, Wed & Fri-Sun, 10am-8pm Thu) A medieval monastery provides a suitably atmospheric backdrop for the city's history museum. The collections plot the region's story from cave dweller to Roman, and medieval trader to 19th-century burgher.

Schottenkirche St Jakob
CHURCH

(Jakobstrasse 3) The sooty 12th-century main portal of the Schottenkirche St Jakob is considered one of the supreme examples of Romanesque architecture in Germany. Its reliefs and sculptures form an iconography that continues to baffle the experts. Sadly it's protected from further pollution by an ageing glass structure that makes the whole thing an eyesore. However, this is more than made up for inside, where pure, tourist-free Romanesque austerity prevails.

Golf Museum
MUSEUM

(Map p169; www.golf-museum.com; Tändlergasse 3; adult/concession €7.50/5; ⊙10am-6pm Mon-Sat) Claiming to be the second most important golf museum in Europe (after the British Golf Museum in Scotland), this unexpected repository of club, tee and score card (including one belonging to King George V of England) backswings its way through golf's illustrious past – interesting, even if you think a green fee is something to do with municipal recycling.

Document Neupfarrplatz
HISTORIC SITE

(Map p169; ✆507 3454; Neupfarrplatz; adult/concession €5/2.50; ⊙tours 2.30pm Thu-Sat Sep-Jun, Thu-Mon Jul & Aug) Excavations in the mid-1990s revealed remains of Regensburg's once-thriving 16th-century Jewish quarter, along with Roman buildings, gold coins and a Nazi bunker. The subterranean Document Neupfarrplatz only provides access to a small portion of the excavated area, but tours feature a nifty multimedia presentation (in German) about the square's history. Back up above, on the square itself, a work by renowned Israeli artist Dani Karavan graces the site of the former synagogue.

Tickets are purchased from Tabak Götz at Neupfarrplatz 3.

Kepler-Gedächtnishaus
MUSEUM

(Kepler Memorial House; Map p169; Keplerstrasse 5; adult/concession €2.20/1.10; ⊙10.30am-4pm Sat & Sun) Disciples of astronomer and mathematician Johannes Kepler should visit the house he lived in while resident in Regensburg.

Alte Kapelle
CHURCH

(Map p169; Alter Kornmarkt 8) South of the Dom, the humble exterior of the graceful Alte Kapelle belies the stunning interior with its rich rococo decorations. The core of the church, however, is about 1000 years old, although the Gothic vaulted ceilings were added in the Middle Ages. The church is open only during services but you can always peek through the wrought-iron grill.

Roman Wall
HISTORIC SITE

The most tangible reminder of the ancient Castra Regina (Regen Fortress), where the name 'Regensburg' comes from, is the remaining Roman wall, which follows Unter den Schwibbögen and veers south onto Dr-Martin-Luther-Strasse. Dating from AD 179 the rough-hewn **Porta Praetoria** (Map p169; Unter den Schwibbögen) arch is a key reminder of the city's heritage.

☞ Tours

Schifffahrt Klinger
BOAT

(Map p169; ✆521 04; www.schifffahrtklinger.de; cruises adult/child from €7.50/4.80) Offers short cruises (50 minutes) on the Danube (available April to late October) and to the Walhalla monument.

Tourist Train Tours
TRAIN

(Map p169; departs Domplatz; adult/family €8/19; ⊙8 tours daily) Multilingual tourist train tours of the city centre take 45 minutes to complete a circuit from the south side of the cathedral. Fares include a free coffee at Haus Heuport.

★☆ Festivals & Events

Dult
BEER

Oktoberfest-style party with beer tents, carousel rides, entertainment and vendors on the Dultplatz, in May and late August/early September.

Weihnachtsmarkt
CHRISTMAS MARKET

The Christmas market has stalls selling roasted almonds, gingerbread and traditional wooden toys. Held at Neupfarrplatz and Schloss Thurn und Taxis during December.

⌷ Sleeping

Regensburg has an unexpectedly wide choice of places to achieve REM, from blue-blooded antique-graced apartments to blood-red suites for fired up honeymooners.

SCHINDLER'S PLAQUE

Oskar Schindler lived in Regensburg for years, and today his house at Watmarkt 5 bears a **plaque** (Map p169) to his achievements commemorated in the Steven Spielberg epic *Schindler's List*.

Hotel Elements
HOTEL €€

(Map p169; ☑3819 8600; www.hotel-elements.de; Alter Kornmarkt 3; apt €135-155) Four elements, four rooms, and what rooms they are! This tiny theme hotel breaks new ground with its imaginative design and is the best-kept secret in Eastern Bavaria. 'Fire' blazes in plush crimson and is just the thing for honeymooning couples, while nautically themed 'Water' is splashed with portholes and a Jacuzzi. 'Air' is spacious and light, as opposed to 'Earth' where colonial chocolate browns and bamboo reign. Reception and breakfast are in the adjoining Caffè Rinaldi.

Petit Hotel Orphée
HOTEL €€

(Map p169; ☑596 020; www.hotel-orphee.de; Wahlenstrasse 1; s €35-125, d €70-135) Behind a humble door in the heart of the city lies a world of genuine charm, unexpected extras and real attention to detail. The striped floors, wrought-iron beds, original sinks and common rooms with soft cushions and well-read books give the feel of a lovingly attended home. Another somewhat grander branch of the hotel is located above the Café Orphée.

Hotel Goldenes Kreuz
HOTEL €€

(Map p169; ☑558 12; www.hotel-goldeneskreuz. de; Haidplatz 7; r €75-125; 🐾) Surely the best deal in town, the nine fairy-tale rooms each bear the name of a crowned head and are fit for a kaiser. Huge mirrors, dark antique and Bauhaus furnishings, four-poster beds, chubby exposed beams and parquet flooring produce a stylishly aristocratic opus in leather, wood, crystal and fabric. Yes, those prices are correct!

Altstadthotel am Pach
HOTEL €€

(Map p169; ☑298 610; www.regensburghotel.de; Untere Bachgasse 9; s €98-124, d €118-144; @🐾) Those who have shaped Regensburg history, from Marcus Aurelius to Emperor Karl V, are commemorated in the 20 rooms of this sleek hotel. Quarters vary in size in size but all are warmly furnished with thick carpets, comfy mattresses and a minibar with complimentary beer and water. If you're tall, you might want to avoid the beamed and slanted rooms in the attic.

Goliath Hotel
HOTEL €€€

(Map p169; ☑200 0900; www.hotel-goliath.de; Goliathstrasse 10; s/d from €125/155; P✳🐾) Right in the heart of the city centre, the 41 rooms at the Goliath are all differently conceived and pristinely serviced. Some have little extras, such as bathroom–bedroom windows and big baths. Funky, but doesn't go the whole boutique hog and staff are surprisingly old school. Parking costs €12.

Brook Lane Hostel
HOSTEL €

(Map p169; ☑696 5521; www.hostel-regensburg.de; Obere Bachgasse 21; dm/s/d from €16/40/50, apt per person €55; 🐾) Regensburg's only backpacker hostel has its very own convenience store, which doubles up as reception; it isn't open 24 hours, so late landers should let staff know in advance. Dorms do the minimum required, but the apartments and doubles here are applaudable deals, especially if you're travelling in a twosome or more. Access to kitchens and washing machines throughout.

Hotel Roter Hahn
HOTEL €€

(Map p169; ☑595 090; www.roter-hahn.com; Rote-Hahnen-Gasse 10; s/d €100/120; P🐾) A bulky beamed ceiling and a glassed-in Roman stone well (of which staff are oblivious) greet you in the lobby of the 'Red Rooster', contrasting with streamlined rooms offering freshly minted amenities. Parking costs €12; request a room on the 2nd floor to access the free wi-fi.

Zum Fröhlichen Türken
HOTEL €€

(Map p169; ☑536 51; www.hotel-zum-froehlichen -tuerken.de; Fröhliche-Türken-Strasse 11; s/d €59/ 84; P) With its comfortable, clean quarters, unstinting breakfast and mild-mannered staff, the 'Jolly Turk' will bring a smile to any budget-minded traveller's face. The pricier rooms have private bathrooms.

Azur-Campingplatz
CAMPGROUND €

(☑270 025; www.azur-camping.de/regensburg; Weinweg 40; per person/tent €8.50/9) A pretty site about 3km from the Altstadt on the southern bank of the Danube. Take bus 6.

DJH Hostel
HOSTEL €

(☑466 2830; www.regensburg.jugendherberge. de; Wöhrdstrasse 60; dm from €21) Regensburg's 186-bed hostel occupies a beautiful old building on a large island about a 10-minute walk north of the Altstadt.

Hotel Am Peterstor
HOTEL €

(Map p169; ☑545 45; www.hotel-am-peterstor.de; Fröhliche-Türken-Strasse 12; s/d €38/48; ⊙reception 7-11am & 4-10.30pm; 🐾) The pale-grey decor might be grim, and the recpetion hours silly, but the location is great, the price is right and staff go out of their way to assist. Make sure you get a non-smoking room as some pong of secondhand smoke. Breakfast is an optional €5 extra.

✗ Eating

'In Regensburg we ate a magnificent lunch, had a divine musical entertainment, an English hostess and a wonderful Moselle wine,' wrote Mozart to his wife Constance in 1790. Available in Mozart's day, but better washed down with a local Kneitinger Pils, is the delectable bratwurst (grilled sausage) and *Händlmaier's Süsser Hausmachersenf*, a distinctive sweet mustard.

Haus Heuport   INTERNATIONAL €€

(Map p169; ☎599 9297; Domplatz 7; mains €7-23; ☺from 9am; ☝) Enter an internal courtyard (flanked by stone blocks where medieval torches were once extinguished) and climb up the grand old wooden staircase to this space-rich Gothic dining hall for eye-to-eye views of the Dom St Peter and an internationally flavoured culinary celebration. The Sunday breakfast buffet runs to a hangover-busting 3pm. Always busy.

Spaghetteria   ITALIAN €

(Map p169; Am Römling 12; dishes €4.50-10; ☺lunch & dinner) Get carbed up at this former 17th-century chapel, where you can splatter six types of pasta with 23 types of sauce, and get out the door for the cost of a cocktail in Munich. The all-you-can-eat buffet (€5 to €6.50) is a cheap way to fill up at lunchtime.

Historische Wurstkuchl   GERMAN €

(Map p169; Thundorfer Strasse 3; 6 sausages €7.80; ☺8am-7pm) Completely submerged several times by the Danube's fickle floods, this titchy eatery has been serving the city's traditional finger-size sausages, grilled over beech wood and dished up with sauerkraut and sweet grainy mustard, since 1135, making it the world's oldest sausage kitchen.

Dicker Mann   BAVARIAN €€

(Map p169; www.dicker-mann.de; Krebsgasse 6; mains €6.50-20; ☺9am-11pm) Stylish, very traditional and serving all the staples of Bavarian sustenance, the 'Chubby Chappy' is one of the oldest restaurants in town, allegedly dating back to the 14th century. On a balmy eve, be sure to bag a table in the lovely beer garden out back.

Vitus   FRENCH €€

(Map p169; ☎526 46; Hinter der Grieb 8; mains €8-18; ☺9am-11pm; ☝) Colourful canvasses mix with ancient beamed ceilings at this bustling place serving provincial French food, including delicious *Flammkuchen* (Alsatian pizza), quiche, salads, meat and fish dishes, as well as a commendable number of meat-free options. Sit in the rustic bar area, the restaurant with linen-draped tables or the child-friendly cafe section.

Café Orphée   FRENCH €€

(Map p169; ☎529 77; Untere Bachgasse 8; mains €7-18; ☺9am-1am) Claiming to be the most French bistro east of the Rhine, you do feel as though you've been teleported to 1920s Paris at this visually pleasing eatery, bedecked in red velvet, dark wood and mirrors aplenty. Pâtés, crêpes, baguettes and other light lunch fare populate a handwritten menu of appetising Gallic favourites with slight Bavarian touches for sturdiness.

Rosenpalais   BAVARIAN €€€

(☎0170-880 1333; Minoritenweg 20; mains €12-32; ☺dinner Tue-Sat) If it's posh nosh you're after, try this refined place occupying a pinkish palace just off Dachauplatz and serving a well-heeled gourmet clientele. Service is first-rate, the admirable edibles as well prepared as they are beautifully presented.

Leerer Beutel   EUROPEAN €€

(Map p169; ☎589 97; Bertoldstrasse 9; mains €10-17; ☺dinner Mon, lunch & dinner Tue-Sat, lunch Sun) Subscriber to the slow-food ethos, the cavernous restaurant at the multi-purpose Leerer Beutel centre offers an imaginatively mixed menu of Bavarian, Tyrolean and Italian dishes, served indoors or out on the car-free cobbles.

Dampfnudel Uli   CAFE €

(Map p169; ☎532 97; Watmarkt 4; dishes under €5; ☺10.01am-6.01pm Wed-Fri, to 3.01pm Sat) This quirky little noshery serves a mean *Dampfnudel* (steamed doughnut) with custard in a photo- and stein-filled Gothic chamber at the base of the Baumburger Tower.

◉ Drinking

Spitalgarten   BEER GARDEN

(St Katharinenplatz 1) A veritable thicket of folding chairs and slatted tables by the Danube, this is one of the best places in town for some alfresco quaffing. It claims to have brewed beer (today's Spital) here since 1350, so it probably knows what it's doing by now.

BAVARIA REGENSBURG

Félix
CAFE

(Map p169; Fröhliche-Türken-Strasse 6; ⊙9am-2am Sun-Thu, 10am-3am Fri & Sat) Early birds break-fast and after-dark trendoids leaf through the lengthy drinks menu behind the curva-ceous neo-baroque frontage of this open-all-hours cafe with a welcoming air.

Kneitinger
PUB

(Map p169; Arnulfsplatz 3) This quintessential Bavarian brewpub is the place to go for some hearty home cooking, delicious house suds and outrageous oompah frolics. It's been in business since 1530.

Hemingway's
CAFE, BAR

(Map p169; Obere Bachgasse 5) Black wood, big mirrors and lots of photos of Papa himself add to the cool atmosphere of this art-deco-style cafe-bar.

Augustiner
BEER GARDEN

(Map p169; Neupfarrplatz 15) This popular fairy-lit beer garden and restaurant is ideally located in the heart of the city. Leave your beer-glass ring and pack away some gor-geous grub in the sprawling garden or cav-ernous interior.

Paletti
CAFE, BAR

(Map p169; Gesandtenstrasse 6, Pustetpassage) Tucked into a covered passageway off Ge-sandtenstrasse, this buzzy Italian cafe-bar is a hip hang-out, with seen-and-be-seen win-dows and art-clad walls.

Cafebar
CAFE, BAR

(Map p169; Gesandtenstrasse 14) This time-warped, tightly squeezed blast from the past in tile, cast iron and stained glass fills with newspaper-reading caffeine fans at first rays and ethanol fans after sundown.

Moritz
BAR

(Map p169; Untere Bachgasse 15) Take some Gothic cross vaulting, paint it high-visibili-ty tunnel orange, throw in some killer cock-tails and invite the iPad crowd – and you got Moritz!

☆ Entertainment

Film Galerie
CINEMA

(Map p169; ☑298 4563; www.filmgalerie.de; Ber-toldstrasse 9) Part of the Leerer Beutel cul-tural centre, this cinema concentrates on art-house films, often shown in the original language (including English).

Garbo-Filmtheater
CINEMA

(Map p169; ☑575 86; Weissgerbergraben 11) This theatre shows German films on general re-lease, as well as mainstream Hollywood and British movies in English.

ⓘ Information

Lok.in (Hauptbahnhof; per hr €4; ⊙6am-11pm Mon-Sat, from 7am Sun) Internet access in the 1st floor of the train station.

Sparkasse City Center (Neupfarrplatz 10)

Post Office (Domplatz) There's another branch next to the Hauptbahnhof.

Regensburg Card (www.regensburgcard.de; 24/48hr €9/17) For free public transport and discounts at local attractions and businesses. Available at the tourist office.

Tourist Office (www.regensburg.de; Altes Rathaus; ⊙9am-6pm Mon-Fri, to 4pm Sat & Sun)

World Heritage Visitors Centre (☑507 4410; www.regensburg-welterbe.de; Weisse-Lamm-Gasse 1; ⊙10am-7pm) Brand-new visitors centre by the Steinerne Brücke focusing on the city's Unesco World Heritage Sites. Interesting interactive multimedia exhibits.

ⓘ Getting There & Away

CAR Regensburg is about an hour's drive south-east of Nuremberg and northwest of Passau via the A3 autobahn. The A93 runs south to Munich.

TRAIN Train connections from Regensburg:

» **Frankfurt am Main** €67, three hours, every two hours or change in Nuremberg

» **Munich** €25.20, 1½ hours, hourly

» **Landshut** €12.20, 40 minutes, hourly

» **Nuremberg** €19, one to two hours, hourly

» **Passau** €22 to €27, one to 1½ hours, hourly or change in Plattling

ⓘ Getting Around

BICYCLE At **Bikehaus** (☑599 8193; www.bike haus.de; Bahnhofstrasse 17; bikes per day €12; ⊙10am-2pm & 3-7pm Mon-Sat) you can hire anything from kiddies' bikes to fully saddled tourers and even a rickshaw for a novel city tour.

BUS On weekdays the **Altstadtbus** (€1) some-how manages to squeeze its way through the narrow streets between the Hauptbahnhof and the Altstadt every 10 minutes between 9am and 7pm. The **bus transfer point** is one block north of the Hauptbahnhof, on Albertstrasse. Tickets for all city buses (except the Altstadtbus) cost €2 for journeys in the centre; an all-day ticket costs €4.40 at ticket machines, €5.90 on the bus and €3.80 at weekends (valid for both days).

CAR & MOTORCYCLE The Steinerne Brücke and much of the Altstadt is closed to private vehicles. Car parks in the centre charge from €1.50 per hour and are well signposted.

Around Regensburg

WALHALLA

Modelled on the Parthenon in Athens, the Walhalla is a breathtaking Ludwig I monument dedicated to the giants of Germanic thought and deed. Marble steps seem to lead up forever from the banks of the Danube to this dazzling marble hall, with a gallery of 127 heroes in marble. It includes a few dubious cases, such as astronomer Copernicus, born in a territory belonging to present-day Poland. The latest addition (2009) was romantic poet Heinrich Heine, whose works were set to music by Strauss, Wagner and Brahms.

To get there take the Danube Valley country road (unnumbered) 10km east from Regensburg to the village of Donaustauf, then follow the signs. Alternatively, you can take a two-hour boat cruise with Schifffahrt Klinger (p171), which includes a one-hour stop at Walhalla, or take bus 5 from Regensburg Hauptbahnhof.

Ingolstadt

🖉 0841 / POP 125,400

Even by Bavaria's standards, Danube-straddling Ingolstadt is astonishingly affluent. Auto manufacturer Audi has its HQ here, flanked by a clutch of oil refineries on the outskirts, but industry has left few marks on the medieval centre, with its cobblestone streets and historic, if slightly over-renovated, buildings. Ingolstadt's museum-church has the largest flat fresco ever made, and few people know that its old medical school figured in the literary birth of Frankenstein, the monster by which all others are judged.

⊙ Sights

Asamkirche Maria de Victoria   CHURCH
(🖉 305 1831; Neubaustrasse 11-12; adult/concession €2/1.50; ⊙9am-noon & 1-5pm Tue-Sun Mar-Oct, 1-4pm Tue-Sun Nov-Feb) The Altstadt's crown jewel is the Asamkirche Maria de Victoria, a baroque masterpiece designed by brothers Cosmas Damian and Egid Quirin Asam between 1732 and 1736. The church's mesmerising trompe l'œil ceiling, painted in just six weeks in 1735, is the world's largest fresco on a flat surface.

Visual illusions abound: stand on the little circle on the diamond tile near the door and look over your left shoulder at the archer with the flaming red turban – wherever you walk, the arrow points right at you. The fresco's Horn of Plenty, Moses' staff and the treasure chest also appear to dramatically alter as you move around the room.

Deutsches Medizinhistorisches Museum   MUSEUM
(German Museum of Medical History; 🖉 305 2860; www.dmm-ingolstadt.de; Anatomiestrasse 18-20; adult/concession €5/2.50; ⊙10am-5pm Tue-Sun) Located in the stately Alte Anatomie (Old Anatomy) at the university, this sometimes rather gory museum chronicles the evolution of medical science as well as the many (scary) instruments and techniques used. Unless you are, or have been, a medical student, pack a strong stomach for the visit.

The ground floor eases you into the exhibition with medical equipment such as birthing chairs, enema syringes, lancets used for bloodletting and other delightful paraphenalia guaranteed to make many go weak at the knees. Upstairs things get closer to the bone with displays of human skeletons, foetuses of conjoined twins, a pregnant uterus and a cyclops.

Neues Schloss   PALACE, MUSEUM
The ostentatious Neues Schloss (New Palace) was built for Duke Ludwig the Bearded in 1418. Fresh from a trip to wealth-laden France, Ludwig borrowed heavily from Gallic design and created a residence with 3m-thick walls, Gothic net vaulting and individually carved doorways. One guest who probably didn't appreciate its architectural merits was future French president Charles de Gaulle, held as a prisoner of war here during WWI.

Today the building houses the **Bayerisches Armeemuseum** (Bavarian Military Museum; 🖉 937 70; www.armeemuseum.de; Paradeplatz 4; adult/concession €3.50/3, Sun €2; combined ticket with Reduit Tilly & Turm Triva €7/5; ⊙9am-5.30pm Tue-Fri, 10am-5.30pm Sat & Sun) with exhibits on long-forgotten battles, armaments dating back to the 14th century and legions of tin soldiers filling the rooms.

The second part of the museum is in the **Reduit Tilly** (adult/concession/child €3.50/3/free, Sun €2; ⊙9am-5.30pm Tue-Fri, 10am-5.30pm Sat & Sun) across the river. This 19th-century fortress has an undeniable aesthetic, having been designed by Ludwig I's chief architect. It was named after Johann Tilly – a field

WORTH A TRIP

STRAUBING

Some 30km southeast of Regensburg, Straubing enjoyed a brief heyday as part of a wonky alliance that formed the short-lived Duchy of Straubing-Holland. As a result, the centre is chock-a-block with historical buildings that opened new horizons in a small town. In August, the demand for folding benches soars during the Gäubodenfest, a 10-day blow-out that once brought together grain farmers in 1812, but now draws over 20,000 drinkers.

Lined with pastel-coloured houses from a variety of periods, the pedestrian square is lorded over by the Gothic **Stadtturm** (1316). It stands next to the richly gabled **Rathaus**, originally two merchant's homes but repackaged in neo-Gothic style in the 19th century. Just east of the tower is the gleaming golden **Dreifaltigkeitssäule** (Trinity Column), erected in 1709 as a nod to Catholic upheavals during the War of the Spanish Succession.

Straubing has about half a dozen historic churches. The most impressive is **St Jakobskirche** (Pfarrplatz), a late-Gothic hall church with original stained-glass windows; it was the recipient of a baroque makeover, courtesy of the frantically productive Asam brothers. The pair also designed the interior of the **Ursulinenkirche** (Burggasse), their final collaboration. Its ceiling fresco depicts the martyrdom of St Ursula surrounded by allegorical representations of the four continents known at the time. Also worth a look is the nearby **Karmelitenkirche** (Hofstatt).

North of here is the former ducal residence **Herzogsschloss** (Schlossplatz), which overlooks the river. This rather austere 14th-century building was once the town's tax office.

One of Germany's most important repositories of Roman treasure is the intimate **Gäubodenmuseum** (✆974 10; www.gaeubodenmuseum.de; Frauenhoferstrasse 23; adult/concession €4/3; ✆10am-4pm Tue-Sun). Displays include imposing armour and masks for both soldiers and horses, probably plundered from a Roman store.

If you fancy staying over, the **tourist office** (✆944 307; www.straubing.de; Theresienplatz 2; ✆9am-5pm Mon-Wed & Fri, 9am-6pm Thu, 10am-2pm Sat) can find rooms.

Straubing has direct train connections to Regensburg (€9.10, 25 minutes, hourly). For Passau (€14.40, one hour and 10 minutes, hourly) and Munich (€24.90, two hours, twice hourly) change at Plattling or Neufahrn.

marshal of the Thirty Years' War who was known as the 'butcher of Magdeburg' – and features exhibits covering the history of WWI and post-WWI Germany.

The newest addition to the museum complex is the **Bayerisches Polizeimuseum** (Donaulände 1; adult/concession €3.50/3; ✆9am-5.30pm Tue-Fri, 10am-5.30pm Sat & Sun), housed in the Turm Triva, which was built at the same time as the Reduit Tilly. Exhibitions trace the story of Bavarian bobbies and their role in various episodes of history such as the Third Reich and the Cold War.

Museum Mobile   MUSEUM
This high-tech car museum is part of the **Audi Forum** (✆893 7575; www.audi.de/foren; Ettinger Strasse 40; adult/child €2/1, tours €4/2; ✆9am-6pm). Exhibits on three floors chart Audi's humble beginnings in 1899 to its latest dream machines, such as the R8. Some 50 cars and 20 motorbikes are on display, including prototypes that glide past visitors on an open lift. Bus 11 and 44 run every 30 minutes from the Hauptbahnhof or central bus station (ZOB) to the Audi complex.

The two-hour tours of the **Audi factory** (adult/concession €7/3.50; ✆tours hourly Mon-Sat, 11am, 1pm & 3pm Sun) take you through the entire production process, from the metal press to the testing station.

Liebfrauenmünster   CHURCH
(Kreuzstrasse; ✆8am-6pm) Ingolstadt's biggest church was established by Duke Ludwig the Bearded in 1425 and enlarged over the next century. This classic Gothic hall church has a pair of strangely oblique square towers that flank the main entrance. Inside, subtle colours and a nave flooded with light intensify the magnificence of the high-lofted vaulting and the blossoming stonework of several side chapels.

The high altar by Hans Mielich (1560) has a rear panel depicting St Katharina debating with the professors at Ingolstadt's new university, ostensibly in a bid to convert the Protestant faculty to Catholicism – a poke at Luther's Reformation. At the rear of the church, there's a small *Schatzkammer* (treasury) displaying precious robes, goblets and monstrances belonging to the diocese.

Museum für Konkrete Kunst　MUSEUM
(Museum of Concrete Art; ⓘ305 1871; Tränktorstrasse 6-8; adult/child €3/1.50; ⓣ10am-5pm Tue-Sun) This unique art museum showcases works and installations from the Concrete Movement, all of a bafflingly abstract nature. The movement was defined and dominated by interwar artists Max Bill and Theo van Doesburg whose works make up a large share of the collection.

Kreuztor　HISTORIC BUILDING
(Kreuzstrasse) The Gothic Kreuztor (1385) was one of the four main gates into the city until the 19th century and its redbrick fairy-tale outline is now the emblem of Ingolstadt. This and the main gate within the Neues Schloss are all that remain of the erstwhile entrances into medieval Ingolstadt, but the former fortifications, now flats, still encircle the city.

Lechner Museum　MUSEUM
(ⓘ305 2250; www.lechner-museum.de; Esplanade 9; adult/concession €3/1.50; ⓣ11am-6pm Thu-Sun) This unusual art museum highlights works cast in steel, a medium that's more expressive than you might think. Exhibits are displayed in a striking glass-covered factory hall from 1953.

🛏 Sleeping

Kult Hotel　DESIGN HOTEL €€€
(ⓘ951 00; www.kult-hotel.de; Theodor-Heuss-Strasse 25; s/d from €120/141; ⓟ🅿@🛜) Aping the Asamkirche, the most eye-catching feature of rooms at this exciting design hotel, 2km northeast of the city centre, are the painted ceilings, each one a work of art. Otherwise fittings and furniture come sleek, room gadgets are the latest toys, and the restaurant is a study in cool elegance.

Hotel Anker　HOTEL €€
(ⓘ300 50; www.hotel-restaurant-anker.de; Tränktorstrasse 1; s/d €58/92) Bright rooms, a touch of surrealist art and a commendably central location make this family-run hotel a good choice, although the lack of English is a slight downside. Try to avoid arriving at mealtimes, when staff are busy serving in the traditional restaurant downstairs.

Enso Hotel　HOTEL €€
(ⓘ885 590; www.enso-hotel.de; Bei der Arena 1; s/d from €79/99; ⓟ🛜) Located just across the Danube from the city centre, the 176 business-standard rooms at Ingolstadt's newest digs come in bold dashes of lip-smacking red and soot black, with acres of retro faux veneer providing a funky feel. Traffic noise is barely audible despite the location at a busy intersection. Amenities include sushi and pasta bars, and a fitness room.

Bayerischer Hof　HOTEL €€
(ⓘ934 060; www.bayerischer-hof-ingolstadt.de; Münzbergstrasse 12; s €59-70, d €82-87) Located around a Bavarian eatery, the 34 rooms are a pretty good deal, and are filled with hardwood furniture, TVs and modern, renovated bathrooms. Rates come down at weekends when business traffic thins out.

DJH Hostel　HOSTEL €
(ⓘ305 1280; www.ingolstadt.jugendherberge.de; Friedhofstrasse 41-42; dm under/over 27yr €16.60/20.60) This beautiful, well-equipped and wheelchair-friendly hostel is in a renovated redbrick fortress (1828), about 150m west of the Kreuztor.

THE BIRTH OF FRANKENSTEIN

Mary Shelley's *Frankenstein*, published in 1818, set a creepy precedent in the world of monster fantasies. The story is well known: young scientist Viktor Frankenstein travels to Ingolstadt to study medicine. He becomes obsessed with the idea of creating a human being and goes shopping for parts at the local cemetery. Unfortunately, his creature is a problem child and sets out to destroy its maker.

Shelley picked Ingolstadt because it was home to a prominent university and medical faculty. In the 19th century, a laboratory for scientists and medical doctors was housed in the Alte Anatomie (now the Deutsches Medizinhistorisches Museum, p175). In the operating theatre, professors and their students carried out experiments on corpses and dead tissue, though perhaps one may have been inspired to work on something a bit scarier...

🍴 Eating & Drinking

Local drinkers are proud that Germany's Beer Purity Law of 1516 was issued in Ingolstadt. To find out why, try a mug of frothy Herrnbräu, Nordbräu or Ingobräu.

For a quick bite head for the Viktualienmarkt, just off Rathausplatz, where fast-food stalls provide international flavour.

Zum Daniel   BAVARIAN €€
(🕿352 72; Roseneckstrasse 1; mains €5-15; ⏱9am-1am Tue-Sun) Ingolstadt's oldest inn is a lovingly run local institution serving what many claim to be the town's best pork roast and seasonal specials.

Weissbräuhaus   PUB €€
(🕿328 90; Dollstrasse 3; mains €4.20-16) This modern beer hall serves standard Bavarian dishes, including the delicious *Weissbräupfändl* (pork fillet with homemade *Spätzle*). There's a beer garden with a charming fountain out back.

Casa Rustica   ITALIAN €€
(🕿333 11; Höllbräugasse 1; mains €6-19; ⏱11.30am-2.30pm & 5-11pm) Most agree that this is Ingolstadt's best Italian restaurant, with a melting cheese and herb aroma in the air and cosy half-circle box seating.

Kuchlbauer   PUB
(🕿335 512; Schäffbräustrasse 11a) This unmissable brewpub, with oodles of brewing and rustic knick-knacks hanging from the walls and ceiling, really rocks (or, should we say, sways) when someone stokes up an accordion. Tipples include the house *Hefeweissbier* or you could try the *Mass Goass*, a 1L jug containing dark beer, cola and 4cL of cherry liqueur!

Neue Galerie Das MO   CAFE, BAR
(🕿339 60; Bergbräustrasse 7; mains €5-21; ⏱from 5pm) This trendy, evening-only place puts on occasional art exhibitions, but it's the walled beer garden in the shade of mature chestnut trees that punters really come for. The international menu offers everything from cheeseburgers to schnitzel and baked potatoes, and vegies are well catered for.

ℹ️ Information

Post Office (Am Stein 8; ⏱8.30am-6pm Mon-Fri, 9am-1pm Sat)
Sparkasse (Rathausplatz 6)

Surfen bei Yorma's (Hauptbahnhof; per hr €2.50) Internet access.
Tourist Office (🕿305 3005; Elisabethstrasse 3; ⏱8.30am-6.30pm Mon-Fri, 9.30am-2pm Sat). The other branch is at **Rathausplatz** (🕿305 3030; Rathausplatz 2; ⏱9am-6pm Mon-Fri, 10am-2pm Sat & Sun, shorter hours Nov-Mar).

ℹ️ Getting There & Away

When arriving by train from the north (from Eichstätt and Nuremberg), Ingolstadt Nord station is nearer to the historical centre than the Hauptbahnhof. Trains from the south arrive at the Hauptbahnhof. Ingolstadt has the following rail connections:

DESTINA-TION	FARE	DURATION	FREQUENCY
Munich	€16.40 to €27	one hour	twice hourly
Nuremberg	€21.80 to €30	30 to 40 minutes	hourly
Regensburg	€14.40	one hour	hourly

ℹ️ Getting Around

Buses 10, 11, 18, 16 and 31 (€1.20) run every few minutes between the city centre and the Hauptbahnhof, 2.5km to the southeast.

Landshut

🕿0871 / POP 63,200

A worthwhile halfway halt between Munich and Regensburg, or a place to kill half a day before a flight from nearby Munich Airport, Landshut (pronounced '*lants*-hoot') was the hereditary seat of the Wittelsbach family in the early 13th century, and capital of the Dukedom of Bavaria-Landshut for over a century. Apart from a brief episode as custodian of the Bavarian University two centuries ago, Landshuters have since been busy retreating into provincial obscurity, but the town's blue-blooded past is still echoed in its grand buildings, a historical pageant with a cast of thousands and one seriously tall church.

👁️ Sights

Coming from the train station, you enter Landshut's historical core through the broken Gothic arch of the stocky **Ländtor**, virtually the only surviving chunk of the town's medieval defences. From here, Theaterstrasse brings you to the 600m-long **Altstadt**, one of Bavaria's most impressive medieval marketplaces. Pastel town houses lining its curving cobbled length hoist elaborate gables, every one a different bell-shaped or saw-toothed creation in brick and plaster.

Burg Trausnitz · CASTLE
(☑924 110; www.burg-trausnitz.de; adult/child €4/ free; ☺9am-6pm Apr-Sep, 10am-4pm Oct-Mar) Roosting high above the Altstadt is Burg Trausnitz, Landshut's top attraction. The 50-minute guided tour (in German with English text) takes you through the Gothic and Renaissance halls and chambers, ending at an alfresco party terrace with bird's-eye views of the town below. The ticket is also good for the **Kunst- und Wunderkammer**, a typical Renaissance-era display of exotic curios assembled by the local dukes.

St Martin Church · CHURCH
(☺7.30am-6pm Apr-Sep, to 5pm Oct-Mar) Rising in Gothic splendour at the southern end of the Altstadt is Landshut's record-breaking St Martin Church; at 130.6m, its spire is the tallest brick structure in the world and it took 55 years to build.

Stadtresidenz · PALACE
(☑924 110; Altstadt 79; adult/concession €3.50/ 2.50; ☺tours in German hourly 9am-6pm Apr-Sep, 10am-4pm Oct-Mar, closed Mon) Gracing the Altstadt is the Stadtresidenz, a Renaissance palace built by Ludwig X which hosts temporary exhibitions on historical themes. Admission is by guided tour only.

✱✱ Festivals & Events

Landshuter Hochzeit · MEDIEVAL
Every four years in July, the town hosts the Landshuter Hochzeit (next held in 2013 and 2017), one of Europe's biggest medieval bashes. It commemorates the marriage of Duke Georg der Reiche of Bavaria-Landshut to Princess Jadwiga of Poland in 1475.

🛏 Sleeping & Eating

Goldene Sonne · HOTEL €€
(☑925 30; www.goldenesonne.de; Neustadt 520; s/d from €89/125; 🅿🛜) True to its name, the 'Golden Sun' fills a magnificently gabled, six-storey town house with light. Rooms sport stylishly lofty ceilings, ornate mirrors, flatscreen TVs and renovated bathrooms. Bus 2 from the train station stops right outside the door.

Zur Insel · HOTEL €€
(☑923 160; www.insel-landshut.de; Badstrasse 16; s €45-90, d €70-95) A good-value place to kip with simple folksy rooms and a wood-panelled restaurant.

DJH Hostel · HOSTEL €
(☑234 49; www.landshut.jugendherberge.de; Richard-Schirrmann-Weg 6; dm from €15) This clean, well-run 100-bed hostel occupies an attractive old villa up by the castle, with views across town.

Alt Landshut · BAVARIAN €€
(Isarpromenade 3; mains €6-14) Sunny days see locals linger over an Augustiner and some neighbourhood nosh outside by the Isar. In winter you can retreat to the simple whitewashed dining room.

Augustiner an der St Martins Kirche · BAVARIAN €€
(Kirchgasse 251; mains €7-17; ☺10am-midnight) This dark wood tavern at the foot of the St Martin's spire is the best place in town to sample a meat–dumpling combo, washed down with a frothy Munich wet one.

ℹ Information
Tourist Office (☑922 050; www.landshut.de; Altstadt 315; ☺9am-6pm Mon-Fri, 10am-4pm Sat Mar-Oct, 9am-5pm Mon-Fri, 10am-2pm Sat Nov-Feb)

ℹ Getting There & Away
TO/FROM THE AIRPORT The airport bus (€11, 35 minutes) leaves almost hourly from near the tourist office and the train station.

TRAIN Landshut is a fairly major stop on the Munich–Regensburg mainline.

» **Munich** €14.40, 45 minutes, twice hourly
» **Passau** €21.50, one hour and 20 minutes, hourly
» **Regensburg** €12.20, 40 minutes, at least hourly

Passau
☑0851 / POP 50,600

Water has quite literally shaped the picturesque town of Passau on the border with Austria. Its Altstadt is stacked atop a narrow peninsula that jabs its sharp end into the confluence of three rivers: the Danube, the Inn and the Ilz. The rivers brought wealth to Passau, which for centuries was an important trading centre, especially for Bohemian salt, central Europe's 'white gold'. Christianity, meanwhile, generated prestige as Passau evolved into the largest bishopric in the Holy Roman Empire. The Altstadt remains pretty much as it was when the powerful prince-bishops built its tight lanes, tunnels and archways with an Italiante flourish, but the western end (around Nibelungenplatz) has received a modern makeover with shopping malls centred around the hang-glider-shaped central bus station (ZOB).

Passau is a Danube river cruise halt and is often bursting with day visitors. It's also the convergence point of several long-distance cycling routes.

◉ Sights

Dom St Stephan CHURCH

(⏷6.30am-7pm) The green onion domes of Passau's Dom St Stephan float serenely above the town's silhouette. There's been a church in this spot since the late 5th century, but what you see today is much younger thanks to the great fire of 1662, which ravaged much of the medieval town, including the ancient cathedral. The rebuilding job went to a team of Italians, notably the architect Carlo Lurago and the stucco master Giovanni Battista Carlone. The result is a rather top-heavy baroque interior with a pious mob of saints and cherubs gazing down at the congregation from countless cornices, capitals and archways.

The building's acoustics are perfect for its pièce de résistance, the world's largest organ above the main entrance, which contains an astonishing 17,974 pipes. Half-hour **organ recitals** take place at noon daily Monday to Saturday (adult/child €4/2) and at 7.30pm on Thursday (adult/child €5/3) from May to October and for a week around Christmas. Show up at least 30 minutes early to ensure you get a seat.

Veste Oberhaus FORTRESS

(www.oberhausmuseum.de; adult/concession €5/4; ⏷9am-5pm Mon-Fri, 10am-6pm Sat & Sun mid-Mar–mid-Nov) A 13th-century defensive fortress, built by the prince-bishops, Veste Oberhaus towers over Passau with patriarchal pomp. Not surprisingly, views of the city and into Austria are superb from up here.

Inside the bastion is the **Oberhausmuseum**, a regional history museum where you can uncover the mysteries of medieval cathedral building, learn what it took to become a knight and explore Passau's period as a centre of the salt trade. Displays are labelled in English.

Altes Rathaus HISTORIC BUILDING

(Rathausplatz 2; Grosser Rathaussaal adult/concession €2/1.50; ⏷Grosser Rathaussaal 10am-4pm Apr-Oct) Passau's Rathaus is a grand Gothic affair topped by a 19th-century landmark painted tower. A carillon chimes several times daily (hours are listed on the wall, alongside historical flood-level markers).

The entrance on Schrottgasse takes you to the **Grosser Rathaussaal** (Great Assembly Room), where large-scale paintings by 19th-century local artist Ferdinand Wagner show scenes from Passau's history with melodramatic flourish. If it's not being used for a wedding or a meeting, also sneak into the adjacent Small Assembly Room for a peek at the ceiling fresco, which again features allegories of the three rivers.

Passauer Glasmuseum MUSEUM

(⏷350 71; www.glasmuseum.de; Hotel Wilder Mann, Am Rathausplatz; adult/concession €5/4; ⏷10am-5pm) Opened by Neil Armstrong, of all people, Passau's warren-like glass museum is filled with some 30,000 priceless pieces of glass and crystal from the baroque, classical, art-nouveau and art-deco periods. Much of what you see hails from the glassworks of Bohemia, but there are also works by Tiffany and famous Viennese producers. Be sure to pick up a floor plan as it's easy to get lost.

Dreiflusseck PENINSULA

The very nib of the Altstadt peninsula, the point where the rivers merge, is known as the Dreiflusseck (Three River Corner). From the north the little Ilz sluices brackish water down from the peat-rich Bavarian Forest, meeting the cloudy brown of the Danube as it flows from the west and the pale jade of the Inn from the south to create a murky tricolour. The effect is best observed from the ramparts of the Veste Oberhaus.

Museum Moderner Kunst ART MUSEUM

(⏷383 8790; www.mmk-passau.de; Bräugasse 17; adult/concession €5/3; ⏷10am-6pm Tue-Sun) Gothic architecture contrasts with 20th- and 21st-century artworks at Passau's Modern Art Museum. The rump of the permanent exhibition is made up of cubist and expressionist works by Georg Philipp Wörlen, who died in Passau in 1954 and whose architect son, Hanns Egon Wörlen, set up the museum in the 1980s. Temporary exhibitions normally showcase big-hitting German artists and native styles and personalities from the world of architecture.

Römermuseum MUSEUM

(⏷347 69; Lederergasse 43; adult/concession €2/1; ⏷10am-4pm Tue-Sun Mar–mid-Nov) Roman Passau can be viewed from the ground up at this Roman fort museum. Civilian and military artefacts unearthed here and elsewhere in Eastern Bavaria are on show and the ruins of **Kastell Boiotro**, which stood here from AD 250 to 400, are still in situ; some of the towers are still inhabited. There's a castle-themed kids' playground nearby.

🏃 Activities

Wurm + Köck BOAT TOUR
(☎929 292; www.donauschiffahrt.de; Höllgasse 26) From March to early November, Wurm + Köck operate cruises to the Dreiflusseck from the docks near Rathausplatz, as well as a whole host of other sailings to places along the Danube. The most spectacular vessel in the fleet is the sparkling Kristallschiff (Crystal Ship) decorated inside and out with Swarovski crystals.

🛏 Sleeping

Hotel Schloss Ort BOUTIQUE HOTEL €€
(☎340 72; www.schlosshotel-passau.de; Im Ort 11; s €68-98, d €97-156; P) This 800-year-old medieval palace by the Inn conceals a tranquil boutique hotel, stylishly done out with polished timber floors, crisp white cotton sheets and wrought-iron bedsteads. Many of the 18 rooms enjoy river views and breakfast is served in the vaulted restaurant.

Pension Rössner GUESTHOUSE €
(☎931 350; www.pension-roessner.de; Bräugasse 19; s/d €35/60; P) This immaculate *Pension*, in a restored mansion near the tip of the peninsula, offers great value for money and a friendly, cosy ambience. Each of the 16 rooms is uniquely decorated and many overlook the fortress. There's bike hire (€10 per day) and parking for €5 a day. Booking recommended.

Hotel König HOTEL €€
(☎3850; www.hotel-koenig.de; Untere Donaulände 1; s €65-100, d €89-140; P🔌) This riverside property puts you smack in the middle of the Altstadt. The 41 timber-rich rooms – many of them enormous – spread out over two buildings and most come with views of the Danube and fortress. One slight disadvantage is the lack of English. Parking is €10 a night.

Hotel Wilder Mann HOTEL €€
(☎350 71; www.wilder-mann.com; Am Rathausplatz 1; s €50-70, d €80-200; P) Sharing space with the glass museum, this historic hotel boasts former guests ranging from Empress Elizabeth (Sisi) of Austria to Mikhail Gorbachev and Yoko Ono. In the rooms, folksy painted furniture sits incongrously with 20th-century telephones and 21st-century TVs. The building is a warren of staircases, passage-

ways and linking doors, so make sure you remember where your room is. Guests receive a miserly discount to the glass museum.

HendlHouseHotel HOTEL €
(☎330 69; www.hendlhousehotel.com; Grosse Klingergasse 17; s/d €55/78) With their light, unfussy decor and well-tended bathrooms, the 15 pristine rooms at this Altstadt new boy offer a high quality to price ratio. Buffet breakfast is served in the downstairs restaurant.

Rotel Inn HOTEL €
(☎951 60; www.rotel-inn.de; Donauufer; s/d €30/50; ⊗closed Oct-Apr; P) An architectural abomination geared up for cyclists, rooms at this no-frills 'cabin hotel' near the train station are literally capsules equipped with an inbuilt futon and basic storage space. However it's not bad considering the bargain price. Breakfast is €6 extra.

Zeltplatz Ilzstadt CAMPGROUND €
(☎414 57; Halser Strasse 34; adult/child €8/6.50; 🅿) Tent-only campground idyllically set on the Ilz River, 15 minutes' walk from the Altstadt. Catch bus 1, 2 or 4 to Kleiner Exerzierplatz-Ilzbrücke.

DJH Hostel HOSTEL €
(☎493 780; www.passau.jugendherberge.de; Veste Oberhaus 125; dm from €20.50) Beautifully renovated 127-bed hostel right in the fortress.

🍴 Eating & Drinking

Heilig-Geist-Stifts-Schenke BAVARIAN €€
(☎2607; Heilig-Geist-Gasse 4; mains €9.50-20; ⊗closed Wed) Not only does the 'Holy Spirit Foundation' have a succession of walnut-panelled rooms, a candlelit cellar (open from 6pm) and a vine-draped garden, but the food is equally inspired. Specialities include *Spiessbraten* (marinated meat licked by a beechwood fire) and fish plucked live from the concrete trough. The garden's apricot tree produces the handmade jam incorporated in the *Marillenpalatschinke* (a rolled-up pancake) and fruit for the *Marillenknödel* (filled yeast dumplings); the schnapps are also homemade.

Diwan CAFE €€
(☎490 3280; Niebelungenplatz 1, Stadtturm; mains €7.20-10.50; ⊗9am-7pm Mon-Thu, to midnight Fri & Sat, 1-6pm Sun) Climb aboard the high-speed lift from street level to get to this trendy, high-perched cafe-lounge at the top of the Stadtturm, with by far the best views in town. From the tangled rattan and plush cappuccino-culture sofas you can see it all –

the Dom St Stephan, the rivers, the Veste Oberhaus – while you tuck into the offerings of the changing seasonal menu.

Zum Grünen Baum
ORGANIC €€

(☑356 35; Höllgasse 7; mains €7.50-16.50; ⊙10am-1am; ⏍) Take a seat under the chandelier made from cutlery to savour risottos, goulash, schnitzel and soups, prepared as far as possible using organic ingredients. Cosy, friendly and tucked away in the atmospherically narrow lanes between the river and the Residenzplatz.

Café Kowalski
CAFE €

(☑2487; Oberer Sand 1; dishes €4-10; ⊙10am-1am; 🠷) Chat flows as freely as the wine and beer at this gregarious cafe, a kicker of a nightspot. The giant burgers, schnitzels and big breakfasts are best consumed on the terrace overlooking the Ilz.

Scharfrichter Haus
ITALIAN, BAVARIAN €€

(☑359 00; Milchgasse 2; mains €11-27; ⊙noon-2pm & 5pm-1am) Cafe, cellar restaurant, jazz club and theatre rolled into one, this Passau institution draws a sophisticated crowd who enjoy seasonal specials on smooth white linen, before retiring to the intimate cabaret theatre with a glass of Austrian wine.

Zi'Teresa Pizzeria
ITALIAN €€

(Theresienstrasse 26; meals €6.40-26; ⊙lunch & dinner) Italian hot spot serving outstanding thin-crust pizzas and tasty pastas, as well as a huge selection of mussel dishes and other seafood.

Andorfer Weissbräu
BEER GARDEN

(☑754 444; Rennweg 2) High on a hill 1.5km north of the Altstadt, this rural beer garden attached to the Andorfer brewery serves filling Bavarian favourites, but the star of the show is the outstanding *Weizen* and *Weizenbock* ales brewed metres away. Take bus 7 from the ZOB to Ries-Rennweg.

❶ Information

Post Office (Bahnhofstrasse 1)

Tourist Office (☑955 980; www.passau.de) Altstadt (Rathausplatz 3; ⊙8.30am-6pm Mon-Fri, 9am-4pm Sat & Sun Easter–mid-Oct, 8.30am-5pm Mon-Thu, 8.30am-4pm Fri mid-Oct–Easter) Hauptbahnhof (Bahnhofstrasse 28; ⊙9am-5pm Mon-Fri, 10.30am-3.30pm Sat & Sun Easter-Sep, reduced hours Oct-Easter) Passau tourist office has a main branch in the Altstadt and another smaller office opposite the Hauptbahnhof. Both branches sell the PassauCard (one day per adult/child €15.50/13, three days €29.50/21), valid

for several attractions, unlimited use of public transport and a city river cruise.

❶ Getting There & Away

BUS Buses leave at 7.45am and 4.45pm to the Czech border village of Železná Ruda (2½ hours), from where there are connections to Prague.

TRAIN Rail connections from Passau:

» **Munich** €32.70, 2¼ hours, hourly

» **Nuremberg** €46, 2¼ hours, every two hours

» **Regensburg** €27, one hour, every two hours or change in Plattling

» **Vienna** €48.20, 2¾ hours, six daily

» **Zwiesel** Change in Plattling; €20.60, 1½ hours, hourly

❶ Getting Around

Central Passau is sufficiently compact to explore on foot. The CityBus links the Bahnhof with the Altstadt (€0.80) up to four times an hour. Longer trips within Passau cost €1.50; a day pass costs €3.50 (€5 for a family).

The walk up the hill to the Veste Oberhaus or the DJH Hostel, via Luitpoldbrücke and Ludwigsteig path, takes about 30 minutes. From April to October, a shuttle bus operates every 30 minutes from Rathausplatz (one-way/return costs €2/2.50).

There are several public car parks near the train station, but only one in the Altstadt at Römerplatz (€0.60/€8.40 per 30 minutes/day).

Bikehaus (⊙Mar-Oct) at the Hauptbahnhof hires out bikes from €12 per day.

Bavarian Forest

Together with the Bohemian Forest on the Czech side of the border, the Bavarian Forest (Bayerischer Wald) forms the largest continuous woodland area in Europe. This inspiring landscape of rolling hills and rounded tree-covered peaks is interspersed with little-disturbed valleys and stretches of virgin woodland, providing a habitat for many species long since vanished from the rest of central Europe. A large area is protected as the wild and remote Bavarian Forest National Park (Nationalpark Bayerischer Wald).

Although incredibly good value, the region sees few international tourists and remains quite traditional. A centuries-old glass-blowing industry is still active in many of the towns along the **Glasstrasse** (Glass Road), a 250km holiday route connecting Waldsassen with Passau. You can visit the

MARKTL AM INN

On a gentle bend in the Inn, some 60km southwest of Passau, sits the drowsy settlement of Marktl am Inn. Few people outside of Germany (or indeed Bavaria) had heard of it before 19 April 2005, the day when its favourite son, Cardinal Joseph Ratzinger, was elected Pope Benedict XVI. Overnight the community was inundated with reporters, devotees and the plain curious, all seeking clues about the pontiff's life and times. Souvenirs like mitre-shaped cakes, 'Papst-Bier' (Pope's Beer) and religious board games flooded the local shops.

The pope's **Geburtshaus** (☏08678-747 680; www.papsthaus.eu; Marktplatz 11; adult/child €3.50/free; ◷10am-noon & 2-6pm Tue-Fri, 10am-6pm Sat & Sun Easter-Oct) is the simple but pretty Bavarian home where Ratzinger was born in 1927 and lived for the first two years of his life before his family moved to Tittmoning. The exhibition kicks off with a film (in English) tracing the pontiff's early life, career and the symbols he selected for his papacy. You then head into the house proper, where exhibits expand on these themes.

The **Heimatmuseum** (Marktplatz 2; adult/child €2/1) is in possession of a golden chalice and a skullcap that was used by Ratzinger in his private chapel in Rome, but is only open to groups of five or more by prior arrangement; visitors should call the **tourist office** (☏08678-748 820; www.marktl.de; Marktplatz 1; ◷10am-noon Mon-Wed & Fri, 2-5pm Thu) at least a day ahead to arrange entry. His baptismal font can be viewed at the **Pfarrkirche St Oswald** (Marktplatz 6), which is open for viewing except during church services.

With immaculate rooms and a superb restaurant, family-run **Pension Hummel** (☏08678-282; www.gasthof-hummel.de; Hauptstrasse 34; s/d €44/63), a few steps from the train station, is the best sleeping spot. Wash down no-nonsense Bavarian fare with a Papst-Bier at **Gasthaus Oberbräu** (☏08678-1040; Bahnhofstrasse 2; mains €6-11; ◷10am-midnight).

Marktl is a brief stop on an Inn-hugging line between Simbach and Mühldorf (€5.50, 20 minutes), from where there are regular direct connections to Munich, Passau and Landshut.

studios, workshops, museums and shops, and stock up on traditional and contemporary designs.

The central town of Zwiesel is a natural base, but other settlements such as Frauenau and Grafenau are also worth considering if relying on public transport.

◉ Sights

Bavarian Forest
National Park
NATIONAL PARK

(www.nationalpark-bayerischer-wald.de) A paradise for outdoor fiends, the Bavarian Forest National Park extends for around 24,250 hectares along the Czech border, from Bayerisch Eisenstein in the north to Finsterau in the south. Its thick forest, most of it mountain spruce, is criss-crossed by hundreds of kilometres of marked hiking, cycling and cross-country skiing trails, some of which now link up with a similar network across the border. The three main mountains, Rachel, Lusen and Grosser Falkenstein, rise up to between 1300m and 1450m and are home to deer, wild boar, fox, otter and countless bird species.

Around 1km northeast of the village of Neuschönau stands the **Hans-Eisenmann-Haus**

(☏08558-961 50; www.nationalpark-bayerischer-wald.de; Böhmstrasse 35), the national park's main visitor centre. The free, but slightly dated, exhibition has hands-on displays designed to shed light on topics such as pollution and tree growth. There's also a children's discovery room, a shop and a library.

Glasmuseum
MUSEUM

(☏09926-941 020; www.glasmuseum-frauenau.de; Am Museumspark 1, Frauenau; adult/concession €5/4.50; ◷9am-5pm Mon-Fri, 10am-4pm Sat & Sun) Frauenau's dazzlingly modern Glasmuseum covers four millennia of glassmaking history. Demonstrations and workshops for kids are regular features.

Museumsdorf Bayerischer Wald
MUSEUM

(☏08504-8482; www.museumsdorf.com; Am Dreiburgensee, Tittling; adult/child €4/free; ◷9am-5pm Apr-Oct) Tittling, on the southern edge of the Bavarian Forest, is home to this 20-hectare open-air museum displaying 150 typical Bavarian Forest timber cottages and farmsteads from the 17th to the 19th centuries. Take frequent RBO bus 6124 to Tittling from Passau Hauptbahnhof.

Waldmuseum
MUSEUM

(☎09922-840 583; www.waldmuseum-zwiesel.de; Stadtplatz 29, Zwiesel; adult/concession €2.50/1; ⊙9am-5pm Mon-Fri, 10am-noon & 2-4pm Sat & Sun mid-May–mid-Oct, reduced hours mid-Oct–mid-May) Housed in a former brewery, Zwiesel's 'Forest Museum' has exhibitions on local customs, flora and fauna, glassmaking and life in the forest.

🏃 Activities

Two long-distance hiking routes cut through the Bavarian Forest: the European Distance Trails E6 (Baltic Sea to the Adriatic Sea) and E8 (North Sea to the Carpathian Mountains). There are mountain huts all along the way. Another popular hiking trail is the Gläserne Steig (Glass Trail) from Lam to Grafenau. Whatever route you're planning, maps produced by Kompass – sheets 185, 195 and 197 – are invaluable companions. They are available from tourist offices and the park visitor centre.

The Bavarian Forest has seven ski areas, but downhill skiing is low-key, even though the area's highest mountain, the Grosser Arber (1456m), occasionally hosts European and World Cup ski races. The major draw here is cross-country skiing, with 2000km of prepared routes through the ranges.

🛌 Sleeping

Accommodation in this region is a bargain; Zwiesel and Grafenau have the best choices.

Hotel Zur Waldbahn
HOTEL €€

(☎09922-8570; www.zurwaldbahn.de; Bahnhofplatz 2, Zwiesel; s €58-64, d €76-96; [P][@][🗢][🐾]) Opposite Zwiesel train station, many of the rooms at this characteristic inn run by three generations of the same family open to balconies with views over the town. The breakfast buffet is an especially generous spread and even includes homemade jams. The restaurant, serving traditional local nosh, is the best in town and is open to non-guests.

Hotel Hubertus
HOTEL €€

(☎08552-964 90; www.hubertus-grafenau.de; Grüb 20, Grafenau; s €66-75, d €108-138) This elegant

hotel in Grafenau offers incredible value for the weary traveller. The rooms are spacious and most have balconies. Guests are treated to a pool and sauna, and delicious buffet meals. Prices are for half-board.

DJH Hostel
HOSTEL €

(☎08553-6000; www.waldhaeuser.jugendherberge.de; Herbergsweg 2, Neuschönau; dm from €19.30) The only hostel right in the Bavarian Forest National Park is an ideal base for hikers, bikers and cross-country skiers.

Ferienpark Arber
CAMPGROUND €

(☎09922-802 595; www.ferienpark-arber.de; Waldesruhweg 34, Zwiesel; per site €19.50) This convenient and well-equipped campground is about 500m north of Zwiesel train station.

ℹ Information

Grafenau Tourist Office (☎08552-962 343; www.grafenau.de; Rathausgasse 1; ⊙8am-5pm Mon-Thu, 8am-1pm Fri, 10-11.30am & 3-5pm Sat, 9.30-11.30am Sun)

Zwiesel Tourist Office (☎09922-840 523; www.zwiesel-tourismus.de; Stadtplatz 27; ⊙8.30am-5pm Mon-Fri, 10am-1pm Sat)

ℹ Getting There & Around

From Munich, Regensburg or Passau, Zwiesel is reached by rail via Plattling; most trains continue to Bayerisch Eisenstein on the Czech border, with connections to Prague. The scenic Waldbahn shuttles directly between Zwiesel and Bodenmais, and Zwiesel and Grafenau.

There's also a network of regional buses, though service can be infrequent. The Igel-Bus, operated by **Ostbayernbus** (www.ostbayern bus.de), navigates around the national park on five routes. A useful one is the Lusen-Bus (€4/10 per one/three days), which leaves from Grafenau Hauptbahnhof and travels to the Hans-Eisenmann-Haus, DJH Hostel and Lusen hiking area.

The best value is usually the **Bayerwald-Ticket** (www.bayerwald-ticket.com; €7), a day pass good for unlimited travel on bus and train throughout the forest area. It's available from the park visitor centre, stations and tourist offices throughout the area.

Salzburg & Around

Includes »

Best Places to Eat

» Magazin (p202)

» Alter Fuchs (p203)

» Gasthof Schloss Aigen (p203)

» Esszimmer (p203)

» Obauer (p212)

Best Places to Stay

» Haus Ballwein (p200)

» Arte Vida (p200)

» Hotel am Dom (p200)

» Hotel & Villa Auersperg (p200)

» Haus Steiner (p200)

Why Go?

One of Austria's smallest provinces, Salzburgerland is proof that size really doesn't matter. Well, not when you have Mozart, Maria von Trapp and the 600-year legacy of the prince-archbishops behind you. This is the land that grabbed the world spotlight and shouted 'visit Austria!' with Julie Andrews skipping joyously down the mountainsides. This is indeed the land of crisp apple strudel, dancing marionettes and high-on-a-hilltop castles. This is the Austria of your wildest childhood dreams.

Salzburg is every bit as grand as you imagine it: a baroque masterpiece, a classical music legend and Austria's spiritual heartland. But it is just the prelude to the region's sensational natural beauty. Just outside of the city, the landscape is etched with deep ravines, glinting ice caves, karst plateaux and mountains of myth – in short, the kind of alpine gorgeousness that no well-orchestrated symphony or yodelling nun could ever quite capture.

When to Go

In January orchestras strike up at Mozart's birthday bash, Mozartwoche. Providing you've booked tickets months ahead, you can partake in the colossal feast of opera, classical music and drama that is the Salzburg Festival from late July to August. Jazz festivals get into full swing in October. Snow lures downhill skiers to the surrounding Alps in winter, while summer is ideal for Alpine hiking and evenings spent lingering in tree-canopied beer gardens. Come in spring or autumn for few crowds, mild days and seasonal colour.

ROCK ME, AMADEUS

Nobody ever rocked Salzburg quite like Mozart. See where the city's most famous son lived, loved and composed on our Mozart walking tour.

Natural Icons

» The limestone turrets and pinnacles of the Tennengebirge (p212).

» The frozen sculptures of Eisriesenwelt (p212).

Fairytale Castles & Palaces

» Salzburg's cliff-top Festung Hohensalzburg (p189), an archetypal fortress with a turbulent 900-year history

» Medieval Burg Hohenwerfen (p212) on its postcard-pretty perch above Werfen

» Whimsical 17th-century palace Schloss Hellbrunn (p210), a summertime escape of the prince-archbishops

Resources

» Salzburg Tourism (www.salzburg.info)

» Salzburgerland (www.salzburgerland.com)

» Salzburger Verkehrsverbund (www.svv-info.at)

» Salzburg Museum (www.salzburgmuseum.at)

Alpine Escapades

Julie Andrews was wrong – these aren't hills, they're mountains; and they aren't alive with the sound of music, but with the sound of footsteps, bicycle bells and swishing skis.

A little preplanning helps whether you plan to freewheel along the Salzach River in Salzburg, rattle along mountain-bike trails threading through Salzburgerland's heights, or flirt with mountaineering in the otherworldly limestone peaks of the Tennengebirge. Salzburg's twin peaks, Gaisberg and Untersberg offer high-altitude escapades such as hiking, biking and paragliding in summer, and modest snow-related fun in winter.

When the flakes start falling, surrounding slopes are given over to cross-country and downhill skiing and tobogganing. Visit www.salzburgerland.com or local tourist offices for details on activities, equipment rental and maps.

MUSICAL LEGENDS

Salzburg is a force to rival Vienna when it comes to classical music and musical classics. This is, after all, the birthplace of such musical royalty as Mozart and Herbert von Karajan; the city that inspired the carol *Silent Night* and Julie Andrews' high-octave vocals.

While you'll need to book tickets weeks ahead for the venerable Salzburg Festival in summer, music fills this city 365 days a year – and we're not talking second-rate stuff. Beyond the obvious, you can watch marionettes perform opera, dine to Mozart's symphonies and attend a chamber concert in Schloss Mirabell's exquisite baroque Marble Hall. The lowdown and ticket agency details are available on www.salzburg.info.

Less high-brow is Salzburg's *Sound of Music* obsession. Twirl in Maria's footsteps on a guided tour, create your own tour of the film locations, or even stay the night at *the* Villa Trapp for the all-singing truth behind the Hollywood legend.

Top Cultural Highs

» The palatial state apartments and Old Master paintings at the Residenz (p193), once home to Salzburg's powerful prince-archbishops.

» The Keltenmuseum (p210) in Hallein, tracing regional heritage through Celtic artefacts and the history of salt extraction.

» Salzburg's Altstadt (p189), an early baroque masterpiece and Unesco World Heritage site, often hailed the 'Rome of the North'.

» The avant-garde art and architecture of Museum der Moderne (p193) atop Mönchsberg's cliffs.

» Salzwelten (p211) near Hallein, a cavernous salt mine that once filled Salzburg's princely coffers with 'white gold'.

SALZBURG

☎ 0662 / POP 149,528 / ELEV 430M

Salzburg is storybook Austria. Standing beside the fast-flowing Salzach River, your gaze is raised inch by inch to the Altstadt's mosaic of graceful domes and spires, the formidable clifftop fortress and the mountains beyond. It's a view that never palls. It's a backdrop that did the lordly prince-archbishops and home-grown genius Mozart proud.

Tempting as it is to spend every minute in the Unesco-listed Altstadt drifting from one baroque church and monumental square to the next in a daze of grandeur, Salzburg rewards those who venture further. Give Getreidegasse's throngs the slip, meander side streets where classical music wafts from open windows, linger decadently over coffee and cake, and let Salzburg slowly, slowly work its magic.

Beyond Salzburg's two biggest money-spinners – Mozart and the *Sound of Music* – hides a city with a burgeoning arts and dining scene, manicured parks and concert halls that uphold musical tradition 365 days a year. Everywhere you go, the scenery, the skyline, the music, the history sends your spirits soaring higher than Julie Andrews octave-leaping vocals.

History

Salzburg has had a tight grip on the region as far back as 15 BC, when the Roman town Iuvavum stood on the site of the present-day city. This Roman stronghold came under constant attack from warlike Celtic tribes and was ultimately destroyed or abandoned due to disease.

The Frankish missionary St Rupert established the first Christian kingdom and founded St Peter's church and monastery in 696. As centuries passed, the successive archbishops of Salzburg gradually increased their power and eventually were given the grandiose titles of princes of the Holy Roman Empire.

Wolf Dietrich von Raitenau, Salzburg's most influential prince-archbishop from 1587 to 1612, spearheaded the total baroque makeover of the city, commissioning many of its most beautiful churches, palaces and gardens. He fell from power after losing a fierce dispute over the salt trade with the powerful rulers of Bavaria, and died a prisoner.

SALZBURG & AROUND

SALZBURG IN...

Two Days

Get up early to see Mozarts Geburtshaus (p194) and boutique-dotted **Getreidegasse** before the crowds arrive. Take in the baroque grandeur of Residenzplatz (p194) and the stately prince-archbishop's palace, Residenz (p193). Coffee and cake in the decadent surrounds of Café Tomaselli (p206) fuels an afternoon absorbing history at the hands-on Salzburg Museum (p189) or monastic heritage at Stiftskirche St Peter (p194). Toast your first day with homebrews and banter in Augustiner Bräustübl's (p205) tree-canopied beer garden.

Begin day two with postcard views from 900-year-old Festung Hohensalzburg's (p189) ramparts, or cutting-edge art exhibitions at Museum der Moderne (p193). Have lunch at M32 (p203) or bag Austrian goodies at the Grüner Markt (p205) for a picnic in Schloss Mirabell's (p195) sculpture-strewn gardens. Chamber music in the palace's sublime **Marble Hall** or enchanting puppetry at Salzburger Marionettentheater (p206) rounds out the day nicely.

Four Days

With another couple of days to explore, you can join a **Mozart** or **Sound of Music tour** (p198). Hire a bike to pedal along the Salzach's villa-studded banks to summer palace Schloss Hellbrunn (p210) and its trick fountains. Dine in old-world Austrian style at Alter Fuchs (p203) before testing the **right-bank nightlife** (p205).

The fun-packed salt mines (p211) of Hallein and the Goliath of ice caves, Eisriesenwelt (p212) in Werfen, both make terrific day trips for day four. Or grab your walking boots or skis and head up to Salzburg's twin peaks: **Untersberg** (p210) and **Gaisberg** (p210).

Salzburg & Around Highlights

① Survey Salzburg's baroque cityscape from the heights of 900-year-old **Festung Hohensalzburg** (p189)

② Go subzero in the frozen depths of **Eisriesenwelt** (p212) in Werfen

③ Tune into the life of a classical genius at Salzburg's **Mozart-Wohnhaus** (p194)

④ Get drenched like a drunken prince-archbishop by fountains at **Schloss Hellbrunn** (p210)

⑤ Do a Julie singing 'Do-Re-Mi' in the fountain-dotted gardens of Salzburg's **Schloss Mirabell** (p195)

⑥ Marvel at puppetry magic at the smaller-

than-life **Salzburger Marionettentheater** (p206)

⑦ Don a boiler suit for a slippery-when-waxed ride at the **Salzwelten** (p211) salt mine in Hallein

⑧ Thank heaven for small breweries and brimful steins at Salzburg's monastery-run **Augustiner Bräustübl** (p205)

Another of the city's archbishops, Paris Lodron (1619–53), managed to keep the principality out of the Europe-wide Thirty Years' War. Salzburg also remained neutral during the War of the Austrian Succession a century later, but bit by bit the province's power gradually waned and Salzburg came under the thumb of France and Bavaria during the Napoleonic Wars. In 1816 Salzburg became part of the Austrian Empire and was on the gradual road to economic recovery.

The early 20th century saw population growth and the founding of the prestigious Salzburg Festival in 1920. Austria was annexed to Nazi Germany in 1938 and during WWII some 40% of the city's buildings were destroyed by Allied bombings. These were restored to their former glory, and in 1997 Salzburg's historic Altstadt became a Unesco World Heritage site.

⊙ Sights

Salzburg's trophy sights huddle in the pedestrianised Altstadt, which straddles both banks of the Salzach River but centres largely on the left bank. Here the tangled lanes are made for a serendipitous wander, leading to hidden courtyards, medieval squares framed by burgher houses and baroque fountains.

Many of the places mentioned below close slightly earlier in winter and open longer – usually an hour or two – during the Salzburg Festival.

TOP CHOICE **Festung Hohensalzburg** FORT
(www.salzburg-burgen.at; Mönchsberg 34; adult/concession/family €7.80/6.90/17.70, with Festungsbahn funicular €11/10.10/25.50; ⊙9-7pm) Salzburg's most visible icon is this mighty 900-year-old clifftop fortress, one of the biggest and best preserved in Europe. It's easy to spend half a day up here, roaming the ramparts for far-reaching views over the Altstadt's spires and squares to the Salzach River and wooded mountains beyond. The fortress is a steep 15-minute jaunt from the centre or a speedy ride in the glass **Festungsbahn funicular** (Festungsgasse 4).

The fortress began life as a humble bailey, built in 1077 by Gebhard von Helffenstein at a time when the Holy Roman Empire was at loggerheads with the papacy. The present structure, however, owes its grandeur to spendthrift Leonard von Keutschach, prince-archbishop of Salzburg from 1495 to 1519 and the city's last feudal ruler.

Highlights of a visit include the **Golden Hall** where lavish banquets were once held, with a gold-studded ceiling imitating a starry night sky. Your ticket also gets you into the **Marionette Museum**, where skeleton-in-a-box Archbishop Wolf Dietrich steals the (puppet) show, as well as the **Fortress Museum** showcasing a 1612 model of Salzburg, medieval instruments, armour and some pretty gruesome torture instruments.

The Golden Hall is the backdrop for year-round **Festungskonzerte** (Fortress Concerts), which often focus on Mozart's works. See www.mozartfestival.at for times and prices.

Salzburg Museum MUSEUM
(www.salzburgmuseum.at; Mozartplatz 1; adult/concession/family €7/6/14; ⊙9am-5pm Tue-Sun, to 8pm Thu) Housed in the baroque Neue Residenz palace, this flagship museum takes you on a fascinating romp through Salzburg's past. A visit starts beneath the courtyard in the strikingly illuminated **Kunsthalle**, presenting rotating exhibitions of art, such as one spotlighting Hohe Tauern landscape paintings. On the 1st floor, **Ars Sacra** zooms in on medieval art treasures, from altarpieces and embroidery to monstrances, chalices, Latin manuscripts and a Romanesque crucifix.

Upstairs, prince-archbishops glower down from the walls at **Mythos Salzburg**, which celebrates the city as a source of artistic and poetic inspiration. Showstoppers include Carl Spitzweg's renowned *Sonntagsspaziergang* (Sunday Stroll; 1841) painting, the portrait-lined prince-archbishop's room and the Ständesaal (Sovereign Chamber), an opulent vision of polychrome stucco curling around frescoes depicting the History of Rome according to Titus Livius. The early 16th-century *Millefiori* tapestry, Archbishop

SALZBURG & AROUND SIGHTS

Salzburg

200 m
0.1 miles

To Bergland
Hotel (150m)

Rupertgasse

65

To Rockhouse
(500m)

Schallmooser Hauptstr

Glockengasse

Kapuzinerberg

Steinhamerstr

29

34

Auerspergstr

Wolf-Dietrich-Str

40 56

Paris-Lodron-Str

Wartlwalerstr

31

Linzer Gasse

Friedhof St
Sebastian

5

84

Kapuzinerberg
Viewpoint

To YOHO
Salzburg (100m)

53

Franz-Josef-Str

Schrannengasse

Bergstr

59

Priesterhausgasse

18

Hubert Sattler Gasse

Bus to
Gaisberg

Dreifaltigkeitsgasse

3

Mozart-Wohnhaus

10

Flight
Bank Bus
Departures

26

85

45

32

Makartplatz

Theatergasse

43

47

23

Rainerstr

22 25

76

74

54 35

Schloss
Mirabell

18

Mirabellplatz

77

Schlosskonzerte
Box Office

Makartsteg

To Jazzit
(550m)

Mirabellgarten

Schwarzstr

24

Elisabethkai

To Bärenwirt (100m);
Esszimmer (250m);
Augustiner Bräustübl (700m)

62

Auerspergstr

Müllner Hauptstr

36

Museumplatz

6

21

Ursulinenplatz

87 9

Gstättengasse

Mönchsberg

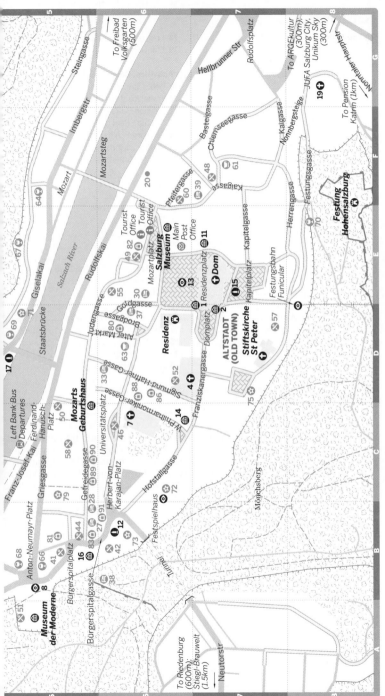

Salzburg

Wolf Dietrich's gold-embroidered pontifical shoe and Flemish tapestries are among other attention-grabbers.

Salzburg's famous 35-bell **glockenspiel**, which chimes daily at 7am, 11am and 6pm, is on the western flank of the Neue Residenz. You can ascend the tower on a behind-the-scenes **tour**. Tickets are sold at the Panorama Museum.

Next door is the **Panorama Museum** (Residenzplatz 9; adult/concession €3/2.50; ⊙9am-5pm), Johann Michael Sattler's 360-degree painting of Salzburg as it was in 1829. The museum plays host to rotating exhibitions such as one on the real life of the Trapp family.

Dom CATHEDRAL
(Domplatz; ⊙8am-7pm Mon-Sat, from 1pm Sun) Gracefully crowned by a bulbous copper dome and twin spires, the Dom stands out as a masterpiece of baroque art. Italian architect Santino Solari redesigned the cathedral during the Thirty Years' War and it was consecrated in 1628. Its origins, though, date to an earlier cathedral founded by Bishop Virgil in 767. Bronze portals symbolising faith, hope and charity lead into the cathedral. In the nave, intricate stucco and Arsenio Mascagni's ceiling frescoes recounting the Passion of Christ guide the eye to the polychrome dome. For more on the history, hook onto one of the free guided tours at 2pm daily.

The adjacent **Dommuseum** (adult/concession €6/2; ⊙10am-5pm Mon-Sat, 11am-6pm Sun) is a treasure trove of sacred art. A visit whisks you past a cabinet of Renaissance curiosities crammed with crystals, coral and oddities like armadillos and pufferfish, through rooms showcasing gem-encrusted monstrances, stained glass and altarpieces, and into the Long Gallery, graced with 17th- and 18th-century paintings, including Paul

SALZBURG & AROUND SIGHTS

Troger's chiaroscuro *Christ on the Mount of Olives* (c1750). From the organ gallery, you get close-ups of the organ Mozart played and a bird's-eye view of the Dom's nave.

Residenz
PALACE
(www.residenzgalerie.at; Residenzplatz 1; adult/concession €9/7; ⊙10am-5pm Tue-Sun) Nowhere is the pomp and circumstance of Salzburg more tangible than at the regal Residenz. A man of grand designs, Wolf Dietrich von Raitenau, prince-archbishop of Salzburg from 1587 to 1612, gave the go-ahead to build this baroque palace on the site of an 11th-century bishop's residence. The prince-archbishops held court here until Salzburg became part of the Hapsburg Empire in the 19th century.

An audio-guide tour takes in the exuberant **state apartments**, a hotchpotch of baroque and neoclassical styles, which are lavishly adorned with tapestries, stucco and frescoes by Johann Michael Rottmayr.

Admission also covers the **Residenz Galerie**. Here the focus is on Flemish and Dutch masters, with must-sees such as Rubens' *Allegory on Emperor Charles V* and Rembrandt's chiaroscuro *Old Woman Praying*. Thomas Ender's alpine landscapes and Heinrich Bürkel's Salzburg scenes are among the 19th-century standouts.

Museum der Moderne
GALLERY
(www.museumdermoderne.at; Mönchsberg 32; adult/concession €8/6, incl Rupertinum €12/8; ⊙10am-6pm Tue-Sun, to 8pm Wed) Straddling Mönchsberg's cliffs, this contemporary glass-and-marble oblong of a gallery stands in stark contrast to the fortress. The gallery shows first-rate temporary exhibitions of 20th- and 21st-century art. The works of Alberto Giacometti, Dieter Roth, Emil Nolde

WALK OF MODERN ART

Eager to slip out of its baroque shoes and show the world that it can do cutting edge, too, Salzburg commissioned a clutch of public artworks between 2002 and 2011, many of which can be seen on a wander through the Altstadt. Internationally renowned artists were drafted in to create contemporary sculptures that provide striking contrast to the city's historic backdrop.

On Mönchsberg you will find Mario Merz' 21 neon-lit **Numbers in the Woods** and James Turrell's elliptical **Sky Space**, the latter creating a play of light and shadow at dawn and dusk. Back in town, you will almost certainly stroll past Stephan Balkenhol's **Sphaera** on Kapitelplatz, a huge golden globe topped by a startlingly realistic-looking man. Tucked away on Ursulinenplatz is Markus Lüpertz' **Mozart - Eine Hommage**, an abstract, one-armed bronze sculpture of the genius, sporting trademark pigtail and the torso of a woman. Another tribute to Mozart stands across the river in the shape of Marina Abramovic's **Spirit of Mozart**, a cluster of chairs surrounding a 15m-high chair, which, as the name suggests, is said to embody the spirit of the composer.

For more, visit the **Salzburg Foundation** (www.salzburgfoundation.at), the driving force behind this display of open-air art installations and sculpture.

and John Cage have previously featured. There's a free guided tour of the gallery at 6.30pm every Wednesday. The **Mönchsberg Lift** (Gstättengasse 13; one-way/rtn €2/3.20, incl gallery ticket €9.70/6.80; ⊘8am-7pm Thu-Tue, to 9pm Wed) whizzes up to the gallery year-round.

Mönchsberg commands broad outlooks across Salzburg's spire-dotted cityscape and its woodland walking trails are great for tip-toeing away from the crowds for an hour or two. While you're up here, take in the far-reaching views over Salzburg over coffee or lunch at **M32** (p203).

Mozarts Geburtshaus   MUSEUM
(Mozart's Birthplace; www.mozarteum.at; Getreide-gasse 9; adult/concession/family €10/8.50/21; ⊘9am-5.30pm) Wolfgang Amadeus Mozart, Salzburg's most famous son, was born in this bright yellow townhouse in 1756 and spent the first 17 years of his life here. Today's museum harbours a collection of instruments, documents and portraits. Highlights include the mini-violin he played as a toddler, plus a lock of his hair and buttons from his jacket. In one room, Mozart is shown as a holy babe beneath a neon blue halo – we'll leave you to draw your own analogies...

Mozart-Wohnhaus   MUSEUM
(Mozart's Residence; www.mozarteum.at; Makart-platz 8; adult/concession/family €10/8.50/21, incl Mozarts Geburtshaus €17/14/36; ⊘9am-5.30pm) Tired of the cramped living conditions on Getreidegasse, the Mozart family moved to this more spacious abode in 1773, where a prolific Mozart composed works such as the *Shepherd King* (K.208) and *Idomeneo* (K.366). Emanuel Schikaneder, a close friend of Mozart and the librettist of *The Magic Flute,* was a regular guest here. An audio guide accompanies your visit, serenading you with opera excerpts. Alongside family portraits and documents, you'll find Mozart's original fortepiano.

Under the same roof and included in your ticket is the **Mozart Ton-und Filmmuseum**, a film and music archive of interest to the ultra-enthusiast, with some 25,000 audio-visual recordings.

Residenzplatz   SQUARE
With its horse-drawn carriages, palace and street entertainers, this stately baroque square is the Salzburg of a thousand post-cards. Its centrepiece is the **Residenzbrun-nen**, an enormous marble fountain ringed by four water-spouting horses and topped by a conch shell–bearing Triton. The plaza is the late-16th-century vision of Prince-Arch-bishop Wolf Dietrich von Raitenau who, inspired by Rome, enlisted Italian architect Vincenzo Scamozzi.

Stiftskirche St Peter   CHURCH
(St Peter's Abbey Church; St Peter Bezirk 1-2; ⊘church 8.30am-noon & 2.30-6.30pm, cemetery 6.30am-7pm daily) A Frankish missionary named Rupert founded this abbey church and monastery in around 700, making it the oldest in the German-speaking world. Though a vaulted Romanesque portal remains, today's church is overwhelmingly baroque, with rococo stucco, statues – including one of archangel Michael shoving

a crucifix through the throat of a goaty demon – and striking altar paintings by Martin Johann Schmidt.

Take a stroll around the **cemetery**, where the graves are mini works of art with their intricate stonework and filigree wrought-iron crosses. Composer Michael Haydn (1737–1806), opera singer Richard Mayr (1877–1935) and renowned Salzburg confectioner Paul Fürst (1856–1941) lie buried here; the last is watched over by skull-bearing cherubs.

The cemetery is home to the **catacombs**, cavelike chapels and crypts hewn out of the Mönchsberg cliff face.

Schloss Mirabell   PALACE
(☺palace 8am-4pm Mon, Wed & Thu, 1-4pm Tue & Fri; gardens dawn-dusk) Prince-Archbishop Wolf Dietrich built this splendid palace in 1606 to impress his beloved mistress Salome Alt. It must have done the trick because

she went on to bear the archbishop some 15 children; sources disagree on the exact number (poor Wolf was presumably too distracted by spiritual matters to keep count himself). Johann Lukas von Hildebrandt, of Schloss Belvedere fame, remodelled the palace in baroque style in 1721. The lavish baroque interior, replete with stucco, marble and frescos, is free to visit. The **Marmorsaal** (Marble Hall) provides a sublime backdrop for evening chamber concerts.

The flowery parterres, rose gardens and leafy arbours are less overrun first thing in the morning and early evening. The lithe *Tänzerin* (dancer) sculpture is a great spot to photograph the gardens with the fortress as a backdrop. *Sound of Music* fans will of course recognise the **Pegasus statue**, the steps and the gnomes of the **Zwerglgarten** (Dwarf Garden), where the mini von Trapps practised 'Do-Re-Mi'.

SALZBURG FOR CHILDREN

With dancing marionettes, chocolate galore and a *big* fairy-tale-like fortress, Salzburg is kid nirvana. If the crowds prove unbearable with tots in tow, take them to the city's adventure **playgrounds** (there are 80 to pick from); the one on **Franz-Josef-Kai** is a central choice.

Salzburg's sights are usually half-price for children and most are free for under-six-year-olds. Many galleries, museums and theatres also have dedicated programs for kids and families. These include the Museum der Moderne (p193), which has regular art workshops at 3pm on Tuesdays (€4), and the matinée performances at the enchanting Salzburger Marionettentheater (p206). The Salzburg Museum (p189) has lots of hands-on displays, from harp-playing to old-fashioned quill writing. Pick up 'Wolf' Dietrich's cartoon guide at the entrance.

Kids will love the **Haus der Natur** (www.hausdernatur.at; Museumsplatz 5; adult/child/family €7.50/5/18.50; ☺9am-5pm), where they can bone up on dinosaurs and alpine crystals in the natural history rooms, gawp at snakes and crocs in the reptile enclosure, and glimpse piranhas and coral reefs in the aquarium. Blink-and-you'll-miss-them baby clownfish splash around in the 'Kinderstube'. Shark-feeding time is 10.30am on Mondays and Thursdays. On the upper levels is a science museum where budding scientists can race rowboats, take a biological tour of the human body and – literally – feel Mozart's music by stepping into a giant violin case.

On the arcaded Bürgerspitalplatz, the **Spielzeugmuseum** (Toy Museum; Bürgerspital-gasse 2; adult/child/family €4/1.50/8; ☺9am-5pm Tue-Sun) takes a nostalgic look at toys, with its collection of doll's houses and *Steiff* teddies. Wednesday afternoon Punch and Judy shows start at 3pm and cost €4. There's also dress-up fun, marble games and a little boy's dream of a Bosch workshop. Parents can hang out in the 'adult parking areas' and at the free tea bar while the little ones let off excess energy.

Outside Salzburg, near Untersberg, the open-air **Freilichtmuseum** (www.freilichtmuseum.com; Hasenweg; adult/child/family €10/5/20; ☺9am-6pm Tue-Sun Apr-Oct) harbours around 100 archetypal Austrian farmhouses and has tractors to clamber over, goats to feed and a huge adventure playground. Kids can come face to face with lions, flamingos and alpine ibex at **Salzburg Zoo** (www.salzburg-zoo.at; Anifer Landesstrasse 1; adult/child/family €9.50/4/21.50; ☺9am-5pm) near Schloss Hellbrunn.

A SUMMER SPLASH

Retreat from the summer madness at one of Salzburg's swimming pools. Here's our pick of the best:

Freibad Leopoldskron (Leopoldskronstrasse 50; adult/concession €4.30/2.80; ⊙9am-7pm May–mid-Sep) Salzburg's biggest lido, with laps for swimmers, kids' splash pools, diving boards, waterslides, table tennis, minigolf and volleyball. Bus 22 to Wartbergweg stops close by.

Waldbad Anif (Waldbadstrasse 1; adult/concession €6/4; ⊙9am-9pm May-Sep) A sylvan beauty of a turquoise, forest-rimmed lake. Go for a quiet dip or activities such as canoeing, climbing, volleyball and table tennis. Take bus 25 or 28 to Maximarkt, a 1km walk from the pool.

Freibad Volksgarten (Hermann-Bahr-Promenade 2; adult/concession €4.30/2.80; ⊙9am-7pm May–mid-Sep) Just south of Kapuzinerberg, this park has decent-sized pools, plenty of space for sunbathing, plus a children's splash pool, table tennis and volleyball. Buses 6, 7 and 20 stop at Volksgarten.

Rupertinum GALLERY
(www.museumdermoderne.at; Wiener-Philhar-moniker-Gasse 9; adult/concession/family €6/4/8; ⊙10am-6pm Tue & Thu-Sun, to 8pm Wed) In the heart of the Altstadt, the Rupertinum is the sister gallery of the **Museum der Moderne** (p193) and is devoted to rotating exhibitions of modern art. There is a strong emphasis on graphic works and photography.

Friedhof St Sebastian CEMETERY
(Nonnberggasse 2; ⊙9am-7pm) Tucked behind the baroque **Sebastianskirche** (St Sebastian's Church), this peaceful cemetery and its cloisters were designed by Andrea Berteleto in Italianate style in 1600. Mozart family members and well-known 16th-century physician Paracelsus are buried here, but outpomping them all is Prince-Archbishop Wolf Dietrich von Raitenau's mosaic-tiled mausoleum, an elaborate memorial to himself.

Stift Nonnberg CHURCH
(Nonnberg Convent; Nonnberggasse 2; ⊙7am-dusk) A short climb up the Nonnbergstiege staircase from Kaigasse or along Festungsgasse brings you to this Benedictine convent, founded 1300 years ago and made famous as *the* nunnery in the *Sound of Music*. You can visit the beautiful rib-vaulted church, but the rest of the convent is off-limits.

Steingasse HISTORIC SITE
On the right bank of the Salzach River, this narrow, cobbled lane was, incredibly, the main trade route to Italy in medieval times. Look out for the 13th-century **Steintor** gate and the house of **Joseph Mohr**, who wrote the lyrics to that all-time classic of a carol

Silent Night. The street is at its most photogenic in the late morning when sunlight illuminates its pastel-coloured townhouses.

Kollegienkirche CHURCH
(Universitätsplatz; ⊙8am-6pm) Johann Bernhard Fischer von Erlach's grandest baroque design is this late-17th-century university church, with a striking bowed facade. The high altar's columns symbolise the Seven Pillars of Wisdom.

Pferdeschwemme PUBLIC ART
(Horse Trough; Herbert-von-Karajan-Platz) Designed by Fischer von Erlach in 1693, this is a horse-lover's delight, with rearing equine pin-ups surrounding Michael Bernhard Mandl's statue of a horse tamer.

Franziskanerkirche CHURCH
(Franziskanergasse 5; ⊙6.30am-7.30pm) A real architectural hotchpotch, Salzburg's Franciscan church has a Romanesque nave, a Gothic choir with rib vaulting and a baroque marble altar (one of Fischer von Erlach's creations).

Dreifältigkeitskirche CHURCH
(Church of the Holy Trinity; Dreifaltigkeitsgasse 14; ⊙6.30am-6.30pm) Baroque master Johann Bernhard Fischer von Erlach designed this graceful right-bank church, famous for Johann Michael Rottmayr's dome fresco of the Holy Trinity.

Domgrabungsmuseum MUSEUM
(Residenzplatz; adult/concession €2.50/2 ; ⊙9am-5pm Jul & Aug, on request Sep-Jun) Map out the city's past with a romp of the rocks at this subterranean archaeology museum beside

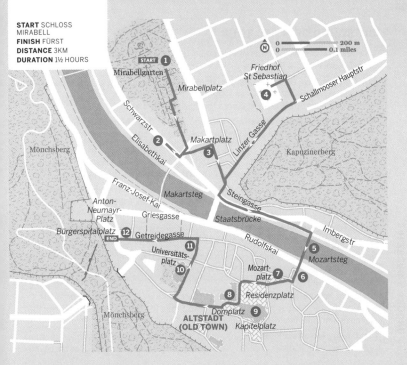

Walking Tour
In Mozart's Footsteps

❯ Mozart was the ultimate musical prodigy: he identified a pig's squeal as G sharp aged two, began to compose when he was five and first performed for Empress Maria Theresia at the age of six. Follow in his footsteps on this classic walking tour.

Begin at baroque **1 Schloss Mirabell**, where the resplendent *Marmorsaal* is often the backdrop for chamber concerts of Mozart's music. Stroll south through the fountain-dotted gardens, passing the strikingly angular **2 Mozarteum**, a foundation honouring Mozart's life and works, and the host of the renowned Mozartwoche festival in January. Just around the corner on Makartplatz is the 17th-century **3 Mozart-Wohnhaus**, where you can see how the Mozart family lived and listen to rare recordings of Mozart's symphonies at the **3 Mozart Ton-und Filmmuseum**. Amble north along Linzer Gasse to **4 Friedhof St Sebastian**, the arcaded cemetery where Wolfgang's father Leopold and wife Constanze lie buried. Retrace your steps towards the Salzach

River, turning left onto medieval Steingasse and crossing the art-nouveau **5 Mozartsteg** (Mozart Bridge). Look out for the **6 memorial plaque** at No 8, the house where Mozart's beloved Constanze died, as you approach **7 Mozartplatz**. On this elegant square, Mozart is literally and metaphorically put on a pedestal. Across the way is the grand **8 Residenz** palace where Mozart gave his first court concert at the ripe old age of six. Beside it rests the baroque **9 Dom**, where Mozart's parents were married in 1747 and Mozart was baptised in 1756. Mozart later composed sacred music here and was cathedral organist. Follow Franziskanergasse to reach the **10 Kollegienkirche** on Universitätsplatz, where Mozart's D Minor Mass, K65, premiered in 1769. On parallel Getreidegasse, stop to contemplate the birthplace of a genius at **11 Mozarts Geburtshaus** and buy some of **12 Fürst's** famous chocolate *Mozartkugeln* (Mozart balls).

DIY SOUND OF MUSIC TOUR

Do a Julie and sing as you stroll your self-guided tour of the *Sound of Music* film locations. OK, let's start at the very beginning:

The Hills are Alive Cut! Make that *proper* mountains. The opening scenes were filmed around the jewel-coloured Salzkammergut lakes. Maria makes her twirling entrance on alpine pastures just across the border in Bavaria.

A Problem like Maria Nuns waltzing on their way to mass at Benedictine Stift Nonnberg (p196) is fiction, but it's fact that the real Maria von Trapp intended to become a nun here before romance struck.

Have Confidence Residenzplatz (p194) is where Maria belts out 'I Have Confidence' and playfully splashes the spouting horses of the Residenzbrunnen fountain.

Do-Re-Mi Oh the Pegasus fountain, the steps with fortress views, the gnomes…the Mirabellgarten (p195) might inspire a rendition of 'Do-Re-Mi', especially if there's a drop of golden sun.

Sixteen Going on Seventeen The loved-up pavilion of the century hides out in Hellbrunn Park, where you can act out those 'oh Liesl', 'oh Rolf' fantasies.

So Long, Farewell The grand rococo palace of Schloss Leopoldskron, a 15-minute walk from Festung Hohensalzburg, is where the lake scene was filmed. Its Venetian Room was the blueprint for the Trapp's lavish ballroom, where the children bid their farewells.

Edelweiss and Adieu The Felsenreitschule (Summer Riding School) is the dramatic backdrop for the Salzburg Festival in the movie, where the Trapp Family Singers win the audience over with 'Edelweiss' and give the Nazis the slip with 'So Long, Farewell'.

Climb Every Mountain To, erm, Switzerland. Or content yourself with alpine views from Untersberg, which appears briefly at the end of the movie when the family flees the country.

the Dom. Particularly of interest are fragments of Roman mosaics, a milestone hewn from Untersberg marble and the brickwork of the former Romanesque cathedral.

🏃 Activities

Salzburg's rival mountains are 540m Mönchsberg and 640m Kapuzinerberg – Julie Andrews and locals used to bigger things call them 'hills'. Both are thickly wooded and crisscrossed by walking trails, with photogenic views of the Altstadt on the right bank and left bank respectively.

There's also an extensive network of cycling routes to explore: from a gentle 20-minute trundle along the Salzach River to Hellbrunn, to the highly scenic 450km Mozart Radweg through Salzburgerland and Bavaria.

👉 Tours

If you would rather go it alone, the **tourist office** (☎889 87-330; www.salzburg.info; Mozartplatz 5; ☉9am-6pm or 6.30pm, closed Sun Sep-Mar) has four-hour iTour audio guides (€9), which take in big-hitters like the Residenz, Mirabellgarten and Mozartplatz.

Fräulein Maria's Bicycle Tours BICYCLE TOURS (www.mariasbicycletours.com; adult/child €24/15; ☉9.30am & 4.30pm May-Sep) Belt out *Sound of Music* faves as you pedal on one of these jolly 3½-hour bike tours, taking in film locations, including the Mirabellgarten, Stift Nonnberg, Schloss Leopoldskron and Hellbrunn. No advance booking is necessary; just turn up at the meeting point on Mirabellplatz.

Segway Tours SEGWAY TOURS (www.segway-salzburg.at; city/Sound of Music tour €33/65 ; ☉tours 9am, noon, 3pm & 5pm) These guided Segway tours take in the big sights by zippy battery-powered scooter. Trundle through the city on a one-hour ride or tick off *Sound of Music* locations on a 2½-hour tour.

Salzburg Schiffsfahrt RIVER CRUISES (www.salzburgschifffahrt.at; adult/child €14/7; ☉Apr-Oct) A boat ride along the Salzach is a leisurely way to pick out Salzburg's sights. Hour-long cruises depart from Makartsteg bridge, with some of them chugging on to Schloss Hellbrunn for adults and children €17 or 10, not including entry to the palace.

Stiegl-Brauwelt BREWERY TOUR
(www.brauwelt.at; Bräuhausstrasse 9; adult/child
€9/4; ◎10am-5pm) Brewing and bottling
since 1492, Stiegl is Austria's largest private
brewery. A tour takes in the different stages
of the brewing process and (woohoo!) the
world's tallest beer tower. A free Stiegl beer
and pretzel are thrown in for the price of a
ticket. The brewery is 1.5km southwest of the
Altstadt; take bus 1 or 8 to Bräuhausstrasse.

Bob's Special Tours COACH TOURS
(✆84 95 11; www.bobstours.com; Rudolfskai 38;
◎office 10am-3pm Mon-Fri, noon-2pm Sat & Sun)
Minibus tours to *Sound of Music* locations
(€45), the Bavarian Alps (€45) and Gross-
glockner (€90). Prices include a free hotel
pick-up for morning tours starting at 9am.
Reservations essential.

Salzburg Panorama Tours COACH TOURS
(✆88 32 11-0; www.panoramatours.com; Mirabellplatz; ◎office 8am-6pm) Boasts the 'original
Sound of Music Tour' (€37) as well as a huge
range of others, including Altstadt walking
tours (€15), Mozart tours (€24) and Bavarian Alps excursions (€37).

Salzburg Sightseeing Tours COACH TOURS
(✆88 16 16; www.salzburg-sightseeingtours.at; Mirabellplatz 2; adult/child €15/7; ◎office 8am-6pm)
Sells a 24-hour ticket for a multilingual hop-
on hop-off bus tour of the city's key sights
and *Sound of Music* locations.

✹ Festivals & Events

Mozartwoche MUSIC FESTIVAL
(Mozart Week; www.mozarteum.at) World-
renowned orchestras, conductors and soloists celebrate Mozart's birthday with a feast
of his music in late January.

Osterfestspiele MUSIC FESTIVAL
(Easter Festival; www.osterfestspiele-salzburg.at)
This springtime shindig brings orchestral
highlights, under Christian Thielemann's
sprightly baton, to the Festspielhaus in
March or April.

SommerSzene CULTURAL FESTIVAL
(www.sommerszene.net) Boundary-crossing
performing arts are the focus of this event
in July.

Jazz & the City JAZZ FESTIVAL
(www.salzburgjazz.com) Salzburg gets its
groove on at some 100 free concerts in the
Altstadt in mid-October.

Christkindlmarkt CHRISTMAS MARKET
(www.christkindlmarkt.co.at) Salzburg is at its
storybook best during Advent, when Christmas markets bring festive sparkle and choirs
to Domplatz and Residenzplatz.

🛏 Sleeping

Salzburg's accommodation is pricey by Austrian standards, but you can get a good deal
if you're willing to go the extra mile or two.
Ask the tourist office for a list of private

FESTIVAL TIME

In 1920, dream trio Hugo von Hofmannsthal, Max Reinhardt and Richard Strauss combined creative forces and the **Salzburg Festival** (www.salzburgerfestspiele.at) was born.
Now, as then, one of the highlights is the staging of Hofmannsthal's morality play *Jedermann* (Everyman) on Domplatz. A trilogy of opera, drama and classical concerts of the
highest calibre have since propelled the five-week summer festival to international renown, attracting some of the world's best conductors, directors, orchestras and singers.

Come festival time, late July and August, Salzburg crackles with excitement, as a
quarter of a million visitors descend on the city for some 200 productions. Theatre
premieres, avant-garde works and the summer-resident Vienna Philharmonic performing Mozart works are all in the mix. The Festival District on Hofstallgasse has a spectacular backdrop, framed by Mönchsberg's cliffs. Most performances are held in the
cavernous **Grosses Festspielhaus** (✆066284 45-579; Hofstallgasse 1) accommodating
2179 theatre-goers, the **Haus für Mozart** in the former royal stables and the baroque
Felsenreitschule.

If you're planning on visiting during the festival, don't leave *anything* to chance –
book your flights, hotel and tickets months in advance. Sometimes last-minute tickets
are available at the **ticket office** (✆80 45-500; info@salzburgfestival.at; Herbert-von-
Karajan-Platz 11; ◎9.30am-1pm & 2-5pm Mon-Sat), but they're like gold dust. Ticket prices
range from €5 to €370.

LOCAL KNOWLEDGE

CHRISTIANA SCHNEEWEISS, SALZBURG GUIDE

Best time to visit May when everything is in bloom and the mountains are still dusted with snow. September is lovely, too, with mild days and fewer crowds than in summer.

Salzburg Festival Even if you don't have tickets, you can still join in the fun! Opera and concert highlights are shown on a big screen against the spectacular backdrop of the fortress illuminated at the free Siemens Festival Nights on Kapitelplatz. If the weather is fine, little beats a performance of Jedermann on Domplatz – it is the very essence of the festival. Last-minute tickets are often available.

Great escapes Kapuzinerberg and Mönchsberg for shady strolls and magnificent panoramas of the Altstadt. For quiet contemplation, head to Friedhof St Sebastian or Stift Nonnberg, where the chapel choir contains wonderful 10th-century Byzantine frescos, which are among Austria's oldest.

Top day trips Gaisberg and Untersberg for hiking in Alpine surrounds; the Bavarian lakes, such as Königsee just across the border; and Waldbad Anif for a swim in beautiful forested surrounds.

Sightseeing tips Avoid the groups by visiting the big sights after 4pm. To feel the true spirit of the Dom, attend Sunday morning mass. Don't overlook lesser-known sights: the Dommuseum, for instance, is fascinating and rarely crowded.

rooms and pensions. Medieval guesthouses oozing history, avant-garde design hotels with river views and chilled-out hostels all huddle in the Altstadt, where booking ahead is advisable.

Bear in mind that the high-season prices below are jacked up another 10% to 20% during the Salzburg Festival. If Salzburg is booked solid, consider staying in Hallein or just across the border in Bavaria.

TOP CHOICE Haus Ballwein GUESTHOUSE €
(☑82 40 29; www.haus-ballwein.at; Moosstrasse 69a; s €35-45, d €58-68, tr €78-85, q €85-98, apt €100-115; ₱⑦₪) Country or city? Why not both at this farmhouse guesthouse, a 10-minute trundle from the Altstadton bus 21. With its bright, pine-filled rooms, mountain views, free bike hire and garden patrolled by duck duo, Rosalee and Clementine, this place is big on charm. The largest, quietest rooms face the back and have balconies and kitchenettes. Breakfast is a wholesome spread of fresh rolls, eggs, fruit, muesli and cold cuts.

Arte Vida GUESTHOUSE €€
(☑87 31 85; www.artevida.at; Dreifaltigkeitsgasse 9; s €55-140, d €80-152; ⑦) Arte Vida has the boho-chic feel of a Marrakech riad, with its lantern-lit salon, communal kitchen and serene garden. Asia and Africa have provided the inspiration for the rich colours and fabrics that dress the individually designed rooms, all with DVD players and iPod docks. Reinhold gives invaluable tips on Salzburg,

and arranges yoga sessions and outdoor activities.

Hotel Am Dom BOUTIQUE HOTEL €€
(☑84 27 65; www.hotelamdom.at; Goldgasse 17; s €90-160, d €130-260; ❀⑦) Antique meets boutique at this Altstadt hotel, where the original vaults and beams of the 800-year-old building contrast with razor-sharp design features. Artworks inspired by the musical legends of the Salzburg Festival grace the rooms, which sport caramel-champagne colour schemes, funky lighting, velvet throws and ultra-glam bathrooms.

Hotel & Villa Auersperg BOUTIQUE HOTEL €€
(☑88 94 40; www.auersperg.at; Auerspergstrasse 61; s €119-145, d €155-195, ste 225-295; ₱@⑦₪) This charismatic villa and hotel duo fuse late-19th-century flair with contemporary design. Guests can relax by the lily pond in the vine-strewn garden or in the rooftop wellness area with a sauna, tea bar and mountain views. Free bike hire is a bonus.

Haus Steiner GUESTHOUSE €
(☑83 00 31; www.haussteiner.com; Moosstrasse 156; s/d/tr €34/56/78; ₱⑦₪) Kind-natured Rosemarie runs a tight ship at this sunny yellow, chalet-style guesthouse, ablaze with flowers in summer. The pick of the petite rooms, furnished in natural wood, come with fridges and balconies with mood-lifting mountain views; family-sized apartments have kitchenettes. Breakfast is copious and the Altstadt is a 15-minute ride away on bus 21.

Hotel Schloss Mönchstein LUXURY HOTEL €€€
(☎84 85 55-0; www.monchstein.at; Mönchsberg Park 26; d €345-580, ste €595-1950; P❄🐾) On a fairy-tale perch atop Mönchsberg and set in hectares of wooded grounds, this 16th-century castle is honeymoon (and second mortgage) material. Persian rugs, oil paintings and Calcutta marble finish the rooms to beautiful effect. A massage in the spa, a candlelit tower dinner for two with Salzburg views, a helicopter ride – just say the word.

Weisse Taube HISTORIC HOTEL €€
(☎84 24 04; www.weissetaube.at; Kaigasse 9; s €88-98, d €139-152; 🐾) Housed in a central 14th-century building in a quiet corner of the Altstadt, the 'white dove' is a solid choice. Staff go out of their way to help and the warm-coloured rooms are large and well kept (some have fortress views). Breakfast is a generous spread.

Wolf Dietrich HISTORIC HOTEL €€
(☎87 12 75; www.salzburg-hotel.at; Wolf-Dietrich-Strasse 7; s €90-130, d €152-222, ste €197-277; P🐾❄🐾) For old-fashioned elegance you can't beat this central hotel, where rooms are dressed in polished wood furnishings and floral fabrics. There's even a suite based on Mozart's *Magic Flute,* with a star-studded ceiling and freestanding bath. By contrast, the spa and indoor pool are ultramodern. Organic produce is served at breakfast.

YOHO Salzburg HOSTEL €
(☎87 96 49; www.yoho.at; Paracelsusstrasse 9; dm €19-23, d €65-75; @🐾) This fun-loving hostel has got it sussed. Free wi-fi, secure lockers, comfy bunks, plenty of cheap beer and good-value schnitzels – what more could a backpacker ask for? Except, perhaps, a merry sing-along with the *Sound of Music* screened daily (yes, *every* day). The friendly crew can arrange tours, adventure sports like rafting and canyoning, and bike hire.

Pension Katrin PENSION €€
(☎83 08 60; www.pensionkatrin.at; Nonntaler Hauptstrasse 49b; s/d/tr/q €59/102/138/156; P🐾) With its flowery garden, bright and cheerful rooms and homemade goodies at breakfast, this pension is one of the homiest in Salzburg. The affable Terler family keep everything spick and span. Be prepared to lug your bags as there's no lift. The pension is 1km south of the Altstadt; take bus 5 to Wäschergasse.

Arthotel Blaue Gans BOUTIQUE HOTEL €€€
(☎84 24 91-0; www.hotel-blaue-gans-salzburg.at; Getreidegasse 41-43; s €125-175, d €159-320; ❄🐾) Contemporary design blends harmoniously with the original vaulting and beams of this 660-year-old hotel. Rooms are pure and simple, with clean lines, lots of white and streamlined furnishings. The restaurant is well worth a visit.

Hotel Elefant HISTORIC HOTEL €€
(☎84 33 97; www.elefant.at; Sigmund-Haffner-Gasse 4; s €86-109, d €102-192, tr €142-245; ❄🐾🐾) Occupying a 700-year-old building and run by the good-natured Mayr family, this central Best Western hotel has loads of charm. Bright colours add a modern touch to the spacious, elegantly furnished rooms. A generous breakfast is available.

Hotel Sacher LUXURY HOTEL €€€
(☎88 97 70; www.sacher.com; Schwarzstrasse 5-7; s €220-335, d €234-393, ste €490-774; P❄🐾🐾) Tom Hanks, the Dalai Lama and Julie Andrews have all stayed at this 19th-century pile on the banks of the Salzach. Scattered with oil paintings and antiques, the rooms have gleaming marble bathrooms, and fortress or river views. Compensate for indulging on chocolate *Sacher Torte* in the health club.

Hotel Mozart HISTORIC HOTEL €€
(☎87 22 74; www.hotel-mozart.at; Franz-Josef-Strasse 27; s/d/tr/q €95/140/160/180; P🐾🐾) An antique-filled lobby gives way to spotless rooms with comfy beds and sizeable bathrooms at the Mozart. You'll have to fork out an extra €10 for breakfast, but it's a good spread with fresh fruit, boiled eggs, cold cuts and pastries.

Goldener Hirsch LUXURY HOTEL €€€
(☎80 84-0; www.goldenerhirschsalzburg.com; Getreidegasse 37; s €190-455, d €220-560; P❄@🐾) A skylight illuminates the arcaded inner courtyard of this 600-year-old Altstadt pile, where famous past guests include Queen Elizabeth and Pavarotti. Countess Harriet Walderdorff tastefully scattered the opulent rooms with objets d'art and hand-printed fabrics. Downstairs are two restaurants: beamed **s'Herzl** (☎8084-0; Getreidegasse 37; mains €11-19; ⏱lunch & dinner) and vaulted Restaurant Goldener Hirsch.

Bergland Hotel BOUTIQUE HOTEL €€
(☎87 23 18; www.berglandhotel.at; Rupertgasse 15; s €60-85, d €80-139, tr €99-149; P🐾) Don't

NO TOURIST TRAPP

Did you know that there were 10, not seven Trapp children, the eldest of whom was Rupert (so long Liesl)? Or that the captain was a gentle, family-loving man and Maria no soft touch? Or, perhaps, that in 1938 the Trapp family left quietly for the United States instead of climbing every mountain to Switzerland? For the truth behind the Hollywood legend, stay the night at **Villa Trapp** (☑63 08 60; www.villa-trapp.com; Traunstrasse 34; d €109-500), tucked away in Salzburg's biggest private park in the Aigen district, 3km east of the Altstadt.

Marianne and Christopher have transformed the original von Trapp family home into a beautiful guesthouse (for guests only, we might add). The 19th-century villa is elegant, if not as palatial as in the movie, with tasteful wood-floored rooms and a balustrade for sweeping down á la Baroness Schräder. Family snapshots and heirlooms, including the baron's model ships and a photo of guest Pink Floyd guitarist David Gilmour strumming 'Edelweiss', grace the dining room. From the main station, take a train or bus 160 to Aigen.

be fooled by the nondescript exterior. In the Kuhn family since 1912, the Bergland is ever so homely inside, with art (courtesy of the owner) on the walls, touches like traditional Austrian hats and painted furnishings in the rooms, and a handsome piano room.

Hotel Amadeus HISTORIC HOTEL €€€
(☑87 14 01; www.hotelamadeus.at; Linzer Gasse 43-45; s/d €92/180; 🕸) Centrally situated on the right bank, this 500-year-old hotel has a boutique feel, with bespoke touches such as chandeliers and four-poster beds in the vibrantly coloured rooms. Guests are treated to free tea or coffee in the afternoon.

Hotel Bristol LUXURY HOTEL €€€
(☑87 35 57; www.bristol-salzburg.at; Makartplatz 4; s/d/ste €240/355/630; 🅿🕸🛜) The Bristol transports you back to a more decadent era. Chandelier-lit salons, champagne at breakfast, exquisitely crafted furniture, service as polished as the marble – this is pure class. Even Emperor Franz Josef and Sigmund Freud felt at home here.

Hotel Rosenvilla GUESTHOUSE €€
(☑62 17 65; www.rosenvilla.com; Höfelgasse 4; s €68-97, d €113-143, ste €146-233; 🅿🛜🛅) This guesthouse goes the extra mile with its sharp-styled contemporary rooms, faultless service and incredible breakfasts with spreads, breads, cereals, eggs and fruit to jump-start your day. Take bus 7 to Finanzamt or walk 15 minutes along the tree-lined riverfront into the centre.

Hotel Zur Goldenen Ente HISTORIC HOTEL €€€
(☑84 56 22; www.ente.at; Goldgasse 10; s/d/apt €125/160/300; 🕸🍴) Bang in the heart of the Altstadt, this 700-year-old townhouse has

oodles of charm – some rooms have four-poster beds, while Emperor Franz Josef guards over others. The sunny terrace overlooks the rooftops of the old town.

JUFA Salzburg City HOSTEL €
(☑05-7083 613; www.jufa.eu; Josef-Preis-Allee 18; dm €21, s €59-69, d €75-119; 🅿🛜🛅) True, its plain, modern facade won't bowl you over, but this budget pick has got plenty going for it: super-clean dorms, bike rental, generous breakfasts (included in rates), the *Sound of Music* shown daily at 8pm and a sun-trap of a cafe terrace with views of Hohensalzburg fortress. It's a five-minute stroll southeast of the Altstadt.

Stadtalm HOSTEL €
(☑84 17 29; www.diestadtalm.com; dm €19) This turreted hostel plopped on top of Mönchsberg takes in the entire Salzburg panorama, from the city's spires and fortress to Kapuzinerberg. There's a good-value restaurant on-site.

✖ Eating

Salzburg's eclectic dining scene skips from the traditional to the super-trendy to the downright touristy. This is a city where schnitzel is served with a slice of history in vaulted taverns, where you can dine in Michelin-starred finery or be serenaded by a warbling Maria wannabe. Save euros by taking advantage of the lunchtime *Tagesmenü* (fixed menu) served at most places.

TOP CHOICE Magazin MODERN EUROPEAN €€€
(☑84 15 84; www.magazin.co.at; Augustinergasse 13a; mains €25-31, tasting menus €57-79, cookery classes €130-150; ⊙Mon-Sat) Chef Richard

Brunnauer's culinary flair and careful sourcing have gastronomes whispering Michelin star. Gathered around a courtyard below Mönchsberg's sheer rock wall, Magazin shelters a deli, wine store, cookery school and restaurant. Menus fizzing with seasonal flavours – scallops with vine-ripened peaches, celery and buttermilk, venison medallions in porcini sauce – are matched with wines from the 850-bottle cellar and served alfresco or in the industro-chic, cavelike interior. Hands-on cookery classes must be pre-booked. Buses 4 and 21 stop at Augustinergasse.

Alter Fuchs   AUSTRIAN €€
([✆]88 20 22; Linzer Gasse 47-49; mains €9.50-16; ☺Mon-Sat; [✎🚶]) This sly old fox prides itself on witty service and old-fashioned Austrian fare – both rarities in the Altstadt. Go for a schnitzel fried to golden perfection or pumpkin seed–coated cordon bleu. Bandana-clad foxes guard the bar in the vaulted interior and there's a courtyard for good-weather dining. In the cosy *Stube* out back, scribbling on the walls (chalk only, please) is positively encouraged.

Gasthof Schloss Aigen   AUSTRIAN €€€
([✆]62 12 84; www.schloss-aigen.at; Schwarzenbergpromenade 37; mains €19-32, menus €32.50-52.50; ☺closed Tue, Wed, lunch Thu) A country manor with an elegantly rustic interior and a chestnut-shaded courtyard, this is Austrian dining at its finest. The Forstner family's house speciality is 'Wiener Melange', different cuts of meltingly tender Pinzgauer beef, served with apple horseradish, chive sauce and roast potatoes, best matched with robust Austrian wines. Bus 7 stops at Bahnhof Aigen, a 10-minute stroll away.

Esszimmer   FRENCH €€€
([✆]87 08 99; www.esszimmer.com; Müllner Hauptstrasse 33; 3-course lunch, tasting menus €68-95; ☺Tue-Sat) Andreas Kaiblinger puts an innovative spin on market-driven French cuisine at Michelin-starred Esszimmer. Eye-catching art, playful backlighting and a glass floor revealing the Almkanal stream keep diners captivated, as do gastronomic showstoppers such as Artic char with calf's head and asparagus. Buses 7, 21 and 28 to Landeskrankenhaus stop close by.

Zum Fidelen Affen   AUSTRIAN €€
([✆]87 73 61; Priesterhausgasse 8; mains €10.50-16.50; ☺dinner Mon-Sat) The jolly monkey lives up to its name with a sociable vibe.

Presuming you've booked ahead, you'll dine heartily under vaults or on the terrace on well-prepared Austrian classics like goulash, *Schlutzkrapfen* (Tyrolean ravioli) and sweet curd dumplings.

Riedenburg   MODERN EUROPEAN €€€
([✆]83 08 15; www.riedenburg.at; Neutorstrasse 31; lunch €18, mains €26-35; ☺Tue-Sat) Martin Pichler mans the stove at this Michelin-starred restaurant with a romantic garden pavilion. His imaginative, seasonally inflected flavours, such as quail breast on asparagus with Bloody Mary and strawberry *Knödel* (dumpling), are expertly matched with top wines. The €18 lunch is a bargain. Riedenburg is a 10-minute walk southwest of the Altstadt along Neutorstrasse; take bus 1, 4 or 5 to Moosstrasse.

M32   FUSION €€
([✆]84 10 00; www.m32.at; Mönchsberg 32; 2-course lunch €13.90, mains €16-26; ☺9am-1am Tue-Sun; [✎🚶]) Bold colours and a veritable forest of stag antlers reveal architect Matteo Thun's imprint at Museum der Moderne's ultra-sleek restaurant. The food goes with the seasons with specialities like tortellini of organic local beef with tomato ragout and tangy green-apple sorbet with cassis. The glass-walled restaurant and terrace take in the full sweep of Salzburg's mountain-backed skyline.

Ikarus   MODERN EUROPEAN €€€
([✆]21 97 77; www.hangar-7.com; tasting menus €150-170; ☺daily) At the space-age Hangar-7 complex at the airport, this glamorous restaurant is the epitome of culinary globe-trotting. Each month, Roland Trettl invites a world-famous chef to cook for a serious foodie crowd.

Bärenwirt   AUSTRIAN €€
([✆]42 24 04; www.baerenwirt-salzburg.at; Müllner Hauptstrasse 8; mains €9-11) Sizzling and stirring since 1663, Bärenwirt is Austrian through and through. Go for hearty *Bierbraten* (beer roast) with dumplings, locally caught trout or organic wild boar bratwurst. A tiled oven warms the woody, hunting-lodge-style interior in winter, while the river-facing terrace is a summer crowd-puller. The restaurant is 500m north of Museumplatz.

Blaue Gans Restaurant   AUSTRIAN €€€
([✆]84 24 91-50; www.blauegans.at; Getreidegasse 43; mains €16-25; ☺Mon-Sat) The 650-year-old

vaults of Arthotel Blaue Gans make a refined setting for this restuarant, serving regional cuisine, such as roast saddle of Hohe Tauern venison and poussin with nettle ravioli and chanterelles married with full-bodied wines. The olive tree–dotted terrace is popular in summer.

Afro Café
AFRICAN €€

(☑84 48 88; www.afrocoffee.com; Bürgerspital-platz 5; lunch €6.70, mains €10-15; ⊙9am-midnight Mon-Sat) Hot-pink walls, butterfly chairs, artworks made from beach junk and *big* hair...this afro-chic cafe is totally groovy. Staff keep the good vibes and food coming – think springbok in a sesame-coriander crust on lentils and lemongrass-zucchini cake.

Triangel
AUSTRIAN €€

(☑84 22 29; Wiener-Philharmoniker-Gasse 7; lunch €4.90, mains €9-21; ⊙Mon-Sat) The menu is market-fresh at this arty bistro, where the picture-clad walls pay tribute to Salzburg Festival luminaries. It does gourmet salads such as saddle of veal with rocket and parmesan, a mean Hungarian goulash with organic beef, and delicious homemade ice cream.

Zwettler's
AUSTRIAN €€

(☑84 41 99; Kaigasse 3; mains €9-11; ⊙Tue-Sun) This gastro pub has a lively buzz on its pavement terrace. Kaiser Karl wheat beers pair nicely with spot-on local grub like schnitzel with parsley potatoes, goulash and *Salzburger Nockerl* (soufflé).

Carpe Diem Finest Finger Food
FUSION €€€

(☑84 88 00; www.carpediemfinestfingerfood.com; Getreidegasse 50; 3-course lunch €19.50, mains €26.50-34.50; ⊙8.30am-midnight daily) This avant-garde, Michelin-starred lounge-restaurant sits in pride of place on Getreidegasse. A food-literate crowd flock here for cocktails and finger-food cones, mini taste sensations with fillings like tomato panna cotta with Jerusalem artichoke and scallop-rhubarb.

Alt Salzburg
AUSTRIAN €€€

(☑84 14 76; Bürgerspitalgasse 2; mains €15-29; ⊙lunch & dinner Tue-Sat, dinner Mon) Tucked into a courtyard at the base of Mönchsberg, this supremely cosy restaurant has attentive service, hearty regional specialities like venison and veal knuckle, and fine Austrian wines.

Saran Essbar
INDIAN €€

(☑84 66 28; Judengasse 10; mains €10-14; ⊙daily) Eat under the vaults or on the pocket-sized terrace at this Austro-Indian restaurant, run by the ever-smiling Mr Saran. This is the only place in Salzburg where you'll find Bengali fish curry, schnitzel and strudel on the same menu.

Wilder Mann
AUSTRIAN €€

(☑84 17 87; Getreidegasse 20; mains €9-17; ⊙daily) Dirndl-clad waitresses bring goulash with dumplings, schnitzels and other light and airy fare to the table at this old-world Austrian tavern in the Altstadt.

Spicy Spices
INDIAN €

(☑87 07 12; Wolf-Dietrich-Strasse 1; mains €6.50; ⊙daily; ☑) 'Healthy heart, lovely soul' is the mantra of this all-organic, all-vegetarian haunt. Service is slow but friendly. It's worth the wait for the good-value *thali* (appetisers) and curries mopped up with *paratha* (flat bread).

Sarastro
INTERNATIONAL €€

(Wiener-Philharmoniker-Gasse 9; mains €11-21.50; ⊙Tue-Sun; ☑✦) Colourful stained glass illuminates this vaulted place at the Rupertinum, opening on to a vine-draped courtyard. The food is Austro-Italian: seafood goulash, summery, herb-dressed salads, parmesan-sprinkled spinach *Knödel* (dumplings) and the like. The two-course lunch is a snip at €7.90.

K+K
AUSTRIAN €€

(☑84 21 56; Waagplatz 2; mains €14-26; ⊙daily; ✦) This buzzy restaurant on the square is a warren of vaulted and wood-panelled rooms. Whether you go for crayfish tails, saddle of venison in morel sauce or good old bratwurst with lashings of potatoes and cabbage – the food here is spot on.

Pescheria Backi
SEAFOOD €€

(Franz-Josef-Strasse 16b; lunch €10.80, mains €9-15; ⊙9am-10pm Mon-Fri, 9am-noon Sat) A clapboard shed of a fishmonger-bistro dishing up fish, fresh and simple, to a hungry crowd of regulars.

Heart of Joy
CAFE €

(Franz-Josef-Strasse 3; lunch €6.90, snacks €3-6; ⊙8am-6pm; ☎☑) Ayurveda-inspired cafe with an all-vegetarian, mostly organic menu. It does great bagels, salads, homemade cakes and juices.

IceZeit
ICE CREAM €

(Chiemseegasse 1; scoop €1.20; ⊙11am-8pm) Grab a cone at Salzburg's best ice-cream parlour, with flavours from poppy seed to passionfruit.

Mensa Toskana
CAFE €

(Sigmund-Haffner-Gasse 11; lunch €4.50-5.40; ⊙lunch Mon-Fri) University cafe in the Altstadt, with courtyard seating and pocket-money priced lunches.

Self-Catering
Grüner Markt
FOOD MARKET €

(Green Market; Universitätsplatz; ⊙Mon-Sat) A one-stop picnic shop on one of Salzburg's grandest squares, for regional cheese, ham, fruit, bread and gigantic pretzels.

Kaslöchl
CHEESE €

(Hagenauerplatz 2) A mouse-sized Austrian cheese shop, crammed with creamy alpine varieties, holey Emmental and fresh cheese with herbs.

Stiftsbäckerei St Peter
BAKERY €

(Mühlenhof; ⊙8am-5.30pm Mon & Tue, 7am-5.30pm Thu & Fri, 7am-1pm Sat) Next to the monastery where the watermill turns, this 700-year-old bakery bakes Salzburg's best sourdough loaves (€3.10 per kilogram) from a wood-fired oven.

🍷 Drinking

A *Stein*-swinging beer hall, a sundowner on the Salzach, an intimate wine bar for appreciating the subtle nuances of Grüner Veltliner wines – all possible ideas for a good night out in Salzburg. Nobody's pretending this is rave city, but the days of lights out by 11pm are long gone. You'll find the biggest concentration of bars along both banks of the Salzach and some of the hippest around Gstättengasse. Rudolfskai can be on the rough side of rowdy at weekends.

[TOP CHOICE] Augustiner Bräustübl
BREWERY

(www.augustinerbier.at; Augustinergasse 4-6; ⊙3-11pm Mon-Fri, 2.30-11pm Sat & Sun) Who says monks can't enjoy themselves? This cheery monastery-run brewery has been serving potent homebrews in traditional ceramic *Stein* mugs since 1621. Fill yours from the pump in the foyer, visit the snack stands and take a pew in the vaulted hall or beneath the chestnut trees in the 1000-seat beer garden.

Republic
BAR

(www.republic-cafe.at; Anton-Neumayr-Platz 2; ⊙8am-1am Sun-Thu, to 4am Fri & Sat) One of Salzburg's most happening haunts, this backlit lounge-bar opens onto a popular terrace on the square. By night, DJs spin to a 20-something, cocktail-sipping crowd in the club. Check the website for free events from jazz, Latin and swing breakfasts to weekly salsa nights (9pm on Tuesdays).

StieglKeller
BEER HALL

(Festungsgasse 10; ⊙11am-midnight Mon-Sat, 10am-midnight Sun) For a 365-day taste of Oktoberfest, try this cavernous Munich-style beer hall, which shares the same architect as Munich's Hofbräuhaus. It has an enormous garden above the city's rooftops and a meaty menu (snacks €6.50 to €11.50). Beer is cheapest from the self-service taps outside. Rollicking events include Sunday morning's post-church, pre-lunch *Frühschoppen* and Thursday evening's *Brauchtumsabend*, when Austrian bands bash out jaunty folk numbers.

Die Weisse
PUB

(www.dieweisse.at; Rupertgasse 10; ⊙pub 10.30am-midnight Mon-Sat, Sudwerk bar 5pm-4am Mon-Sat) The cavernous brewpub of the Salzburger Weissbierbrauerei, this is the place to guzzle cloudy wheat beers in the wood-floored pub and the shady beer garden out back. DJs work the decks in Sudwerk bar, especially at the monthly Almrausch when locals party in skimpy dirndls and strapping lederhosen.

Steinterrasse
COCKTAIL BAR

(Giselakai 3; ⊙3pm-midnight Sun-Thu, to 1am Fri & Sat) Hotel Stein's chichi 7th-floor terrace attracts Salzburg's Moët-sipping socialites and anyone who loves a good view. It isn't cheap, but it is the best spot to see the Altstadt light up against the theatrical backdrop of the fortress.

Humboldt Stub'n
BAR

(Gstättengasse 4-6; ⊙10am-2am, to 4am Fri & Sat) Cartoons deck the walls and a nail-studded Mozart punk guards this upbeat bar opposite Republic. Try a Mozart cocktail, a sickly composition of liqueur, cherry juice, cream and chocolate. Wednesday is student night, with beers a snip at €2.50.

Unikum Sky
CAFE

(Unipark Nonntal; ⊙10am-7pm Mon-Fri, 8am-7pm Sat) For knockout fortress views and a full-on Salzburg panorama, head up to this

CAFE CULTURE

You can make yourself pretty *gemütlich* (comfy) over coffee and people-watching in Salzburg's cafes. Expect to pay around €4 for a slice of cake and €8 for a day special. Here are our six favourites:

Café Tomaselli (www.tomaselli.at; Alter Markt 9; ⊙7am-9pm Mon-Sat, 8am-9pm Sun) Going strong since 1705, this marble and wood-panelled cafe is a former Mozart haunt. It's famous for having Salzburg's flakiest strudels, best *Einspänner* (coffee with whipped cream) and grumpiest waiters.

Sacher (www.sacher.com; Schwarzstrasse 5-7; ⊙7.30am-midnight) Nowhere is the chocolate richer, the apricot jam tangier and cream lighter than at the home of the legendary *Sacher Torte*. The cafe is pure old-world grandeur, with its picture-lined walls and ruby-red banquettes. Sit on the terrace by the Salzach for fortress views.

220 Grad (Chiemseegasse 5; ⊙9am-7pm Tue-Sat) Famous for freshly ground coffee, this retro-chic cafe serves probably the best espresso in town.

Fingerlos (Franz-Josef-Strasse 9; ⊙7.30am-7.30pm Tue-Sun) Salzburgers rave about the dainty petits fours, flaky pastries and creamy tortes served at this high-ceilinged cafe. Join a well-dressed crowd for breakfast or a lazy afternoon of coffee and newspapers.

Café am Kai (Müllner Hauptstrasse 4; ⊙9am-9pm daily) On the banks of the Salzach River, this is a pleasantly low-key cafe to kick back over coffee and cake, ice cream or a cold beer.

Café Bazar (www.cafe-bazar.at; Schwarzstrasse 3; ⊙7.30am-11pm Mon-Sat, 9am-6pm Sat) All chandeliers and polished wood, locals enjoy the same river views today over breakfast, cake and intelligent conversation, as Marlene Dietrich did in 1936.

sun-kissed terrace atop the new Unipark Nonntal campus, 300m south of Schanzl-gasse in the Altstadt. It's a relaxed spot to chill over drinks and inexpensive snacks.

Köchelverzeichnis   WINE BAR
(Steingasse 27; ⊙5-11pm Tue-Sat) This is a real neighbourhood bar with jazzy music, antipasti and great selection of wines. Taste citrusy Grüner Veltliners and rieslings from the family's vineyards in the Wachau.

Mayday Bar   COCKTAIL BAR
(www.hangar-7.com; ⊙noon-midnight Sun-Thu, to 1am Fri & Sat) Peer down at Flying Bulls' aircraft through the glass walls at this crystalline bar, part of the airport's futuristic Hangar-7 complex. Strikingly illuminated by night, it's a unique place for a fresh fruit cocktail or 'smart food' appetisers served in Bodum glasses.

Cave le Robinet   WINE BAR
(Steingasse 41; ⊙2-6pm Tue-Sat) This historic vaulted cellar has an excellent range of Austrian and European wines, including pinots from the owner's vineyard in Burgundy. Open wines start at €2.50 a glass.

☆ Entertainment

TOP CHOICE **Salzburger Marionettentheater**   THEATRE
(☎87 24 06; www.marionetten.at; Schwarzstrasse 24; ⊙May-Sep, Christmas, Easter; ⊛) The red curtain goes up on a miniature stage at this marionette theatre, a lavish stucco, cherub and chandelier-lit affair. The repertoire star is the *Sound of Music*, with a life-sized Mother Superior and a marionette-packed finale. Other enchanting productions include Mozart's the *Magic Flute*, Tchaikovsky's the *Nutcracker* and Strauss' *Die Fledermaus*. All have multilingual surtitles.

Landestheater   THEATER
(☎87 15 12-0; www.salzburger-landestheater.at; Schwarzstrasse 22; ⊛) Opera, operetta, ballet and musicals dominate the stage at this elegant 18th-century playhouse. There's a strong emphasis on Mozart's music, with the Mozarteum Salzburg Orchestra often in the pit. There are dedicated performances for kids, and the *Sound of Music* musical is a winner with all ages.

Schlosskonzerte
CLASSICAL MUSIC

(☑84 85 86; www.salzburger-schlosskonzerte.at; Theatergasse 2; ☺8pm) A fantasy of coloured marble, stucco and frescoes, Schloss Mirabell's baroque *Marmorsaal* (Marble Hall) is the exquisite setting for chamber music concerts. Internationally renowned soloists and ensembles perform works by Mozart and other well-known composers such as Haydn and Chopin. Tickets cost between €29 and €35.

Mozarteum
CLASSICAL MUSIC

(☑88 94 0-0; www.mozarteum.at; Schwarzstrasse 26-28) Opened in 1880 and revered for its supreme acoustics, the Mozarteum highlights the life and works of Mozart through chamber music (October to June), concerts and opera. The annual highlight is Mozart Week in January.

ARGEkultur
CONCERT VENUE

(www.argekultur.at; Ulrike-Gschwandtner-Strasse 5) This alternative cultural venue was born out of protests against the Salzburg Festival in the 1980s. Today it's a bar and performing-arts hybrid. Traversing the entire arts spectrum, the line-up features concerts, cabaret, DJ nights, dance, poetry slams and world music. It's at the Unipark Nonntal campus, a five-minute walk east of the Altstadt.

Rockhouse
LIVE MUSIC

(www.rockhouse.at; Schallmooser Hauptstrasse 46) Salzburg's hottest live music venue, Rockhouse presents first-rate rock, pop, jazz, folk, metal and reggae concerts – see the website for details. There's also a tunnel-shaped bar that has DJs (usually free) and bands. Rockhouse is 1km northeast of the Altstadt; take bus 4 to Canavalstrasse.

Jazzit
JAZZ CLUB

(☑88 32 64; www.jazzit.at; Elisabethstrasse 11; ☺Tue-Sat) Hosts regular concerts from tango to electro alongside workshops and club nights. Don't miss the free Tuesday-night jam sessions in Jazzit:Bar. It's 600m north of the Mirabellgarten along Elisabethstrasse.

Salzburg Arena
CONCERT VENUE

(☑24 04-0; www.salzburgarena.at; Am Messezentrum 1) Under a domed wooden roof, this is Salzburg's premier stage for sporting events, musicals and big-name concerts (Santana and Bob Dylan have played here). The arena is 3km north of town; take bus 1 to Messe.

Das Kino
CINEMA

(www.daskino.at; Giselakai 11) Shows independent and art-house films from Austria and across the globe in their original language. The cinema hosts the mountain-focused Bergfilmfestival in November.

Sound of Salzburg Show
SHOW

(☑82 66 17; www.soundofsalzburgshow.com; Griesgasse 23; tickets with/without dinner €48/33; ☺7.30pm May-Oct) This all-singing show at Sternbräu is a triple bill of Mozart, the *Sound of Music* and operetta faves performed in traditional costume. Kitsch but fun.

Mozart Dinner
CONCERT SHOW

(☑82 86 95; www.mozartdinnerconcert.com; Sankt-Peter-Bezirk 1; ☺8.30pm) You'll love or hate this themed dinner, with Mozart music, costumed performers and (mediocre) 18th-century-style food. It's held in Stiftskeller St Peter's lavish baroque hall.

🔒 Shopping

Traditional wrought-iron signs hang above the shops on Getreidegasse, which has everything from designer fashion to hats. Goldgasse has accessories, antiques and porcelain. A popular street for a shop and stroll is Linzer Gasse.

TOP CHOICE Fürst
FOOD

(www.original-mozartkugel.com; Getreidegasse 47; ☺10am-6.30pm Mon-Sat, 11am-5pm Sun) Pistachio, nougat and dark chocolate dreams, the *Mozartkugeln* (Mozart balls) here are still handmade to Paul Fürst's original 1890 recipe and cost €1 per mouthful. Other specialities include cube-shaped Bach Würfel – coffee, nut and marzipan truffles dedicated to yet another great composer.

Johann Nagy & Söhne
GIFTS

(Linzer Gasse 32) Since it opened in 1870, this family-run store has been doing a brisk trade in hand-painted candles, wax figurines and gingerbread; there are around 40 different kinds of gingerbread to choose from.

Musikhaus Katholnigg
MUSIC

(Sigmund-Haffner-Gasse 16) Housed in a 16th-century townhouse and a music shop since 1847, this is the place to pick up high-quality recordings of the Salzburg Festival. There's a huge selection of classical, jazz, chanson and folk CDs and DVDs.

RETURN OF THE TRACHT

Ever thought about purchasing a tight-fitting dirndl or a pair strapping lederhosen? No? Well, Salzburg might just change your mind with its *Trachten* (traditional costume) stores adding alpine oomph to your wardrobe. If you have visions of old maids in gingham and men in feathered hats, you might be surprised. Walk the streets where 20-somethings flaunt the latest styles or hit the dance-floor at Die Weisse's Almrausch club night and you'll see that hemlines have risen and necklines have plunged over the years; that young Salzburger are reinventing the style by teaming lederhosen with T-shirts and trainers or pairing slinky off-the-shoulder numbers with ballet pumps. Their message? *Trachten* can be cool, even sexy.

Embracing the trend is **Ploom** (www.ploom.at; Ursulinenplatz 5; ⊙11am-6pm Thu & Fri, 11am-5pm Sat), where designer Pflaum has playfully and successfully reinvented the dirndl; her boutique is a wonderland of floaty femininity: a sky-blue bodice here, a frothy cotton blouse, a wisp of a turquoise *Schürze* (apron) or silk evening gown there.

For a more classic look, there's **Lanz Trachten** (www.lanztrachten.at; Schwarzstrasse 4) and upscale **Stassny** (www.stassny.at; Getreidegasse 30), combining *Tracht*-making know-how with high-quality fabrics and age-old patterns (stag prints, polka dots, gingham etc). For a fusion of modern and traditional *Trachten* in myriad colours, try mid-range **Forstenlechner** (www.salzburg-trachtenmode.at; Mozartplatz 4) and **Wenger** (www.wenger.at; Getreidegasse 29); the latter stocks figure-hugging lederhosen for ladies and dirndls from below-the-knee Heidi to thigh-flashing diva creations trimmed with ribbons and lace.

Zotter
FOOD

(Herbert-von-Karajan-Platz 4) Made in Austria, Zotter's organic, Fairtrade chocolate – including unusual varieties like Styrian pumpkin, ginger-carrot and mountain cheese-walnut – is divine. Dip a spoon into the choc fountain and try samples from the conveyor belt.

Alte Hofapotheke
PHARMACY

(Alte Markt 6) For a whiff of nostalgia and a packet of sage throat pastilles, nip into this wonderfully old-fashioned, wood-panelled pharmacy, Salzburg's oldest, founded in 1591.

Salzburg Salz
GIFTS

(Wiener-Philharmoniker-Gasse 6) Pure salt from Salzburgerland and the Himalaya, herbal salts and rock-salt tea lights are among the high-sodium wonders here.

Drechslerei Lackner
GIFTS

(Badergasse 2) The hand-carved nutcrackers, nativity figurines and filigree Christmas stars are the real deal at this traditional craft shop.

Spirituosen Sporer
WINE

(Getreidegasse 39) In Getreidegasse's narrowest house, family-run Sporer has been intoxicating local folk with Austrian wines, herbal liqueurs and famous *Vogelbeer* (rowan berry) schnapps since 1903.

❶ Information

EMERGENCY Hospital (☏44 82; Müllner Hauptstrasse 48) Just north of Mönchsberg. **Police Headquarters** (☏63 83; Alpenstrasse 90)

INTERNET ACCESS There are several cheap internet cafes near the train station. A more central choice is **City Net Café** (Gstättengasse 11; per hr €2; ⊙10am-10pm), also offering discount calls.

MONEY *Bankomaten* (ATMs) are all over the place. Many hotels, bars and cafes offer free wi-fi. Exchange booths are open all day every day at the airport. There are also plenty of exchange offices downtown, but beware of potentially high commission rates.

POST Main Post Office (Residenzplatz 9; ⊙8am-6pm Mon-Fri, 9am-noon Sat) **Station Post Office** (Südtiroler Platz 1)

TOURIST INFORMATION The main **tourist office** (☏889 87-330; www.salzburg.info; Mozartplatz 5; ⊙9am-6pm or 6.30pm, closed Sun Sep-Mar) has plenty of information about the city and its immediate surrounds. There's a **ticket booking agency** (www.salzburgticket.com) in the same building. For information on the rest of the province, visit **Salzburgerland Tourismus** (www.salzburgerland.com)

TRAVEL AGENCIES STA Travel (www.statravel.at; Rainerstrasse 2) Student and budget travel agency.

ⓘ Getting There & Away

Air

Salzburg airport (www.salzburg-airport.com), a 20-minute bus ride from the centre, has regular scheduled flights to destinations all over Austria and Europe. Low-cost flights from the UK are provided by **Ryanair** (www.ryanair.com) and **EasyJet** (www.easyjet.com). Other airlines include **British Airways** (www.britishairways. com) and **Jet2** (www.jet2.com).

Bus

Buses depart from just outside the Hauptbahnhof on Südtiroler Platz, where timetables are displayed. Bus information and tickets are available from the information points on the main concourse. For more information on buses in and around Salzburg and an online timetable see www.svv-info.at and www.postbus.at.

Car & Motorcycle

Three motorways converge on Salzburg to form a loop around the city: the A1/E60 from Linz, Vienna and the east; the A8/E52 from Munich and the west; and the A10/E55 from Villach and the south. The quickest way to Tyrol is to take the road to Bad Reichenhall in Germany and continue to Lofer (B178) and St Johann in Tyrol.

Train

Salzburg has excellent rail connections with neighbouring Bavaria in Germany and the rest of Austria, though the Hauptbahnhof is undergoing extensive renovation until 2014.

Direct EC trains run at least hourly to Munich (€34, 1¾ hours) and every two hours to Stuttgart (€77, four hours). S-Bahn (suburban metro railway) trains operate twice hourly between the Hauptbahnhof and Bad Reichenhall (€5.10, 37 minutes). Reaching Berchtesgaden (€8.10, 1½ hours, hourly) by S-Bahn involves a change at Freilassing. For timetables, see www.svv-info.at.

The quickest way to Innsbruck is by the 'corridor' train through Germany; trains depart at least every two hours (€41.30, two hours) and stop at Kufstein. Trains leave frequently to Vienna (€49.90, three hours) and Linz (€23.70, 1¼ hours). There is a two-hourly express service to Klagenfurt (€38.70, three hours).

There are also several trains daily to Berlin (€134, eight hours), Budapest (€76, 5¾ hours), Prague (€79.60, seven hours) and Venice (€49, 6½ to nine hours).

ⓘ Getting Around

To/From the Airport

Salzburg airport is around 5.5km west of the centre along Innsbrucker Bundesstrasse. Buses 2, 8 and 27 (€2.30) depart from outside the terminal roughly every 10 minutes and make several central stops near the Altstadt; buses 2 and 27 terminate at the Hauptbahnhof. Services operate roughly from 5.30am to 11pm. A taxi between the airport and the centre costs €15 to €20.

Bicycle

Salzburg is one of Austria's most bike-friendly cities, with an extensive network of scenic cycling trails heading off in all directions, including along the banks of the Salzach River. See www.movelo.com (in German) for a list of places renting out electric bikes.

A Velo (Mozartplatz; 1hr/half-/full day €4.50/10/16, e-bike €6/16/22; ☺9am-6pm mid-Apr–Oct) Just across the way from the tourist office.

Top Bike (www.topbike.at; Staatsbrücke; ☺10am-5pm) Rents bikes for around €15 per day (half-price for kids). The Salzburg Card yields a 20% discount.

Bus

Bus drivers sell single (€2.30) and 24-hour (€5.20) tickets. If you're planning on making several trips, *Tabak* (tobacconist) shops sell tickets even cheaper still (€1.60 each), but only in units of five. Week tickets (€13.60) can be purchased from machines and *Tabak* shops. Children under six travel free, while all other children pay half-price.

Bus routes are shown at bus stops and on some city maps; bus 1 starts from the Hauptbahnhof and skirts the pedestrian-only Altstadt. Another central stop is Hanuschplatz.

Bus Taxi

'Bus taxis' operate from 11.30pm to 1.30am (3am on weekends) on fixed routes, dropping off and picking up along the way, for a cost of €4.50. Ferdinand-Hanusch-Platz is the departure point for suburban routes on the left bank, and Theatergasse for routes on the right bank.

Car & Motorcycle

Parking places are limited and much of the Altstadt is only accessible on foot, so it's easier to leave your car at one of three park-and-ride points to the west, north and south of the city. The largest car park in the centre is the Altstadt Garage under Mönchsberg (€14 per day); some restaurants in the centre will stamp your ticket for a reduction. Rates are lower on streets with automatic ticket machines (blue zones); a three-hour maximum applies (€3, or €0.50 for 30 minutes) from 9am to 7pm on weekdays.

Avis (www.avis.com; Ferdinand-Porsche-Strasse 7)

Europcar (www.europcar.com; Gniglerstrasse 12)

Hertz (www.hertz.com; Ferdinand-Porsche-Strasse 7)

Fiaker

A *Fiaker* (horse-drawn carriage) for up to four people costs €40 for 25 minutes. The drivers line up on Residenzplatz. Not all speak English, so don't expect a guided tour.

AROUND SALZBURG

Schloss Hellbrunn

A prince-archbishop with a wicked sense of humour, Markus Sittikus built **Schloss Hellbrunn** (www.hellbrunn.at; Fürstenweg 37; adult/concession/family €9.50/6.50/24; ⊙9am-5.30pm, to 9pm Jul & Aug; 🚌) in the early 17th century as a summer palace and an escape from his functions at the Residenz. The Italianate villa became a beloved retreat for rulers of state who flocked here to eat, drink and make merry. It was a Garden of Eden to all who beheld its exotic fauna, citrus trees and trick fountains – designed to sober up the clergy without dampening their spirits. Domenico Gisberti, poet to the court of Munich, once gushed: 'I see the epitome of Venice in these waters, Rome reduced to a brief outline.'

While the whimsical palace interior – especially the oriental-style Chinese Room and frescoed Festsaal – is worth a peek, the eccentric **Wasserspiele** (trick fountains) are the big draw in summer. Be prepared to get soaked in the mock Roman theatre, the shell-clad Neptune Grotto and the twittering Bird Grotto. No statue here is quite as it seems, including the emblematic tongue-poking-out Germaul mask (Sittikus' answer to his critics). The tour rounds out at the 18th-century water-powered Mechanical Theatre, where 200 limewood figurines depict life in a baroque city. Tours run every 30 minutes.

Studded with ponds, sculptures and leafy avenues, the palace **gardens** are free and open until dusk year-round. Here you'll find the *Sound of Music* pavilion of 'Sixteen Going on Seventeen' fame.

❶ Getting There & Away

Hellbrunn is 4.5km south of Salzburg, a scenic 20-minute bike ride (mostly along the Salzach River) or a 12-minute ride on bus 25 (€2.30, every 20 minutes) from Mozartsteg/Rudolfskai in the Altstadt.

Untersberg

Rising above Salzburg and straddling the German border, the rugged 1853m peak of Untersberg affords a spectacular panorama of the city, the Rositten Valley and the Tyrolean, Salzburg and Bavarian alpine ranges. The mountain is a magnet to local skiers in winter, and hikers, climbers and paragliders in summer. A cable car to the top (up/down/return €13/11.50/21) runs every half-hour, but is closed from 1 November to mid-December. Take bus 25 from Salzburg's Hauptbahnhof or Mirabellplatz to St Leonhard and the valley station.

Gaisberg

A road snakes up to 1287m Gaisberg, where stellar views of the Salzburg Valley, Salzkammergut lakes, the limestone Tennengebirge range and neighbouring Bavaria await. The best way to appreciate all this is on the 5km around-the-mountain circuit trail. Salzburgers also head up here for outdoor pursuits from mountain biking to cross-country skiing. Bus 151 (€3.10) operates a twice daily direct service from Mirabellplatz to Gaisberg in summer; or take the hourly bus number 2 (€4.20) from Mirabellplatz, which involves a change at Obergnigl. The journey takes around 40 minutes. From November to March the bus only goes as far as Zistelalpe, 1.5km short of the summit.

Hallein & Bad Dürrnberg

📞06245 / POP 20,022 / ELEV 460M

Too few people visit Hallein and Bad Dürrnberg, but those who do are pleasantly surprised. Beyond its industrial outskirts lies a pristine late-medieval town, where narrow lanes are punctuated by courtyards, art galleries and boho cafes.

◉ Sights

Keltenmuseum TOP CHOICE MUSEUM

(Celtic Museum; www.keltenmuseum.at; Pflegerplatz 5; adult/child €6/2.50; ⊙9am-5pm; 🚌) Overlooking the Salzach, the glass-fronted Keltenmuseum runs chronologically through the region's heritage in a series of beautiful vaulted rooms. It begins with Celtic artefacts,

SILENT NIGHT

Hallein's festive claim to fame is as the one-time home of Franz Xaver Gruber (1787–1863) who, together with Joseph Mohr, composed the carol 'Stille Nacht' (Silent Night). Mohr penned the poem in 1816 and Gruber, a schoolteacher at the time, came up with the melody on his guitar. You can see that fabled guitar in Gruber's former residence, now the **Stille Nacht Museum** (www .stillenachthallein.at; Gruberplatz 1; adult/ child €2/0.70; ☺3-5pm) next to Hallein's parish church. The museum tells the story of the carol through documents and personal belongings.

including Asterix-style helmets, an impressively reconstructed chariot and a selection of bronze brooches, pendants and buckles. The 1st floor traces the history of salt extraction in Hallein, featuring high points such as a miniature slide and the mummified *Mannes im Salz* (man in salt) unearthed in 1577. There is a pamphlet with English explanations (€2.50).

Salzwelten   SALT MINE
(www.salzwelten.at; Ramsaustrasse 3, Bad Dürrnberg; adult/child/family €18/9/46; ☺9am-5pm; ⚐) The sale of salt filled Salzburg's coffers during its princely heyday. At Austria's biggest show mine, you can slip into a boiler suit to descend to the bowels of the earth. The tour aboard a rickety train passes through a maze of claustrophobic passageways, over the border to Germany and down a 27m slide – don't brake, lift your legs and ask the guide to wax for extra speed! After crossing a salt lake on a wooden raft, a 42m slide brings you to the lowest point (210m underground) and back to good old Austria. Guided tours depart every half-hour. Bus 41 runs from Hallein train station hourly on weekdays, less often at weekends.

✸ Festivals & Events

First-rate musicians and artists draw crowds to the two-week **Halleiner Stadtfestwoche** in June. The festival is one of the headliners on the summer events program in Salzburgerland, with everything from classical concerts to live jazz, theatre, comedy acts, readings and exhibitions. For more details, see www.forum-hallein.at (in German).

⌨ Sleeping & Eating

Hallein can be visited on a day trip from Salzburg, but there are lots of value-for-money places to stay if you'd rather base yourself here, a point worth considering during the Salzburg Festival.. The tourist office helps book private rooms.

Pension Sommerauer   GUESTHOUSE €
(☑800 30; www.pension-hallein.at; Tschusistrasse 71; s/d €41/65; P☀⚐) Housed in a 300-year-old farmhouse, the rustic rooms at this guesthouse are a bargain. There's a heated pool and conservatory as well as kiddie stuff including a playroom, sandpit and swings.

Pension Hochdürrnberg   GUESTHOUSE €
(☑751 83; Rumpelgasse 14, Bad Dürrnberg; d/tr €60/70; P⚐) Surrounded by meadows, this farmhouse in Bad Dürrnberg has countrified rooms with warm pine furnishings and downy bedding. The furry residents (rabbits, sheep and cows) keep children amused.

Bistro Barock   ITALIAN €€
(Gollinger-Tor-Gasse 1; lunch €7.30-8.60, mains €7-16; ☺Mon-Sat; ⚐) Hidden down an old-town backstreet, the cobbled terrace at this art-strewn bistro is a magnet to lunching locals. Its good-value menu emphasises bright, herby Italian flavours such as celery-apple soup and grilled sea bass with rosemary potatoes.

❶ Information

The post office is opposite the train station. The **tourist office** (☑853 94; www.hallein.com; Mauttorpromenade 6; ☺8.30am-5.30pm Mon-Fri) is on the narrow Pernerinsel island adjoining the Stadtbrücke.

❶ Getting There & Away

Hallein is close to the German border, 18km south of Salzburg via the B150 and A10/E55 direction Graz/Villach. It's a 25-minute bus or

> ### ❶ SALZ ERLEBNIS TICKET
>
> All train stations in the region sell the money-saving **Salz Erlebnis Ticket**, which covers a return train journey to Hallein, a bus transfer to Bad Dürrnberg, plus entry to Salzwelten, the Keltenmuseum and the Stille Nacht Museum. From Salzburg, the ticket costs €23.80/12.80 for adults/children.

SALZBURG & AROUND HALLEIN & BAD DÜRRNBERG

train journey from Salzburg, with departures roughly every 30 minutes (€3.10).

Werfen

📞06468 / POP 2999 / ELEV 525M

The world's largest accessible ice caves, the soaring limestone turrets of the Tennengebirge range and a formidable medieval fortress are but the tip of the superlative iceberg in Werfen. Such salacious natural beauty hasn't escaped Hollywood producers, Werfen stars in WWII action film *Where Eagles Dare* (1968) and makes a cameo appearance in the picnic scene of the *Sound of Music*.

◎ Sights & Activities

TOP CHOICE **Eisriesenwelt**   ICE CAVE

(www.eisriesenwelt.at; adult/concession €9/8, cable car €20/18; ◎9am-3.30pm May-Oct; ⛟) Billed as the world's largest accessible ice caves, Eisriesenwelt is a glittering ice empire spanning 30,000 sq m and 42km of narrow passages burrowing deep into the heart of the mountains. Even if it's hot outside, entering the caves in any season is like stepping into a deep freeze – bring warm clothing and sturdy footwear.

A tour through these Narnia-esque chambers of blue ice is a unique experience. As you climb up wooden steps and down pitch-black passages, with carbide lamps aglow, otherworldly ice sculptures shaped like polar bears and elephants, frozen columns and lakes emerge from the shadows. A highlight is the cavernous **Eispalast** (ice palace), where the frost crystals twinkle when a magnesium flare is held up to them. A womblike tunnel leads to a flight of 700 steps, which descends back to the entrance.

In summer, minibuses (single/return €3.10/6.10) operate every 25 minutes between Eisriesenstrasse in Werfen and the car park, which is a 20-minute walk from the bottom station of the cable car. The last bus departs at 3.50pm. Allow roughly three hours for the return trip (including tour). You can walk the whole route, but it's a challenging four-hour ascent, rising 1100m above the village.

Burg Hohenwerfen   CASTLE

(adult/concession/family €14/12/33; ◎9am-5pm Apr-Oct; ⛟) Slung high on a wooded clifftop and cowering beneath the majestic peaks of the Tennengebirge range, Burg Hohenwerfen is visible from afar. For 900 years this fortress has kept watch over the Salzach Valley, its current appearance dating to 1570. The big draw is the far-reaching view over Werfen from the 16th-century belfry, though the dungeons (displaying the usual nasties such as the iron maiden and thumb screw) are also worth a look. The entry fee also covers a **falconry show** in the grounds (11.15am and 2.15pm or 3.15pm), where falconers in medieval costume release eagles, owls, falcons and vultures to wheel in front of the ramparts. There is commentary in English and German.

Both the fortress and the ice caves can be squeezed into a day trip from Salzburg; start early, visit the caves first and be at the fortress for the last falconry show. The brisk walk up from the village takes 20 minutes.

🛏 Sleeping & Eating

Nip into the tourist office for a list of nearby B&Bs, private rooms and campgrounds.

Pension Obauer   PENSION €

(📞52 24-0; www.obauer.at; s/d €45/75; P🛜) Not to be confused with the smart restaurant of the same name, this pension has spotless wood-floored rooms with comfy beds and scatter rugs. The family runs the deli next door, so you'll sample their cheese and homemade sausages at breakfast.

TOP CHOICE **Obauer**   MODERN AUSTRIAN €€€

(📞52 12-0; www.obauer.com; Markt 46; mains €15-45, set menus €58-110; ⛟) Culinary dream duo Karl and Rudi Obauer run the show at this highly-regarded, ingredient-focused restaurant. Sit in the rustic-chic restaurant or the garden, where most of the fruit and herbs are grown. Signatures like meltingly tender Werfen lamb and flaky trout strudel are matched with the finest of Austrian wines.

ℹ Information

The **tourist office** (📞53 88; www.werfen.at; Markt 24; ◎9am-12.30pm & 1-6pm Mon-Fri year-round, 2-4pm Sat May-Sep) hands out information and maps, and makes hotel bookings free of charge.

ℹ Getting There & Away

Werfen is 45km south of Salzburg on the A10/E55 motorway. Trains run frequently to Salzburg (€10, 40 minutes).

Stuttgart & the Black Forest

Best Places to Eat

» Irma la Douce (p221)

» Schwarzwaldstube (p245)

» Zur Forelle (p234)

» Rizzi (p239)

» Rindenmühle (p261)

Best Places to Stay

» Parkhotel Wehrle (p258)

» Hotel Schiefes Haus (p233)

» Die Halde (p254)

» Hotel am Schloss (p228)

» Villa Barleben (p266)

Why Go?

If one word could sum up Germany's southwesternmost region, it would be inventive. Baden-Württemberg gave the world relativity (Einstein), DNA (Miescher) and the astronomical telescope (Kepler). It was here that Bosch invented the spark plug; Gottlieb Daimler, the gas engine; and Count Ferdinand, the zeppelin. And where would we be without black forest gateau, cuckoo clocks and the ultimate beer food, the pretzel?

Beyond the high-tech, urbanite pleasures of 21st-century Stuttgart lies a region still ripe for discovery. On the city fringes, country lanes roll to vineyards and lordly baroque palaces, spa towns and castles steeped in medieval myth. Swinging south, the Black Forest (*Schwarzwald* in German) looks every inch the Grimm fairy-tale blueprint. Hills rise steep and wooded above church steeples, half-timbered villages and a crochet of tightly woven valleys. It is a perfectly etched picture of sylvan beauty, a landscape refreshingly oblivious to time and trends.

When to Go

Snow dusts the heights from January to late February and pre-Lenten *Fasnacht* brings carnival shenanigans to the region's towns and villages. Enjoy cool forest hikes, riverside bike rides, splashy fun on Lake Constance and open-air festivals galore during summer. From late September to October the golden autumn days can be spent rambling in woods, mushrooming and snuggling up in Black Forest farmhouses.

HAVE YOUR CAKE

True, there's more to the Black Forest than gateau but try saying that after a cherry-chocolate-cream fest at Café Schäfer in Triberg, guardian of the original 1915 recipe.

Need to Know

» Many museums close on Mondays.

» Family in tow? *Ferienwohnungen* (holiday apartments) are often a better deal than hotels. Tourist offices have lists.

» Save on train fares with the good-value Baden-Württemberg Ticket.

Spa Time

» **Friedrichsbad** (p238) A palatial 19th-century spa for a Roman-style scrub-a-dub-dub.

» **Sanitas Spa** (p258) Broad forest views, few crowds, luscious treatments. Bliss.

» **Badeparadies** (p257) Palms, lagoons and Caribbean cocktails lift rainy-day moods.

Resources

» **Schwarzwaldverein** (www.schwarzwaldverein. de)

» **Farmstays** (www.bauern hofurlaub.de)

» **Baden-Württemberg Tourism** (www.tourism-bw. com)

» **Local news and weather** (www.swr.de)

Outdoor Adventures

Oh, we have nothing but fresh air, plenty of forest and peace and quiet, the self-effacing locals tell you with a shrug. One whiff of that cold piny air and a glimpse of those emerald forested hills and you'll be itching to grab your walking boots or cross-country skis and strike into the wilderness of the Black Forest. Great waterways like Lake Constance and the Danube invite languid days spent exploring by bike or kayak.

Baden-Württemberg practically coined the word 'wanderlust' as the founding father of the Schwarzwaldverein (www. schwarzwaldverein.de), whose well-marked paths crisscross the darkest depths of the Black Forest.

DRIVE TIME

The Schwarzwald (Black Forest) may be a forest but it sure is a big 'un and you'll need a car to reach its out-of-the-way corners.

Schwarzwald-Hochstrasse (Black Forest Hwy; www.schwarzwaldhochstrasse.de) Swoon over views of the mist-wreathed Vosges Mountains, heather-flecked forests and glacial lakes like Mummelsee on this high-altitude road, meandering 60km from Baden-Baden to Freudenstadt on the B500.

Badische Weinstrasse (Baden Wine Rd; www. deutsche-weinstrassen.de) From Baden-Baden to Lörrach, this 160km route corkscrews through the vineyards of Ortenau, Kaiserstuhl, Tuniberg and Markgräflerland.

Schwarzwald-Tälerstrasse (Black Forest Valley Rd) What scenery! Twisting 100km from Rastatt to Alpirsbach, this road dips into the forest-cloaked hills and half-timbered towns of the Murg and Kinzig valleys.

Deutsche Uhrenstrasse (German Clock Rd; www. deutscheuhrenstrasse.de) A 320km loop starting in Villingen-Schwenningen that revolves around the story of clockmaking in the Black Forest. Stops include Furtwangen and cuckoo-crazy Triberg.

Grüne Strasse (Green Rd; www.gruene-strasse. de) Linking the Black Forest with the Rhine Valley and French Vosges, this 160km route zips through Kirchzarten, Freiburg, Breisach, Colmar and Münster.

Discount Passes

Check into almost any hotel in Baden-Württemberg, pay the nominal *Kurtaxe* (holiday tax) and you automatically receive the money-saving **Gästekarte** (Guest Card), often entitling you to free entry to local swimming pools and attractions, plus hefty discounts on everything from bike hire and spas to ski lifts and boat trips. Versions with the **Konus** symbol offer free use of public transport.

Most tourist offices in the Black Forest sell the three-day **SchwarzwaldCard** for admission to around 150 attractions. For details, visit www.blackforest-tourism.com.

ℹ Getting There & Around

Flights to the region serve Stuttgart airport (STG; www.stuttgart-airport.com), a major hub for Germanwings; **Karlsruhe-Baden-Baden airport** (Baden Airpark; www.badenairpark. de), a Ryanair base; and **Basel-Mulhouse Euro-Airport** (BSL; www.euroairport.com), where easyJet operates.

Trains, trams and/or buses serve almost every town and village, though public transport across

the Black Forest can be slow, and long-distance trips (for instance, Freiburg to Konstanz) may involve several changes. Plan your journey with the help of www.efa-bw.de and www.bahn.de.

By road, motorways blazing through the region include the A5 from Baden-Baden south to Freiburg and Basel, which can get hellishly congested because of ongoing roadworks; www.swr .de (in German) has up-to-date traffic news. The A81 runs south from Stuttgart to Lake Constance

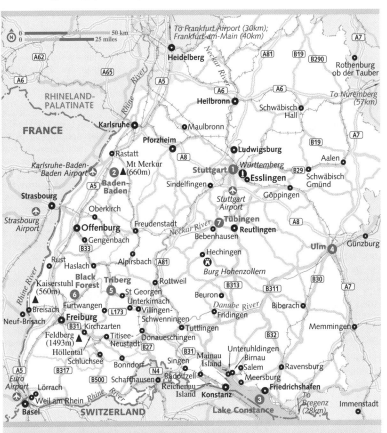

STUTTGART & THE BLACK FOREST

Stuttgart & the Black Forest Highlights

❶ Tune into modern-day **Stuttgart** (p216)

❷ Wallow in thermal waters and art nouveau grandeur in **Baden-Baden**, belle of the Black Forest (p235)

❸ Hop between borders on **Lake Constance** (p262),

straddling Switzerland, Germany and Austria

❹ Be amazed by Einstein's birthplace, **Ulm**, crowned by the world's tallest cathedral steeple (p231)

❺ Go cuckoo for clocks, black forest gateau and waterfalls in **Triberg** (p258)

❻ Roam hill, dale and kilometre after pristine kilometre of woodland in the **Black Forest** (p235)

❼ Boat along the Neckar and live it up Goethe-style in postcard-pretty **Tübingen** (p226)

ⓘ **BADEN-WÜRTTEMBERG TICKET**

Available at all train stations and online (www.bahn.de), the great-value **Baden-Württemberg Ticket** allows unlimited 2nd-class travel on IRE, RE, RB, S-Bahn trains and buses in the region. The one-day ticket costs €21 for an individual, plus €4 per extra person. Children aged 14 and under travel for free when accompanied by an adult.

---

via Villingen-Schwenningen, while the A8 links Stuttgart to Karlsruhe, Ulm and Munich.

STUTTGART

📞 0711 / POP 581,100

Ask many Germans their opinion of Stuttgarters and they will go off on a tangent: they are road hogs speeding along the autobahn; they are sharp-dressed executives with a Swabian drawl; they are tight-fisted homebodies who slave away to *schaffe, schaffe, Häusle baue* (work, work, build a house). So much for the stereotypes.

The real Stuttgart is less superficial than legend. True, some good-living locals like their cars fast and their restaurants fancy but most are just as happy getting their boots dirty in the surrounding vine-clad hills and hanging out with friends in the rustic confines of a *Weinstube* (wine tavern). In the capital of Baden-Württemberg, city slickers and down-to-earth country kids walk hand in hand.

History

Whether with trusty steeds or turbocharged engines, Stuttgart was born to ride, founded as the stud farm Stuotgarten around 950 AD. Progress was swift: by the 12th century Stuttgart was a trade centre, by the 13th century a blossoming city and by the early 14th century the seat of the Württemberg royal family. Count Eberhard im Bart added sheen to Swabian suburbia by introducing the *Kehrwoche* in 1492, the communal cleaning rota still revered today.

The early 16th century brought hardship, peasant wars, plague and Austrian rulers (1520–34). A century later, the Thirty Years' War devastated Stuttgart and killed half its population.

In 1818, King Wilhelm I launched the first the Cannstatter Volksfest to celebrate the end of a dreadful famine. An age of industrialisation dawned in the late 19th and early 20th centuries, with Bosch inventing the spark plug and Daimler pioneering the gas engine. Heavily bombed in WWII, Stuttgart was painstakingly reconstructed and became the capital of the new state of Baden-Württemberg in 1953. Today it is one of Germany's greenest and most affluent cities.

◉ Sights

Stuttgart's main artery is the shopping boulevard Königstrasse, running south from the Hauptbahnhof. Steep grades are common on Stuttgart's hillsides: more than 500 city streets end in *Stäffele* (staircases).

Schlossplatz SQUARE
(Map p218) This regal plaza is crowned by the **König Wilhelm Jubilee Column** (Map p218), topped by a statue of winged Concordia and flanked by two fountains representing the eight rivers of Baden-Württemberg.

Rising majestically above the square is the exuberant three-winged **Neues Schloss**. Duke Karl Eugen von Württemberg's answer to Versailles, the baroque-neoclassical royal residence now houses state government ministries. A bronze statue of Emperor Wilhelm I graces nearby **Karlsplatz**.

TOP CHOICE **Staatsgalerie** GALLERY
(Map p218; www.staatsgalerie-stuttgart.de; Konrad-Adenauer-Strasse 30-32; adult/concession €5.50/4, special exhibitions €10/8, Wed & Sat free; ⊙10am-6pm Tue-Sun, to 8pm Tue & Thu) The neoclassical-meets-contemporary Staatsgalerie bears British architect James Stirling's curvy, colourful imprint. Alongside big-name exhibitions, the gallery harbours a phenomenal collection of 20th-century art, showcasing works by Rembrandt, Picasso, Monet, Dalí and pop idols Warhol and Lichtenstein.

Kunstmuseum Stuttgart GALLERY
(Map p218; www.kunstmuseum-stuttgart.de; Kleiner Schlossplatz 1; adult/concession €5/3.50; ⊙10am-6pm Tue-Sun, to 9pm Wed & Fri) Occupying a shimmering glass cube, this gallery is a romp through modern and contemporary art, with works by Otto Dix and Dieter Roth. For a 360-degree view over Stuttgart, head up to the Cube cafe. Out front, the primary colours and geometric forms of **Alexander Calder's mobile** (Map p218) catch the eye.

Schlossgarten   GARDEN
(Map p218) The fountain-dotted **Mittlerer Schlossgarten** (Middle Palace Garden; Map p218) draws thirsty crowds to its beer garden in summer. The **Unterer Schlossgarten** (Lower Palace Garden) is a ribbon of greenery rambling northeast to the Neckar River and the **Rosensteinpark**, home to the zoo. Sitting south, the **Oberer Schlossgarten** (Upper Palace Garden) is framed by eye-catching landmarks like the columned **Staatstheater** (State Theatre; Map p218) and the ultramodern glass-clad **Landtag** (State Parliament; Map p218).

FREE **Aussichtsplatform**   VIEWPOINT
(Viewing Platform; Map p218; ☉10am-6pm Fri-Wed, to 8pm Thu) A lift races up to the Hauptbahnhof's 9th floor, where a staircase spirals up to this viewing platform. You'll get closeups of the revolving Mercedes logo and far-reaching views over Stuttgart, from the bauble-topped **Fernsehturm** (TV Tower) to vine-cloaked hills on the city fringes.

You also get a bird's-eye view of developments taking shape for Stuttgart 21, a huge – and hugely controversial – project to revamp the main train station and extend the city's high-speed rail network. Costing €4.5 billion, the project is due for completion in 2021.

Mercedes-Benz Museum   MUSEUM
(www.museum-mercedes-benz.com; Mercedesstrasse 100; adult/concession €8/4; ☉9am-6pm Tue-Sun; 🚃Neckarpark) A futuristic swirl on the cityscape, the Mercedes-Benz Museum takes a chronological spin through the Mercedes empire. Look out for legends like the 1885 Daimler Riding Car, the world's first gasoline-powered vehicle, and the record-breaking Lightning Benz that hit 228km/h at Daytona Beach in 1909. There's a free guided tour in English at 11am.

Porsche Museum   MUSEUM
(www.porsche.com; Porscheplatz 1; adult/concession €8/4; ☉9am-6pm Tue-Sun; 🚃Neuwirtshaus) Like a pearly white spaceship preparing for lift-off, the barrier-free Porsche Museum is every little boy's dream. Groovy audio-guides race you through the history of Porsche from its 1948 beginnings. Break to glimpse the 911 GT1 that won Le Mans in 1998.

Landesmuseum Württemberg   MUSEUM
(Map p218; www.landesmuseum-stuttgart.de; Schillerplatz 6; adult/concession €5.50/4.50; ☉10am-5pm Tue-Sun) An archway leads to the turreted 10th-century Altes Schloss, where this museum homes in on regional archaeology and architecture. The historic booty comprises Celtic jewellery, neolithic pottery, diamond-encrusted crown jewels and rare artefacts. Time your visit to see, from the arcaded courtyard, the rams above the clock tower lock horns on the hour.

Wilhelma Zoologisch-Botanischer Garten   GARDEN, ZOO
(www.wilhelma.de; Rosensteinpark; adult/concession €12/6, after 4pm & in winter €8/4; ☉8.15am-nightfall; ⑤Wilhelma) Wilhelma Zoologisch-Botanischer Garten is a quirky mix of zoo and botanical gardens. Kid magnets include semi-striped okapis, elephants, penguins and a petting farm. Greenhouses sheltering tree ferns, camellias and Amazonian species are among the botanical highlights. Sniff out the gigantic bloom of the malodorous titan arum in the Moorish Villa.

Württembergischer Kunstverein   GALLERY
(Map p218; www.wkv-stuttgart.de; Schlossplatz 2; adult/concession €5/3; ☉11am-6pm Tue-Sun, to 8pm Wed) Identified by its copper cupola, this gallery stages thought-provoking contemporary art exhibitions.

Schillerplatz   SQUARE
(Map p218) On the other side of the Renaissance **Alte Kanzlei** (Old Chancellery; Map p218), south of Schlossplatz, lies cobbled Schillerplatz, where the poet-dramatist **Friedrich Schiller** (Map p218) is immortalised in bronze.

FREE **Stiftskirche**   CHURCH
(Collegiate Church; Map p218; Stiftstrasse 12; ☉10am-7pm Mon & Thu, to 4pm Fri & Sat, to 6pm Sun) Topped by two mismatched towers, this largely 15th-century church has Romanesque origins.

☞ Tours

Sightseeing tours feature **Hop-on, Hop-off Bus Tours** (adult/concession € 18/15; ☉11am Apr-Oct), which depart roughly hourly from 11am to 6pm from Schlossplatz and trundle past icons like the Fernsehturm and Mercedes-Benz Museum. Pop into the tourist office for details on German-language guided tours, from vineyard ambles to after-work 'walk and view' strolls.

From May to October, **Neckar-Käpt'n** (www.neckar-kaeptn.de) runs boat excursions on the Neckar River (€9 to €31), departing from its dock at Wilhelma in Bad Cannstatt on the U14.

Stuttgart

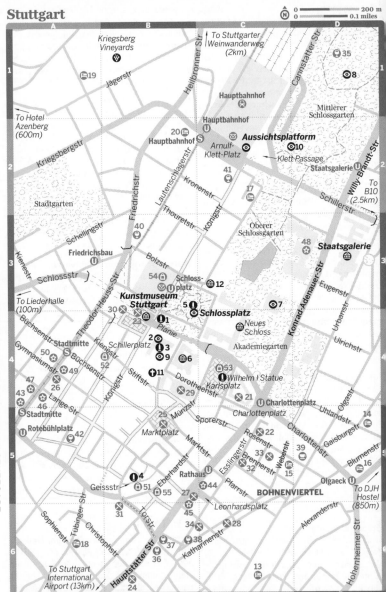

Map labels:

Kriegsberg Vineyards
🍷 19
Jägerstr
To Stuttgarter Weinwanderweg (2km)
Heilbronner Str
Cannstatter Str
35
8
To Hotel Azenberg (600m)
Kriegsbergstr
Hauptbahnhof
Hauptbahnhof
20
Hauptbahnhof
Arnulf-Klett-Platz
Mittlerer Schlossgarten
Aussichtsplatform
10
Klett Passage
Staatsgalerie
To B10 (2.5km)
Stadtgarten
Schellingstr
Kronenstr
41
17
Oberer Schlossgarten
Schillerstr
Willy-Brandt-Str
Friedrichstr
Lautenschlagerstr
Thouretstr
Königstr
40
Bolzstr
48
Staatsgalerie
Friedrichsbau
Schlossstr
Schloss-platz
54
12
Kunstmuseum Stuttgart
5
Schlossplatz
7
To Liederhalle (100m)
30
1
Planie
Neues Schloss
Akademiegarten
Eugenstr
Konrad-Adenauer-Str
Urbanstr
Ulrichstr
Büchsenstr
Theodor-Heuss-Str
Schillerplatz
2
3
9
6
Stadtmitte
Kienestr
Stiftstr
Gymnasiumstr
50
49
52
11
53
Wilhelm I Statue
Karlsplatz
21
Charlottenplatz
Uhlandstr
Gaisburgstr
47
26
43
46
Lange Str
Königstr
Dorotheenstr
29
Charlottenplatz
14
Stadtmitte
25
Münzstr
Sporerstr
Charlottenstr
Olgastr
Rotebühlplatz
42
Marktplatz
Marktstr
Rosenstr
22
33
Brennerstr
Esslingerstr
Weberstr
39
15
32
Blumenstr
16
Olgaeck
To DJH Hostel (850m)
4
51
Eberhardstr
Rathaus
44
Pfarrstr
BOHNENVIERTEL
Geissstr
55
27
Leonhardsplatz
45
31
Torstr
34
28
Sophienstr
Tübingerstr
Christophstr
37
38
Katharinenstr
18
36
13
To Stuttgart International Airport (13km)
Hauptstätter Str
24
Hohenheimerstr

N 0 —————— 200 m
   0 —————— 0.1 miles

✨ Festivals & Events

Sommerfest FESTIVAL
(www.sommerfest-stuttgart.de) Riverside parties, open-air gigs and alfresco feasting are what this four-day August shindig is all about.

Weindorf WINE FESTIVA[l]
(www.stuttgarter-weindorf.de) A 10-day even[t] where winemakers sell the year's vintag[e] from hundreds of booths on Schlossplat[z] and the Oberer Schlossgarten. Begins on th[e] last weekend in August.

Stuttgart

Cannstatter Volksfest   BEER FESTIVAL
(www.cannstatter-volksfest.de) Stuttgart's answer to Oktoberfest, this beer-guzzling bash, held over three consecutive weekends from late September to mid-October, lifts spirits with oompah music, fairground rides and fireworks.

Weihnachtsmarkt   CHRISTMAS MARKET
(www.stuttgarter-weihnachtsmarkt.de) One of Germany's biggest Christmas markets brings festive twinkle to Marktplatz, Schillerplatz and Schlossplatz from late November to 23 December.

🛏 Sleeping

Stuttgart is gradually upping the ante in slumberland but nondescript chains still reign supreme. Expect weekend discounts of 10% to 20% at hotels targeting business travellers. If you're seeking individual flair and a family welcome, stop by the tourist office for a list of private guesthouses and apartments.

Kronen Hotel   HOTEL €€€
(Map p218; ☎225 10; www.kronenhotel-stuttgart.
de; Kronenstrasse 48; s €108-120, d €149-180;
P✳@☎) Right on the lap of Königstrasse, this outclasses most of Stuttgart's hotels

with its terrific location, good-natured team, well-appointed rooms and funkily lit sauna. Breakfast is above par, with fresh fruit, egg and bacon, smoked fish and pastries to keep you going.

Hostel Alex 30 HOSTEL €
(Map p218; ☑838 8950; www.alex30-hostel.de; Alexanderstrasse 30; dm/s/d/q €24/36/58/100, breakfast €8; P🐾🛜) Backpackers find a relaxed base in these mellow digs with a bar, sun deck and communal kitchen. The spotless, citrus-bright rooms are light and contemporary.

Hotel Azenberg HOTEL €€
(☑225 5040; www.hotelazenberg.de; Seestrasse 114-116; s €70-105, d €85-120; P🐾🛏🖥43) This family-run pick has individually designed quarters with themes swinging from English country manor to Picasso. There's a pool, tree-shaded garden and mini spa for relaxing moments. Take bus 43 from Stadtmitte to Hölderlinstrasse.

Hotel am Schlossgarten LUXURY HOTEL €€€
(Map p218; ☑202 60; www.hotelschlossgarten .com; Schillerstrasse 23; s €132-167, d €167-187, tasting menus €109-139; P🍴🛜) Sidling up to the Schloss, this hotel has handsome, park-facing rooms, which flaunt the luxuries that justify the price tag. Book a table at Michelin-starred Zirbelstube for classy

---

DON'T MISS

BOHEMIAN BEANS

To really slip under Stuttgart's skin, mosey through one of the city's lesser-known neighbourhoods. Walk south to **Hans-im-Glück Platz**, centred on a fountain depicting the caged Grimm's fairy-tale character **Lucky Hans** (Map p218), and you'll soon reach the boho-flavoured **Bohnenviertel** (Bean District; www.bohnenviertel.net), named after beans that were introduced in the 16th century. Back then they were grown everywhere as the staple food of the poor tanners, dyers and craftsmen who lived here.

A recent facelift has restored the neighbourhood's cobbled lanes and gabled houses, which harbour idiosyncratic galleries, workshops, bookshops, wine taverns and cafes. The villagey atmosphere is a refreshing tonic to the big-city feel of central Stuttgart.

French dining in subtly lit, pine-panelled surrounds.

City Hotel HOTEL €€
(Map p218; ☑210 810; www.cityhotel-stuttgart .de; Uhlandstrasse 18; s €79-89, d €99-115; P🛜) Eschew the anonymity of Stuttgart's cookie-cutter chains for this intimate hotel just off Charlottenplatz. Rooms are light, clean and modern, if slightly lacklustre. Breakfast on the terrace in summer is a bonus.

Interhostel HOSTEL €
(Map p218; ☑6648 2797; www.inter-hostel.com; Paulinenstrasse 16; dm/s/d €25/42/64; 🛜) A short toddle from Stadtmitte station, this hostel makes backpackers' hearts sing with its free coffee and wi-fi, bright and characterful digs, relaxed lounge and chipper team, plus handy stuff like luggage storage and a shared kitchen.

Der Zauberlehrling BOUTIQUE HOTEL €€€
(Map p218; ☑237 7770; www.zauberlehrling.de; Rosenstrasse 38; s €135-180, d €180-290, ste €195-320; P🛜) The self-consciously cool Sorcerer's Apprentice reveals design-driven rooms, from Titanic and its waterbed to the high-tech wizardry of the Media Suite. Yet the place lacks a little soul. Nice, but not quite magic.

Steigenberger Graf Zeppelin LUXURY HOTEL €€€
(Map p218; ☑204 80; www.stuttgart.steigenberger .de; Arnulf-Klett-Platz 7; r €170-260; P🍴🛜🛏) While its concrete facade won't bowl you over, inside is a different story. This five-star pad facing the Hauptbahnhof is luxury all the way with its snazzy rooms, Zen-style spa and Michelin-starred restaurant, Olivo.

Ochsen Hotel HISTORIC HOTEL €€
(☑407 0500; www.ochsen-online.de; Ulmer Strasse 323; s €89-99, d €119-129; P🛜; Ⓢ Inselstrasse) It's worth going the extra mile to this charismatic 18th-century hotel. Some of the spacious, warm-hued rooms have whirlpool tubs for a post-sightseeing bubble. The wood-panelled restaurant dishes up appetising local fare.

Abalon Hotel HOTEL €€
(Map p218; ☑217 10; www.abalon.de; Zimmermannstrasse 7-9; s €74-89, d €89-112; P🛜) Affable staff, a top location and wallet-friendly rates make Abalon a great pick. The bright parquet-floored rooms are large and spotless.

DJH Hostel HOSTEL €
(☑6647470; www.jugendherberge-stuttgart.de; Haussmannstrasse 27; dm 1st/subsequent night €24.50/21.20; @🛜; Ⓢ Eugensplatz) This DJH hostel is

a step above most others. Its squeaky-clean dorms have private bathrooms and a lounge and a terrace with fab city views add to the sociable vibe. It's 800m southeast of the Hauptbahnhof.

 Eating

Stuttgart has raised the bar in the kitchen, with chefs putting an imaginative spin on local, seasonal ingredients. The city's half-dozen Michelin-starred restaurants prepare cuisine with enough gourmet panache to satisfy a food-literate crowd. For intimate bistro-style dining, explore the backstreets and the alley-woven Bohnenviertel.

Self-caterers make for the **food market** (Map p218; Marktplatz; ⊘7.30am-1pm Tue, Thu & Sat) and the **Markthalle** (Map p218; Dorotheen-strasse 4, Market Hall; ⊘7am-6.30pm Mon-Fri, to 4pm Sat), which sells picnic fixings and has Italian and Swabian restaurants.

TOP CHOICE **Irma la Douce** MEDITERRANEAN €€€
(Map p218; ☐470 4320; www.irmaladouce.de; Katharinenstrasse 21b; lunch €11-14, dinner €25-39.50; ⊘closed lunch Sat & Sun) An ornate fireplace and chandeliers cast flattering light across the polished wood, book shelves and paintings at this 19th-century bistro. Inspired by the seasons and herby Mediterranean flavours, the menu might star quail breast on wild garlic and roast Iberian pork with spinach gnocchi – all beautifully cooked and expertly matched with wine.

Ochs'n'Willi SWABIAN €€€
(Map p218; ☐226 5191; www.ochsn-willi.de; Kleiner Schlossplatz 4; mains €10-22.50; ⊘daily) A warm, woody hunter's cottage of a restaurant just this side of twee, Ochs'n'Willi delivers gutsy portions of Swabian and Bavarian fare. Dig into pork knuckles with lashings of dumplings and kraut, spot-on *Maultaschen* (pasta pockets) or rich, brothy *Gaisburger Marsch*. There's a terrace for warm-weather dining.

Olivo MODERN EUROPEAN €€€
(Map p218; ☐204 8277; www.olivo-restaurant.de; Arnulf-Klett-Platz 7; mains €35-44, 4-course lunch/dinner €68/98; ⊘Tue-Sat) Young, sparky chef Nico Burkhardt works his stuff at Steigenberger's Michelin-starred restaurant. The minimalist-chic restaurant is lauded for

DON'T MISS

GOING THE WHOLE HOG

Billing itself as the world's biggest pig museum, the **Schweinemuseum** (www.schweinemuseum.de; Schlachthof-strasse 2a; adult/concession €4.90/4; ⊘11am-7.30pm daily; ☐56) is one heck of a pigsty: 45,000 paintings, lucky trinkets, antiques, cartoons, piggy banks and a veritable mountain of cuddly toys cover the entire porcine spectrum. Since opening in 2010 in the city's 100-year-old former slaughterhouse, the kitsch-cool museum has drawn crowds to its exhibits spotlighting everything from pig worship to wild boar hunt rituals. In the adjacent beer garden (mains €12 to €19), you can pig out on schnitzel, fat stubby pork knuckles and more.

THE WAY TO A SWABIAN'S HEART...

As the Swabian saying goes: *Was der Bauer net kennt, frisst er net* (What the farmer doesn't know, he doesn't eat), so find out before you dig in:

Bubespitzle Officially called *Schupfnudeln*, these short, thick potato noodles – vaguely reminiscent of gnocchi – are browned in butter and tossed with sauerkraut. Sounds appetising until you discover that *Bubespitzle* means 'little boys' penises'.

Gaisburger Marsch A strong beef stew served with potatoes and *Spätzle*.

Maultaschen Giant ravioli pockets, stuffed with leftover ground pork, spinach, onions and bread mush. The dish is nicknamed *Herrgottsbeschieserle* (God trickster) because it was a sly way to eat meat during Lent.

Saure Kuddle So who is for sour tripe? If you haven't got the stomach, try potato-based, meat-free *saure Rädle* (sour wheels) instead.

Spätzle Stubby egg-based noodles. These are fried with onions and topped with cheese in the calorific treat *Käsespätzle*.

Zwiebelkuche Autumnal onion tart with bacon, cream and caraway seeds, which pairs nicely with *neuer Süsser* (new wine) or *Moschd* (cider).

exquisitely presented, French-inspired specialities such as Breton turbot with celery, peanuts and Champagne foam.

Weinhaus Stetter
SWABIAN €€

(Map p218; ☑240 163; Rosenstrasse 32; mains €8.50-13.50; ☺3-11pm Mon-Fri, noon-3pm & 5.30-11pm Sat) No-nonsense Swabian cooking, such as flavoursome *Linsen und Saiten* (lentils with sausage), and wines are the mainstay of this Bohnenviertel tavern. The attached wine shop sells 650 different vintages.

Cube
INTERNATIONAL €€€

(Map p218; ☑280 4441; Kleiner Schlossplatz 1; mains lunch €9-17, dinner €28-31; ☺daily) The food is good but it plays second fiddle to the dazzling view at this glass-fronted cube on Kleiner Schlossplatz. Bag a window table to see Stuttgart twinkle over winningly fresh dishes like yellow-fin tuna with wasabi-pepper crumble and black bean risotto. Come at lunchtime for a more relaxed vibe.

Weinstube Fröhlich
SWABIAN €€

(Map p218; ☑242 471; www.weinstube-froehlich .de; Leonhardstrasse 5; mains €12-23; ☺5.30pm-12.30am daily) True, it's in the heart of the red-light district, but don't be put off. This softly lit, dark-wood-panelled restaurant is an atmospheric choice for well-executed Swabian fare (cheese-rich *Käsespätzle*, *Maultaschen* with potato salad) and regional wines.

Délice
MODERN EUROPEAN €€€

(Map p218; ☑640 3222; www.restaurant-delice .de; Hauptstätter Strasse 61; 5-course tasting menu €90; ☺6.30pm-midnight Mon-Fri) At this vaulted Michelin-starred restaurant, natural, integral flavours sing in specialities like medley of tuna with lemon vinaigrette and fried egg with parsnips and Périgord truffles. The sommelier will talk you through the award-winning riesling selection.

Amadeus
SWABIAN €€

(Map p218; ☑292 678; Charlottenplatz 17; mains €9.50-22.50; ☺daily) Once an 18th-century orphanage dishing up gruel, this chic, bustling restaurant now serves glorious Swabian food such as *Maultaschen* and riesling-laced *Kutteln* (tripe). The terrace is a big draw in summer.

Alte Kanzlei
GERMAN €€

(Map p218; ☑294 457; Schillerplatz 5a; mains €10.50-20.50; ☺daily) Empty tables are gold-dust rare at this convivial, high-ceilinged restaurant on Schillerplatz. Feast on Swabian favourites like *Spannpferkel* (roast suckling pig) and *Flädlesuppe* (pancake soup), washed down with regional tipples.

Takeshii's
VIETNAMESE €€

(Map p218; ☑2483 9559; Esslinger Strasse 12; mains €10.90-13.90; ☺Tue-Sat) Subtly lit Vietnamese bolt-hole, rustling up faves like shrimp-and-herb summer rolls with hoisin sauce.

Café Nast
CAFE €

(Map p218; Esslingerstrasse 40; snacks €1.50-3.50; ☺7am-6.30pm Mon-Sat) Great bakery for freshly prepared sandwiches or coffee and cake.

Reiskorn
INTERNATIONAL €

(Map p218; ☑664 7633; Torstrasse 27; mains €5.50-12.90; ☺closed Sun lunch; ☑) With an easy-going vibe and bamboo-green retro interior, this culinary globetrotter serves everything from tangy Caribbean prawn salad to dim sum.

Forum Café
CAFE €

(Map p218; Gymnasiumstrasse 21; snacks €4-7.50; ☺Mon-Sat; ☑) Wholesomely hip, kid-friendly cafe in the Forum Theatre, with yogi teas and organic snacks on the menu.

Imbiss Zum Brunnenwirt
FAST FOOD €

(Map p218; Leonhardsplatz 25; snacks €2.70-3.50; ☺11am-2am Mon-Thu, to 3am Fri & Sat, 4pm-2am Sun) Join hungry Stuttgarter to chomp on wurst and fries at this hole-in-the-wall joint.

Drinking

Ciba Mato
LOUNGE

(Map p218; www.ciba-mato.de; Wilhelmsplatz 11; ☺5pm-3am Mon-Sat, 10am-3am Sun) There's more than a hint of Buddha Bar about this scarlet-walled, Asia-infused space. It's a slinky spot to sip a gingertini or pisco punch, hang out Bedouin-style in the shisha tent and nibble on fusion food. The decked terrace is a summertime magnet.

Sky Beach
BAR

(Map p218; www.skybeach.de; Königstrasse 6, Galeria Kaufhof, top floor; ☺noon-12.30am Mon-Sat, 11am-midnight Sun Easter-Sep) When the sun comes out, Stuttgarters live it up at this urban beach, complete with sand, cabana beds, DJs spinning mellow lounge beats and grandstand city views.

Biergarten im Schlossgarten
BEER GARDEN

(Map p218; www.biergarten-chlossgarten.de; ☺10.30am-1am May-Oct; ☎) Toast summer with beer and pretzels at Stuttgart's best-loved, 2000-seat beer garden in the green heart of the Schlossgarten. Regular live music gets steins a-swinging.

Hüftengold
CAFE

(Map p218; Olgastrasse 44; ⊘7am-midnight Mon-Thu, to 1am Fri & Sat, 10am-8pm Sun) Work on your own *Hüftengold* (love handles) with cake and locally roasted coffee at this sylvan wonderland of a cafe. The log stool and sheepskins create a wonderfully cosy vibe for brunch or evening chats by candlelight.

Zum Paulaner
PUB

(Map p218; Calwerstrasse 45; ⊘10am-midnight daily, to 1am Fri & Sat) Freshly tapped Paulaner brews in a buzzy, tree-shaded beer garden.

Fou Fou
COCKTAIL BAR

(Map p218; Leonhardstrasse 13; ⊘5pm-1am Mon-Wed, 6pm-2am Thu, 8pm-3am Fri & Sat) Intimate bar with expertly mixed cocktails.

Palast der Republik
BAR

(Map p218 Friedrichstrasse 27; ⊘3pm-1am) Bar staff didn't graduate from charm school but this public toilet reborn as a kiosk bar is still a pleasingly laid-back spot for a beer.

☆ Entertainment

For the events low-down, grab a copy of German-language monthly **Lift Stuttgart** (www.lift-online.de) from the tourist office or news kiosks, or listings magazine **Prinz** (www.prinz.de/stuttgart.html). Events tickets can be purchased at the **i-Punkt desk** (☑222 8243; Königstrasse 1a; ⊘9am-8pm Mon-Fri, to 6pm Sat, 11am-6pm Sun).

Liederhalle
CONCERT VENUE

(☑202 7710; www.liederhalle-stuttgart.de; Berliner Platz 1) Jimi Hendrix and Sting are among the stars who have performed at this culture and congress centre. The 1950s venue stages big-name classical and pop concerts, cabaret and comedy.

Staatstheater
PERFORMING ARTS

(Map p218; ☑203 20; www.staatstheater-stuttgart .de; Oberer Schlossgarten 6) Stuttgart's grandest theatre presents a top-drawer program of ballet, opera, theatre and classical music. The **Stuttgart Ballet** (www.stuttgart-ballet.de) is hailed one of Europe's best companies.

Bix Jazzclub
LIVE MUSIC

(Map p218; ☑2384 0997; www.bix-stuttgart.de; Leonhardsplatz 28; ⊘7pm-2am Tue-Wed, to 3am Thu-Sat) Suave chocolate-gold tones and soft

THROUGH THE GRAPEVINE

To taste the region's fruity Trollingers and citrusy rieslings, factor in a stroll through the vineyards surrounding Stuttgart. The **Stuttgarter Weinwanderweg** (www.stuttgarter-weinwanderweg .de) comprises several walking trails that thread through winegrowing villages. One begins at Pragsattel station (on the U5 or U6 line) and meanders northeast to Max-Eyth-See, affording fine views from Burgholzhofturm. Visit the website for alternative routes, maps and distances.

From October to March, look out for a broom above the door of **Besenwirtschaften** (*Besa* for short). Run by winegrowers, these rustic bolt-holes are atmospheric places to chat with locals while sampling the new vintage and Swabian home cooking. Some operate every year but most don't. Check the Besen Kalender website (www. besenkalender.de) during vintage times. Stuttgart-area *Besenwirtschaften* that open annually include the central **City-Besen** (Map p218; ☑470 4248; Wilhelmsplatz 1; ⊘daily), an atmospheric vaulted cellar serving home-grown wines.

lighting set the scene for first-rate jazz acts at Bix, swinging from big bands to soul and blues.

Kiste
LIVE MUSIC

(Map p218; www.kiste-stuttgart.de; Hauptstätter Strasse 35; ⊘6pm-1am Mon-Thu, to 2am Fri & Sat) Jam-packed at weekends, this hole-in-the-wall bar is Stuttgart's leading jazz venue, with nightly concerts starting at 9pm or 10pm.

Wagenhallen
CLUB

(www.wagenhallen.de; Innerer Nordbahnhof 1; Eckhardtshaldenweg) Swim away from the mainstream at this post-industrial space, where club nights, gigs and workshops skip from Balkan beat parties to poetry slams. There's a relaxed beer garden for summertime quaffing.

Theaterhaus
THEATRE

(☑402 0720; www.theaterhaus.com; Siemensstrasse 11; Maybachstrasse) This dynamic theatre stages live rock, jazz and other music genres, plus theatre and comedy performances.

DON'T MISS

THEODOR-HEUSS-STRASSE BAR CRAWL

Packed with clubs and hipper-than-thou lounges, Theodor-Heuss-Strasse is perfect for a late-night bar crawl. DJs spin house and electro at charcoal-black **7 Grad** (Map p218; Theodor-Heuss-Strasse 32). Next door **Barcode** (Map p218; Theodor-Heuss-Strasse 30) fuels the party with decadent cocktails in streamlined surrounds, while neighbouring **Rohbau** (Map p218; Theodor-Heuss-Strasse 26) pumps out '80s disco and rock in retro-cool surrounds. Good-looking Stuttgarters dance to soul and funk at nouveau Alpine chic **Muttermilch** (Map p218; Theodor-Heuss-Strasse 23) and ice-cool **Suite 212** (Map p218; Theodor-Heuss-Strasse 23). Further along is spacily lit, monochromatic **T-O12** (Map p218; Theodor-Heuss-Strasse 12), where RnB, house and electro dominate the decks.

Shopping

Mooch around plane-tree-lined Königstrasse, Germany's longest shopping mile, for high-street brands and department stores, Calwer Strasse for boutiques and Stifftstrasse for designer labels. The casual Bohnenviertel is the go-to quarter for antiques, galleries, vintage garb and Stuttgart-made crafts and jewellery.

Just north of Schlossplatz is the classical, colonnaded Königsbau, reborn as an upmarket shopping mall, the **Königsbau Passagen** (Map p218). For outdoor shopping, there's a bustling **flower market** (Map p218; Schillerplatz; 7am-1pm Tue, Thu & Sat) and a **flea market** (Map p218; Karlsplatz; 8am-4pm Sat).

Tausche
ACCESSORIES
(Map p218; Eberhardstrasse 51; 11am-7pm Mon-Fri, to 6pm Sat) Berlin's snazziest messenger bags have winged their way south. Tausche's walls are a technicolour mosaic of exchangeable flaps: from *die blöde Kuh* (the silly cow) to Stuttgart's iconic Fernsehturm (TV Tower). Pick one to match your outfit and mood.

Brunnenhannes
FASHION
(Map p218; Geissstrasse 15; 11am-7pm Tue-Fri, to 4pm Sat) Nothing to wear to Oktoberfest? Biker-meets-Bavaria Brunnenhannes has the solution, with lederhosen for strapping lads, dirndls for buxom dames and gingham lingerie that is half kitsch, half cool.

Feinkost Böhm
FOOD
(Map p218; Kronprinzstrasse 6) Böhm is a foodie one-stop shop with regional wine, beer, chocolate and preserves, and an appetising deli.

Stilwerk
DESIGN
(Map p218; www.stilwerk.de; Königsbau-Passagen) Some of Germany's top design stores cluster under an elliptical glass roof at Stilwerk, doing trade in everything from futuristic bathrooms to stylish rattan creations.

Information

Königstrasse has many ATMs, including one in the tourist office. **ReiseBank & Western Union** (Hauptbahnhof, opposite track 11; 8am-8.30pm) offers currency exchange.

City Call Internet Center (Eberhardstrasse 14; per hr €2; 10am-midnight Mon-Sat, 11am-midnight Sun)

Coffee Fellows (per 10min €0.50; 8am-9pm;) Up the stairs opposite track 4 in the Hauptbahnhof. Free wi-fi.

I-Punkt Tourist Information (222 8100; www.stuttgart-tourist.de; Königstrasse 1a; 9am-8pm Mon-Fri, to 6pm Sat, 11am-6pm Sun) The staff can help with room bookings (for a €3 fee) and public transport enquiries. Has a list of vineyards open for tastings.

Klinikum Stuttgart (278 01; Kriegsbergstrasse 60) The city's largest hospital.

Post office (inside Königsbau Passagen) Slightly northwest of the Schlossplatz. There's also a branch in the **Hauptbahnhof**, up the stairs behind track 4.

StuttCard (72hr with/without VVS ticket €18/9.70) Free entry to most museums, plus discounts on events, activities and guided tours. Sold at the tourist office and some hotels.

Tourist office (8am-7pm Mon-Fri, 9am-1pm & 2-6pm Sat & Sun) The tourist office branch at Stuttgart International Airport. Situated in Terminal 3, Level 2 (Arrivals).

VVS 3-Day Ticket (72hr inner city/metropolitan area €10.60/14.50) Three-day pass for unlimited use of public transport, available to guests with a hotel reservation.

Getting There & Away

AIR **Stuttgart International Airport** (STG; www.stuttgart-airport.com), a major hub for **Germanwings** (www.germanwings.com), is 13km south of the city. There are four terminals, all within easy walking distance of each other.

CAR & MOTORCYCLE The A8 from Munich to Karlsruhe passes Stuttgart (often abbreviated to 'S' on highway signs) as does the A81 from Singen (near Lake Constance) to Heilbronn and Mannheim. Stuttgart is an **Umweltzone** (Green Zone; www.umwelt-plakette.de), where vehicles are graded according to their emissions levels. Expect to pay €6 to €10 for an *Umweltplakette* (environment sticker), which is obligatory in green zones and can be ordered online.

TRAIN IC and ICE destinations include Berlin (€135, 5½ hours), Frankfurt (€59, 1¼ hours) and Munich (€49 to €54, 2¼ hours). There are frequent regional services to Tübingen (€12.20, one hour), Schwäbisch Hall (€16.40, 70 minutes) and Ulm (€18.10 to €25, one hour).

❶ Getting Around

TO/FROM THE AIRPORT S2 and S3 trains take about 30 minutes to get from the airport to the Hauptbahnhof (€3.50).

BICYCLE **Rent a Bike** (www.rentabike-stuttgart. de; Lautenschlagerstrasse 22; adult 6½hr/full day €12/18, concession €9/14) delivers and picks up bikes. Stuttgart has 50 **Call-a-Bike** (☎0700 0522 2222; www.callabike.de) stands. The first 30 minutes are free and rental costs €4.80 per hour thereafter (€15 per day). Visit the website for maps and details.

It's free to take your bike on *Stadtbahn* lines, except from 6am to 8.30am and 4pm to 6.30pm Monday to Friday. Bikes are allowed on S-Bahn trains (S1 to S6) but you have to buy a *Kinderticket* (child's ticket) from 6am to 8.30am Monday to Friday. You can't take bikes on buses or the *Strassenbahn* (tramway).

CAR & MOTORCYCLE Underground parking costs about €2.50 for the first hour and €2 for each subsequent hour. See www.parkinfo.com (in German) for a list of car parks. The Park & Ride ('P+R') options in Stuttgart's suburbs afford cheap parking; convenient lots include Degerloch Albstrasse (on the B27; take the U5 or U6 into town), which is 4km south of the centre; and Österfeld (on the A81; take the S1, S2 or S3 into the centre).

Avis, Budget, Europcar, Hertz, National and Sixt have offices at the airport (Terminal 2, Level 2). Europcar, Hertz and Avis have offices at the Hauptbahnhof (opposite track 16).

PUBLIC TRANSPORT From slowest to fastest, Stuttgart's **public transport network** (www .vvs.de) consists of a *Zahnradbahn* (rack railway), buses, the *Strassenbahn* (tramway), *Stadtbahn* lines (light-rail lines beginning with U; underground in the city centre), S-Bahn lines (suburban rail lines S1 through to S6) and *Regionalbahn* lines (regional trains beginning with R). On Friday and Saturday there are night buses (beginning with N) with departures from Schlossplatz at 1.11am, 2.22am and 3.33am.

For travel within the city, single tickets are €2.10 and four-ride tickets *(Mehrfahrtenkarte)* cost €7.90. A day pass, good for two zones (including, for instance, the Mercedes-Benz and Porsche Museums), is better value at €6.10 for one person and €10.50 for a group of between two and five.

TAXI To order a taxi call ☎194 10 or ☎566 061.

Around Stuttgart

MAX-EYTH-SEE

When temperatures soar, Stuttgarters head to Max-Eyth-See, for pedalo fun on the lake and picnicking beside the Neckar River. Murky water rules out swimming but there's a worthwhile bike path, part of the Neckar-Radweg (www.neckar-radweg.com). The terraced-style vineyards rising above the river are scattered with *Wengerter-Häuschen* (tool sheds); some are over 200 years old and protected landmarks.

The lake is 9km northeast of Stuttgart Hauptbahnhof on the U14 line.

GRABKAPELLE WÜRTTEMBERG

When King Wilhelm I of Württemberg's beloved wife Katharina Pavlovna, daughter of a Russian tsar, died at the age of 30 in 1819, the king tore down the family castle and built this domed **burial chapel** (adult/ concession €2.20/1.10; ⊙10am-noon & 1-5pm Tue-Sat, 10am-noon & 1-6pm Sun Mar-Oct). The king was also interred in the classical-style Russian Orthodox chapel decades later. Scenically perched on a vine-strewn hill, the grounds afford long views down to the valley.

Grapkapelle Württemberg is 10km southeast of Stuttgart's centre. Take bus 61 from Stuttgart-Untertürkheim station, served by the S1.

LUDWIGSBURG
☎07141 / POP 87,740

This neat, cultured town is the childhood home of the dramatist Friedrich Schiller. Duke Eberhard Ludwig put it on the global map in the 18th century by erecting a chateau to out-pomp them all: the sublime, Versailles-inspired Residenzschloss. With its whimsical palaces and gardens, Ludwigsburg is baroque in overdrive and a flashback to when princes wore powdered wigs and lords went a-hunting.

◉ Sights & Activities

Residenzschloss   PALACE
(www.schloss-ludwigsburg.de; 30min tour adult/
concession €6.50/3.30, museums incl audioguide
€3.50/1.80; ☉10am-5pm) Nicknamed the Swabian Versailles, the Residenzschloss is an
extravagant 452-room baroque, rococo and
Empire affair. The 90-minute chateau tours
(in German; English tour at 1.30pm) begin
half-hourly.

The 18th-century feast continues with a
spin of the staggeringly ornate, scarlet and
gold **Karl Eugen Apartment**, and three
museums showcasing everything from exquisite baroque paintings to fashion accessories and majolica.

Blühendes Barock   GARDEN
(Mömpelgardstrasse 28; adult/concession €8/3.90;
☉gardens 7.30am-8.30pm, Märchengarten 9am-
6pm, both closed early Nov–mid-Mar) More appealing in summer is a fragrant stroll amid
the herbs, rhododendrons and gushing
fountains of the Blühendes Barock gardens.
Included in the admission price is entry
to the **Märchengarten** (☉9am-6pm), a fairy-
tale theme park. Take your kids to see the
witch with a Swabian cackle at the gingerbread house and admire their fairness in
Snow White's magic mirror. Should you want
Rapunzel to let down her hair at the tower,
get practising: *Rapunzel, lass deinen Zopf
herunter.* (The gold-tressed diva only under-
stands German – accurately pronounced!).

Schloss Favorite   PALACE
(30min tour adult/concession €3.50/1.80; ☉10am-
noon & 1.30-5pm mid-Mar–Oct, 10am-noon & 1.30-
4pm Tue-Sun Nov–mid-Mar) Sitting in parkland,
a five-minute walk north of the Residenzschloss, is the petit baroque palace Schloss
Favorite, graced with Empire-style furniture.
Duke Eugen held glittering parties here.

❶ Information

Ludwigsburg's **tourist office** (☎910 2252; www
.ludwigsburg.de; Marktplatz 6; ☉9am-6pm
Mon-Fri, to 2pm Sat) has excellent material in
English on lodgings, festivals and events such as
the baroque Christmas market.

❶ Getting There & Around

S-Bahn trains from Stuttgart serve the Hauptbahnhof, 750m southwest of the centre. The
Residenzschloss, on Schlossstrasse (the B27)
lies 400m northeast of the central Marktplatz.

Stuttgart's S4 and S5 S-Bahn lines go directly
to Ludwigsburg's Hauptbahnhof (€3.50), frequently linked to the chateau by buses 421, 425
and 427. On foot, the chateau is 1km from the
train station.

There are two large car parks 500m south of
the Residenzschloss, just off the B27.

MAULBRONN

Billed as the best-preserved medieval monastery north of the Alps, the one-time Cistercian
monastery **Kloster Maulbronn** (☎07043-926
610; www.schloesser-und-gaerten.de; adult/con-
cession/family €6/3/15; ☉9am-5.30pm Mar-Oct,
9.30am-5pm Tue-Sun Nov-Feb) was founded
by Alsatian monks in 1147, born again as a
Protestant school in 1556 and designated
a Unesco World Heritage Site in 1993. Its
famous graduates include the astronomer Johannes Kepler. Aside from the Romanesque-
Gothic portico in the monastery church and
the weblike vaulting of the cloister, it's the
insights into monastic life that make this
place so culturally stimulating.

Maulbronn is 30km east of Karlsruhe
and 33km northwest of Stuttgart, near the
Pforzheim Ost exit on the A8. From Karlsruhe, take the S4 to Bretten Bahnhof and
from there bus 700; from Stuttgart, take the
train to Mühlacker and then bus 700.

SWABIAN ALPS & AROUND

Tübingen

☑07071 / POP 88,360
Liberal students and deeply traditional *Bur-
schenschaften* (fraternities) singing ditties
for beloved Germania, eco-warriors, artists and punks – all have a soft spot for this
bewitchingly pretty Swabian city, where cobbled lanes twist up to a turreted castle. It was
here that Joseph Ratzinger, now Pope Benedict XVI, lectured theology in the late 1960s;
and here that Friedrich Hölderlin studied
stanzas; Johannes Kepler planetary motions;
and Goethe, the bottom of a beer glass.

The finest days unfold slowly in Tübingen: lingering in Altstadt cafes, punting on
the plane-tree-lined Neckar River and pretending, as the students so diligently do, to
work your brain cells in a chestnut-shaded
beer garden.

⊙ Sights & Activities

TOP
CHOICE **Schloss Hohentübingen** CASTLE
(Burgsteige 11; museum adult/concession €5/3;
⊙castle 7am-8pm daily, museum 10am-5pm Wed-
Sun, to 7pm Thu) On its perch above Tübingen, this turreted 16th-century castle has
a terrace overlooking the Neckar and the
Altstadt's triangular rooftops to the vine-
streaked hills beyond. An ornate Renaissance gate leads to the courtyard and the
laboratory where Friedrich Miescher discovered DNA in 1869.

Inside, the **archaeology museum** hides
the 35,000-year-old Vogelherd figurines, the
world's oldest figurative artworks. These
thumb-sized ivory carvings of mammoths
and lions were unearthed in the Vogelherd-
höhle caves in the Swabian Alps.

Am Markt SQUARE
Half-timbered town houses frame the Altstadt's main plaza Am Markt, a much-loved
student hang-out. Rising above it is the 15th-
century **Rathaus**, with a riotous baroque
facade and an astronomical clock. Statues of
four women representing the seasons grace
the **Neptune Fountain** opposite. Keep an
eye out for **No 15**, where a white window
frame identifies a secret room where Jews
hid in WWII.

Cottahaus LANDMARK
The Cottahaus is the one-time home of Johann Friedrich Cotta, who first published
the works of Schiller and Goethe. A bit of
a lad, Goethe conducted detailed research
on Tübingen's pubs during his weeklong
stay in 1797. The party-loving genius is commemorated by the plaque '*Hier wohnte
Goethe*' (Goethe lived here). On the wall of
the grungy student digs next door is the
perhaps more insightful sign '*Hier kotzte
Goethe*' (Goethe puked here).

FREE **Stiftskirche St Georg** CHURCH
(Am Holzmarkt; ⊙9am-5pm) The late-Gothic
Stiftskirche shelters the tombs of the Württemberg dukes and some dazzling late-
medieval stained-glass windows.

Platanenallee PROMENADE
Steps lead down from Eberhardsbrücke
bridge to Platanenallee, a leafy islet on the
Neckar River canopied by sycamore trees,
with views up to half-timbered houses in a
fresco painter's palette of pastels and turreted villas nestled on the hillsides.

Hölderlinturm MUSEUM
(Bursagasse 6; adult/concession €2.50/1.50;
⊙10am-noon & 3-5pm Tue & Fri, 2-5pm Sat & Sun)
You can see how the dreamy Neckar views
from this silver-turreted tower fired the
imagination of Romantic poet Friedrich
Hölderlin, resident here from 1807 to 1843.
It now contains a museum tracing his life
and work.

Kunsthalle GALLERY
(www.kunsthalle-tuebingen.de; Philosophenweg
76; adult/concession €9/7; ⊙10am-6pm Tue-Sun)
The streamlined Kunsthalle stages first-rate
exhibitions of mostly contemporary art. At
the time of writing, Beuys, Polke and Warhol
were in the spotlight. Buses 5, 13 and 17 stop
here.

FREE **Botanischer Garten** GARDEN
(Hartmeyerstrasse 123; ⊙8am-4.45pm daily, to
7pm Sat & Sun in summer) Green-fingered students tend to the Himalayan cedars, swamp
cypresses and rhododendrons in the gardens
and hothouses of the serene Botanischer
Garten, 2km northwest of the centre. Take
bus 5, 13, 15 or 17.

> **DON'T MISS**
>
> ## MESSING ABOUT ON THE RIVER
>
> There's nothing like a languid paddle
> along the sun-dappled Neckar River
> in summer. At **Bootsvermietung
> Märkle** (Eberhardsbrücke 1; ⊙11am-6pm
> Apr-Oct, to 9pm in summer), an hour of
> splashy fun in a rowboat, canoe, pedalo
> or 12-person *Stocherkähne* (punt)
> costs €9, €9, €12 and €48 respectively.
>
> Or sign up at the tourist office for
> an hour's **punting** (adult/child €6/3;
> ⊙1pm Sat & Sun May-Sep) around the
> Neckarinsel, beginning at the Hölder-
> linturm.
>
> Students in fancy dress do battle
> on the Neckar at June's hilarious **Sto-
> cherkahnrennen** (www.stocherkahn
> rennen.com) punt race, where jostling,
> dunking and even snapping your rival's
> oar are permitted. The first team to
> reach the Neckarbrücke wins the race,
> the title and as much beer as they can
> sink. The losers have to down half a litre
> of cod-liver oil. Arrive early to snag a
> prime spot on Platanenallee.

Wurmlinger Kapelle — CHURCH, WALK

(⊙10am-4pm May-Oct) A great hike is the *Kreuzweg* (way of the cross) to the 17th-century Wurmlinger Kapelle, 6km south-west of Tübingen. A footpath loops up through well-tended vineyards to the white-washed pilgrimage chapel, where there are long views across the Ammer and Neckar Valleys. The tourist office has leaflets (€1).

🛌 Sleeping

The tourist office has a free booklet listing private rooms, holiday homes, youth hostels and camping grounds in the area.

TOP CHOICE Hotel am Schloss — HISTORIC HOTEL €€

(☑929 40; www.hotelamschloss.de; Burgsteige 18; s €75, d €108-135; P 🐾) So close to the castle you can almost touch it, this flower-bedecked hotel has dapper rooms ensconced in a 16th-century building. Rumour has it Kepler was partial to the wine here; try a drop yourself before attempting the tongue twister above the bench outside: *dohoggeddiadiaemmerdohogged* (the same people sit in the same spot). And a very nice spot it is, too.

Hotel La Casa — HOTEL €€€

(☑946 66; www.lacasa-tuebingen.de; Hechinger Strasse 59; d €156-182; 🐾) Tübingen's swishest digs are a 15-minute stroll south of the Altstadt. Contemporary rooms designed

---

DON'T MISS

TOP SNACK SPOTS

Eating on the hoof? Try these informal nosh spots.

» **Die Kichererbse** (Metzgergasse 2; snacks €3-5; ⊙closed Sun; 🖉) All hail the 'chickpea' for its scrummy falafel. Grab a table to chomp on a classic (€3).

» **X** (Kornhausstrasse 6; snacks €1.50-3; ⊙11am-1am) Hole-in-the-wall joint rustling up Tübingen's crispiest fries, bratwurst and burgers.

» **Wochenmarkt** (⊙7am-1pm Mon, Wed & Fri) Bag glossy fruit and veg, oven-fresh bread, local honey and herbs at Tübingen's farmers market.

» **Eiscafé San Marco** (Nonnengasse 14; ice cream cone €1; ⊙8.30am-11pm Mon-Sat, 10.30am-11pm Sun) Italian-run, with hands-down the best gelati in town.

---

with panache come with welcome tea, coffee and soft drinks. Breakfast is a smorgasbord of mostly organic goodies. The crowning glory is the top-floor spa with tremendous city views.

Hotel Hospiz — GUESTHOUSE €€

(☑9240; www.hotel-hospiz.de; Neckarhalde 2; s/d €70/105; 🐾) Huddled away in the Altstadt, this candyfloss-pink guesthouse has old-school, immaculately kept rooms, many looking across Tübingen's gables. Pastries, smoked fish and eggs are nice additions to the breakfast buffet.

🍴 Eating

Mauganeschtle — SWABIAN €€€

(☑929 40; Burgsteige 18; mains €10-19.50; ⊙daily) It's a stiff climb up to this restaurant at Hotel am Schloss but worth every step. Suspended above the rooftops of Tübingen, the terrace is a scenic spot for the house speciality, *Maultaschen*, with fillings like lamb, trout, porcini and veal.

Neckarmüller — BREWPUB €€

(☑278 48; Gartenstrasse 4; mains €7.50-15; ⊙10am-1am) Overlooking the Neckar, this cavernous microbrewery is a summertime magnet for its chestnut-shaded beer garden. Come for home brews by the metre and beer-laced dishes from (tasty) Swabian roast to (interesting) tripe stew.

Alte Weinstube Göhner — SWABIAN €€€

(☑551 668; Schmiedtorstrasse 5; mains €10-17; ⊙closed Mon lunch, Sun) As down-to-earth and comfy as a Swabian farmer's boots, this 175-year-old haunt is Tübingen's oldest wine tavern. Join the high-spirited regulars to discuss the merits of *Maultaschen,* sip a glass of Trollinger and, if you're lucky, hear someone bashing out golden oldies on the piano.

Wurstküche — GERMAN €€€

(☑927 50; Am Lustnauer Tor 8; mains €9-17.50; ⊙11am-midnight daily) The rustic, wood-panelled Wurstküche brims with locals quaffing wine and contentedly munching *Schupfnudeln* (potato noodles) and *Spanferkel* (roast suckling pig).

🍷 Drinking

Tangente-Night — BAR

(Pfleghofstrasse 10; ⊙6pm-3am, to 5am Fri & Sat) Totally chilled Tangente-Night enjoys a fierce student following. Belt out a classic at Monday's karaoke party under the motto 'drink faster and sing for your life'. The vibe is clubbier at weekends, with music skipping from rock to electro.

Weinhaus Beck BAR
(Am Markt 1; ⊘9am-11pm) There's rarely an empty table at this wine tavern beside the Rathaus, a convivial place to enjoy a local tipple or coffee and cake.

Storchen CAFE
(Ammergasse 3; ⊘3pm-1am, from 11am Sat) Mind your head climbing the stairs to this easy-going student hang-out, serving enormous mugs of milky coffee and cheap local brews under wood beams.

Schwärzlocher Hof BEER GARDEN
(Schwarzloch 1; ⊘11am-10pm Wed-Sun; 🔊) Scenically perched above the Ammer Valley, a 20-minute trudge west of town, this creaking farmhouse is famous for its beer garden and home-pressed *Most* (cider). Kids love the resident horses, rabbits and peacocks.

ℹ Information

Find ATMs around the Hauptbahnhof, Eberhardsbrücke and Am Markt.
Post office (cnr Hafengasse & Neue Strasse) In the Altstadt.
Tourist office (⊉913 60; www.tuebingen-info.de; An der Neckarbrücke 1; ⊘9am-7pm Mon-Fri, 10am-4pm Sat, plus 11am-4pm Sun May-Sep) South of Eberhardsbrücke. Has a hotel board outside and can provide details on hiking options (for example, to Bebenhausen or Wurmlinger Kapelle).

ℹ Getting There & Around

The Neckar River divides Tübingen from east to west. Karlstrasse leads south to the Hauptbahnhof (500m) from Eberhardsbrücke.

Tübingen is an easy train ride from Stuttgart (€12.20, one hour, at least two per hour) and Villingen (€21, 1½ to two hours, hourly) in the Black Forest.

The centre is a maze of one-way streets with residents-only parking, so head for a multistorey car park. To drive into Tübingen, you need to purchase an environmentally friendly *Umwelt-plaketten* (emissions sticker).

Radlager (Lazarettgasse 19-21; ⊘9.30am-6.30pm Mon, Wed & Fri, 2-6.30pm Tue & Thu, 9.30am-2.30pm Sat) rents bikes for €10 per day.

If you'd rather let someone else do the pedalling, **Riksch-Radsch** (⊉300 449; Aixer Strasse 198) organise a three-hour spin to Bebenhausen (€59 for a two-person rickshaw).

Naturpark Schönbuch

For back-to-nature hiking and cycling, make for this 156-sq-km **nature reserve** (www.naturpark-schoenbuch.de), 8km north of Tübingen. With a bit of luck you might catch a glimpse of black woodpeckers and yellow-bellied toads.

The nature reserve's beech and oak woods fringe the village of **Bebenhausen** and its well-preserved **Cistercian Abbey** (www.kloster-bebenhausen.de; adult/concession €4.50/2.30; ⊘guided tours hourly 11am-5pm Tue-Sun). Founded in 1183 by Count Rudolph von Tübingen, the complex became a royal hunting retreat post-Reformation. A visit takes in the frescoed **summer refectory**, the Gothic **abbey church** and intricate star vaulting and half-timbered facades in the **cloister**.

Bebenhausen, 3km north of Tübingen, is the gateway to Naturpark Schönbuch. Buses run at least twice hourly (€2.20, 15 minutes).

Burg Hohenzollern

Rising dramatically from an exposed crag, its medieval battlements and silver turrets often veiled in mist, **Burg Hohenzollern** (www.burg-hohenzollern.com; tour adult/concession €10/8, grounds admission without tour adult/concession €5/4; ⊘tour 10am-5.30pm, to 4.30pm Nov–mid-Mar) is impressive from a distance but up close it looks more contrived. Dating to 1867, this neo-Gothic castle is the ancestral seat of the Hohenzollern family, the first and last monarchical rulers of the short-lived second German empire (1871–1918).

History fans should take a 35-minute German-language **tour**, which takes in towers, overblown salons replete with stained glass and frescoes, and the dazzling *Schatzkammer* (treasury). The **grounds** command tremendous views over the Swabian Alps.

Frequent trains link Tübingen, 28km distant, with Hechingen (€4.40, 25 minutes, one or two per hour), about 4km northwest of the castle.

Schwäbisch Hall

⊉0791 / POP 37,140

Out on its rural lonesome near the Bavarian border, Schwäbisch Hall is an unsung gem. This medieval time-capsule of higgledy-piggledy lanes, soaring half-timbered houses built high on the riches of salt, and covered

STUTTGART & THE BLACK FOREST NATURPARK SCHÖNBUCH

bridges that criss-cross the Kocher River is storybook stuff.

Buzzy cafes and first-rate museums add to the appeal of this town, known for its rare black-spotted pigs and the jangling piggy banks of its nationwide building society.

◉ Sights & Activities

Altstadt   NEIGHBOURHOOD
A leisurely Altstadt saunter takes you along narrow alleys, among half-timbered hillside houses and up slopes overlooking the Kocher River. The islands and riverbank parks are great for picnics.

Am Markt springs to life with a farmers market every Wednesday and Saturday morning. On the square, your gaze is drawn to the baroque-style **Rathaus**, festooned with coats of arms and cherubs, and to the terracotta-hued **Widmanhaus** at No 4, a remnant of a 13th-century Franciscan monastery. The centrepiece is the late-Gothic **Kirche St Michael**.

Note the **Gotischer Fischbrunnen** (1509), next to the tourist office, a large iron tub once used for storing fish before sale.

Towering above Pfarrgasse is the steep-roofed, 16th-century **Neubau**, built as an arsenal and granary and now used as a theatre. Ascend the stone staircase for dreamy views over red-roofed houses to the former city fortifications, the covered **Roter Steg** bridge and the **Henkerbrücke** (Hangman's Bridge).

FREE Kunsthalle Würth   GALLERY
(www.kunst.wuerth.com; Lange Strasse 35; ⊙11am-6pm) The brainchild of industrialist Reinhold Würth, this contemporary gallery is housed in a striking limestone building that preserves part of a century-old brewery. Stellar temporary exhibitions have previously spotlighted the work of artists such as David Hockney, Edvard Munch and Georg Baselitz.

Hällisch-Fränkisches Museum   MUSEUM
(adult/student €2.50/1.50; ⊙10am-5pm Tue-Sun) Down by the river, this well-curated museum traces Schwäbisch Hall's history with its collection of shooting targets, Roman figurines, and rarities including an exquisite hand-painted wooden synagogue interior from 1738 and a 19th-century mouse guillotine.

Hohenloher Freilandmuseum   MUSEUM
(Wackershofen; adult/concession €6/4; ⊙9am-6pm daily; ⊞) One place you can be guaranteed of seeing a black-spotted pig is this open-air farming museum, a sure-fire hit with the kids with its traditional farmhouses, orchards and animals. It's 6km northwest of Schwäbisch Hall and served by bus 7.

🛏 Sleeping & Eating

Hotel Scholl   HOTEL €€
(☎975 50; www.hotel-scholl.de; Klosterstrasse 2-4; s/d €74/99; ⊛) A charming pick behind Am Markt, this family-run hotel has rustic-chic rooms with parquet floors, flat-screen TVs, granite bathrooms and free wi-fi.

Der Adelshof   HISTORIC HOTEL €€
(☎758 90; www.hotel-adelshof.de; Am Markt 12; s €80-100, d €110-150, mains €18-32; P⊛) This centuries-old pad is as posh as it gets in Schwäbisch Hall, with a wellness area and plush quarters, from the blue-and-white Wedgwood room to the four-poster Turmzimmer. Its beamed Ratskeller serves seasonally inspired French fare.

TOP CHOICE Rebers Pflug   GASTRONOMIC €€€
(☎931 230; www.rebers-pflug.de; Weckriedener Strasse 2; mains €17.50-36; ⊙closed lunch Mon & Tue, dinner Sun) Hans-Harald Reber mans the stove at this 19th-century country house, one of Schwäbisch Hall's two Michelin-starred haunts. Signatures such as veal in an oxtail crust are exquisitely cooked and presented. Dine in the chestnut-shaded garden in summer.

Entenbäck   BISTRO €€
(☎9782 9182; Steinerner Steg 1; mains €10-15.50; ⊙noon-2.30pm & 5-10pm Tue-Fri, 11am-10pm Sat & Sun) This inviting bistro receives high praise for its Swabian-meets-Mediterranean menu, from satisfying roast beef with Spätzle to salmon roulade with riesling sauce. Lunch is a snip at €7.50.

Brauerei-Ausschank
Zum Löwen   BREWPUB €€
(☎2041 622; Mauerstrasse 17; mains €8-14.50; ⊙5-11pm Thu, 11.30am-2pm & 5-11pm Fri-Tue) Down by the river, this brewpub attracts a jovial bunch of locals, who come for freshly tapped Haller Löwenbrauerei brews and hearty nosh like pork cooked in beer-cumin sauce.

ℹ Information

Tourist office (☎0791 751 246; www.schwae bischhall.de; Am Markt 9; ⊙9am-6pm Mon-Fri, 10am-3pm Sat & Sun May-Sep, 9am-5pm Mon-Fri Oct-Apr) On the Altstadt's main square.

ℹ Getting There & Around

The town has two train stations: trains from Stuttgart (€14.40, 1¼ hours, hourly) arrive at Hessental, on the right bank about 7km south of the centre and linked to the Altstadt by bus 1; trains from Heilbronn go to the left-bank Bahnhof Schwäbisch Hall, a short walk along Bahnhofstrasse from the centre.

Ulm

♪ 0731 / POP 122,800

Starting with the statistics, Ulm has the crookedest house (as listed in *Guinness World Records*) and one of the narrowest (4.5m wide), the world's oldest zoomorphic sculpture (aged 30,000 years) and tallest cathedral steeple (161.5m high), and is the birthplace of the physicist Albert Einstein. Relatively speaking, of course.

This idiosyncratic city will win your affection with everyday encounters, particularly in summer as you pedal along the Danube and the Fischerviertel's beer gardens hum with animated chatter. One *Helles* too many and you may decide to impress the locals by attempting the tongue twister: '*In Ulm, um Ulm, und um Ulm herum.*'

◉ Sights & Activities

FREE Münster   CATHEDRAL
(Map p232; www.ulmer-muenster.de; Münsterplatz; organ concerts €3.50-6, tower adult/concession €4/2.50; ⊙9am-7.45pm, to 4.45pm in winter)
Ooh, it's so big... first-time visitors gush as they strain their neck muscles gazing up to the Münster. It is. And rather beautiful. Celebrated for its 161.5m-high steeple, the world's tallest, this Goliath of cathedrals took a staggering 500 years to build from the first stone laid in 1377. Note the hallmarks on each stone, inscribed by cutters who were paid by the block. Those intent on cramming the Münster into one photo, filigree spire and all, should lie down on the cobbles.

Only by puffing up 768 spiral steps to the 143m-high viewing platform of the **tower** can you appreciate the Münster's dizzying height. Up top there are terrific views of the Black Forest and, on cloud-free days, the Alps.

The **Israelfenster**, a stained-glass window above the west door, commemorates Jews killed during the Holocaust. The Gothic-style wooden pulpit canopy eliminates echoes during sermons. Biblical figures and historical characters such as Pythagoras embellish the 15th-century oak **choir stalls**. The Münster's regular organ concerts are a musical treat.

Marktplatz   SQUARE
Lording it over the Marktplatz, the 14th-century, step-gabled **Rathaus** (Town Hall; Map p232) sports an ornately painted Renaissance facade and a gilded astrological clock. Inside is a replica of Albrecht Berblinger's flying machine. In front is the **Fischkastenbrunnen** (Map p232; Marktplatz), a fountain where fishmongers kept their catch alive on market days. The 36m-high glass pyramid behind the Rathaus is the city's main library, the **Zentralbibliothek** (Map p232; Marktplatz), designed by Gottfried Böhm.

Stadtmauer   WALL
(Map p232) South of the Fischerviertel, along the Danube's north bank, runs the red-brick *Stadtmauer* (city wall), the height of which was reduced in the 19th century after Napoleon decided that a heavily fortified Ulm was against his best interests. Walk it for fine views over the river, the Altstadt and the colourful tile-roofed **Metzgerturm** (Butcher's Tower; Map p232), doing a Pisa by leaning 2m off-centre.

East of the Herdbrücke, the bridge to Neu-Ulm, a bronze **plaque** (Map p232) marks where Albrecht Berblinger, a tailor who invented a flying machine, attempted to fly over the Danube in 1811. The so-called 'Tailor of Ulm' made an embarrassing splash landing but his design was later shown to be workable (his failure was caused by a lack of thermals on that day).

Fischerviertel   NEIGHBOURHOOD
(Map p232) The charming Fischerviertel, Ulm's old fishers' and tanners' quarter, is slightly southwest. Here beautifully restored half-timbered houses huddle along the two channels of the Blau River. Harbouring art galleries, rustic restaurants, courtyards and

ℹ CITY SAVER

If you're planning on ticking off most of the major sights, consider investing in a good-value **UlmCard** (1/2 days €12/18), which covers public transport in Ulm and Neu-Ulm, a free city tour or rental of the itour audioguide and entry to all museums, plus numerous other discounts on tours, attractions and restaurants.

Ulm

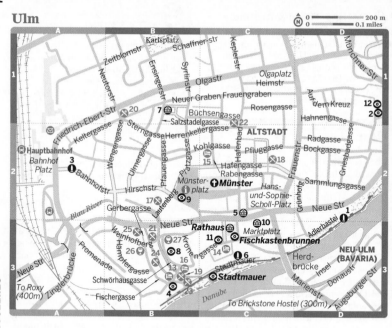

Ulm

◎ Top Sights

◎ Sights

⬚ Sleeping

⊗ Eating

◉ Drinking

the crookedest house in the world – as well as one of the narrowest – the cobbled lanes are ideal for a leisurely saunter.

Ulmer Museum MUSEUM

(Map p232; www.ulmer-museum.ulm.de; Marktplatz 9; adult/concession €5/3.50, Fri free; ☺11am-5pm Tue-Sun, to 8pm Thu) This museum is a fascinating romp through ancient and modern art, history and archaeology. Standouts are the 20th-century **Kurt Fried Collection**, starring Klee, Picasso and Lichtenstein works. Archaeological highlights include tiny Upper Palaeolithic figurines, unearthed in caves in the Swabian Alps, including the 30,000-year-old ivory *Löwenmensch* (lion man), the world's oldest zoomorphic sculpture.

Kunsthalle Weishaupt   GALLERY
(Map p232; www.kunsthalle-weishaupt.de; Hans-und-Sophie-Scholl-Platz 1; adult/concession €6/4; ☉11am-5pm Tue-Sun, to 8pm Thu) The glass-fronted Kunsthalle Weishaupt unveils the private collection of Siegfried Weishaupt. The accent is on modern and pop art, with bold paintings by Klein, Warhol and Haring.

Museum der Brotkultur   MUSEUM
(Map p232; www.museum-brotkultur.de; Salzstadel-gasse 10; adult/concession €3.50/2.50; ☉10am-5pm) How grain grows, what makes a good dough and other bread-related mysteries are unravelled at the Museum of Bread Culture. The collection celebrates bread as the stuff of life over millennia and across cultures, displaying curios from mills to Egyptian corn mummies.

Stadthaus   LANDMARK
(Map p232) Designed by Richard Meier, the contemporary aesthetic of the concrete-and-glass Stadthaus is a dramatic contrast to the Münster. The American architect caused uproar by erecting a postmodern building alongside the city's Gothic giant but the result is striking. The edifice stages exhibitions and events, and houses the tourist office and a cafe.

Schwörhaus   LANDMARK
(Oath House; Map p232) On the third Monday of July, the mayor swears allegiance to the town's 1397 constitution from the 1st-floor loggia of the early 17th-century baroque Schwörhaus (Oath House), three blocks west of the Rathaus.

Einstein Fountain & Monument   LANDMARK
(Map p232) A nod to Ulm's most famous son, Jürgen Goertz's fiendishly funny bronze fountain shows a wild-haired, tongue-poking-out Albert Einstein, who was born in Ulm but left when he was one year old. Standing in front of the 16th-century **Zeughaus** (arsenal; Map p232), the rocket-snail creation is a satirical play on humanity's attempts to manipulate evolution for its own self-interest. Nearby, at Zeughaus 14, is a single stone bearing the inscription *Ein Stein* (One Stone).

On Bahnhofstrasse sits Max Bill's 1979 **monument** (Map p232) to the great physicist, a stack of red-granite pillars marking the spot where Einstein was born.

Legoland   THEME PARK
(www.legoland.de; adult/concession €38/34; ☉10am-btwn 6pm & 8pm Apr-early Nov) A sure-fire kid-pleaser, Legoland Deutschland is a pricey Lego-themed amusement park, with shows, splashy rides and a miniature world built from 25 million Lego bricks. It's in Günz-burg, 37km east of Ulm, just off the A8.

🛏 Sleeping

The tourist office lists apartments and guest-houses charging around €25 per person.

TOP CHOICE / **Hotel Schiefes Haus**   B&B €€€
(Map p232; ☎967 930; www.hotelschiefeshausulm.de; Schwörhausgasse 6; s €125, d €148-160; 🛜) There was a crooked man and he walked a crooked mile...presumably to the world's most crooked hotel. But fear not, ye of little wonkiness, this early-16th-century, half-timbered rarity is not about to topple into the Blau River. And up those creaking wood stairs, in your snug, beamed room, you won't have to buckle yourself to the bed thanks to spirit levels and specially made height adjusters. If you're feeling *really* crooked, plump straight for room No 6.

Brickstone Hostel   HOSTEL €
(☎708 2559; www.brickstone-hostel.de; Schützen-strasse 42; dm €18-22, s/d €30/44; 🛜) We love the homely vibe at this beautifully restored art nouveau house in Neu-Ulm. The high-ceilinged rooms are kept spotless and back-packer perks include a self-catering kitchen with free coffee and tea, bike rental and a cosy lounge with book exchange. Take bus 7 to Schützenstrasse from the Hauptbahnhof.

Das Schmale Haus   B&B €€
(Map p232; ☎175 4940; Fischergasse 27; s/d €81/104) Measuring just 4.5m across, the half-timbered 'narrow house' is a one-off. The affable Heides have transformed this slender 16th-century pad into a gorgeous B&B, with exposed beams, downy bedding and wood floors in all three rooms.

Hotel Restaurant Löwen   HOTEL €€
(☎388 5880; www.hotel-loewen-ulm.de; Klosterhof 41; s €81-91, d €116-122; 🅿🛜) It's amazing what

---

DON'T MISS

SPOT THE SPARROW

You can't move for *Spatzen* (sparrows) in the German language. You can eat like one (*essen wie ein Spatz*) and swear like one (*schimpfen wie ein Rohrspatz*); there are *Spatzenschleuder* (catapults), *Spätzles* (little darlings) and *Spatzenhirne* (bird brains). Nicknamed *Spatzen*, Ulm residents are, according to legend, indebted to the titchy bird for the construction of their fabulous Münster.

The story goes that the half-baked builders tried in vain to shove the wooden beams for the minster sideways through the city gate. They struggled, until suddenly a sparrow fluttered past with straw for its nest. Enlightened, the builders carried the beams lengthways, completed the job and placed a bronze statue of a sparrow at the top to honour the bird.

Today there are sparrows everywhere in Ulm: on postcards, in patisseries, at football matches (team SSV Ulm are dubbed *die Spatzen*) and, above all, in the colourful sculptures dotting the Altstadt.

---

you can do with a former monastery and an eye for design. Exposed beams and stone add historic edge to streamlined rooms with parquet floors and flat-screen TVs. The chestnut-canopied beer garden is a boon in summer. Take tram 1 from central Ulm to Söflingen.

Hotel Bäumle HISTORIC HOTEL €€
(Map p232; ☑622 87; www.hotel-baeumle.de; Kohlgasse 6; s €70-89, d €90-103, tr €130; 🛜) Big on old-world flair, the Bäumle can trace its history way back to 1522 and houses smart, immaculately kept rooms. Unless you class cathedral bells as 'noise', you're going to love the location. No lift.

**Hotel am Rathaus &
Hotel Reblaus** HOTEL €€
(Map p232; ☑968 490; www.rathausulm.de; Kronengasse 10; s €70-110, d €88-130, q €130-170, s/d without bathroom €52/72; 🛜) Just paces from the Rathaus, these family-run twins ooze individual charm in rooms with flourishes like stucco and Biedermeier furnishings. Light sleepers take note: the walls are thin and the street can be noisy.

✗ Eating

Zur Forelle GERMAN €€€
(Map p232; ☑639 24; Fischergasse 25; mains €12-22; ☺daily) Since 1626, this low-ceilinged tavern has been convincing wayfarers (Einstein included) of the joys of seasonal Swabian cuisine. Ablaze with flowers in summer, this wood-panelled haunt by the Blau prides itself on its namesake *Forelle* (trout), kept fresh under the bridge.

Barfüsser BREWPUB €€
(Map p232; ☑602 1110; Lautenberg 1; mains €9-16.50; ☺10am-1am Sun-Wed, to 2am Thu-Sat) Hearty fare like *Käsespätzle* (cheese noodles) and pork roast soak up the prize-winning beer, microbrewed in Neu-Ulm, at this brewpub.

Da Franco ITALIAN €€€
(Map p232; ☑305 85; Neuer Graben 23; mains €13-24.50; ☺closed Mon) If you fancy a break from the norm, why not give this little Italian a whirl. There is a seasonal touch to authentic dishes like swordfish with clams and veal escalope with asparagus, which are cooked and presented with style.

Gerberhaus MEDITERRANEAN €€€
(Map p232; ☑677 17; Weinhofberg 9; mains €10-18; ☺daily) This warm, inviting woodcutter's cottage of a restaurant hits the mark with its Med-inspired dishes. Plump for a river-facing table for clean, bright flavours like home-smoked salmon carpaccio and lemongrass crème brûlée. Day specials go for as little as €7.

Zunfthaus der Schiffleute GERMAN €€€
(Map p232; ☑755 771; www.zunfthaus-ulm.com; Fischergasse 31; mains €10-19; ☺daily) Looking proudly back on a 600-year tradition, this timber-framed restaurant sits by the river. The menu speaks of a chef who loves the region, with Swabian faves like *Katzagschroi* (beef, onions, egg and fried potatoes) and meaty one-pot *Schwäbisches Hochzeitssüppchen*.

Zur Lochmühle GERMAN €€€
(Map p232; ☑673 05; Gerbergasse 6; mains €8.50-18.50; ☺daily; 👪) The watermill has been churning the Blau since 1356 at this rustic

half-timbered pile. Plant yourself in the riverside beer garden for Swabian classics like crispy roast pork, *Schupfnudeln* and brook trout with lashings of potato salad.

Cafe Ulmer Münz   CAFE €€
(Map p232; Schwörhausgasse 4; light meals €7-12; ⊘closed Mon) Fischerviertel cafe with a happy buzz on the cobbled patio, daily specials and homemade cakes.

Yamas   GREEK €€€
(Map p232; ☑407 8614; Herrenkellergasse 29; mains €12-23; ⊘daily) Classy Greek food with a market-driven menu, lots of fresh seafood and a bulging wine cellar.

Café im Kornhauskeller   CAFE €
(Map p232; Hafengasse 19; breakfast & snacks €4-8; ⊘8am-midnight Mon-Sat, 9am-10pm Sun) Arty cafe with an inner courtyard for drinks, breakfast, light bites or ice cream.

Café im Stadthaus   CAFE €
(Map p232; Münsterplatz 50; lunch special €8.40; ⊘8am-midnight, to 1am Fri & Sat) Go for coffee or a good-value lunch special; linger for the mesmerising cathedral views at this glass cube opposite.

Drinking & Entertainment

Zur Zill   BAR
(Map p232; Schwörhausgasse 19; ⊘10am-2am daily, to 4am Fri & Sat) Join a happy-go-lucky crowd for a cold beer or cocktail by the river.

Wilder Mann   PUB
(Map p232; Fischergasse 2; ⊘11am-1am Mon-Thu, to 3am Fri-Sun) Service is a lucky dip and the food is mediocre but by all means head to the people-watching terrace for a drink.

Roxy   ARTS CENTRE
(www.roxy.ulm.de; Schillerstrasse 1) A huge cultural venue, housed in a former industrial plant 1km south of the Hauptbahnhof, with a concert hall, cinema, disco, bar and special-event forum. Take tram line 1 to Ehinger Tor.

❶ Information

Internet cafe (Herdbruckerstrasse 26; per hr €1; ⊘10am-9pm)

Post office (Bahnhofplatz 2) To the left as you exit the Hauptbahnhof.

Tourist office (☑161 2830; www.tourismus. ulm.de; Münsterplatz 50, Stadthaus; ⊘9am-6pm Mon-Fri, to 4pm Sat, 11am-3pm Sun) Sells the Ulm Card and events tickets and has a free room-booking service.

❶ Getting There & Away

Ulm, about 90km southeast of Stuttgart and 150km west of Munich, is near the intersection of the north–south A7 and the east–west A8.

Ulm is well-served by ICE and EC trains; major destinations include Stuttgart (€18.10 to €25, 56 minutes to 1¼ hours, several hourly) and Munich (€30 to €36, 1¼ hours, several hourly).

❶ Getting Around

Ulm's ecofriendly trams run on renewable energy. There's a **local transport information counter** (www.swu-verkehr.de) in the tourist office. A single/day ticket for the bus and tram network in Ulm and Neu-Ulm costs €1.95/4.40.

Except in parking garages (€0.60 per 30 minutes), the whole city centre is metered; many areas are limited to one hour (€1.80). There's a Park & Ride lot at Donaustadion, a stadium 1.5km northeast of the Münster and on tram line 1.

You can hire bikes from **Fahrradhandlung Ralf Reich** (☑211 790 231; Frauenstrasse 34; per day €9; ⊘9am-12.30pm & 2-6.30pm Mon-Fri, 9am-2pm Sat), a five-minute stroll northeast of the Münsterplatz. Bike paths shadow the Danube.

THE BLACK FOREST

Baden-Baden

☑07221 / POP 54,500

'So nice that you have to name it twice', enthused Bill Clinton about Baden-Baden, whose air of old-world luxury and curative waters have attracted royals, the rich and celebrities over the years – Obama and Bismarck, Queen Victoria and Victoria Beckham included. 'Nice', however, could never convey the amazing grace of this Black Forest town, with its grand colonnaded buildings and whimsically turreted art nouveau villas spread across the hillsides and framed by forested mountains.

The bon-vivant spirit of France, just across the border, is tangible in the town's open-air cafes, chic boutiques and pristine gardens fringing the Oos River. And with its temple-like thermal baths – which put the *Baden* (bathe) in Baden – and palatial casino, the allure of this grand dame of German spa towns is timeless as it is enduring.

Black Forest

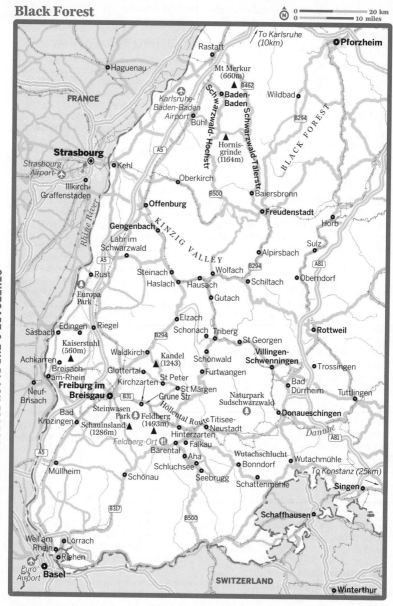

⊙ Sights

Trinkhalle   LANDMARK

(Pump Room; Map p238; Kaiserallee 3; ⊙10am-5pm Mon-Sat, 2-5pm Sun) Standing proud above a manicured park, this neoclassical pump room was built in 1839 as an attractive addition to the Kurhaus. The 90m-long portico is embellished with 19th-century frescoes of local legends. Baden-Baden's elixir of youth, some say, is the free curative mineral water that gushes from a faucet linked to the

Friedrichsbad spring. A cafe sells cups for €0.20, or bring your own bottle.

Kurhaus & Casino   LANDMARK
(Map p238; www.kurhaus-baden-baden.de; Kaiserallee 1; guided tour €5; ☉guided tour 9.30am–11.30am daily) Corinthian columns and a frieze of mythical griffins grace the belle époque facade of the Kurhaus, which towers above well-groomed gardens. An alley of chestnut trees, flanked by two rows of boutiques, links the Kurhaus with Kaiserallee.

Inside is the sublime **casino** (www.casino-baden-baden.de; admission €5; ☉2pm–2am Sun-Thu, to 3am Fri & Sat), which seeks to emulate the gilded splendour of Versailles. Marlene Dietrich called it 'the most beautiful casino in the world'. Gents must wear a jacket and tie, rentable for €8 and €3 respectively. If you're not a gambler and don't fancy dressing up, join a 25-minute **guided tour** of the opulent interior.

Lichtentaler Allee   GARDENS
This 2.3km ribbon of greenery, threading from Goetheplatz to Kloster Lichtenthal, is quite a picture: studded with fountains and sculptures and carpeted with flowers (crocuses and daffodils in spring, magnolias and azaleas in summer). Shadowing the sprightly Oosbach, its promenade and bridges are made for aimless ambling.

The gateway to Lichtentaler Allee is **Baden-Baden Theater** (Map p238), a neo-baroque confection whose grandiose interior resembles the Opéra-Garnier in Paris. About 1km south is the **Gönneranlage** (Map p238), a rose garden ablaze with more than 400 varieties. Almost Siberian is the **Russische Kirche** (Russian Church; Map p238; Maria-Victoria-Strasse; admission €1; ☉10am-6pm), slightly to the east. Built in the Byzantine style in 1882, it's topped with a brilliantly golden onion dome.

Lichtentaler Allee concludes at the **Kloster Lichtenthal**, a Cistercian abbey founded in 1245, with an abbey church, open daily, where generations of the margraves of Baden lie buried.

Museum Frieder Burda   GALLERY
(Map p238; www.museum-frieder-burda.de; Lichtentaler Allee 8b; adult/concession €10/8; ☉10am-6pm Tue-Sun) A Joan Miró sculpture guards the front of this architecturally innovative gallery, designed by Richard Meier. The star-studded collection of modern and contemporary art, featuring works by Picasso, Gerhard Richter and Jackson Pollock, is complemented by temporary exhibitions, such as the recent retrospective of American surrealist William Copley.

Staatliche Kunsthalle   GALLERY
(Map p238; www.kunsthalle-baden-baden.de; Lichtentaler Allee 8a; adult/concession €5/4; ☉10am-6pm Tue-Sun) Sidling up to the Museum Frieda Burda is this sky-lit gallery, which showcases rotating exhibitions of contemporary art in neoclassical surrounds. Recently it zoomed in on Belgian visual artist Jan de Cock, postmodern painter Georg Baselitz and the collage-style works of Kenyan artist Wangechi Mut.

Stiftskirche   CHURCH
(Map p238; Marktplatz; ☉8am-6pm daily) The centrepiece of cobbled Marktplatz is this pink church, a hotchpotch of Romanesque, late Gothic and, to a lesser extent, baroque styles. Its foundations incorporate some ruins of the former Roman baths. Come in the early afternoon to see its stained-glass windows cast rainbow patterns across the nave.

Römische Badruinen   ARCHAEOLOGICAL SITE
(Map p238; Römerplatz; adult/concession €2.50/1; ☉11am-noon & 3-4pm mid-Mar–mid-Nov) The beauty-conscious Romans were the first to discover the healing properties of Baden-Baden's springs in the city they called Aquae Aureliae. Slip back 2000 years on a tour of the well-preserved ruins of their baths.

🏃 Activities
Baden-Baden is criss-crossed by scenic walking trails. Footpaths lead to the crumbling 11th-century **Altes Schloss**, 3km north of the centre, with Rhine Valley views; the **Geroldsauer waterfalls**, 6km south of

STUTTGART & THE BLACK FOREST BADEN-BADEN

DON'T MISS

TEN YEARS YOUNGER

Rheumatism, arthritis, respiratory complaints, skin problems – all this and a host of other ailments can, apparently, be cured by Baden-Baden's mineral-rich spring water. If you'd rather drink the stuff than bathe in it, head to the **Fettquelle** fountain at the base of a flight of steps near Römerplatz, where you can fill your bottle for free. It might taste like lukewarm bath water but who cares if it makes you feel 10 years younger?

Baden-Baden

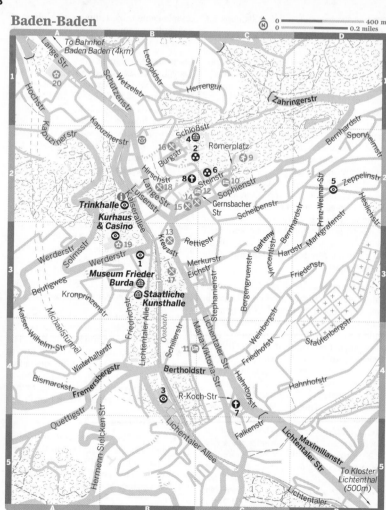

Leopoldsplatz; and the overgrown **Yburg** castle ruins, in the vineyards southwest of town. The 40km **Panoramaweg** is an above-the-city delight.

Friedrichsbad
TOP CHOICE
SPA

(Map p238; ☏275 920; www.roemisch-irisches-bad .de; Römerplatz 1; 3hr ticket €23, incl soap-and-brush massage €33; ⊗9am-10pm, last admission 7pm) If it's the body of Venus and the complexion of Cleopatra you desire, abandon modesty (and clothing) to wallow in thermal waters at this sumptuous 19th-century spa.

As Mark Twain put it, 'after 10 minutes you forget time; after 20 minutes, the world' as you slip into the regime of steaming, scrubbing, hot-cold bathing and dunking in the Roman-Irish bath. With its cupola, mosaics and Carrera marble pool, the bathhouse is the vision of a neo-Renaissance palace.

Caracalla Therme
SPA

(Map p238; www.caracalla.de; Römerplatz 11; 2/3/4hr €14/17/20; ⊗8am-10pm, last admission 8pm) If you would prefer to keep your bathing togs on, this glass-fronted spa has a cluster of indoor and outdoor pools, grottos and

Baden-Baden

◎ Top Sights
Kurhaus & Casino B3
Museum Frieder Burda B3
Staatliche Kunsthalle B3
Trinkhalle...B2

◎ Sights
1 Baden-Baden Theater........................B3
2 Florentinerberg...................................B2
3 Gönneranlage B4
4 Neues Schloss B2
5 Paradies am Annaberg.......................D2
6 Römische Badruinen..........................C2
7 Russische Kirche C4
8 Stiftskirche..B2

◎ Activities, Courses & Tours
9 Caracalla Therme C2
Friedrichsbad............................. (see 6)

◎ Sleeping
Hotel am Markt .... (see 8)
10 Hotel Beek..C2
11 Hotel Belle Epoque B4
12 Rathausglöckel B2

◎ Eating
13 Café König...B3
14 Kaffeehaus Baden-Baden...................B2
15 La Casserole B2
16 La Provence B2
17 Rizzi B3
18 Weinstube im Baldreit.........................B2

◎ Entertainment
19 Baden-Badener Philharmonie............B3
20 Festspielhaus.......................................A1

surge channels, making the most of the mineral-rich spring water. For those who dare to bare, saunas range from the rustic 'forest' to the roasting 95°C 'fire' variety.

🛏 Sleeping

Baden-Baden is crammed with hotels but bargains are rare. The tourist office has a room-reservation service, for which a 10% fee is deducted from the cost of the room.

Hotel am Markt   HISTORIC HOTEL €
(Map p238; ☑270 40; www.hotel-am-markt-baden.de; Marktplatz 18; s €37-53 d €70-92; P@🛜) Sitting pretty in front of the Stiftskirche, this 250-year-old hotel has 23 homely, well-kept rooms. It's quiet up here apart from your

wake-up call of church bells, but then you wouldn't want to miss out on the great breakfast.

Heiligenstein   HOTEL €€
(☑07223-961 40; www.hotel-heiligenstein.de; Heiligensteinstrasse 19a; s €78-82, d €113-118; P) It's worth going the extra mile (or seven) to this sweet hotel overlooking vineyards. Slick, earthy-hued rooms come with balconies and guests can put their feet up in the spa and gardens. The highly regarded **restaurant** (mains €15 to €27) serves local, seasonally inspired fare, from homemade *Maultaschen* to venison ragout.

Rathausglöckel   HOTEL €€
(Map p238; ☑906 10; www.rathausgloeckel.de; Steinstrasse 7; s €77-100, €110-139; @🛜) Down the hill from the Stiftskirche, this family-run hotel occupies a 16th-century town house. The recently renovated rooms (some with rooftop views) are dressed in muted tones with pine furniture.

Hotel Belle Epoque   LUXURY HOTEL €€€
(Map p238; ☑300 660; www.hotel-belle-epoque.de; Maria-Viktoria-Strasse 2c; s €170-245, d €225-299; 🛜) Nestling in manicured parkland, this neo-Renaissance villa is one of Baden-Baden's most characterful five-star pads. Antiques lend a dash of old-world opulence to the individually designed rooms. Rates include high tea, with scones and cakes and fine brews served on the terrace or by the fireplace.

Hotel Beek   B&B €€
(Map p238; ☑367 60; www.hotel-beek.de; Gernsbacherstrasse 44-46; s €85-95, d €109-119; @) On a tree-fringed street in the heart of town, this pretty-in-pink hotel doubles as an excellent patisserie, going strong since 1885. Facing either a courtyard or the Neues Schloss, the bright rooms sport comfy beds; the best ones (for a price hike) come with balconies.

🍴 Eating

Rizzi   ITALIAN €€€
(Map p238; ☑258 38; Augustaplatz 1; mains €18-25; ⏰noon-1am) A summertime favourite, this pink villa's tree-shaded patio faces Lichtentaler Allee. Italian-influenced dishes like osso buco (veal shanks braised with vegetables, garlic and wine) and scallops with truffle mash pair well with local wines. The €7.90 lunch is a steal.

SILENT HEIGHTS

Escape the crowds and enjoy the view at these Baden-Baden lookouts.

Neues Schloss (Map p238; Schlossstrasse) Vine-swathed steps lead from Marktplatz to the 15th-century Neues Schloss, the former residence of the Baden-Baden margraves, which is set to reopen as a luxury hotel in 2013. The lookout affords far-reaching views over Baden-Baden's rooftops and spires to the Black Forest beyond.

Mt Merkur Though modest in height, this 668m peak commands wide-screen views of Baden-Baden and the Murg Valley. It's a popular spot for paragliding, gentle hiking and family picnics. Buses 204 and 205 stop near the **funicular** (one-way/rtn €2/4 ⏰10am-10pm), which has been trundling to the top since 1913.

Florentinerberg (Map p238) The Romans used to cool off here; check out the ruins of the original baths at the foot of the hill. Nowadays, the serene botanical gardens nurture wisteria, cypress trees, orange and lemon groves.

Paradies am Annaberg (Map p238) These Italianate gardens are the perfect spot to unwind in, with their soothing fountains and waterfalls. There are fine views of the Altstadt and wooded hills from these heights. Bus 205 to Friedrichshöhe runs nearby.

La Provence FRENCH €€€
(Map p238; ☎216 515; Schlossstrasse 20; mains €13.50-25; ⏰5pm-1am Mon-Fri, noon-1am Sat & Sun) Housed in the Neues Schloss wine cellar, the vaulted ceilings, art nouveau mirrors and sense of humour at La Provence complement the French cuisine. Specialities like garlicky snails, frogs' legs and chateaubriand are spot-on.

Café König CAFE €
(Map p238; Lichtentaler Strasse 12; cake €3.50-5; ⏰9.30am-6.30pm Mon-Sat, 10.30am-6.30pm Sun) Liszt and Tolstoy once sipped coffee at this venerable cafe, which has been doing a brisk trade in Baden-Baden's finest cakes, tortes, pralines and truffles for 250 years. Black forest gateau topped with clouds of cream, fresh berry tarts, moist nut cakes – oh, decisions!

La Casserole FRENCH €€€
(Map p238; ☎222 21; Gernsbacherstrasse 18; mains €12-18; ⏰closed Mon, Sun lunch) Lace curtains, cheek-by-jowl tables and flickering candles create the classic bistro tableau at intimate La Casserole. Go for satisfying Alsatian specialities like beef cheeks braised in Pinot noir until tender, served with *Spätzle* (thick egg-based noodles).

Weinstube im Baldreit GERMAN €€€
(Map p238; ☎231 36; Küferstrasse 3; mains €12.50-19; ⏰5-10pm Mon-Sat) Tucked down cobbled lanes, this wine cellar restaurant is tricky to find, but persevere. Baden-Alsatian fare such as *Flammkuchen* topped with Black Forest ham, Roquefort and pears is expertly matched with local wines. Eat in the ivy-swathed courtyard in summer, the vaulted interior in winter.

Rathausglöckl GERMAN €€
(☎906 10; Steinstrasse 7; mains €10-16; ⏰6-11pm Mon-Sat, 11.30am-2pm & 6-11pm Sun, closed Wed; 🕹🐾) Strong on old-school charm, this low-beamed tavern is cosily clad in dark wood and oil paintings. Historic regional and German dishes are on the menu, from *Himmel und Erde* (black pudding, mashed potatoes, apple sauce and fried onions) to stuffed quail with *Schupfnudeln* (stubby potato noodles with sauerkraut).

Kaffeehaus Baden-Baden CAFE €
(Map p238; Gernsbacherstrasse 24; snacks €3-6; ⏰9.30am-6pm Mon-Fri, 10.30am-6pm Sat, 1-6pm Sun) The aroma of freshly roasted coffee fills this artsy cafe, a laid-back spot for an espresso and slice of tart. Its shop sells organic preserves and handmade ceramics.

☆ Entertainment

Ensconced in an historic train station and fabled for its acoustics, the **Festspielhaus** (Map p238; ☎301 3101; www.festspielhaus.de; Beim Alten Bahnhof 2, Robert-Schumann-Platz) is Europe's second biggest concert hall, seating 2500 theatre-goers, and a lavish tribute to Baden-Baden's musical heritage. Under the direction of Andreas Mölich-Zebhauser, the grand venue hosts a world-class program of concerts, opera and ballet.

The revered **Baden-Badener Philharmonie** (Map p238; ☎932 791; www.philharmonie

.baden-baden.de; Solms-Strasse 1) frequently performs in the Kurhaus.

ℹ Information

Branch tourist office (Kaiserallee 3; ⊘10am-5pm Mon-Sat, 2-5pm Sun) In the Trinkhalle. Sells events tickets.

Main tourist office (☑275 200; www.baden -baden.com; Schwarzwaldstrasse 52; ⊘9am-6pm Mon-Sat, to 1pm Sun) Situated 2km northwest of the centre. If you're driving from the northwest (from the A5) this place is on the way into town. Sells events tickets.

Post office (Lange Strasse 44) Inside Kaufhaus Wagener.

ℹ Getting There & Away

Karlsruhe-Baden-Baden airport (p215), 15km west of town, is linked to London and other European cities by Ryanair.

Buses to Black Forest destinations depart from the bus station, next to the Bahnhof.

Baden-Baden is close to the A5 (Frankfurt–Basel autobahn) and is the northern starting point of the zigzagging Schwarzwald-Hochstrasse, which follows the B500.

Baden-Baden is on a major north–south rail corridor. Twice-hourly destinations include Freiburg (€19.20 to €28, 45 to 90 minutes) and Karlsruhe (€10 to €15, 15 to 30 minutes).

ℹ Getting Around

BUS Local buses run by **Stadtwerke Baden-Baden** (www.stadtwerke-baden-baden.de) cost €2.20/5.20 for a single/24-hour ticket. A day pass for up to five people is €8.20. Bus 201 (every 10 minutes) and other lines link the Bahnhof with Leopoldsplatz. Bus 205 runs roughly hourly between the Bahnhof and the airport, less frequently at weekends.

CAR & MOTORCYLE The centre is mostly pedestrianised, so it's best to park and walk. There is a free Park & Ride at the Bahnhof. Closer to the centre, the cheapest car park is at the Festspielhaus (€0.70 per hour). Michaelstunnel on the D500 routes traffic away from the centre, ducking underground west of the Festspielhaus and resurfacing just south of the Russische Kirche.

Karlsruhe

☑0721 / POP 294,760

When planning this radial city in 1715, the Margraves of Baden placed a mighty baroque palace smack in the middle – an urban layout so impressive it became the blueprint for Washington DC.

Laid-back and cultured, Karlsruhe will grow on you the longer you linger, with its rambling parks, museums crammed with futuristic gizmos and French Impressionist paintings. The suburbs dotted with art nouveau town houses are a reminder that France is just 15km away. Some 20,000 students keep the beer cheap and the vibe upbeat in the pubs and the wheels of innovation in culture and technology turning.

◉ Sights & Activities

TOP CHOICE **Schloss**　　　　　　　　　　PALACE
From the baroque-meets-neoclassical Schloss, Karlsruhe's 32 streets radiate like the spokes of a wheel. Karl Wilhelm Margrave of Baden-Durlach named his epicentral palace Karlsruhe (Karl's retreat) when founding the city in 1715. Destroyed in the war, the grand palace was sensitively rebuilt. In warm weather, locals play pétanque on the fountain-strewn **Schlossplatz** parterre.

The treasure-trove **Badisches Landesmuseum** (www.landesmuseum.de; adult/concession €4/3, after 2pm Fri free; ⊘10am-5pm Tue-Thu, to 6pm Fri-Sun), inside the Schloss, shelters the jewel-encrusted crown of Baden's granducal ruling family, and spoils of war from victorious battles against the Turks in the 17th century. Scale the **tower** for a better look at Karlsruhe's circular layout and for views to the Black Forest.

Edging north, the **Schlossgarten** is a popular student hang-out and a relaxed spot for walks and picnics.

Kunsthalle Karlsruhe　　　　　　　GALLERY
(www.kunsthalle-karlsruhe.de; Hans-Thoma-Strasse 2-6; adult/concession €8/6, Orangerie €4/2.50; ⊘10am-5pm Tue-Fri, to 6pm Sat & Sun) The outstanding State Art Gallery presents a world-class collection; from the canvases of late-Gothic German masters like Matthias Grünewald and Lucas Cranach the Elder to Impressionist paintings by Degas, Monet and Renoir. Step across to the **Orangerie** to view works by German artists like Georg Baselitz and Gerhard Richter.

Marktplatz　　　　　　　　　　　　SQUARE
The grand neoclassical Marktplatz is dominated by the Ionic portico of the 19th-century **Evangelische Stadtkirche** and the dusky-pink **Rathaus**. The iconic red-stone **pyramid** is an incongruous tribute to Karl Wilhelm Margrave of Baden-Durlach and marks his tomb.

DON'T MISS

A WALK IN THE BLACK FOREST

As locals will tell you, you need to hit the trail to really see the **Black Forest** (www.black forest-tourism.com; SchwarzwaldCard adult/child/family €37/€27/€113). From gentle half-day strolls to multi-day treks, we've cherry-picked the region for a few of our favourites.

Panoramaweg (40km) If you want to appreciate Baden-Baden and the northern Black Forest from its most photogenic angles, walk all or part of this high-level ridge trail, weaving past waterfalls and viewpoints through orchards and woodlands.

Gütenbach-Simonswäldertal (13km) Tucked-away Gütenbach, 22km south of Triberg, is the trailhead for one of the Black Forest's most beautiful half-day hikes. From here a forest trail threads to Balzer Herrgott, where a sandstone figure of Christ has grown into a tree. Walking downhill from here to Simonswälder Valley, fir-draped hills rise like a curtain before you. Return by veering north to Teichsschlucht gorge, where a brook cascades through primeval forest lined by sheer cliffs and moss-strewn boulders. Head upstream to return to Gütenbach.

Westweg (280km) Up for an adventure? This famous long-distance trail, marked with a red diamond, stretches from Pforzheim in the Northern Black Forest to Basel, Switzerland. Highlights feature the steep Murg Valley, Titisee and Feldberg. See www.westweg.de (in German) for maps and details.

Wutachschlucht (13km) This wild gorge, carved out by a fast-flowing river and flanked by near-vertical rock faces, lies near Bonndorf, close to the Swiss border and 15km east of Schluchsee. The best way to experience its unique microclimate, where you might spot orchids, ferns, rare butterflies and lizards, is on this trail leading from Schattenmühle to Wutachmühle. For more details, visit the website www.wutachschlucht.de (in German).

Feldberg Steig (12km) Orbiting Feldberg, the Black Forest's highest peak at 1493m, this walk traverses a nature reserve that's home to chamois and wildflowers. On clear days, the views of the Alps are glorious. It's possible to snowshoe part of this route in winter.

Martinskapelle (10km) A scenic and easygoing walk, this 10km loop begins at hilltop chapel Martinskapelle, which sits 11km southwest of Triberg. The well-marked path wriggles through forest to tower-topped Brendturm (1149m) which affords views reaching from Feldberg to the Vosges and Alps on cloud-free days. Continue via Brendhäusle and Rosseck for a stunning vista of overlapping mountains and forest.

At its northern tip, **Museum beim Markt** (Karl-Friedrich-Strasse 6; adult/concession €2/1, after 2pm Fri free; ⊘11am-5pm Tue-Thu, 10am-6pm Fri-Sun) contains a stash of post-1900 applied arts, from art nouveau to Bauhaus.

Zentrum für Kunst und Medientechnologie   MUSEUM
Set in a historic munitions factory, the **ZKM** (www.zkm.de; Lorenzstrasse 19; ⊘10am-6pm Wed-Fri, 11am-6pm Sat & Sun) is a mammoth exhibition and research complex fusing art and emerging electronic media technologies.

The interactive **Medienmuseum** (Media Museum; adult/concession €5/3, after 2pm Fri free) has media art displays, including a computer-generated 'legible city' and real-time bubble simulations. The **Museum für Neue Kunst** (adult/concession €5/3, incl the Me-

dienmuseum €8/5, after 2pm Fri free) hosts first-rate temporary exhibitions of post-1960 art.

Served by tram 2E, the ZKM is 2km southwest of the Schloss and a similar distance northwest of the Hauptbahnhof.

Botanischer Garten   GARDEN
(Hans-Thoma-Strasse 6; garden admission free, greenhouses adult/concession €2.20/1.10; ⊘10am-6pm) Lush with exotic foliage, the Botanischer Garten is speckled with greenhouses – one with a giant Victoria waterlily.

Museum in der Majolika   MUSEUM
(Ahaweg 6; adult/concession €2/1; ⊘10am-1pm & 2-5pm Tue-Sun) A line of 1645 blue majolica tiles, called the **Blaue Linie**, connects the Schloss to the Museum in der Majolika,

exhibiting glazed ceramics made in Karlsruhe since 1901.

🛌 Sleeping

Mainly geared towards corporate functions, Karlsruhe's hotels don't rank too highly on the charm-o-meter. Ask the tourist office for a list of private guesthouses.

Hotel Rio HOTEL €€

(☑840 80; www.hotel-rio.de; Hans-Sachs-Strasse 2; s €70-108, d €86-125; P🛜) Service can be brusque but this is still one of your best bets for spotless, contemporary quarters in Karlsruhe. Breakfast is worth the extra €6 – eggs, salmon, the works. Take the tram to Mühlburger Tor.

Acora Hotel HOTEL €€€

(☑850 90; www.acora.de; Sophienstrasse 69-71; s €99-144, d €119-179; P🛜) Chirpy staff make you feel right at home at this apartment-hotel, featuring bright, modern rooms equipped with kitchenettes.

Hotel Avisa HOTEL €€

(☑349 77; www.hotel-avisa.de; Am Stadtgarten 5; s/d from €85/120; P🛜) Spruce rooms with free wi-fi are the deal at this family-run hotel, two blocks northeast of the Hauptbahnhof.

🍴 Eating & Drinking

Vogelbräu BREWPUB €€

(Kapellenstrasse 50; mains €6.50-13; ☺10am-midnight Sun-Thu, to 1am Fri & Sat) Quaff a cold one with regulars by the copper vats or in the leafy beer garden of this microbrewery. The unfiltered house pils washes down hale and hearty food like Berlin-style beef liver with mash and onions.

Oberländer Weinstuben GERMAN €€€

(☑250 66; www.oberlaender-weinstube.de; Akademiestrasse 7; 3-course lunch €35, mains €34-37; ☺Tue-Sat) Special occasion? Book a table at this Michelin-starred restaurant, combining a cosy wood-panelled tavern and a flowery courtyard. Fine wines marry perfectly with signatures like meltingly tender lamb with aubergines and peppers – cooked with flair, served with finesse.

Die Kippe PUB €

(Gottesauer Strasse 23; daily special €3.90; ☺8am-1am, to 2am Fri & Sat) Every student has a tale about the 'dog end', named after the free tobacco behind the bar. Wallet-friendly daily specials skip from schnitzel to plaice with potato salad. There's live music a couple of times weekly, as well as bingo and quiz nights. The beer garden has a great buzz in summer. Take tram 1 or 2 to Durlacher Tor.

Moccasin CAFE €

(Ritterstrasse 6; snacks €2-5; ☺daily) Go for a mango smoothie, bagel or coffee with a cherry-studded Black Forest muffin.

Bray Head PUB €

(Kapellenstrasse 40; mains €5.90-7.90; ☺4pm-btwn 1am & 3am; 🛜) Home-brewed stout goes down a treat with grub such as Irish stew and fish and chips at this convivial pub, with regular live music and quiz nights.

ℹ️ Information

Hauptbahnhof tourist office (☑3720 5383; www.karlsruhe-tourism.de; Bahnhofplatz 6; ☺8.30am-6pm Mon-Fri, 9am-1pm Sat) Across the street from the Hauptbahnhof. The iGuide (€7.50) is a self-guided audiovisual walking tour of the centre lasting four hours. Also sells the Karlsruher WelcomeCard (24-/48-/72-hour card €5.50/10.50/15.50) for free or discounted entry to museums and other attractions.

Post office (Poststrasse) Just east of the Hauptbahnhof.

ℹ️ Getting There & Away

Destinations well-served by train include Baden-Baden (€10 to €15, 15 to 30 minutes) and Freiburg (€24.70 to €34, one to two hours).

Karlsruhe is on the A5 (Frankfurt–Basel) and is the starting point of the A8 to Munich. There are Park & Ride options outside of the city centre; look for 'P+R' signs.

ℹ️ Getting Around

The Hauptbahnhof is linked to the Marktplatz, 2km north, by tram and light-rail lines 2, 3, S1, S11, S4 and S41. Single tickets cost €2.20; a 24-Stunden-Karte costs €5.20 (€8.20 for up to five people).

A relaxed and ecofriendly way to explore Karlsruhe is by bike. Deutsche Bahn has Call-a-Bike stands across the city.

Freudenstadt

☑07441 / POP 23,550

Duke Friedrich I of Württemberg built a new capital here in 1599, which was bombed to bits in WWII. The upshot is that Freudenstadt's centre is underwhelming, though its magnificent setting in the Black Forest is anything but. That said, statistic lovers will delight in ticking off Germany's biggest square (216m by 219m, for the record), dislocated by a T-junction of heavily trafficked roads.

Freudenstadt marks the southern end of the Schwarzwald-Hochstrasse and is a terminus of the gorgeous Schwarzwald-Tälerstrasse, which runs from Rastatt via Alpirsbach.

◎ Sights

Stadtkirche   CHURCH
(◎10am-5pm) In the southwest corner of Marktplatz looms the 17th-century red-sandstone Stadtkirche, with an ornate 12th-century Cluniac-style baptismal font, Gothic windows, Renaissance portals and baroque towers. The two naves are at right angles to each other, an unusual design by the geometrically minded duke.

🏃 Activities

While you won't linger for Freudenstadt's sights, the deep forested valleys on its fringes are worth exploring. Scenic hiking trails include a 12km uphill walk to **Kniebis** on the Schwarzwald-Hochstrasse, where there are superb Kinzig Valley views. Ask the tourist office for details.

Jump on a mountain bike to tackle routes like the 85km **Kinzigtal-Radweg**, taking in dreamy landscapes and half-timbered villages, or the 60km **Murgtal-Radweg** over hill and dale to Rastatt. Both valleys have bike trails and it's possible to return to Freudenstadt by train.

Intersport Glaser   BICYCLE RENTAL
(Katharinenstrasse 8; bike rental per day €14-20; ◎9.30am-6.30am Mon-Fri, to 4pm Sat) A couple of blocks north of Marktplatz, this outlet hires mountain bikes.

Panorama-Bad   SWIMMING
(www.panorama-bad.de; Ludwig-Jahn-Strasse 60; 3hr pass adult/concession €6.70/5.80; ◎9am-10pm Mon-Sat, to 8pm Sun) The glass-fronted Panorama-Bad is a relaxation magnet with pools, steam baths and saunas.

🛏 Sleeping & Eating

At the heart of Freudenstadt, the sprawling, arcaded Marktplatz harbours rows of shops and cafes with alfresco seating.

Warteck   HOTEL €€
(📞919 20; www.warteck-freudenstadt.de; Stuttgarterstrasse 14; s €55-70, d €88-98, mains €14.50-39; 🐕) In the capable hands of the Glässel

family since 1894, this hotel sports modern, gleamingly clean rooms. The real draw, however, is the wood-panelled restaurant, serving market-fresh fare like beetroot tortellini and rack of venison with wild mushrooms.

Hotel Adler   HOTEL €€
(📞915 20; www.adler-fds.de; Forststrasse 15-17; s €45-53, d €74-90, mains €12 to €17; P🐕) This family-run hotel near Marktplace has well-kept, recently renovated rooms and rents out e-bikes for €9/16 per half/full day. The restaurant dishes up appetising regional grub such as *Zwiebelrostbraten* (roast beef with onions).

Camping Langenwald   CAMPGROUND €
(📞2862; www.camping-langenwald.de; Strasburger Strasse 167; per person/tent €7/8.50; ◎Easter-Oct; 🐕) With a solar-heated pool and nature trail, this leafy site has impeccable eco credentials. It's served by bus 12 to Kniebis.

Turmbräu   GERMAN €€
(Marktplatz 64; mains €7-17; ◎11am-midnight, to 3am Fri & Sat) This lively microbrewery doubles as a beer garden. Pull up a chair in ye-olde barn to munch *Maultaschen* and guzzle brews – a 5L barrel costs €14.

❶ Information

Tourist office (📞8640; www.freudenstadt.de; Marktplatz 64; ◎9am-6pm Mon-Fri, 10am-3pm Sat & Sun; 🐕) Has an internet terminal (per 5/60min €0.50/6). Hotel reservations are free.

❶ Getting There & Away

Freudenstadt's focal point is the Marktplatz on the B28. The town has two train stations: the Stadtbahnhof, five minutes' walk north of Marktplatz, and the Hauptbahnhof, 2km southeast of Marktplatz at the end of Bahnhofstrasse.

Trains on the Ortenau line, serving Offenburg and Strasbourg, depart hourly from the Hauptbahnhof and are covered by the 24-hour **Europass**. The pass represents excellent value, costing €10.40 for individuals and €16.70 for families. Trains go roughly hourly to Karlsruhe (€16.40, 1½ to two hours) from the Stadtbahnhof and Hauptbahnhof.

Kinzigtal

Shaped like a horseshoe, the Kinzigtal (Kinzig Valley) begins south of Freudenstadt and shadows the babbling Kinzig River south to Schiltach, west to Haslach and north to Offenburg. Near Strasbourg, 95km downriver, the

REACH FOR THE STARS

Swinging along country lanes 6km north of Freudenstadt brings you to Baiersbronn. It looks like any other Black Forest town, snuggled among meadows and wooded hills. But on its fringes sit two of Germany's finest restaurants, both holders of the coveted three Michelin stars.

First up is the **Schwarzwaldstube** (☑07442-4920; www.traube-tonbach.de; Tonbach-strasse 237, Baiersbronn-Tonbach; menus €155-189; ⊘closed Mon, Tue, lunch Wed), with big forest views from its rustically elegant dining room. Here Harald Wohlfahrt performs culinary magic, staying true to the best traditions of French cooking, sourcing carefully and adding his own creative flourishes. The tasting menu goes with the seasons but you might begin with a palate-awakening carpaccio of wild salmon and scallops with ginger-lime marinade, say, followed by saddle of venison served two ways. If you fancy getting behind the stove, sign up for one of the **cookery classes** (€140-180; ⊘10am Mon & Tue), which revolve around a theme such as cooking with crustaceans, asparagus, goose or truffles, or techniques like pasta-making and preparing pâtés.

Equally legendary is the **Restaurant Bareiss** (☑07442-470; www.bareiss.com; Gärten-bühlweg 14, Baiersbronn-Mitteltal; menus €125-185; ⊘Wed-Sun). Claus-Peter Lumpp has consistently won plaudits for his brilliantly composed, French-inflected menus. On paper, dishes such as braised Bresse chicken with nut-butter foam and almond maca-roon with pineapple and dill seem deceptively simple; on the plate they become things of beauty, rich in textures and aromas and presented with an artist's eye for detail.

Kinzig is swallowed up by the mighty Rhine. The valley's inhabitants survived for centuries on mining and shipping goods by raft.

This Black Forest valley is astonishingly pretty, its hills brushed with thick larch and spruce forest and its half-timbered villages looking freshly minted for a fairy-tale. For seasonal colour, come in in autumn (foliage) or spring (fruit blossom).

❶ Getting There & Away

The B294 follows the Kinzig from Freudenstadt to Haslach, from where the B33 leads north to Offenburg. If you're going south, pick up the B33 to Triberg and beyond in Hausach.

An hourly train line links Freudenstadt with Offenburg (€14.40, 1¼ hours), stopping in Alpirsbach (€3.25, 16 minutes), Schiltach (€5.50, 27 minutes), Hausach (€7.50, 43 minutes), Haslach (€9.10, 49 minutes) and Gengenbach (€12.20, one hour). From Hausach, trains run roughly hourly southeast to Triberg (€5.50, 22 minutes), Villingen (€11.10, 47 minutes) and Konstanz (€27.10, two hours).

Alpirsbach

☑07444 / POP 6580

Lore has it that Alpirsbach is named after a quaffing cleric who, when a glass of beer slipped clumsily from his hand and rolled into the river, exclaimed: *All Bier ist in den Bach!* (All the beer is in the stream!). A prophecy, it seems, as today Alpirsbacher Klosterbräu is brewed from pure spring water. **Brewery tours** (☑670; www.alpirsbacher .com; Marktplatz 1; tours €6.90; ⊘2.30pm daily) are in German, though guides may speak English. Two beers are thrown in for the price of a ticket.

A few paces north, you can watch chocolate being made and scoff delectable beer-filled pralines at **Schau-Confiserie Heinzelmann** (Ambrosius-Blarer-Platz 2; ⊘9am-12pm & 2-6pm Mon-Fri, to 5pm Sat).

All the more evocative for its lack of adornment, the 11th-century former Bene-dictine **Kloster Alpirsbach** (adult/concession €4/3.30; ⊘10am-5.30pm Mon-Sat & 11am-5.30pm Sun) sits opposite. The monastery effectively conveys the simple, spiritual life in its flat-roofed church, spartan cells and Gothic cloister, which hosts candlelit concerts (www.kreuzgangkonzerte.de) from June to August. It's amazing what you can find under the floorboards, as the museum re-veals with its stash of 16th-century clothing, caricatures (of artistic scholars) and lines (of misbehaving ones).

The **tourist office** (☑951 6281; www.stadt -alpirsbach.de; Krähenbadstrasse 2; ⊘10am-noon & 2-5pm Mon-Fri, closed Wed afternoon) can supply hiking maps and, for cyclists, information on the 85km Kinzigtalradweg from Offenburg to Lossburg.

Schiltach

📞07836 / POP 3880

Sitting smugly at the foot of wooded hills and on the banks of the Kinzig and Schiltach Rivers, medieval Schiltach looks too perfect to be true. The meticulously restored half-timbered houses, which once belonged to tanners, merchants and raft builders, are a riot of crimson geraniums in summer.

◎ Sights & Activities

Altstadt   NEIGHBOURHOOD

Centred on a trickling fountain, the sloping, triangular **Marktplatz** is Schiltach at its picture-book best. The frescoes of the stepgabled, 16th-century **Rathaus** opposite depict scenes from local history. Clamber south up **Schlossbergstrasse**, pausing to notice the plaques that denote the trades of one-time residents, such as the *Strumpfstricker* (stocking weaver) at No 6, and the sloping roofs where tanners once dried their skins. Up top there are views over Schiltach's red rooftops. Because Schiltach is at the confluence of the **Kinzig** and **Schiltach Rivers**, logging was big business until the 19th century and huge rafts were built to ship timber as far as the Netherlands. The willow-fringed banks now attract grey herons and kids who come to splash in the shallows when the sun is shining.

FREE Museum am Markt   MUSEUM

(Marktplatz 13; ⊙11am-5pm daily Apr-Oct, Sat & Sun only Nov-Mar) Museum am Markt is crammed with everything from antique spinning wheels to Biedermeier costumes. Highlights include the cobbler's workshop and an interactive display recounting the tale of the devilish Teufel von Schiltach.

FREE Schüttesäge Museum   MUSEUM

(Gerbegasse; ⊙11am-5pm daily Apr-Oct, Sat & Sun only Nov-Mar) The Schüttesäge Museum focuses on Schiltach's rafting tradition with reconstructed workshops, a watermill generating hydroelectric power for many homes in the area and touchy-feely exhibits for kids, from different kinds of bark to forest animals.

🛏 Sleeping & Eating

TOP CHOICE Weysses Rössle   GUESTHOUSE €

(📞387; www.weysses-roessle.de; Schenkenzeller Strasse 42; s/d €52/75; P🛜) Rosemarie and Ulrich continue the tradition of 19 generations in this 16th-century inn. Countrified rooms decorated with rosewood and floral fabrics also feature snazzy bathrooms and wi-fi. Its restaurant uses locally sourced, organic fare.

Zur Alten Brücke   GUESTHOUSE €€

(📞20 36; www.altebruecke.de; Schramberger Strasse 13; s/d/apt €59/89/109; P🛜) You'll receive a warm welcome from Michael, Lisa and dog Max at this riverside guest house. The pick of the bright, cheery rooms overlook the Schiltach. Michael cooks up seasonal, regional fare in the kitchen and there's a terrace for summer imbibing.

Campingplatz Schiltach   CAMPGROUND €

(📞7289; Bahnhofstrasse 6; per person/tent/car €5/3.50/3; ⊙Apr-Oct) Beautifully positioned on the banks of the Kinzig, this campground has impeccable eco credentials and a playground and sandpit for kids.

❶ Information

The **tourist office** (📞5850; www.schiltach.de; Marktplatz 6; ⊙9am-noon & 2-4pm Mon-Thu, 9am-noon Fri) in the Rathaus can help find accommodation and offers free internet access. Hiking options are marked on an enamel sign just opposite.

Gutach

📞07831 / POP 2180

Worth the 4km detour south of the Kinzig Valley, the **Schwarzwälder Freilichtmuseum** (www.vogtsbauernhof.org; adult/concession/child/family €8/7/4.50/18; ⊙9am-6pm late Mar-early Nov, to 7pm Aug) spirals around the Vogtsbauernhof, an early-17th-century farmstead. Farmhouses shifted from their original locations have been painstakingly reconstructed, using techniques such as thatching and panelling, to create this authentic farming hamlet and preserve age-old Black Forest traditions.

Explore barns filled with wagons and horn sleds, *Rauchküchen* (kitchens for smoking fish and meat) and the Hippenseppenhof (1599), with its chapel and massive hipped roof constructed from 400 trees. It's a great place for families, with inquisitive farmyard animals to pet, artisans on hand to explain their crafts and frequent demonstrations from sheep shearing to butter-making.

The self-controlled bobs of the **Schwarzwald Rodelbahn** (Black Forest Toboggan Run; Singersbach 4; adult/child €2.50/2; ☺9am-6pm Mar-early Nov), 1.5km north of Gutach, are faster than they look. Lay off the brakes for extra speed.

Haslach

☑07832 / POP 6980

Back in the Kinzig Valley, Haslach's 17th-century former Capuchin monastery lodges the **Schwarzwälder Trachtenmuseum** (Black Forest Costume Museum; Im Alten Kapuzinerkloster; adult/concession €2/1.50; ☺10am-12.30pm & 1.30-5pm Tue-Sun), showcasing flamboyant costumes and outrageous hats, the must-have accessories for the well-dressed Fräulein of the 1850s. Look out for the Black Forest *Bollenhut*, a straw bonnet topped with pompons (red for unmarried women, black for married) and the *Schäppel*, a fragile-looking crown made from hundreds of beads and weighing up to 5kg.

Gengenbach

☑07803 / POP 11,020

If ever a Black Forest town could be described as chocolate box, it would surely be Gengenbach, with its scrumptious Altstadt of half-timbered town houses framed by vineyards and orchards. It's fitting, then, that director Tim Burton made this the home of gluttonous Augustus Gloop in the 2005 blockbuster *Charlie and the Chocolate Factory* (though less so that he called it Düsseldorf).

◉ Sights & Activities

The best way to discover Gengenbach's historic centre is with a saunter through its narrow backstreets, such as the gently curving **Engelgasse**, off Hauptstrasse, lined with listed half-timbered houses draped in vines and bedecked with scarlet geraniums. Between the town's two tower-topped gates sits the triangular **Marktplatz**, dominated by the **Rathaus**, an 18th-century, pink-and-cream confection. The fountain bears a statue of a knight, a symbol of Gengenbach's medieval status as a Free Imperial City. Amble east along Klosterstrasse to spy the former **Benedictine monastery**. Opposite, the stuck-in-time **Holzofen-Bäckerei Klostermühle** (Klosterstrasse 7; ☺7am-6pm Mon-Fri,

BEHOLD THE SUPER BOG

If giant cuckoo clocks and black forest gateau no longer thrill, how about a trip to the world's largest loo? Drive a couple of minutes south of Gutach on the B33 to Hornberg and there, in all its lavatorial glory, stands the titanic toilet dreamed up by Philippe Starck. Even if you have no interest in designer urinals or home jacuzzis, it's worth visiting the **Duravit Design Centre** (www.duravit. de; Werderstrasse 36; ☺8am-6pm Mon-Fri, 12-4pm Sat) for the tremendous view across the Black Forest from the 12m-high ceramic loo.

to noon Sat) fills the lanes with wafts of freshly baked bread from its wood-fired oven. Buy a loaf to munch in the calm **Kräutergarten** (Herb Garden; Benedikt-von-Nursia-Strasse) or stroll east to the flowery park.

The tourist office has info on the hour-long **Weinpfad**, a wine trail beginning in the Altstadt that threads through terraced vineyards to the Jakobskapelle, a 13th-century chapel commanding views that reach as far as Strasbourg on clear days. The free, lantern-lit **Nachtwächterrundgang** (night watchman's tour) starts at the Rathaus on Wednesday and Saturday at 10pm from May to July and at 9pm from August to October.

⎘ Sleeping & Eating

Pfeffermühle   B&B €

(☑933 50; www.pfeffermuehle-gengenbach.de; Oberdorfstrasse 24; s/d €50/78, mains €14-22) In a snug half-timbered house dating to 1476, close to one of the Altstadt gate towers, this neat-and-tidy B&B is a bargain. Decorated with antique knick-knacks, the wood-panelled restaurant features among the town's best, dishing out regional favourites like Black Forest trout and *Sauerbraten* (sweet-sour pot roast).

DJH Hostel   HOSTEL €

(☑0781-317 49; www.jugendherberge-schloss-ortenberg.de; Burgweg 21; dm €21.70) The Hogwarts gang would feel at home in 12th-century Schloss Ortenberg, rebuilt in whimsical neo-Gothic style complete with lookout tower and wood-panelled dining hall. A staircase sweeps up to dorms with Kinzig

STUTTGART & THE BLACK FOREST FREIBURG

DON'T MISS

CHRISTMAS COUNTDOWN

Every December, Gengenbach rekindles childhood memories of opening tiny windows when the Rathaus morphs into the world's biggest advent calendar. At 6pm daily, one of 24 windows is opened to reveal a festive scene. In the past, the tableaux have been painted by well-known artists and children's-book illustrators such as Marc Chagall and Tomi Ungerer. From late November to 23 December, a Christmas market brings extra yuletide sparkle, mulled wine and carols to the Marktplatz.

Valley views. Take bus 7134 to Ortenberger Hof, 500m from the hostel.

Pfeffer & Salz B&B €

(☑934 80; www.pfefferundsalz-gengenbach.de; Mattenhofweg 3; s/d €52/78) This forest farmhouse is a peaceful hideaway 10 minutes' stroll north of the Altstadt. The modern rooms are quite a bargain, jazzed up with warm colours and flat-screen TVs.

Winzerstüble GERMAN €

(Hauptstrasse 18; Flammkuchen €6.50-9) In the cobbled courtyard next to the tourist office, this wine tavern serves local produce and wine. Visitors can sample light, crisp *Flammkuchen* with Müller-Thurgau and riesling wines.

❶ Information

The **tourist office** (☑930 143; www.stadt-gengenbach.de; Im Winzerhof; ☺9am-5pm Mon-Fri) is in a courtyard just off Hauptstrasse.

Freiburg

 0761 / POP 224,190

Sitting plump at the foot of the Black Forest's wooded slopes and vineyards, Freiburg is a sunny, cheerful university town, its medieval Altstadt a story-book tableau of gabled town houses, cobblestone lanes and cafe-rimmed plazas. Party-loving students spice up the local nightlife.

Blessed with 2000 hours of annual sunshine, this is Germany's warmest city. Indeed, while neighbouring hilltop villages are still shovelling snow, the trees in Freiburg are clouds of white blossom, and locals are already imbibing in canalside beer gardens. This eco-trailblazer has shrewdly tapped into that natural energy to generate nearly as much solar power as the whole of Britain, making it one of the country's greenest cities.

◉ Sights

Freiburg's medieval past is tangible in backstreets like wisteria-draped Konviktstrasse and in the canalside Fischerau and Gerberau, the former fishing and tanning quarters. The Dreisam River runs along the Altstadt's southern edge.

Keep an eye out for the cheerful pavement mosaics in front of many shops – a cow is for a butcher, a pretzel for a baker, a diamond marks a jewellery shop, and so on.

⌈TOP⌉
⌊CHOICE⌋ Münster CATHEDRAL

(Map p250; Münsterplatz; tower adult/concession €1.50/1; ☺10am-5pm Mon-Sat, 1pm-7.30pm Sun, tower 9.30am-5pm Mon-Sat, 1-5pm Sun) Freiburg's 11th-century Münster is the monster of all minsters, a red-sandstone giant that looms above the half-timbered facades framing the square. Its riot of punctured spires and gargoyles flush scarlet in the dusk light.

The main portal is adorned with sculptures depicting scenes from the Old and New Testaments. Nearby are medieval wall markings used to ensure that merchandise (eg loaves of bread) were of the requisite size.

Square at the base, the sturdy tower becomes an octagon higher up and is crowned by a filigreed 116m-high spire. Ascend the tower for an excellent view of the church's intricate construction; on clear days you can spy the Vosges Mountains in France.

Inside the Münster, the kaleidoscopic stained-glass windows dazzle. Many were financed by various guilds – in the bottom panels look for a pretzel, scissors and other symbols of medieval trades. The high altar features a masterful triptych of the coronation of the Virgin Mary by Hans Baldung.

Augustinermuseum MUSEUM

(Map p250; Augustinerplatz 1; adult/concession €6/4; ☺10am-5pm Tue-Sun) Following a recent makeover, this beautiful Augustinian monastery, with origins dating back to 1278, once again showcases a prized collection of medieval, baroque and 19th-century art. Baldung, Matthias Grünewald and Cranach masterpieces grace the gallery and the medieval stained glass ranks among Germany's finest.

There is a cafe overlooking the cloister where you can sip a drink and soak up the monastic vibe.

Historisches Kaufhaus   LANDMARK
(Map p250; Münsterplatz) Facing the Münster's south side and embellished with polychrome tiled turrets is the arcaded brick-red Historisches Kaufhaus, an early 16th-century merchants' hall. The coats of arms on the oriels and the four figures above the balcony symbolise Freiburg's allegiance to the House of Habsburg.

City Gates   HISTORIC BUILDING
Freiburg has two intact medieval gates, one of which is the **Martinstor** (Martin's Gate; Map p250; Kaiser-Joseph-Strasse) rising above Kaiser-Joseph-Strasse. A block east of the Museum of Modern Art is the 13th-century **Schwabentor** (Map p250) on the Schwabenring, a massive city gate with a mural of St George slaying the dragon and tram tracks running under its arches.

Schlossberg   VIEWPOINT, WALK
(Schlossbergring; cable car one way/return €2.80/5; ☺9am-10pm, shorter hours in winter) The forested Schlossberg dominates Freiburg. Take the footpath opposite the Schwabentor, leading up through sun-dappled woods, or hitch a ride on the recently restored Schlossbergbahn **cable car**. If you're keen to do some serious hiking, several trails begin here, including those to St Peter (17km) and Kandel (25km).

The little peak is topped by the ice-cream-cone-shaped **Aussichtsturm** (lookout tower). From here, Freiburg spreads photogenically before you – the spire of the Münster soaring above a jumble of red gables, framed by the dark hills of the Black Forest.

Rathausplatz   SQUARE
(Town Hall Square; Map p250) Freiburg locals hang out by the fountain in chestnut-shaded Rathausplatz. On its western side, note the red-sandstone, step-gabled **Neues Rathaus** (New City Hall; Map p250).

Across the way is the mid–16th-century **Altes Rathaus** (Old City Hall; Map p250; Universitatstrasse), a flamboyant, ox-blood-red edifice, embellished with gilt swirls and crowned by a clock and a fresco of the twin-headed Habsburg eagle.

On its northern side, the medieval **Martinskirche** (Map p250) demands attention with its covered cloister. Once part of a Franciscan monastery, the church was severely damaged in WWII; it was rebuilt in the ascetic style typical of this mendicant order.

Haus zum Walfisch   LANDMARK
(House of the Whale; Map p250; Franziskanerstrasse) Across the street from the Martinskirche is its architectural antithesis, the marvellously extravagant Haus zum Walfisch, whose late-Gothic oriel is garnished with two impish gargoyles.

Archäologisches Museum   MUSEUM
(Map p250; www.museen.freiburg.de; Rotteckring 5; adult/concession €2/1; ☺10am-5pm Tue-Sun) In a sculpture-dotted park sits the neo-Gothic **Colombischlössle**. Built for the Countess of Colombi in 1859, the whimsical red-sandstone villa now harbours this archaeology-focused museum. From the skylit marble entrance, a cast-iron staircase ascends to a stash of finds, from Celtic grave offerings to Roman artefacts.

Museum für Stadtgeschichte   MUSEUM
(Map p250; Münsterplatz 30; adult/concession €2/1; ☺10am-5pm Tue-Sun) The sculptor Christian Wentzinger's baroque town house, east of the Historisches Kaufhaus, now shelters this museum, spelling out in artefacts Freiburg's eventful past. Inside, a wrought-iron staircase guides the eye to an elaborate ceiling fresco.

Museum für Neue Kunst   GALLERY
(Map p250; Marienstrasse 10; adult/concession €2/1; ☺10am-5pm Tue-Sun) Across the Gewerbekanal, this gallery highlights 20th-century expressionist and abstract art, including emotive works by Oskar Kokoschka and Otto Dix.

COLD FEET OR WEDDED BLISS?

As you wander Freiburg's Altstadt, watch out for the gurgling *Bächle*, streamlets once used to water livestock and extinguish fires. Today they provide welcome relief for hot feet on sweltering summer days. Just be aware that you could get more than you bargained for: legend has it that if you accidentally step into the Bächle, you'll marry a Freiburger or a Freiburgerin.

Freiburg

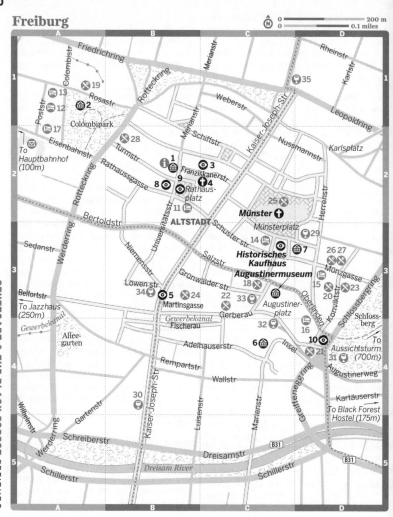

Tours

If you want to explore the Altstadt at your own pace, two-and-a-half-hour audioguides are available at the tourist office for €9.

Freiburg Kultour   GUIDED TOUR
(Map p250; www.freiburg-kultour.com; Rathausplatz 2-4; adult/concession €8/6; ⊙11.30am Sat) Based in the tourist office, Kultour offers 1½- to two-hour walking tours of the Altstadt and Münster in English. The website lists times for the more frequent tours in German.

Fahrradtaxi   GUIDED TOUR
(☑947 9595; www.fahrradtaxi-freiburg.de; An der Höhlgasse 5; ⊙mid-Apr–Oct) Fahrradtaxi charges €7.50 for a 15-minute, two-person spin of the Altstadt in a pedicab. Call ahead or look for one on Rathausplatz or Münsterplatz.

Sleeping

Charismatic hotels abound in the Altstadt but it's wise to book ahead in summer. The tourist office offers a booking service (€3) and has a list of good-value private guesthouses.

Freiburg

Hotel Oberkirch TOP CHOICE HISTORIC HOTEL €€€
(Map p250; ☎202 6868; www.hotel-oberkirch.de; Münsterplatz 22; s €102-123, d €155-169, mains €13-23; P) Wake up to Münster views at this green-shuttered hotel. The country-style rooms feature floral wallpaper and half-canopies over the beds. Oberkirch has an intoxicating 250-year history; during a fire in WWII the hotelier doused the blaze with wine from his cellar. The dark-wood **tavern** downstairs does a roaring trade in hearty Badisch fare like venison ragout with *Knödel* (dumplings).

Park Hotel Post HISTORIC HOTEL €€€
(Map p250; ☎385 480; www.park-hotel-post.de; Am Colombipark; s €99-159, d €129-199; P🖃) Slip back to the more graceful age of art nouveau at this refined pile overlooking Colombipark, with summery rooms decorated in pastel blues and yellows. Attentive service and generous breakfasts sweeten the deal.

Hotel Schwarzwälder Hof HOTEL €€
(Map p250; ☎380 30; www.schwarzwaelder-hof.eu; Herrenstrasse 43; s/d/tr €65/99/120; @) This bijou hotel has an unrivalled style-for-euro ratio. A wrought-iron staircase sweeps up to snazzy rooms that are temples to chalk whites and chocolate browns. Some have postcard views of the Altstadt.

Hotel am Rathaus HOTEL €€
(Map p250; ☎296 160; www.am-rathaus.de; Rathausgasse 4-8; s €85-95, d €119-129; P🖃) Just a step away from the bustle of Rathausplatz, this neat-and-tidy hotel has spacious, neutral-toned rooms with homely touches like CD and DVD players; ask for a back-facing room if you're a light sleeper. Breakfast is a treat, with smoked salmon and a wide array of bread, cheese and fruit.

Hotel Minerva HOTEL €€
(Map p250; ☎386 490; www.minerva-freiburg.de; Poststrasse 8; s €85-100, d €115-150; P🖃) All curvaceous windows and polished wood, this art nouveau charmer is five minutes' trudge from the Altstadt. The convivial rooms are painted in sunny shades and feature free wi-fi. The sauna is another plus.

Hotel zum Roten Bären HISTORIC HOTEL €€€
(Map p250; ☎387 870; www.roter-baeren.de; Oberlinden 12; s €90-133, d €129-184; P@) Billed as Germany's oldest guesthouse, this bubblegum-pink hotel near Schwabentor

dates to 1120. Though the vaulted cellar is medieval, rooms are modern, with sleek wood furnishings.

Hotel Barbara
HISTORIC HOTEL €€

(Map p250; ☑296 250; www.hotel-barbara.de; Poststrasse 4; s €74-86, d €102-129, apt €124-189; ☞) A grandfather clock, curvy staircases and high ceilings give this art nouveau town house a nostalgic feel. It's a homely, family-run place with old-fashioned, pastel-hued rooms and homemade jams at breakfast.

Black Forest Hostel
HOSTEL €

(☑881 7870; www.blackforest-hostel.de; Kartäuserstrasse 33; dm €14-23, s/d €30/50; @) Funky budget digs with chilled common areas, a shared kitchen, bike rental and spacey stainless-steel showers. It's a five-minute walk from the centre of town.

Hirzberg Camping
CAMPGROUND €

(☑350 54; www.freiburg-camping.de; Kartäuserstrasse 99; sites per adult/tent/car €7.80/5/2.50; P☞) This year-round campground sits in a quiet woodland spot 1.5km east of Schwabentor. It has cooking facilities and bike rental. Take tram 1 to Musikhochschule.

Eating

The Altstadt is stacked with cafes, wine taverns, brewpubs and restaurants, many spilling out onto pavement terraces. You can find cheap bites on Martinstor and Kartäuserstrasse.

Zirbelstube
FRENCH €€€

(Map p250; ☑210 60; www.colombi.de; Rotteckring 16; mains €32-49; ☺Wed-Sun) Freiburg's bastion of fine dining is this candlelit restaurant, decorated in warm Swiss pine. A chef of exacting standards, Alfred Klink allows each ingredient to shine in specialities like poussin with Périgord truffles and Dover sole with caramelised capers, perfectly matched with top wines.

Drexlers
BRASSERIE €€€

(Map p250; ☑595 7203; www.drexlers-restaurant .de; Rosastrasse 9; mains €10-26; ☺closed Sat lunch, Sun; ☞) There's a great lunchtime buzz at this contemporary, high-ceilinged brasserie behind Colombipark. It's an unpretentious, kid-friendly choice, with an ingredient-focused menu homing in on dishes from homemade pasta to herb-crusted lamb.

Kreuzblume
FUSION €€€

(Map p250; ☑311 94; Konviktstrasse 31; mains €22.50-24.50, 3-course menu €36; ☺Wed-Sun) Clever backlighting and a menu fizzing with bright, sunny flavours attract a food-literate clientele to Kreuzblume. Dishes like homesmoked cod with beetroot and anise and zingy lemongrass tart with chilli, mango and yoghurt pack a taste-bud punch.

Wolfshöhle
MEDITERRANEAN €€€

(Map p250; ☑303 03; Konviktstrasse 8; mains €16-27; ☺closed Mon lunch, Sun) With tables set up on a pretty square, Wolfshöhle is a summerevening magnet. The menu whisks you off on a gastro tour of the Mediterranean, with well-executed dishes like Iberian pork with wild-garlic purée and scampi with saffroninfused risotto.

Englers Weinkrügle
GERMAN €€

(Map p250; ☑383 115; Konviktstrasse 12; mains €9-16; ☺Tue-Sun) A warm, woody Badenstyle *Weinstube* (wine tavern) with wisteria growing out front and regional flavours on the menu. The trout in various guises (for instance, with riesling or almond-butter sauce) is delicious.

Enoteca Trattoria
ITALIAN €€€

(Map p250; ☑389 9130; www.enoteca-freiburg .de; Schwabentorplatz 6; mains €15-28; ☺dinner Mon-Sat) This is the trattoria of the two Enoteca twins (the more formal restaurant is at Gerberau 21). The chef here always hits the mark, with authentic Italian dishes such as Taleggio ravioli with Frascati sauce and glazed pear.

Harem
TURKISH €€

(Map p250; Gerberau 7c; mains €6-12; ☺closed Sun) Friendly spot for good-value Turkish specialities such as crisp *börek* (filled pastries).

Chang
THAI €€

(Map p250; Grünwälderstrasse 21; mains €6-9.50; ☺daily) Sweet little Thai for inexpensive daily specials, from green curry to pad thai.

Martin's Bräu
MICROBREWERY €€

(Map p250; Fressgässle 1; mains €9-18; ☺11ammidnight, to 2am Fri & Sat) Homebrewed pilsners wash down meaty snacks like ox tongue salad and half-metre bratwursts.

Münsterplatz Food Market
MARKET €

(Map p250; ☺until 1pm Mon-Fri, to 1.30pm Sat) Bag local goodies sold here (honey, cheese, fruit and the like), or snack on a wurst-in-abun topped with fried onions.

Markthalle
FOOD HALL €

(Map p250; Martinsgasse 235; light meals €3-6; ⊗8am-8pm, closed Sun) A food court whose Mexican, Italian, Indian, Korean and French counters offer fast, tasty lunches.

Rücker Käse und Wein
DELI €

(Map p250; Münzgasse 1; ⊗10am-6.30pm Mon-Fri, 9am-3pm Sat) For wine and cheese.

Drinking & Entertainment

Freiburg's restless student population keep steins a-swinging in the beer gardens and bars and clubs pumping until the wee hours.

Schlappen
PUB

(Map p250; Löwenstrasse 2; ⊗11am-btwn 1am & 3am Mon-Sat, 3pm-1am Sun) With its jazz-themed back room and poster-plastered walls, this pub is a perennial favourite. Try one of 10 absinthe varieties and you'll be away with the green fairies. Punters spill onto the terrace in summer.

Alte Wache
WINE BAR

(Map p250; Münsterplatz 38; ⊗10am-7pm Mon-Fri, to 4pm Sat) Right on the square, this 18th-century guardhouse serves local Müller-Thurgau and Pinot noir wines at the tasting tables. If they sharpen your appetite, order a tasting plate of cheese and olives.

Freiburg Bar
BAR

(Map p250 Kaiser-Joseph-Strasse 278; ⊗daily) This retro-cool bar attracts a mixed, fun-loving crowd with everything from karaoke and quiz nights to '80s and *Schlager* (German pop) parties. If you get hungry, you can also order decent grub here (mains €9 to €15).

Hausbrauerei Feierling
BEER GARDEN

(Map p250; Gerberau 46; ⊗11am-midnight, to 1am Fri & Sat Mar-Oct) This stream-side beer garden is a relaxed spot to quaff a cold one under the chestnut trees in summer. Pretzels and sausages (snacks €3 to €7) soak up the malty brews.

Greiffenegg-Schlössle
BEER GARDEN

(Map p250; Schlossbergring 3; ⊗11am-midnight Mar-Oct) All of Freiburg is at your feet from this chestnut-shaded beer garden atop Schlossberg. Perfect sunset spot.

Isle of Innisfree
PUB

(Map p250; Atrium Augustinerplatz; ⊗daily) Find Guinness and the craic at this lively Irish watering hole, with a weekly line-up of quizzes, karaoke and live music.

White Rabbit Club
CLUB

(Map p250; www.white-rabbit-club.de; Leopoldring 1) A student wonderland of cheap beers, DJs and gigs. Things get even curiouser at Wednesday night's open jam sessions.

Jazzhaus
LIVE MUSIC

(⊘349 73; www.jazzhaus.de; Schnewlinstrasse 1) Under the brick arches of a wine cellar, this venue hosts first-rate jazz, rock and world-music concerts (€15 to €25) at 7.30pm or 8pm at least three nights a week (see the website for details). It morphs into a club from 11pm to 3am on Friday and Saturday nights.

❶ Information

Police station (Rotteckring)

Post office (Eisenbahnstrasse 58-62)

Tourist office (⊘388 1880; www.freiburg. de; Rathausplatz 2-4; ⊗8am-8pm Mon-Fri, 9.30am-5pm Sat, 11am-4pm Sun) Well stocked with 1:50,000-scale cycling maps, city maps (€1) and the useful booklet *Freiburg – Official Guide* (€4.90). Can make room bookings (€3).

❶ Getting There & Around

AIR Freiburg shares EuroAirport (p215) with Basel (Switzerland) and Mulhouse (France). Low-cost airline easyJet flies from here to destinations including London, Berlin, Rome and Alicante.

BICYCLE Bike paths run along the Dreisam River, leading westward to Breisach and then into France.

Mobile (Wentzingerstrasse 15; city bike 4hr/day €8/15, mountain/e-bike day €20/25; ⊗9am-7pm), in a glass-enclosed pavilion across the bridge from the Hauptbahnhof, rents bikes and sells cycling maps.

BUS The **airport bus** (⊘500 500; www. freiburger-reisedienst.de; one-way/rtn €23/39) goes hourly from Freiburg's bus station to EuroAirport (55 minutes).

Südbaden Bus (www.suedbadenbus.de) and **RVF** (www.rvf.de) operate bus and train links to towns and villages throughout the southern Black Forest. Single tickets for one/two/three zones cost €2.10/3.60/5.10; a 24-hour Regio24 ticket costs €5.30 for one person and €9.50 for two to five people.

Bus and tram travel within Freiburg is operated by **VAG** (www.vag-freiburg.de) and charged at the one-zone rate. Buy tickets from the vending machines or from the driver and validate upon boarding.

CAR & MOTORCYCLE The Frankfurt–Basel A5 passes just west of Freiburg. The scenic B31 leads east through the Höllen Valley to Lake Constance. The B294 goes north into the Black Forest.

Car-hire agencies include **Europcar** (☑515 100; Lörracher Strasse 10) and **Avis** (☑197 19; St Georgener Strasse 7).

About 1.5km south of Martinstor, there's unmetered parking on some side streets (eg Türkenlouisstrasse). Otherwise, your best bet is to park at a free Park & Ride, such as the one at Bissierstrasse, a 10-minute ride from the centre on tram 1.

TRAIN Freiburg is on a major north–south rail corridor, with frequent departures for destinations such as Basel (€16.40 to €24.20, 42 to 69 minutes) and Baden-Baden (€19.20 to €28, 45 minutes to 1½ hours). Freiburg is also the western terminus of the Höllentalbahn to Donaueschingen via Titisee-Neustadt (€5.10, 38 minutes, twice an hour). There's a local connection to Breisach (€5.10, 26 minutes, at least hourly).

Schauinsland

Freiburg seems tiny as you drift up above the city and a tapestry of meadows and forest on the **Schauinslandbahn** (adult/concession return €12/11, one-way €8.50/8; ⊙9am-5pm, to 6pm Jul-Sep) to the 1284m **Schauinsland peak** (www.bergwelt-schauinsland.de). The lift provides a speedy link between Freiburg and the Black Forest highlands.

Up top there's a lookout tower commanding astounding views to the Rhine Valley and Alps, plus walking, cross-country and cycling trails that allow you to capture the scenery from many angles. Or you can bounce downhill on the 8km off-road **scooter track** (www.rollerstrecke.de; €20; ⊙2pm & 5pm Sun May-Jun, Sat & Sun Jul & Sep-Oct, Wed-Sun Aug), one of Europe's longest; it takes around an hour from top to bottom station. To reach Schauinslandbahn from Freiburg, take tram 2 to Günterstal and then bus 21 to Talstation.

On its quiet perch above the rippling hills of the Black Forest, **Die Halde** (☑07602-944 70; www.halde.com; Oberried-Hofsgrund; d €124-157, mains €16-26.50; ℗@☲) is a rustic-chic retreat, with an open fire crackling in the bar, calm rooms dressed in local wood and a glass-walled spa overlooking the valley. Martin Hegar cooks market-fresh dishes from trout to wild boar with panache in the wood-panelled restaurant.

Steinwasen Park

Buried deep in the forest, the nature-focused **Steinwasen Park** (www.steinwasen-park.de; Steinwasen 1; adult/concession €19/16; ⊙9am-6pm, closed early Nov-late Mar) is a big hit with families. A trail weaves past animal-friendly enclosures home to wild boar, ibex and burrowing marmots. One of the top attractions is a 218m-long **hanging bridge**, one of the world's longest. Not to be outdone by its rival, Europa-Park, Steinwasen has introduced whizzy rides such as Gletscherblitz and River Splash.

Todtnauer Wasserfall

Heading south on the Freiburg–Feldberg road, you'll glimpse the roaring **Todtnauer Wasserfall** (admission free; ⊙daylight hrs). While the 97m falls are not as high as those in Triberg, they're every bit as spectacular, tumbling down sheer rock faces and illuminating the velvety hills with their brilliance. Hike the circular 9km trail to **Aftersteg** for precipitous views over the cataract. Take care on paths in winter when the falls often freeze solid. The waterfall car park is on the L126.

St Peter

☑07660 / POP 2550

The folk of the bucolic village of St Peter, on the southern slopes of Mt Kandel (1243m), are deeply committed to time-honoured traditions. On religious holidays, villagers (from toddlers to pensioners) still proudly don colourful, handmade Trachten (folkloric costumes).

The most outstanding landmark is the **Ehemaliges Benedikterkloster** (Former Benedictine Abbey; guided tours adult/concession €6/2; ⊙tours 11.30am Sun, 11am Tue, 2.30pm Thu), a rococo jewel designed by Peter Thumb of Vorarlberg. Many of the period's top artists collaborated on the sumptuous interior of the twin-towered red-sandstone **church**, including Joseph Anton Feuchtmayer, who carved the gilded Zähringer duke statues affixed to pillars. Guided tours (in German) to the monastery complex include the rococo library.

The **tourist office** (☑910 224; www.st-peter-schwarzwald.de; Klosterhof 11; ⊙9am-noon & 3-5pm Mon-Fri) is under the archway leading to the Klosterhof (the abbey courtyard). A nearby information panel shows room availability.

By public transport, the best way to get from Freiburg to St Peter is to take the train to Kirchzarten (13 minutes, twice hourly) and then bus 7216 (23 minutes, twice hourly).

St Peter is on the **Schwarzwald Panoramastrasse**, a 70km-long route from Waldkirch (17km northeast of Freiburg) to Feldberg with giddy mountain views.

Breisach

⚑07667 / POP 14,500

Rising above vineyards and the Rhine, Breisach is where the Black Forest spills into Alsace. Given its geographical and cultural proximity to France, it's little surprise that the locals share their neighbours' passion for a good bottle of plonk.

From the cobbled streets lined with pastel-painted houses you'd never guess that 85% of the town was flattened in WWII, so successful has been the reconstruction. Vauban's star-shaped French fortress-town of Neuf-Brisach (New Breisach), which made the Unesco World Heritage list in 2008, sits 4km west of Breisach.

High above the centre, the Romanesque and Gothic **St Stephansmünster** shelters a faded fresco cycle, Martin Schongauer's *The Last Judgment* (1491), and a magnificent altar triptych (1526) carved from linden wood. From the tree-shaded square outside, the Schänzletreppe leads down to **Gutgesellentor**, the gate where Pope John XXIII was scandalously caught fleeing the Council of Constance in 1415.

Boat excursions along the Rhine are run by **BFS** (www.bfs-info.de; Rheinuferstrasse; ◷Apr-Sep); the dock is 500m southwest of the tourist office.

Some of Breisach's hotels have seen better days but there is a great **DJH hostel** (⚑7665; www.jugendherberge-breisach.de; Rheinuferstrasse 12; dm 1st/subsequent night €23/19.70) on the banks of the Rhine, whose facilities include a barbecue hut and volleyball court.

The **tourist office** (⚑940 155; Marktplatz 16; ◷9am-12.30pm & 1.30-6pm Mon & Wed-Fri, 10am-3pm Sat) can advise on wine tasting and private rooms in the area. You'll find the pick of the restaurants along Rheinuferstrasse and Richard-Müller-Strasse.

ⓘ Getting There & Around

Breisach's train station, 500m southeast of Marktplatz, serves Freiburg (€4.80, 25 minutes, at least hourly) and towns in the Kaiserstuhl. Buses go to Colmar, 22km west.

Breisach is a terrific base for free-wheeling over borders. Great rides include crossing the Rhine to the delightful French town of Colmar, or pedalling through terraced vineyards to Freiburg. Hire wheels from **Funbike** (⚑7733; Metzgergasse 1; 1/3 days €10/25; ◷9am-noon or on request) opposite the tourist office.

Kaiserstuhl

Squeezed between the Black Forest and French Vosges, these low-lying volcanic hills in the Upper Rhine Valley yield highly quaffable wines, including fruity *Spätburgunder* (Pinot noir) and *Grauburgunder* (Pinot gris) varieties.

The grapes owe their quality to a unique microclimate, hailed as Germany's sunniest, and fertile loess (clay and silt) soil that retains heat during the night. Nature enthusiasts should look out for rarities like sand lizards, praying mantis and European bee-eaters.

The Breisach tourist office can advise on cellar tours, wine tastings, bike paths like the 55km **Kaiserstuhl-Tour** circuit, and trails such as the **Winzerweg** (Wine Growers' Trail), an intoxicating 15km hike from Achkarren to Riegel.

The Kaiserstuhlbahn does a loop around the Kaiserstuhl. Stops (where you may have to change trains) include Sasbach, Endingen, Riegel and Gottenheim.

◉ Sights & Activities

Vitra Design Museum   MUSEUM
(www.design-museum.de; Charles-Eames-Strasse 1, Weil am Rhein; adult/concession €8/6.50, architectural tour €10.50; ◷10am-6pm, to 8pm Wed) Sharp angles contrast with graceful swirls on Frank Gehry's strikingly postmodern Vitra Design Museum. The blindingly white edifice hosts thought-provoking contemporary design exhibitions. Buildings on the nearby Vitra campus, designed by prominent architects like Nicholas Grimshaw, Zaha Hadid and Alvaro Siza, can be visited on a two-hour architectural tour, held in English at noon and 2pm daily.

Europa-Park   THEME PARK
(www.europapark.de; adult/concession €37.50/33; ◷9am-6pm Apr-early Nov, 11am-7pm late Nov-early Jan) Germany's largest theme park, 35km north of Freiburg near Rust, is Europe in miniature. Get soaked fjord-rafting in Scandinavia before nipping across to England to race at Silverstone, or Greece to unravel the mysteries of Atlantis. Aside from white-knuckle thrills, Welt der Kinder amuses tots with labyrinths and Viking ships. When

Mickey waltzed off to Paris, Europa-Park even got their own mousy mascot, Euromaus.

Shuttle buses (hourly in the morning) link Ringsheim train station, on the Freiburg-Offenburg line, with the park. By car, take the A5 exit Rust (57b).

Feldberg

📞 07655 / POP 1880

At 1493m Feldberg is the Black Forest's highest mountain and one of the few places here with downhill skiing. The actual mountaintop is treeless and not particularly attractive but on clear days the view southward towards the Alps is mesmerising.

Feldberg is also the name given to a cluster of five villages, of which **Altglashütten** is the hub. Its Rathaus houses the **tourist office** (Kirchgasse 1; ⊗8am -12pm & 1-5pm Mon-Fri), which has the low-down on activities in the area and rents Nordic walking poles.

Sitting 2km north is the lushly wooded **Bärental**, where traditional Black Forest farmhouses snuggle against the hillsides. East of Bärental in the Haslach Valley is **Falkau**, a family-friendly resort with a small waterfall. **Windgfällweiher**, an attractive lake for a swim or picnic, is 1km southeast of Altglashütten.

Around 9km west of Altglashütten is **Feldberg-Ort**, in the heart of the 42-sq-km nature reserve that covers much of the mountain. Most of the ski lifts are here, including the scenic Feldbergbahn chairlift to the **Bismarckdenkmal** (Bismarck monument).

🏃 Activities

The eco-conscious **Haus der Natur** (📞 07676-933 610; www.naturpark-suedschwarzwald.de; Dr-Pilet-Spur 4; ⊗10am-5pm, closed Mon) can advise on some of the area's great hiking opportunities, such as the rewarding 12km **Feldberg-Steig** to Feldberg summit.

The Feldberg ski area comprises 28 lifts, accessible with the same ticket. Four groomed cross-country trails are also available. To hire skis, look for signs reading 'Skiverleih'. A reliable outlet is Skiverleih Schubnell.

Come winter Feldberg's snowy heights are ideal for a stomp through twinkling woods. Strap on snowshoes to tackle the pretty 3km **Seebuck-Trail** or the more challenging 9km **Gipfel-Trail**. The Haus der Natur rents lightweight snowshoes for €10/5 per day for adults/children.

🛏 Sleeping

Landhotel Sonneck   HOTEL €€
(📞 211; www.sonneck-feldberg.de; Schwarzenbachweg 5; d €90-100) Immaculate, light-filled rooms with pine furnishings and balconies are the deal at this hotel. The quaint restaurant (mains €8 to €15) rolls out hearty local fare.

Naturfreundehaus   HOSTEL €
(📞 07676-336; www.jugendherberge-feldberg.de; Am Baldenweger Buck; dm €14.50) Lodged in a Black Forest farmhouse a 30-minute walk from Feldberg's summit, this back-to-nature hostel uses renewable energy and serves fair-trade and organic produce at breakfast. Surrounding views of wooded hills and comfy, pine-clad dorms make this a great spot for hiking in summer, and skiing and snowshoeing in winter.

ℹ Getting There & Away

Bärental and Altglashütten are stops on the Dreiseenbahn, linking Titisee with Seebrugg (Schluchsee). From the train station in Bärental, bus 7300 makes trips at least hourly to Feldberg-Ort (€2.10, 10 minutes).

From late December until the end of the season, shuttle buses run by Feldberg SBG link Feldberg and Titisee with the ski lifts (free with a lift ticket or Gästekarte).

If you're driving, take the B31 (Freiburg-Donaueschingen) to Titisee, then the B317. To get to Altglashütten, head down the B500 from Bärental.

Titisee-Neustadt

📞 07651 / POP 11,860

Titisee is a cheerful summertime playground with a name that makes English-speaking travellers giggle and a shimmering blue-green glacial lake, ringed by forest, which has them diving for their cameras.

◉ Sights & Activities

Sure, the village is touristy but tiptoe south along the flowery **Seestrasse** promenade and you'll soon leave the crowds and made-in-China cuckoo clocks behind to find secluded bays ideal for swimming and picnicking. For giddy views, head up to 1192m **Hochfirst** tower, which overlooks Titisee from the east.

A laid-back way to appreciate the lake's soothing beauty is to hire a **rowing boat** or pedalo at one of the set-ups along the lakefront; expect to pay around €6 per hour.

The forest trails around Titisee are hugely popular for **Nordic walking** which, for the uninitiated, is walking briskly with poles to simultaneously exercise the upper body and legs.

Snow transforms Titisee into a winter wonderland and a **cross-country skiing** magnet, with *Loipen* (tracks) threading through the hills and woods, including a 3km floodlit track for a starlit skate. The tourist office map pinpoints cross-country and Nordic walking trails in the area.

Badeparadies   DAY SPA

(www.badeparadies-schwarzwald.de; Am Badeparadies 1; 3hr €17, incl sauna complex €21; ⊙10am-10pm Mon-Thu, to 11pm Fri, 9am-10pm Sat & Sun) This huge glass-canopied leisure and wellness centre made a splash when it opened in December 2010. You can lounge, cocktail in hand, by palm-fringed lagoons in Palmenoase, race white-knuckle slides with gaggles of overexcited kids in Galaxy, or strip off in themed saunas with waterfalls and Black Forest views in the adults-only Wellnessoase.

🛏 Sleeping & Eating

Alemannenhof   HOTEL €€€

(☑911 80; www.hotel-alemannenhof.de; d €120-250, mains €22-34; P🐾🛜🌊) A pool, private beach and contemporary rooms with transparent shower stalls and balconies overlooking Titisee await at this farmhouse-style hotel. Opening onto a lakefront terrace, the all-pine restaurant serves regional cuisine with a twist, such as local beef with potato-rosemary puree and wild-garlic pasta.

Neubierhäusle   PENSION €

(☑8230; www.neubierhaeusle.de; Neustädterstrasse 79; d €64-82; P) Big forest views, piny air and pastures on the doorstep – this farmhouse is the perfect country retreat. Dressed in local wood, the light-filled rooms are supremely comfy. The hosts lay on a hearty spread at breakfast and you can help yourself any time to free tea and fruit. It's on the L156, 3km northeast of the station.

Bergseeblick   PENSION €

(☑8257; www.bergseeblick-titisee.de; Erlenweg 3; s €27-33, d €52-78, q €70; P) This welcoming, family-run cheapie near the church offers peaceful slumber in humble rooms decorated in pine and floral fabrics.

ℹ Information

The **tourist office** (☑07652-1206 8120; www.titisee-neustadt.de; Strandbadstrasse 4; ⊙9am-6pm Mon-Fri, 10am-1pm Sat & Sun) in the Kurhaus, 500m southwest of the train station, stocks walking and cycling maps.

ℹ Getting There & Around

Train routes include the twice-hourly Höllentalbahn to Freiburg (€5.10, 40 minutes) and hourly services to Donaueschingen (€9.10, 50 minutes), Feldberg (€2.10, 12 minutes) and Schluchsee (€2.10, 22 minutes).

From Titisee train station, there are frequent services on bus 7257 to Schluchsee (€2.10, 40 minutes) and bus 7300 to Feldberg–Bärental (€2.10, 13 minutes).

Ski-Hirt (☑922 80; Titiseestrasse 26) rents reliable bikes and ski equipment, and can supply details on local cycling options.

Schluchsee

☑07656 / POP 2540

Photogenically poised above its namesake petrol-blue lake – the Black Forest's largest – and rimmed by forest, Schluchsee tempts you outdoors with pursuits like swimming, windsurfing, hiking, cycling and, ahem, skinny-dipping from the western shore's secluded bays. The otherwise sleepy resort jolts to life with sun-seekers in summer and cross-country skiers in winter.

Popular with families, the lakefront lido, **Aqua Fun Strandbad** (Strandbadstrasse; adult/concession €4/2.70; ⊙9am-7pm Jun-Aug) has a heated pool, a sandy beach, a volleyball court and waterslides.

T Toth (www.seerundfahrten.de) runs boat tours around Schluchsee, with stops in Aha, Seebrugg and the Strandbad. An hour-long round trip costs €7.50 (less for single stops). You can hire rowing boats and pedalos for €4/6 per half/full hour.

🛏 Sleeping & Eating

Decent beds are pretty slim in Schluchsee, though there are a few good-value pensions and farmstays – ask the tourist office.

Gasthof Hirschen   GUESTHOUSE €

(☑989 40; www.hirschen-fischbach.de; Schluchseestrasse 9; s €45, d €54-80, mains €13-21) It's worth going the extra mile to this farmhouse prettily perched on a hillside in Fischbach, 4km north of Schluchsee. The simple, quiet rooms are a good-value base for summer hiking and modest winter skiing. There's also a sauna, playground and a restaurant dishing up regional fare.

Seehof INTERNATIONAL €€€
(📞988 9965; Kirchsteige 4; mains €8-18; ⏱11.30am-10.30pm Mon-Sun) An inviting spot for a bite to eat, with a terrace overlooking the lake, Seehof has a menu packed with local fish and meat mains, salads, pizzas and ice cream.

ℹ Information

The train tracks and the B500 shadow the lake's eastern shore between the lakefront and the Schluchsee's town centre. The lake's western shore is accessible only by bike or on foot.

Tourist office (📞07652-1206 8500; www. schluchsee.de; Fischbacher Strasse 7, Haus des Gastes; ⏱8am-5pm Mon-Thu, 9am-5pm Fri) Situated 150m uphill from the church, with maps and info on activities and accommodation.

ℹ Getting There & Around

Trains go hourly to Feldberg–Altglashütten (€2.10, 11 minutes) and Titisee (€2.10, 22 minutes). Bus 7257 links Schluchsee three or four times daily with the Neustadt and Titisee train stations (€2.10, 40 minutes).

City, mountain and e-bikes can be rented for €9/10/22 per day at **Müllers** (An der Staumauer 1; ⏱10am-6pm Apr-Oct). An hour's pedalo/motor boat/rowing boat hire costs €6/15/6.

Triberg

📞0722 / POP 5000

Home to Germany's highest waterfall, heir to the original 1915 black forest gateau recipe and nesting ground of the world's biggest cuckoos, Triberg leaves visitors reeling with superlatives. It was here that in bleak winters past folk huddled in snowbound farmhouses to carve the clocks that would drive the world cuckoo, and here that in a flash of brilliance the waterfall was harnessed to power the country's first electric street lamps in 1884.

◎ Sights & Activities

TOP CHOICE **Triberger Wasserfälle** WATERFALL
(adult/concession €3.50/3; ⏱Mar-early Nov & 25-30 Dec) Niagara they ain't but Germany's highest waterfalls do exude their own wild romanticism. The Gutach River feeds the seven-tiered falls, which drop a total of 163m. It's annoying to have to pay to experience nature but the fee is at least worth it. The trail up through the wooded gorge is

guarded by tribes of red squirrels after the bags of nuts (€1) sold at the entrance.

Weltgrösste Kuckucksuhr LANDMARK
Triberg is Germany's undisputed cuckoo-clock capital. Two timepieces claim the title of world's largest cuckoo clock, giving rise to the battle of the birds.

To the casual observer, the biggest is undeniably the commercially savvy **Eble Uhren-Park** (www.uhren-park.de; Schonachbach 27; admission €2; ⏱9am-6pm Mon-Sat, 10am-6pm Sun), listed in *Guinness World Records*, on the B33 between Triberg and Hornberg.

At the other end of town in Schonach is its underdog **rival clock** (Untertalstrasse 28; adult/concession €1.20/0.60; ⏱9am-noon & 1-6pm), nestled inside a snug chalet and complete with gear-driven innards. This giant timepiece – unable to compete in size alone – has taken to calling itself the world's oldest, largest cuckoo clock. It was built in the 1980s.

Haus der 1000 Uhren LANDMARK
(House of 1000 clocks; www.hausder1000uhren.de; Hauptstrasse 79; ⏱9am-5pm Sat, 10am-5pm Sun) A glockenspiel bashes out melodies and a cuckoo greets his fans with a hopelessly croaky squawk on the hour at the kitschy House of 1000 Clocks, a wonderland of clocks from traditional to trendy. The latest quartz models feature a sensor that sends the cuckoo to sleep after dark!

Sanitas Spa SPA
(📞860 20; www.sanitas-spa.de; Gartenstrasse 24; admission half-/full-day €24/40; ⏱9.30am-8pm) Fronted by wrap-around windows overlooking Triberg's forested hills, Parkhotel Wehrle's day spa is gorgeous. This is a serene spot to wind down, with its spacily lit kidney-shaped pool, exquisitely tiled hammams, steam rooms, whirlpool and waterbed meditation room. Treatments vary from rhassoul clay wraps to reiki.

🛏 Sleeping & Eating

TOP CHOICE **Parkhotel Wehrle** HISTORIC HOTEL €€€
(📞860 20; www.parkhotel-wehrle.de; Hauptstrasse 51; s €95-105, d €149-169, mains €12-23; P 🛜 ❄) Hemingway once waxed lyrical about this 400-year-old hotel and it remains a rustically elegant place to stay today. Often with a baroque or Biedermeier touch, quarters are roomy and beautifully furnished with antiques; the best have Duravit whirlpool tubs. All guests get free entry to the hotel's

CLAUS SCHÄFER, CONFECTIONER

Want to whip up your own black forest gateau back home? Claus Schäfer reveals how.

All About Cake Baking a black forest gateau isn't rocket science but it involves time, practice and top-quality ingredients. Eat the cake the day you make it, when it is freshest, and never freeze it or you will lose the aroma.

Secrets in the Mix Whip the cream until silky, blend in gelatine and two shots of quality kirsch. Mine comes from a local distillery and is 56% proof. The compote needs tangy cherries, sugar, cherry juice and a pinch of cinnamon. The bottom layer of sponge should be twice as thick as the other two, so it can support the compote without collapsing.

Finishing Touches These are important: spread the gateau with cream, then decorate with piped cream, cherries, chocolate shavings and a dusting of icing sugar.

Other Regional Flavours When in the Black Forest, try the fresh trout, smoked ham and *Kirsch* sold locally by farmers. Their quality is higher and prices lower than elsewhere.

Sanitas Spa. The well-regarded restaurant serves seasonal delicacies like gilthead sea bream with market-fresh veg and oxtail jus in wood-panelled, softly lit surrounds.

Kukucksnest　　　　　　　　　B&B €
(☑869 487; Wallfahrtstrasse 15; d €58) Below is the shop of master woodcarver Gerald Burger, above is the beautiful nest he has carved for his guests, featuring blonde-wood rooms with flat-screen TVs. The *Wurzelsepp* (faces carved into fir tree roots) by the entrance supposedly ward off evil spirits.

Café Schäfer　　　　　　　　　BAKERY €
(www.cafe-schaefer-triberg.de; Hauptstrasse 33; cake €3-4; ☺9am-6pm Mon-Fri, 8am-6pm Sat, 11am-6pm Sun, closed Wed) The black forest gateau here is the real deal and confectioner Claus Schäfer has Josef Keller's original 1915 recipe for *Schwarzwälder Kirschtorte* to prove it. The aroma draws you to the glass counter showcasing the masterpiece: layers of moist sponge, fresh cream and sour cherries, with a mere suggestion of *Kirsch* (cherry brandy) and heavenly dusting of chocolate.

❶ Information

Triberg's main drag is the B500, which runs more or less parallel to the Gutach River. The town's focal point is the Marktplatz, a steep 1.2km uphill walk from the Bahnhof.

Triberg markets itself as **Das Ferienland** (The Holiday Region; www.dasferienland.de) to visitors.

Tourist office (☑866 490; www.triberg.de; Wahlfahrtstrasse 4; ☺10am-5pm Oct-Apr,

to 6pm May-Sep) Inside the Schwarzwald-Museum, 50m uphill from the river.

❶ Getting There & Away

The Schwarzwaldbahn train line loops southeast to Konstanz (€23.30, 1½ hours, hourly), and northwest to Offenburg (€11.10, 46 minutes, hourly).

Bus 7150 travels north through the Gutach and Kinzig Valleys to Offenburg; bus 7265 heads south to Villingen via St Georgen. Local buses operate between the Bahnhof and Marktplatz, and to the nearby town of Schonach (hourly).

Stöcklewaldturm

Triberg's waterfall is the trailhead for an attractive 6.5km walk to Stöcklewaldturm (1070m). A steady trudge through spruce forest and pastures brings you to this 19th-century lookout tower (admission €0.50), where the 360-degree views stretch from the Swabian Alps to the snowcapped Alps. Footpaths head off in all directions from the summit, where the woodsy cafe (snacks €2.50-7; ☺10am-8pm, closed Tue) is an inviting spot for a beer and snack or, in winter, hot chocolate. The car park on the L175 is a 10-minute stroll from the tower.

Martinskapelle

Named after the tiny chapel at the head of the Bregtal (Breg Valley), Martinskapelle attracts cross-country skiers to its forested trails in winter and hikers when the snow melts. The steep road up to the 1100m peak negotiates some pretty hairy switchbacks, swinging past wood-shingle farmhouses that cling to forested slopes.

Höhengasthaus Kolmenhof (☎07723-931 00; www.kolmenhof.de; An der Donauquelle; mains €9.50-16; ☺closed Wed dinner, Thu) fills up with ruddy-cheeked skiers and walkers, who pile into this rustic bolt-hole for *Glüh-wein* (mulled wine) and soul food. Despite what critics (who have argued until blue in the face since 1544) may say, the Danube's main source is right here. This accounts for the freshness of the trout, served smoked, roasted in almond butter, or poached in white wine.

Bus 7270 runs roughly hourly from the Marktplatz in Triberg to Escheck (€1.90, 25 minutes); from here it's a 4.5km walk to Martinskapelle. If you're driving, take the B500 from Triberg following signs to Schwarzenbach, Weissenbach and the K5730 to Martinskapelle.

Villingen-Schwenningen

☎07221 / POP 81,020

Villingen and Schwenningen trip simultaneously off the tongue, yet each town has its own flavour and history. Villingen once belonged to the Grand Duchy of Baden and Schwenningen to the duchy of Württemberg, conflicting allegiances that apparently can't be reconciled. Villingen, it must

be said, is the more attractive of the twin towns.

Encircled by impenetrable walls that look as though they were built by the mythical local giant, Romäus, Villingen's Altstadt is a late medieval time capsule, with cobbled streets and handsome patrician houses. Though locals nickname it the *Städtle* (little town), the name seems inappropriate during February's mammoth weeklong *Fasnet* celebrations.

◉ Sights & Activities

Münsterplatz   SQUARE

The main crowd-puller in Villingen's Altstadt is the red-sandstone **Münster** with disparate spires: one overlaid with coloured tiles, the other spiky and festooned with gargoyles. The Romanesque portals with haut-relief doors depict dramatic biblical scenes.

Right opposite is the step-gabled **Altes Rathaus** (Old Town Hall) and Klaus Ringwald's **Münsterbrunnen**, a bronze fountain and a tongue-in-cheek portrayal of characters that have shaped Villingen's history. The square throngs with activity on Wednesday and Saturday mornings when market stalls are piled high with local bread, meat, cheese, fruit and flowers.

Franziskaner Museum   MUSEUM

(Rietgasse 2; adult/concession €3/2; ☺1-5pm Tue-Sat, 11am-5pm Sun) Next to the 13th-century Riettor and occupying a former Franciscan

---

WORTH A TRIP

NATURPARK OBERE DONAU

Theatrically set against cave-riddled limestone cliffs, dappled with pine and beech woods that are burnished gold in autumn, and hugging the Danube's banks, the **Upper Danube Valley Nature Reserve** (www.naturpark-obere-donau.de) bombards you with rugged splendour. Stick to the autobahn, however, and you'll be none the wiser. To explore the nature reserve, slip into a bicycle saddle or walking boots and hit the trail.

One of the finest stretches is between **Fridingen** and **Beuron**, a 12.5km ridge-top walk of three to four hours. The signposted, easy-to-navigate trail runs above ragged cliffs, affording eagle's-eye views of the meandering Danube, which has almost 2850km to go before emptying into the Black Sea. The vertigo-inducing outcrop of **Laibfelsen** is a great picnic spot. From here, the path dips in and out of woodlands and meadows flecked with purple thistles. In Beuron the big draw is the working **Benedictine abbey**, one of Germany's oldest, dating to 1077. The lavish stucco-and-fresco **church** (☺5am-8pm daily) is open to visitors. See the website www.beuron.de (in German) for sleeping options.

Fridingen and Beuron lie on the L277, 45km east of Villingen. Frequent trains link Beuron to Villingen (€7.50, one hour).

monastery, the Franziskaner Museum skips merrily through Villingen's history and heritage. Standouts include Celtic artefacts unearthed at Magdalenenberg, 30 minutes' walk south of Villingen's centre. Dating to 616 BC, the mystery-enshrouded site is one of the largest Hallstatt burial chambers ever discovered in Central Europe and is shaded by a 1000-year-old oak tree.

Spitalgarten
GARDEN

Tucked behind the Franziskaner is the Spitalgarten, a park flanked by the original city walls. Here your gaze will be drawn to **Romäusturm**, a lofty 13th-century thieves' tower named after fabled local leviathan Remigius Mans (Romäus for short).

Kneippbad
SWIMMING

(Am Kneippbad 1; adult/child €3.70/2.50; ⊙6.30am-8pm Mon-Fri, 8am-8pm Sat & Sun mid-May–early Sep) If the sun's out, take a 3km walk northwest of the Altstadt to this forest lido, a family magnet with its outdoor pools, slides and volleyball courts.

🛏 Sleeping & Eating

Rindenmühle
HOTEL €€

(🖉886 80; www.rindenmuehle.de; Am Kneippbad 9; r €99-125, mains €16-32; Ⓟ🛜) Next to the Kneippbad, this converted watermill houses one of Villingen's smartest hotels, with forest walks right on its doorstep. Rooms are slick and decorated in muted hues. In the kitchen, Martin Weisser creates award-winning flavours using home-grown organic produce, including chicken, geese and herbs from his garden.

Haus Bächle
GUESTHOUSE €

(🖉597 29; Am Kneippbad 5; s/d €15/32; Ⓟ) This half-timbered house overlooks the flowery Kurgarten. The tidy rooms are an absolute bargain and the Kneippbad is next door for early-morning swims.

Kapuzinerhof
ITALIAN €€€

(🖉506 084; Färberstrasse 18; mains €10-24; ⊙11.30am-10pm Sun-Thu, to 11pm Fri & Sat, closed Wed) Gathered around a courtyard in a restored 17th-century Capuchin monastery, this Altstadt restaurant emphasises Italian flavours, from antipasti to sea bass.

Zampolli
CAFE €

(Rietstrasse 33; ice cream cone €0.80; ⊙9.30am-11pm Mon-Sat, 10.30am-11pm Sun Feb–mid-Nov) For an espresso or creamy gelati, make for this Italian-run cafe. By night, the pavement terrace facing Riettor is a laid-back spot for a drink.

❶ Information

Post office (Bahnhofstrasse 6)

Villingen Tourist Office (🖉822 525; www.tourismus-vs.de; Rietgasse 2; ⊙9am-5pm Mon-Sat, 11am-5pm Sun) In the Franziskaner Museum. You can pick up the itour audio guide in English; two hours costs €5.

❶ Getting There & Around

Villingen's Bahnhof is on the scenic Schwarzwaldbahn train line from Konstanz (€18.10, 70 minutes) to Triberg (€7.50, 23 minutes) and Offenburg (€16.40, 70 minutes). Trains to Stuttgart (€28.50, 1¾ hours) involve a change in Rottweil, and to Freiburg (€18.10 to €27.10, two hours) a change in Donaueschingen.

From Villingen, buses 7265 and 7270 make regular trips north to Triberg. Frequent buses (for example, line 1) link Villingen with Schwenningen.

Villingen-Schwenningen is just west of the A81 Stuttgart–Singen motorway and is also crossed by the B33 to Triberg and the B27 to Rottweil.

Rottweil

🖉0741 / POP 25,660

Baden-Württemberg's oldest town is the strapline of Roman-rooted Rottweil, founded in AD 73. Yet a torrent of bad press about the woofer with a nasty nip means that most folk readily associate it with the Rottweiler, which was indeed bred here as a hardy butchers' dog until recently. Fear not, the Rottweiler locals are much tamer.

The sturdy 13th-century **Schwarzes Tor** is the gateway to Hauptstrasse and the well-preserved Altstadt, a cluster of red-roofed, pastel-painted houses. Nearby at No 6, the curvaceous **Hübschen Winkel** will make you look twice with its 45-degree kink. Just west on Münsterplatz, the late Romanesque **Münster-Heiliges-Kreuz** features some striking Gothic stonework and ribbed vaulting. Equally worth a peek about 1km south is the **Roman bath** (Hölderstrasse; admission free; ⊙daylight hrs), a 45m-by-42m bathing complex unearthed in 1967.

The **tourist office** (🖉494 280; www.rottweil.de; Hauptstrasse 21; ⊙9.30am-5.30pm Mon-Fri, to 12.30pm Sat) can advise on accommodation, tours and biking the **Neckartal-Radweg**.

Rottweil is just off the A81 Stuttgart–Singen motorway. Trains run at least hourly to Villingen (€3, 25 minutes) and Stuttgart (€20.80, 1½ hours).

CELEBRATE THE FIFTH SEASON

Boisterous and totally bonkers, the **Swabian-Alemannic Fasnacht** or *Fasnet* (not to be confused with Carnival) is a 500-year-old rite to banish winter and indulge in pre-Lenten feasting, parades, flirting and all-night drinkathons. Starting on Epiphany, festivities reach a crescendo the week before Ash Wednesday. Dress up to join the party, memorise a few sayings to dodge the witches, and catch the flying sausages – anything's possible, we swear. For *Fasnacht* at its traditional best, try the following:

Rottweil (www.narrenzunft.rottweil.de) At Monday's 8am *Narrensprung*, thousands of jester-like Narros in baroque masques ring through Baden-Württemberg's oldest town. Look out for the devil-like *Federhannes* and the *Guller* riding a cockerel.

Schramberg (www.narrenzunft-schramberg.de) Protagonists include the *hoorige Katz* (hairy cat) and the hopping *Hans*.

Elzach (www.schuttig.com) *Trallaho!* Wearing a hand-carved mask and a tricorn hat adorned with snail shells, *Schuttige* dash through Elzach's streets cracking *Saublodere* (pig bladders) – dodge them unless you wish for many children! Sunday's torchlit parade and Shrove Tuesday's afternoon *Schuttigumzug* are the must-sees.

Unterkirnach

☑ 07721 / POP 2730

Nestled among velvety green hills, low-key Unterkirnach appeals to families and outdoorsy types. Kids can slide and climb to their heart's content at the all-weather **Spielscheune** (Schlossbergweg 4; admission €4; ☺1-7pm Mon-Fri, 11am-7pm Sat & Sun), or toddle uphill to the **farm** to meet inquisitive goats and Highland cattle (feeding time is 3pm). In summer, the village is a great starting point for **forest hikes**, combed with 130km of marked walking trails, while in winter there are 50km of *Loipen* (**cross-country ski tracks**) and some terrific slopes to sledge.

Picturesquely perched above Unterkirnach, **Ackerloch Grillschopf** (www.ackerloch.de; Unteres Ackerloch; light meals €4-11; ☺11.30am-midnight, closed Tue) is a rickety barn, brimming with rustic warmth in winter and with a beer garden overlooking a broad valley in summer. Occasionally there is a suckling pig roasting on the spit and you can grill your own steaks and sausages on the barbecue.

Bus 61 runs roughly hourly between Unterkirnach and Villingen (€3, 18 minutes).

LAKE CONSTANCE

Nicknamed the *schwäbische Meer* (Swabian Sea), Lake Constance is Central Europe's third largest lake and it straddles three countries: Germany, Austria and Switzerland. Formed by the Rhine Glacier during the last ice age and fed and drained by that same sprightly river today, this whopper of a lake measures 63km long, 14km wide and up to 250m deep. Vital statistics aside, there is definite novelty effect in the fact that this is the only place in the world where you can wake up in Germany, cycle across to Switzerland for lunch and make it to Austria in time for afternoon tea, strudel and snapshots of the Alps.

Taking in meadows and vineyards, orchards and wetlands, beaches and Alpine foothills, the lake's landscapes are like a 'greatest hits' of European scenery. Culture? It's all here, from baroque churches to Benedictine abbeys, Stone Age dwellings to Roman forts, medieval castles to zeppelins.

BODENSEE ERLEBNISKARTE

The three-day **Bodensee Erlebniskarte** (adult/child €72/36, not incl ferries €40/21), available at area tourist and ferry offices from early April to mid-October, allows free travel on almost all boats and mountain cableways on and around Lake Constance (including its Austrian and Swiss shores) and gets you free entry to around 180 tourist attractions and museums. There are also seven-day (adult/child €92/46) and 14-day (adult/child €130/66) versions.

Come in spring for blossom and autumn for new wine, fewer crowds and top visibility when the warm *Föhn* blows. Summers are crowded, but best for swimming and camping. Almost everything shuts from November to February, when fog descends and the first snowflakes dust the Alps.

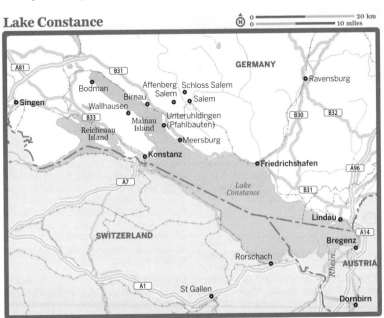 Getting There & Around

The most enjoyable way to cross the lake is by ferry. Konstanz is the main hub but Meersburg and Friedrichshafen also have plentiful ferry options.

Although most towns have a train station (Meersburg is an exception), in some cases buses provide the only land connections. **Euregio Bodensee** (www.euregiokarte.com), which groups all Lake Constance–area public transport, publishes a free *Fahrplan* with schedules for all train, bus and ferry services.

The **Euregio Bodensee Tageskarte** (www.euregiokarte.com) gets you all-day access to land transport around Lake Constance, including areas in Austria and Switzerland. It's sold at train stations and ferry docks and costs €16.50/22/29 for one/two/all zones.

CAR FERRIES The roll-on-roll-off **Konstanz–Meersburg car ferry** (www.sw.konstanz.de; car up to 4m incl driver/bicycle/pedestrian €8.40/2.20/2.60) runs 24 hours a day, except when high water levels prevent it from docking. The ferry runs is every 15 minutes from 5.30am to 9pm, every 30 minutes from 9pm to midnight and every hour from midnight to 5.30am. The crossing, affording superb views from the top deck, takes 15 minutes.

The dock in Konstanz, served by local bus 1, is 4km northeast of the centre along Mainaustrasse. In Meersburg, car ferries leave from a dock 400m northwest of the old town.

PASSENGER FERRIES The most useful lines, run by German **BSB** (www.bsb-online.com) and Austrian **OBB** (www.bodenseeschifffahrt.at), link Konstanz with ports such as Meersburg (€5.30, 30 minutes), Friedrichshafen (€11.70, 1¾ hours), Lindau (€15.40, three hours) and Bregenz (€16.40, 3½ hours); children aged six to 15 years pay half-price. The website lists full timetables.

Der Katamaran (www.der-katamaran.de; adult/6-14yr €9.80/4.90) is a sleek passenger service that takes 50 minutes to make the Konstanz–Friedrichshafen crossing (hourly from 6am to 7pm, plus hourly from 8pm to midnight on Fridays and Saturdays from mid-May to early October).

Konstanz

📞07531 / POP 84,690

Sidling up to the Swiss border, bisected by the Rhine and outlined by the Alps, Konstanz sits prettily on the northwestern shore of Lake Constance. Roman emperors,

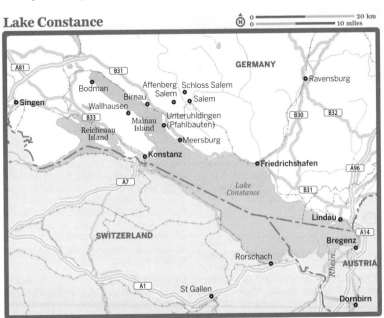

Lake Constance

0 — 20 km
0 — 10 miles

Konstanz

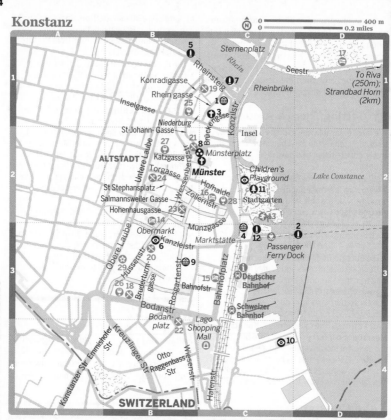

medieval traders and the bishops of the 15th-century Council of Constance have all left their mark on this alley-woven town, mercifully spared from the WWII bombings that obliterated other German cities.

When the sun comes out to play, Konstanz is a feel-good university town with a lively buzz and upbeat bar scene, particularly in the cobbled Altstadt and the harbour where the voluptuous *Imperia* turns. In summer the locals, nicknamed *Seehasen* (lake hares), head outdoors to the leafy promenade and enjoy lazy days in lakefront lidos.

◉ Sights

TOP CHOICE **Münster** CATHEDRAL
(Map p264; tower adult/child €2/1; ⊙10am-6pm Mon-Sat, to 6pm Sun, tower 10am-5pm Mon-Sat, 12.30am-5.30pm Sun) Crowned by a filigree spire and looking proudly back on 1000 years of history, the sandstone Münster was the church of the diocese of Konstanz until 1821. Its interior is an architectural potpourri of Romanesque, Gothic, Renaissance and baroque styles. Standouts include the 15th-century **Schnegg**, an ornate spiral staircase in the northern transept, to the left of which a door leads to the 1000-year-old **crypt**. From the crypt's polychrome chapel, you enter the sublime **Gothic cloister**.

On cloudless days, it's worth ascending the **tower** for broad views over the city and lake.

The glass pyramid in front of the Münster shelters the **Römersiedlung** (Map p264; tour €1; ⊙6pm Sun), the 3rd-century-AD remains of the Roman fort Constantia, which gave the city its name. The ruins can be visited on a brief guided tour – there's no need to book; just turn up.

Lakefront HARBOUR
At the merest hint of a sunray, the tree-fringed, sculpture-dotted lakefront prom-

Konstanz

enade lures inline skaters, cyclists, walkers and ice-cream-licking crowds.

Look for the white dormered **Konzilge-bäude** (Council Building; Map p264), built in 1388, which served as a granary and warehouse before Pope Martin V was elected here in 1417. Today it's a conference and concert hall.

The nearby **Zeppelin Monument** (Map p264) shows the airship inventor Count Ferdinand von Zeppelin in an Icarus-like pose. He was born in 1838 on the Insel, an islet a short stroll north through the flowery **Stadtgarten** (Map p264) park, where there's a **children's playground**.

Niederburg NEIGHBOURHOOD
Best explored on foot, Niederburg, Konstanz' cobbled heart, stretches north from the Münster to the Rhine. The twisting lanes lined with half-timbered town houses are the place to snoop around galleries, antique shops and 13th-century **Kloster Zoffingen** (Map p264; Brückengasse 15), Konstanz' only remaining convent, still in the hands of Dominican nuns.

On the Rheinsteig is the medieval **Rhein-torturm** (Rhine Gate Tower; Map p264), a defensive tower with a pyramid-shaped red-tile roof. About 200m west along the river is the more squat, 14th-century **Pulverturm** (Gunpowder Tower; Map p264, with 2m-thick walls.

Cross the street to the orange-red, baroque **Domprobstei** (Map p264; Rheingasse 20), once the residence of the cathedral provosts.

Rathaus LANDMARK
(City Hall; Map p264; Kanzleistrasse) Slightly south of the Münster, the flamboyantly frescoed Renaissance Rathaus occupies the former linen weavers' guildhall. Behind you'll find a peaceful arcaded courtyard.

Rosgartenmuseum MUSEUM
(Map p264; www.rosgartenmuseum-konstanz.de; Rosgartenstrasse 3-5; adult/concession €3/1.50, 1st Sun of the month & after 2pm Wed free; ⊙10am-6pm Tue-Fri, to 5pm Sat & Sun) The one-time butchers' guildhall now harbours the Rosgartenmuseum, spotlighting regional art and history, with an emphasis on medieval panel painting and sculpture.

Sea Life AQUARIUM
(Map p264; www.visitsealife.com/konstanz; Hafenstrasse 9; adult/child €15.95/10.95; ⊙10am-btwn 5pm & 7pm) Running a dragnet through your wallet, the borderline-kitsch Sea Life immerses you in an underwater world. Highlights include a shipwreck where you can handle starfish and get stingray close-ups, a shark tunnel, penguins, and a creepy corner

ONE LAKE, TWO WHEELS, THREE COUNTRIES

When the weather warms, there is no better way to explore Bodensee (Lake Constance) than with your bum in a saddle. The well-marked **Bodensee Cycle Path** (www .bodensee-radweg.com) cycling path makes a 273km loop of Lake Constance, taking in vineyards, meadows, orchards, wetlands and historic towns. There are plenty of small beaches where you can stop for a refreshing dip in the lake. See the website for itineraries and maps. Bike hire is available in most towns for between €10 and €20 per day. While the entire route takes roughly a week, ferries and trains make it possible to cover shorter chunks, such as Friedrichshafen–Konstanz–Meersburg, in a weekend.

A day suffices to cover some highlights in three countries on a 30km stretch of the route. Begin in **Lindau's** storybook old town in Germany, then pedal along the lakeshore to **Bregenz**, in Austria, famous for its **Festpiele** (www.bregenzerfestspiele.com), an open-air opera festival held on the lake from mid-July to mid-August. Rearing above the town is the 1064m peak of **Pfänder**, which commands a breathtaking panorama of Lake Constance and the not-so-distant Alps. A **cable car** (round-trip adult/concession €11/8.80; ⊗8am-7pm) glides to the summit. Continue southwest along a woodland path to the broad banks of the **Bregenzerach**, a beautiful meltwater river where locals bathe and fly-fish on hot days. From here it's just a short pedal to the Rheindelta wetlands and the wide bay of **Rorschach** in Switzerland, where you can stop for Swiss chocolate before catching a ferry back to Lindau.

blubbing with oddities like frogfish and, ugh, giant isopods.

🏃 Activities

For some ozone-enriched summer fun, grab your bathers and head to the lake.

FREE Strandbad Horn
BEACH

(Eichhornstrasse 100; ⊗mid-May–Sep) This lakefront beach, 4km northeast of the centre, has sunbathing lawns, a kiddie pool, playground, volleyball courts and even a naturist area.

La Canoa
BOAT HIRE

(www.lacanoa.com; Robert-Bosch-Strasse 4; canoe/kayak 3 hr €14/18, per day €21/27; ⊗10am-12.30pm & 2-6pm Tue-Fri, 10am-4pm Sat) Rents high-quality canoes and kayaks in Konstanz and from various other Lake Constance locations, including Lindau and Friedrichshafen. Visit the website for canoe tour details.

Bootsvermietung Konstanz
BOAT HIRE

(Map p264; per hr €9-17; ⊗11am-sunset Easter–mid-Oct) This boat rental in the Stadtgarten has pedalos for trundling across the lake.

🛏 Sleeping

Rock up between November and mid-March and you may find some places closed. The tourist office has a free booking service and a list of private rooms.

Villa Barleben
HISTORIC HOTEL €€€

(Map p264; ☑942 330; www.hotel-barleben.de; Seestrasse 15; s €135-230, d €195-255; ☺) Gregariously elegant, this 19th-century villa's sunny rooms and corridors are sprinkled with antiques and ethnic art. The rambling lakefront gardens are ideal for dozing in a *Strandkorb* (wicker beach lounger), G&T in hand, or enjoying lunch on the terrace.

Hotel Barbarossa
HISTORIC HOTEL €€

(Map p264; ☑128 990; www.barbarossa-hotel.com; Obermarkt 8-12; s €55-75, d €95-130; ☺) This 600-year-old patrician house harbours parquet-floored, individually decorated rooms, which are bright and appealing, if a tad on the small side. The terrace has views over Konstanz' rooftops and spires.

Riva
BOUTIQUE HOTEL €€€

(☑363 090; www.hotel-riva.de; Seestrasse 25; s €110-150, d €200-240; P☺☺☺) This ultra-chic contender has crisp white spaces, glass walls and a snail-like stairwell. Zen-like rooms with hardwood floors feature perks such as (like it!) free minibars. The rooftop pool and Mediterranean-style restaurant (mains €18 to €25) overlook the lake.

Pension Gretel
B&B €€

(Map p264; ☑455 825; www.hotel-gretel.de; Zollernstrasse 6-8; s €45, d €60-98, tr/q €126/180) Sure, the rooms are basic, but they are light, tidy and a snip given the Altstadt location.

There's a cosy *Weinstube* if you fancy a glass of wine and bite to eat, and handy bike storage for cyclists.

Hotel Halm
HOTEL €€

(Map p264; ☑12 10; www.hotel-halm-konstanz.de; Bahnhofplatz 6; s/d €110-130; ☎) A joyous hop and skip from the lake and Altstadt, this late 19th-century pile has warm, elegantly furnished rooms with marble bathrooms; upgrade if you want a balcony with lake view. Skip the €16 breakfast and hit a nearby bakery instead.

✖ Eating

Münsterplatz and Markstätte are peppered with pizzerias, snack bars and gelaterias. Watch out for rip-offs around Stadtgarten.

Münsterhof
GERMAN €€€

(Map p264; ☑3638 427; Münsterplatz 3; mains €8.50-17; ☺daily; ☑☟) Tables set up in front of the Münster, a slick bistro interior and a lunchtime buzz have earned Münsterhof a loyal local following. The two-course €6.90 lunch is a bargain. Dishes from cordon bleu with pan-fried potatoes to asparagus-filled *Maultaschen* in creamy chive sauce are substantial and satisfying.

Tolle Knolle
INTERNATIONAL €€€

(Map p264; ☑175 75; Bodanplatz 9; mains €9-17; ☺daily) On a fountain-dotted square with alfresco seating, this art-slung restaurant lives up to its 'great potato' moniker. Potatoes come in various guises: with *Wiener Schnitzel*, beer-battered fish and on the signature pizza. There's always a good-value €5.50 lunch special.

Voglhaus
CAFE €

(Map p264; Wessenbergstrasse 8; light meals €2.50-6; ☺9am-6.30pm Mon-Sat, 11am-6pm Sun; ☑) Locals flock to the 'bird house' for its chilled vibe and contemporary wood-and-stone interior, warmed by an open fire in winter. Wood-oven bread with spreads, wholegrain bagels and cupcakes pair nicely with smoothies and speciality coffees like Hansel and Gretel (with gingerbread syrup).

Zeitlos
GERMAN €

(Map p264; St Stephansplatz 25; snacks €4-10; ☺10am-1am Mon-Sat, to 6pm Sun) Behind Stephanskirche, this beamed, stone-walled bistro overflows with regulars. It's a cosy spot for brunch or filling snacks like *Wurstsalat* (sausage salad) and *Maultaschen*, the

local take on ravioli. Sit in the ivy-draped courtyard in summer.

La Bodega
TAPAS €€

(Map p264; ☑277 88; Schreibergasse 40; tapas €3.50-10.50; ☺dinner Tue-Sat) Squirrelled away in Niederburg, this candy-bright bodega with a pocket-sized terrace whips up tapas from *papas canarias* (Canarian potatoes) to stuffed calamari.

Hexenkuche
STEAKHOUSE €€

(Map p264; ☑245 60; Bodanstrasse 30; mains €10-23; ☺dinner Wed-Mon) Rump, fillet and Charolais – the rustic-look 'witches' kitchen' hits the mark with well-seasoned steaks.

Maximilian's
DELI €

(Map p264; Hussenstrasse 9; cake around €2.50; ☺10am-7pm Mon-Fri, to 6.30pm Sat) Fancy a picnic by the lake? Stop by this central deli for fresh bread, cheese, ham, wine and other goodies. It's also a snug spot for coffee and cake.

☕ Drinking & Entertainment

A vibrant student population fuels Konstanz' after-dark scene. For the low-down, see www.party-news.de (in German). Head to the harbour for drinks with a lake view.

K9
CULTURAL CENTRE

(Map p264; www.k9-kulturzentrum.de; Obere Laube 71) Once a medieval church, this is now Konstanz' most happening cultural venue, with a line-up skipping from salsa nights and film screenings to gigs, club nights and jive nights. See the website for times.

Klimperkasten
BAR

(Map p264; Bodanstrasse 40; ☺10am-1am, to 3am Sat) Indie kids, garage and old-school fans

---

DON'T MISS

IMPERIA RULES

At the end of the pier in Konstanz, giving ferry passengers a come-hither look from her rotating pedestal, stands **Imperia** (Map p264). Peter Lenk's 9m-high sculpture of a buxom prostitute, said to have plied her trade in the days of the Council of Constance, is immortalised in a novel by Honoré de Balzac. In her clutches are hilarious sculptures of a naked (and sagging) Pope Martin V and Holy Roman Emperor Sigismund, symbolising religious and imperial power.

all hail this retro cafe, which gets clubbier after dark when DJs work the decks. Occasionally hosts gigs.

Schwarze Katz BAR
(Map p264; Katzgasse 8; ⊙6pm-1am Mon-Thu, to 2am Fri & Sat) Found the 'black cat'? You're in luck. A relaxed mood, friendly crowd and reasonably priced drinks (including Black Forest Alpirsbacher beer) make this a Konstanz favourite.

Brauhaus Johann Albrecht BREWPUB
(Map p264; Konradigasse 2; ⊙11.30am-1pm) This step-gabled microbrewery is a relaxed haunt for quaffing wheat beer or hoppy lager by the glass or metre, with a terrace for summer imbibing.

Seekuh PUB
(Map p264; Konzilstrasse 1; ⊙6pm-btwn 1am & 3am) The rough and ready 'lake cow' is a Konstanz favourite for its beer garden, cheapish drinks and occasional gigs.

❶ Information

ReiseBank (Hauptbahnhof; ⊙8am-12.30pm & 1.30-6pm Mon-Fri, 8am-3pm Sat) Currency exchange, including Swiss francs.

Tourist office (☑133 030; www.konstanz -tourismus.de; Bahnhofplatz 43; ⊙9am-6.30pm Mon-Fri, to 4pm Sat, 10am-1pm Sun Apr-Oct, 9.30am-6pm Mon-Fri Nov-Mar) Just north of the train stations. Inside you can pick up a walking-tour brochure (€1) and city map (€0.50); outside there's a hotel reservation board and free hotel telephone.

❶ Getting There & Away

Konstanz is Lake Constance's main ferry hub.

By car, Konstanz can be reached via the B33, which links up with the A81 to and from Stuttgart near Singen. Or you can take the B31 to Meersburg and then catch a car ferry.

Konstanz' Hauptbahnhof is the southern terminus of the scenic Schwarzwaldbahn, which trundles hourly through the Black Forest, linking Offenburg with towns such as Triberg and Villingen. To reach Lake Constance's northern shore, you usually have to change in Radolfzell. The Schweizer Bahnhof has connections to destinations throughout Switzerland.

❶ Getting Around

The city centre is a traffic headache, especially at weekends. Your best bet is the free Park & Ride lot 3km northwest of the Altstadt, near the airfield on Byk-Gulden-Strasse, where your only outlay will be for a bus ticket.

Local buses (www.sw.konstanz.de) cost €2.10 for a single ticket; day passes are €4/6.80 for an individual/family. Bus 1 links the Meersburg car-ferry dock with the Altstadt. If you stay in Konstanz for at least two nights, your hotelier will give you a Gästekarte entitling you to free local bus travel.

Bicycles can be hired from **Kultur-Rädle** (☑273 10; Bahnhofplatz 29; per day €12; ⊙9am-12.30pm & 2.30-6pm Mon-Fri, 10am-4pm Sat year-round, plus 10am-12.30pm Sun Easter-Sep), close to the tourist office.

Mainau Island

Jutting out over the lake and bursting with flowers, the lusciously green islet of **Mainau** (www.mainau.de; adult/concession €18/10.50; ⊙dawn-dusk) is a 45-hectare Mediterranean garden dreamed up by the Bernadotte family, relatives of the royal house of Sweden.

Around two million visitors flock here every year to admire sparkly lake and mountain views from the **baroque castle**, and wander sequoia-shaded avenues and hothouses bristling with palms and orchids. Crowd-pullers include the **Butterfly House**, where hundreds of vivid butterflies flit amid the dewy foliage, an **Italian Cascade** integrating patterned flowers with waterfalls, and a **petting zoo**. Tulips and rhododendrons bloom in spring, hibiscus and roses in summer. Avoid weekends, when the gardens get crowded.

You can drive, walk or cycle to Mainau, 8km north of Konstanz. Take bus 4 from Konstanz' train station or hop aboard a passenger ferry.

Reichenau Island

☑07534 / POP 3200
In AD 724 a missionary named Pirmin founded a Benedictine monastery on **Reichenau** (www.reichenau.de), a 4.5km-by-1.5km island (Lake Constance's largest) about 11km west of Konstanz. During its heyday, from 820 to 1050, the so-called Reichenauer School produced stunning illuminated manuscripts and vivid frescoes. Today, three surviving churches provide silent testimony to Reichenau's Golden Age. Thanks to them, the island was declared a Unesco World Heritage Site in 2000.

Bring walking boots and binoculars, as this fertile isle of orchards and wineries is home to **Wollmatinger Ried** (www.nabu -wollmatingerried.de), a marshy nature reserve whose reed wetlands attract butterflies, migratory birds including kingfishers, grey herons and cuckoos, and even the odd beaver.

A 2km-long tree-lined causeway connects the mainland with the island, which is served by bus 7372 from Konstanz. The Konstanz–Schaffhausen and Konstanz–Radolfzell ferries stop off at Reichenau.

Marienschlucht

Well worth the 15km trek north of Konstanz, Marienschlucht (⊙daylight hrs) is a deep ravine wedged between the villages of Bodman and Wallhausen. A wooden staircase zigzags up through the chasm, past a babbling stream and 30m-high cliffs thick with lichen and ferns. The top rewards you with snapshot views of Lake Constance through the beech trees. Bear left to follow the trail along the ridge and back down to Wallhausen. There are picnic areas and a kiosk en route, as well as pebbly bays for refreshing dips in the lake.

Coming from Konstanz, Wallhausen is the best place to access the gorge, either by bicycle or bus 4 from the Hauptbahnhof (€2.30, 30 minutes). From Wallhausen it's a 3km walk to Marienschlucht.

Meersburg

📞07532 / POP 5630

Tumbling down vine-streaked slopes to Lake Constance and crowned by a perkily turreted medieval castle, Meersburg lives up to all those clichéd knights-in-armour, damsel-in-distress fantasies. And if its tangle of cobbled lanes and half-timbered houses filled with jovial banter doesn't sweep you off your feet, the local Pinot noir served in its cosy *Weinstuben* (wine taverns) will, we swear.

⊙ Sights & Activities

Altes Schloss   CASTLE
(adult/concession €8.50/6.50; ⊙9am-6.30pm Mar-Oct, 10am-6pm Nov-Feb) Looking across the Lake Constance from its lofty perch, the Altes Schloss is an archetypal medieval stronghold, complete with keep, drawbridge, knights' hall and dungeons. Founded by Merovingian king Dagobert I in the 7th century, the fortress is among Germany's oldest, which is no mean feat in a country with a *lot* of castles. The bishops of Konstanz used it as a summer residence between 1268 and 1803.

Neues Schloss   CASTLE
(www.schloesser-und-gaerten.de; adult/concession €5/2.50; ⊙9am-6.30pm May-Oct, 11am-4pm Sat & Sun Nov-Apr) In 1710 Prince-Bishop Johann Franz Schenk von Stauffenberg, perhaps tired of the dinginess and rising damp, swapped the Altes Schloss for the dusky-pink, lavishly baroque Neues Schloss. A visit to the now state-owned palace takes in the extravagant bishops' apartments replete with stucco work and frescoes, Bathasar Neumann's elegant staircase, and gardens with inspirational lake views.

Lakefront   HARBOUR
Stroll the harbour for classic snaps of Lake Constance or to hire a pedalo. On the jetty, you can't miss – though the pious might prefer to – Peter Lenk's satirical **Magische Säule** (Magic Column). The sculpture is a hilarious satirical depiction of characters who have shaped Meersburg's history, including buxom wine-wench Wendelgart and poet Annette von Droste-Hülshoff (the seagull).

Meersburg Therme   DAY SPA
(📞440 2850; www.meersburg-therme.de; Uferpromenade 12; thermal baths 3hr adult/concession €9/8.50, incl sauna 3hr €16.50/16; ⊙10am-10pm Mon-Thu, to 11pm Fri & Sat, 9am-10pm Sun) It's a five-minute walk east along the Uferpromenade to this lakefront spa, where the 34°C thermal waters, water jets and Swiss Alp views are soothing. Those who dare to bare all can skinny-dip in the lake and steam in saunas that are replicas of Unteruhldingen's Stone Age dwellings.

🛏 Sleeping & Eating

Meersburg goes with the seasons, with most places closing from November to Easter. Pick up a brochure listing good-value apartments and private rooms at the tourist office.

Characterful wine taverns line Unterstadtstrasse, while the lakefront Seepromenade has wall-to-wall pizzerias, cafes and gelaterias with alfresco seating.

Gasthof zum Bären   GUESTHOUSE €€
(📞432 20; www.baeren-meersburg.de; Marktplatz 11; s €49, d €98-110, mains €9-17.50) Straddling three 13th- to 17th-century buildings, this guest house near Obertor receives glowing reviews for its classic rooms, spruced up with stucco work, ornate wardrobes and lustrous wood; corner rooms No 13 and 23 are the most romantic. The rustic tavern

serves Lake Constance fare like *Felchen* (whitefish).

Romantik Residenz
am See LUXURY HOTEL €€€

(⌨800 40; www.hotel-residenz-meersburg.com; Uferpromenade 11; s €80-120, d €150-200; tasting menus €80-135; ☏) Sitting aplomb the promenade, this romantic hotel is a class act. The higher you go, the better the view in the warm-hued rooms facing the vineyards or lake. In the hotel's Michelin-starred restaurant, **Casala**, chef Markus Philippi brings sophisticated Mediterranean cuisine to the table.

Aurichs GUESTHOUSE €

(⌨445 9855; www.aurichs.com; Steigstrasse 28; s €44, d €72-76, mains €16.50-32) Choose from lake or castle views in stylish rooms with flourishes like slanted beams and wool rugs. In the art-filled restaurant, chef Christian Aurich pairs market-fresh dishes such as wild boar with chestnut purée and Lake Constance lamb with rosehip jus with Meersburg wines.

Gasthaus zum Letzten Heller GUESTHOUSE €

(⌨6149; www.zum-letzten-heller.de; Daisendorfer Strasse 41; s/d €38/58, mains €9-12.50) This family-friendly guest house keeps it sweet 'n' simple in bright, cottage-like rooms with pine trappings. The restaurant serving home-grown food and wine has a tree-shaded patio. It's 1km north of the old town.

Winzerstube zum Becher GERMAN €€€

(⌨9009; Höllgasse 4; mains €10.50-25.80; ☺closed Mon) Vines drape the facade of this wood-panelled bolt-hole, run by the same family since 1884. Home-grown Pinot noirs accompany Lake Constance classics such as whitefish in almond-butter sauce. The terrace affords Altes Schloss views.

Weinhaus Hanser GERMAN €

(⌨9128; Unterstadtstrasse 28; Flammkuchen €7-8) Exposed red-brick and barrel tables create a cosy vibe at this 500-year-old *Torkel* (wine press), where you can taste local wines and chomp pizza-like *Flammkuchen*.

Gutsschänke GERMAN €€

(⌨807 630; Seminarstrassse 6; mains €10-15; ☺daily) On a perch above the lake and vineyards, this restaurant's terrace is a beautiful spot to sip a glass of Meersburg Pinot noir or blanc or dig into hearty mains like *Zwiebelrostbraten* (beef and onions in gravy).

ⓘ Information

Tourist office (⌨440 400; www.meersburg .de; Kirchstrasse 4; ☺9am-12.30pm & 2-6pm Mon-Fri, 10am-3pm Sat, 10am-1pm Sun, shorter hours in winter) Housed in a one-time Dominican monastery. Internet access costs €3 per hour.

ⓘ Getting There & Away

Meersburg, which lacks a train station, is 18km west of Friedrichshafen.

From Monday to Friday, eight times a day, express bus 7394 makes the trip to Konstanz (€3.25, 40 minutes) and Friedrichshafen (€3.10, 26 minutes). Bus 7373 connects Meersburg with Ravensburg (€5, 40 minutes, four daily Monday to Friday, two Saturday). Meersburg's main bus stop is next to the church.

ⓘ Getting Around

The best and only way to get around Meersburg is on foot. Even the large pay car park near the car-ferry port (€1.20 per hour) is often full in high season. You might find free parking north of the old town along Daisendorfer Strasse.

Hire bikes at **Hermann Dreher** (⌨5176; Stadtgraben 5; per day €4.50; ☺rental 9am-noon), down the alley next to the tourist office.

Pfahlbauten

Awarded Unesco World Heritage status in 2011, the **Pfahlbauten** (Pile Dwellings; www .pfahlbauten.de; Strandpromenade 6, Unteruhldingen; adult/concession €7/5; ☺9am-btwn 5pm & 7pm; ♿) 6km north of Meersburg, represent one of 111 Prehistoric Pile dwellings around the Alps. Based on the findings of local excavations, the carefully reconstructed pile dwellings catapult you back to the Stone and Bronze Age, from 4000 to 850 BC. A spin of the lakefront complex takes in stilt dwellings that give an insight into the prehistoric lives of farmers, fishermen and craftsmen. Kids love the hands-on activities, from axe-making to starting fires using flints.

Birnau

The exuberant, powder-pink **Wahllfahrtskirche Birnau** (Pilgrimage Church; Uhldingen-Mühlhofen; ☺7.30am-btwn 5.30pm & 7pm) is one of Lake Constance's architectural highlights. It was built by the rococo master Peter Thumb of Vorarlberg in 1746. When you walk in, the decor is so intricate and profuse that you don't know where to look first. At some point your gaze will be drawn to the ceiling, where Gottfried Bernhard Göz worked his usual fresco magic. It's situated 9km north of Meersburg on the B31.

Affenberg Salem

No zoo-like cages, no circus antics – just happy Barbary macaques free to roam in a near-to-natural habitat is the concept behind the conservation-oriented **Affenberg Salem** (www.affenberg-salem.de; adult/child €8/5; ⊙9am-btwn 5pm & 6pm). Trails interweave the 20-hectare woodlands, where you can feed tail-less monkeys one piece of special popcorn at a time, observe their behaviour (you scratch my back, I'll scratch yours...) and get primate close-ups at hourly feedings. The park is also home to storks: listen for bill clattering and look out for their nests near the entrance. The Affenburg is on the K7765, 10km north of Meersburg.

Schloss Salem

Founded as a Cistercian monastery in 1134, the immense estate known as **Schloss Salem** (www.salem.de; adult/concession €7/3.50; ⊙9.30am-6pm Mon-Sat, 10.30am-6pm Sun Apr-Oct) was once the largest and richest of its kind in southern Germany. The Grand Duchy of Baden sold out to the state recently but you can still picture the royals swanning around the hedge maze, gardens and extravagant rococo apartments dripping with stucco. The west wing shelters an elite boarding school, briefly attended by Prince Philip (Duke of Edinburgh and husband of Queen Elizabeth II). Schloss Salem sits 12km north of Meersburg.

Friedrichshafen

📞07541 / POP 59,000

Zeppelins, the cigar-shaped airships that first took flight in 1900 under the stewardship of high-flying Count Ferdinand von Zeppelin, will forever be associated with Friedrichshafen. An amble along the flowery lakefront promenade and a visit to the museum that celebrates the behemoth of the skies are the biggest draws of this industrial town, which was heavily bombed in WWII and rebuilt in the 1950s.

⊙ Sights & Activities

TOP CHOICE **Zeppelin Museum** MUSEUM
(www.zeppelin-museum.de; Seestrasse 22; adult/concession €7.50/4; ⊙9am-5pm daily May-Oct, 10am-5pm Tue-Sun Nov-Apr) Near the eastern end of Friedrichshafen's lakefront promenade, Seestrasse, is the Zeppelin Museum, housed in the Bauhaus-style former Hafenbahnhof, built in 1932.

The centrepiece is a full-scale mock-up of a 33m section of the *Hindenburg* (LZ 129), the largest airship ever built, measuring an incredible 245m long and outfitted as luxuriously as an ocean liner. The hydrogen-filled craft tragically burst into flames, killing 36, while landing in New Jersey in 1937.

Other exhibits provide technical and historical insights, including an original motor gondola from the famous *Graf Zeppelin*, which made 590 trips and travelled around the world in 21 days in 1929.

The top-floor art collection stars brutally realistic works by Otto Dix.

Lakefront PROMENADE
A promenade runs through the lakefront, sculpture-dotted **Stadtgarten** park along Uferstrasse, a great spot for a picnic or stroll. Pedal and electric boats can be rented at the Gondelhafen (€9 to €23 per hour).

The western end of Friedrichshafen's promenade is anchored by the twin-onion-towered, baroque **Schlosskirche**. It's the only accessible part of the Schloss and is still inhabited by the ducal family of Württemberg.

DON'T MISS

COME FLY WITH ME

Real airship fans will justify the splurge on a trip in a high-tech, 12-passenger **Zeppelin NT** (📞590 00; www.zeppelinflug.de). Flights lasting 30/45/60/90/120 minutes cost €200/295/395/565/745. Shorter trips cover lake destinations such as Schloss Salem and Lindau, while longer ones drift across to Austria or Switzerland. Take-off and landing are in Friedrichshafen. The flights aren't cheap but little beats floating over Lake Constance with the Alps on the horizon, so slowly that you can make the most of legendary photo ops.

🍴 Sleeping & Eating

The tourist office has a free booking terminal. For lake-view snacks, hit Seestrasse's beer gardens, pizzerias and ice-cream parlours.

Hotel Restaurant Maier   HOTEL €€
(📞4040; www.hotel-maier.de; Poststrasse 1-3, Friedrichshafen-Fischbach; s €59-95, d €89-120; P🅿🛜) The contemporary, light-drenched rooms are immaculately kept at this family-run hotel, 5km west of Friedrichshafen and an eight-minute hop on the train. The mini spa invites relaxing moments, with its lake-facing terrace, steam room and sauna.

Gasthof Rebstock   GUESTHOUSE €
(📞950 1640; www.gasthof-rebstock-fn.de; Werastrasse 35; s/d/tr/q €55/75/90/100; 🛜) Geared up for cyclists and offering bike rental (€7 per day), this family-run hotel has a beer garden and humble but tidy rooms with pine furnishings. It's situated 750m northwest of the Stadtbahnhof.

Brot, Kaffee, Wein   CAFE €
(Karlstrasse 38; snacks €3-8; ⊙8.30am-8pm Mon-Fri, 9am-8pm Sat, 9.30am-8pm Sun) Slick and monochrome, this deli-cafe has a lakeside terrace for lingering over a speciality coffee, breakfast, homemade ice cream or sourdough bread sandwich.

Beach Club   LOUNGE BAR €
(Uferstrasse 1; snacks €6-8; ⊙11am-midnight Apr-Oct) This lakefront shack is the place to unwind on the deck, mai tai in hand, and admire the *Klangschiff* sculpture and the not-so-distant Alps. Revive over tapas, salads and antipasti.

ℹ Information

Post office (Bahnhofplatz) To the right as you exit the Stadtbahnhof.
Tourist office (📞300 10; www.friedrichshafen.info; Bahnhofplatz 2; ⊙9am-1pm & 1-6pm Mon-Fri, 9am-1pm Sat) On the square outside the Stadtbahnhof. Has a free internet terminal. Can book accommodation and zeppelin flights.

ℹ Getting There & Around

There are ferry options, including a catamaran to Konstanz. Sailing times are posted on the waterfront just outside the Zeppelin Museum.

From Monday to Friday, seven times a day, express bus 7394 makes the trip to Konstanz (1¼ hours) via Meersburg (30 minutes). Birnau and Meersburg are also served almost hourly by bus 7395.

Friedrichshafen is on the Bodensee–Gürtelbahn train line, which runs along the lake's northern shore from Radolfzell to Lindau. There are also regular services on the Bodensee–Oberschwaben–Bahn, which runs to Ravensburg (€3.95, 20 minutes).

Ravensburg

📞0751 / POP 49,780
Ravensburg has puzzled the world for the past 125 years with its jigsaws and board games. The medieval Altstadt has toy-town appeal, studded with turrets, robber-knight towers and gabled patrician houses. For centuries dukes and wealthy merchants polished the cobbles of this Free Imperial City – now it's your turn.

◉ Sights

Marienplatz   SQUARE
The heart of Altstadt is the elongated, pedestrianised Marienplatz, framed by sturdy towers, frescoed patrician houses and cafes.

The 51m-high **Blaserturm** (adult/concession €1.50/1; ⊙2-5pm Mon-Fri, 10am-3pm Sat Apr-early Nov), part of the original fortifications, has superb views over the Altstadt from up top. Next door is the late-Gothic, step-gabled **Waaghaus**, while on the opposite side of Marienplatz sits the 15th-century **Lederhaus**, with its elaborate Renaissance facade, once the domain of tanners and shoemakers.

At the northern end of Marienplatz is the round **Grüner Turm**, with its lustrous tiled roof, and the weighty, late-Gothic church **Liebfrauenkirche**.

Ravensburger Spieleland   THEME PARK
(www.spieleland.de; Mecklenbeuren; adult/concession €25.50/23.50; ⊙10am-6pm Apr-Oct) Kids in tow? Take them to this board-game-inspired theme park, with attractions from giant-rubber-duck racing and cow milking against the clock to rodeo and Alpine rafting. It is a 10-minute drive south of Ravensburg on the B467.

Museum Humpis   MUSEUM
(www.museum-humpis-quartier.de; Marktstrasse 45; adult/concession €4/2; ⊙11am-6pm Tue-Sun, to 8pm Thu) Seven exceptional late-medieval houses set around a glass-covered courtyard shelter a permanent collection and rotating exhibitions focusing on Ravensburg's past as a trade centre.

Mehlsack   TOWER
The all-white Mehlsack (Flour Sack) is a tower marking the Altstadt's southern edge. From there a steep staircase leads up to the **Veitsburg**, a quaint baroque castle, which

now harbours the restaurant of the same name, with outlooks over Ravensburg's mosaic of red-tiled roofs.

🛏 Sleeping & Eating

Waldhorn   HISTORIC HOTEL €€
(☑361 20; http://waldhorn.de; Marienplatz 15; s €75-125, d €135-150, mains €12-25; 🛜) The Waldhorn creaks with history and its light, appealingly restored rooms make a great base for exploring the Altstadt. Lodged in the 15th-century vintners' guildhall, its wood-beamed restaurant, **Rebleutehaus**, turns out spot-on seasonal dishes like tender corn-fed chicken with herb gnocchi. The three-course lunch is a bargain at €19.80.

Gasthof Obertor   GUESTHOUSE €€
(☑366 70; www.hotelobertor.de; Marktstrasse 67; s €72-90, d €112-125; 🅿🛜) The affable Rimpps take pride in their lemon-fronted patrician house. Obertor stands head and shoulders above most Altstadt guesthouses, with spotless rooms, a sauna area and generous breakfasts.

Veitsburg   INTERNATIONAL €€€
(☑366 1990; www.restaurant-veitsburg.de; Veitsburg 2; mains €11-18; ⊙11am-midnight, closed Wed Oct-Mar; 🖉🚍) Welf and Hohenstaufen dukes once lorded it over this castle, now a highly atmospheric restaurant. Gaze across Ravensburg to the hills beyond while tucking into dishes like Bavarian pork roast in dark beer sauce and tagliatelle in wild mushroom sauce.

❶ Information

Tourist office (☑828 00; www.ravensburg.de; Kirchstrasse 16; ⊙9am-5.30pm Mon-Fri, 10am-1pm Sat) A block northeast of Marienplatz.

❶ Getting There & Away

The train station is six blocks to the west along Eisenbahnstrasse. Ravensburg is on the train line linking Friedrichshafen (€3.95, 16 minutes, at least twice hourly) with Ulm (€16.40, 57 minutes, at least hourly) and Stuttgart (€38, two hours, at least hourly).

Lindau

☑08382 / POP 24,800

Brochures rhapsodise about Lindau being Germany's 'Garden of Eden' and the 'Bavarian Riviera'. Paradise and southern France it ain't but it is, well, pretty special. Cradled in the southern crook of Lake Constance and almost dipping its toes into Austria, this is

a good-looking, outgoing little town, with a candy-coloured postcard of an Altstadt, clear-day Alpine views and lakefront cafes that use every sunray to the max.

◉ Sights

Seepromenade   PROMENADE
In summer the harbourside promenade has a happy-go-lucky air, with its palms, bobbing boats and folk sunning themselves in pavement cafes.

Out at the harbour gates, looking across to the Alps, is Lindau's signature 33m-high **Neuer Leuchtturm** (New Lighthouse) and, just in case you forget which state you're in, a statue of the Bavarian lion. The square tile-roofed, 13th-century **Mangturm** (Old Lighthouse) guards the northern edge of the sheltered port.

Altes Rathaus   LANDMARK
(Old Town Hall; Bismarckplatz) Lindau's biggest architectural stunner is the 15th-century step-gabled Altes Rathaus, a frescoed frenzy of cherubs, merry minstrels and galleons.

Stadtmuseum   MUSEUM
(Marktplatz 6; adult/concession €3/1.50; ⊙11am-5pm Tue-Fri & Sun, 2-5pm Sat) Lions and voluptuous dames dance across the trompe l'oeil facade of the flamboyantly baroque Haus zum Cavazzen, which contains this museum, showcasing a fine collection of furniture, weapons and paintings.

Peterskirche   CHURCH
(Schrannenplatz; ⊙daily) Looking back on a 1000-year history, this enigmatic church is now a war memorial, hiding exquisite time-faded frescoes of the Passion of Christ by Hans Holbein the Elder. The cool, dimly lit interior is a quiet spot for contemplation. Next door is the turreted 14th-century **Diebsturm**, once a tiny jail.

🛏 Sleeping

Lindau virtually goes into hibernation from November to February, when many hotels close. Nip into the tourist office for a list of good-value holiday apartments.

Hotel Garni-Brugger   HISTORIC HOTEL €€
(☑934 10; www.hotel-garni-brugger.de; Bei der Heidenmauer 11; s €56-78, d €92-106; @) Our readers rave about this 18th-century hotel, with bright rooms done up in floral fabrics and pine. The family bends over backwards to please. Guests can unwind in the little spa with steam room and sauna (€10) in the cooler months.

Reutemann & Seegarten
LUXURY HOTEL €€€

(☑9150; www.reutemann-lindau.de; Seepromenade; s €87-240, d €138-342; ☎☀) Wow, what a view! Facing the harbour, lighthouse and lion statue, this hotel has plush, spacious rooms done out in sunny shades, as well as a pool big enough to swim laps, a spa, gym and refined restaurant.

Hotel Anker
GUESTHOUSE €

(☑260 9844; www.anker-lindau.de; Bindergasse 15; s/d €55/78; ☎) Shiny parquet floors, citrus colours and artwork have spruced up the bargain rooms at this peach-coloured guesthouse. Rates include a hearty breakfast.

Alte Post
HOTEL €€

(☑934 60; www.alte-post-lindau.de; Fischergasse 3; s €60-75, d €120-150, mains €8-15) Sitting on cobbled Fischergasse, this 300-year-old coaching inn was once a stop on the Frankfurt–Milan mail run. Well-kept, light and spacious, the rooms have chunky pine furnishings and perks like free tea. Downstairs is a beer garden and a dark-wood tavern pairing dishes like *Tafelspitz* (boiled beef) and *Maultaschen* with fruity local wines.

Hotel Medusa
GUESTHOUSE €€

(☑932 20; www.medusa-hotel.com; Schafgasse 10; s €49-69, d €98-138) The Greek mythology link is tenuous, but this guesthouse pleases with lovingly renovated, high-ceilinged rooms, jazzed up with bursts of red or aquamarine and flat-screen TVs.

✗ Eating & Drinking

For a drink with a cool view, head to Seepromenade. The crowds on the main thoroughfare, Maximilianstrasse, can be dodged in nearby backstreets, where your euro will stretch further.

Valentin
MEDITERRANEAN €€€

(☑504 3740; In der Grub 28; mains €8-23.50; ☉Tue-Sat) Markus Allgaier carefully sources the local ingredients that go into his Med-style dishes at this sleek vaulted restaurant. Signatures like leg of lamb with parmesan beans and pistachio-plum risotto and grilled scallops on balsamic-beluga lentils are beautifully cooked and presented.

37°
CAFE €€

(Bahnhofplatz 1; snacks €4-11; ☉10am-8pm Tue-Wed & Sun, to 11pm Thu-Sat) Part boutique, part boho-chic cafe, 37° combines a high-ceilinged interior with a lake-facing pavement terrace. Pull up a chair for cold drinks and light bites like tapas, quiche and soups.

Weinstube Frey
GERMAN €€€

(☑947 9676; Maximilianstrasse 15; mains €13-22; ☉closed Mon) This 500-year-old wine tavern oozes Bavarian charm in its wood-panelled tavern full of cosy nooks. Dirndl-clad waitresses serve up regional wines and fare such as beer-battered Lake Constance trout. Sit on the terrace when the sun's out.

Marmor Saal
BAR

(Bahnhofplatz 1e; ☉9am-2am or 3am) The lakefront 'marble hall' once welcomed royalty and still has a feel of grandeur with its soaring columns, chandeliers and Biedermeier flourishes. Nowadays it's a relaxed cafe-bar with occasional live music and a chilled terrace.

❶ Information

Post office (cnr Maximilianstrasse & Bahnhofplatz)

Tourist office (☑260 030; www.lindau.de; Alfred-Nobel-Platz 1; ☉10am-6pm Mon-Sat, to 1pm Sun, shorter hours in low season) Can make hotel bookings.

❶ Getting There & Away

Lindau is on the B31 and connects to Munich by the A96. The precipitous **Deutsche Alpenstrasse** (German Alpine Rd), which winds giddily eastward to Berchtesgaden, begins here.

Lindau is at the eastern terminus of the train line, which goes along the lake's north shore via Friedrichshafen (€5.50, 20 minutes) westward to Radolfzell and the southern terminus of the Südbahn to Ulm (€23.50, 1¾ hours) via Ravensburg (€9.10, 44 minutes).

❶ Getting Around

The compact, walkable Insel (island), home to the town centre and harbour, is connected to the mainland by the Seebrücke, a road bridge at its northeastern tip, and by the Eisenbahndamm, a rail bridge open to cyclists and pedestrians. The Hauptbahnhof lies to the east of the island, a block south of the pedestrianised, shop-lined Maximilianstrasse.

Buses 1 and 2 link the Hauptbahnhof to the main bus hub, known as ZUP. A single ticket costs €2, a 24-hour pass is €5.20.

To get to the island by car follow the signs to 'Lindau-Insel'. It's easiest and cheapest to park at the large metered car park (€0.60 per hour) just before you cross the bridge to the island.

Bikes and tandems can be rented at **Unger's Fahrradverleih** (Inselgraben 14; per day €6-12; ☉9am-1pm & 3-6pm Mon-Fri, 9am-1pm Sat & Sun).

Understand
Munich, Bavaria &
the Black Forest

population per sq km

BADEN-WURRTEMBERG   BAVARIA   GERMANY

≈ 180 people

Munich, Bavaria & the Black Forest Today

It's the Economy, Stupid!

Even the most militant anti-capitalist might shut down Facebook and blow out the Molotov, just for a moment, to agree that Bavaria is a rampant success story of post-war free enterprise. Just one stat says it all – if Bavaria was an independent country (and not a small number of locals secretly wish it were), its economy would be the world's 19th largest (equally affluent Baden-Württemberg would rank around 22nd), bigger than Sweden or Austria and more than twice the size of neighbouring Czech Republic. Germany's economic California is cooking with gas, and probably on an eco-friendly stove of sturdy design, proudly stamped with *'Hergestellt in Bayern'* (Made in Bavaria). Even as it looked as though Germany's economy was losing momentum in late 2012, Bavaria and the rest of southern Germany still seemed like a pretty good investment.

So what underpins the south's economic triumph? Good 'ole manufacturing seems to be the 'secret', with a motor industry second to none leading the way. The most desirable names of the Teutonic luxury car world – BMW, Audi, Porsche and Mercedes – are all based in the south, pumping billions of euros into the economy and employing hundreds of thousands. Other local corporate behemoths include Siemens, Allianz, Grundig and Adidas.

Tourism also generates a solid chunk of the south's wealth. In 2010 Munich alone saw well over five million foreign guests crumple hotel bed sheets, and blockbuster sights such as Schloss Neuschwanstein and Regensburg's Unesco-listed city centre attract millions. Visitor numbers continue to swell with arrivals from the so-called BRIC countries responsible for a good share of the increases.

Fast Facts: Munich & Bavaria

» Area: 70,549 sq km

» Population: 12.6 million

» GDP: €446 billion

» Per capita income: €2650 per month (blue-collar), €3600 per month (white-collar)

» Unemployment rate: 3.8%

» Annual per capita beer consumption: 170L

» Kilometres of autobahn: 2506

» Museums: 1150

Top Books

Massacre in Munich: Manhunt for the Killers Behind the 1972 Olympics Massacre (Michael Bar Bar-Zohar and Eitan Haber, 2005) The title says it all really.
Lola Montez: A Life (Bruce Seymour, 1998) A superbly written account of the life of Bavaria's

most outrageous courtesan who brought down a king.
Ludwig II of Bavaria (Martha Schad, 2001) One of the most readable and compact biographies of Bavaria's most flamboyant monarch and available throughout the state.

Dos & Don'ts

» In pubs and beer halls never sit at the *Stammtisch* (usually clearly marked) as this is permanently reserved for regular local drinkers.

» Do emit a cheery *'Gruss Gott'* or *'Guten Morgen'* when entering

belief systems
(% of population)

54.4 Catholic

4 Muslim

21.2 Other

20.4 Evangelical

if Southern Germany were 100 people

92 would be German
3 would be Turkish
2 would be from the former Yugoslavia
1 would be Italian
2 would be other

Green Giant

With local plants boxing up everything from R8s to locos, you'd expect a toxic murk to envelope you at the airplane door. But it doesn't. In fact by 2025 Munich is set to become the world's first major city powered solely using renewable energy sources, and in the countryside some small towns look very different from one direction than from the other as south-facing roofs bear the weight of millions of solar panels (you see this odd phenomenon best from trains). Farmers have turned over considerable acreage to accommodate vast swathes of buzzing solar panels, wind turbines are a common sight and biking has been in fashion for decades. Germany is even planning to switch off its nuclear power stations by 2020, unless Berlin's politicians devise a crafty U-turn.

Fast Facts: Baden-Württemberg

» Area: 35,751 sq km
» Population: 10.73 million
» GDP: €376 billion
» Unemployment rate: 5.5%

Traditional Success Story

It must feel good to be a German from the south – a high-octane economy, sun and wind powering your latest gadgetry, the cultural and historic delights of Germany's secret capital (Munich) and an Alpine playground a swift train ride away; your country top of the Continent's (shaky) europile and even a Bavarian pope in the Vatican. So why all the glum faces on the S-Bahn you may wonder; what do these people have to be grumpy about? As throughout the Western world, even flourishing southern Germany is not immune to an underlying angst about the future. But the difference here may be that on the evenings and weekends, locals retreat to the unglobalised world of thigh-slapping tradition – the beer hall, the Alpine tavern, a Baroque theatre or a folk bash – to celebrate their astounding successes, whatever the future may bring.

Bavaria has its own obscure internet suffix – .by – but you'll rarely see it used. Most businesses prefer the German .de or the more international -looking .com.

small shops, offices, trains and hotel receptions.
» Don't ask for tap water in restaurants – central Europeans simply don't drink the stuff.
» Don't leave food on your plate if you can help it – it's seen as an insult to the eatery/chef/host.

Top Films

Sophie Scholl – The Final Days (Marc Rothmund, 2005) Extremely moving account of the capture, trial and execution of members of the White Rose anti-Nazi group.
Ludwig (Luchino Visconti, 1973) The reign of Ludwig II.

Hierankl (Hans Steinbichler, 2003) Family drama set against the backdrop of the Alps.
The Nasty Girl (Michael Verhoeven, 1990) A woman digging up her town's Nazi past gets more than she bargains for.

History

One of Europe's oldest states, with origins dating back to the 6th century, it's safe to say that Bavaria, Germany's largest and southernmost *Land*, has enjoyed a long and eventful past, one populated by a weird-and-*wunderbar* cast of oddball kings, scandalous courtesans and infamous Nazis.

However, the Bavaria of today is a relatively new territorial entity, its three distinct tribes – the Bajuwaren (Bavarians), the Franken (Franconians) and the Schwaben (Swabians) – each having developed quite separately until thrown in together by Napoleon as the Kingdom of Bavaria in 1806. Munich was founded in 1158 by Duke Heinrich der Löwe (Henry the Lion), granted town rights in 1175 and declared capital of Bavaria in 1506. Although never really at the centre of European power, Bavaria was a key player in continental politics for centuries. Governed by the same family, the colourful Wittelsbachs, for over 700 years, it was able to form a distinct culture that continues to shape its image and identity to this day. The most famous member of the House of Wittelsbach was King Ludwig II, who frittered away the family silver on blockbuster castles, thus creating Bavaria's modern tourist industry.

Of course Bavaria of the 20th century is synonymous with the rise of Hitler and the Nazis who found fertile ground for their ideas in the working class neighbourhoods of Munich and Nuremberg. The area is littered with reminders of those stormy decades when mass rallies were held in Nuremberg, and Dachau became the Nazis' first concentration camp.

After WWII Bavaria firmly established itself as Germany's economic engine, with high-tech industries and car production in particular making this region one of Europe's most prosperous. In more recent times Bavaria has given the world an Olympic games, which ended in tragedy, and a controversial pope, as well as playing a memorable part in the 2006 FIFA World Cup soccer championships.

TIMELINE	15 BC	AD 555–788	7th–8th centuries
	Nero Claudius Drusus and Tiberius Claudius Nero, stepsons of Roman emperor Augustus, conquer the Celtic tribes north of the Alps, calling their new colony Raetia. Augusta Vindelicorum (today's Augsburg) is capital.	The Agilofinges dynasty founds the first Bavarian duchy with Garibald I (r 555–91) its first-known duke. They remain in power until absorbed into the Frankish Empire in 788 by Charlemagne.	Christianity takes hold as roving missionaries arrive in Bavaria from Ireland, Scotland and the Frankish Empire. In 738 St Boniface creates the dioceses of Salzburg, Freising, Passau and Regensburg.

Tribal Melting Pot

The first recorded inhabitants of Bavaria were the Celts, who proved to be a pushover for the Romans who began swarming across the Alps in the 1st century AD. The invaders founded the province of Raetia with Augusta Vindelicorum (Augsburg) as its capital. By the 5th century the tables were turned on the Romans by marauding eastern Germanic tribes pushing up the Danube Valley in search of pastures new.

As with all central Europe's peoples, the precise origin of the Bavarian tribe is obscure, but it's widely assumed that it coalesced from the remaining Romans, Romanised Celts and the newcomers from the east. The name 'Bajuwaren' may be derived from 'men from Bohemia', the neighbouring region of today's Czech Republic.

The Franken began forming in the 3rd century AD from several western Germanic tribes who settled along the central and lower Rhine, on the border with the Roman Empire. The Schwaben, meanwhile, are a subtribe of the population group of the Alemannen (Alemannic tribes) who spread across the southwestern corner of Germany around the 2nd century AD. In the 3rd century they took on the Romans, eventually pushing as far east as the Lech River.

For a comprehensive overview of Bavarian history (partly in English) see the website of the government-financed Haus der Bayerischen Geschichte at www.hdbg.de.

Church Dominance

Religion, especially of the Roman Catholic variety, has shaped all aspects of Bavarian history and culture for nearly two millennia. Following the decline of the Roman Empire, missionaries from Ireland and Scotland swarmed across Europe to spread the gospel. They found open arms and minds among the Agilofinges, the dynasty who had founded the first Bavarian duchy in the 6th century. They adopted the faith eagerly and Christianity quickly took root. By 739 there were bishoprics in Regensburg, Passau, Freising and Salzburg, and monasteries had been founded in Tegernsee, Benediktbeuern, Weltenburg and several other locations.

For almost the next 800 years, the Church dominated daily life as the only major religion in the land. Until 1517, that is. That's when a monk and theology professor named Martin Luther sparked the Reformation with his 95 theses critiquing papal infallibility, clerical celibacy, selling indulgences and other elements of Catholic doctrine.

Despite the Church's attempt to quash Luther, his teachings resonated widely, especially in Franconia and Swabia, though not in Bavaria proper where local rulers instantly clamped down on anyone toying with conversion. They also encouraged the newly founded Jesuit order to make Ingolstadt the hub of the Counter-Reformation. The religious strife eventually escalated into the Thirty Years' War (1618–48), which left Europe's soil drenched with the blood of millions. During the conflict, Bavaria's

On Bavaria's coat of arms, 'Old Bavaria' is represented by a blue panther, the Franconians by a red-and-white rake, the Swabians by three black lions, and the Upper Palatinate (no longer part of today's Bavaria) by a golden lion.

962	1158	1180	1214
The pope crowns the Saxon King Otto I to *Kaiser* (emperor), marking the beginning of the Holy Roman Empire, which remains a major force in European history until 1806.	Duke Heinrich der Löwe establishes Munich as a market town in a bid to take control of the lucrative central European trade in salt, known then as 'white gold'.	The Wittelsbachs' 738-year reign begins with Otto von Wittelsbach's appointment as duke of Bavaria by Emperor Friedrich Barbarossa, marking the transition from tribal duchy to territorial state.	Emperor Friedrich II grants the fiefdom of the Palatinate along the Rhine River to Duke Otto II von Wittelsbach, thereby significantly enlarging the family's territory and increasing its power.

Top Five Wittelsbach Residences:

» Schloss Neuschwanstein

» Munich Residenz

» Schloss Herrenchiemsee

» Schloss Nymphenburg

» Schloss Linderhof

Duke Maximilian I (r 1598–1651) fought firmly on the side of Catholic emperor Ferdinand II of Habsburg, who thanked him by expanding Max's territory and promoting him to *Kurfürst* (prince-elector). With calm restored in 1648 following the signing of the Peace of Westphalia, Bavaria – along with much of the rest of central Europe – lay in ruins.

The treaty permitted each local ruler to determine the religion of his territory and essentially put the Catholic and Lutheran churches on equal legal footing. Bavaria, of course, remained staunchly Catholic. In fact, if the baroque church-building boom of the 17th century is any indication, it seemed to positively revel in its religious zeal.

But beyond Bavaria times were a-changing. The Enlightenment spawned reforms throughout Europe, first leading to the French Revolution, then the Napoleonic Wars and ultimately to the demise of the Holy Roman Empire. The ancient Church structure collapsed along with it, prompting the secularisation of Bavarian monasteries after 1803 and, finally, religious parity. Although Ludwig I restored the monasteries, Protestants have since enjoyed equal rights throughout Bavaria, even though it remains predominantly Catholic to this day.

Much to the delight and pride of the population, Bavarian-born Joseph Cardinal Ratzinger was elected Pope Benedict XVI in 2005. The last German pope was Adrian VI who ruled from 1522 to 1523.

Keep it in the Family – the Wittelsbachs

From 1180 to 1918, a single family held Bavaria in its grip, the House of Wittelsbach. Otto von Wittelsbach was a distant relative of Emperor Friedrich Barbarossa who, in 1180, appointed him duke of Bavaria, which at that time was a fairly small and insignificant territory. Ensuing generations of Wittelsbachs focused on expanding their land – and with it their sphere of influence – through wheeling and dealing, marriage, inheritance and war.

The most prominent Wittelsbach descendant is Prince Luitpold of Bavaria who runs his own brewery, the Schlossbrauerei Kaltenberg, and hosts a popular jousting tournament, the Kaltenberger Ritterturnier. Learn more at www .kaltenberg.com.

Being granted the fiefdom of the Palatinate, an area along the Rhine River northwest of present-day boundaries, was a good start back in 1214, but the family's fortunes peaked when one of their own, Ludwig the Bavarian, became Holy Roman Emperor in 1328. As the first Wittelsbach on the imperial throne, Ludwig used his powerful position to bring various far-flung territories, including the March of Brandenburg (around Berlin), the Tyrol (part of today's Austria) and several Dutch provinces, under Bavarian control.

The Thirty Years' War brought widespread devastation but, by aligning themselves with Catholic emperor Ferdinand II, the Wittelsbachs managed not only to further expand their territory but to score a promotion from duchy to *Kurfürstentum* (electorate), giving them a say in the election of future emperors.

1506	1516	1517	1555
To further prevent Bavaria from being split into ever-smaller territories, Duke Albrecht the Wise introduces the law of primogeniture. Possessions now pass automatically to first-born sons.	On 23 April the *Reinheitsgebot* (Purity Law) is passed in Ingolstadt, which limits the ingredients used in the production of beer to water, barley and hops.	Martin Luther splits the Christian church by kicking off the Reformation with his 95 theses posted on the door of the cathedral in the eastern German town of Wittenberg.	Emperor Karl V signs the Peace of Augsburg allowing each local ruler to decide which religion to adopt in their principality, ending decades of religious strife and officially recognising Lutherism.

Not all alliances paid off so handsomely. In the 1680s Maximilian II Emanuel (r 1679–1726) – a man of great ambition but poor judgement – battled the Turks alongside the Habsburg Kaiser in an attempt to topple the Ottoman Empire. Much to his dismay, his allegiance did not lead to the rewards he had expected. So he tried again, this time switching sides and fighting with France against Austria in the War of the Spanish Succession (1701–14). The conflict ended in a disastrous Franco-Bavarian loss and a 10-year occupation of Bavaria by Habsburg troops. Not only had Max Emanuel failed to achieve his personal goals, his flip-flop policies had also seriously weakened Bavaria's political strength.

Max Emanuel's son, Karl Albrecht (r 1726–45), was determined to avenge his father's double humiliation. Through some fancy political manoeuvring, he managed to take advantage of the confusion caused by the War of Succession and, with the backing of Prussia and France, ended up on the imperial throne as Karl VII in 1742. His triumph, however, was

> Germany's first ever postage stamp was issued in Bavaria in November 1849 and was called the *Schwarze Einser* (Black Penny). Not as rare as Britain's Penny Black, a used copy only fetches around €1300 when auctioned.

WE ARE POPE!

'*Habemus papam*.' It was a balmy spring evening in Rome when the world – Catholics and non-Catholics – held its collective breath. Who would follow in the footsteps of the charismatic Pope John Paul II who had led the church for 27 years? The man was Cardinal Joseph Ratzinger, henceforth known as Benedict XVI and born on 16 April 1927 in Bavaria's Marktl am Inn. For the first time in nearly 500 years a German had been elected pope. The following day the headline of the tabloid German daily *Bild* screamed proudly: '*Wir sind Papst!*' (*We are Pope!*).

Ratzinger's election met with a mix of elation and disappointment. Those who had hoped for a more progressive and liberal church leader were stunned to find that the job had gone to this fierce and uncompromising cardinal who for 24 years had been John Paul II's enforcer of church doctrine. He was known to be opposed to abortion, homosexuality and contraception, and ruthless in his crackdowns on dissident priests. 'Panzer cardinal' and 'God's Rottweiler' were just two of his nicknames.

Yet, even his staunchest critics could not deny that Ratzinger was well prepared for the papal post. A distinguished theologian, he speaks seven languages and has written more than 50 books. He looks back on a long career as a university professor, archbishop of Freising and Munich, and 24 years as John Paul II's main man.

As Pope Benedict XVI, he has declared that stemming the tide of secularisation, especially in Europe, and a return to Christian values, is his major priority. He considers interfaith dialogue another important mission but has at times been clumsy in going about accomplishing it. In his first seven years 'in office' he has managed to peeve Muslims, the State of Israel, Jews, South America's indigenous population and China (for meeting the Dalai Lama) but remains popular among more conservative Catholic bishops.

1618–48	1806	1810
The Thirty Years' War involves most European nations, but is fought mainly on German soil, bringing murder, starvation and disease, and decimating Europe's population from 21 million to 13.5 million.	Bavaria becomes a kingdom and nearly doubles its size when handed Franconia and Swabia. Sweeping reforms result in the passage of the state's first constitution in 1808.	Ludwig I marries Princess Therese von Sachsen-Hildburghausen with a horse race and lavish festivities that mark the beginning of the tradition of the annual Munich Oktoberfest.

KRZYSZTOF DYDYNSKI/GETTY IMAGES©

» Statue of King Ludwig I

short-lived as Bavaria was quickly reoccupied by Austrian troops. Upon Karl Albrecht's death in 1745, his son Maximilian III Joseph (r 1745–77) was forced to renounce the Wittelsbachs' claims to the imperial crown forever.

The Accidental Kingdom

Bruce Seymour's *Lola Montez: A Life* is a highly entertaining and comprehensive romp through the life of Bavaria's ultimate courtesan, whose affair with Ludwig I changed the course of history.

Modern Bavaria, more or less as we know it today, was established in the early 19th century by Napoleon. At the onset of the Napoleonic Wars (1799–1815), Bavaria initially found itself on the losing side against France. Tired of war and spurred on by his powerful minister Maximilian Graf von Montgelas, Maximilian IV Joseph (r 1799–1825) decided to put his territory under Napoleon's protection.

In 1803, after victories over Austria and Prussia, Napoleon set about remapping much of Europe. Bavaria fared rather well, nearly doubling its size when it received control over Franconia and Swabia. In 1806 Napoleon created the kingdom of Bavaria and made Maximilian I his new best buddy.

Alas, keeping allegiances had never been Bavaria's strong suit and, in 1813, with Napoleon's fortunes waning, Montgelas shrewdly threw the new kingdom's support behind Austria and Prussia. After France's defeat, the victorious allies again reshaped European boundaries at the Congress of Vienna (1814–15) and Bavaria got to keep most of the territory it had obtained with Napoleon's help.

Reluctant Reformers

At economic odds today, Bavaria and Greece once shared a ruler when Otto I of Bavaria became modern Greece's first monarch in 1832. The biggest headache of his reign – Greece's ailing economy.

During the 18th century, the ideas of the Enlightenment that had swept through other parts of Europe had largely been ignored in Bavaria. Until Elector Maximilian III Joseph (r 1745–77) arrived on the scene, that is. Tired of waging war like his predecessors, he made peace with Austria and busied himself with reforming his country from within. He updated the legal system, founded the Bavarian Academy of Sciences and made school attendance compulsory. Max Joseph's reign also saw the creation of the Nymphenburg porcelain factory and the construction of the Cuvilliés-Theater at the Munich Residenz.

Now that the reforms had begun, there was no going back, especially after Bavaria became a kingdom in 1806. The architect of modern Bavaria was King Maximilian I's minister, Maximilian Graf von Montgelas. He worked feverishly to forge a united state from the mosaic of 'old Bavaria', Franconia and Swabia, by introducing sweeping political, administrative and social changes, including the secularisation of the monasteries. The reforms ultimately led to Bavaria's first constitution in 1808, which was based on rights of freedom, equality and property ownership, and the

1835	1848	1865	1869
Drawn by a steam locomotive called *Adler* (Eagle), Germany's first railway commences operations between Nuremberg and nearby Fürth, transporting newspapers, beer and people. It ploughs on until 1922.	A man with a weakness for the arts and beautiful women, King Ludwig I is forced to resign after his affair with Lola Montez causes a public scandal.	Wagner's opera *Tristan and Isolde* was premiered at Munich's Nationaltheater on 10 June during the composer's 18 months in the city under the patronage of Ludwig II.	Building work on Neuschwanstein castle is begun by architect Eduard Riedel. Due to lack of funds work was halted in 1892 and Ludwig II's fairytale pile was never completed.

promise of representative government. Ten years later Bavaria got its first *Landtag* (two-chamber parliament).

Under Max I's son, Ludwig I (r 1825–48), Bavaria flourished into an artistic and cultural centre, an 'Athens on the Isar'. Painters, poets and philosophers gathered in Munich, where Leo von Klenze and Friedrich von Gärtner were creating a showcase of neoclassical architecture. Königsplatz with the Glyptothek and Propyläen, flashy Ludwigstrasse with the Siegestor triumphal arch, and the Ludwig Maximilian University were all

MILESTONES IN BLACK FOREST HISTORY

In the beginning the Black Forest was just that: a huge, dark, dense clump of trees so impenetrable that even the Romans didn't dare colonise it, although they couldn't resist taking advantage of the thermal mineral springs in Baden-Baden on the forest's edge. Around the 7th century, a band of intrepid monks took a stab at taming the area, but it would be another few centuries until the ruling Zähringer clan founded Freiburg in 1120. In order to solidify their claim on the land, they moved farmers into the valleys to clear the trees and create small settlements. This led to the discovery of natural resources and, up until the 15th century, the extraction of iron, zinc, lead and even silver were major industries.

While their feudal lords enjoyed the spoils of their subjects' labour, the lot of the miners and farmers steadily deteriorated. In the 16th century unrest fomenting in the Black Forest eventually grew into the Peasant Rebellion that swept through much of southern Germany. Poorly equipped and haphazardly organised, the farmers were, of course, no match for the authorities who brought the uprising to a bloody conclusion.

In the following centuries the people of the Black Forest experienced a series of hardships of Biblical proportions. The Thirty Years' War left about 70% of the population dead, and plague and crop failures did much the same for the rest. Unsurprisingly, many of the survivors left for greener pastures in other parts of Europe.

The Black Forest stayed out of the spotlight for well over a century until the Baden Revolution of 1848–49. Inspired by the democratic movement in France and the declaration of the French Republic in February 1848, local radical democratic leaders Friedrich Hecker and Gustav von Struve led an armed rebellion against the arch-duke of Baden in April 1848, demanding freedom of expression, universal education, popular suffrage and other democratic ideals. Struve was arrested and Hecker fled into exile, but their struggle inspired the population and spilled over into other parts of Germany. Eventually Prussian troops cracked down on the revolutionaries in a fiery showdown at Rastatt in July 1849.

Nearly 100 years later, Freudenstadt and Freiburg were among the regional cities bombed to bits during WWII. In 1952 the Black Forest became part of the newly formed German state of Baden-Württemberg. Still largely agrarian, tourism is the single biggest source of income today.

1870-71	1886	1914–18	1919
Through brilliant diplomacy and the Franco-Prussian War, Bismarck creates a unified Germany. However, Bavaria keeps much of its sovereignty and many of its own institutions.	King Ludwig II is declared mentally unfit and confined to Schloss Berg (Berg Palace) on Lake Starnberg where he drowns in mysterious circumstances in shallow water, alongside his doctor.	WWI: Germany, Austria, Hungary and Turkey go to war against Britain, France, Italy and Russia. Germany is defeated, the monarchy overthrown and Bavaria declared a 'free state'.	Left-leaning intellectuals proclaim the Münchner Räterepublik on 4 April, hoping to create a Soviet-style regime. The movement never spreads beyond Munich and is quashed by government forces on 3 May.

built on Ludwig I's watch, as was the Alte Pinakothek. The king was also keen on new technology and heavily supported the idea of a nationwide railway. The first short line from Nuremberg to Fürth opened during his reign in 1835.

Politically though, Ludwig I brought a return to authority from the top as revolutionary rumblings in other parts of Europe coaxed out his reactionary streak. An arch-Catholic, he restored the monasteries, introduced press censorship and authorised arrests of students, journalists and university professors whom he judged subversive. Bavaria was becoming restrictive, even as French and American democratic ideas flourished elsewhere in Germany.

On 22 March 1848 Ludwig I abdicated in favour of his son, Maximilian II (r 1848–64), who finally put into place many of the constitutional reforms his father had ignored, such as abolishing censorship and introducing the right to assemble. Further progressive measures passed by his son Ludwig II (r 1864–86) early in his reign included welfare for the poor, liberalised marriage laws and free trade.

Ludwig, a 1973 flick directed by Luchino Visconti, is a lush, epic and sensitive Oscar-nominated portrayal of the life of Ludwig II, a highly emotional and tormented king out of step with his time.

The Mystique of Ludwig II

No other Bavarian king stirs the imagination quite as much as Ludwig II, the fairy-tale king so tragically at odds with a modern world that had no longer any use for an absolutist, if enlightened, monarch. Ludwig was a sensitive soul, fascinated by romantic epics, architecture and the music of Richard Wagner. When he became king at 18, he was at first a rather enthusiastic leader; however, Bavaria's days as a sovereign state were numbered. After it was absorbed into the Prussian-led German Reich in 1871, Ludwig became little more than a puppet king (albeit one receiving regular hefty allowances from Berlin).

Disillusioned, the king retreated to the Bavarian Alps to drink, draw castle plans, and enjoy private concerts and operas. His obsession with French culture and the Sun King, Louis XIV, inspired the fantastical palaces of Neuschwanstein, Linderhof and Herrenchiemsee – lavish projects that spelt his undoing.

In 1923 a postage stamp cost 50 billion marks, a loaf of bread cost 140 billion marks and US$1 was worth 4.2 trillion marks. In November the new Rentenmark was traded in for one trillion old marks.

In January 1886 several ministers and relatives arranged a hasty psychiatric test that diagnosed Ludwig as mentally unfit to rule. He was dethroned and taken to Schloss Berg on Lake Starnberg (Starnbergersee). Then, one evening, the dejected bachelor and his doctor took a lakeside walk and several hours later were found dead – mysteriously drowned in just a few feet of water.

No-one knows with certainty what happened that night. There was no eyewitness or proper criminal investigation. The circumstantial evidence was conflicting and incomplete. Reports and documents were tampered with, destroyed or lost. Conspiracy theories abound. That summer the

1923	1932	1933	1938
Hitler's failed *putsch* attempt lands him in jail where he takes just nine months to pen his vitriolic rant, *Mein Kampf*. It sells between eight and nine million copies.	Hitler and Churchill almost meet when the latter is researching his family history in Munich. Hitler calls off the meeting, considering a washed up politician such as Churchill unworthy of his time.	Hitler becomes chancellor of Germany and creates a dictatorship, making Munich the 'capital of the movement' and Obersalzberg, near Berchtesgaden, a second seat of government.	The Munich Agreement allows Hitler to annex the Sudetenlands, a mostly German-speaking region of Czechoslovakia. British Prime Minister Neville Chamberlain declares there will be 'peace in our time'.

authorities opened Neuschwanstein to the public to help pay off Ludwig's huge debts. King Ludwig II was dead, but a tourist industry was just being born.

Nazi Legacy

If Berlin was the head of the Nazi government, its heart beat in Bavaria. This was the birthplace of the movement, born out of the chaos and volatility of a post-WWI Germany wracked by revolution, crippling reparations and runaway inflation. Right-wing agitation resonated especially among Bavarians who deeply resented losing much of their sovereignty to a centralised national government in Berlin.

In Munich, a failed artist and WWI corporal from Austria – Adolf Hitler – had quickly risen to the top of the extreme right-wing Nationalsozialistische Arbeiterpartei (NSDAP). On 8 November 1923 he led his supporters in a revolt aimed at overthrowing the central government following a political rally in the Bürgerbräukeller (near today's Gasteig arts centre). The so-called Beer Hall Putsch was an abysmal failure, poorly planned and amateurishly executed. The following day a ragtag bunch of would-be armed revolutionaries marched through Munich's streets but only got as far as the Feldherrnhalle where a shoot-out with police left 16 Nazis and four policemen dead.

The NSDAP was banned and Hitler was sentenced to five years in prison for high treason. While in Landsberg jail, west of Munich, he began work on *Mein Kampf* (*My Struggle*), dictated in extended ramblings to his secretary Rudolf Hess. Incredibly, Hitler was released after only nine months in 1924 on grounds of 'good behaviour'.

After Hitler took control of Germany in January 1933, Bavaria was assigned a special status. Munich was declared the 'Capital of the Movement' and Nuremberg became the site of the Nazi party's mass rallies. In 1935 the party brass enacted the Nuremberg Laws, which ushered in the systematic repression of the Jews. In Dachau, north of Munich, Germany's first concentration camp was built in 1933. In addition, many Nazi honchos hailed from Bavaria, including *Sturmabteilung* (SA) chief Ernst Röhm (later killed by Hitler), Heinrich Himmler and Hermann Göring. Hitler himself was born just across the border, in Austria's Braunau. The Nazis enjoyed almost universal support in Bavaria, but there were also some pockets of resistance, most famously the Munich-based group Die Weisse Rose (The White Rose).

In 1938 Hitler's troops met no resistance when they marched into Austria and annexed it to Nazi Germany. The same year, the UK's Neville Chamberlain, Italy's Benito Mussolini and France's Édouard Daladier, in an attempt to avoid another war, continued their policy of appeasement by handing Hitler control over large portions of Czechoslovakia in the

Hitler called his regime the 'Third Reich' because he thought of the Holy Roman Empire and Bismarck's German empire as the first and second Reichs, respectively.

The Academy Award–nominated *Sophie Scholl – The Final Days* (2005) re-creates in harrowing detail the last six days in the life of this courageous Nazi resistance fighter, who was executed aged 21.

1939–45	**1943**	**1945**	
WWII: Hitler invades Poland; Britain, France and, in 1941, the US, declare war on Germany; Jews are murdered en masse in concentration camps throughout Eastern Europe during the Holocaust.	Members of the Nazi resistance group, *Die Weisse Rose* (White Rose), are caught distributing anti-Nazi leaflets at Ludwig Maximilian University and executed a few days later, following a sham trial.	Hitler commits suicide in his Berlin bunker. A broken Germany surrenders to the Allies and is divided into four zones. Bavaria falls into the US Zone.	

ANDREA SCHULTE-PEEVERS/GETTY IMAGES©

» Dachau concentration camp

LOLA MONTEZ, FEMME FATALE BY JEREMY GRAY

A whip-toting dominatrix and seductress of royalty, Lola Montez (1818–61) would show today's celebs what sex scandals are all about. Born as Eliza Gilbert in Ireland, to a young British army officer and a 13-year-old Creole chorus girl, Lola claimed to be the illegitimate daughter of poet Lord Byron (or, depending on her mood, of a matador). When her actual father died of cholera in India, her mother remarried and then shipped the seven-year-old Eliza off to Scotland. During her time in Scotland she was occasionally seen running stark naked through the streets. She then finished her schooling in Paris and after an unsuccessful stab at acting, reinvented herself as the Spanish dancer Lola Montez.

She couldn't dance either but her beauty fascinated men, who fell at her feet – sometimes under the lash of her ever-present riding crop. One time she fired a pistol at a lover who'd underperformed, but he managed to escape with his trousers around his knees.

Those succumbing to her charms included the tsar of Russia, who paid her 1000 roubles for a 'private audience'; novelist Alexandre Dumas; and composer Franz Liszt. Liszt eventually tired of Lola's incendiary temper, locked his sleeping mistress in their hotel room and fled – leaving a deposit for the furniture Lola would demolish when she awoke.

When fired by a Munich theatre manager, Lola took her appeal to the court of Ludwig I himself. As the tale goes, Ludwig asked casually whether her lovely figure was a work of nature or art. The direct gal she was, Lola seized a pair of scissors and slit open the front of her dress, leaving the ageing monarch to judge for himself. Predictably, she was rehired (and the manager sacked).

The king fell head over heels for Lola, giving her a huge allowance, a lavish palace and even the doubtful title of Countess of Landsfeld. Her ladyship virtually began running the country, too, and when Munich students rioted during the 1848 revolution, Lola had Ludwig shut down the university. This was too much for the townsfolk, who joined the students in revolt. Ludwig was forced to abdicate and Lola was chased out of town.

Lola cancanned her way around the world; her increasingly lurid show was very popular with gold miners in California and Australia. Next came a book of 'beauty secrets' and a lecture tour featuring topics such as 'Heroines of History and Strong-Minded Women'. She shed her Spanish identity, but in doing so, Lola – who had long publicly denied any link to her alter ego, Eliza – became a schizophrenic wreck. She spent her final two years as a pauper in New York, dying of pneumonia and a stroke aged 43.

Munich Agreement. Chamberlain's naive hope that such a move would bring 'peace in our time' was destroyed on 1 September 1939 when Nazi troops marched into Poland, kicking off WWII.

1945–46	**1972**	**1974**	**1992**
The Allies hold a series of trials against Nazi leaders accused of crimes against peace and humanity in a courthouse at Nuremberg. Ten of the accused are executed by hanging.	Bavaria shows off its friendliness – and cutting-edge architecture – during the Olympic Games, but the event is overshadowed by the so-called Munich Massacre, a deadly terrorist attack on Israeli athletes.	Just two years after the tragic events of the Munich Olympics, the city hosts the final of the FIFA World Cup. West Germany defeat Holland 2:1 at the Olympic Stadium.	The state-of-the-art Munich airport opens quickly becoming the second-busiest airport in Germany. It's named after former Bavarian minister-president Franz Josef Strauss, who helped establish Airbus.

A State Apart

Modern Bavaria may be integrated thoroughly within the German political construct, but its people take great pride in their distinctiveness. Its history, traditions, attitudes, political priorities and culture are, in many ways, quite different from the rest of Germany.

After WWII Bavaria became part of the American occupation zone and was allowed to pass its own constitution in December 1946. In 1949 it became the only German state that didn't ratify the German constitution because, in its opinion, it put unacceptable limitations on state powers. Bavaria did, however, agree to honour and abide by the federal constitution and has always done so. However, to underscore its independent streak it calls itself 'Freistaat' (free state) Bayern, even though this has no political meaning.

Since 1946 a single party, the archconservative Christlich-Soziale Union (CSU; Christian Social Union) has dominated Bavarian politics at every level of government, from communal to state. Although peculiar to Bavaria, it is closely aligned with its national sister party, the Christlich-Demokratische Union (CDU; Christian Democratic Union).

Powerful CSU figures include Franz-Josef Strauss, who served as Bavarian *Ministerpräsident* (minister-president, ie governor) from 1978 until his death in 1988, and his protégé, Edmund Stoiber, who clung to the job from 1999 until 2007. Although hugely popular and successful in Bavaria, both failed in their attempts to become federal chancellor: Strauss when losing to Helmut Schmidt in 1980, and Stoiber when outmanoeuvred by Gerhard Schröder in 2002. Since October 2008, Bavaria has been led by Horst Seehofer.

No other German state has been more successful in its postwar economic recovery than Bavaria. Within decades, it transformed from an essentially agrarian society into a progressive, high-tech state. The upturn was at least in part fuelled by the arrival of two million ethnic German expellees mainly from the Sudetelands of Bohemia and Moravia, who brought much-needed manpower.

Bavaria's Top Five Nazi Sites

» Eagle's Nest, Berchtesgaden

» Dachau concentration camp

» Reichsparteitagsgelände, Nuremberg

» Nuremberg Trials courtroom, Nuremberg

» Dokumentation Obersalzberg, Berchtesgaden

In *Massacre in Munich: The Manhunt for the Killers Behind the 1972 Olympics Massacre* (2005) Michael Bar Bar-Zohar and Eitan Haber describe the events in haunting detail and in a style as fast-paced and engrossing as a novel.

2005	2006	2007	2016
Cardinal Joseph Ratzinger, who was born in 1927 in the town of Marktl am Inn near the Austrian border, is elected Pope Benedict XVI.	Munich's new Allianz Arena hosts the first match of the FIFA World Cup soccer championships. Hosts Germany beat Costa Rica 4:2 in an exciting curtain raiser.	After 14 years, Edmund Stoiber steps down as minister-president of Bavaria and party chairman of the CSU, having seen his leadership skills called into question.	The Free State of Bavaria's rights to Hitler's *Mein Kampf* are set to run out. The text can then be reproduced freely by any publishing house in the world.

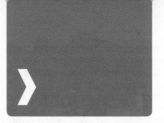

Bavarian Culture & Traditions

Regional Identity

Few other states in Germany can claim as distinct an identity as Bavaria. The country's southernmost state has always been a crossroads of trading routes to the Mediterranean and southeast Europe, and as the Alps never formed a truly impassable barrier, Bavaria absorbed the influences of Mediterranean culture early on. This gave the Bavarian character an easygoing outlook but one tempered with a Germanic respect for law and order. Patriotic feeling runs high, and at any hint of an affront, Bavarians close ranks, at least until the next party or festival. People here claim to be Bavarians first, Germans second, though this feeling weakens the further north into Franconia you head.

For outsiders the marriage of traditional rural Bavaria with modern-day industrial efficiency and wealth are hard to see as one entity – the two just don't seem to fit together. A popular slogan once coined by the state government dubbed Bavaria 'the land of lederhosen and laptops', conjuring up images of farmers and computer scientists happily working hand-in-virtual-hand. Modern Bavaria is indeed the land of Oktoberfest, beer and tradition, but it's also about cutting-edge glass-and-steel architecture, bright-lights nightlife, hipster fashion, sophisticated dining and world-class sport. It's youthful and almost completely without the brooding introspection you may encounter elsewhere in Germany.

> Indigenous Bavarians still strongly identify with their tribal heritage and call everyone not born in this neck of the *Wald* a *Zuagroaste* ('newcomer' in Bavarian dialect).

Lifestyle

So who exactly is the average Bavarian? Statistically speaking, he (or she) is in his early thirties, white and married, has at least some higher education and lives in a 90-sq-metre rented apartment in a midsize town. He and his partner drive a midsize car, but use public transport to commute to work in the service industry, where he earns about €3000 per month. About 40% of that evaporates in tax and social security deductions. Our average Bavarian tends to vote conservative, but would not rule out giving another party the nod. Sorting and recycling his rubbish is done religiously and, speaking of religion, he is, of course, Roman Catholic, though definitely not a regular churchgoer. He feels comfortable on the hiking trail and ski slopes, but is not fitness obsessed and could actually lose a few pounds. When he and his wife decide to have a family, they will have 1.38 children.

> Catholic Bavaria has produced few Jewish writers of note. A major exception is Jakob Wassermann (1873–1934), a popular novelist of the early 20th century. Many of his works grapple with Jewish identity, but he's best known for his sentimental take on Kaspar Hauser.

Religion

Southern Germany is overwhelmingly Roman Catholic but pockets of Lutherans can be found in such cities as Munich, Augsburg and Nuremberg, and in the northeastern Black Forest. Munich has a growing

MULTICULTURALISM

Every 12th resident of Bavaria is of non-German origin, with most of them setting up shop in the bigger cities where economic opportunities are greater and xenophobia less likely. In fact, almost 24% of people in Munich and around 18% in Nuremberg are of foreign descent. The largest groups are those from Turkey, the former states of Yugoslavia and Italy.

Despite a high level of tolerance, few groups mix on a day-to-day basis and racial tensions are increasing, at least in the cities. Government 'integration courses' for immigrants on welfare payments have done little to break down barriers and neo-Nazism is on the rise with a growing number of cases of intimidation of non-white foreigners reported.

A setback for integration was the passage of the so-called *Kopftuchgesetz*, a law that forbids female Muslim teachers to wear head scarves at school on the grounds that it's a symbol of non-integration. Both Bavaria and Baden-Württemberg adopted the law in 2004.

Jewish community of around 10,000 people, most of them recent arrivals from former Soviet republics. Muslims account for about 2.5% of the population.

Conventions

Bavarians (and their counterparts in the Black Forest) are a culturally conservative bunch. When in business mode, at fancy social gatherings or at high-brow cultural events, such as opera and theatre performances, you'll probably feel more comfortable if dressed in smart casual clothes. However chic threads may be needed to get past face control at fancier Munich nightclubs.

Locals are generally accommodating and fairly helpful towards visitors, and many will volunteer assistance if you look lost. This politeness does not necessarily extend to friendliness, however, and in public, people usually maintain a degree of reserve towards strangers – you won't find many conversations striking up on the bus or in the supermarket checkout queue. On the other hand, in younger company it's easy to chat with just about anyone, particularly in studenty hang-outs.

Shaking hands is common among both men and women, as is a hug or a kiss on the cheek, especially among young people. When making a phone call, start by giving your name (eg 'Smith, Grüss Gott'). Not doing so is considered impolite.

Importance is placed on the formal '*Sie*' form of address, especially in business situations. Among younger people and in social settings, though, people are much more relaxed about using '*Sie*' and '*Du*'.

> The website www .kulturportal -bayern.de is your guide to Bavarian culture, with sections on fine arts, film, museums, traditions and much, much more.

Sport
Football

Mention *Fussball* (football, soccer) in Bavaria and passions will flare. FC Bayern München has dominated the Bundesliga on and off for the past two decades and has won the German championship 21 times, most recently in 2010. It's also had some success in the UEFA Champion's League, reaching the final four times, but winning the competition only once. The team packs plenty of actual and financial muscle and attracts some of Europe's best players. The other Bavarian teams in the Bundesliga as of 2013 are 1 FC Nürnberg, FC Augsburg and SpVgg Greuther Fürth.

The football season runs from September to June, with a winter break from Christmas to mid-February.

> The Goethe Institut website (www.goethe .de) is a superb place to start for detailed info on all aspects of German culture.

Skiing

Bavarian slopes still lure the sport's elite to annual World Cup races held in such resorts as Garmisch-Partenkirchen, Reit im Winkl and Berchtesgaden. On New Year's Day, Garmisch-Partenkirchen is also a stop on the four-part Vierschanzen-Tournee, the World Cup ski-jumping competition. Famous female champions from Bavaria include Rosi Mittermaier, a two-time Olympic gold-medal winner in 1976, and more recently Martina Ertl and Hilde Gerg. In early 2005 Alois Vogl ended the men's drought by snagging the World Cup for slalom.

If you want to follow the thrills, spills and manager tantrums in Germany's top soccer league, it's all online at www .bundesliga.de (in English).

Arts
Literature

Quite a few German writers of the 18th and 19th centuries, including Jean Paul and ETA Hoffmann, lived in southern Germany, but the golden age of Bavarian literature kicked off in the second half of the 19th century. Some of the finest writers of the time, Thomas Mann and Frank Wedekind (famous for his coming-of-age tale *Spring Awakening,* 1891) among them, contributed to *Simplicissimus,* a satirical magazine founded in 1896 with a cover bearing a trademark red bulldog. A few of its barbs about Emperor Wilhelm II were so biting that the magazine was censored and some of its writers (Wedekind among them) were sent to jail. During his 40 years in Munich, Thomas Mann wrote a bookcase of acclaimed works and picked up a Nobel prize in the process. His Bavarian gems include the short story *Gladius Dei* (1902), a clever parody of Munich's pretensions to being the Florence of Bavaria.

Germany's most successful golfer, Bernhard Langer, is the son of a Russian prisoner of war who jumped off a Siberia-bound train and settled in Bavaria.

Today's leading literary lights are an eclectic, label-defying bunch. Herbert Rosendorfer (b 1934), a former Munich judge, has a long list of credits, including a legal satire, a history of the Thirty Years' War and travel guides. Anna Rosmus (b 1960) has turned her investigation of the Third Reich period in Passau, her birthplace, into several best-selling novels, including *Against the Stream: Growing Up Where Hitler Used to Live* (2002). Munich-based Patrick Süskind (b 1949) achieved international acclaim with *Das Parfum* (*Perfume;* 1985), his extraordinary tale of a psychotic 18th-century perfume-maker, which was made into a film by Tom Tykwer in 2006.

Although he lived mostly in Switzerland, Nobel Prize–winner Hermann Hesse (1877–1962) is originally a Black Forest boy whose most famous novels, *Siddhartha* and *Steppenwolf,* became hippie-era favourites. The philosopher Martin Heidegger (1889–1976), author of *Being and Time,* one of the seminal works of German existentialism, also hailed

TRACHTEN

If the tourist bumf is to be believed, Bavaria is full of locals cavorting around in *Trachten* (folk costume), the men in lederhosen, the women in figure-hugging, cleavage-baring, aproned dresses called dirndl. You may not see many such exotic folk on the streets of Nuremberg, Ingolstadt or Passau, but travel to the Alpine region, and you'll be in cliché heaven. Many young Munich city dwellers own these traditional outfits, but most only leave the closet for Oktoberfest and special occasions, but things are different in rural areas, especially among older generations. If you want to see real *Trachten* on parade, go to any folk festival or even just a Sunday morning church service in Oberammergau or Berchtesgaden.

Munich has several traditional costume emporia selling everything from the real hand-embroidered deal to made-heaven-knows-where imitations untouched by human hand. Getting garbed up for a beer festival or a night in a beer hall is an essential part of the fun in the Bavarian capital.

HEIMATFILM

Southern Germany's dreamy Alpine landscapes help spawn the *Heimatfilm* (homeland film), the only film genre to have been created in Germany. It reached its zenith in the 1950s and helped spread many of today's cosy clichés about Bavaria.

Most *Heimatfilms* show a world at peace with itself, focusing on basic themes such as love, family and the delights of traditional rural life. An interloper, such as a priest, creates some kind of conflict for the main characters – perhaps a milkmaid and her boyfriend or a poacher fighting local laws – who then invoke traditional values to solve the problem. Stories are set in the mountains of Austria, Bavaria or Switzerland, with predictable plots and schmaltzy film scores.

If you'd like to experience the *Heimatfilm* genre, titles to look out for include *Die Fischerin vom Bodensee* (*The Fisher Girl of Lake Constance*; 1956), *Hoch Droben auf dem Berg* (*High Up On the Mountain*; 1957) and *Die Landärztin von Tegernsee* (*Lady Country Doctor*; 1958) though these often cheap flicks were made by the dozen.

from the Black Forest, as did Hans Jacob Christoffel von Grimmelshausen (1622–76), a 17th-century literary genius and author of the earliest German adventure novel, *Simplicissimus* (*Adventures of a Simpleton*; 1668), which later inspired the name of the aforementioned satirical magazine.

Bavaria's greatest playwright of international stature was the ever-abrasive Bertolt Brecht (1898–1956) from Augsburg. After WWII, writers throughout Germany either dropped out of sight ('inner exile' was the favoured term) or, as Hans Carossa and Ernst Wiechert did, attempted some kind of political and intellectual renewal.

Cinema & Television

OK, so Germany's last true international success, the Oscar-winning *Das Leben der Anderen* (*Lives of Others*; 2006), was filmed in Berlin, but Munich's Bavaria Film studio is no slouch in the movie scene. Successes cranked out this side of the millennium include Marc Rothemund's Oscar-nominated *Sophie Scholl – The Final Days* (2005) and Tom Twyker's *Perfume: Story of a Murderer* (2006).

The studio pegs its pedigree back to 1919 and has lured many well-known directors, including Alfred Hitchcock (*Pleasure Garden;* 1925), Billy Wilder (*Fedora*; 1978), Rainer Werner Fassbinder (*Bolwieser;* 1977) and, most famously, Wolfgang Petersen (*Boat*, 1979, and *Neverending Story,* 1984). Many made-for-German-TV features, detective series such as *Polizeiruf 110* and popular soaps such as *Marienhof,* are also produced in Munich. Part of the studio complex is Bavaria Filmstadt, a movie-themed film park with original sets and props from *Das Boot* and other famous flicks.

Florian von Donnersmarck, director of the Oscar-winning *The Lives of Others* (2006), learned his craft at the Munich film school.

Music

Ironically, the composer most commonly associated with Bavaria wasn't Bavarian at all. Richard Wagner (1813–83) was born in Leipzig and died in Venice but his career took a dramatic turn when King Ludwig II became his patron in 1864 and financed the *Festspielhaus* (opera house) in Bayreuth, which was completed in 1872. Strongly influenced by Beethoven and Mozart, Wagner is most famous for his operas, many of which dealt with mythological themes (eg *Lohengrin* or *Tristan und Isolde*). His great achievement was a synthesis of visual, musical, poetic and dramatic components into a *Gesamtkunstwerk* (single work of art). Wagner's presence also drew other composers to Bayreuth, most notably Anton Bruckner and Franz Liszt, Wagner's father-in-law.

In Anna Rosmus' *Against the Stream: Growing Up Where Hitler Used to Live,* a teenage girl writes an essay and uncovers shocking crimes in prewar Passau.

BAVARIAN CULTURE & TRADITIONS CINEMA & TELEVISION

As the scores for symphonies became more complex, not the least thanks to Wagner, Bavarian composers hastened to join in. Richard Strauss (1864–1949), who hailed from Munich, created such famous symphonies as *Don Juan* and *Macbeth* but later focused on operas, including the successful *Der Rosenkavalier* (*The Knight of the Rose*).

Last, but not least, there's Munich-born Carl Orff (1895–1982), who achieved lasting fame with just one work: his life-embracing 1935 cantata *Carmina Burana*, a work characterised by simple harmonies, rhythms and hypnotic repetition. Kloster Andechs, where he is buried, holds an annual Orff festival.

The most illustrious name in music to emerge from just across the border in Austria was Wolfgang Amadeus Mozart, born in Salzburg in 1756. On their travels, the Mozart family visited several places in Bavaria and played at the court of the prince-elector Maximilian III in Munich in 1762. Mozart's birthplace and his family house can both be visited in Salzburg.

First stop for fans of 'serious music' should be Munich where the Münchner Philharmoniker are the chart toppers thanks to music director Lorin Maazel. Equally respected is the Bayerische Staatsoper, currently helmed by California wunderkind Kent Nagano. Nuremberg's highbrow scene perked up in 2005 when the Bavarian state government elevated the municipal theatre to the Staatstheater Nuremberg, whose opera, concert and ballet productions also get high marks.

Southern Germany maintains a busy festival schedule, but the granddaddy of them all is the Richard Wagner Festival in Bayreuth. Opened by the maestro himself in 1876 with the *Ring des Nibelungen* opera marathon, it was run by the composer's grandson, Wolfgang Wagner from 1951 until his death in 2010. Although still a major societal and artistic event, the festival stagnated under his long leadership and is just beginning to emerge from his shadow with a recent shake-up of the ticket allocation system and number of other improvements to the visitor experience.

Bavaria's 'Oscar' is the porcelain 'Pierrot', which is handed out to winners of the annual Bavarian Film Prize at a glitzy ceremony on the stage of Munich's Cuvilliés-Theatre. Past recipients include Wim Wenders, Tom Tykwer and Marc Rothemund.

VOLKSMUSIK

No other musical genre is as closely associated with Bavaria as *Volksmusik* (folk music). Every village has its own proud brass band or choir, and the state government puts serious euros into preserving this traditional music. More than 600,000 Bavarians, mostly lay musicians, belong to some 11,000 music groups, most of them in the Alpine regions. The basic musical form is the ¾-time *Landler*, which is also a dance involving plenty of hopping and stomping; men sometimes slap themselves on their knees in what is called *Platteln*. Typical instruments are the accordion and the zither and some songs end in a yodel. Popular performers of traditional *Volksmusik* are the Rehm Buam, Sepp Eibl and Ruperti Blech.

In the 1970s and '80s, small stages in Munich such as the Fraunhofer pub gave birth to a new style of *Volksmusik*. Performers infused the folklore concept with a political edge, freed it from conservative ideology and merged it with folk music from countries as diverse as Ireland and Ghana. Among the pioneers was the Biermösl Blosn, a band known for its satirical and provocative songs. Also keep an ear out for the Fraunhofer Saitenmusik, a chamber folk music ensemble that plays traditional tunes on acoustic instruments and which used to be the Fraunhofer pub's house band.

Since the '90s the scene has gone even further and now champions wacky crossovers of Bavarian folk with pop, rock, punk, hip-hop and techno in what has been dubbed 'Alpine New Wave'. Look for the folk rockers Hundsbuam, or the jazzy Munich trio Die Interpreten. Rudi Zapf uses the hammered dulcimer to take you on a musical journey around the world. The wildest band of them all, according to our sources, is the hardcore folk-punk band Attwenger.

Painting & Sculpture

EARLY WORKS

Frescos and manuscript illumination were early art forms popular between the 9th and 13th centuries. The oldest frescos in Bavaria are in the crypt of the Benedictine Abbey of St Mang in Füssen. Stained glass emerged around 1100; the 'Prophet's Windows' in Augsburg's cathedral are the earliest example in Central Europe.

GOTHIC

Portraiture and altar painting hit the artistic stage around 1300 AD. Top dog here was Jan Polack, whose work can be admired in such churches as Munich's Schloss Blutenburg.

A major Gothic sculptor was Erasmus Grasser, whose masterpieces include the St Peter altar in St Peterskirche in Munich and the *Morris Dancers* in the Munich Stadtmuseum. Another is Veit Stoss, a Franconian who imbued his sculptures with dramatic realism. In 1503 Stoss spent a stint in jail for forgery, but restored his reputation with the main altar in Bamberg's cathedral, his crowning achievement.

RENAISSANCE

The Renaissance saw the rise of human elements in painting: religious figures were now depicted alongside mere mortals. The heavyweight – quite literally – in Germany was the Nuremberg-born Albrecht Dürer, who excelled both as a painter and graphic artist. His subjects ranged from mythology to religion to animals, all in fantastic anatomical detail, natural perspective and vivid colours. The Alte Pinakothek in Munich has several famous works, and his Nuremberg house is now a museum.

Dürer influenced Lucas Cranach the Elder, a major artist of the Reformation. Cranach's approach to landscape painting, though, grew out of the *Donauschule* (Danube School), an artistic movement based in Passau and Regensburg. The amazing details of these landscapes seethed with dark movement, making them the focal point of the painting rather than a mere backdrop.

The brightest star among Renaissance sculptors was Tilman Riemenschneider. His skills were formidable, allowing his stone to mimic wood and featuring compositions playing on light and shadow. Must-sees include the altars in the Jakobskirche in Rothenburg ob der Tauber and in the Herrgottskirche in Creglingen, both on the Romantic Road. The Mainfränkisches Museum in Würzburg also has an outstanding Riemenschneider collection.

BAROQUE & ROCOCO

The sugary styles of the baroque and rococo periods left their mark throughout Bavaria, especially in church art. Illusionary effects and contrast between light and shadow are typical features, and surfaces are often bewilderingly ornate.

Arguably the finest and most prolific artists of the period, the brothers Cosmas and Egid Asam, were of a generation of Germans educated in Rome in the Italian baroque tradition. Their father, Hans Georg, was a master fresco artist who transformed the Basilika St Benedikt in Benediktbeuern. Word of their supreme talent, along with the family's connections in the Benedictine order, meant the duo were always swamped with work. Cosmas was primarily a fresco painter while Egid used his considerable talents as an architect and stucco sculptor. Examples of their brilliant collaboration can be found throughout Bavaria, mostly notably in the Asamkirche in Munich and the Asamkirche Maria de Victoria in Ingolstadt.

Another set of brothers dominating the baroque period was Dominikus and Johann Baptist Zimmermann, whose collaboration reached its pinnacle in the Unesco-listed Wieskirche, a stop on the Romantic Road. Johann Baptist also worked on Munich's St Peterskirche and Schloss Nymphenburg. Both were members of the so-called Wessobrunner School, which counted architect and stucco artist Josef Schmuzer among its founding members. Schmuzer's work can be admired at Kloster Ettal and in the Alte St Martinskirche in Garmisch-Partenkirchen.

THE 19TH CENTURY

Heart-on-your-sleeve Romanticism that drew heavily on emotion and a dreamy idealism dominated the 19th century. Austria-born Moritz von Schwind is noted for his moody scenes of German legends and fairy tales. His teacher, Peter Cornelius, was a follower of the Nazarenes, a group of religious painters who drew from the old masters for inspiration. There's a giant fresco of his in Munich's Ludwigskirche, although for the full survey of Romantic art you should swing by the nearby Sammlung Schack.

Romanticism gradually gave way to the sharp edges of realism and, later on, the meticulous detail of naturalism. Major practitioners were Wilhelm Leibl, who specialised in painting Bavarian country scenes, and Hans Thoma, who joined Leibl in Munich, but favoured the landscapes of his native Black Forest. Look for their works in Munich's Städtische Galerie im Lenbachhaus (when it reopens in 2013).

MUNICH SECESSION & JUGENDSTIL

During the 1890s a group of about 100 artists shook up the art establishment when they split from Munich's *Künstlergesellschaft* (Artists' Society), a traditionalist organisation led by portrait artist Franz von Lenbach. Secessionists were not linked by a common artistic style, but by a rejection of reactionary attitudes towards the arts that stifled new forms of expression. They preferred scenes from daily life to historical and religious themes, shunned studios in favour of natural outdoor light and were hugely influential in inspiring new styles.

One of them was Jugendstil (art nouveau), inspired by printmaking and drawing on functional, linear ornamentation partly inspired by Japanese art. The term originated from the weekly trendsetting art-and-literature magazine *Die Jugend,* published in Munich from 1896 until 1940. In Munich the Neue Pinakothek is the place to head for some fine examples of this most elegant of styles.

EXPRESSIONISM

In the early 20th century German artists looked for a purer, freer approach to painting through abstraction, vivid colours and expression. In Bavaria the trailblazer was the artist group *Der Blaue Reiter* (Blue Rider), founded by Wassily Kandinsky and Franz Marc in 1911, and joined later by Paul Klee, Gabriele Münter and other top artists. The Städtische Galerie im Lenbachhaus has the most comprehensive collection, much of it donated by Münter, who managed to hide her colleagues' paintings from the Nazis. A good selection of Münter's own paintings are on view at the Schlossmuseum Murnau, a town in the Alps. At the Buchheim Museum on Starnberger See, the focus is on the equally avant-garde artist group called *Die Brücke* (Bridge), founded in 1905 in Dresden by Ernst Ludwig Kirchner, Erich Heckel and Karl Schmidt-Rottluff.

NAZI ERA

After the creative surge in the 1920s, the big chill of Nazi conformity sent Germany into an artistic deep freeze in the 1930s and '40s. Many internationally famous artists, including Paul Klee and Max Beckmann, were classified as 'degenerate' and their paintings confiscated, sold off or burned.

MODERN & CONTEMPORARY

Post-1945 creativity revived the influence of Nolde, Kandinsky and Schmidt-Rottluff, but also spawned a new abstract expressionism in the work of Willi Baumeister. The completely revamped and enlarged Franz Marc Museum in Kochel am See traces the evolution of pre- and post-WWII expressionism.

An edgy genre that has found major representation in Bavaria is concrete art, which emerged in the 1950s and takes abstract art to its extreme, rejecting any natural form and using only planes and colours. See what this is all about at the Museum für Konkrete Kunst in Ingolstadt and the Museum im Kulturspeicher in Würzburg.

The Bavarian photorealist Florian Thomas is among the influential artists whose work is now in the Museum Frieder Burda in Baden-Baden. Other good spots to plug into the contemporary art scene are the Neues Museum in Nuremberg, and the Pinakothek der Moderne and the superb Museum Brandhorst in Munich.

Theatre

Theatre in its various forms enjoys a wide following in Bavaria, especially in Munich, which has the famous Münchener Kammerspiele, but also in Nuremberg, Regensburg and Bamberg. Bavaria's longest-running drama is the *Passionsspiele* (*Passion Play*), which has been performed in Oberammergau once every decade since the 17th century.

For a dose of local colour, head to a *Bauerntheater* (literally, 'peasant theatre'), which usually presents silly and rustic tales in dialect so thick that it's basically incomprehensible to all non-Bavarians. But never mind, because the story lines are so simplistic, you'll probably be able to follow the plot anyway. The oldest *Bauerntheater* is in Garmisch-Partenkirchen.

If you're travelling with kids, don't miss one of the many excellent marionette theatres starring endearing and often handmade puppets. The most famous is the Augsburger Puppenkiste in Augsburg, but the Marionettentheater Bad Tölz and the Münchener Marionetten Theater will also take you on a magic carpet ride.

The website www .theaterparadies -deutschland. de (in German) is the ultimate thespian's portal with links to hundreds of theatres throughout the German-speaking world.

BAVARIAN CULTURE & TRADITIONS THEATRE

Food & Drink

Sausages with foaming wheat beer in rollicking Munich beer halls, snowball-sized dumplings with an avalanche of sauerkraut and roast pork in the Alps, black forest gateau slathered in chocolate, cream and cherries – everyone has a tale of calorific excess when it comes to dining in southern Germany. And the rural *Gaststätte* (pubs) you've heard about do indeed exist; brimming with low beams, old-fashioned bonhomie and dirndl-clad fräuleins dishing up enormous platters of solid home cooking.

But while the classics still star on many a country menu, in the cities things are changing fast. In the blink of an eye, Munich can switch from pig trotter–chomping rusticity to the retro-chic surrounds of two Michelin-starred Tantris, where chef Hans Haas works culinary magic with clean, bright Mediterranean flavours. Here and in other bigger cities like Nuremberg and Freiburg, menus go way beyond the obvious, with a world of street food, vegetarian menus with oomph and new generation chefs wowing critics with their avant-garde take on German fare.

In many restaurants here today, chefs take great pride in carefully sourcing the finest regional and seasonal ingredients to create dishes that sing with natural, integral flavours. Dishes that may well surprise you.

Regional & Seasonal
Classic Mains

The Chinese say you can eat every part of the pig bar the 'oink', and Bavarian chefs seem to be in full agreement. No part of the animal is spared their attention as they cook up its *Schweinshaxe* (knuckles), *Rippchen* (ribs), *Züngerl* (tongue) and *Wammerl* (belly). Pork also appears as *Schweinebraten* (roast pork) and the misleadingly named *Leberkäse* (liver cheese), a savoury meatloaf that contains neither liver nor cheese.

SEASON'S GREETINGS

May is peak season for *Spargel* (white asparagus), which is classically paired with boiled potatoes, hollandaise sauce and sometimes *Schinken* (smoked or cooked ham). In spring, look for *Bärlauch*, a wild-growing garlic that is often turned into a delicious pesto sauce. Wild mushrooms peak in late summer and early autumn when you find many dishes revolving around *Pfifferlinge* (chanterelles) and *Steinpilze* (cep or porcini). Other autumn delights include pumpkins, game and *Zwiebelkuchen* (onion tart), especially in rural Swabia, where it is paired with sweet *Neuer Süsser* (new wine) or *Most* (cider).

Bavaria is beer festival country. At Oktoberfest in September, 6.9 million partygoers wash down entire farms of pigs, oxen and chickens with *Mass* (litres) of beer. In March, the city throws festivals for pre-Lenten *Starkbier* (strong beer), where you can quaff the malty 7.5% brews monks once dubbed *flüssiges Brot* (liquid bread).

WEISSWURST ETIQUETTE

Bavarians love sausage and there is no sausage more Bavarian than the *Weisswurst*. It's so Bavarian, in fact, that there's even an imaginary boundary (the *Weisswurst* equator) beyond which it is no longer served (ie, roughly north of Frankfurt). Unlike most sausages, which are pork-based, this one's made from veal and, before refrigeration, had to be eaten before noon to prevent spoilage. Now they're available all day. They're brought to the table still swimming in hot water. Discard the skin and eat only with fresh pretzels, sweet mustard and, preferably, paired with a mug of Helles. Enjoy!

The Black Forest contributes the famous *Schwarzwälder Schinken* – ham that's been salted, seasoned and cured for around two weeks.

Non-pork-based dishes include *Hendl* (roast chicken) and *Fleischpflanzerl*, the Bavarian spin on the hamburger. Fish is often caught fresh from the lakes. *Forelle* (trout) is especially popular in the Black Forest and served either *Forelle Müllerin* (baked), *Forelle Blau* (boiled) or *Räucherforelle* (smoked). In Bavarian beer gardens, you'll often find *Steckerlfisch* – skewers of grilled mackerel.

Originating in Swabia but now served throughout southern Germany are *Maultaschen*, which are ravioli-like stuffed pasta pockets, and *Kässpätzle*, stubby noodle-dumpling hybrids topped with melted cheese.

Bavarians like to 'pig out' and the numbers prove it: of the 60kg of meat consumed by the average resident each year, about two-thirds are pork. Oink!

Sausages & Side Orders

Wurst (sausage) is traditionally served with *süsser Senf* (sweet mustard) alongside sauerkraut or potato salad and a slice of bread. Bavaria's flagship link is the *Weisswurst*. In Eastern Bavaria and Franconia the mildly spicy *Bratwurst* rules. Nuremberg and Regensburg make the most famous versions: finger-sized and eaten by the half dozen or dozen. Other sausages you may encounter include the spicy *Krakauer* and the hot dog–like *Wiener*.

The *Kartoffel* (potato) is 'Vegetable *Nummer Eins*' in any meat-and-three-veg dish and can be served as *Salzkartoffeln* (boiled), *Bratkartoffeln* (fried), *Kartoffelpüree* (mashed) or shaped into *Knödel* (dumplings). Dumplings can be made of bread (*Semmelknödel*) and there's also a meaty version made with liver (*Leberknödel*). Pickled cabbage is another common vegetable companion and comes as either sauerkraut (white) or *Rotkohl* and *Blaukraut* (red).

Just Desserts

You will never forget your first forkful of real *Schwarzwälder Kirschtorte* (black forest gateau): a three-layered chocolate sponge cake filled with cream, morello cherries and *Kirsch* (cherry liqueur). Read our interview with the Triberg baker who holds the original recipe on p259.

Usually served with a dollop of ice cream is *Apfelstrudel* (apple strudel), which actually originated in Austria but is now eaten all over southern Germany. Tasty alternatives include *Dampfnudeln,* steamed doughy dumplings drenched in custard sauce, and Allgäu's *Apfelkrapfen*, sugar-sprinkled apple fritters. Nuremberg is famous for its *Lebkuchen* (gingerbread) made with nuts, fruit peel, honey and spices, while in Rothenburg ob der Tauber, chocolate-coated pastry *Schneeballen* (snowballs) come with a variety of creamy fillings.

If you want to train your tummy for your trip to Bavaria, try any of the recipes (roast pork to liver dumplings) detailed on www.bavarian-online.de, in German.

Cookery Schools

The region's fledgling cookery school scene has started to spread its wings of late. On average, anticipate paying between €140 and €240 for a day at the stove, which usually includes lunch and recipes to take home.

We've picked three favourites, but you can search by region for a course to suit you on www.kochschule.de or www.die-kochschulen.de (both in German).

Schwarzwaldstube (☎07442-4920; www.traube-tonbach.de; Tonbachstrasse 237, Baiersbronn-Tonbach; menus €155-189; ☺closed Mon, Tue, lunch Wed) Three Michelin–starred legend in Baiersbronn in the Black Forest. Classes revolve around a theme such as cooking with asparagus or pasta making.

Wirthaus in der Au (☎089-448 14 00; http://wirtshausinderau.de; Lilienstrasse 51) Munich's king of *Knödel* since 1901 runs an English-language dumpling-making workshop.

Magazin (p202) Hop over the border to Salzburg for hands-on, small-group classes spotlighting cookery themes from fish and crustaceans to Austrian desserts.

Grape & Grain
Here's to Beer!

Bavarians have made beer-making a science, and not just since the passage of the *Reinheitsgebot* (Purity Law) in Ingolstadt in 1516, which stipulates brewers may use only four ingredients – malt, yeast, hops and water. It stopped being a legal requirement in 1987 when the EU struck it down as uncompetitive, but many Bavarian brewers still conform to it anyway, making local brews among the best in the world. Many traditional family-run concerns have been swallowed up by the big brewers, but some smaller operations have survived, including those set up in monasteries. Kloster Weltenburg in the Altmühltal and Kloster Andechs near Munich are especially famous.

Beer aficionados face a bewildering choice of labels. The following is a small glossary of the most commonly encountered varieties. Note that most Bavarian beer has an alcohol content between 5% and 5.5%, although some can be as strong as 8%.

For an in-depth study of what's pouring at Munich's beer halls and gardens, Larry Hawthorne's the *Beer Drinker's Guide to Munich* is an indispensable tool that will take you far beyond the Hofbräuhaus.

For more information about German grape varieties, growing regions, wine festivals and courses, check out the pages of the German Wine Institute at www .deutscheweine.de.

BEER GLOSSARY

» **Alkoholfreies Bier** – nonalcoholic beer

» **Bockbier/Doppelbock** – strong beer (*doppel* meaning even more so), either pale, amber or dark in colour with a bittersweet flavour

» **Dampfbier (steam beer)** – originating from Bayreuth, it's top-fermented (this means the yeast rises to the top during the fermentation process) and has a fruity flavour

» **Dunkles (dark lager)** – a reddish-brown, full-bodied lager, malty and lightly hopped

» **Helles (pale lager)** – a lightly hopped lager with strong malt aromas and a slightly sweet taste

» **Hofbräu** – type of brewery belonging to a royal court

DARE TO TRY

Feeling daring? Why not give these three regional faves a whirl.

» **sauere Kutteln/Nierle/Lüngerl** (sour tripe/kidneys/lung) No beer fest would be complete without these offal faves, simmered in vinegar or wine, bay, laurel, juniper and spices.

» **Bubespitzle** Otherwise known as *Schupfnudeln*, this Swabian dish's ingredients are innocuous: potato noodles tossed in butter, served with sauerkraut and speck. But the name (literally, 'little boys' penises') certainly isn't.

» **Leberknödelsuppe** Hearty beef broth with beef, veal or pork liver dumplings, flavoured with onions, parsley and marjoram.

BEER GARDEN GRUB

In beer gardens, tables laid with a cloth and utensils are reserved for people ordering food. If you're only planning to down a mug of beer, or have brought along a picnic, don't sit there.

If you do decide to order food, you'll find very similar menus at all beer gardens. Typical dishes include roast chicken, spare ribs, *Schweinebraten* (roast pork) and schnitzel.

Radi is a huge, mild radish that's eaten with beer; you can buy prepared radish or buy a radish at the market and a *Radimesser* at any department store; stick it down in the centre and twist the handle round and round, creating a radish spiral. If you do it yourself, smother the cut end of the radish with salt until it weeps to reduce the bitterness (and increase your thirst!).

Obatzda (oh-batsdah) is Bavarian for 'mixed up'. This cream cheese–like speciality is made of butter, ripe Camembert, onion and caraway. Spread it on *Brezn* (a pretzel) or bread.

» **Klosterbräu** – type of brewery belonging to a monastery
» **Malzbier** – sweet, aromatic, full-bodied malt beer
» **Märzen** – full bodied with strong malt aromas and traditionally brewed in March
» **Pils (pilsener)** – a bottom-fermented lager with strong hop flavour
» **Rauchbier (smoke beer)** – dark beer with a fresh, spicy or 'smoky' flavour
» **Weissbier/Weizen (wheat beer)** – around 5.4% alcohol. A cloudy *Hefeweizen* has a layer of still-fermenting yeast on the bottom of the bottle, whereas *Kristallweizen* is clearer with more fizz. These wheat beers are fruity and spicy, often recalling bananas and cloves. Decline offers of a slice of lemon as it ruins the head and – beer purists say – the flavour.

> In Bavaria beer is officially defined not as alcohol but as a staple food, just like bread.

If you want to go easy on the booze, order a sweetish *Radler,* which comes in half or full litres and mixes *Helles Lagerbier* and lemonade. A *Russe* (Russian) is generally a litre-sized concoction of *Helles Weissbier* and lemonade.

Riesling to Pinot

Bavaria's only wine-growing region is located in Franconia in and around Würzburg. Growers here produce some exceptional dry white wines, which are bottled in distinctive green flagons called *Bocksbeutel*. If *Silvaner* is the king of the grape here, then *Müller-Thurgau* is the prince, and riesling, *Weissburgunder* (pinot grigio) and *Bacchus* the courtiers. The latter three thrive especially on the steep slopes flanking the Main River. Red wines play merely a supporting role. Nearly 80% of all wine produced is consumed within the region.

Kaiserstuhl is the major wine-growing area in the Black Forest. It produces mainly *Spätburgunder* (pinot noir) and *Grauburgunder* (pinot gris).

Kaffee und Kuchen

Anyone who has spent any length of time in Bavaria or the Black Forest knows the reverence bestowed on the three o'clock weekend ritual of *Kaffee und Kuchen* (coffee and cake). More than just a chance to devour delectable cakes and tortes – though it's certainly that, too – locals see it as a social event. You'll find *Cafe-Konditoreien* (cafe–cake shops) pretty much everywhere – in castles, in the middle of the forest, even plopped on top of mountains. Track down the best by asking sweet-toothed locals where the cake is *hausgemacht* (homemade). Coffee is usually brewed

> With roughly 14,000 distillers, the Black Forest has the highest density of schnapps makers in the world.

fresh and all the usual varieties are on offer, including cappuccinos, espressos and milky coffee called *Milchkaffee*.

Except in posh cafes, tea is usually a teabag in a glass or pot of hot water, served with a slice of lemon. If you want milk, ask for *Tee mit Milch*.

Festive Food

Prost! (with beer) or *Zum Wohl!* (with wine) are typical drinking toasts.

Major holidays are feast days and usually spent at home with family, gorging and guzzling way more than everyone knows is good for them. At Easter roast lamb is often the star of the show. Easter is preceded by Lent, a period of fasting when sweet dishes such as *Rohrnudeln* (browned yeasty buns served with plum compote and vanilla sauce) are enjoyed and fish replaces meat in Catholic households. Carp, served boiled, baked or fried, is popular at Christmas time, although more people roast up a goose or a turkey as the main event. *Lebkuchen* (gingerbread) and *Spekulatius* (spicy cookies) are both sweet staples of *Advent* (the pre-Christmas season). For drinks, *Glühwein* (spicy mulled wine), best consumed at a Christmas market, is a favoured seasonal indulgence.

Where To Eat & Drink

» **Gastätte & Gasthöfe** Rural inns with a laid-back feel, local crowd and solid menu of *gutbürgerliche Küche* (home cooking). There's sometimes a beer garden out the back.

» **Eiscafé** Italian or Italian-style cafes, where you can grab an ice cream or cappuccino and head outside to slurp and sip.

» **Stehcafé** A stand-up cafe for coffee and snacks at speed and on the cheap.

» **Cafe-Konditorei** A traditional cake shop doubling as a cafe.

» **Ratskeller** Atmospheric town-hall basement restaurant, generally more frequented by tourists than locals nowadays.

» **Restaurant** These serve everything from informal meals to *gehobene Küche* (gourmet meals). The *Tagesmenü* (fixed daily menu) often represents good value.

» **Bierkeller & Weinkeller** The emphasis is on beer and wine respectively, with a little food (sausages and pretzels, cold cuts etc) on the side.

» **Imbiss** Handy speed-feed stops for savoury fodder from wurst-in-a-bun to kebabs and pizza.

When to Eat

Traditionally *Frühstück* (breakfast) is a sweet and savoury smorgasbord of bread, cheese, salami, wurst, preserves, yoghurt and muesli. At weekends, it's an altogether more leisurely, family-oriented affair. Many cafes have embraced the brunch trend, serving all-you-can-eat buffets with fresh rolls, eggs, smoked fish, fruit salad and even prosecco.

Traditionally, *Mittagessen* (lunch) has been the main meal of the day, but modern working practices have changed this considerably, at least in the cities. However, many restaurants still tout lunch-time dishes or a fixed lunch menu (*Mittagsmenü* or *Tagesmenü*), which can be an affordable way of dining even at upscale restaurants.

WHAT'S HOT

» All-you-can-eat weekend brunches.

» Asian lifestyle eateries with designer edge.

» Vegan and vegetarian food done creatively.

» NYC–style gourmet delis – cheesecake, bagels and cupcakes galore.

» Locavore movement (locally produced food).

DOS & DON'TS

» Do bring a small gift – flowers or a bottle of wine – when invited to a meal.

» Do say *Guten Appetit!* (*bon appetit!*) before starting to eat.

» Do offer to help with the dishes afterwards.

» Don't start eating until everyone has been served.

» Don't expect to get a glass of tap water at a restaurant.

» Don't assume you can pay by credit card when eating out.

Dinner is dished up at home around 7pm. For those who have already eaten heartily at midday, there is *Abendbrot*, bread with cold cuts. Bar the cities with their late-night dining scenes, Germans head to restaurants earlier than elsewhere in Europe, and many kitchens in rural areas stop serving around 9pm. At home, meals are relaxed and require few airs and graces beyond the obligatory '*Guten Appetit*' (literally 'good appetite'), exchanged before eating.

Dining Etiquette

On the Menu

English menus are not a given, even in big cities, though the waiter or waitress will almost invariably be able to translate for you. The more rural and remote you go, the less likely it is that the restaurant will have an English menu, or multilingual staff for that matter. It helps to know a few words of German.

Paying the Bill

Sometimes the person who invites pays, but generally locals go Dutch and split the bill evenly. This might mean everyone chipping in at the end of a meal or asking to pay separately (*getrennte Rechnung*). Buying rounds in bars British-style is not usually the done thing, though friends might buy each other the odd drink. In bars and beer halls, table service is still quite common and waiting staff often come around to *abkassieren* (cash up).

Table Reservations

If you want to dine at formal or popular restaurants, it is wise to make table reservations a day or two ahead. Michelin-starred restaurants are often booked up weeks in advance, especially at weekends. Most *Gasthöfe*, *Gaststätten*, cafes and beer halls should be able to squeeze you in at a moment's notice.

Tipping

Tipping is quite an individual matter, but as a rule of thumb, most Germans will tip between 5% and 10% in restaurants, and simply round to the nearest euro in cafes and bars. Do whatever you're comfortable with, given the service and setting. Give any tip directly to the server when paying your bill. Say either the amount you want to pay, or '*Stimmt so*' if you don't want change.

From *Allerseelenzopf* (a sweet bread loaf) to *Zwickelbier* (unfiltered beer), all of the mysteries behind Bavaria's regional culinary secrets are revealed on www.food-from-bavaria.com.

Landscapes & Wildlife

The Land

In Bavaria and the Black Forest nature has been as prolific and creative as Picasso in his prime. The most dramatic region is the Bavarian Alps, a phalanx of craggy peaks created by tectonic uplift some 770 million years ago and chiselled and gouged by glaciers and erosion ever since. Several limestone ranges stand sentinel above the rest of the land, including, west to east, the Allgäuer Alps, the glaciated Wetterstein/Karwendel Alps (with Germany's highest mountain, the Zugspitze at 2962m) and the Berchtesgadener Alps. Many peaks tower well above 2000m.

North of here, the Alpine Foothills are a lush mosaic of moorland, rolling hills, gravel plains and pine forests dappled with glacial lakes, including the vast Chiemsee, Starnberger See and the Ammersee. The foothills are book-ended by Lake Constance in the west and the Inn and Salzach Rivers in the east.

The Bavarian Forest in eastern Bavaria is a classic *Mittelgebirge*, a midsize mountain range, and one of Germany's greatest unknowns. Its highest peak, the Grosse Arber (1456m), juts out like the tall kid in your school photo. Much of it is blanketed by dark, dense forests that fade into the thinly populated Frankenwald and Fichtelgebirge areas further north.

The Black Forest, in Germany's southwestern corner, is another *Mittelgebirge*, a storied quilt that enwraps waterfalls, rolling hills, sparkling lakes, lush vineyards, and oak, pine and beech forests into one mystique-laden package. The little Kinzig River divides the north from the much higher south, where the Feldberg is the highest elevation at 1493m.

Much of Franconia and Swabia is a complex patchwork of low ranges, rifts and deep meandering valleys. A Jurassic limestone range is responsible for bizarre rock formations, such as those in the Franconian Switzerland region north of Nuremberg.

Southern Germany is traversed by several major rivers, of which the Danube, which originates in the Black Forest, and the Main are the longest. The Inn and the Isar flow down from the Alps into the Danube, the former at Passau, the latter near Deggendorf on the edge of the Bavarian Forest. Germany's main south–north river, the mighty Rhine, divides the Black Forest from France and Switzerland.

Wildlife

The most common large forest mammal is the red deer, a quick-footed fellow with skinny legs supporting a chunky body. Encounters with wild boar, a type of wild pig with a keen sense of smell but poor eyesight, are also possible, especially in the Bavarian Forest.

Beavers faced extinction in the 19th century not only because they were coveted for their precious pelts (beaver hats were all the rage), but also because they were cooked up in strict Catholic households each Friday since the good people considered them to be 'fish'. Reintroduced in the mid-1960s, beavers are thriving once again, especially along the Danube, between Ingolstadt and Kelheim, and its tributaries.

Lynxes actually died out in Germany in the 19th century but in the 1980s Czech authorities released 17 lynxes in the Bohemian Forest, and a small group of brave souls have since tried their luck again in the Bavarian Forest right across the border. There have even been rare sightings around the Feldberg in the southern Black Forest.

In the Alps, the Alpine marmot, a sociable chap that looks like a fat squirrel, lives in burrows below the tree line, while wild goats make their home in the upper mountains. The snow hare, whose fur is white in winter, is also a common Alpine denizen. The endangered *Auerhuhn* (capercaillie), a grouselike bird, also makes its home here and in the Bavarian Forest. Lizards, praying mantids and European bee-eaters live in the sunny Kaiserstuhl area.

Local skies are home to over 400 bird species, from white-backed woodpeckers and pygmy owls to sparrowhawks, grey herons, jays and black redstarts. The Wutach Gorge in the Black Forest is a unique habitat that supports such rare birds as treecreepers and kingfishers, as well as many species of butterflies, beetles and lizards.

The Black Forest straddles the Continental Divide. Water either drains into the north-flowing Rhine, which empties into the Atlantic Ocean, or into the east-flowing Danube, which empties into the Black Sea.

Plants

Despite environmental pressures, southern German forests remain beautiful places to escape the crowds. At lower altitudes, they usually consist of a potpourri of beech, oak, birch, chestnut, lime, maple and ash that erupt into a riot of colour in autumn. Up in the higher elevations, fir, pine, spruce and other conifers are more prevalent. Canopies often shade low-growing ferns, heather, clover and foxglove.

In spring, Alpine regions burst with wildflowers – orchid, cyclamen, gentian, pulsatilla, Alpine roses, edelweiss and buttercups – which brighten meadows. Minimise your impact by sticking to trails.

The true king of the skies is the golden eagle. If you're lucky, you might spot one patrolling the mountain peaks in Nationalpark Berchtesgaden (p123).

Wild Food

Bavaria and the Black Forest's woods brim with berries, herbs and mushrooms, many of which are perfectly edible. Summer and autumn yield rich forest pickings, with bilberries, raspberries, blackberries and strawberries; wild herbs like bear's garlic, dandelion, dill, buckhorn and sorrel fringe meadows and woodlands. The fungi-foraging season kicks off with apricot-hued, trumpet-shaped *Pfifferlinge* (chanterelles) in June/July, peaks with the prized *Steinpilz* (cep or porcini) around August and ends with autumnal delights like button-topped *Maronen* (Bay Bolete).

Tourist offices can point you towards local *Kräuterwanderungen* and *Pilzwanderung* (herb and mushroom walks), such as those run by the German Alpine Club (www.alpenverein.de) or Schwarzwaldverein (www.schwarzwaldverein.de); you'll need to join as a member first.

For the inside scoop on the region's nature and national parks, surf German-language www.naturparke.de and www.nationalpark-deutschland.com.

National & Nature Parks

Bavaria is home to Germany's oldest national park, the Nationalpark Bayerischer Wald, which was founded in 1970. There is only one more of Germany's 14 national parks in Bavaria but it's a good one: the Nationalpark Berchtesgaden on the Austrian border, a ravishing mountainscape of big-shouldered Alps and jewel-coloured, fjordlike lakes. Both parks preserve places of outstanding natural beauty, rare geographical features and various wildlife species.

NATIONAL & NATURE PARKS

PARK	FEATURES	ACTIVITIES	BEST TIME TO VISIT	WEBSITE
Nationalpark Bayerischer Wald (p183)	mountain forest, bogs, streams, (243 sq km); deer, hazel grouse, fox, otter, pygmy owl, three-toe woodpecker	hiking, mountain biking, cross-country skiing	year-round	www.national park-bayerischer-wald.de
Nationalpark Berchtesgaden (p124)	lakes, mixed forest, cliffs, meadows (210 sq km); eagle, chamois, marmot, blue hare, salamander	hiking, skiing, wildlife-watching	year-round	www.nationalpark -berchtesgaden.de
Naturpark Altmühltal (p163)	mixed forest, streams, rock formations, Roman ruins (2962 sq km)	hiking, cycling, canoeing, kayaking, rock climbing, cross-country skiing, fossil digging	late spring to autumn	www.naturpark -altmuehltal.de
Naturpark Bayerischer Wald	largest continuous forest in Germany (includes the smaller Nationalpark Bayerischer Wald), moorland, meadows, rolling hills (3077 sq km)	hiking, cycling, cross-country skiing, Nordic walking	late spring to autumn	www.naturpark -bayer-wald.de
Naturpark Schwarzwald Mitte/Nord	mixed forest, deep valleys, lakes (3750 sq km); deer, wild boar, raven, capercaillie	hiking, Nordic walking, mountain biking	late spring to autumn	www.naturpark schwarzwald.de
Naturpark Südschwarzwald	mixed forest, pastures, vineyards, lake, moorland (3700 sq km); capercaillie, deer, lynx	hiking, Nordic walking, snow-shoeing, mountain biking	year-round	www.naturpark -suedschwarz wald.de

The Black Forest has two nature parks, which enjoy a lower degree of environmental protection and are essentially outdoor playgrounds. These are sprawling rural landscapes criss-crossed by roads and dotted with villages. Selective logging (no clear-cutting) and agriculture here is done in a controlled and environmentally friendly fashion.

Sylvan wilderness though it may be, the Black Forest has no national parks, though plans are in the pipeline to create the Nationalpark Nordschwarzwald (www.nationalparknordschwarzwald.de), which environmentalists hope will be given the green light in early 2013.

Survival Guide

Directory A–Z

Accommodation

Bavaria and the Black Forest offer all types of places to unpack your suitcase, from hostels, campsites and traditional taverns to chains, business hotels and luxury resorts. Reservations are a good idea between June and September, around major holidays and festivals and, in business-oriented cities, during trade shows.

» Online booking services include www.venere.com, www.booking.com and www.hotel.de. For best last-minute rates try www.hrs.com.

» The website www.sightsleeping.by is a booking portal for rooms in some of Bavaria's most magnificent properties such as castles, palaces and other historical buildings.

» Many tourist office and hotel websites let you check room availability and make reservations. Staff can also help you in person or, if you arrive after office hours, have vacancies posted in the window or a display case.

» Electronic reservation boards, especially common in the Alps, connect you directly to local properties for free, but don't always work reliably.

» Properties with designated nonsmoking rooms are now the norm, but before committing to a room at midrange and budget level, go and smell it first.

» If heading to the region in late September (during Oktoberfest) accommodation of any kind may be very difficult to book at short notice.

» Rooms with air-con are rare.

» Wherever you stay, breakfast always appears on price lists as a separate item, not included in room rates. This is due to finicky local tax laws.

» Another extra charge is the Kurtaxe (resort tax), particularly common in the Alps. Between €1 and €3, it's not included in the room rate but does often gain you a discount card for local transport and sights.

» Wi-fi at every standard of accommodation is increasingly widespread, but is not free. Gratis web connection is more common at hostels than at establishments further up the hotel food chain.

Camping

Almost every town in southern Germany has a campsite a short bus ride away. German campsites are normally well maintained and offer a wide range of facilities.

» The core season runs from May to September with only a few campsites open year-round. July and August are the busiest months.

» There are usually separate charges per person, tent and car, and additional fees for resort tax, electricity and sewage disposal.

» A Camping Card International may yield some savings.

» The *ADAC Camping & Caravanning Führer*, available from bookshops, is a comprehensive camping guide, in German. Other handy sources include www.alanrogers.com and www.eurocampings.eu.

» It's a grey area, but wild camping in Germany is illegal. Farmers may be willing to let you camp on their land if you ask permission first.

BOOK YOUR STAY ONLINE

For more accommodation reviews by Lonely Planet authors, check out http://hotels.lonelyplanet.com. You'll find independent reviews, as well as recommendations on the best places to stay. Best of all, you can book online.

Farm Stays

A holiday on a working farm is a big hit with kids who love interacting with their favourite barnyard animals and helping with everyday chores. Accommodation ranges from barebones rooms with shared facilities to fully furnished holiday flats. Minimum stays of three days are common. For details, check www .landtourismus.de or www .bauernhofurlaub.com (both in German).

Hostels

Bavaria has many hostels of both the indie and youth varieties. While dorm rooms are the cheapest form of accommodation available (even cheaper than camping at certain times of the week/year), private rooms can cost the same or even more than midrange hotel rooms booked online or last minute.

» There are backpacker hostels across the region, though fewer in Baden-Württemberg than Bavaria. This type of hostel attracts a convivial, international crowd to mixed dorms and private rooms. Facilities usually include communal kitchens, lockers, internet access, laundry and a common room.

» The German hostel site www.backpackernetwork .de lists affiliated hostels, but the best places to start are international booking systems such as www.hostelworld.com and www.hostelbookers.com.

» Most hostels offer inexpensive sightseeing and themed tours.

» Classic Hostelling International–affiliated hostels are run by the **Deutsches Jugendherbergswerk** (DJH; www.jugendherberge.de) and cater primarily to German school groups and families.

» Most of DJH hostels have been modernised but can't quite shake that institutional feel. Some can be noisy with harried, grumpy staff.

» Rates in gender-segregated dorms or in family rooms range from €15 to €25 per person, including linen and breakfast. People over 27 are charged an extra €4. If space is tight, priority is given to people under 27, except for those travelling as a family.

» Unless you're a member of your home country's HI association, you either need to buy a Hostelling International Card for €15.50 (valid for one year) or six individual stamps costing €3.10 per night. Both are available at any DJH hostel.

» DJH hostels can now be booked online.

Hotels

Hotels range from small family-run establishments to comfortable midsized properties to luxurious international chains. Expect even budget establishments to be well run and clean. In most older, privately run hotels rooms may vary dramatically in terms of size, décor and amenities. The cheapest share bathroom facilities, while others may come with a shower cubicle installed but no private toilet; only pricier ones have ensuite bathrooms. If possible, ask to see several rooms before committing.

Top-end establishments offer deluxe amenities, perhaps a scenic location, special décor or historical ambience. Many also have pools, saunas, business centres and other upmarket facilities.

Standards of service across the board may be lower than those you are used to back home.

Pensions, Inns & Private Rooms

» *Pensionen* (guesthouses) and *Gasthöfe* or *Gasthäuser* (inns) are smaller, less formal and cheaper than hotels; the latter usually have a restaurant. Expect clean rooms but only minimal amenities – maybe a radio, sometimes a small TV, almost never a phone. Facilities may be shared. What rooms lack in amenities, they often make up for in charm and authenticity.

» *Privatzimmer* (essentially guest rooms in private homes) are ubiquitous and great for catching a glimpse into how locals live, although privacy seekers may find these places a bit too intimate. Tourist offices list rooms available, or look for *Zimmer Frei* (rooms available) signs in house or shop windows. Per person prices range from €20 to €40.

Rental Accommodation

Renting a *Ferienwohnung* (furnished flat) for a week or longer is a sensible option for self-caterers, families and small groups. Stays under a week usually incur a surcharge, and there's almost always a 'cleaning fee' payable at the end.

PRACTICALITIES

» **Newspapers** The Monday edition of *Süddeutsche Zeitung* has a *New York Times* supplement; the *International Herald Tribune* is also available, mainly in cities.

» **Magazines** *Der Spiegel* and *Focus* magazines are popular German news weeklies, which, along with the *Economist, Time* and *Newsweek,* are sold at train stations and major newsstands.

» **Radio** Stations are regional with most featuring a mix of news, talk and music.

» **Weights & Measures** Germany uses the metric system.

» **Smoking** As of 2010 a proper smoking ban in all public indoor spaces took effect in Bavaria. Baden-Württemberg has had a ban since 2007.

Business Hours

Museums usually take Monday off but stay open late one evening a week. Many eateries observe a *Ruhetag* (day of rest), usually Monday or Tuesday.

Banks	8.30am-4pm Mon-Wed & Fri, 8.30am-5.30pm or 6pm Thu
Bars	around 6pm-1am minimum
Clubs	around 11pm-early morning hours
Post offices	9am-6pm Mon-Fri, 9am-1pm Sat
Restaurants	11am-11pm (varies widely)
Major stores and supermarkets	9.30am-8pm Mon-Sat (varies)

Customs

Most articles that you take into Germany for your personal use may be imported free of duty and tax. The following allowances apply to duty-free goods purchased in a non-European Union country. In addition, you can bring in other products up to a value of €430, including tea, coffee and perfume. Bringing meat and milk, as well as products made from them, into the EU is prohibited.

» **Alcohol** 1L of strong liquor or 2L of less than 22% alcohol by volume and 4L of wine.

» **Tobacco** 200 cigarettes or 100 cigarillos or 50 cigars or 250g of loose tobacco.

Electricity

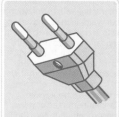

230V/50Hz

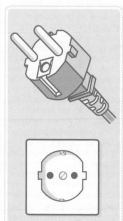

230V/50Hz

Climate

Freiburg

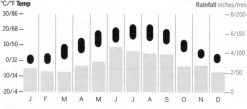

Munich

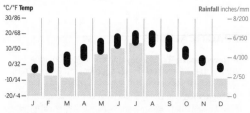

Zugspitze

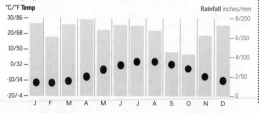

Embassies & Consulates

Most foreign embassies are in Berlin but many countries have consular offices in Munich (only New Zealand in the list below doesn't). For other foreign missions in Germany as well as German missions around the world, see www.auswaertiges-amt.de.

Australia (☑0308 800 880;
Pranner Strasse 8)

Austria (☑089-998 150;
Ismaninger Strasse 136)

Belgium (☑089-2104 1603;
Pacellistrasse 16)

Canada (☑089-219 9570;
Tal 29)

Czech Republic (☑089-
9583 7232; Libellenstrasse 1)

France (☑089-419 4110;
Heimeranstrasse 10)

Ireland (☑089-2080 5990;
Denninger Strasse 15)

Netherlands (☑089-206
026 710; Nymphenburger Str
20a)

New Zealand (☑030-206
210; www.nzembassy.com;
Friedrichstrasse 60; S Stadtmitte, Berlin)

Poland (☑089-418 6080;
Röntgenstrasse 5)

UK (☑089-211 090; Möhlstrasse 5)

USA (☑089-288 80; Königin-
strasse 5)

Gay & Lesbian Travellers

Homosexuality is legal in
Bavaria and the Black Forest, but the scene, even in
Munich, is tiny compared
to, say, Berlin or Cologne.
Nuremberg, Regensburg
and Freiburg are a little more
relaxed as well, but in rural
areas gays and lesbians tend
to keep a low profile. There
are websites aplenty but
most are in German only. Try
www.gayscape.com, www
.gay-web.de or, for women,
www.lesarion.de.

Insurance

No matter how long or short
your trip, make sure you have
adequate travel insurance
covering you for medical
expenses, luggage theft or
loss, and against cancella-
tions or delays of your travel
arrangements. Check your
existing insurance policies at
home (medical, homeowners
etc), since some policies may

already provide worldwide
coverage.

Worldwide travel insurance
is available at www.lonely
planet.com/travel_services.
You can buy, extend and
claim online anytime – even if
you're already on the road.

Internet Access

Getting online is fairly easy
in Germany's south, though
as is the case across Europe
internet cafes are almost a
thing of the past, with perhaps a sole survivor hanging
on in each town.

» Public libraries offer free
terminals and sometimes
wi-fi access, but downsides
may include time limits,
reservation requirements
and queues.

» Some tourist informa-
tion centres lay on free web
access.

» Internet access is available
at slightly seedy telephone
call shops, which cluster near
train stations.

» Hotels and hostels often
have high-speed access and
wi-fi (W-LAN in German – the
word wi-fi is not generally understood) but it's not always
free. That said, an increasing
number of midrange hotels
are dropping their W-LAN
charges.

» Some cafes and pubs offer
wi-fi access, sometimes at no
charge with purchase.

» If you're in the region for
longer than a week or so,
consider investing in a 'don-
gle' (a wireless Internet USB
adaptor) which allows you
surf the net with your laptop
using the mobile phone
network. They're available
off the shelf at mobile phone
shops and electrical goods
outlets for around €30.

Language Courses

The following Munich schools
offer quality German lan-
guage courses:

DESK (Map p48; ☑089-263
334; www.desk-sprachkurse.
de; Blumenstrasse 1) Tried and

tested school with almost
three decades of experi-
ence behind it and a central
location.

Deutschakademie (Map
p48; ☑089-2601 8989; www.
deutschakademie.de; Son-
nenstrasse 8) Small groups,
qualified teachers and
courses running throughout
the day.

Inlingua (Map p48;
☑089-231 1530; www.inlingua
-muenchen.de; Sendlinger-
Tor-Platz 6) A national chain
serving a more corporate
clientele.

**Ludwig-Maximilians-
Universität München**
(☑089-2180 2143; www.
sprachenzentrum.uni
-muenchen.de; Schellingstrasse
3) Summer and term-time
courses at the university.

Legal Matters

By law, you must carry photo
identification such as your
passport or national identity
card (a driving licence may or
may not be acceptable to the
police). If you are arrested,
you have the right to make a
phone call and are presumed
innocent until proven guilty.
If you don't know a lawyer,
contact your nearest consulate for a referral.

Maps

Most tourist offices distrib-
ute free (but often very basic) city maps, but for driving
around you'll need a detailed
road map or atlas such as
those published by Falkplan,
Freytag & Berndt, RV Verlag
or ADAC. Look for them in
bookshops, tourist offices,
newsagents and petrol stations. Find downloadable
maps and driving directions
at www.viamichelin.de and
www.stadtplandienst.de.

Money

» Germany is one of the 17
countries in the European
Union that uses the euro

as its national currency. No other currency is accepted.

» Euros come in seven notes (five, 10, 20, 50, 100, 200 and 500 euros) and eight coins (one and two euro coins, and one, two, five, 10, 20 and 50 cent coins). You're unlikely ever to set eyes on a 200 or 500 euro note.

Exchange money at airports, some banks and currency exchange offices, such as Reisebank, American Express and TravelEx. In rural areas, such facilities are rare, so make sure you have plenty of cash.

ATMs

ATMs linked to international networks such as Cirrus, Plus, Star and Maestro are ubiquitous, accessible 24/7 and the easiest and quickest way to obtain cash. Check with your bank or credit-card company about fees.

Cash

Bavaria is still very much a cash culture and making sure you have ample supply of the stuff will avoid embarrassing situations, such as trying to pay for a beer in a pub or a sausage at the railway station with your credit card. Even at the supermarket cashiers (and the queue behind you) can get a bit huffy if you don't have readies.

Credit Cards

Despite its limited use in Germany to actually pay for anything, a piece of plastic can be vital in emergencies and occasionally also useful for phone or internet bookings. Avoid getting cash on your credit card via ATMs since fees are steep and you'll be charged interest immediately (in other words, there's no grace period as with purchases). Report lost or stolen cards to the following:

American Express (☏069-9797 1000)

MasterCard (☏0800-819 1040)

Visa (☏0800-814 9100)

Travellers Cheques

Travellers cheques are really not worth the hassle for the security they offer and have become virtually obsolete in the age of network-linked ATMs. German businesses generally don't accept them, even if denominated in euros, and banks charge exorbitant fees for cashing them (currency exchange offices are usually better). American Express offices cash Amex cheques free or for a very low commission rate.

Post

» The postal service in Germany is operated by Deutsche Post (www.deutschepost.de) and is very reliable.

» Main post offices are often near train stations.

» Busy offices often have a dedicated desk/window for letters and postcards, avoiding the need to stand in lengthy queues with locals paying bills etc.

» Avoid the post office altogether by printing out *Internetmarke* (internet stamps) from the Deutsche Post website.

Public Holidays

Businesses and offices are closed on the following public holidays:

» **Neujahrstag** (New Year's Day) 1 January

» **Heilige Drei Könige** (Epiphany) 6 January

» **Ostern** (Easter) March/April – Good Friday, Easter Sunday and Easter Monday

» **Maifeiertag** (Labour Day) 1 May

» **Christi Himmelfahrt** (Ascension Day) 40 days after Easter

» **Pfingsten** (Whitsun/Pentecost) mid-May to mid-June – Whit Sunday and Whit Monday

» **Fronleichnam** (Corpus Christi) 10 days after Pentecost

» **Mariä Himmelfahrt** (Assumption Day, Bavaria only) 15 August

» **Tag der Deutschen Einheit** (Day of German Unity) 3 October

» **Allerheiligen** (All Saints Day) 1 November

» **Weihnachtstag** (Christmas Day) 25 December

» **Weihnachtstag** (Boxing/St Stephen's Day) 26 December

Telephone

Domestic & International Calls

German phone numbers consist of an area code, which starts with 0, and the local number. Area codes can be up to six numbers and local numbers up to nine digits long. If dialling from a landline within the same city, you don't need to dial the area code. If using a mobile, you must dial it.

» If calling Germany from abroad, first dial your country's international access code, then 49 (Germany's country code), the area code (dropping the initial 0) and the local number. Germany's international access code is 00.

» Numbers starting with 0800 are toll-free but numbers starting with 0190 or 900 are charged at exorbitant rates. Direct-dialled calls made from hotel rooms are also usually charged at a premium.

» If you have access to a private phone, you can benefit from cheaper rates by using a call-by-call access code. Rates can be found online at www.billigertelefonieren.de.

» With a high-speed internet connection, you can talk PC to PC for free via **Skype** (www.skype.com), or, for a small per-minute charge, to landlines and mobiles direct from your computer.

Mobile Phones

Mobile phones operate on GSM 900/1800. If your

home country uses a different standard, you'll need a multiband GSM phone in Germany. If you have an unlocked multiband phone, a prepaid rechargeable SIM card from a German telecom provider will always work out cheaper than using your own network. Cards are available at any mobile phone store (eg T-Mobile, Vodafone, E-Plus or O2) and will give you a local number without signing a contract.

Phonecards

Most public payphones only work with Deutsche Telecom (DT) phonecards, available in denominations of €5, €10 and €20 from DT stores, post offices, newsagents and tourist offices.

For long-distance and international calls, prepaid calling cards issued by other providers tend to offer better rates. Look for them at newsagents and telephone call shops. There may be a connection fee. Most cards work with payphones with a surcharge.

Time

Clocks in Germany are set to central European time (GMT/ UTC plus one hour). Daylight-saving time kicks in at 2am on the last Sunday in March and ends on the last Sunday in October. The use of the 24-hour clock (eg where 6.30pm is 18.30) is common.

Toilets

» Men's toilets are marked 'Herren' (or just 'H'), the ladies' 'Damen' (or just 'D').
» Public toilets in southern Germany's city centres are almost non-existent. Instead use facilities in department stores, railway stations, markets, beer halls and other public places.
» Toilets are rarely free and those at large railway stations can charge a silly €1

to spend a penny. At some facilities payment is by donation, thus you pay as much as you like. At others there's a price list.
» Toilets are normally clean, well maintained and not of the squat variety, though some are of the slightly off-putting 'reverse bowl design', not common in the UK or US.

Tourist Information

Every reasonable-sized town in southern Germany (even those with no tourists) has a municipally-funded tourist information centre, some of which are stand-alone operations, while others are twinned with a kind of local residents' information point. Only very occasionally will you come across staff who don't speak English and the vast majority of those charged with aiding tourists on their way are knowledgeable, friendly and efficient. Websites operated by tourist boards vary wildly in quality.

Good websites for your pre-trip research are www.bayern.by and www.germany-tourism.de.

Each *Land* (region) also has its own dedicated website:

Black Forest Tourism Association (www.schwarzwald-tourismus.info)

Baden-Württemberg Tourist Association (www.tourism-bw.com)

Eastern Bavarian Tourism Association (www.ostbayern-tourismus.de)

Franconian Tourism Association (www.frankentourismus.org)

Tourism Association Allgäu-Bavarian Swabia (www.bavarian-alps.info)

Upper Bavarian Tourism Association (www.oberbayern-tourismus.de)

Romantic Road Tourism Association (www.romantischestrasse.de)

Travellers with Disabilities

» Generally speaking, southern Germany caters well for the needs of the *Behinderte* (disabled), especially the wheelchair-bound.
» You'll find access ramps and/or lifts in many public buildings, including train stations, museums, theatres and cinemas.
» New hotels and some renovated establishments have lifts and rooms with extra-wide doors and spacious, accessible bathrooms.
» Nearly all trains are accessible, and local buses and U-Bahns are becoming increasingly so. Seeing-eye dogs are allowed on all forms of public transport.
» Many local and regional tourism offices have special brochures for people with disabilities, although usually in German. Good general resources include the following:

Deutsche Bahn Mobility Service Centre (www.bahn.com) Train access information and route planning assistance. The website has useful information in English (search for 'barrier-free travel').

German National Tourism Office (www.deutschland-tourismus.de) Has information about barrier-free travel in Germany.

Munich for Physically Challenged Tourists (www.munich.de) Searching the official Munich tourism website will produce gigabytes of info on everything for travellers with disabilities from Oktoberfest to local clubs and organisations to special ride services.

Natko (www.natko.de) Central clearing house for enquiries about barrier-free travel in Germany.

Visas

Most EU nationals only need their national identity card or passport to enter, stay and work in Germany. Citizens of Australia, Canada, Israel, Japan, New Zealand and the US are among those countries that need only a valid passport (no visa) if entering as tourists for up to three months within a six-month period. Passports should be valid for at least another four months from the planned date of departure from Germany.

Nationals from other countries need a so-called Schengen Visa, named after the 1995 Schengen Agreement that enables passport controls between most countries in the Europe Union to be abolished (all except the UK and Ireland have signed up). For full details, see www.auswaertiges-amt.de or check with a German consulate in your country.

Transport

GETTING THERE & AWAY

If coming from anywhere in Europe, southern Germany's central position means excellent transport connections to the rest of the Continent. Air, rail and bus are all options and Germany's excellent, toll-free motorways (autobahn) make car journeys fast and inexpensive when compared to other countries. From other continents, air is the best option with many big-name flag-carrier airlines operating in and out of Munich airport.

Flights, cars and tours can all be booked online at www .lonelyplanet.com.

Entering the Country

Entering Germany is normally a straightforward procedure. Citizens of most Western countries don't need a visa, but even if you do, you'll be through checks swiftly.

When arriving in Germany from any of the Schengen countries (all Germany's neighbours), you no longer have to go through passport and customs checks, regardless of your nationality.

Air

Airports

Southern Germany is served by several airports:

» The main regional hub is **Flughafen München** (Munich International Airport; MUC; www.munich-airport.de), 30km northeast of Munich's city centre.

» Although Munich is well served by transcontinental flights, most land at **Frankfurt Airport** (FRA; www .frankfurt-airport.com), which is closer to northern Bavaria and the beginning of the Romantic Road.

» **Salzburg Airport** (SZG; www.salzburg-airport.com) is convenient for the southeast of the region and the Alps.

» Despite the name, **Frankfurt-Hahn** (HHN; www .hahn-airport.de) is about 100km west of Frankfurt, not at all convenient for southern Germany.

» The main airport in Franconia is **Nuremberg** (NUE; www .airport-nuernberg.de).

» The two airports serving the Black Forest are **Karlsruhe-Baden-Baden** (Baden Airpark; FKB; www. badenairpark.de) for the north and **EuroAirport Basel-Mulhouse-Freiburg** (BSL; www.euroairport.com) for Freiburg and the south.

Airlines

The main airline serving Germany, **Lufthansa** (LH; www.lufthansa.com), operates a huge network of domestic and international flights and has one of the worlds best safety records. Munich is also a major hub for **Air Berlin** (AB; www.airberlin.com) and **Germanwings** (4U; www. germanwings.com).

Many of the world's major national carriers fly into Munich while budget airlines prefer the region's smaller airports.

Tickets

» Bagging a flight any time around Oktoberfest (late September to early October) is nigh impossible, even well in advance. Other busy times include late August, Christmas and New Year.

» When flights to Munich are unavailable or beyond budget, many travellers buy cheaper tickets to other airports such as Frankfurt, Salzburg or Nuremberg, then hop on a train to their final destination.

» Don't assume budget airline tickets to Germany will be cheaper than those offered by other airlines. Lufthansa often have some great deals and don't charge for all those extras like luggage and credit card payment as the no-frills carriers usually do.

» If travelling from North America, Australia or Asia via Frankfurt, save money (and time) and take the train south, rather than another domestic flight to Munich. Frankfurt airport has it's own train station.

Land

Border Crossings

Germany is bordered (anticlockwise) by Denmark, the Netherlands, Belgium, Luxembourg, France, Switzerland, Austria, the Czech Republic and Poland. The Schengen Agreement abolished passport and customs formalities between Germany and all bordering countries.

Bus

* **Eurolines** (www.eurolines. com) is the umbrella organisation of European coach operators connecting over 500 destinations across Europe. Its website has links to each national company's site, with detailed fare and route information, promotional offers, contact numbers and, in many cases, an online booking system. In Germany, Eurolines is represented by **Deutsche Touring** (www.touring.de).

» If Germany's south is part of your European-wide itinerary, a **Eurolines Pass** (www .eurolines-pass.com; 15-/30-day peak-travel pass travellers over 26 €350/460, under 26 €295/380) can save you money. It allows for unlimited travel between 51 European cities within a 15- or 30-day period. Buy online or from travel agents.

» **Busabout** (www.busabout. com; one loop £399) is a hop-on, hop-off service that runs coaches along several interlocking European loops between May and October.

Stops include Munich, Stuttgart and Salzburg.

Boat

The Romanshorn-Friedrichshafen ferry provides the quickest way across Lake Constance between Switzerland and Germany. Ferries operated by **SBS Schifffahrt** (www.sbsag.ch; per person €8.60, bicycles €5.70, cars €18.20) take 40 minutes.

Car & Motorcycle

» When bringing your own vehicle to Germany, you need a valid driving licence, your car registration certificate and proof of insurance.

» Foreign cars must display a nationality sticker unless they have official Euro-plates.

» Equipment you need to have in your car by law includes a first-aid kit, spare bulbs and a warning triangle.

» In winter, even away from the Alps, make sure your vehicle is fitted with winter tyres and carry snow chains in the boot. Spiked tyres are prohibited.

» Be aware that if driving to Germany via France, you must now have a breathalyser approved by the French authorities in the car, as well as other equipment not required in Germany. The Czech Republic also has some finicky requirements, so see www.theaa.com (click through to Driving, then Driving Abroad) for the full rundown.

Train

» Long-distance trains connecting major German

cities with those in other countries are called EuroCity (EC) trains. Seat reservations are highly recommended, especially during the peak summer season and around major holidays.

» Linking the UK with continental Europe, the **Eurostar** (www.eurostar.com) takes less than three hours from London–St Pancras to Paris, where you can get a high-speed TGV service to Munich taking another six hours.

» There are direct overnight trains to Munich from Amsterdam, Copenhagen, Belgrade, Budapest, Bucharest, Florence, Milan, Rome, Venice and Vienna.

» Use the Deutsche Bahn website (www.bahn.de) or The Man in Seat 61 site (www.seat61.com) to plan your journey to southern Germany.

GETTING AROUND

Getting around Bavaria and the Black Forest is most efficient by car or by train. Regional bus services fill the gaps in areas not well served by the rail network.

Air

Although it is possible to fly, say, from Frankfurt to Munich or Salzburg, the time and cost involved don't make air travel a sensible way to get around southern Germany.

Unless you're travelling to Bavaria or the Black Forest from northern Germany,

---

CLIMATE CHANGE & TRAVEL

Every form of transport that relies on carbon-based fuel generates CO_2, the main cause of human-induced climate change. Modern travel is dependent on aeroplanes, which might use less fuel per kilometer per person than most cars but travel much greater distances. The altitude at which aircraft emit gases (including CO_2) and particles also contributes to their climate change impact. Many websites offer 'carbon calculators' that allow people to estimate the carbon emissions generated by their journey and, for those who wish to do so, to offset the impact of the greenhouse gases emitted with contributions to portfolios of climate-friendly initiatives throughout the world. Lonely Planet offsets the carbon footprint of all staff and author travel.

planes are only marginally faster than trains if you factor in the time it takes to travel to and from the airports. **Lufthansa** (LH; www.lufthansa.com), **Air Berlin** (AB; www.airberlin.com) and **Germanwings** (4U; www.germanwings.com) are among the airlines flying domestically.

ROMANTIC ROAD BUS

Europabus coach services is run by **Deutsche Touring** (www.touring.de) and geared towards individual travellers on the Romantic Road (p127) between Würzburg and Füssen from April to October.

There's one coach in either direction daily. Tickets can be purchased by phone or online and are available either for the entire distance or for segments between any of the stops. Various discounts are available.

Bicycle

Cycling is one of the most popular ways to get around for both locals and visitors, making southern Germany one of Europe's most bike-friendly regions.

» Cycling is allowed on all roads and highways but not on the autobahns (motorways). Cyclists must follow the same rules of the road as vehicles.

» Cycle paths are ubiquitous in large cities.

» Lights are compulsory but helmets aren't, not even for children. Wearing one is still a good idea, though.

» Bicycles may be taken on most trains but usually require a separate *Fahrradkarte* (bicycle ticket). However, they're not allowed on high-speed ICE trains. For specifics inquire at a local station or call Deutsche Bahn (DB) on the **DB Radfahrer-Hotline** (Bicycle Hotline; ☏0180-599 6633; ⏲8am-8pm).

» Many regional bus companies use vehicles with special bike racks. Bicycles are also allowed on practically all lake and river boats.

» Around 250 train stations throughout the country hire bikes. All information can be found at www.bahn.de.

» Cycle hire centres are common – rates range between €10 and €25 per day.

» **Bett & Bike** (www.bettundbike.de; Bed & Bike) lists accommodation with facilities for bikes (storage, tools, washing amenities).

Bus

Basically, wherever there is a train, take it. Buses are generally slower, less dependable and more polluting than trains, but in some rural areas they may be your only option. This is especially true of the Bavarian Forest and the Black Forest, sections of the Alpine foothills and the Alpine region. Separate bus companies, each with its own tariffs and schedules, operate in the different regions, but with a bit of practice all timetables (though not fares) can be looked up using the Deutsche Bahn website (www.bahn.de).

In cities, buses generally converge at the *Busbahnhof* or *Zentraler Omnibus Bahnhof/ZOB* (central bus station), often near the Hauptbahnhof (main train station). The frequency of service varies from 'rarely' to 'constantly'. Commuter-geared routes offer limited or no service in the evenings and on weekends. Always ask about special fare deals, such as day or weekly passes or tourist tickets.

Car & Motorcycle

» German autobahns (motorways) are of a good standard though they do possess some quirks such as excessively bendy slip roads and many two-lane sections.

» The extensive network of *Bundesstrassen* (secondary 'A' and 'B' roads) is also good, though perhaps not up to the standard you are used to back home.

» No tolls are charged on public roads.

» Traffic can be heavy on *Bundesstrassen* at busy times of the day.

» Up-to-the-minute travel and roadwork information in English is available at www .bayerninfo.de. Traffic reports on the radio (in German) usually follow on-the-hour news summaries.

» Well-equipped service areas appear every 40km to 60km on autobahns with petrol stations, toilet facilities and restaurants; some are open 24 hours. In between are *Rastplätze* (rest stops), which usually have picnic tables and toilet facilities.

Automobile Associations

Germany's main motoring organisation, the **Allgemeiner Deutscher Automobil-Club** (ADAC; ☏for roadside assistance 0180-222 2222, from mobile phone 222 222; www.adac.de) has offices in all major cities and many smaller ones. Its roadside assistance is also available to members of its affiliates, including the British AA and American AAA.

Driving Licence

Drivers need a valid driving licence. International Driving Permits (IDP; issued by your local automobile association) for non-EU drivers are not compulsory but having one may help Germans make sense of your home licence (always carry that one too)

TRAIN PASSES

If residing permanently outside Europe, you qualify for the German Rail Pass, which entitles you to unlimited travel for four to 10 days within a one-month period. Sample prices for four/seven/10 days of travel are €249/323/408 in 2nd class (half-price for children ages six to 11). The pass is valid on all trains within Germany, plus Salzburg and Basel as well as some river services, and entitles you to discounts on the Europabus along the Romantic Road and the Bayerische Zugspitzbahn.

The German Rail Youth Pass for people between 12 and 25, and the German Rail Twin Pass for two adults travelling together are variations on the scheme. If Bavaria is part of a wider European itinerary, look into a **Eurail Pass** (www.eurail.com).

A great resource for rail passes wherever you live is **Rail Europe** (www.raileurope.com), a major agency specialising in train travel around Europe.

and may simplify the car hire process.

Hire

» Southern Germany has an excellent public transport system meaning car hire isn't absolutely necessary. One exception is the trip along the Romantic Road where a car makes travel a lot easier.

» As anywhere, rates for car hire vary quite considerably by model, pick-up date and location.

» Mini-economy class vehicles start from around €35 per day, but expect surcharges for additional drivers and one-way hire.

» Pre-booking through websites such as www .auto-europe.co.uk, www .rentalcars.com and www .holidayautos.com can bring daily rates down to less than €20 depending on how long you need the car.

» Child or infant seats are usually available for free or for a symbolic charge. Satellite-navigation units can be hired for a small fee per day. Both should be reserved at the time of booking.

» To pick up your car you'll probably need to be at least 21 years old with a valid driv-ing licence as well as a major credit card.

» Taking your car into an Eastern European country, such as the Czech Republic or Poland, is often not al-lowed. Check in advance if that's where you're heading.

» All the main international companies maintain branches at airports, major train stations and in large towns.

Insurance

» German law requires that all registered vehicles carry minimum third-party liability insurance. Don't even think of driving uninsured or under-insured.

» When hiring a vehicle, make sure your contract includes adequate liability insurance at the very minimum.

» Optional Collision Damage Waiver (CDW) for hire cars is extra and is charged when you pick up the vehicle.

Road Rules

» Driving is on the right-hand side of the road and standard international signs are in use. If you're unfamiliar with these, contact your local motoring organisation.

» Obey the road rules care-fully: speed and red-light cameras are common and no-tices are sent to the car's reg-istration address, wherever that may be. If you're renting a car, the police will obtain your home address from the rental agency and fines may be chased up by debt collec-tors where you live.

» There's a long list of other actions that may incur a fine, including using abusive language or gestures and running out of petrol on the autobahn.

» Speed limits are 50km/h in built up areas and 100km/h on highways and country roads unless oth-erwise indicated. There are sections of autobahns where there's no speed limit, but always keep an eye out for signs indicating that slower speeds must be observed.

» Drivers unaccustomed to the high speeds on autobahns should be extra careful when passing another vehicle. It takes only seconds for a car in the rear-view mir-ror to close in at 200km/h. Pass as quickly as possible, then quickly return to the right lane.

» Ignore drivers who flash their headlights to make you drive faster and get out of the way. It's an illegal practice, as is passing on the right.

» If you break down, pull over to the side of the road immediately and set up your warning triangle about 100m behind the car. Emergency call boxes are spaced about 2km apart or, if you have a mobile phone, call the ADAC and wait for assistance.

» The highest permissible blood-alcohol level for drivers is 0.05%, which for most people equates to roughly one glass of wine or two small beers. The limit for drivers under 21 and for those who have held their license for less than two years is 0%.

» Pedestrians at crossings have right of way over all

motor vehicles. Always watch out for cyclists when turning right; they too have the right of way. Right turns at a red light are only legal if there's also a green arrow pointing to the right.

Hitching & Ride-Share

Trampen (hitching) is never entirely safe and, frankly, we don't recommend it. That said, in some remote parts of Bavaria and the Black Forest – such as sections of the Alpine foothills and the Bavarian Forest – that are poorly served by public transport, you will occasionally see people thumbing for a ride. Remember that it's safer to travel in pairs and be sure to let someone know where you're planning to go.

A safer and more predictable form of travelling is ride-shares, where you travel as a passenger in exchange for some petrol money. Most arrangements are now made via online ride-boards at www.mitfahrzentrale.de, www.mitfahrgelegenheit.de or www.drive2day.de. You can advertise a ride yourself or link up with a driver going to your destination.

Local Transport

» Most towns have efficient public transport systems. Bigger cities, such as Munich and Nuremberg, integrate buses, trams, and U-Bahn (underground) and S-Bahn (suburban) trains into a single network.

» Tickets are generally bought in advance from ticket machines before boarding any mode of transport and must be stamped before or upon boarding in order to be valid.

» Fares are either determined by zones or time travelled, or sometimes by both. *Tageskarten* (day passes) generally offer better value than single-ride tickets.

» The fine if you're caught without a valid ticket is €40.

» Taxis are metered and charged at a base rate (flag fall) plus a per-kilometre fee. These are fixed but vary across cities. Some charge extra for bulky luggage or night-time rides. Rarely can you flag down a taxi. Rather, you board at a taxi rank or order one by phone (look their numbers up under *Taxiruf* in the phonebook).

Train

Germany's rail system is operated almost entirely by **Deutsche Bahn** (www.bahn .com) with a bamboozling 'alphabet soup' of train types serving just about every corner of the country. The system is efficient, but largely automated and unmanned. This can cause problems when things go wrong as there are often no staff members around to whom you can turn for information.

Most train stations have coin-operated lockers charging from €1.50 to €4 for 24 hours.

» Long-distance trains are either called ICE (InterCity Express), which travel at high speeds, or the only slightly slower IC (InterCity) or EC (EuroCity) trains. Both run at hourly or bi-hourly intervals.

» Regional service is provided by the IRE (InterRegio Express), the RB (Regional-Bahn), the SE (StadtExpress) and the S-Bahn.

SAMPLE FARES

Permanent rail deals include:

TICKET	COST	VALIDITY
Bayern-Ticket	€22+€4 per extra person	Mon-Fri 9am-3am, weekends midnight-3am of next day
Baden-Württemberg-Ticket	€21+€4 per extra person	Mon-Fri 9am-3am, weekends midnight-3am of next day
Bayern-Ticket Nacht	€22+€2 per extra person	6pm-6am
Baden-Württemberg-Ticket Nacht	€17+€4 per extra person	6pm-6am

All of the above tickets are good for second class travel on IRE, SE, RB and S-Bahn trains, as well as all public buses, trams, U-Bahns and privately run railways across the given *Land* for which they are valid. They're now available from vending machines; buying from ticket windows incurs an extra charge. Remember, with the daytime tickets you can save tens of euros by putting off your journey until after 9am, especially when travelling long distances within Bavaria. The Bayern-Ticket is also valid as far as Salzburg Hauptbahnhof.

Tickets

» Large train stations have a *Reisezentrum* (travel centre) where staff sell tickets and can help you plan an itinerary (ask for an English-speaking agent). Smaller stations may only have a few ticket windows or no staff at all.

» Sometimes you will have no choice but to buy your ticket from a vending machine. These are plentiful at staffed and unstaffed stations and convenient if you don't want to queue at a ticket counter. Instructions are in English and the ticket purchasing system has been greatly simplified.

» Both ticket windows and machines accept major credit cards, but machines don't take €50 notes. Tickets sold on board (cash only) incur a service fee (€3 to €8) unless the station where you boarded was unstaffed or had a broken vending machine.

» Tickets are also available online up to 10 minutes before departure but need to be printed out.

» Tickets and passes are almost always checked. The fine for not holding a valid travel document is €40.

» Standard, non-discounted train tickets are expensive, but promotions, discount tickets and special offers become available all the time. Check the website or ask at the train station.

ON BOARD

German trains have 1st- and 2nd-class cars, both of them modern and comfortable. Seating is either in compartments of up to six people or in open-plan carriages with panoramic windows. Trains are now completely nonsmoking. ICE, IC and EC trains are air-conditioned and have a restaurant or self-service bistro.

RESERVATIONS

Seat reservations (€4 per person) for long-distance travel are highly recommended, especially on a Friday or Sunday afternoon, around holidays or in summer. They can be made up to 10 minutes before departure by phone, online or at ticket counters.

WANT MORE?

For in-depth language information and handy phrases, check out Lonely Planet's *German Phrasebook*. You'll find it at **shop.lonely planet.com**, or you can buy Lonely Planet's iPhone phrasebooks at the Apple App Store.

Language

German belongs to the West Germanic language family, with English and Dutch as close relatives, and has around 100 million speakers. It is commonly divided into two forms – Low German *(Plattdeutsch)* and High German *(Hochdeutsch)*. Low German is an umbrella term used for the dialects spoken in Northern Germany. High German is considered the standard form and is understood throughout German-speaking communities; it's also the variety used in this chapter.

German is easy for English speakers to pronounce because almost all of its sounds are also found in English. If you read our coloured pronunciation guides as if they were English, you'll have no problems being understood. Note that kh is like the 'ch' in 'Bach' or the Scottish 'loch' (pronounced at the back of the throat), r is also pronounced at the back of the throat (almost like a g, but with some friction), zh is pronounced as the 's' in 'measure', and ü as the 'ee' in 'see' but with rounded lips. The stressed syllables are indicated with italics.

BASICS

Hello.	*Guten Tag.*	*goo*·ten tahk
Goodbye.	*Auf Wiedersehen.*	owf *vee*·der·zay·en
Yes./No.	*Ja./Nein.*	yah/nain
Please.	*Bitte.*	*bi*·te
Thank you.	*Danke.*	*dang*·ke
You're welcome.	*Bitte.*	*bi*·te
Excuse me.	*Entschuldigung.*	ent·*shul*·di·gung
Sorry.	*Entschuldigung.*	ent·*shul*·di·gung

How are you?
Wie geht es Ihnen/dir? (pol/inf)	vee gayt es *ee*·nen/deer

Fine. And you?
Danke, gut. Und Ihnen/dir? (pol/inf)	*dang*·ke goot unt *ee*·nen/deer

What's your name?
Wie ist Ihr Name? (pol)	vee ist eer *nah*·me
Wie heißt du? (inf)	vee haist doo

My name is ...
Mein Name ist ... (pol)	main *nah*·me ist ...
Ich heiße ... (inf)	ikh *hai*·se ...

Do you speak English?
Sprechen Sie Englisch? (pol)	*shpre*·khen zee *eng*·lish
Sprichst du Englisch? (inf)	shprikhst doo *eng*·lish

I don't understand.
Ich verstehe nicht.	ikh fer·*shtay*·e nikht

ACCOMMODATION

campsite	*Campingplatz*	*kem*·ping·plats
guesthouse	*Pension*	pahng·*zyawn*
hotel	*Hotel*	ho·*tel*
inn	*Gasthof*	*gast*·hawf
room in a private home	*Privatzimmer*	pri·*vaht*·tsi·mer
youth hostel	*Jugend-herberge*	*yoo*·gent·her·ber·ge
Do you have a ... room?	*Haben Sie ein ...?*	*hah*·ben zee ain ...
double	*Doppelzimmer*	*do*·pel·tsi·mer
single	*Einzelzimmer*	*ain*·tsel·tsi·mer

How much is it per ...?	Wie viel kostet es pro ...?	vee feel kos·tet es praw ...
night	Nacht	nakht
person	Person	per·zawn

Is breakfast included?
Ist das Frühstück inklusive? — ist das frü·shtük in·kloo·zee·ve

DIRECTIONS

Where's ...?
Wo ist ...? — vaw ist ...

What's the address?
Wie ist die Adresse? — vee ist dee a·dre·se

How far is it?
Wie weit ist es? — vee vait ist es

Can you show me (on the map)?
Können Sie es mir (auf der Karte) zeigen? — ker·nen zee es meer (owf dair kar·te) tsai·gen

How can I get there?
Wie kann ich da hinkommen? — vee kan ikh dah hin·ko·men

Turn ...	Biegen Sie ... ab.	bee·gen zee ... ab
at the corner	an der Ecke	an dair e·ke
at the traffic lights	bei der Ampel	bai dair am·pel
left	links	lingks
right	rechts	rekhts

EATING & DRINKING

I'd like to reserve a table for ...	Ich möchte einen Tisch für ... reservieren.	ikh merkh·te ai·nen tish für ... re·zer·vee·ren
(eight) o'clock	(acht) Uhr	(akht) oor
(two) people	(zwei) Personen	(tsvai) per·zaw·nen

I'd like the menu, please.
Ich hätte gern die Speisekarte, bitte. — ikh he·te gern dee shpai·ze·kar·te bi·te

What would you recommend?
Was empfehlen Sie? — vas emp·fay·len zee

What's in that dish?
Was ist in diesem Gericht? — vas ist in dee·zem ge·rikht

I'm a vegetarian.
Ich bin Vegetarier/Vegetarierin. (m/f) — ikh bin ve·ge·tah·ri·er/ve·ge·tah·ri·e·rin

That was delicious.
Das hat hervorragend geschmeckt. — das hat her·fawr·rah·gent ge·shmekt

Cheers!
Prost! — prawst

KEY PATTERNS

To get by in German, mix and match these simple patterns with words of your choice:

When's (the next flight)?
Wann ist (der nächste Flug)? — van ist (dair naykhs·te flook)

Where's (the station)?
Wo ist (der Bahnhof)? — vaw ist (dair bahn·hawf)

Where can I (buy a ticket)?
Wo kann ich (eine Fahrkarte kaufen)? — vaw kan ikh (ai·ne fahr·kar·te kow·fen)

Do you have (a map)?
Haben Sie (eine Karte)? — hah·ben zee (ai·ne kar·te)

Is there (a toilet)?
Gibt es (eine Toilette)? — gipt es (ai·ne to·a·le·te)

I'd like (a coffee).
Ich möchte (einen Kaffee). — ikh merkh·te (ai·nen ka·fay)

I'd like (to hire a car).
Ich möchte (ein Auto mieten). — ikh merkh·te (ain ow·to mee·ten)

Can I (enter)?
Darf ich (hereinkommen)? — darf ikh (her·ein·ko·men)

Could you please (help me)?
Könnten Sie (mir helfen)? — kern·ten zee (meer hel·fen)

Do I have to (book a seat)?
Muss ich (einen Platz reservieren lassen)? — mus ikh (ai·nen plats re·zer·vee·ren la·sen)

Please bring the bill.
Bitte bringen Sie die Rechnung. — bi·te bring·en zee dee rekh·nung

Key Words

bar (pub)	Kneipe	knai·pe
bottle	Flasche	fla·she
bowl	Schüssel	shü·sel
breakfast	Frühstück	frü·shtük
cold	kalt	kalt
cup	Tasse	ta·se
daily special	Gericht des Tages	ge·rikht des tah·ges
delicatessen	Feinkostgeschäft	fain·kost·ge·sheft
desserts	Nachspeisen	nahkh·shpai·zen
dinner	Abendessen	ah·bent·e·sen
drink list	Getränkekarte	ge·treng·ke·kar·te

fork	*Gabel*	*gah*·bel
glass	*Glas*	glahs
grocery store	*Lebensmittel-laden*	*lay*·bens·mi·tel·lah·den
hot (warm)	*warm*	warm
knife	*Messer*	*me*·ser
lunch	*Mittagessen*	*mi*·tahk·e·sen
market	*Markt*	markt
plate	*Teller*	*te*·ler
restaurant	*Restaurant*	res·to·*rahng*
set menu	*Menü*	may·*nü*
spicy	*würzig*	*vür*·tsikh
spoon	*Löffel*	*ler*·fel
with/without	*mit/ohne*	mit/*aw*·ne

Meat & Fish

beef	*Rindfleisch*	*rint*·flaish
carp	*Karpfen*	*karp*·fen
fish	*Fisch*	fish
herring	*Hering*	*hay*·ring
lamb	*Lammfleisch*	*lam*·flaish
meat	*Fleisch*	flaish
pork	*Schweinefleisch*	*shvai*·ne·flaish
poultry	*Geflügelfleisch*	ge·*flü*·gel·flaish
salmon	*Lachs*	laks
sausage	*Wurst*	vurst
seafood	*Meeresfrüchte*	*mair*·res·frükh·te
shellfish	*Schaltiere*	*shahl*·tee·re
trout	*Forelle*	fo·*re*·le
veal	*Kalbfleisch*	*kalp*·flaish

Fruit & Vegetables

apple	*Apfel*	*ap*·fel
banana	*Banane*	ba·*nah*·ne
bean	*Bohne*	*baw*·ne
cabbage	*Kraut*	krowt
capsicum	*Paprika*	*pap*·ri·kah
carrot	*Mohrrübe*	*mawr*·rü·be
cucumber	*Gurke*	*gur*·ke
fruit	*Frucht/Obst*	frukht/awpst
grapes	*Weintrauben*	*vain*·trow·ben
lemon	*Zitrone*	tsi·*traw*·ne
lentil	*Linse*	*lin*·ze
lettuce	*Kopfsalat*	*kopf*·za·laht
mushroom	*Pilz*	pilts
nuts	*Nüsse*	*nü*·se
onion	*Zwiebel*	*tsvee*·bel

orange	*Orange*	o·*rahng*·zhe
pea	*Erbse*	*erp*·se
plum	*Pflaume*	*pflow*·me
potato	*Kartoffel*	kar·*to*·fel
spinach	*Spinat*	shpi·*naht*
strawberry	*Erdbeere*	*ert*·bair·re
tomato	*Tomate*	to·*mah*·te
vegetable	*Gemüse*	ge·*mü*·ze
watermelon	*Wasser-melone*	*va*·ser·me·law·ne

Other

bread	*Brot*	brawt
butter	*Butter*	*bu*·ter
cheese	*Käse*	*kay*·ze
egg/eggs	*Ei/Eier*	ai/*ai*·er
honey	*Honig*	*haw*·nikh
jam	*Marmelade*	mar·me·*lah*·de
pasta	*Nudeln*	*noo*·deln
pepper	*Pfeffer*	*pfe*·fer
rice	*Reis*	rais
salt	*Salz*	zalts
soup	*Suppe*	*zu*·pe
sugar	*Zucker*	*tsu*·ker

Drinks

beer	*Bier*	beer
coffee	*Kaffee*	*ka*·fay
juice	*Saft*	zaft
milk	*Milch*	milkh
orange juice	*Orangensaft*	o·*rang*·zhen·zaft
red wine	*Rotwein*	*rawt*·vain
sparkling wine	*Sekt*	zekt
tea	*Tee*	tay
water	*Wasser*	*va*·ser
white wine	*Weißwein*	*vais*·vain

Signs

Ausgang	Exit
Damen	Women
Eingang	Entrance
Geschlossen	Closed
Herren	Men
Toiletten (WC)	Toilets
Offen	Open
Verboten	Prohibited

EMERGENCIES

Help!
Hilfe! — *hil·fe*

Go away!
Gehen Sie weg! — *gay·en zee vek*

Call the police!
Rufen Sie die Polizei! — *roo·fen zee dee po·li·tsai*

Call a doctor!
Rufen Sie einen Arzt! — *roo·fen zee ai·nen artst*

Where are the toilets?
Wo ist die Toilette? — *vo ist dee to·a·le·te*

I'm lost.
Ich habe mich verirrt. — *ikh hah·be mikh fer·irt*

I'm sick.
Ich bin krank. — *ikh bin krangk*

It hurts here.
Es tut hier weh. — *es toot heer vay*

I'm allergic to ...
Ich bin allergisch — *ikh bin a·lair·gish*
gegen ... — *gay·gen ...*

SHOPPING & SERVICES

I'd like to buy ...
Ich möchte ... kaufen. — *ikh merkh·te ... kow·fen*

I'm just looking.
Ich schaue mich nur um. — *ikh show·e mikh noor um*

Can I look at it?
Können Sie es mir — *ker·nen zee es meer*
zeigen? — *tsai·gen*

How much is this?
Wie viel kostet das? — *vee feel kos·tet das*

That's too expensive.
Das ist zu teuer. — *das ist tsoo toy·er*

Can you lower the price?
Können Sie mit dem — *ker·nen zee mit dem*
Preis heruntergehen? — *prais he·run·ter·gay·en*

There's a mistake in the bill.
Da ist ein Fehler — *dah ist ain fay·ler*
in der Rechnung. — *in dair rekh·nung*

ATM	*Geldautomat*	*gelt·ow·to·maht*
post office	*Postamt*	*post·amt*
tourist office	*Fremden-verkehrsbüro*	*frem·den·fer·kairs·bü·raw*

Question Words		
How?	*Wie?*	vee
What?	*Was?*	vas
When?	*Wann?*	van
Where?	*Wo?*	vaw
Who?	*Wer?*	vair
Why?	*Warum?*	va·rum

TIME & DATES

What time is it? *Wie spät ist es?* — vee shpayt ist es

It's (10) o'clock. *Es ist (zehn) Uhr.* — es ist (tsayn) oor

At what time? *Um wie viel Uhr?* — um vee feel oor

At ... *Um ...* — um ...

morning	*Morgen*	*mor·gen*
afternoon	*Nachmittag*	*nahkh·mi·tahk*
evening	*Abend*	*ah·bent*
yesterday	*gestern*	*ges·tern*
today	*heute*	*hoy·te*
tomorrow	*morgen*	*mor·gen*
Monday	*Montag*	*mawn·tahk*
Tuesday	*Dienstag*	*deens·tahk*
Wednesday	*Mittwoch*	*mit·vokh*
Thursday	*Donnerstag*	*do·ners·tahk*
Friday	*Freitag*	*frai·tahk*
Saturday	*Samstag*	*zams·tahk*
Sunday	*Sonntag*	*zon·tahk*
January	*Januar*	*yan·u·ahr*
February	*Februar*	*fay·bru·ahr*
March	*März*	merts
April	*April*	*a·pril*
May	*Mai*	mai
June	*Juni*	*yoo·ni*
July	*Juli*	*yoo·li*
August	*August*	*ow·gust*
September	*September*	*zep·tem·ber*
October	*Oktober*	*ok·taw·ber*
November	*November*	*no·vem·ber*
December	*Dezember*	*de·tsem·ber*

TRANSPORT

Public Transport

boat	*Boot*	bawt
bus	*Bus*	bus
metro	*U-Bahn*	*oo·bahn*
plane	*Flugzeug*	*flook·tsoyk*
train	*Zug*	tsook

At what time's the ... bus?	*Wann fährt der ... Bus?*	van fairt dair ... bus
first	*erste*	*ers·te*
last	*letzte*	*lets·te*

Numbers

1	eins	ains
2	zwei	tsvai
3	drei	drai
4	vier	feer
5	fünf	fünf
6	sechs	zeks
7	sieben	zee·ben
8	acht	akht
9	neun	noyn
10	zehn	tsayn
20	zwanzig	tsvan·tsikh
30	dreißig	drai·tsikh
40	vierzig	feer·tsikh
50	fünfzig	fünf·tsikh
60	sechzig	zekh·tsikh
70	siebzig	zeep·tsikh
80	achtzig	akht·tsikh
90	neunzig	noyn·tsikh
100	hundert	hun·dert
1000	tausend	tow·sent

A ... to (Berlin).	Eine ... nach (Berlin).	ai·ne ... nahkh (ber·leen)
1st-class ticket	Fahrkarte erster Klasse	fahr·kar·te ers·ter kla·se
2nd-class ticket	Fahrkarte zweiter Klasse	fahr·kar·te tsvai·ter kla·se
one-way ticket	einfache Fahrkarte	ain·fa·khe fahr·kar·te
return ticket	Rückfahrkarte	rük·fahr·kar·te

At what time does it arrive?
Wann kommt es an? — van komt es an

Is it a direct route?
Ist es eine direkte Verbindung? — ist es ai·ne di·rek·te fer·bin·dung

Does it stop at (Freiburg)?
Hält es in (Freiburg)? — helt es in (frai·boorg)

What station is this?
Welcher Bahnhof ist das? — vel·kher bahn·hawf ist das

What's the next stop?
Welches ist der nächste Halt? — vel·khes ist dair naykh·ste halt

I want to get off here.
Ich möchte hier aussteigen. — ikh merkh·te heer ows·shtai·gen

Please tell me when we get to (Kiel).
Könnten Sie mir bitte sagen, wann wir in (Kiel) ankommen? — kern·ten zee meer bi·te zah·gen van veer in (keel) an·ko·men

Please take me to (this address).
Bitte bringen Sie mich zu (dieser Adresse). — bi·te bring·en zee mikh tsoo (dee·zer a·dre·se)

platform	Bahnsteig	bahn·shtaik
ticket office	Fahrkartenverkauf	fahr·kar·ten·fer·kowf
timetable	Fahrplan	fahr·plan

Driving & Cycling

I'd like to hire a ...	Ich möchte ein ... mieten.	ikh merkh·te ain ... mee·ten
4WD	Allradfahrzeug	al·raht·fahr·tsoyk
bicycle	Fahrrad	fahr·raht
car	Auto	ow·to
motorbike	Motorrad	maw·tor·raht

How much is it per ...?	Wie viel kostet es pro ...?	vee feel kos·tet es praw ...
day	Tag	tahk
week	Woche	vo·khe

bicycle pump	Fahrradpumpe	fahr·raht·pum·pe
child seat	Kindersitz	kin·der·zits
helmet	Helm	helm
petrol	Benzin	ben·tseen

Does this road go to ...?
Führt diese Straße nach ...? — fürt dee·ze shtrah·se nahkh ...

(How long) Can I park here?
(Wie lange) Kann ich hier parken? — (vee lang·e) kan ikh heer par·ken

Where's a petrol station?
Wo ist eine Tankstelle? — vaw ist ai·ne tangk·shte·le

I need a mechanic.
Ich brauche einen Mechaniker. — ikh brow·khe ai·nen me·khah·ni·ker

My car/motorbike has broken down (at ...).
Ich habe (in ...) eine Panne mit meinem Auto/Motorrad. — ikh hah·be (in ...) ai·ne pa·ne mit mai·nem ow·to/maw·tor·raht

I've run out of petrol.
Ich habe kein Benzin mehr. — ikh hah·be kain ben·tseen mair

I have a flat tyre.
Ich habe eine Reifenpanne. — ikh hah·be ai·ne rai·fen·pa·ne

Are there cycling paths?
Gibt es Fahrradwege? — geept es fahr·raht·vay·ge

Is there bicycle parking?
Gibt es FahrradParkplätze? — geept es fahr·raht·park·ple·tse

GLOSSARY

(pl) indicates plural

Abtei – abbey
ADAC – Allgemeiner Deutscher Automobil Club (German Automobile Association)
Allee – avenue
Altstadt – old town
Apotheke – pharmacy
Ärzt – doctor
Ausgang – exit

Bad – spa, bath
Bahnhof – train station
Basilika – basilica
Bedienung – service; service charge
Berg – mountain
Bibliothek – library
Biergarten – beer garden
Bierkeller – cellar pub
Brauerei – brewery
Brotzeit – literally bread time, typically an afternoon snack featuring bread with cold cuts, cheeses or sausages
Brücke – bridge
Brunnen – fountain, well
Burg – castle
Busbahnhof – bus station

Christkindlmarkt – Christmas food and craft market; sometimes spelt *Christkindlesmarkt*

DB – Deutsche Bahn (German national railway)
Denkmal – memorial
Deutsche Reich – German empire; refers to the period 1871–1918
DJH – Deutsches Jugendherbergswerk (German youth hostel association)
Dom – cathedral
Dorf – village

Eingang – entrance

Fahrrad – bicycle
Ferienwohnung, Ferienwohnungen (pl) – holiday flat or apartment
Fest – festival
Flohmarkt – flea market
Flughafen – airport

Krankenhaus – hospital
Kunst – art
Kurhaus – literally spa house, but usually a spa towns central building, used for social gatherings and events
Kurort – spa resort
Kurtaxe – resort tax
Kurverwaltung – spa resort administration
Kurzentrum – spa centre

Land, Länder (pl) – state
Landtag – state parliament

Markgraf – margrave; German nobleman ranking above a count
Markt – market; often used instead of *Marktplatz*
Marktplatz – marketplace or square; often abbreviated to *Markt*
Mass – 1L tankard or stein of beer
Mensa – university cafeteria
Milchcafé – coffee with milk
Münster – minster, large church, cathedral

Nord – north
Notdienst – emergency service
NSDAP – National Socialist German Workers Party, Nazi party

Ost – east

Pension, Pensionen (pl) – inexpensive boarding house
Pfarrkirche – parish church
Platz – square
Postamt – post office

Radwandern – bicycle touring
Rathaus – town hall
Ratskeller – town hall restaurant
Reisezentrum – travel centre in train or bus stations
Ruhetag – rest day; closing day at a shop or restaurant

Saal, Säle (pl) – hall, room
Sammlung – collection
S-Bahn – *Schnellbahn*; suburban-metropolitan trains
Schatzkammer – treasury
Schloss – palace
Schnellimbiss – fast-food stall or restaurants
See – lake
Seilbahn – cable car
Speisekarte – menu
Stadt – city, town
Stadtbad, Stadtbäder (pl) – public pool
Staumauer – dam
Strasse – street; often abbreviated to Str
Süd – south

Tal – valley
Tor – gate
Tracht, Trachten (pl) – traditional costume
Turm – tower

U-Bahn – underground (subway) train

Verboten – forbidden
Viertel – quarter, district
Volksmusik – folk music

Wald – forest
Wasserfall – waterfall
Weg – way, path
Weinstube – traditional wine bar or tavern
West – west

Zimmer Frei – room available (for accommodation purposes)

behind the scenes

SEND US YOUR FEEDBACK

We love to hear from travellers – your comments keep us on our toes and help make our books better. Our well-travelled team reads every word on what you loved or loathed about this book. Although we cannot reply individually to postal submissions, we always guarantee that your feedback goes straight to the appropriate authors, in time for the next edition. Each person who sends us information is thanked in the next edition – the most useful submissions are rewarded with a selection of digital PDF chapters.

Visit **lonelyplanet.com/contact** to submit your updates and suggestions or to ask for help. Our award-winning website also features inspirational travel stories, news and discussions.

Note: We may edit, reproduce and incorporate your comments in Lonely Planet products such as guidebooks, websites and digital products, so let us know if you don't want your comments reproduced or your name acknowledged. For a copy of our privacy policy visit lonelyplanet.com/privacy.

OUR READERS

Many thanks to the travellers who used the last edition and wrote to us with helpful hints, useful advice and interesting anecdotes:
Anja Bauriedel, Angela Burgin, Beth Cade, Cliff Gathercole, Tom Green, Aleksandra Grzenda, Stefan Hilpert, Stefano Mezzato, Matt Pinches, Cinzia Gloria Redaelli, Christiane Scheuer, James Siddle, Isobel Williams, Gordon Woods, Sonya Zwolinski

AUTHOR THANKS

Marc Di Duca

Firstly a big thank you to Oleksandr Kalinin for the use of his apartment in Erding and all the nights out researching in the company of Mr Weissbier, and to my parents-in-law Mykola and Vira for taking care of my son Taras while I was on the road. Thanks also go to my outstanding fellow author Kerry Christiani; Alan Wissenberg, for his help in Munich and fascinating rail-related background info; Deustche Bahn, for their valued assistance; Karoline Graf and Tanja Olszak of the Munich Tourist Board; all the staff at the London Branch of the German National Tourism Office as well as all the local tourist offices

around Bavaria, in particular the guys in Coburg, Donauwörth and Nuremberg. And last, but certainly not least, heartfelt gratitude must go to my wife, Tanya, for all those long days we spend apart.

Kerry Christiani

A heartfelt *Dankeschön* to friends and family in the *Schwarzwald*, especially Hans and Monika. Enormous thanks to Claus Schäfer in Triberg and Christiana Schneeweiss in Salzburg for their invaluable tips. Thank you, too, to all the tourist board pros who smoothed the road to research, including Maria Altendorfer and colleagues in Salzburg, and to Marc Di Duca for being a brilliant coordinating author. Finally, special thanks to my Black Forest-born husband for being with me every step of the way.

ACKNOWLEDGMENTS

Climate map data adapted from Peel MC, Finlayson BL & McMahon TA (2007) 'Updated World Map of the Köppen-Geiger Climate Classification', Hydrology and Earth System Sciences, 11, 163344.

Cover photograph: Schloss Neuschwanstein with Schloss Hohenschwangau in Bavaria, Reinhard Schmid/AWL.

This Book

This 4th edition of Lonely Planet's Munich, Bavaria & the Black Forest guidebook was written and researched by Marc Di Duca and Kerry Christiani. The 3rd edition was written by Kerry, Andrea Schulte-Peevers and Catherine Le Nevez; the 2nd edition (titled Munich & Bavaria) was written by Andrea, Catherine and Jeremy Gray, and the 1st edition of this book (titled Bavaria) was written by Andrea. This guidebook was commissioned in Lonely Planet's London office, and produced by the following:

Commissioning Editor
Katie O'Connell

Coordinating Editors
Lauren Hunt, Tasmin Waby

Coordinating Cartographer Laura Matthewman

Coordinating Layout Designer Sandra Helou

Managing Editor Angela Tinson

Senior Editor Andi Jones

Managing Cartographers
Anita Banh, Adrian Persoglia

Managing Layout Designer Chris Girdler

Assisting Editors
Luna Soo

Assisting Layout Designers Carol Jackson, Katherine Marsh

Cover Research Naomi Parker

Internal Image Research
Aude Vauconsant, Frank Diem

Language Content Branislava Vladisavljevic

Thanks to Imogen Bannister, David Carroll, Daniel Corbett, Melanie Dankel, Bruce Evans, Ryan Evans, Samantha Forge, Larissa Frost, Jouve India, Trent Paton, Raphael Richards, Jacqui Saunders, John Taufa, Gerard Walker, Juan Winata

index

how to use this book

These symbols will help you find the listings you want:

👁	Sights	👆	Tours	🍷	Drinking
🏄	Beaches	🎉	Festivals & Events	⭐	Entertainment
🏃	Activities	🛏	Sleeping	🛍	Shopping
🎓	Courses	✖	Eating	ℹ	Information/Transport

These symbols give you the vital information for each listing:

📞	Telephone Numbers	📶	Wi-Fi Access	🚌	Bus
🕐	Opening Hours	🏊	Swimming Pool	🛥	Ferry
Ⓟ	Parking	🥗	Vegetarian Selection	Ⓢ	U-Bahn
🚭	Nonsmoking	📋	English-Language Menu	🚋	Tram
❄	Air-Conditioning	👨‍👩‍👧	Family-Friendly	🚆	Train
@	Internet Access	🐾	Pet-Friendly		

Reviews are organised by author preference.

Look out for these icons:

TOP CHOICE	Our author's recommendation
FREE	No payment required
🌿	A green or sustainable option

Our authors have nominated these places as demonstrating a strong commitment to sustainability – for example by supporting local communities and producers, operating in an environmentally friendly way, or supporting conservation projects.

Map Legend

Sights
- 🏖 Beach
- 🛕 Buddhist
- 🏰 Castle
- ✝ Christian
- 🕉 Hindu
- ☪ Islamic
- ✡ Jewish
- 🗿 Monument
- 🏛 Museum/Gallery
- 🏚 Ruin
- 🍇 Winery/Vineyard
- 🐘 Zoo
- 👁 Other Sight

Activities, Courses & Tours
- 🤿 Diving/Snorkelling
- 🛶 Canoeing/Kayaking
- ⛷ Skiing
- 🏄 Surfing
- 🏊 Swimming/Pool
- 🚶 Walking
- 🏄 Windsurfing
- 🎯 Other Activity/Course/Tour

Sleeping
- 🛏 Sleeping
- ⛺ Camping

Eating
- ✖ Eating

Drinking
- ☕ Drinking
- ☕ Cafe

Entertainment
- 🎭 Entertainment

Shopping
- 🛍 Shopping

Information
- 📮 Post Office
- ℹ Tourist Information

Transport
- ✈ Airport
- ⊗ Border Crossing
- 🚌 Bus
- Cable Car/Funicular
- Cycling
- Ferry
- Monorail
- Ⓟ Parking
- Ⓢ S-Bahn
- 🚕 Taxi
- Train/Railway
- Tram
- Ⓣ Tube Station
- Ⓤ U-Bahn
- Ⓜ Underground Train Station
- Other Transport

Routes
- Tollway
- Freeway
- Primary
- Secondary
- Tertiary
- Lane
- Unsealed Road
- Plaza/Mall
- Steps
- Tunnel
- Pedestrian Overpass
- Walking Tour
- Walking Tour Detour
- Path

Boundaries
- International
- State/Province
- Disputed
- Regional/Suburb
- Marine Park
- Cliff
- Wall

Population
- ★ Capital (National)
- ◉ Capital (State/Province)
- ● City/Large Town
- • Town/Village

Geographic
- 🛖 Hut/Shelter
- 🚨 Lighthouse
- 🔭 Lookout
- ▲ Mountain/Volcano
- 🌴 Oasis
- 🌳 Park
-)(Pass
- ⛱ Picnic Area
- 💧 Waterfall

Hydrography
- River/Creek
- Intermittent River
- Swamp/Mangrove
- Reef
- Canal
- Water
- Dry/Salt/Intermittent Lake
- Glacier

Areas
- Beach/Desert
- + + + Cemetery (Christian)
- × × × Cemetery (Other)
- Park/Forest
- Sportsground
- Sight (Building)
- Top Sight (Building)

OUR STORY

A beat-up old car, a few dollars in the pocket and a sense of adventure. In 1972 that's all Tony and Maureen Wheeler needed for the trip of a lifetime – across Europe and Asia overland to Australia. It took several months, and at the end – broke but inspired – they sat at their kitchen table writing and stapling together their first travel guide, *Across Asia on the Cheap*. Within a week they'd sold 1500 copies. Lonely Planet was born.

Today, Lonely Planet has offices in Melbourne, London and Oakland, with more than 600 staff and writers. We share Tony's belief that 'a great guidebook should do three things: inform, educate and amuse'.

OUR WRITERS

Marc Di Duca

Coordinating Author, Munich, Bavaria From a library job in the Ruhrgebiet during that summer of '89 to scrambling around the Alps for this guide, German and Germany have been with Marc throughout his adult life. A well-established travel guide author, Marc has explored many corners of Germany over the last 20 years but it's to the quirky variety and laid-back openness of Bavaria that he returns most willingly. When not eating snowballs in Rothenburg ob der Tauber, brewery hopping in Bamberg or pedantically correcting railway museum staff in Nuremberg, he can be found in Sandwich, Kent, where he lives with his Kievite wife, Tanya, and their two sons. *Munich, Bavaria and the Black Forest* is Marc's 22nd Lonely Planet title.

Read more about Marc Di Duca at:
lonelyplanet.com/members/madidu

Kerry Christiani

Stuttgart & the Black Forest, Salzburg & Around Having lived for six years in Germany's Black Forest, Kerry jumped at the chance to return to her second home – and family – to write her chapters. Cycling around Lake Constance, road-testing Black forest gateau in Triberg (it's a hard life) and going behind the scenes to discover the truth about the von Trapps in Salzburg kept her busy for this edition. Kerry has authored some 20 guidebooks and frequently contributes to print and online magazines, including *Olive*, *Lonely Planet Magazine* and bbc.com/travel. She tweets @kerrychristiani and lists her latest work at www.kerrychristiani.com. Kerry also wrote the Outdoor Activities, Landscapes & Wildlife and Food & Drink chapters.

Published by Lonely Planet Publications Pty Ltd
ABN 36 005 607 983
4th edition – March 2013
ISBN 978 1 74179 409 0
© Lonely Planet 2013   Photographs © as indicated 2013
10 9 8 7 6 5 4
Printed in China